THE FLETCHER JONES FOUNDATION

HUMANITIES IMPRINT

The Fletcher Jones Foundation has endowed this imprint to foster innovative and enduring scholarship in the humanities.

D1567336

THE PUBLISHER AND THE UNIVERSITY OF CALIFORNIA PRESS
FOUNDATION GRATEFULLY ACKNOWLEDGE THE GENEROUS
SUPPORT OF THE FLETCHER JONES FOUNDATION IMPRINT
IN HUMANITIES.

UNDERSTANDING RELIGION

UNDERSTANDING
RELIGION

Theories and Methods for Studying
Religiously Diverse Societies

Paul Hedges

 UNIVERSITY OF CALIFORNIA PRESS

University of California Press
Oakland, California

© 2021 by Paul Hedges

Library of Congress Cataloging-in-Publication Data

Names: Hedges, Paul (Paul Michael), 1970– author.
Title: Understanding religion : theories and methods for studying
    religiously diverse societies / Paul Hedges.
Description: Oakland, California : University of California Press, [2021] |
    Includes bibliographical references and index.
Identifiers: LCCN 2020032939 (print) | LCCN 2020032940 (ebook) |
    ISBN 9780520298897 (hardcover) | ISBN 9780520298910 (paperback) |
    ISBN 9780520970861 (ebook)
Subjects: LCSH: Religious pluralism—Case studies. | Religions—
    Relations—Case studies. | Religion and sociology—Case studies.
Classification: LCC BL410 .H46 2021 (print) | LCC BL410 (ebook) |
    DDC 200.71—dc23
LC record available at https://lccn.loc.gov/2020032939
LC ebook record available at https://lccn.loc.gov/2020032940

29 28 27 26 25 24 23 22 21
10 9 8 7 6 5 4 3 2 1

CONTENTS

ILLUSTRATIONS

All pictures are the author's own photographs.

BOXES

ACKNOWLEDGMENTS AND DEDICATIONS

This book is dedicated to my teachers and my students. The two are, of course, not distinctly demarcated as I have learned from both.

The names I must thank for advice, suggestions, patient reading, and support in the production of this book are almost too numerous to mention. However, I wish to particularly name the following (with all due apologies to any I have overlooked): Abdullah Saeed, Craig Martin, Farish Noor, Nelly van Doorn-Harder, Wendy Dossett, Alana Vincent, Nursheila Muez, Diyanah Yahya, Gavin Flood, Tenzan Eaghll, Grace Davie, Luca Farrow, Neil Messer, Mohamed Salihin, Daan Oostveen, Will Sweetman, Orlando Woods, Cheryl Lim, and Junaidah Jaffar. While not direct contributors to this book, I would also acknowledge intellectual inspiration, ideas, and/or support over the years from Paul Badham, Diana Eck, Timothy Fitzgerald, Julius Lipner, Kevin Schilbrack, Marianne Moyaert, Alami Musa, Mohamed Bin Ali, Mohamed Imran Mohamed Taib, Chris Arthur, Richard King, Biko Agozino, Syed Farid Alatas, Jonathan Z. Smith, Lily Kong, Christina Welch, Liz Stuart, Alan Race, Russell McCutcheon, Jayne Svenungsson, Perry Schmidt-Leukel, and Bruce Lincoln—and because I must stop this list somewhere, I stop here. This has sometimes involved simply reading their work. Many of the figures will find themselves named inside the pages of this book, but it is no guarantee that they will agree with what I have said. Also, my thanks go to the several anonymous reviewers of the manuscript. But most especial thanks are due to my various students in AS6028, HA4071, and AS6035 at Nanyang Technological University, who have been the guinea pigs for the draft versions. Students from both Winchester University and the ISC

(Queen's University, Canada) at Herstmonceux Castle, as well as various institutions in China, including Heilongjiang University and the Harbin Institute of Technology, have also been my interlocutors along the way as I have struggled to become a better teacher and educator—and learner. At the University of California Press my enduring thanks must go to Eric Schmidt, who supported this project to the utmost from the beginning and graciously put up with my tardiness, as well as Archna Patel, Kate Hoffman, and Austin Lim for their support. The whole production and copyediting team must also be mentioned, especially Sue Carter, who has picked up on my infelicities with great care. Without these people and their support, this book would be much poorer; any failures and errors that do remain are solely the responsibility of myself as an author.

INTRODUCTION

TO THE STUDENT

I hope that you will both learn from and enjoy reading this book. I have tried to make it not just another ho-hum, run-of-the-mill introduction to . . . (yawn) . . . type of book. Rather, I address debates between scholars and give you the skills and knowledge to comprehend the world around you. That means this book is about—and it sounds scary—methodology and theory. Theory and method are not just dry, abstract concepts, but principles relating to life and society. Indeed, giving you new ways to look at the world is a major aim of this book.

So, this book is not *about* "religions." Rather, it is a book about *how to study* religions. Reading this book first, or alongside, other books on specific religions will help you understand them (the books and the religions!) better.

Furthermore, religions are not separate from our embodiment and social life. We should not study religion as isolated ideas, texts, or rituals, but as part of human life. This is why the following issues are core to this text:

Politics: I do not mean being party political. However, all scholarship is political: it makes choices about what we study, who gets funding, what subjects are worth studying, and so on. Why the study of religion looks the way it does will be addressed.

Commitment: You may have been told that academic study should be neutral and uncommitted; however, there are academic traditions committed to justice, the oppressed, and the welfare of all humanity (and sentient beings, other-than-human-persons, and the planet we live on). These debates will be addressed.

Voices: Western scholarship comes from Western traditions and the Enlightenment. While this has always been in conversation with global voices, much of the outside legacy has been hidden or sidelined. This has affected how the concept "religion" is conceived. Less fully represented voices, in terms of gender, race, and class, which challenge the standard construction of religion are explored.

Decolonizing: I will bring in insights from nonwhite and non-Western scholarship. This book will fail miserably to be truly decolonial and include all possible voices; there are just too many. But it will try.

Enlightenment values: Such values as equality, reason, and justice are key to this book, and the Western heritage behind the study of religion is part of how we have come to study as we do. But, as noted above, we cannot take it as the only voice; we must understand that scholarship has a political heritage and that various stances will help us see differently.

The rest of this introduction will do a few things, which you can read or skip. I have an introduction to instructors (what do I tell them but not you?); some notes on teaching theory (pedagogy) and scholarly choices; and a methodological introduction (or rant) which helps put some ideas in context. Although this last section is more directed at fellow scholars, it addresses concepts that are fundamental to this book.

TO THE INSTRUCTOR

If you are reading this, there is a good chance that you are thinking of adopting this book. I should therefore follow this with a sales pitch. However, I will do something more mundane and outline some key aspects of this text (which is, of course, simply a subtler sales pitch):

Student-centered: A trendy buzzword, but I use it here meaningfully in at least two ways. First, the writing and style is accessible. Second, it aims to give students practical skills, tools, and knowledge to examine the varied phenomena we term "religion."

Case study methodology: Often seen in business schools, this approach has not been widely adopted in the study of religion. I say more about this later, but I believe case studies are of benefit to both students and teachers.

Theory and method approach: This book does not address theory and method in the traditional ways of particular approaches (e.g., "sociology," "anthropology," "feminism," etc.), but focuses on helping students understand religion in society as discourse and practice.

Critical approach: The book is underlain by a range of central theories and methods. I can name these as critical theory (broadly construed): concern with gender representation and theory; a postcolonial and decolonizing approach; an awareness of class and political issues; and, a critical hermeneutical phenomenology. However, I do not take any of these approaches uncritically. There is more on this below.

Flexibility: By this I mean three things. First, a wide range of theory and method is covered. Second, this book can be used from introductory undergraduate courses up to graduate-level teaching. This is partly through the case studies, which can be explored at many levels of complexity. It is written assuming no knowledge, so can suit absolute beginners, but because it enters areas of dispute and critical discussion it can lead into discussion with graduate students (used alongside primary texts). Third, this book can be used for method and theory classes, courses on specific religions (with specific case studies) for a methodological approach, or in sociology/history (etc.) of religion courses that focus on methodology.

Author's positionality: This book comes out of my own teaching across over twenty years and several continents, so it is about what has worked for me. While mostly teaching in religious studies contexts, I currently find myself in a graduate school of international relations with students who normally have no background in the study of religion. This book comes from me finding no adequate text to make religious studies method and theory relevant and coherent to them. However, it is also very much for pure religious studies students. Below, I address further why I think a scholar's own stance is important.

Hopefully my non-sales-pitch has convinced you, but you may still feel "Nah, it's not for me." I hope you at least read the next section before deciding; it may still convince you.

PEDAGOGICAL APPROACHES AND SCHOLARLY CHOICES
WHY DID YOU DO THAT?

I will start off noting a few (but not all) key stylistic and pedagogical choices:

Focus: The book's concern is contemporary religion and its role in society. While this book takes contemporary criticism of the concept of "religion" very seriously—and agrees with much of it—I argue throughout the book that we can still employ the term; you will find out more in chapter 1.

No diacritics: As an introduction, the book is student-centered and not off-putting. While some see using diacritics as showing a certain scholarly rigor, they do little to help an introductory student, and experts do not need them. However, I do use accents where they normally appear in languages which use Roman characters and retain diacritics where they appear in quotations and book titles.

"We": This book stresses a learning model that emphasizes the "expert" and student as colearners, rather than an information delivery model.[1] As such, I normally use "we" to speak about the authorial voice and reader learning together. "I" is only used when I very consciously want to emphasize my choices (it appears much more here in the introduction than elsewhere). In other words, it seeks dialogue toward knowledge, rather than emphasizing a depository of ideas to be imparted[2]—something developed in the case study method.

Chapters: Space means there is an inevitable arbitrary cutoff on what is, and is not, included. I will not justify every choice, but some points can be made. "Race" was not included as a chapter; however, it is central to the book, and chapters 7 and 18 cover it significantly. It is a theme not limited to one primary location. "Fundamentalism" and "violence" are covered together, which does not suggest that I see them as inherently linked. I did not want to leave either out, and commonly perceived associations made it logical to cover them together. I have not included fieldwork or research methodologies. They are important but did not seem to fit; the questions of the book are more, "Why do people collect data the way they do?" "Why do they interpret it the way they do?" Rather than, "How do they collect it?"

Intertextuality: The book aims to show that many topics, issues, methods, and theories are not discrete units but are deeply connected. Chapters, terms, and discussions are referenced back and forth. The final section of each chapter, "Questions and Connecting Thoughts," makes such links. Boxes are, in part, used to make it easier for students to find some key ideas in other chapters if they illuminate something covered in another chapter. This is also seen in the recurring usage of a number of issues in specific religions to help provide different insights on particular issues.

Structure: There are three sections. The first three chapters deal with what I see as two fundamentals: what we think religion is, and some core methodology in approaching it. While the rest of the book can be read without reading these, they lay out some fundamental issues. The next section is primarily particular methods and theories, some of which are fairly central to the whole book, but none is essential to understanding other chapters. The final section turns to religion in society today.

Theory and method: This book seeks to bring together both methodological tools and theoretical lenses. My reasons should become clear, but we must reflect (theory) on why we think as we do (method, or "action").[3] To understand what is meant by theory here: "To theorize is to look at something in a special way, one that achieves its perspective by distancing or by probing beneath a surface."[4]

History: This book is about contemporary religion, but I often engage history. My PhD was in the history of religion, and I believe that we cannot understand the contemporary world, or why things are as they are, without understanding how they came about. As such, one chapter engages historical methods and many chapters delve back hundreds, sometimes thousands, of years. However, in general, our focus remains on how this history affects us today.

Technical/foreign terms: Generally, English-language terms are used. This reflects a desire to be accessible to students at different stages, although foreign/technical terms often follow in parenthesis. These may be glossed or further explained in the glossary; definitions there normally appear under the technical/foreign term to stress their particular meanings. The book's focus, though, is method and theory, so it does not generally delve deeply into tradition-specific terms. Occasionally, a foreign/technical term is used in the text where the reader should be alert to a very distinct meaning for a pedagogical purpose, even if that term is elsewhere rendered in English. My guiding principle is ease of usage for the reader while alerting them to further complexities; where and how instructors supply further details will, of course, vary depending on course objectives, level of students, and so on. Further, given that terms come from Arabic, Chinese, Latin, Greek, Pali, Sanskrit, and a range of other languages, it should be clear why this book avoids deep engagement with specific terms, whose meanings may also be the subject of ongoing scholarly disputes.

Text boxes: Heavy use is made of boxes, which do at least three things. One is to provide introductions to key theories, issues, and concepts which can be cross-referenced from other chapters when relevant. Another is to provide examples without interrupting the flow of the main text, so readers can stop to check them or carry on and come back to them later. A third is to provide key background knowledge which may be known to some readers but not others, so those to whom it is familiar can keep with the flow of the text, while others can read them. In some cases, one box may serve more than one of these purposes.

OPPRESSION, JUSTICE, AND THE POLITICS OF SCHOLARSHIP

This book expressly addresses a number of issues which affect the way that scholarship is written and how we are able to think about the world. This has made this book deeply political in that it asks questions about who controls scholarship, and what voices have been silenced or marginalized in scholarship. This means that questions of class, race, and gender frequently arise as they have shaped our categories. This also means that this is a book deeply concerned with questions of justice and oppression. This is both a personal and an academic choice; such questions have been raised both as personal expressions and as academic choices by various academics.[5]

The contemporary study of religion has a history, in part as a tool of colonial classification and control. We cannot simply jump to a place of pure and objective criticism of this without asking where we stand. The notion of standing apart from such questions, or even simply offering some supposedly external critique without being grounded in a concept of justice, is a stance that is viable only for those who support the unjust status quo. Therefore, as Desmond Tutu and others have noted, to refuse to seek justice against the status quo is an act that continues to support oppression.[6] It should be noted in this regard that this book is influenced by Paulo Freire's *Pedagogy of the Oppressed,* including his notion that the oppressors can be liberated by the oppressed.[7] That is to say, it is sometimes hard for those in positions of privilege to see views from elsewhere, and it takes hard work to recognize the validity of the stance of our "Others."

To address some potential criticisms that may arise and clarify some issues, I will raise three points:

> *"Theses on method":* Bruce Lincoln's famous statement on method largely aligns with my own stance and opinions.[8] It is often one of the first texts I give to my students. However, I do not tell them they have to accept it all. When it comes to the thirteenth thesis, I believe there are good reasons why scholars may be advocates in certain circumstances. This is discussed in chapters 5, 7, 10, and 18. However, I raise it as a point of debate, rather than asserting my own position as correct.

> *Does this book tell people what to think?* I am stating my own stance here because I believe that, as students and scholars, we need to be reflexive about our own stances, biases, and prejudices, as discussed in chapter 2. Autobiography can become part of our scholarship.[9] However, I am very clear in asking readers to question the claims of this book.

> *Is this book an SJW (social justice warrior) manifesto?* Many assert that academia is full of "cultural Marxists" who have stopped looking at evidence and only assert politically correct ideologies. My commitment to justice, decolonizing methods, and a concern with race, gender, and class may lead to this accusation. However, I would argue that objective and rational academic study will show that oppression is a real factor that shapes our world. My stance comes from evidence, not ideology. I do not, though, prescribe a single form of action nor what we could describe as a political agenda: those are questions I leave to the reader. This book also does not dismiss what the Western world and elite white males have contributed to our knowledge and understanding, which has been considerable. However, there are more voices to listen to, and hearing them will widen our knowledge and understanding further.

This book is written in my role as a scholar who identifies with interreligious studies.[10] Interreligious studies is a fairly new term in academia, and refers to several things:

- A multidisciplinary or interdisciplinary approach (respectively, using or learning from many distinct disciplines, and combining the disciplines in study or research).
- An interest in situations of religious diversity, so that rather than studying religions in isolation, we seek to understand the "dynamic encounters and interactions" that occur between different traditions, including secular traditions and non-religious worldviews.[11] See especially chapters 2, 13, 14.
- The recognition that scholars are part of the creation of the discourse and cannot pretend to sit back as impartial observers who only examine other people's discourse or practices. Many scholars of interreligious studies are scholar-activists and do not see this as inherently controversial or contradictory.[12]
- An acknowledgment, following from the above point, that theological approaches and the secular academic study of religion are not strictly separate; secularism is discussed in chapter 16. Rather, we see a continuum of approaches. This book is definitely not a confessional theological one.[13] However, it is open to learning from theologians when they have something to tell us. Theologians are sources of data for the scholar of religion, but can also be sources of theory, an issue discussed in chapter 2, but also raised in chapter 7.

This book focuses on contemporary society and diverse societies, and critically explores attitudes toward religious diversity and the practice of interreligious dialogue, the latter two in chapters 13 and 14, respectively. However, it does not advocate for dialogue nor any specific view on this.

CASE STUDIES

The sustained use of case studies is rarely found in the study of religion. Even when it is, it is not normally approached in the way it is here. The model here draws from what is seen as good practice in other disciplines,[14] and is influenced by the pioneer efforts of Diana Eck in the study of religion.[15] I will briefly explain the method and key features.

The case study is a way to bring theory or method to life for students. In particular, it shows that we are not simply discussing abstract concepts but issues that relate to and apply to the real world outside the classroom. Indeed, this interaction with real-world issues allows theory and method to be applied directly, and therefore understood better because it becomes an active method of learning. It also emphasizes that there are not necessarily right or wrong answers.

A successful case study generally should accomplish the following:

· Involve a personal or existential aspect. Students may be asked to put themselves into the context of somebody in the scenario, or see things from another point of view. This helps highlight that answers are partly perspectival. Further, considering the effect the issues have on people will help develop an element of "genuine choice," or crisis, in that a decision needs to be made.

· Raise at least one or more aspects of theory and/or method to allow students to think about its application.

· Not have a single answer. Students should be able to see why, in different situations, from different perspectives, or at differing times and places, the situation may be thought about or answered differently. This encourages a reflexive approach (see box 2.7).

The case study approach also makes this text flexible as a teaching tool. While I have deliberately used case studies from global situations and a range of different traditions, an instructor could devise their own case studies for a single religion or regional context. The diversity here is seen as a virtue, because it is partly by engaging differing worldviews that students will hopefully be asked to think outside their normal boxes. However, it is not essential. Indeed, asking students to see another person's point of view from another strand of their own religion (if they have one, but this is equally applicable to students with no religion) can be challenging and eye-opening. Scholarly study is enriched through asking existential questions that engage diverse points of view and potentially give greater depth of understanding.

CRITICAL HERMENEUTICAL PHENOMENOLOGY AND METHODOLOGICAL POLYMORPHISM

No academic standpoint floats free of history and context, and I have already suggested certain things that inform this study. In this section, I will engage two areas. First, I address some reasons for the wide engagement with differing theories and methods. Second, I outline my own particular theoretical framework. I do not provide a fully developed theoretical platform (partly because if I had written a 60,000-word introduction I think the publishers would have had something to say about it!), but merely sketch some key issues. This section is addressed more to my fellow scholars, so I hope other readers will bear with me if parts seem opaque or obscure at this stage.[16]

METHODOLOGICAL POLYMORPHISM: OR, BEING PROMISCUOUS WITH METHOD

Whatever "religion" may be (and taking seriously critiques that suggest we abandon the term altogether), it is neither monolithic, sui generis, nor clearly definable. Therefore, being multidisciplinary, or even interdisciplinary, is essential. We should have a diverse toolkit. This I term methodological polymorphism, which is to say that our method must take on a variety of forms in differing circumstances. This is needed for at least three reasons:

1. The range of phenomena under investigation are themselves plural, and thus our methods of investigation, to get a suitable angle, must also be plural.

2. Our ways of looking affect what we see, and thus varied lenses will help us gain insights from different angles and prevent us from assuming any is the "Truth."

3. Extending from the last point, multiple perspectives will help us see better. Assuming we cannot attain "Truth" does not mean that we cannot seek for more coherent, more consistent, or more plausible theories and explanations with a hope to approximate "truth."

Employing many approaches may mean that our methods and theories are not always consistent. Sometimes, taking insights from varied—even from potentially conflicting—methods and theories may be beneficial. This is why I have subtitled this section "being promiscuous with method." For many, this may seem illicit; however, I suggest that promiscuity may at times be a virtue. Through it all, this book hopes to weave a central narrative that makes sense of how we understand the theoretical basis.

SKETCHES TOWARD A CRITICAL HERMENEUTICAL PHENOMENOLOGY

The theoretical basis I am advancing here is termed a critical hermeneutical phenomenology. In a fuller sense, I might term it a critical, embodied, feminist, postcolonial, decolonizing, philosophical hermeneutical phenomenology. That, however, is too much of a mouthful and so the shorter term may stand in. It will be useful to clarify the terms:

Critical: Connoting critical theory and social constructionism. This is dealt with more fully in chapter 5. Critical theory may draw from many sources (see box 0.1), but in broad terms it is a scholarly and investigative suspicion of claims to knowledge, power, and authority. Importantly, it is not (necessarily—and certainly not here) a claim that all knowledge is relative. However, it does historicize how we see the world, showing that what we see as obvious, commonsense, or taken for granted may simply be cultural formations that are more or less arbitrary. In the broad sense taken here, it includes both feminist and postcolonial approaches that question, respectively, male-centric and Western-centric ways of seeing the world.

Hermeneutical: Meaning hermeneutical philosophy, which names a particular lineage of thought that has explored how humans make sense of the world around us through language and interpretation (see boxes 0.2 and 2.6).

Phenomenology: Originating in the early twentieth century (see chapter 2, especially box 2.3), phenomenology is—as the name suggests—the study of phenomena. Heavily critiqued via critical theory, it can nevertheless be seen as a viable approach combined with a reflexive awareness of our own preconceptions (see box 2.7). Further, it helps underpin our method through an embodied awareness that takes materiality seriously (see box 9.10).

First off, we need to deal with what will no doubt be a charge of undue promiscuity. Phenomenology has come under criticism from critical theory. This is discussed in chapter 2. But hermeneutical philosophy has also come under fire from a range of critical thinkers, including Jürgen Habermas, who is linked to the Frankfurt school, as well as Jacques Derrida (1930–2004). Habermas's arguments I think misconstrue Gadamer's thought,[17] and the same can be said for Derrida.[18] However, some hold that Michel Foucault's (1926–1984) work also undermines Gadamer's ideas. As substantial usage is made of parts of Foucault's work—though I would not describe my method as Foucauldian, nor Gadamerian, come to that—we should address this. Hubert Dreyfus and Paul Rabinow claim that when Foucault said "For centuries we have waited in vain for the decision of the Word," he discredited Gadamer's hermeneutical endeavors.[19] However, this has been disputed, with Foucault, Dreyfus, and Rabinow seemingly misunderstanding the nature and intent of Gadamer's philosophical hermeneutics.[20] Indeed, we should be suspicious of claims that sophisticated scholars can be so readily declared irrelevant by this "magic wand" approach, whereby a simple phrase (or incantation) makes a whole school of thought disappear in an instant. It is, I would argue, a problem to which many scholars in the critical theory camp are prone. However, equally, the naysayers of critical theory also seem prone to assuming that some errors (and admittedly some incoherence) in the writings of certain theorists means that everything they say is meaningless.[21]

Why do I advance a critical hermeneutical phenomenology (that is also postcolonial, feminist, and embodied) here? First, I draw strongly from the way that both critical theory and philosophical hermeneutics have a strong focus in language as the basis of human interpretation of the world. This can be related to what is often termed the "linguistic turn" in the humanities and social sciences, which also relies on the work of Ludwig Wittgenstein (1889–1951). Older theories of knowledge (epistemology) assumed that we spoke about the world as something we directly experienced—as "facts" out there. But things are not this simple. The linguistic turn recognizes that our experience of the world is based in language (our cultural and social conditioning), which determines to some degree what we can know, understand, and experience. We never consciously experience or understand the world directly, but always and only through language. Now this may sound quite radical—and, indeed, some critics have suggested that such theories are primarily political in nature[22]—but there are solid reasons why these theories took root. For example:

WHAT IS CRITICAL THEORY?

"Critical theory" can be defined narrowly or widely. Here, it is used widely to describe a range of approaches which variously trace their heritage from (to note a few figures): Edmund Husserl (1859–1938) and Martin Heidegger (1889–1976) (phenomenology); Theodore Adorno (1903–1969) and Max Horkheimer (1895–1973) (the Frankfurt School); Jacques Derrida (1930–2004), Michel Foucault (1926–1984), Jean Baudrillard (1929–2007), Judith Butler, and Pierre Bourdieu (1930–2002) (broadly, but inadequately, postmodernism [see box 2.5] and/or poststructuralism); Peter Berger and Sally Haslanger (social constructionism); and, Walter Mignolo, Syed Hussein Alatas (1928–2008), Frantz Fanon (1925–1961), and Gayatri Chakravorty Spivak (postcolonialism/decolonization). To roughly draw a common "critical" stance:

- Dominant ways of seeing the world are not the only ways we can see it.
- Many groups are suppressed (oppressed) in social and cultural discourse.
- Methods such as the archaeology/genealogy of knowledge, the historization of ideas, social constructionism, or deconstruction help question our concepts and ideas.

Notably, we are not discussing a single school of thought or set of ideas. This is a broad drawing of a "critical theory" approach. Chapter 5 explores this more fully, though focusing on only certain strands of critical theory; chapter 7 focuses on postcolonial and decolonization theory; and chapter 10 on feminist theory.

WHAT IS PHILOSOPHICAL HERMENEUTICS?

Originally, hermeneutics meant the interpretation of Christian scripture. But it also refers to any textual or literary interpretation, including in legal contexts. Codified through figures such as Friedrich Schleiermacher (1768–1834), Wilhelm Dilthey (1833–1911), and Martin Heidegger (1889–1976), it started to become part of a wider discussion about how humans come to understand, or interpret, anything at all. Hans-Georg Gadamer (1900–2002) is often seen as the father of hermeneutical philosophy, which is a systematic investigation into the nature of human interpretation and understanding. His ideas and hermeneutical philosophy were further developed by Paul Ricoeur (1913–2005). Together, their ideas have been influential in various fields, especially in terms of how humans interpret language.

- In English, we demarcate a range of colors, such as green, red, blue, brown, and so on. However, some linguistic groups, especially from jungle environments, have a multitude of words that equate to what we call green, with each being its own separate "color." This is not simply a linguistic fact; tests indicate that speakers of these languages can distinguish between a range of what we would call "shades" of green that English-language speakers cannot discern.

- Some languages have words for emotions or experiences that we do not possess in English, and it seems credible to claim that this may equally affect the limits of what we can and cannot experience in certain ways.

- Some cultures do not speak of left and right, but of the cardinal directions (north, south, east, and west). They orientate themselves in the world this way. So, if a speaker of such a language says move your leg on the southeast side one step forward, other speakers of that language will be able to do this and orientate themselves in ways that English speakers are simply not able to do.[23]

Now, and this is very important, one consequence for some people who follow critical theory and take the linguistic turn is support for non-realist epistemologies. That is to say, theories of knowledge which assert that, as it is often phrased: "it is discourse all the way down." In other words, the only reality we ever come to know is the cultural, social, and linguistic one. Sophisticated non-realisms do not assert that there is no "reality," but only that we simply cannot "know" it directly for it always comes discursively conditioned. I discuss in chapters 5 and 9 the reasons why I would advocate instead for a critical realism (which aligns with the current scientific, philosophical, and social scientific consensus), and which overlaps with a sophisticated non-realism (sometimes anti-realism; see box 5.8).[24] Notably, I do not want to directly contrast as absolutely different the variety of things which get termed "non-realism" or "anti-realism," or sometimes get termed "post-structuralist" views, with the variety of things which get termed "critical realism." This is partly because each includes a variety of standpoints, and sometimes there is much overlap. For instance, many of the theorists who inform non-realism also inform critical realism, such that both may be said to be poststructuralist—and so I see "poststructuralism" as an empty term to bandy around here—with some differences depending on varying readings of the theorists (my readings, I would argue, accord with the mainstream philosophical readings and align with legitimate critique raised by such areas as feminist or decolonial scholarship).[25] Recognizing that these terms are used differently, within this text non-realism will stand for approaches where the social construction of reality is seen to take priority over the experience of "reality," and in which we are primarily faced only with differing interpretations of experiences. Meanwhile, critical realism stands for approaches which see "reality" as being—while socially constructed in our discursive experience of it—too powerful an influence to be merely a secondary component to social construction, for it determines our discourse and lived realities. From a critical realist stance, it "is possible for social science to refine and improve its knowledge about the real world over time, and to make claims about reality which are relatively justified, while still being historical, contingent, and changing."[26] The latter is favored here partly because we should also take account of the "material turn" and not just the "linguistic turn" in contemporary thought, discussed briefly in what follows. But it can be noted here that Wittgenstein's work accords with my arguments.[27] Five key insights from hermeneutical philosophy also supplement my theory:

1. A basic premise of philosophical hermeneutics is the fact that understanding and interpretation are always combined. We do not first understand something and subsequently interpret it; rather, all our acts of understanding are already and always interpretations of the data we have received. This necessitates having a reflexive attitude to understanding. There is not, and never can be, some free-floating reason or critique which is above the fray. As such, hermeneutics extends beyond arguments which contend that reason is pure and neutral (one interpretation of modernity), on the one hand, and unreflexive critical theory which sees itself as having no ideological foundation, on the other (one interpretation of " postmodernity"; see box 2.5[28]): there is no such thing as a nonfoundational theorist, when this is erroneously used to deny an embodied and socially conditioned perspective.

2. Developing this idea, Gadamer seeks to rehabilitate the term "prejudice" as something positive. Our prejudices are our preunderstandings and form the basis of all new possibilities of understanding. An important feminist criticism of Gadamer to keep in mind here characterizes his stress on prejudice as reinforcing patriarchal and traditional norms. However, as I read hermeneutical philosophy, this is not entailed. Prejudice informs our starting point, which may lead to an opening of our horizons; it is not the endpoint, or limit, as discussed below.[29]

3. Inherent in what we have said above is the linguistic nature of all understanding. However, this does not mean that we can never understand another culture, language, or worldview. For Gadamer—and Wittgenstein—the commonality of language is the possibility of communication, not an unsurpassable barrier. It is also important to have an embodied focus on materiality which prevents logocentrism (see box 9.1), as discussed in chapter 9. Our being-in-the-world—thrown as we are into a certain context that is not of our choosing (see box 9.2)—and our socially and linguistically constructed discourse must be held in balance; we go astray when we emphasize one without the other. We are interpreting (hermeneutical) and embodied beings. Our materiality and embodiment shape us before we ever linguistically construct our world (see box 9.10).

4. This brings us to the concept of translation. Hermeneutical philosophers such as Gadamer and Ricoeur have argued for what may variously be termed the "agony of translation" or the "im/possibility" of translation. These figures are not naive, and certainly recognize that even between closely related languages we do not see a one-for-one correspondence of words. Nevertheless, translation does take place. When you visit France, India, Botswana, or Mexico, you can find the language to get you to the museum, eat the food you are looking for, or navigate your way to the lavatory (or is it the toilet, loo, or cesspit?). William Shakespeare's *Romeo and Juliet* can be translated into Romanian, Hindi, and Korean, while Sunzi's *Art of War* can be translated into English, Spanish, and Malay. There may be some things we do not quite get in translation, but this does not mean that translation is impossible. Indeed, translation also occurs within one language: many speakers of contemporary English struggle with Shakespeare's Tudor English and need a "modern translation"; not to mention when we read some contemporary theorists! Importantly, we are not simply speaking about words here, because all language embodies a culture, and cultures are embodied in words and actions. We may never become a "native speaker," but we can find our way. Or, stressing the possibility of translation, as Souleymane Bachir Diagne has put it, "The language of the universal is translation."[30] In other words, we understand always and only through seeing that which is beyond ourselves. So, we must always translate (from our own language, from another language, from the gestures, touch, and actions of another, or even from seeing ourselves in a mirror) that which is beyond us into meanings that we can interpret in terms we understand.

5. We come now to one of Gadamer's key concepts: the "fusion of horizons." I prefer to term this the "opening of horizons," as I think it is less liable to misunderstanding.[31] Now, our present knowledge (our current set of prejudices) forms our horizons: it forms the limits of what we see/know. However, the analogy of the horizon is apt because as we walk from one place to another the skyline that we can see (our horizon) shifts with us. In short, it is a basic facet of human understanding that our knowledge changes (grows, expands—though we may also forget or become more closed) with time and experience. Our horizons (generally) expand naturally. An important part of this, for Gadamer, is the way that when two people (worldviews, cultures, systems of thought) intersect or come together we can have new learning: the opening of horizons. We can understand the other, while new perspectives that neither had thought of before may arise. However, this is not about creating a new thought realm, or horizon, shared by each participant; rather, we see each participant in the learning experience

having their horizons opened in new, and sometimes unexpected, ways. In Freire's terms, we can overcome our "limit-situation."[32]

This brief survey of five key points is neither definitive nor comprehensive of hermeneutical philosophy. They do, nevertheless, provide a basis for helping us move forward in theorizing religion. Such a stance moves beyond the problematic binary of either a naive realism or radical non-realism. The possibility of our understanding can, and must, be held in tension with the problematic "agony" of translation, which means we can never entirely enter another's worldview. In one sense, we remain forever, as Derrida would suggest, in a state of *différance* where a final and absolute meaning/meeting is never attained; indeed, Derrida would have suggested that the final, fixed, truth is a fiction, as standpoints and the world always change. Yet it does not suggest we are forever stuck unable to speak. Derrida himself maintained that we must speak and act, and his deconstruction was aimed, in part, at justice.[33] We may seek "truth" even if we see "Truth" as an unobtainable and false goal. This accords with Freire's balance of subjectivity and objectivity.[34] The lineage traced is primarily concerned with elite Western male thinkers (though we have noted some others), which may seem to go against the concern with gender, class, race, and a decolonizing lens.[35] Space does not allow us to extend on this here, but how such perspectives can add to theory appears through this book.

This may all seem somewhat abstract theory now, but especially through chapters 1, 2, 5, 7, 8, 9, 10, 11, and 18, we will see why these debates matter and how they help us understand and think about what "religion" may (or may not) be, as well as to coherently interpret the world. The reader may freely reject or critique this theoretical basis. It is not essential to deploying the various methodologies contained herein. For instance, social identity theory, the cognitive science of religion, decolonial perspectives, and lived religion do not rely upon a critical hermeneutical phenomenology. Nevertheless, I hope that readers will find it a compelling stance that helps make sense of the complex realities and social structures we associate with religious traditions and how we think about the world.

PART I

WHAT IS RELIGION AND HOW TO APPROACH IT?

RELIGION
Language, Law, and Legacies

IN WHICH WE EXPLORE:

Definitions of the term "religion," and critical problems with the category religion

The world religions paradigm (WRP) and its colonial, Western, and Christian legacy

Issues in the legal, political, and social deployment of "religion"

Case studies exploring Falun Gong and legal-political issues, and the distinction of culture and religion in Christian-Confucian encounters

INTRODUCTION: DO WE KNOW WHAT RELIGIONS ARE?

"Religion" may seem like a straightforward term. We can name religions (e.g., Buddhism, Christianity, Hinduism, Islam, Jainism, Sikhism, etc.), or give terms that define it (transcendence, community, supernatural beings, scriptures, etc.). Further, we tend to know what it is not. For instance, it is contrasted with "secular," and so it is distinguished from economics, philosophy, politics, and so on. However, when we start to contemplate these categories and definitions, we soon find ourselves facing a range of problems, including, but not limited to, the following:

- What about traditions like Confucianism, which look and act quite a lot like religion in many situations, but are said to be a "philosophy" or a "secular humanist tradition"?

- Some Buddhists will insist that there are no supernatural beings in their tradition—the Buddha was simply a human who came to an insight attainable by anyone.
- Religious traditions inform the way people vote, spend their money, and have been inspirational for philosophers.

Actually, the question is so problematic that some scholars suggest we should abandon the category "religion." They argue that a modern, Western, Christian (specifically European Protestant) and Enlightenment (see box 16.1) paradigm has, via a history of colonialism (see chapter 7), become a global norm. Therefore, complex aspects of culture have been distorted and misrepresented. In this chapter, we will explore criticisms of the concept "religion," look at potential defenses, and then note how and why the concept is used in this book. We will conclude with two case studies. By the end of this chapter, we will see that definitions of religion are inherently political, and often hide more than they reveal.

HISTORICIZING RELIGION

We begin by looking at some of the deep problems with the term and concept "religion" through six main themes.

THE PROBLEM OF TRANSLATION

In 1962, Wilfred Cantwell Smith (1916–2000) argued that the concept of religion as we know it is a modern English (or, more broadly, Western) notion which does not occur in other languages or historical contexts.[1] The origins of the term are very different from current conceptions (see box 1.1). Typically, "religion(s)" today signifies a range of traditions found throughout the world which share many similar features. This, it has been argued, distorts our view of the world and history.

One way "religion" distorts is when we translate words into English. The Indian term "*dharma*" is often translated as "religion." However, the most common usage is closer to "duty." Traditionally, in India, people were born into a specific caste (see box 4.6) which defined their occupation, so you might come from a family of butchers, weavers, warriors, or priests. To fulfil your *dharma* is to live out your caste station. Moreover, British colonial officials in India found what they saw as the distinct questions of religion and caste conflated and struggled to understand the connections. Another usage of the term *dharma* is "tradition," or "teaching lineage." One could follow Shankaradharma (Shankara's tradition) or Ramanujadharma (Ramanuja's tradition), but the meaning still differs from the English "religion." Both traditions are classed as Hindu today. This list does not exhaust *Dharma*'s numerous meanings.[2] Rendering it as "religion" is problematic.

THE ETYMOLOGY OF RELIGION

Religion stems from the Latin *religio*, for which we have two different etymologies. The most commonly known is that of Lactantius (ca. 250–325 CE), who claimed it came from *religere* meaning "to yoke" or "to bind." For Lactantius, it was the bond between the human and (the Christian) God. However, Lactantius's etymology tried to replace an older one from Cicero (106–43 BCE). For Cicero, *religio* came from *relegere*, meaning to "retrace" or "reread." It was about repeating or continuing the rites of your ancestors. Religion was therefore about following the customs of your community, family, and particular location. In Cicero's understanding, *religio* was:

- tolerant—each has their own (the only limit is non-interference with civic duties);
- pluralistic—there can never be only one religio (variation is inevitable);
- ritualistic—it concerns practices and homage; and
- human—it involves rituals developed by your ancestors.

In Lactantius's conception, by contrast, *religio* was:

- intolerant—there is one true religion, and others must therefore be false;
- exclusive—truth is singular;
- faith-centric—belief rather than ritual is key; and
- divine—it is not a human product.

We cannot draw a straight line from Lactantius to all forms of Christianity (some are pluralistic and tolerant or very focused on ritual). Nevertheless, Lactantius's definition laid important foundations that still shape Western thinking. Moreover, the etymology is political, not descriptive. Using anachronistic language, Cicero's *religio* meant Christians were "atheists": they lacked a tradition; they did not accept the pluralism of *religio*; and their tradition disrupted civic duties, that is, they would not worship the emperor. Lactantius's definition was therefore not a simple description, but an agenda to make Christianity not just acceptable as *religio*, but to be *religio*.[1]

---

1 See S. N. Balagangadhara, *"The Heathen in His Blindness": Asia, the West and the Dynamic of Religion* (Leiden: Brill, 1994).

Likewise, the Arabic *"deen"* is often translated as "religion," but looking at how this is translated in Quran 5.3 will show why this is problematic:[3]

This day I have perfected your *religion* [*deen*] for you, completed My favour to you. I have chosen *Islam* [*islam*] to be your *faith* [*deen*].[4]

This standard modern translation suggests that there is a specific religious tradition called "Islam," translating *deen* as "religion" and "faith" (we often assume religions need faith), and treating "Islam" as a noun. However, in Arabic, *deen* signifies "custom" or "judgment." Therefore, following Arabic usage, we can adjust the translation as follows:

> This day I have perfected your *customs* [*deen*] for you, completed My favour to you. I have chosen *submission* [*islam*] to be your *behaviour* [*deen*].[5]

This rendering looks both at what *deen* and *islam* mean in Arabic, translating the latter literally as "submission" (see box 13.2). Hence rather than naming a particular religious tradition, Islam, it gives a traditional Arabic and Islamic understanding of *"islam"* as submission (to the will of God). The emphasis is on the practices and behavior rather than adhering to a specific named religion and its tenets of faith.

When we find near equivalents to "religion," like the Chinese *zongjiao*, we find a modern term created to provide an equivalent to Western usage (see box 1.2 and case study 1A).

THE NAMING AND CLASSIFICATION OF TRADITIONS

The names by which we know most religious traditions have been imposed by Western scholars and classifiers. The consequences of this vary. For instance, the English term "Confucianism" replaces the Chinese *"rujiao,"* or "the tradition of the scholars." Confucians never saw Confucius as the founder of their tradition; his significance is in editing and codifying a more ancient textual tradition (the *ru*/scholar's tradition). Hence this name misrepresents Confucianism by implying he is the founder.[6] What we call "Buddhism" may variously have been termed "*buddhadharma*" in India or "*fojiao*" in China. Both, more or less literally, mean "Buddha tradition/teachings." It is therefore not as misleading as Confucianism, though the "-ism" stresses ideology more than practice or lineage transmission. Islam, W. C. Smith claimed, is the only tradition which we describe by its own self-designation. However, in English, it becomes a distinct tradition rather than those submitting to God's will (see box 13.2). The most widely discussed naming as alleged creation is Hinduism (see case study 7A). "Hindu" originally indicated the land beyond the Indus (River). In time, it came to refer to the people and culture of South Asia, then finally the "religion" of the region: Hinduism. Indeed, Sikhism, Jainism, Buddhism, and tribal traditions have been included under the label of Hinduism. Let us reflect on how significant this is: we do not see natural divisions between religions, such that it is obvious that something is one and not another. Playing with this, Syed Farid Alatas asks us to imagine that the advance of conquests by Islamic empires over eastern Europe around the sixteenth century had not been stopped but had continued to the Rhine with subsequent conversions, and if therefore Muslims had created their own terminology to group together the "religious" traditions of western Europe in a similar way as Westerners did in India:

> The term *nahr al-rayn* [those beyond the Rhine], from which Nahraynianism, denoting the Catholic, Lutheran, Orthodox and Jewish sects of Western Eurasia, was in all likelihood employed by the Arabs to the Rhine river in northern Eurasia. . . . It was only after the arrival of the Safavid Iranians in the sixteenth century that the term Nahraynianism came to refer to those peoples of Western Eurasia, who did not convert to Shi'ism.
>
> We would be in error though to suggest, however, that there is no naturally occurring *religio* that can be designated by the term Nahrayianism. This religion consists of Catholic, Lutheran, Orthodox and Jewish sects which all trace their origins to a Hellenized rendition of the faith of Abraham. They profess belief in an immanent and yet transcendent personal God, and believe in a common set of scriptures, variously known as Torah, Talmud and Bible.[7]

Here, Alatas skillfully shows that, for outsiders (see chapter 2), the borders of traditions can be variously imagined.

THE WORLD RELIGIONS PARADIGM

Lactantius's etymology (box 1.1.) did not lead directly to our modern usage. Various twists in the story bring us to that. First, through the medieval period, *religio* denoted what we would today call "piety." With the Reformation, for the first time, *religio* could be pluralized: Catholic piety and Protestant piety (two traditions); existing diversity was often subsumed under the heading of "heresy" and so seen as intra-Christian diversity (see chapter 13). This period coincided with the beginnings of European colonialism, when, for the first time, Christian Europe came face to face with the reality of other religious traditions. In Asia and elsewhere, European Christians had to deal with people who believed very differently and could not be set into the narratives which existed.[8] Thus, from about the seventeenth century (various arguments are made for the first usage), we see the term "religion" being applied not simply to two forms of Christianity, but to a range of different traditions around the world.

The Western world was also changing. This period saw a growing split between political power and church institutions, termed "secularization" (see chapter 16). There-fore, in (northwestern) Europe and North America, a sense developed that religion was separate from politics, economics, philosophy, and other spheres; it concerned the private realm—the beliefs and personal convictions of individuals.

Thus a range of factors and impulses gave rise to what, by the nineteenth century, can be spoken of as the "world religions paradigm" (WRP), which dominates the way we think about religion today.[9] Some key points of the WRP can be noted:

- There are a range of different religions which are essentially subspecies of a common genus.
- They share facets in common, typically scriptures, founders, beliefs, rituals, institutional organizations, and a priesthood.
- They concern personal belief and the private sphere, and do not (properly) concern politics, economics, and so forth.

There are many problems with these assumptions. For instance, Islam's religious elite (*ulama*) are legal scholars more than "priests," while "scripture" is not central to all religions (see box 1.3). Nevertheless, the WRP is powerfully influential: it is normally what is taught in schools and universities;[10] it determines how politicians, media commentators, community leaders, and religious leaders speak of "religion." It is simply how most of us are conditioned to think about the concept as a "natural" part of the world (see chapter 5).

THE SUI GENERIS AND EMPTY SIGNIFIER ISSUES

Rudolf Otto (1869–1937) and Mircea Eliade (1907–1986) both believed there was a distinctive religious experience or sphere (see box 8.5). This, they held, was separate from any other aspect of human culture or experience and so unique, or sui generis (see box 1.4). Otto wrote a book called *The Idea of the Holy* (*Das Heilige* in the original German), which set out to describe the nature of religious experience.[11] Eliade sought to identify common patterns of religious experience and narrative across cultures, and spoke of humanity as *homo religiosus* ("the religious human"), meaning that religious sentiment is innate.[12] For both, there was a clearly identifiable arena of religion (including experience and symbols) which could be isolated and studied apart from other spheres of human

DO ALL RELIGIONS HAVE SCRIPTURE?

Saying that all religions have "scripture" is common, but it is a problem (see chapter 11):

- Scripture typically denotes texts considered to be divine revelation. But Confucians claim their texts are human products, while "revelation" is understood very differently between traditions (see box 11.4).
- We often assume, based on a Protestant dynamic, that scriptures define the norms of a religion or are the foundational source. But early Buddhists believed that real knowledge had to be passed person to person. Written texts were considered inadequate or secondary. However, around the second century BCE, a major famine in Sri Lanka made many fear that the oral record would be lost because so many monks were dying. The texts, originally a temporary measure, became central only later.
- We assume that all religions have texts. But Australian Aborigines and others do not, yet are among those we typically define as having a "religion."

WHAT IS A SUI GENERIS CATEGORY?

"Sui generis" derives from the Latin term meaning "of its own kind." It refers to something of a distinct type, not reliant on anything else. To speak of religion, or religious experience, as sui generis suggests it is distinct from other areas of life or other experiences. However, it is hard to see how those traditions we call religious are distinct from the arenas of politics, culture more broadly, philosophy, and many other areas. Even religious experiences are not clearly distinct (see box 8.5).

culture. However, critics have noted that, far from being clear and distinct, we actually find we cannot clearly locate religion as a phenomenon. There is an unclear border between what is and what is not religion.

If we say religion needs a god (or gods), we exclude some forms of Buddhism, as well as traditions which see the divine as some transcendent impersonal reality. When we talk of a supernatural or transcendent category, it is unclear what this may mean: if we describe it as something outside the general physical world which cannot be seen, touched, or experienced normally, then Marxist claims about the force of history as leading us toward the inevitable victory of the proletariat may fit as a nonphenomenal claim. Again, capitalism informs us that we must let the economy be run by "market forces," which are an unseen, untouchable force (see box 8.3). Whether we regard Marxism or capitalism as religions, they arguably have religious elements (though we are yet to define what "religious" is). It is hard to define religion in a way that distinguishes it from other worldviews, unless we have sharply prescriptive borders—which cause their own problems, as just noted with Buddhism.[13] Maybe we should not try?

Such problems lead to the argument that "religion" is variously filled with so many meanings that it is in effect completely meaningless. It has been termed an "empty signifier" (see box 9.11),[14] used here to imply a word which means almost whatever the user wants, with McCutcheon even asking, "What might not also be called religion if soccer is?"[15] Is Buddhism a religion? You can answer yes or no. Is Marxism a religion? You can answer yes or no. Even if we ask if Christianity is a religion, people can answer yes or no: some Christians claim that Christianity is "revelation" or a "relationship." Does any definition of religion do more than tell us about the cultural expectations or agenda of the person using the word? "Religion" is a "shifting signifier" (see box 9.11), a term that is part of wider networks of meaning, but certain critics of religion arguably neglect that this is true of almost all terms, and fail to see the problems when this one term is singled out; this is discussed further below.

THE SECULAR-RELIGIOUS DIVIDE

If you lived in fourteenth-century England, you would not see the distinction we make today between "religion" and the "secular." Monarchs ruled by a God-given right combining religious and political legitimacy. In imperial China, the emperor was the Son of Heaven, ruling under the Mandate of Heaven (*tianming*). In almost every traditional society, those things we term religion and politics have been coterminous. Only around the eighteenth century, in northwestern Europe and North America, did the conception arise that we could separate these two. This brief survey is just a rough guide to issues we explore elsewhere (see chapter 16). However, we can note some key points:

- Applied historically, speaking of two "natural" realms of the religious and secular is anachronistic, and separates the thought world of the people examined. It provides a problem when we look at many contemporary contexts, too.
- Many conceptual terms which we use to classify the contemporary world gained their current meanings over the last few centuries.[16] As such, words like "politics," "economics," "religion," and "secular" only make sense because we have divided the world into arbitrary, or culturally specific, boxes.
- To some extent, calling one area of life "religious" only makes sense because we call another area "secular" (see chapter 16), but these distinctions are always social and contingent rather than "natural" (see chapter 5).

THE POLITICS OF THE WORD

"Religion" has been employed politically in many ways. Today, the status of being a religion often grants a tradition/community various benefits such as tax breaks, charitable status,

WHAT IS A CULT, OR *XIEJIAO*?

Max Weber (1864–1920) described a cult as a religion which was newly founded and seeking its place in society. However, this is not an adequate definition, leading to a joke among historians of religion: "What is the difference between a cult and a religion?" Answer: "About 100 years." While "cult" is used among scholars of religion to refer to specific practices of devotion within a religion—for instance in Christianity there is the cult of the Virgin Mary, and Mahayana Buddhists have the cult of Guanyin (see box 2.9)—its popular usage is pejorative. In the media it refers to a religion that people do not approve of, often newly formed ones, or what scholars might call "new religious movements." In this sense, the Chinese government translates an indigenous term, *xiejiao*, as "evil cult," especially to refer to traditions such as Falun Gong (see case study 1A). The term is also variously translated as "cult," "evil religion," or "heterodox tradition."

Xiejiao goes back to the Ming Dynasty (1368–1644) to identify "unacceptable traditions." The Chinese characters are *xie*, meaning "false," "erroneous," "unorthodox"; and *jiao*, meaning "tradition/teaching." Decisions as to what is xiejiao, that is, "heterodoxy/heresy," are not normally theological, and the classification has been the government's prerogative. The main criterion is a group that threatens public order. Historically, one primary use was for White Lotus Societies, anti–Qing Dynasty (1644–1912) revolutionaries. It was the revolutionary character of such movements that marked them as xiejiao. However, the decision lay with the Ministry of Rites and nearly always included discussion of erroneous beliefs and practices. The White Lotus Societies tended to be apocalyptic or messianic movements, that is, they spoke of the end of the world and/or proclaimed a coming savior figure. We are hard-pressed to find a xiejiao which is not also "religious." Notably, Christianity was declared a xiejiao in the eighteenth century; see case study 1B.

protection under the law, and so on. Contrarily, denying the category religion can stigmatize or delegitimize a tradition, as do such terms as "superstition," "magic" (see boxes 7.8, 9.4, and 12.2), and "cult" (see box 1.5). To most people, these may seem distinct from religion; however, the dividing lines are somewhat arbitrary (see case studies 1A and 7B).

"Religion" is so loaded politically that some scholars suggest we should only study how it is used, but never use it, because scholars cannot control how it is used to advantage or disadvantage certain groups and so should not be so presumptuous as to say what it "really means"; further, it is argued, the word carries rewards or punishments in society so it is not responsible for scholars to use it.[17] Certainly, religion's definition is not simply academic, but (like many other terms) is debated by politicians, lawyers, religious groups, and others. Indeed, the legal questions are often primary (see case study 1A). Human rights declarations and laws enshrine freedom of religion and belief as a fundamental right (see chapter 16). Often courts arbitrate what is classified as a religion. Considerations include whether the group/tradition calls itself a "religion (legally speaking, "subjective criteria") and whether it has such things as doctrines, rituals, or scripture (legally speaking, "objective criteria"). The latter often maps onto the WRP, though increasingly courts are taking notice of scholarly arguments about the flaws of this approach.

CAN WE SPEAK OF RELIGION TODAY?
HARD AND SOFT DECONSTRUCTION

W. C. Smith suggested we abandon the term "religion," arguing we should use "faith" for the internal aspects and "cumulative tradition" for the external factors.[18] But Jonathan Z. Smith (1938–2017) argued: "Religion is solely the creation of the scholar's study. It is created for the scholar's analytic purposes by his imaginative acts of comparison and generalization."[19] In other words, not just the term but the very concept is a problem. This may result in a "hard deconstructivist" stance:[20] the manifold problems with religion are held to prove it is biased, distorted, and not analytically useful.[21] However, we could argue for a "soft deconstructivist" stance: this accepts the historicizing project (all words have a history), but sees problems with the wholesale rejection of the term. This may not involve rebuttals of the points above, but may add a deeper scholarly analysis. Moreover, while there are costs to using "religion," there are also benefits, which will be shown below, but in brief: it helps us speak about a historically and cross-culturally recognized, and recurring, social reality and aspect of human culture that critics try and fill with often more problematic terms, especially when looking at contemporary society, because we find a legal, social, and political entity. So, we can contest how it is constructed, but cannot deny its social reality (see box 1.9). (The terms "hard" and "soft" "deconstructivist" stances are used here for convenience; it is not how those in the disputes typically self-identify.)

THE HISTORICAL DATA FOR RELIGION

Part of the hard deconstructivist argument is that only modern Western scholars have bracketed together those traditions we today call religions. Certainly, at no other time in history could we have classified quite the same group of traditions together in the way we do. However, those things we today call religions have been relating to each other in ways that suggest they recognized some similarities:

- Buddhist monks and Catholic priests in sixteenth- to seventeenth-century Thailand recognized each other as inhabiting similar territory (as religious specialists).[22]
- When Muslims traveled eastward across Asia, they debated whether Zoroastrians, Hindus, and Buddhists should be included in the category of

"People of the Book" (*ahl al-kitab*), which would put them in the same group as Christians and Jews (see box 13.2).

· Buddhists arriving in China from India (via Central Asia) had the most heated contestations with Daoists, and related debates with Confucians.

Historically, those traditions which today are grouped together as religions have, for centuries, been in contestation and debate due to recognition of similarities. Rhetorically we can ask:

· Why did Christian missionaries in Thailand not relate to fishermen as their closest rivals?
· Why did Muslims arriving in India not classify hairdressers as People of the Book?
· Why did Buddhists going to China not set up in opposition to the postal service?

Grouping some things as religious traditions is not simply a bizarre facet of the modern scholarly imagination; it is not entirely arbitrary. Of course, this does not show it is a sui generis category. Nevertheless, we can meaningfully say that throughout history those things we tend to think of as religions have engaged in ways which suggest recognition of similarity, even if this was sometimes apologetically to deny that others are truly religions.

ESSENTIALLY CONTESTED CONCEPTS

Walter Gallie (1912–1998) noticed that some words cannot be adequately defined: there may be disagreements about what fits into a category; particular historical trajectories mean a word has a certain employment which does not fit other contexts; or we simply cannot agree on a definition. Gallie noted this applied to "art," "social justice," "democracy," and "Christianity." Many of these terms are deeply political, with society rewarding some and neglecting others; for instance, who defines what is "high" art and so displayed in certain galleries? Are the works of indigenous tribes "art" in the same way that Italian Renaissance paintings are considered to be art?

Gallie developed the notion of "essentially contested concepts" to refer to terms for which we cannot find universally agreed meanings. It can be argued that "religion" is an essentially contested concept.[23] Importantly, Gallie's point is that we do not abandon words simply because we cannot agree how to use them or what they mean. This is the nature of language. Critics of religion often seem to assume that it is a uniquely bad word, but it is arguably no worse than, for example, democracy. Athenian democracy is often claimed as a foundation of our modern systems, but neither women nor slaves could vote. Today, in many countries, powerful media moguls and online news outlets, alongside lobbyists from special interest groups and industry, can sway voters and elected politicians and so subvert elections. What counts as a democracy?

RELIGION AND CULTURE

The distinction between "religion" and "culture" is a commonplace. It normally distinguishes between "religion" as the supposed core elements of a tradition, with "culture" as localized, or nonessential, customs or beliefs. It may distinguish between terms seen within a social order as signifying something "religious" ("worship"), and those which are "non-religious" ("veneration") (see case study 1B). However, it is not an academic distinction. Every religious tradition involves interpretation, and what at any place or time may be considered the (changeable) "cultural" aspects, may elsewhere be seen as "religious" (unchangeable); varying religious authorities debate what falls into each category.

Notably, some scholars suggest that because "religion" is an empty signifier it should be replaced by "culture," arguing "religion" is only an arbitrarily defined aspect of culture.[1] However, our modern English usage of "culture," which developed in the nineteenth century, is also embedded in the modern Western social order. It can be critiqued in ways similar to religion, as scholars in cultural studies have long noted.[2] While some scholars today define "culture" as those aspects of human life which are not biologically determined, this is not analytic. For one thing, it encapsulates almost every conceivable activity that we (and many primates and other animals) engage in, and hence does not help us understand things better. For another, the distinction between what is and is not biologically given is contested and unstable, so while language would be seen as part of "culture" in these terms, it is also clear that humans have an inbuilt propensity to learn languages, thus problematizing this binary.

---

1 McCutcheon, *Manufacturing Religion*.

2 See John Baldwin, Sandra Faulkner, and Michael Hecht, "A Moving Target: The Illusive Definition of Culture," in *Redefining Culture: Perspectives across the Disciplines*, ed. John Baldwin, Sandra Faulkner, Michael Hecht, and Sheryl Lindsley (Mahwah, NJ: Erlbaum, 2006); and Chris Barker, *The Sage Dictionary of Cultural Studies* (London: Sage, 2004).

Particular terms/spheres where "religion" overlaps or intersects include philosophy, literature, art, politics, culture, and economics—themselves also essentially contested concepts. Sometimes particular work is done by making such distinctions, notably between "religion" and "culture" (see box 1.6). Gallie made an insightful point: essentially contested terms must be meaningful; that is, we are better off with the term than without it. Does this apply to religion?

THE PROBLEM OF TRANSLATION

W. C. Smith was right that other languages do not (traditionally) have words that match the modern English "religion." However, we are mistaken if we assume that most words have a one-to-one correspondence. Even with something as basic as color, this is not the case. Some languages have a variety of words signifying different colors for what in English we would see as different shades of green (see introduction); indeed, it seems that partly because of this people from those cultures can spot and recognize differences that native English speakers cannot: language does make us see the world differently.[24] That the English "religion" does not map exactly onto a single word in other languages is therefore not actually surprising or significant.

We discussed above how *dharma, deen,* and *zongjiao* are often translated into English as "religion," and noted the confusion this can cause. However, this does not mean that they are entirely unrelated. Words such as "pain," "suffering," "anguish," or "hurt" do not necessarily match directly onto words in another language, but this does not mean that only English speakers know what pain is (see box 1.7).

The lack of exact terms does not mean that translation can never occur: how else could Chinese people read Shakespeare's *Romeo and Juliet,* or English speakers read Sun Zi's *Art of War?* Hans-Georg Gadamer (1900–2002) and Paul Ricoeur (1913–2005) have theorized what they term the problem or "agony" of translation; while difficult, and generally never capable of one-to-one transference, translation does and can happen in both theory and practice (see introduction).[25] We must always beware of what is lost or hidden, though, when we translate. Critics of religion discuss its problems as somehow uniquely bad, or the only word we have trouble translating. Many words, certainly concepts, such as philosophy, politics, or slavery (see box 1.8), have no equivalents in some languages.

Of course, we are not simply translating words. Cultural systems are embedded into networks of linguistic meanings. We noted a problem with assuming *dharma* meant religion. Likewise, when we call Shinto a religion, what do we fail to see in that tradition if we assume that our notion of religion encapsulates what it means and what it entails in a Japanese context?[26]

Religion has a specific history and ideology that has arisen in a Western (mainly Protestant) Christian context in the transition into what is generally known as secular modernity. Most terminology that we use conceptually, when speaking English, has the same heritage. It is not a neutral description of the way the world is. Michel Foucault

BOX 1.8 **WERE THERE SLAVES IN ANCIENT GREECE?**

Ancient Greek had no word that directly relates to the modern English "slave," nor did it have a concept that equates to "slavery." Does this mean there were no slaves? Those people we speak of as slaves were treated in other linguistic ways.[1] We could say that

- they had no word for it and so it did not exist;
- it is a meaningless concept applied to their world; or
- we have named a conception, which they spoke of differently, but still has a useful application in that context.

To say a word can only be used in the context it arose, or only means what it originally meant when it was created, is what philosophers term the "etymological fallacy" (see box 11.2).

---

1 See Giorgio Agamben, *The Use of Bodies,* trans. Adam Kotso (Stanford: Stanford University Press, 2015).

(1926–1984) is generally credited with the insight that all language and classification is political: we shape that which is other than us into boxes which we have made. This insight means we must be aware of the problems of all our language and classifications. If we use the terminology and theory, we must do so with caution and an awareness of its limitations.

THE CATEGORY OF THE RELIGIOUS

When we quoted J. Z. Smith, above, we missed his first line: "There is a staggering amount of data, of phenomena, of human experiences and expressions that might be characterized in one culture or another, by one criterion or another, as religious."[27] He argues we can speak about things which are "religious" but we have problems when we speak about "religions," because we assume they fit the WRP. Likewise, Timothy Fitzgerald suggested that we should get rid of "religion" and instead use "sacred" to speak about the same spheres of culture.[28] We see here a fissure in the hard deconstructivist argument: how to speak of those areas where we historically see "religions." One cannot argue that "religion" should be abandoned as a term, but then agree that temples and post offices are clearly different in ways that invoke "religious" language to clarify this. It is a word that helps us, as Jeppe Sinding Jensen says: "It [religion] is a handy term, one that helps getting a grip on complex ideas, one could call it an 'epistemic placeholder.'"[29] To introduce an idea I develop elsewhere, we can distinguish between analytic categories and descriptive categories.[30] While religion may not be a higher-order analytic category (something which we can classify as a discrete class in its own right), this does not mean it is not a definitional category (a subcategory of an analytical category which helps us clarify between specifically delineated concepts). Indeed, descriptive categories remain analytically useful by helping us see things more clearly. In relation to religion, the concept of the sacred (in its sociological usage; see chapter 18, especially box 18.7, as concepts to which we apply absolute value) is an analytical category, with such things (when invested with absolute value) as religion, nationalism, Marxism, human rights, and so on, being definitional categories within its remit. Though one could also suggest that if culture were taken as an analytic category (notwithstanding the issues noted in box 1.6 of its overly broad usage), then religion could be a definitional category that assists us in narrowing that down for analytic purposes.

Indeed, many scholars who criticize the WRP do not abandon religion. Talal Asad, Tomoko Masuzawa, Richard King, and others have spoken powerfully about the problem of "religion" but suggest we can use it strategically, or at least do not advocate its total abandonment. Moreover, other scholars offer powerful arguments about how we can meaningfully employ religion:

- Martin Riesebrodt (1948–2014) argues that the theme of salvation provides an analytically powerful tool to conceptualize religion.[31]
- Gavin Flood has undertaken very sophisticated comparative studies of patterns across religions (see chapter 11).[32]
- The cognitive science of religion strongly indicates that, at a species level, commonalities which relate to "religion" exist (see chapter 8).

EPISTEMOLOGY: OR, HOW DO WE KNOW ANYTHING?

Our final issue concerns the way we know things (epistemology). This may seem obscure, but Kevin Schilbrack has shown that the hard deconstructivist stance often relies on a particular form of "non-realism" (see box 5.8).[33] Roughly, this version of non-realism contends that all meaning is linguistic and contingent; if everything is only linguistic, "religion" cannot relate directly to any reality outside of discourse. Schilbrack, however, argues that this hard deconstructivist stance misconstrues the arguments.[34] This debate is tackled elsewhere in this book (see, primarily, introduction, box 5.8, and chapters 2, 5, 8, and 9), but some points can be noted briefly. This text employs a critical hermeneutical phenomenology holding that while religion is a social construction, it is not entirely arbitrary because it is part of wider cultural forms related to human embodiment and materiality. Further, "religion" *exists* in human social and cultural worlds as a social reality (see box 1.9).

SPEAKING OF RELIGION?

Having looked at the arguments, we need to decide whether we can still employ the term "religion." While readers must decide for themselves, we note below six reasons why, and how, the term "religion" is employed throughout this book:

1. There are traditions around the world which have, historically and in the contemporary context, related as somewhat similar domains. These we will term "religions," but we do not apply a WRP approach assuming commonality of function, organization, or modes of behavior. Religion is simply a useful classifier and an essentially contested concept.

2. There seems to be a realm of "culture" we can usefully speak of as "religious." This broadly indicates realms of thought, life, and interaction that deal with what may be broadly termed "transcendence" (see box 1.10).

3. What we call religion is not a separate sphere from philosophy, politics, economics, art, or even the secular. These realms, which we can usefully distinguish for strategic purposes (as definitional categories), overlap and are not static.

4. We must stay alert to what is hidden when we employ the term "religion." It will conjure certain things to our mind, not other things.

5. We must never forget that "religion" is not a neutral descriptor. No word is. The very fact that our discussion of the term is in English shapes the arguments, how we frame those arguments, and even how we think (see chapters 2 and 7, and box 18.1).

6. As our concern is contemporary "religion" in society, many traditions claim and relate to this label today, while it is also a political and legal reality. Traditions are, or have become, "religions" in multiple ways.

· · ·

TRANSCENDENCE/TRANSCENDENT

"Transcendence" here refers to concepts/beings/spheres/posited realities which are seen as beyond the phenomenal/physical world. These transcendent referents may be diverse and do not clearly relate to any unifying concept. Traditions which relate to transcendence are commonly termed "religions." However, they are not clearly demarcated from certain supposedly "secular" systems. For instance, Marxism, capitalism, and other worldviews may posit nonphysical realities (see box 8.3). "Religion" is not the only term that can usefully speak of such traditions.

Importantly, this use of "transcendence" does not imply that whatever is referred to either exists or is "transcendent" ontologically (i.e., actually above, beyond, or outside the world). Furthermore, it is not, in some terminology, distinct from "immanence" (i.e., claims that the "divine" is within the world or the self). "Transcendence" should be read simply as a signifying marker of the claims noted. Whether the claim is that there is an all-powerful (omnipotent) creator deity, that trees are our ancestors, that "supernatural" powers/forces within the world direct our lives, or whatever else, all are here captured by transcendence as a conceptual category.

CASE STUDY 1A. FALUN GONG: RELIGION OR SELF-CULTIVATION PRACTICE?

Falun Gong (or Falun Dafa) is a Chinese tradition that teaches a form of *qigong* (often Chi Gung), slow rhythmic movements designed to promote physical and moral well-being. It was suppressed by the Chinese government as an "evil cult." While the suppression is often framed, by Western commentators, as violating freedom of religion and belief, Falun Gong members normally do not accept that they are a religion, preferring the term "self-cultivation tradition."

WHAT IS FALUN GONG?

In the 1980s, the Chinese government started promoting scientific investigations into the health benefits of *qigong*. This resulted in a huge upsurge, which the Chinese media termed "*qigong* fever." Falun Gong, founded by Li Hongzhi in 1994, became perhaps the largest of the *qigong* movements. As for the name:

· *Falun* alludes to Buddhist teachings.
· *Gong* signifies "hard work" or "practice."
· *Dafa* means "great law."

Therefore, Falun Gong/Dafa refers to the practice/effort of cultivating spiritual laws or truths.

As Li's following grew, he emphasized moral development over health practice, but both were integral. His teachings drew from Buddhism, Daoism, folk religion, and *qigong*. It involved reincarnation and a cosmic worldview with buddhas, daos, and gods as teachers, but Li himself was the greatest teacher. The Chinese government became framed as an evil spirit when it started to suppress Falun Gong. The central ideas can be found in Li's main book, *Zhuan Falun* (*Revolving Dharma Wheel*).

THE POLITICAL CONTEXT

By the late 1990s, the Chinese government had started suppressing *qigong* fever for promoting "superstition." Support changed to derision. Falun Gong was often singled out for attack, with events coming to a head in 1999. In response to a critical TV program in the city of Tianjin, Falun Gong protesters demanded an apology at the TV station. This was a fairly well-known routine, a demand for an apology was met with one, and both sides were satisfied. However, this time, police beat back the protesters. Seeking recompense, it seems the Falun Gong protesters were told to appeal to the central government in Beijing. What happened next changed everything.

Rather than a small protest, ten thousand members of the movement sat in silent meditation outside the central government headquarters, just next to Tiananmen Square. They were probably met by Premier Zhu Rongji, who told them that their complaints would be dealt with, and they dispersed. However, shortly afterward, President Jiang Zemin issued an announcement calling Falun Gong an "evil cult," outlawing the movement. Many members were arrested and sent to prison or labor camps for "deconversion." There are also allegations of torture. From a huge movement, with more members than the Communist Party, it declined.

Falun Gong members protested the suppression, while the world press took up their cause. Notably, one alleged Falun Gong protest involved seven members who attempted self-immolation in 2001. It is not clear whether they were Falun Gong practitioners, or whether this event had any sanction from leaders, but it marked a turning point in perceptions of Falun Gong from being an unfairly suppressed group to being a movement that was radical and dangerous.[35]

TERMINOLOGY AND THE CHINESE CONTEXT

Falun Gong members do not normally claim they belong to a religion, preferring "self-cultivation practice." This is partly because, in China, religion (*zongjiao*) refers to five specific traditions (see box 1.2). Moreover, *zongjiao* does not denote "self-cultivation practice," which signifies activities such as *qigong* and Tai Chi—simplified and popularized practices derived from Daoist practices of biospiritual cultivation ("internal alchemy").[36] All are based in Chinese cosmology, which is linked to this concept of self-cultivation (see box 1.11). Therefore, calling something a self-cultivation practice is not

CHINESE COSMOLOGY AND SELF-CULTIVATION

Chinese cosmology makes no distinction between the body and the soul/spirit. Rather, the self is seen as a microcosm of the universe, and so physical techniques are seen as capable of helping to purify/align the self with the universal Way (*Dao*). In Chinese thought, the whole cosmos (physical, mental, and spiritual) is composed of the same "stuff": psychospiritual matter (*qi,* often translated as "breath"). The "spiritual" is simply more refined *qi;* "matter" is less refined *qi.* Indeed, ethics is related to this. Having pure *qi* relates to good moral character, and darkened *qi* indicates the opposite.[1] Therefore, self-cultivation practice denotes things we perhaps would not normally see as part of a religion: physical practice and health (but linked to spirituality and morality); not being necessarily tied to beliefs or doctrines (though rooted in concepts of *qi* and a wider cosmological schema); martial arts practice (e.g., Tai Chi or Kung Fu). Given the connection of body and spiritual transformation in Chinese thought, the practices discussed here are sometimes termed "biospiritual cultivation" in English. "Self-cultivation" can refer to a variety of practices which may be more focused upon bodily movements and health practices to those more focused on meditation. In general, they are simplified forms of originally Daoist practices of "internal alchemy" (*neidan*), which from around the eighteenth century became taught in practices and lineages beyond Daoist traditions.[2]

---

1 See Paul Hedges, "China," in *Religion and Everyday Life and Culture,* ed. Richard Hecht and Vincent Biondo, vol. 1 (Santa Barbara: Praeger, 2010): 45–82, 47–48.

2 See Vincent Goosaert, "Daoists in the Modern Chinese Self-Cultivation Market: The Case of Beijing, 1850–1949," in *Daoism in the 20th Century: Between Eternity and Modernity,* ed. David Palmer and Liu Xun (Berkeley: California University Press, 2012): 123–53.

simply a different classification, but presupposes a very different form of practice and activity. The fundamental assumptions of self-cultivation are very different from those of the WRP.

Once suppressed, Falun Gong was referred to as an "evil cult," or *xiejiao* (see box 1.5), which put it in the category of a public order concern. Benjamin Penny has argued that Falun Gong fits our typical conception of a "religion," as it:[37]

- draws from Daoism, Buddhism, and Chinese folk religion;
- has a pantheon of deities and supernatural beings;
- involves belief in reincarnation and the laws of *karma* (retribution in future lives for bad deeds, and reward for good);
- portrays a cosmic battle between good and evil;
- has some form of "salvation" offered through Li and the practice of Falun Gong;

- has a form of scripture;
- has a messianic teacher (Li); and
- has an organization with various levels or initiations.

THE POLITICAL AND LEGAL CASE

While Falun Gong is a *xiejiao* in China by government decree, elsewhere courts have had to determine whether it is a religion. Two Asian jurisdictions with comparable traditions of law, Hong Kong and Singapore (due to colonialism, their systems evolved from British Common Law), have reached different conclusions. The Hong Kong Court of First Instance in Chu Woan Chyi v. Director of Immigration considered the question. In the ruling, Judge Hartmann noted that although described as "a spiritual movement" by "practitioners," they "do not classify it as a 'religion'"; the judge looked to guidelines from an Australian High Court case:

> One of the more important indicia of "a religion" involves belief in the supernatural . . . that really extends beyond that which is capable of perception by the sense . . . . Another is that the ideas relate to man's nature and place in the universe and his relation to things supernatural. A third is that the ideas are accepted by adherents as requiring or encouraging them to observe particular standards or codes of conduct or to participate in specific practices having supernatural significance. A fourth is that . . . adherents . . . constitute an identifiable group or identifiable groups.[38]

Weighting "objective" over "subjective" criteria, Hartmann decided that Falun Gong was a religion, giving it legal protections in Hong Kong. In the Singapore High Court, in Ng Chye Huay v. PP, the "subjective" criteria of the self-declaration of Falun Gong was given greater weight. Therefore, in Singapore, Falun Gong is, legally speaking, not a religion but a self-cultivation practice. A different outcome was reached in each case even though the same legal standards were applied.

REFLECTION

Some questions can help us think through these issues:

1. If you were an advocate of Falun Gong, would you want to speak about it as a religion or not? Think about what consequences and meanings would follow from this, for yourself and others, in your country and globally.
2. Considering the legal disagreements, would you favor the approach taken by Hong Kong or Singapore? Why?
3. Are there analytic benefits in calling Falun Gong a religion? What aspects of the practice, belief, behavior, or nature of it and its followers are likely to be brought out or hidden? How convinced are you by Penny's characterization?

4. Does the concept of "self-cultivation practice" provide an alternative to "religion"? Could we imagine other traditions in this way? Try using the concept of "self-cultivation practice" to classify Buddhism or Christianity (or another "religion"; see box 9.6). See what aspects of the tradition are highlighted or hidden.

CASE STUDY 1B. CHRISTIANS AND ANCESTOR VENERATION: RELIGION OR CULTURE?

One common distinction is between "religion" and "culture" (see box 1.6). To consider this distinction, we discuss ways that Christians in Asia have made sense of ancestral sacrifices, something that tears families apart both in the past and today.

BEING A FAITHFUL CHILD AND ANCESTRAL VENERATION

Across much of Asia, a fundamental virtue is filial piety—the respect a child owes to their parents. Because the parent gave life to the child, sons and daughters should be obedient, and do their utmost to repay the debt of life. This is linked to ancestor veneration—performing sacrifices and rituals to remember and honor parents, grandparents, and significant forebears.[39] The question of whether a convert to Christianity can engage in ancestral sacrifices has serious social and personal implications. A child who refuses to engage in such rites can be disowned by their parents and families. To not perform them is to disrespect parents, family, and essentially the whole culture.

While ancestor veneration is often linked to Confucianism, it is a common part of East Asian religiosity. Confucian texts merely codified various practices, especially those related to imperial ancestral rites.

CHRISTIANS MEET THE ANCESTORS

Depending on where you are, and what form of Christianity, Christians in Asia may or may not practice ancestral veneration. A key factor is whether the practice is seen as "religious" or "cultural." In Christian theological terms, the debate concerns "worship" and "veneration."

- Worship assumes ancestors are seen as supernatural entities, even deities, capable of responding to intercessions or punishing those who do not make the correct sacrifices. For Christians, worship can only be offered to God.
- Veneration means paying due respect to honored descendants. As respect, it can be linked to Christian veneration of saints, or simply to "honor your father and mother" (Ex. 20:12).

Matteo Ricci (1552–1610) and other Jesuit missionaries who dressed as Confucian scholars, argued that rituals to honor Confucius and the ancestors were veneration.

A Confucian ancestral shrine containing the tablet that represents the founding ancestor of the lineage, Andong, South Korea.

They made high-profile converts to Catholic Christianity at the Chinese imperial court. However, other missionaries argued the sacrifices to Confucius and ancestors were worship. To try to help mediate, Emperor Kangxi (1654–1722) wrote to the Pope explaining that these rituals were merely respect, reflecting how many elite Confucian scholars understood them. However, following reports from other missionaries of what they perceived as "worship" among ordinary people, the Pope decreed, in 1704, against the Jesuits. Vehement disputes between rival Catholic Christians led Emperor Yongzheng (1678–1735) to declare Christianity an "evil cult" (*xiejiao;* see box 1.5) in 1724. The debate still rages.

FUNERALS, INCENSE, BOWING

Differing ideas about ancestral veneration persist today.

- Many Daoists in Singapore say funerary practices such as lighting incense and bowing to ancestral tablets (small, traditionally wooden, tablets with the names of the deceased) are religious acts.
- Many Confucian lineage heads in Korea will say these acts are not religious but only cultural.

Differing and changing Christian allegiances, theologies, and locations are also important. Today, most Catholics understand ancestral sacrifices as veneration, and allow devotees to bow to ancestral tablets and use incense sticks at Buddhist or Daoist funerals to respect/venerate the dead. They see this as part of Chinese culture. Indeed, in Taiwan, Catholic funerals often resemble those of other Chinese religions, with incense sticks and ancestral tablets, although Catholic funerals in Singapore look more like Western ones. However, Protestants in Korea and Singapore tend to see lighting incense sticks or bowing to ancestral tablets as a religious act and therefore as worship, although Protestants in Hong Kong typically see it as veneration and cultural.

REFLECTIONS

We can ask various questions about this from different angles:

1. If you were a Protestant Christian from a traditional Confucian household in Korea, how would you choose between honoring your parents and family (a biblical as well as a Confucian/Korean virtue), and following your Christian tradition (your pastor says ancestral sacrifice is worship)? Think about the following: What social effects follow? Does being a Christian mean also leaving your culture and family? Put another way, is being Confucian and Christian a contradiction?

2. Do you agree that making a religion/culture divide can never be a matter of academic analysis? Is it always a theological debate? Do scholars simply report on how religious insiders (see chapter 2) make these distinctions?

.   .   .

QUESTIONS AND CONNECTING THOUGHTS

The questions raised in this chapter permeate the whole book. What we think religion is, and whether the concept is meaningful, determines how and what we study; issues further explored in chapters 2, 3, and 9. Some scholars, and perhaps some readers, will argue we should abandon religion. However, other scholars, and maybe other readers, will argue that, while imperfect, the concept can help us think about society and human activity. This book works on the basis of the latter, which is linked to various arguments we make throughout (see introduction and chapters 5, 8, and 9). Nevertheless, we should stop and think every time we see or use the word "religion." Some issues touched upon here are discussed more thoroughly elsewhere; especially notable are the themes of religion's relationship to elite, colonial, and male norms (see, respectively, chapters 3, 7, and 10), and connections to politics and the secular (chapters 18, and 16, respectively).

We conclude with some questions to help think through the issues raised:

1. Do you think we can use the category "religion" as an academic category? Why or why not?

2. How do you, or your culture/society, define religion? More particularly: Why are certain things classified as religion, and why are other things not so classified?

3. Which potentially controversial groups are classified in your country as religions? By whom and when were these decisions made? Who makes these decisions? Think about such traditions as Jediism, Scientology, yoga, Wicca, Falun Gong, ISKCON/the Hare Krishna movement, the Church of the Flying Spaghetti Monster (you can Google these if you are not familiar with them). Note: In nations there may be regional variations; for example, in the US, state courts have differing rulings on whether yoga is a religion.

4. We have raised related terms such as "cult," "magic," and "superstition" (see boxes 1.5, 7.8, 9.4, and 12.2; see also chapter 3). How, in traditions or countries you are familiar with, are divisions made between acceptable beliefs and practices (probably labeled "religion") and unacceptable ones (possibly labeled "superstitions" or "cults")?

FURTHER READING
THEORY

Fitzgerald, Timothy. *Discourse on Civility and Barbarity: A Critical History of Religion and Related Categories* (Oxford: Oxford University Press, 2007).

Flood, Gavin. *The Importance of Religion: Meaning and Action in Our Strange World* (Chichester: Wiley-Blackwell, 2012).

King, Anna, and Paul Hedges. "What Is Religion? Or What Is It We're Talking About?," in *Controversies in Contemporary Religion,* ed. Paul Hedges, vol. 1 (Santa Barbara: Praeger, 2014), 1–30.

Masuzawa, Tomoko. *The Invention of World Religions* (Chicago: Chicago University Press, 2005).

McCutcheon, Russell. *Manufacturing Religion: The Discourse on Sui Generis Religion and the Politics of Nostalgia* (Oxford: Oxford University Press, 1997).

McLeod, Sean. "Religions Are Belief Systems," in *Stereotyping Religion: Critiquing Clichés,* ed. Craig Martin and Brad Stoodart (London: Bloomsbury, 2017), 11–22.

Nongbri, Brent. *Before Religion: A History of a Modern Concept* (New Haven: Yale University Press, 2013).

Smith, Christian. *Religion: What It Is, How It Works, and Why It Matters* (Princeton: Princeton University Press, 2017).

Smith, Jonathan Z. "Religion, Religions, Religious," in *Critical Terms for Religious Studies,* ed. Mark C. Taylor (Chicago: Chicago University Press, 1998), 269–84.

Smith, Wilfred Cantwell. *The Meaning and End of Religion* (London: SPCK, 1978).

CASE STUDY 1A. FALUN GONG: RELIGION OR SELF-CULTIVATION PRACTICE?

Adams, Ryan J. T. "New Religious Movements, 'Cults,' and the State," in Hedges, *Controversies in Contemporary Religion,* vol. 3, 145–68.

Hedges, Paul. "Burning for a Cause: Four Factors in Successful Political (and Religious) Self-Immolation Examined in Relation to Alleged Falun Gong 'Fanatics' in Tiananmen Square," *Politics and Religion* 8 (2015): 797–815.

Penny, Benjamin. *The Religion of Falun Gong* (Chicago: University of Chicago Press, 2012).

ter Haar, Barend. "Falun Gong: Evaluation and Further Resources" (2002/2013), https://bjterhaa.home.xs4all.nl/falun.htm#top%20page.

CASE STUDY 1B. CHRISTIANS AND ANCESTOR VENERATION: RELIGION OR CULTURE?

Bays, Daniel H. *A New History of Christianity in China* (Chichester: Wiley-Blackwell, 2012), 21–33.

BBC. "Confucian Ancestor Worship" video, BBC Radio 4, www.youtube.com/watch?v=2dZfaU5tsDY.

Hedges, Paul. "The Harmony of Confucianism and Christianity? Reflections on a Dialogue in South Korea," *Interreligious Insight* 16.1 (2018): 18–31.

Min, Anselm, ed. *Korean Religions in Relation: Buddhism, Confucianism, Christianity* (New York: State University of New York Press, 2016).

Sun, Anna. *Confucianism as a World Religion: Contested Histories and Contemporary Realities* (Princeton: Princeton University Press, 2013), 32–38.

2

METHOD
Insider-Outsider Debates, Phenomenology, and Reflexivity

IN WHICH WE EXPLORE:

The insider-outsider debate in the study of religion
Debates around phenomenology in the study of religion
Questions about how we know and understand
The reflexive turn
Case studies of conversion and reconversion, and multiple religious belonging

INTRODUCTION

The distinction between people who are members of religious communities (insiders) and those who are not members of those religious communities, often scholars studying them (outsiders), may seem straightforward. However, when we start to push at this concept we soon see cracks appearing. We can note four questions:

- If somebody brought up within a religion leaves her religion, can she retain an understanding of what it "feels" like to be an insider?
- If a scholar studies her own religion, can she be both an insider and an outsider?
- Are nominal believers/practitioners as much of an insider as those deeply committed?

- Are religious "professionals" (priest/nun/leader) more of an insider than an ordinary member or layperson?

These four simple questions show that imagining insider and outsider as two clear and distinct positions is mistaken. Nevertheless, these terms can help us think about how we conceive religious and non-religious boundaries and identities. We will use these questions as starting points for considering some methods in the study of religion. We begin by looking at the typical world religions paradigm (WRP, see chapter 1) and how this shapes how we think about the territory. This leads us directly to discussing the insider-outsider debate, and from there we will discuss phenomenology and what is termed the "reflexive turn." This more theoretical discussion will lead us back to looking again at the insider-outsider debate and challenging some distinctions, partly by asking questions about the "spiritual but not religious" (SBNR) designation as well as the possibility of having multiple religious identities (MRI). We conclude with two case studies.

THE PROBLEMATIC CONCEPT OF RELIGION
THE WORLD RELIGIONS PARADIGM, RELIGIOUS BOUNDARIES, AND AUTHORITY

The world religions paradigm (WRP) shapes the way we think about religion (see box 2.1). We can certainly ask whether the way we normally think about religion affects our concepts of identity and belonging (chapter 6), or what it means to be an insider or outsider. So, what does the WRP mean for religious identity/belonging?

Arguably, scholars have inherited many aspects of a Christian, or more particularly modern Protestant, conception of religion. This manifests in the WRP. We can summarize some key assumptions of the WRP that are relevant for us here:

- Religions are bounded territories of belonging. Therefore, each religion is a distinct and discrete unit to which sole allegiance is required.
- Religion is primarily about belief in a set of principles. Therefore, you cannot adhere to more than one set of beliefs at a time.
- Every religious tradition has its own set of meanings leading to a clearly defined set of beliefs and practices. Therefore, you can only practice as an "insider" of one religion (at a time).

These features could be seen as reflecting an Abrahamic paradigm (see box 2.2). That is, on the whole, they fit the three traditions which trace their roots to Abraham (Judaism, Christianity, Islam). However, it may not be the way we see religion operating elsewhere in the world. For instance, in South Asian Hindu and Sikh traditions, people have more readily crossed boundaries, as has often also been the case with Islam in that part of the world.[1] This is also especially common in East Asia (see below and boxes 13.1 and 16.7).

The idea that we can only be an insider to one "religion" is, globally and historically, neither natural nor normative.

Another related factor is whether religion is primarily a matter of belief, practice, or something else (see chapters 3, 9, and 12). Indeed, we can pick out three areas:[2]

- Religions which emphasize orthodoxy (correct/standard doctrine/belief).
- Religions which emphasize orthopraxy (correct/standard practice/ritual).
- Religions which emphasize cultural authenticity (correct/standard forms of roles/norms).

It is sometimes suggested that certain religions emphasize one or the other:

- Christianity emphasizes orthodoxy; that is, you are an insider if you accept the correct beliefs.
- Judaism emphasizes orthopraxy; that is, differences of belief can exist. A well-known joke is that if you have three rabbis, you will find four different opinions. You are an insider as long as rituals are observed.
- Thai Buddhism stresses cultural performance or authenticity; that is, you are an insider if you fulfill roles determined by social and cultural factors which go beyond both scriptural/doctrinal injunctions (orthodoxy) and prescribed ritual actions (orthopraxy).[3]

However, all three areas exist as interacting poles that determine normative practices and assumptions.[4] Orthodoxy is not unrelated to orthopraxy and cultural authenticity. Even within one religious tradition, what is deemed "correct" belief, ritual, or behavior may differ across time and geographical locations (see chapter 4). This raises questions about what acts as markers of identity or "insiderness" in any specific context.

KEY THEORETICAL ISSUES
INSIDER-OUTSIDER AND EMIC-ETIC

Some specific terminology and theory can help us think through some of the emerging issues. Insider and outsider can be seen as giving rise to two specific ways of talking about religion:

Insider accounts: Descriptions by a member about their own tradition.

Outsider accounts: Descriptions by a nonmember about another person's tradition.

We need, when speaking of these, to take care not to always see these as distinct poles. This is highlighted by the terms "emic" and "etic," coined by Kenneth Pike (1912–2000). Both refer to outsider accounts (though many mistakenly see them as synonyms of insider and outsider) as ways that scholars may speak of religions:

Emic accounts: Descriptions given in terms meaningful to a believer, that is, using terms native to the tradition being described.

Etic accounts: Description given in external theoretical terms devised by scholars.

This brings us into a further debate of who understands a tradition "better": the insider, who knows what it "means" and "feels" like from the inside, or the outsider, who may be seen to bring objectivity? We may then ask what we mean by the term "better." Anthropologists, whether looking at religion or cultures, have often suggested that we actually need both. While an outsider can bring a sense of objectivity and classificatory tools and

UNDERSTANDING PHENOMENOLOGY

Phenomenology as a philosophical position goes back to Edmund Husserl (1859–1938), who saw it as a way to grasp the "essence" of things. It passed into the study of religion especially in the mid to late twentieth century.[1] To give a broad brushstroke description, the method of phenomenology involves two steps:

- First, we undertake the act of *epoché*, which means a suspension of judgment. We put aside our existing understanding and preconceptions, so we can come to the thing as it is in itself (i.e., the phenomenon, hence phenomenology).
- Second, having done this, we then use *eidetic* vision, which is to say seeing things as a whole. In other words, not just to see the surface but to dig down to know something as an "essence."

This may sound vague, but Husserl gave a very straightforward example. Suppose we walk into a room and see a chair. However, as we enter, we do not see the whole chair, only the back. Husserl suggests, though, that we commonly use *eidetic* vision so that, in our mind, we see/know that it has a seat, four legs (if we only see two), and so forth. While this is a specific skill to be cultivated by the scholar, Husserl believed that we could all understand the practice.

---

1 See George Chryssides, "Phenomenology and its Critics," in Chryssides and Geaves, *Insider/ Outsider Debate*, 157–82, James Cox, *An Introduction to the Phenomenology of Religion* (London: Continuum, 2010); and Gavin Flood, *Beyond Phenomenology: Rethinking the Study of Religion* (London: Cassell, 1999), 91–116.

modes of analysis not native to the tradition, this will only be a partial account. That is to say, without understanding what specific rituals, teachings, or practices mean to insiders, and how they operate within a wider system, such understanding will be incomplete and unrepresentative.[5]

We will find it useful here to take a short methodological detour into a bigger debate that goes to the very basis of the study of religion.

PHENOMENOLOGY IN THE STUDY OF RELIGION

Through much of the twentieth century, phenomenology was the primary mode of conducting religious studies. Rudolf Otto (1869–1937), Mircea Eliade (1907–1986), Ninian Smart (1927–2001), and Wilfred Cantwell Smith (1916–2000) propounded and practiced phenomenology. We can describe it briefly as a method that tries to understand the nature of the world through objective study by simply looking at and describing phenomena (see box 2.3).

In the study of religion, phenomenology was often coupled with an empathetic approach, which meant, as Smart put it, walking a mile in another person's moccasins. That is to say, you were meant to approach things by putting aside own your preconcep-

METHODOLOGICAL AGNOSTICISM

Methodological agnosticism is often seen as a value free and neutral, even secular (see chapter 16), approach to the study of religion. It suspends any judgment on the truth, or otherwise, of transcendent claims, for example, whether deities exist, afterlife claims, and so on. As such, it ceases to be a theological enterprise based within confessional (insider) claims. Rather, one simply studies the human phenomena (linking to phenomenology). Some critical scholarship, however, suggests that it does not ask difficult questions about the maintenance of power structures and the way that all claims are part of the discourse that supports power structures (see chapter 5, especially boxes 5.1 and 5.2; see also box 2.7). For some, bracketing out certain questions may be overly deferential to religion, especially when associated with an empathetic approach that seeks to understand insider perspectives. This is indeed a danger, so must be held alongside a more critical perspective. However, some critical perspectives seem to advocate a methodological atheism (an implicit even if not explicit assumption that religious claims are "false"), which presupposes knowledge on cosmological/transcendent questions (see box 1.10 and case study 8A). Herein, it is suggested that a critical methodological agnosticism is the most tenable approach in the study of religion. This links with the arguments for methodological polymorphism in the introduction. However, it does not mean that claims are taken at face value or treated with reverence. We critically study the human claims and traditions that surround claims about the transcendent, variously envisaged.

tions, to see where the other came from, to allow a value-free description. This was often said to be combined with what was termed a methodological agnosticism (see box 2.4), so you made no judgments about the truth or falsity of the beliefs described. It was often held that phenomenology went alongside the possibility of actually knowing the other through the method of empathetic understanding. Such a method, in the German philosophical tradition, concerns " reliving" another's experience (*verstehen*, roughly, "understanding"). We address this issue further in the next section, but it becomes part of the critique of phenomenology to which we now turn.

SOME CRITICISMS OF PHENOMENOLOGY

Phenomenology has been subject to much criticism, especially from critical theory (see box 0.1 and chapter 5) and postmodernism (see box 2.5). Here, we will only note points useful for our discussion on the insider-outsider debate. One line of criticism is that there is no objective stance. We all come from somewhere, have certain beliefs (about the world, even if not religious beliefs per se), assume certain things are more natural than others, or have preferences for certain things over others. This cannot be put aside. In particular,

WHAT ON EARTH IS POSTMODERNISM (AND WHY SHOULD WE CARE)?

Postmodernism has no single meaning and is found across a wide range of disciplines from architecture to linguistics, the social sciences to philosophy. It is often suggested that any definition says more about the person defining it than about whatever "post-modernism" may be. Nevertheless, here we attempt a partial and relatively descriptive definition as systems of thought that see themselves as coming after, or "transcend-ing/overcoming," modernity. This follows Jean-Francois Lyotard's (1924–1998) argu-ment that whereas modernity/Enlightenment paradigms (see box 16.1) sought grand or universal explanations of the world and humanity (what he termed metanarratives), we now live in a time of "suspicion" against all such grand narratives of explanation.[1] We prefer localized and partial explanations, and stress the deferral of truth claims. (Stressing this definition as partial and inadequate amounts to a postmodern defini-tion of postmodernism.) However, there is no single school of postmodernism (as is true of every school of thought).[2] Further, few thinkers these days claim to be postmod-ernists. However, it is important to understand that we live after (post)modernity. That is to say, claims about universal explanations are generally treated with suspicion, in the humanities and social sciences at least, though the physical sciences sometimes seek a unifying theory of everything. For some, living after (post)modernity manifests in what we term a (naive) "folk postmodernism" which advocates relativism. This assumes that the deferral of truth and localized knowing means any truth claims are "false." This is, however, incoherent: if it is "correct," then its own claims are not correct.[3] Other parts of this book demonstrate philosophical (see introduction and chapters 5 and 9) and theoretical (see chapters 7, 10, and 18) reasons behind this.

---

1 Jean-Francois Lyotard, *The Postmodern Condition: A Report on the Knowledge,* trans. Geoff Ben-nington and Brian Massumi (Minneapolis: University of Minnesota Press, 1984).

2 See Thomas Docherty, ed., *Postmodernism: A Reader* (New York: Harvester Wheatsheaf, 1993); Terry Eagleton, *The Illusions of Postmodernism* (Oxford: Blackwell, 1996); and Keith Tester, *The Life and Times of Post-Modernity* (New York: Routledge, 1993).

3 See Eagleton, *Illusions of Postmodernism.*

we should note that methodological atheism is itself a standpoint. Likewise, to assume that religion can be explained through a specific lens (sociological, psychological, scien-tific, etc.) means that we approach it with a perspective and tools that will emphasize certain things and not others, make us see certain things and not others, and prefer certain things and not others. There has also been a criticism of the way that many think-ers practiced phenomenology, especially figures like Otto and Eliade, whose theories were distinctly religious.[6] Their supposed neutrality of description often meant seeing, or privileging, particular aspects of traditions; their intent was to discern existing patterns in the data, but they may have created patterns instead (see chapter 11).

This discussion of phenomenology is relevant to our previous discussion on the insider-outsider because it leads us to ask questions about how we can know the other. This in turn involves asking questions about an abstract area of philosophy: epistemology (theories of knowledge). We need to address ways of knowing when we study religion. We will briefly see why:

- We may claim that outsider accounts are more objective as they will not have any confessional bias. However, everybody comes with their own worldview and preconceptions, so they will have some bias.
- We may claim that insider accounts are more reliable as they know what it feels like to be a member of that religion. However, all such accounts may be affected by their position due to gender (chapter 10), race (chapter 7 and box 18.6), or class (chapters 3 and 18). There is never only one insider account.
- We may therefore say that every account is relative, that there is no "truth," because it depends where you stand. However, there are many problems with this stance (see box 2.5 and chapter 9).

While raising quite abstract areas of philosophical thought about how we know things, it is essential to even think about what might have seemed a very basic question (but which we now know is not straightforward at all): whether somebody is a member of a religion (an insider), or not a member of that religion (an outsider).[7] Indeed, the question of who is, or is not, an insider of one religion may even be debated ("policed") by various insiders (and sometimes outsiders too), that is, whether all forms of belief, practice, or tradition are accepted.

Having raised these questions, we can ask where we stand on the issue of whether it is possible for us ever to come to an understanding of other religions (for those without one, then all religions are "other" to us)—and other cultures, nations (or states/regions), and so on. We can note the assumptions underlying three different ways of looking at the world:[8]

Open book: We can readily know people and cultures different from ourselves; we simply need to read them as we do everything around us. There are common human experiences which we can relate to. This represents a traditional way of thinking about knowledge and understanding. It assumes that reason, common sense, and human nature are reliable and simple guides.

Hidden codes: Other people and cultures are not readily obvious to us, but we can decipher them; people's outer beliefs or ideas may be based upon internal/psychological motivations which may even be unknown to them. We can discover structures in their society or thinking. This stance arose in the late nineteenth and early twentieth century with social scientific and psychological approaches. It suggests that human nature is not an open book, but can be opened with expert knowledge or skills.

Mirror of the self: We can never understand other people or cultures; our study actually misunderstands and imposes our own biases and prejudices. This represents late twentieth-century scholarly moves toward postmodern and critical stances which suggest that our cultural prejudice affects our knowledge (see box 7.3). It is often seen as a sophisticated and critical approach, but it may lead to incoherent relativism (see box 2.5).

We may not agree wholly with any one of these sets of assumptions. Or, depending on the context, we may find ourselves drawn to certain ones at different times. It goes beyond the intentions and possibility of this book to develop a complete theory of human understanding, but ad hoc discussions of hermeneutical philosophy (see box 2.6; see also box 0.2), materiality (chapter 9, especially boxes 9.1, 9.2, and 9.10), social constructionism (chapter 5, especially box 5.8), postcolonialism (chapter 7), and feminist thought (chapter 10) are used to build a theory of critical hermeneutical phenomenology (see the introduction). In brief, this means we do not naively adopt the "open book" stance, wholly endorse a "hidden codes" approach, or accept the relativism of an extreme "mirror of the self" approach. However, we may find in all three approaches valuable epistemological tools and lessons.

Importantly, the idea that we make mistakes does not show that all understanding is false or impossible. We can see this from our own experience. An example from my own life may be useful. When I first arrived in China, where I lived for several years, I often saw groups of people engaged in, what seemed to me, arguments at the end of the meal. I assumed that either nobody wanted to pay the bill, or else there was always an argument about how much each should pay according to who drank more beer (this was in a city called Harbin, famous for its excellent beer) or how much each had eaten. It was only later, as I came to better understand Chinese culture (and language), that I realized it was an argument about "face." That is to say, it was not an argument about not paying, but a competition of everyone wanting to pay. They would show their "seniority" within a group by being the one picking up the tab!

We can probably all think of similar misunderstandings we have had—at home or overseas—when we do not know what is going on. As an important theoretical note, the question of language and bodies is key here. For often when we do not understand the words, we may try and interpret the body language, which can lead to us stereotyping or reading our own preconceptions into the way that others behave (see box 9.8; see also 7.4).[9] However, in my example, I only knew my initial idea was mistaken because I later actually understood what the arguments were about. A failure to understand, or imperfect understandings, do not mean that all understanding is always wrong! Indeed, the claim that all understanding is false assumes the person making that claim has some bird's-eye position beyond the world whereby they can make this judgment—how

BOX 2.6 **PHILOSOPHICAL HERMENEUTICS AND UNDERSTANDING**

Philosophical hermeneutics (see box 0.2) emphasizes human understanding and interpretation.[1] Importantly, Hans-Georg Gadamer (1900–2002) argued that "prejudices" do not have to be seen as negative. Rather, he suggests, they are the basis for our knowing anything. We put new information in relation to things we already know; otherwise we would simply be unable to comprehend anything. Our prejudices can sometimes be seen as positive forms of preconceptions. For instance, if we have seen horses, we have some context into which we can make sense of a zebra when we see one. If we have never seen any four-legged animal, or an animal which eats grass, then we would surely struggle to conceptualize a zebra (or a horse). Gadamer, though, sees some prejudices as more helpful than others, because some can close down new knowledge (if we already assume we know everything about a subject) or cause us to misinterpret (if we put new things only in relation to what we know, rather than expanding our knowledge and understanding). If, for instance, we said the zebra must be a horse which someone had painted, we would not understand it very well. Meanwhile, both Gadamer and Paul Ricoeur (1913–2005) have theorized the issue of translation, that is, how not just words, but concepts, from another language/culture can be interpreted in our own. Ricoeur speaks of the "agony of translation," yet notes its possibility: understanding does occur across worldviews and languages (see introduction and chapter 1, especially boxes 1.7 and 1.8).[2] This barely touches the surface of hermeneutical philosophy, but indicates that our limited capacity as humans to get beyond our prejudices does not mean we must be relativist (see introduction, boxes 2.5, 5.8, and chapter 9). Importantly, "prejudice" is used, in this case, very differently from its general usage to talk about attitudes linked to stereotyping and discrimination.[3]

---

1 See Jeff Malpas and Hans-Helmuth Gander, eds, *The Routledge Companion to Hermeneutics* (New York: Routledge, 2015); and Hans-Georg Gadamer, *Philosophical Hermeneutics*, trans. David Linge (Berkeley: University of California Press, 2008 [1976]).

2 See Hans-Georg Gadamer, *Theory and Method*, trans. William Glen-Doepl (London: Sheed and Ward, 1979); Paul Ricoeur, *Hermeneutics and the Human Sciences*, ed. and trans. John B. Thompson (Cambridge: Cambridge University Press, 2016); Paul Hedges, "Deconstructing Religion: Where We Go from Here—A Hermeneutical Proposal," *Exchange* 47.1 (2018): 5–24; Paul Hedges, "Gadamer, Play, and Interreligious Dialogue as the Opening of Horizons," *Journal of Dialogue Studies* 4 (2016): 5–26; and Marianne Moyaert, *In Response to the Religious Other: Ricoeur and the Fragility of Interreligious Encounters* (Lanham, MD: Lexington, 2014), 119–56.

3 On the scholarship on prejudice, relating specifically to religion, see Paul Hedges, *Religious Hatred: Prejudice, Islamophobia, and Antisemitism in Global Context* (London: Bloomsbury, 2021), especially chapter 1.

else would they know? Certainly, it may be suggested we always have partial knowledge, never reaching a final determination, such that we always defer absolute claims. But this is very different from suggesting that all knowledge or claims are entirely, or equally, inadequate. Rather, we must be questioning, even of ourselves, our societies, and our sources of knowledge (including questioning the claims of this book!).

BEING REFLEXIVE PRACTITIONERS

The moves from what are often seen as modern and Enlightenment worldviews (see box 16.1) toward those which come afterwards, sometimes dubbed postmodernity, have impacted how we think we know (epistemology). We can note two positions:

Positivism: Positivists generally assert that pure reason, and our language about it, can examine readily available phenomena in the world and provide accurate and transparent descriptions of that reality.

Relativism: Relativists hold that rather than being universal, reason is always particular and bound to cultural and linguistic traditions. Our upbringing, language, and culture give us preconceptions, which means we are always culturally bound, and so cannot describe the world in a neutral way.

To mediate between these, we can speak about the need to be reflexive. This means to be aware of the cultural and linguistic baggage and prejudice which we all carry with us.[10] Meanwhile, we also exercise what is often called a hermeneutics of suspicion (see box 2.7). We ask questions about both our own categories and those of others. This is not to say that we never understand across linguistic, cultural, and religious boundaries, as stressed earlier.

Oddbjørn Leirvik has argued that we need always to recognize "the researcher's, the teacher's and the student's role as *agents* in the spaces between. Agency means being implicated in negotiations of power, both within the religious traditions and between them."[11] His point is that there is not some clear "outsider" space which is not involved in creating discourse about religion and what this means. Therefore, Leirvik continues, "self-critical reflection on one's own agency is called for."[12] We all come laden with cultural and personal baggage, epistemological views, and preconceptions which color our understandings. We can never simply sit back and look at other people's position from some vantage point that makes things clear to us. We are all insiders to some other discourse or standpoint.

A FURTHER REFLECTION ON WHERE WE STAND

Mentioned at a number of points in this text is the question of language. Here, it is worth thinking how a particular English, and more broadly European, heritage is part of how we know and think. Our language, to some extent at least, shapes our world (see introduc-

THE REFLEXIVE TURN AND THE HERMENEUTICS OF SUSPICION

It is often asserted that traditional modes of knowledge, especially those associated with the European Enlightenment/modernity (see box 16.1), assumed that the world was straightforward for us: our words related directly to the world out there as-it-is. Pure and universal language and reason took us to assured and certain knowledge. Often associated with thinkers such as Immanuel Kant (1724–1804), it is something of a stereotype (see box 5.2). Contrasting with this, from at least the late twentieth century (but relying on earlier work), various thinkers have suggested we should be suspicious of our assumptions about what reason is, what cultural norms affect our thinking, and our own preconceptions, particularly concerning the possibility that we can ever be neutral or objective. This is associated with a range of trends such as social constructionism (see chapter 5), feminist critiques of the gender bias in the construction of knowledge (see chapter 10), and postcolonial critiques of Western norms (see chapter 7), as well as postmodernism (see box 2.5). The requirement for us to be reflexive, to critically question our own experiences, as a trend in thought, has been dubbed the reflexive turn. It is our questioning of our thought and suspicion about what seems natural or obvious to us. We can link it to a term coined by Paul Ricoeur (1913–2005): the hermeneutics of suspicion. This means that our interpretation of the world (our hermeneutical strategy) is marked by questioning and seeking to look behind the immediate, "natural," or "commonsense" answers we have. Although associated by Ricoeur with his so-called masters of suspicion, who challenged our ways of thinking around the late nineteenth century (see box 5.2), one scholar suggests that the hermeneutics of suspicion is nothing but "a tautological way of saying what thoughtful people have always known, that words may not always mean what they seem to mean."[1] This is partly true, and in broad terms, it has correlations with the ideas of such figures as Socrates and Kant (see box 5.2). But the hermeneutics of suspicion implies more than simply questioning. It names an approach that seeks to unmask the assumptions and power dynamics in concepts and assertions.[2]

---

1 Christopher Bryan, "The Hermeneutics of Suspicion," in *Listening to the Bible: The Art of Faithful Biblical Interpretation*, ed. Christopher Bryan and David Landon (Oxford: Oxford University Press, 2013), 23–39, 23.

2 See Rita Felski, "Critique and the Hermeneutics of Suspicion," *M/C Journal* 15.1 (2012), http://journal.media-culture.org.au/index.php/mcjournal/article/view/431.

tion and chapters 1, 5, 7, and 9). In relation to this, Boaventura de Sousa Santos has noted that a classical statement of Western philosophy, "I think, therefore I am" (*cogito ergo sum*), which relies upon the notion of "thinking" in a particular way, cannot be stated in the African Akan philosophical tradition. Drawing from Kwasi Wiredu, he notes that "thinking" means "measuring something" in the Akan tradition, which cannot be tied to "being" (I am) in the same way. In Akan, the closest linguistic equivalent would be something like "I am there," implying not the solitary "I" of internal experience, but an embodied self in relation to a wider world.[13] As such, a certain lineage has shaped our world, requiring what Wiredu has termed a "conceptual decolonization."[14] This dominance of knowledge is not simply about English/Western dominance in the last couple of centuries (see chapter 7), for Western working-class or non-elite knowledge and practices have also been dismissed (see chapter 3), and gender bias is evident (see chapter 10). The term "kyriarchy," the dominance of elites, may help express this (see box 10.9). Knowledge of such perspectives can help us see what we may not currently be able to see, and keep aware of the perspectival nature of our own standpoints.

SUMMATION

This detour through phenomenology, theories of knowledge (epistemology), and theories and methods of interpretation (hermeneutics) has been necessary for us to come back to our questions on the insider-outsider debate. Let us briefly set out some key points:

- We cannot, without any qualification or justification, claim that an outsider approach is more objective (unbiased) than an insider one.
- We cannot simply be relativist and say that any insider's or any outsider's stance is simply as good, or bad, as any other. Some positions make more sense.
- We can credibly claim that it is possible to understand another person or tradition. Not perfectly, but at least adequately. The claim that we cannot supposes that the person making that claim fully understands that other person, and so can be the ultimate judge of other people's misunderstanding!
- We can have meaningful discussions and understanding across not just insider and outsider claims, but also across differing insider and outsider claims.
- A reflexive approach is needed, in which we are self-questioning toward our own preconceptions, but we do not deny the possibility of adequate knowledge.

BEING INSIDE AND OUTSIDE
CHALLENGING INSIDER-OUTSIDER DISTINCTIONS

As discussed above, insider and outsider are not necessarily distinct poles, despite the fact that people very often identify very strongly with one or the other. For instance, if asked, many people will typically say "I am a Christian," "I am a Buddhist," "I am an atheist," or "I am spiritual but not religious" (SBNR) (see box 2.8). However, we can further complicate this by asking whether we see polar opposites between those who are religious and those who are not religious.

- Do *all* Daoists, Muslims, Buddhists, Confucians, Jains, Pagans, and Sikhs similarly fit into one class of religious insiders while *all* atheists, freethinkers, and Humanists belong to another class of non-religious outsiders?

BOX 2.8 **THE SPIRITUAL BUT NOT RELIGIOUS (SBNR) AND (RELIGIOUS) "NONES"**

Increasingly, many people globally do not identify with any religious tradition but, nevertheless, may not identify as either atheist or agnostic.[1] These people are often identified as "spiritual but not religious" (SBNR), a category that overlaps with those termed the (religious) "nones." Nones are those who, for census purposes, list their religion as "none" (of the above), but may not be non-religious (see case study 8A). Nones often represent a significant number of people who are recording, on censuses and surveys, their religious affiliation as unaffiliated to any particular religious tradition. Neither the SBNR nor the "nones" are opposed to everything we may categorize as "religion" or "religious," though they may prefer to identify as "spiritual."[2] In this context, "spiritual" implies a rejection of institutional traditions, that is, "religion," but often an acceptance of such things as meditation, yoga, or forms of ecological spirituality (see box 5.6). The data suggests that the decline of religious belonging may not therefore be a decline of religiosity per se (see chapter 16). This clearly relates to debates on how we frame such terms as religion (see chapter 1).

---

1 See Becka Alper, "Why America's 'Nones' Don't Identify with a Religion," *Pew Research Center* (8 August 2018), www.pewresearch.org/fact-tank/2018/08/08/why-americas-nones-dont-identify-with-a-religion/.

2 See Graham Harvey, *Food, Sex and Strangers: Understanding Religion as Everyday Life* (Durham: Acumen, 2013), 23–42, 55–56; Andie Alexander and Russell McCutcheon, "I Am Spiritual but Not Religious," in *Stereotyping Religion: Critiquing Clichés*, ed. Craig Martin and Brad Stoddard (London: Bloomsbury, 2017), 97–112; and Lois Lee, *Recognising the Non-Religious* (Oxford: Oxford University Press, 2015).

- What about the spiritual but not religious (SBNR)?
- What about the Buddhist who insists her tradition is an atheist one that has no God, and claims Buddhism is a philosophy? Who must be seen alongside the Buddhist who reveres the Bodhisattva Guanyin and treats her as a deity (see box 2.9)?
- What about the Confucian who says her tradition has no "supernatural" elements and is simply a philosophy, but which historically has related to cosmological concepts like Heaven (*tian*) and the Supreme Ultimate (*taiji*)?

We have many problems coming to a definition of religion, with many gray border areas (see chapter 1), which makes the insider-outsider division itself murkier than we first assumed.

A further issue is that being an insider or an outsider is not simply about things we define as "religion." We are all inside or outside many communities, identities, or groups. These may involve gender, class, ethnicity, nationality, political allegiance, and so on. Do working-class Catholics and working-class atheists have more in common

BOX 2.9 **WHO IS GUANYIN?**

Guanyin (in Sanskrit, Avalokiteshvara; in Japanese, Kwannon) is the most revered figure of East Asian religiosity. Technically a bodhisattva (according to Mahayana Buddhism an awakened being who puts off entry to nirvana to assist others), she is generally seen as a Chinese goddess in popular devotion. She is, in orthodox elite representations, an assistant to Amida Buddha (technically buddhas outrank bodhisattvas), but in most temples her shrine is more revered than his. Notably, since about the twelfth century, she has (almost universally) been portrayed (in the Sinitic Buddhist world) as female, but is understood as male, even though in elite Buddhism a bodhisattva is beyond gender. Devotion to her is found outside Buddhism and throughout East and Southeast Asia.[1]

A Chinese goddess and/or the Bodhisattva Guanyin, Lian Shan Shuang Lin Temple, Singapore.

---

1 See Chün-fang Yü, *Kuan-yin: The Chinese Transformation of Avalokiteśhvara* (New York: Columbia University Press, 2001); Paul Hedges, "The Identity of Guanyin: Religion, Convention, and Subversion," *Culture and Religion* 13.1 (2012): 91–106; and C.N. Tay, "Kuan-yin: The Cult of Half Asia," *History of Religions* 16.2 (1976): 147–77.

with each other than the former have with middle-class Hindus, and the latter with middle-class Humanists? These and other factors need to be considered:

> Variables such as gender, ethnicity, region, class and other matters all play a part. For instance, a Western scholar who seeks an emic understanding of the religious culture of a Hindu (ex)-untouchable, or Dalit . . . will find himself an Outsider . . . on account of religion . . . class and ethnicity. . . . If we consider a movement like Santeria, a fusion of Roman Catholicism and African traditional religions . . . we may find that many Insiders within Roman Catholicism . . . may experience greater difficulties relating to and understanding this system than many others, perhaps those who share the cultural and social origins that gave rise to Santeria even if they do not practise it (i.e. black slaves).[15]

This quote suggests that some types of "insiderness" may actually make it less easy to understand other "insiders." Indeed, some have noted that often splits and divisions within traditions can be more bitter than those between traditions.[16] For instance, many Christians do not recognize Jehovah's Witnesses' claims to be Christians, while Catholic and Protestant Christians are sometimes in violent antagonism. Some divisions within Islam can lead to animosity, whether this is between Sunni and Shia, or both of these with Ahmadiyya, who many Muslims say are not Muslims.

CONVERSION AND INSIDER KNOWLEDGE

Questions of mission, conversion, and interreligious (including non-religious) relations are also places where insider-outsider debates occur. Sometimes converts' narratives are used to highlight perceived failings of their original home tradition. For instance, for some, criticisms by former Muslims like Ayaan Hirsi Ali are found to be particularly compelling.[17] Her critique suggests that Islam is inherently repressive of women and non-Muslims. Do such figures carry "greater insider insight," or should we apply a hermeneutics of suspicion (see box 2.7) to their narratives? Converts (or ex-members) may well want to explain why they converted (left), therefore criticizing their old tradition, which, obviously, they found in some ways inadequate. Such accounts are quite common in many traditions, where converts from another religion are used to reinforce narratives of the superiority of the religion converted to (or to atheism) to existing insiders, as well as to glean missionary information, that is, how to make appeals to others in the convert's old religion.

MULTIPLE RELIGIOUS IDENTITIES

Another issue to raise in relation to the standard conception of the insider and outsider as dichotomous poles is what is variously termed multiple religious belonging or identity (or dual religious belonging, hybrid identities, etc.). This is the phenomenon of belonging to, or identifying with, more than one religion. Here, we will call this "multiple religious identity" (MRI). The world religions paradigm makes it appear natural to assume that people can only (properly) belong to just one religion. However, this does not reflect the way that much of the world has made sense of being religious. In East Asia, the vast majority of people do not claim a single religious identity. Rather, they have engaged in what has been termed strategic religious participation (SRP) (see box 13.1). They employ the resources of a range of religious traditions as seems most beneficial, or is culturally determined.[18] Within medieval China, someone in need of an exorcist may have sought out a Daoist from the Celestial Masters lineage, a Buddhist monk for funerals, or any passing itinerant ritual expert for rites at the village shrine. This phenomenon seems to be becoming increasingly common in contemporary Western contexts today as well.[19] We see different patterns globally.

.   .   .

CASE STUDY 2A. LIVING BETWEEN RELIGIOUS WORLDS: CONVERSION AND RECONVERSION

The question of conversion, and even multiple conversions or reconversion, raises a specific issue for imagining a binary between insider and outsider. If somebody converts to another religious tradition, or becomes an atheist, do they still have some insider perspective to their original tradition? If we defined insider-outsider as simply allegiance/belonging, the answer would be no. However, we may hold that being an insider has some qualitative aspect. Certainly, the convert may be held to have some "authority" to demonstrate the inadequacy of their original tradition. They can say why it is inadequate even from an "insider" point of view.

INTRODUCING PAUL WILLIAMS

Paul Williams is professor emeritus (retired) of Indian and Tibetan philosophy at the University of Bristol, UK. As an academic, he is best known for his work on the Buddhist tradition, especially Mahayana Buddhist philosophy. In his youth, he was brought up within the Anglican (Episcopalian) Christian tradition, but he converted to Buddhism in his twenties and remained a Buddhist for over twenty years before converting to Catholic Christianity. We could either speak of his reconversion to Christianity, or, as he seems to do, of his conversion to a new denomination. The question of Williams's insider or outsider status to various traditions is therefore an interesting case. Coupled with the fact that he is also a scholar of Buddhism, we can ask how his academic work intersects with his religious insider and outsider statuses.

Williams was born in Exeter, a city in the southwest of England. He was a nominal Anglican who did not take his tradition and its beliefs and practices seriously, though he participated in his church choir. This raises an issue within insider-outsider debates about what claims to affiliation or membership actually mean. He studied philosophy at the University of Sussex and developed a particular interest in non-Western philosophy. This led him to Oxford University, where he undertook a doctorate in Indian and Buddhist philosophy.

Williams found Buddhism more than intellectually stimulating; he drifted toward a religious affiliation. In his accounts of this period, Williams suggests that this was something of a journey. He remained a Buddhist for around twenty-eight years, specifically in a Tibetan Buddhist lineage. This raises another query about the insider-outsider issue; normally conversions do not happen overnight or in an instant, though there are reports of sudden conversions. Rather, Williams's insider relationship to Buddhism was a gradually developing one, without us being able to say at a specific point that he was not Buddhist one day, but was the next day.

As an academic, Williams wrote some excellent research on Buddhism, and one of his books, *Buddhist Thought: A Complete Introduction to the Indian Tradition*, is a standard work.[20] It shows a deep and sophisticated understanding of the tradition. Therefore, we can speak of Williams's work as exhibiting an outsider stance: scholarly analysis. His insider status, though, was of interest to some students, including Buddhist monks, who came to study under him (particularly at the PhD level) because he was both a significant scholar of Buddhism and a well-known Buddhist, leading meditation retreats, but not holding any formal religious leadership position.

AN UNEXPECTED JOURNEY

Williams describes a religious need which was not met within Buddhism; hence his conversion to Catholicism. Like his conversion to Buddhism, this was not an overnight decision, but involved several years of deliberation. We may therefore ask questions about his status as an insider or outsider to both Buddhism and Christianity during this period. Certainly, as he moved toward feeling that Catholicism had what he yearned for, and that Buddhism did not, we do not see a simple jump from one to the other. The insider-outsider position does not switch at some clear point. Rather, at some point, could we say he was an insider to both traditions? Of course, there was a formal initiation—confirmation into the Catholic tradition. However, before this Williams no longer understood himself as a Buddhist. Formal initiations, such as confirmation into Christianity, or taking the Buddhist Three Refuges (*triratna*), do not necessarily mark the move from "outsiderness" to "insiderness." They may mark a formal point of entry, but rest upon (assuming they are sincere) a prior sense of commitment to the tradition. Nevertheless, we must not underestimate them as performative and enacting a social change (see chapter 12).

Williams retained his academic role, teaching and researching Indian and Tibetan Buddhism. Would the conversion to Catholicism make any difference to him as a scholar? Academically, it would seem not. The second edition of *Buddhist Thought*, published after his conversion to Catholicism, does not mark a change in his interpretation of that tradition. However, when he speaks of Buddhism as a Catholic, his description of

Buddhism seems to shift dramatically from his scholarly presentations.[21] In this mode, it can be argued, he presents a "negative" view of Buddhism based on an "antiquated" interpretation of that tradition, making claims that

- Buddhism is essentially pessimistic—a view propagated by some Western philosophers in the nineteenth century, but widely refuted.
- Buddhism is self-centered and noncommunal—a problematic representation which does not account for the central place of the community (*sangha*) in Buddhism.
- Buddhism is simply subjective (all based in your own mind and so is introverted and solipsistic)—a claim refuted by Williams's academic work.

We could surmise why he speaks this way, but we cannot access Williams's own personal thoughts. Notably, though, some of his former Buddhist students have been personally hurt, or even feel betrayed, by him leaving Buddhism and his new depictions of it.

REFLECTIONS

It would be useful to ask some questions to consider the issues:

1. As a student, would you prefer to study (at undergraduate or postgraduate level) with a scholar who did or did not share your religion (or non-religious option), or identified with the religion taught? Does the professor's affiliation affect their academic credibility or understanding?
2. Can we speak of Williams being both an insider and an outsider to specific traditions leading up to and around his various conversions? What does this mean for how we think about these terms?
3. Should we see varying degrees of "insiderness" and "outsiderness" as being a better way of speaking, rather than simply being an insider or an outsider?
4. Does conversion mean that you can no longer look objectively at a tradition you were previously an insider to? Think about this in relation to the way that Williams speaks about Buddhism when speaking as an insider to Catholicism. But also consider his work as a scholar.

CASE STUDY 2B. HINDU AND CHRISTIAN?
MULTIPLE RELIGIOUS IDENTITIES

That people may belong to, or identify with, several different religious traditions is simply an empirical fact. However, many scholars inspired by the world religions paradigm (WRP) model have assumed that such multiple religious identities (MRI) are somehow doing religion wrong. Here, we will explore the case of the Catholic Christian monastic Bede Griffiths (1906–1993), who comes from a tradition that traditionally considers such MRI as impossible. We also briefly consider the contemporary context.

Griffiths lived a fairly conventional English middle-class life, developing a deep interest in his Anglican Christian identity under the influence of C. S. Lewis (1898–1963) while a student at Oxford University. However, in 1931, he became a Catholic Christian, after reading John Henry Newman's (1801–1890) work, and became a monk at Prinknash Abbey the following year. Various events saw him going, in 1955, to India, and there he became greatly influenced by monks who had already started living in ways typical of Hindu holy men (*sadhu*). This involved wearing saffron robes rather than a Western monk's habit, living in an *ashram* (traditional Hindu ascetic communities), studying Hindu philosophy, and even engaging in Hindu-inspired forms of practice and meditation.[22] In 1958, Griffiths established a Christian *ashram* called Kurisumala. However, he was best known for his role at the *ashram* of Shantivanam, where he arrived in 1968. It was founded by a monk known as Abhistikananda (Henri Le Saux, 1910–1973), whose teachings were influential for Griffiths and others. Abhistikananda's description of an experience while practicing Advaita Vedanta meditation is famous.[23] He had the "*advaita* experience": feeling his own self/soul merging with God/the divine such that they were one and undifferentiated. For a Christian monk who believed in God as the Trinity and creator of humanity, this was hard for Abhistikananda to reconcile on an intellectual level. Nevertheless, he could not deny his experience of union with the divine.

For Griffiths, a dramatic experience occurred in 1990 when he suffered a stroke, and had what he termed an experience of the divine feminine. He spoke of this as being linked to Hindu goddesses but also in Christian terms as relating to Mary and the Holy Spirit. While both Griffiths and Abhistikananda remained firm in their Christian identity, both were also deeply imbued within Hindu thought and practice. Could they be spoken of as Hindus and Christians? Notably, this is distinct from the Chinese context, where people would not see any dissonance or conflict in using, or in some sense belonging to, different traditions (see box 13.1). However, in their context, both these monks were aware that they were seeking reconciliation between what are seen as two separate and distinct religions, and even conflicting ways of experiencing what it means to be religious.

MRI TODAY

The cases of Griffiths and Abhistikananda are far from unique. Increasingly, Christians around the world practice forms of Hindu or Buddhist meditation or contemplation. Some describe themselves in dual terms (e.g., as Buddhist Christians), and some are initiated into both traditions and are recognized as members (insiders) of each tradition by other insiders.[24] Others, who may identify by such terms as spiritual but not religious (SBNR), see no problem with identifying with, or using practices from, a range of different traditions. Yet they may not see themselves as insiders to any specific tradition. In such situations, how do we think about the concepts of insider and outsider?

Some questions may help clarify specific issues:

1. Griffiths had both Hindu critics (who thought he was using his *ashram* as a covert way to make converts by tricking them into becoming Christians) and Christian critics (who thought he had betrayed his Christian faith by becoming too Hindu). Assuming a stance opposing such views, show how you would seek to answer critics. Or, take the stance of one such critic, and show how you would advance these arguments in a substantive way.

2. Can somebody be an insider to two traditions at the same time? If you say no, how do you account for the simple fact that some people do this? If you say yes, how do you account for the fact that today many traditions say it is not possible?

3. Bede and Abhistikananda remained primarily Christians, so insiders to that tradition. To what extent may we also speak of them as insiders to Hinduism?

4. In something like the Chinese context, or with the contemporary SBNR phenomenon, where somebody may make use of particular rituals, practices, or religious professionals but not have a confessional sense of identity or belonging to a tradition, should we speak of that person as an insider to the traditions with which they engage? Or do they have any "insiderness"? If not, what is going on?

. . .

QUESTIONS AND CONNECTING THOUGHTS

The terminology of insider-outsider has been imagined as a natural and simple conceptualization to explain the situation of devotees/religious practitioners as opposed to "nonbelievers"/scholars. However, on many levels, the simple dichotomy does not work. A female atheist doctor may find she has much in common with a female Baha'i lawyer based on a shared sense of being an insider to the category of gender, or perhaps a shared LGBTQI identity. This also raises a range of questions which intersect with other chapters, including how our conception of religion affects how we imagine religious borders (chapter 1), which in turn will include issues about interreligious relations (chapter 13). We have also raised questions about how we know or understand across boundaries, which intersects with issues in social constructionism (chapter 5), gender and feminist thought (chapter 10), materiality (chapter 9), colonialism (chapter 7), and politics (chapter 18). Indeed, the fundamental nature of these questions about how we know, and therefore how we understand religion and its borders, can be seen as relating to all aspects of this text. Hence, they are placed in the first section of this book, where we deal with some foundational questions about what religion is and how we study it. To help think through some of the issues raised, we can ask the following questions:

1. What is your own experience of being an insider/outsider in relation to a religious tradition you belong to or are familiar with?

2. Do you think we should keep the terms "insider-outsider" as useful markers despite their problems, abandon them altogether, or modify them to speak about things like degrees of insiderness and outsiderness?

3. How can you apply a hermeneutics of suspicion and reflexivity to your own prejudices? (Remember that Gadamer does not see "prejudice" as "negative," because it also represents the possibility of our learning, see box 2.6.)

4. Is the notion of insider-outsider a clear divide between being a member of a religious group (insider) and not being a member of a religious group (outsider)? Or, are we always inside and outside many different standpoints, traditions, and worldviews? If so, how significant is this distinction?

5. Giving examples to clarify your position, argue whether it is possible for someone in a particular religion to ever understand someone in another religion.

6. Can outsiders sometimes understand things better, or more clearly, than an insider, and vice versa?

FURTHER READING

THEORY

Chryssides, George, and Stephen Gregg, eds. *The Insider/Outsider Debate: New Perspectives in the Study of Religion* (Sheffield: Equinox, 2019).

Cox, James. *An Introduction to the Phenomenology of Religion* (London: Continuum, 2010).

Flood, Gavin. *Beyond Phenomenology: Rethinking the Study of Religion* (London: Cassell, 1999), 91–116.

Hedges, Paul. "Multiple Religious Belonging after Modernity: Theorising Strategic Religious Participation in a Shared Religious Landscape as a Chinese Model," *Open Theology* 3.1 (2017): 48–72.

Hedges, Paul, and Anna King. "Is the Study of Religion Religious? How to Study Religion, and Who Studies Religion?" in *Controversies in Contemporary Religion*, ed. Paul Hedges, vol. 1 (Santa Barbara: Praeger, 2014), 31–56.

McCutcheon, Russell. "General Introduction," in *The Insider/ Outsider Problem in the Study of Religion: A Reader*, ed. Russell McCutcheon (London: Cassell, 1999), 1–11.

CASE STUDY 2A. LIVING BETWEEN RELIGIOUS WORLDS: CONVERSION AND RECONVERSION

Coming Home Network. "Dr. Paul Williams: Buddhist Who Became a Catholic Christian," *The Coming Home Network International*, interview (2014), www.youtube.com /watch?v=dUPC_s3i8zU.

Kong, Choy Fah. *A Response to a Notable Christian Convert's Presentation on Buddhism* (Singapore: self-published via Amazon.com, 2015).

Schmidt-Leukel, Perry. "'Light and Darkness' or 'Looking through a Dim Mirror?': A Reply to Paul Williams from a Christian Perspective," in *Converging Ways? Conversion and Belonging in Buddhism and Christianity,* ed. John D'Arcy May (Sant Ottilien: EOS Verlag, 2007), 67–88. See also the papers by José Ignacio Cabezón giving a Buddhist response, and Williams's reply to Schmidt-Leukel and Cabezón, in the same volume.

Williams, Paul. *The Unexpected Way: On Converting from Buddhism to Catholicism* (London: T. & T. Clark, 2002).

CASE STUDY 2B. HINDU AND CHRISTIAN?
MULTIPLE RELIGIOUS IDENTITIES

Coles, Laura. "Hindu-Christian Dialogue and the Blurred Boundaries of Religious Identity" (PhD diss., Canterbury Christchurch University, 2013), 198–207, https://repository .canterbury.ac.uk/download/1c682ff9b963e0bb608fe2e2fa22704db686a4ac8c810d37f905 b075c35768f3/2723508/Coles_Laura.pdf.

Drew, Rose. "Christian and Hindu, Jewish and Buddhist: Can You Have a Multiple Religious Identity?," in *Controversies in Contemporary Religion,* ed. Paul Hedges, vol. 1 (Santa Barbara: Praeger, 2014), 247–72.

Griffiths, Bede. "Bede Griffiths: Surrender to the Mother," *Lance's Religion Blog* (2018), http://lancereligion.blogspot.com/2018/07/bede-griffiths-surrender-to-mother.html.

Griffiths, Bede. *The Golden String: An Autobiography* (London: Fount, 1994).

Griffiths, Bede. *The Marriage of East and West* (London: Collins, 1982).

Hedges, Paul. "Strategic Religious Participation in a Shared Religious Landscape: A Model for Westerners?," in *Theology without Walls,* ed. Jerry Martin (New York: Routledge, 2020), 165–71.

Laksana, Albertus. "Multiple Religious Belonging or Complex Identity?: An Asian Way of Being Religious," in *The Oxford Handbook of Christianity in Asia,* ed. Felix Wilfred (Oxford: Oxford University Press, 2014), 493–510.

3

LIFE
Lived Religion, Syncretism, and Hybridity

IN WHICH WE EXPLORE:

The lived practice of people versus the idealized representations of traditions

The question of hybridity and syncretism in religion

Case studies of popular Mexican American Catholic Christianity in the United States, and Theravada Buddhism and spirit medium cults in Thailand

INTRODUCTION

Here, we will ask a set of questions about how we think about religion: Why do we think religion is mainly about texts, rules, or doctrines? Or, in reverse, why do we not think religion is primarily concerned with, or defined by, behavior, rituals, and day-to-day practices? If you have already read chapter 1, you will have seen part of the answer. Our modern conception of "religion" has come to be defined by certain predominant elite and textual Protestant Christian cultural assumptions. This is manifested in the world religions paradigm (WRP), which has dominated scholarly and popular images of religion (see chapter 1 and box 2.1).

The concept of lived religion switches the focus from belief and texts to practice and behavior. Religion is more about what people do than what they think. However, we should see it as much more than simply changing our focus of study from generally cognitive to embodied practices. It is also about challenging what we think religion is, what it does, and how it operates. Indeed, the very modes we use to think about religion will change, as will the questions we ask. When you hear about another religion, or meet somebody from a religion different from your own (assuming you have one), do you typically ask: "What are your beliefs?" Or "What do you believe?" But is this how we should start off? Maybe we should ask: "What do you do?" or "What is your practice?" or "What rituals do you perform?" Why are these not our normative thoughts and questions?

We will begin by looking at the concept of lived religion before passing on to the issue of understanding religion as syncretic/hybrid in all its forms. Next we look at some ways in which everyday practice is part of religion, and we conclude as usual with our two case studies.

THE CONCEPT OF LIVED RELIGION
WHAT PEOPLE DO AND WHAT RELIGIONS SAY

Meredith McGuire tells us how, as a student, she found that common ways of thinking about religion were inadequate when she encountered real people:

> Like other sociologists, I assumed that individuals' religious worlds would be linked . . . with the beliefs, moral norms, and religious practices promoted by the particular religious organizations of which they were members. Early in my dissertation research . . . however, I discovered how dramatically complicated my interviewees' religions were. . . . As I and many other researchers have discovered, those standard notions of religion are wholly inadequate.[1]

McGuire brings to light a number of other key points:

- a difference between elite/organized institutions and systems, and the practice of individual members;
- the dissonance between beliefs and norms, and everyday manifestations of people's religious or social behavior; and
- the simple messiness of religion, or even life as a whole.

We should lay out here some particular issues that arise in the way that scholars have thought about religion, and what a lived religion approach tells us.

What Is "Proper" Religion?

Is religion about some type of "spiritual" or "transcendent" reality (see box 1.10) separate from our daily life and the mundane world? The argument here is that this is not the case. Whatever we imagine religion to be, it is often about the mundane—everyday things and our practical experiences in life. This is not to say that people do not relate these to the transcendent or divine (variously conceptualized), but the two are not separate.

What Are the Sources of Religion?

Many introductions to religion talk about the scriptures and doctrines of religion, but these only have significance in terms of how they are put into practice by individuals (within a communal context). Reading a text does not tell you what other people think it means; almost every "religious scripture" has elements which are contradictory, and so which ones are prioritized, or given authority, is significant.

Everyday Interpretation and Praxis

We need to think about how any injunction or doctrine from texts, or some official form of religion, is actually understood and practiced. Most religions, for instance, have been seen to have some form of what is called "the Golden Rule," to treat others as you want them to treat you (see box 14.5), but how that is practiced in day-to-day regulations or expectations can be very diverse.[2]

The Relationship of Institutions and Individuals

By the very nature of almost any institution, elite teachings and positions are often inevitably restricted to a minority. To understand how a religion is actually practiced by the majority of its practitioners involves a very different approach: looking at what ordinary people really do. This challenges the assumption that the "elite" teachings or injunctions are the "correct" form. Given the interest of this book with various oppressed or sidelined groups, whether via race, gender, or class, we can see that elite religion often reflects the voice of a powerful minority.

LIVED RELIGION AND ELITE OR INSTITUTIONAL RELIGION

McGuire argues that "instead of looking at affiliation or organizational participation," we should focus on "individuals, the experiences they consider most important, and the concrete practices that make up their personal religious experience and expression."[3] In other words, if we want to know what a particular Theravada Buddhist or Baptist Christian actually does or believes, we should not start off by assuming that presumed "elite" or "textual" prescriptions will give us the answers. How any community, or individual, practices their religion is often quite distinct. And, most importantly, we have to remember: This does not mean that they are getting their religion "wrong."

It is a particular ideological and cultural set of assumptions that lead us to assume that any particular version is "correct," "right," "real," or "true." Indeed, in what we might define as one "religion" we will see that there are actually many different versions. For instance, in Christianity we see Roman Catholic, Methodist, Syriac, Mar Thomas, Southern Baptist, Pentecostal, Coptic, Old Catholic, Anglican, Mennonite, Quaker, Lightning from the East, Seventh Day Adventist, Brethren, Charismatic Evangelical—and an estimated twenty (maybe thirty) thousand other variations.

Further, the beliefs or practices of many of these will vary from country to country, region to region, or decade to decade. Is only one "correct"? Some Christians certainly think only their way of doing Christianity is correct: maybe "my denomination," or "my congregation" (of perhaps twenty people) is the only "true" one. From a scholarly position, though, we simply see variety. Moreover, when we take the lens of lived religion we do not prioritize or give normative status to any, but take seriously the variety not only among elites, but among everyday expressions too. However, scholars have often dismissed what they see as nontextual or non-elite traditions as "lesser." For instance, Melford Spiro (1914–2014) distinguished between the elite practices of Buddhism (often textual norms) and what he termed "apotropaic" Buddhism. "Apotropaic" literally means "warding off evil," but it is often used more widely. As such, the distinction Spiro makes is related to "ultimate" and "proximate" goals:

> *Elite/ultimate:* The pursuit of what is seen as the elite/textual tradition; in Buddhism, for example, awakening/nirvana and release from the cycles of reincarnation (*samsara*).
>
> *Apotropaic/proximate:* Practices aimed at, variously, securing a more fortunate rebirth and/or seeking particular gains in this life, for example, a good harvest, a healthy child, wealth, or the avoidance of various forms of evil or misfortune.

To take another quotation from McGuire: "Religion[s] . . . [are] an ever-changing, multifaceted, often messy—even contradictory—amalgam of beliefs and practices that are not necessarily those religious institutions consider important."[4] The apotropaic may be more widely significant than the elite conceptions.

We should also note that institutional (i.e., structures demarcating authority, hierarchy, prestige, or dominance in some form) and lived religion are not necessarily distinct. Every individual does not simply create their own religion. Indeed, the notion of individual autonomy is pretty problematic as it is created within a social context (see chapter 6). Part of studying lived religion is seeing how people interact with institutional forms of religion. But we must also problematize the notion of "institutional religion" (see box 3.1).

THINKING ABOUT HOW PEOPLE THEORIZE RELIGION

It is worth thinking about how and why we theorize religion the way we do. According to a lived religion theoretical approach, what we typically define as religion is really a very small aspect of a wider phenomenon: "Only a small and unrepresentative proportion struggle to achieve tight consistency among their wide-ranging beliefs, perceptions, experiences, practices, and actions."[5]

However, this "small" and "unrepresentative" group typically represents the most educated, resource-rich, and scholarly groups. Throughout history, elite literate groups have had their literature taken seriously. The non-elites, or subalterns (see box 7.6), were

ARE THERE "LEVELS" OF INSTITUTIONAL RELIGION?

While some religions have fairly clear hierarchies, others do not. Some leadership structures are very tight, and others are far looser. This can be the case where the "priest" plays varying functions. Further, there can be tensions or differences between the upper echelons of any elite, or hierarchy, and the local manifestations of community leadership. We can note some examples:

- The Catholic Christian tradition is probably the best example of a clear global chain of command: from the Pope, via cardinals, archbishops, and bishops to parish priests and the laity; with religious orders (monks, nuns, friars, etc.) alongside this. The magisterium (teaching authority) of the papacy and Vatican is meant to be binding on all.

- Within the global Anglican (Episcopalian) Communion, each national church is autonomous. The symbolically central Archbishop of Canterbury (head of the Church of England) has no direct authority over other archbishops. Even within the Church of England, the archbishops and the doctrinal teachings from the central bodies have no absolute authority, and act more as guidelines. Even individual priests can be relatively autonomous from their local bishop in some situations, as historically, and still sometimes today, a parish appointment may lie in the hands of a local landowner.

- In modern Singapore, leadership of the Hindu community may be said to lie with the Hindu Endowment Board (HEB), a government statutory body that runs several temples. However, its leaders are lay community leaders, not priests (brahmins). The brahmins are primarily ritual experts who do temple rituals, with no particular pastoral role. Many ordinary Hindus look to specific gurus for "spiritual" guidance. Most temples are also independent of the HEB. Therefore, speaking about the hierarchy, or institutional aspects, of this tradition is complicated.

typically illiterate and so produced no texts. The study of religion began as a primarily literary study, and took as normative the worldview of such elites, whose texts and lineages were considered significant (see boxes 4.13 and 14.2). The nexus of such elites and the WRP reinforced the rationalist and textual Protestant Christian model as definitive of religion (see also chapter 7), especially in academic thought through figures such as Friedrich Max Müller (1823–1900).[6]

McGuire argues that the period when our theory of religion was generated represents a "historical blip."[7] From ca. 1850 to the 1950s, the West (northwestern Europe and North America) saw rising levels of literacy and mass communications via pamphlets. Later, other forms of communication (e.g., radio) became available, and a tightening and strengthening of government control over swathes of nations was partly made possible via new modes of transportation. This control and institutionalization also occurred within religion, enabling a "church-authorized" religion. This involved a "gentility" in religiosity, due to a rising middle-class identity becoming seen as "normative" or "ideal."[8] How we think about "religion" is shaped by a particular Western set of dynamics, and does not tell us what "religion" is in any "natural" or "normative" sense; indeed, theory in academia has been dominated traditionally by Germany, France, and the UK.[9] We must always therefore exercise a hermeneutics of suspicion (see box 2.7) toward our perceptions of religion.

SYNCRETISM AND HYBRIDITY
HOW THE WRP MAKES US MISUNDERSTAND THE SYNCRETIC NATURE OF RELIGION

The term "syncretism" is a loaded and contested term. We need to unpack what may be some of our natural expectations about religion which come from the WRP:

- Religions are bounded entities (clearly marked and discrete).
- Religion is primarily about belief in a set of principles (believing, not doing).
- Every religious tradition has clearly defined doctrines and practices.
- Therefore, each religion sets out what its believers/devotees think and do.
- Consequently, religion is an outworking of a particular authoritative set of religious ideas.

We have dealt with a number of these assumptions already. Therefore, our focus is primarily on the first: each religion is a clearly bounded and discrete territory, marked out as a separate entity—Hinduism, Buddhism, Sikhism, Jainism, Judaism, Wicca, Shinto, and so on. This, however, is almost entirely historically and conceptually wrong. No religion is a cultural and conceptual island.

The names we have for religions, and the typical way they are taught in academic books as separate units, hides the fact that religions are, and always have been, syncretic. We may assume each has its own "founder," distinct "scriptures," and specific "beliefs" and "rituals" stemming from this particular religious identity. But such a view is very misleading. Religions in both mainstream/orthodox and folk/popular/lived expressions have always been syncretic (we will define this below). Some examples of the origins of different religions help demonstrate this:

- The first Christians were all Jews, as was Jesus. The texts of the early Jesus movement (see box 4.11) were Jewish, and were concerned primarily with bringing non-Jews within the covenant.[10] While Judaism and Christianity had become somewhat distinct by the second century CE, texts from as late as the fourth century exist which we cannot readily identify as either Jewish or Christian.[11]

- We often speak of Buddhism and Jainism growing out of Hinduism (ca. sixth to fifth centuries BCE). However, much of what we call Hinduism today did not exist then, including temple worship, a structured caste system, and the devotional (*bhakti*) tradition. Even the major deities worshipped now (Vishnu, Shiva, and the Goddess) were not central, while reincarnation was still new, emerging in the Upanishads, Buddhism, and Jainism. Further, the concept of nonviolence (*ahimsa*) was probably developed first in Buddhism and Jainism, then adopted by what becomes Hinduism (see case study 7A).[12]
- Sikhism developed in sixteenth-century northern India, when dominant Hindu devotional (*bhakti*) and Islamic Sufi traditions were meeting in the Sant tradition. Figures such as the devotional poet and philosopher Kabir (fifteenth century) were revered by Muslims, Hindus, and Sikhs. In this context, Guru Nanak claimed: "There is no Hindu, there is no Muslim." His teachings brought together the Sant tradition in a specific form among his students (Sikh means "student").[13]

Almost no institutional religious authority today would accept that their tradition is syncretic, but historically, syncretism is inescapable:

- Daoism adopted reincarnation from Buddhism.[14]
- Confucianism adopted Daoist and Buddhist meditation.[15]
- Buddhism adopted Hindu deities; Vishnu is the protector deity of Buddhism in Sri Lanka.[16]
- Islam and Christianity seemingly adopted prayer beads from South Asian traditions.[17]
- Judaism, Christianity, and Islam borrowed heavily from Zoroastrianism (see box 3.2).

SYNCRETISM: A CONTESTED TERM

The term "syncretism" is theologically negative in many traditions; after funding a professorship in Sikh studies, a Canadian Sikh community was outraged when the person appointed argued for what they saw as claims that Sikhism was syncretic.[18] Religious traditions tend to stress their purity, which, especially today, often rests on supposed original texts, but many religions traditionally saw tradition or oral teachings as having equivalence or greater value than texts (see boxes 1.3 and 11.3). Though today some Christian theologians argue for syncretism being perceived as a positive aspect of their traditions,[19] this negative theological connotation of "syncretism" has passed into scholarly work, as Graham Harvey notes: "The label 'syncretism' often functions as a condemnation of people who are deemed to wrongly and foolishly blend, for example, Catholic

BOX 3.2 ZOROASTRIANISM'S INFLUENCE ON THE "ABRAHAMIC" RELIGIONS

Judaism, Christianity, and Islam would almost certainly look very different if it were not for borrowings from Zoroastrianism. One key concept is resurrection.[1] The early Hebrew Bible spoke of a shadowy place called Sheol where souls went after death, but contemporaneously with the exile of some elite Jews in Babylon (fifth century BCE), resurrection appears. (The Hebrew Bible was heavily edited and added to around this period.) This was the accepted belief of the Zoroastrians of Persia, who held them captive. Indeed, one of the first descriptions of what appears to be resurrection in Jewish texts, the image of a field of dry bones in Ezekiel (Ez:37:1–14), is an exact description of a Zoroastrian graveyard of this period. This then passed to Christianity and Islam. Again, the concept of millennialism (thousand-year realms) found prominently in many early Jewish and Christian texts also arose in Zoroastrian thought. The notion of a messiah as a figure who will come again at the end of time and usher in God's reign is also Zoroastrian; the older Hebrew term for messiah simply means "anointed" (with oil) and referred to kings and others with God's favor. A particular Islamic borrowing was the Chinvat Bridge, the idea that in the afterlife you would cross a bridge to paradise above the flames of torment. Only if your deeds merited it would you pass, led by a maiden; otherwise the bridge would narrow to a razor's edge and you would fall to the flames below. It is also likely that Zoroaster was the first teacher of monotheism, a belief in only one god (Zoroastrianism's dualism of good and evil deities seemingly developed later). A direct borrowing from Zoroastrianism is unclear, but the earliest Hebrew Bible is suggestive of polytheism, including goddess worship, or perhaps henotheism (belief in one supreme deity among a pantheon of other deities).[2]

---

1 See Colleen McDannell and Bernhard Lang, *Heaven: A History* (New Haven: Yale University Press, 1990), 11–14.

2 See Mary Boyce, *Zoroastrians: Their Religious Beliefs and Practices*, 2nd ed. (New York: Routledge, 2001); John Hinnells, "The Zoroastrian Saviour Imagery and Its Influence on the New Testament," *Numen* 16.3 (1969): 161–85; Marieeta Stepaniants, "The Encounter of Zoroastrianism with Islam," *Philosophy East and West* 52.2 (2002): 159–72; and Werner Sundermann, "Zoroastrian Motifs in Non-Zoroastrian Traditions," *Journal of the Royal Asiatic Society of Great Britain and Ireland* 18.2 (2008): 155–65.

Christianity, Yoruba traditionalism and Amazonian animism into something like Candomblé or Santo Daime."[20]

Within the study of religion, these "unhelpful hangovers of elite imaginings" linger.[21] Syncretism is viewed as suspect or "inauthentic," and various dynamics in the field have aided the theological prejudice that mainstream religions are "pure":

· Scholars often specialize in only one religion. Hence syncretic features are less likely to be registered.

- There is a continued focus on textual and elite traditions. Elites (scholars and religious leaders) typically decry what seem like the syncretic aspects as marginal, or "folk/popular" religion.
- Syncretic elements are often hidden in plain site by being part of normative texts and so assumed to be original parts of a religion (see box 3.2).
- The prejudice against the term "syncretism"—even outside theological contexts—continues as an unquestioned assumption.
- Scholars may be (elite) members of a religion and so are invested in "not seeing" syncretic elements of their own tradition. However, many scholars who are not members of religions have perceptions of "mainstream" religions as nonsyncretic.

THEORIZING SYNCRETISM, FUSION, AND HYBRIDITY

Given the negative connotations of syncretism, some scholars argue that we should use other terms, such as "hybridity." Here, though, we will employ "syncretic/syncretism" as a default descriptive marker. We will see why arguments against syncretism are problematic by viewing some theory on hybridity. Here we will follow the useful set of arguments advanced by Pattana Kitiarsa, who views "hybridity" as "a keyword in postcolonial discourse" to go "beyond syncretism," drawing on Mikhail Bakhtin (1895–1975), Homi Bhabha, and Peter Jackson.[22] However, against Kitiarsa, we will argue that hybridity is not a better term or concept, and understand both as terms for essentially the same processes. Before discussing those, we will briefly consider the mestiza/nepantla theory of Gloria Anzaldúa (1942–2004).

For Anzaldúa, being situated within the border between identities was a part of who she was, being born near the US-Mexico border, and she used the "language of the mestiza and the related notion of nepantla, which is a Nahuatl term for middle or in-between-ness."[23] This language of being mixed speaks about a readiness to embrace ambivalence and can be seen in contrast to expectations that our identities or traditions will be fixed, monolithic, or rigidly demarcated. It speaks about a way of seeing the world in which we have a different view about the norms it presents to us.

Mikhail Bakhtin stressed the inevitably syncretic nature of all human social and linguistic realities and structures. For him, hybridization is "a mixture of two social languages within the limits of a single utterance, an encounter, within the arena of an utterance, between two different linguistic consciousnesses, separated from one another by an epoch, by social differentiation or by some other factor."[24] Bakhtin suggests hybridity can be either intentional or organic, that is, done by either consciously fusing two traditions (intentional) or without direct intent in the meeting of traditions, cultures, or other systems (organic). It is, though, a normal process.

However, a problematic assumption in Bakhtin is that we have two "pure" entities which get mixed to form a hybrid. The hybrid remains problematically seen as dependent

HOMI BHABHA'S HYBRIDITY AND THIRD SPACE

For Bhabha, the hybrid is something which challenges elite representations of power, theorized from a postcolonial perspective: "Hybridity is a problematic of colonial representation . . . that reverses the effects of the colonialist disavowal, so that other 'denied' knowledges enter upon the dominant discourse and estranges the basis of its authority."[1]

In other words, hybridity uses aspects of the colonizer's own system, but in new ways leading to what may be termed a double-voicedness. This leads to the loss of "univocal grip on meaning" wherein the powerful becomes "open to the trace . . . of the other."[2] The notion of hybridity has roots in the ideas of the French theorist Michel Foucault (1926–1984), and is a form of counterpower, or counterdiscourse, resistant to a dominant authority. It relates to Bhabha's widely cited concept of "Third Space" and his related discussions of hybridity and mimicry.[3] This Third Space is where a dominant power is contested and pushed back against. Bhabha sees it as a new creation that is neither the colonizer's space (or that of the powerful elite), nor the colonized's (or, the oppressed or less dominant) space; but a place in which change and a new creation can open up, or, as Bhabha puts it, a "something else besides."[4]

Like Bakhtin's notion, Bhabha's hybridity appears as only an epiphenomenon, something created merely as derivative of other existing things. Some postcolonial critics have argued that Bhabha's more political notions of hybridity as a space of mimicry and resistance are essentially ineffective in challenging hegemonic powers.[5]

---

1 Homi Bhabha, "Art and National Identity: A Critics Symposium," (Interview with Brian Wallis), *Art in America* 79.9 (1991): 70–91, 82.

2 Bhabha, cited from Young, *Colonial Desire*, 21–22, in Kitiarsa, "Beyond Syncretism," 467.

3 See Homi Bhabha, *The Location of Culture* (New York: Routledge, 1994), 36–39, 85–92, 112–15.

4 Homi Bhabha, "The Commitment to Theory," *New Formations* 5 (1988): 13, cited in Kitiarsa, "Beyond Syncretism," 468.

5 See Richard King, *Orientalism and Religion: Postcolonial Theory, India, and "The Mystic East"* (New York: Routledge, 1999), 204, 254 n. 81.

on existing entities; however, these entities are already syncretic admixtures of previous elements.

Kitiarsa also looks at Homi Bhabha's well-known representation of hybridity (see box 3.3).

Peter Jackson, the third theorist referenced by Kitiarsa, makes a distinction between the supposed cultural periods of modernity and postmodernity (see box 2.5). Speaking of Thailand, Jackson says that modernity meant doctrinal rationalization, centralization, and bureaucratization. By contrast, Thai postmodernity means the resurgence of the supernatural, efflorescence, decentralization, localization, and a contestation of disenchantment by reenchantment; that is, a modernized and secular world is made

COMMODITIZATION AND RELIGION

The assumption that commoditization or consumerism is not part of religion is probably inherited from the WRP. This suggests that such "mundane" matters are not "religious" (see case study 5B). However, throughout history, "religion" has been sold, packaged, and monetized in countless ways, including

- the effective selling of indulgences (remission of sins and time in purgatory) by the Catholic Church in medieval Europe;[1]
- priests asking for money from pilgrims for access to shrines in India;
- today's Prosperity Gospel preaching in American, Asian, and African Protestant and Pentecostal churches (see box 16.9);[2] and
- priests selling fake mummy animals as offerings in ancient Egypt.[3]

Imagining that commoditization is something new is a common mistake of many scholars. Nevertheless, there are particular ways that religion and spirituality (see box 5.6) have been commoditized and sold in the contemporary context, often tied in to exoticized notions of Asian "mystical" (see box 8.5) practices (see box 5.4).[4]

---

1 Johann Tetzel, "Sermon on Indulgences," GBHI (n.d. [1964/ca. 1517]), http://ghdi.ghi-dc.org /sub_document.cfm?document_id=4207.

2 Vicky Baker, "The Preachers Getting Rich from poor Americans," *BBC* (29 May 2019), www.bbc .com/news/stories-47675301.

3 Eliza Anyangwe, "Could Egypt's Empty Animal Mummies Reveal an Ancient Scam?," CNN (22 May 2015), https://edition.cnn.com/2015/05/22/africa/ancient-egypt-animal-mummies-empty/index .html.

4 See Sophia Rose Arjana, *Buying Buddha, Selling Rumi: Orientalism and the Mystical Marketplace* (Oxford: Oneworld, 2020); Jeremy Carrette and Richard King, *Selling Spirituality: The Silent Takeover of Religion* (New York: Routledge, 2004); and Martin, Craig, *Capitalizing Religion: Ideology and the Opiate of the Bourgeoisie* (London: Bloomsbury, 2014).

once again full of supernatural or spiritual elements (see chapter 16). For Kitiarsa, this is important because in a context where we see religion becoming commoditized (see box 3.4) and part of consumer culture, we can see hybrid forms of spirit medium cults appear. Hybridity is therefore an essentially new and novel form of religious development.

However, we can contest Jackson's conception. The terms "modern" and "postmodern" are not always meaningful, simply providing sweeping generic overviews of patterns in society. Certainly, we can grant that to some degree what we often term modernity and the Enlightenment paradigm (see box 16.1) tend to emphasize rationality over the supernatural. though they are not as opposed as we might suspect—for one thing, commoditization is not simply new and "postmodern." Moreover, Jackson's argument may overemphasize certain differences and make problematic claims about how we view religion (see box 3.4). McGuire makes the point that what we might call an enchanted worldview (see box 16.10)—where what we can roughly term "magic," the supernatural, and religious realms form part of the everyday (see boxes 7.8 and 9.4)—did not disappear with modernity,[25] though these elements may have become less obvious. Their "return" may not therefore be a move from modernity to postmodernity, but simply a change of emphasis on what we study or perceive (see chapter 16).

Kitiarsa's overview favors the term "hybridity" over "syncretism." Kitiarsa argues that syncretism implies, in the context of a dominant religion, a "harmonious" blending, not a "rupture," but a blending which is "contentious, unauthenticated, and impure."[26] However, this phrasing seems to assume that "syncretism" is inherently bad (i.e., "impure" or "unauthenticated"). Moreover, Kitiarsa's argument that hybridization is different, being "a temporal moment and site of contestation, or 'rupture' for spiritual meanings and relevance,"[27] does not show any analytic distinction. Rather, we can suggest that "syncretism," "hybridity," and "fusion" are all terms that can be used as synonyms to talk about the blending of religions.

Let us look at some reasons. First, while the theorists cited by Kitiarsa see hybridity as based in dominant traditions, they do not necessarily imply a "rupture." This is implied by Bhabha, yet he also shows a place where the two traditions may meet and become, arguably, "harmonious." Further, Kitiarsa assumes that "syncretism" carries inherent negative connotations. Indeed, Graham Harvey argues both syncretism and hybridity are "heavy" terms for a very natural process and suggests that "fusion" may serve equally well.[28] Certainly, Kitiarsa's concept of hybridity as a special moment of contestation seems to give extra weight to this as something special, rather than simply a very ordinary part of all religious expression. The term "hybridity" also, coming from biology, carries some very negative overtones for some. In some contexts, children born across the boundaries of "race" (itself a problematic construct; see chapter 7 and box 18.6) have been described as "hybrid" to suggest an illegitimate crossover. Therefore, we do not argue that a particular term is better; every term carries problems. Each is given specific meanings by different authors, and may in certain contexts be preferable or problematic. Nevertheless, Kitiarsa's discussion of theorists of hybridity gives us these helpful insights, which we can summarize here with some other points, using "syncretism" as a catchall term:

- Syncretism is often lost sight of and needs to be kept in mind. Every tradition, even at its purported origin, is syncretic; Bakhtin reminds us that this is normal.
- Anzaldúa also reminds us that we can be comfortable with syncretic forms, which will also allow us to see and experience the world differently.
- Bakhtin usefully discusses intentional and organic syncretism.
- Bhabha reminds us that the meeting may be a point of contestation against a dominant power, a Third Space, though this may have limited effectiveness.

- As Kitiarsa reminds us, referencing Jackson, syncretism can be about new formations in distinct and changing social contexts.
- Related to the last point, Kitiarsa's notion of "relevance" suggests a new syncretism may be compelling in a way an old tradition was not.
- Harvey reminds us, by the term "fusion," not to invest too much weight in the very normal and natural process of syncretism.

RELIGION AND THE EVERYDAY
FOOD, SEX, AND STRANGERS

From a lived religion perspective, one obvious place for study is everyday or mundane activities. Indeed, religious traditions regulate things we (mostly) do regularly.[29] Max Weber (1864–1920) noted that communities and societies typically regulate who you can eat with (commensality), have sex with or marry (connubium), and interact with (inclusion and exclusion; see chapters 6 and 13).

Such regulation often falls into the purview of religious traditions or injunctions. In medieval Europe, there were strictures relating to whether Jews, Christians, and Muslims could eat together, while Hindu traditions also regulate food purity.[30] If we focus on connubium (who one is allowed to have sexual intercourse with), some of these regulations concern close family members, while others regulate the rituals of marriage and sexual ethics (see box 3.5). For some traditions, a boundary to be patrolled is marriage outside one's own religion. Contemporary Evangelical Protestant Christians use a biblical phrase, to be "unequally yoked" (2 Cor. 6:4), to denote the undesirability of marrying non-(Protestant)Christians.[31]

RELIGION AS DAILY LIFE

Jayeel Serrano Cornelio's research in the Philippines has shown that for many young Catholic Christians, contrary to official church teaching that weekly mass attendance is compulsory, many see simply being good people and engaging in charity work as the key components of their Christian identity.[32] Importantly, it does not seem that these young people are simply "nominal" Christians or take their religion less seriously. Rather, they are often deeply committed, and this commitment is what can lead to social work. A similar example is seen in one of McGuire's case studies, where she says of one figure, "Peter considered his extensive social activism to be the most important part of his spirituality. He emphasized that activism for peace and social justice is not merely a byproduct of his religion; it is at the core."[33]

In lived religion, religious identity may be played out in ways different from what official teaching demands and expects. It concerns what matters most to people: in the language of Paul Tillich (1886–1965), religion is people's "ultimate concern."[34] Indeed, as

Robert Orsi noted in a study of Italian American Catholics, they distinguished between "religion" and "church," the former being what mattered to them, and the latter relating to institutional expectations.[35] Elite/institutional religion, in these terms, may not be people's "ultimate concern."

One case study from McGuire, whose work Harvey says shows "lived religion is far more interesting than the imaginary religion defined by texts of creeds,"[36] concerns Margaret, who was brought up as a Lutheran Christian in small-town Ohio, but after high school stopped going to church. Nevertheless, she was "highly engaged in religious practices and experiences not connected with any religious group."[37] But where did she find her religion?

As she talked about her experiences with healing, it became clear that Margaret engaged in deeply meaningful and moving spiritual practices that many would not recognize as "religious." For example, she described gardening as her daily "worship service." She had begun practicing organic gardening years earlier . . . But as she got "into" gardening, she came to think of it as a valuable spiritual discipline, requiring patience, hope, and "nurturing love." She engages meditatively in even such prosaic practices as preparing the compost.[38]

This brief example helps show that if we simply looked at what we termed the official or textual teachings of somebody's religion, we would get very little sense of what people actually do. Likewise, Monica Miller has questioned what gets to count as religion when we explore the lyrics and lifestyle of hip hop artists.[39] People's practices are not, as it were, simply part of a label that they wear. We cannot meet somebody and say, "Oh, you are a Hasidic Jew, and so you believe so-and-so and do such-and-such," or, "Oh, you are a Mahayana Buddhist, and so you believe so-and-so and do such-and-such." Studying texts, elite philosophical belief systems, and normative official statements only gets you so far.

·　　·　　·

CASE STUDY 3A. MEXICAN AMERICAN CATHOLIC CHRISTIANITY AND OUR LADY OF GUADALUPE

We will take a tradition which has a very clear hierarchical structure and official belief structure, Catholic Christianity, and see how it operates in the lives of ordinary Mexican American Catholic women.

THE VIRGIN OF GUADALUPE

On 9 December 1531, an indigenous man named Juan Diego was walking across the hill of Tepeyac, which was sacred to the Aztec goddess known as Tonantzin to the Nahua people, when he reportedly received a vision of the Christian saint the Virgin Mary. She commanded him to tell the bishop to erect a shrine for her. Fearing that the new Spanish conquistadors would not believe an indigenous man like him, for they were often regarded as less than human by the conquerors (see chapter 7), he nevertheless went, but was dismissed. Subsequent visions over the following days culminated in what is seen as the miracle that confirmed the truth of his vision. This took place on 12 December, now the feast day of Our Lady of Guadalupe, when he allegedly took Castilian roses—growing miraculously during winter—to the local bishop, but as he let them drop from his *tilma* (cloak) they disappeared and, in their place, an astounding image of the saint was found upon his *tilma*. This figure of Mary, but in the likeness of a native woman, became recognized as the patron saint of New Spain in 1746, and has become a figure bound up in mestizo culture and politics. She was a key figure invoked in Mexican struggles for self-determination and remains a central figure in the political and cultural identity of many Mexicans at home and abroad.[40] Moreover, the image on the *tilma* is believed to have been beyond human construction and to have demonstrated miraculous powers.[41]

THE EXPERIENCE OF MEXICAN AMERICAN WOMEN

The most revered figure of Mexican Catholicism, Our Lady of Guadalupe is revered far beyond Mexico, but receives particular devotion from Mexican women. Many women carry an image of her with them at all times, and the scholar María Del Socorro Castañenda-Liles recounts that during her fieldwork she was surprised when one elderly lady reached

THE DEVOTIONAL TRIANGLE

The devotional triangle describes the movement of passing tradition across generations that relates both to human-to-human encounters (horizontal, and forming the
bottom edge of the triangle), and a divine-human encounter (vertical, and with the two
bottom corners of the triangle intersecting with the top corner). The devotion/rela-
tionship that the mother has with Our Lady is Guadalupe is passed on to the daughter, not simply as a narrative, but in a way that instills this devotion in the receiver,
hence creating the triangle, where the relationship is not simply horizontal (human to
human), or vertical (divine to human), but where the horizontal informs and reaffirms
the vertical axis.[1] Importantly, the context of passing this on is significant: we do not
simply see a human-to-human transmission, or an individual and their relationship
to some postulated deity. Rather, the relationship is more complex. The divine relationship is imbued through the human relationship, and this in turn strengthens the
human bond because of the shared devotion to the postulated transcendent.

---

1 See Castañenda-Liles, *Our Lady of Everyday Life*, 57–59; and Robert Orsi, *Thank You, St. Jude:
Women's Devotion to the Patron Saint of Hopeless Causes* (New Haven: Yale University Press, 1996).

---

into her blouse and withdrew a laminated picture of Our Lady of Guadalupe from her
brassiere, telling her: "I keep her here all the time, and I even talk to her."[42] This devotion
is typically passed from mothers to daughters,[43] relating to what Robert Orsi termed the
"devotional triangle" (see box 3.6).

Understandings of Our Lady of Guadalupe often mirror official Catholic teachings,
seeing her as a local instantiation of Jesus's mother, Mary. However, she is not just perceived as the "Mother of God"; Mexican women see her as their mother, and the mother
of the Mexican people. An example from Castañenda-Liles's fieldwork: a thirty-one-year-
old mother recounts a story from her childhood where she stole candy from the home
altar built for the saint's feast day because she knew that, as her mother, Our Lady of
Guadalupe would not mind sharing candy with her and would forgive her.[44] Further, in
some instances, such as when considering abortion, women would also pray to the saint
rather than God because they believed that, as a woman, she would be more compassionate and understanding. This reflects a lived religion understanding in which God
is not seen as all-compassionate and all-loving (omnibenevolent); rather, these qualities
are found only (more prominently?) in Our Lady of Guadalupe.

MEXICAN AMERICAN COLLEGE STUDENTS' DEVOTION

In her fieldwork, Castañenda-Liles notes that devotion to Our Lady of Guadalupe differed
among the three cohorts she studied: elderly women (ca. 60s–80s), younger married

women (ca. 30s–40s), and college students (ca. 19–20). This shows the changing nature of tradition (see chapter 4) and also how attitudes change over the life course.

Across the cohorts, Our Lady of Guadalupe was sometimes considered equal to God, though far less among the oldest women, who were more in tune with orthodoxy. Among those women who saw Mary as equal to God, she was understood as the mother of God, itself an orthodox Catholic Christian term for Mary. They saw her not simply as Jesus's mother, however, but as equal with God. This was most marked among the college students. Moreover, inspired by Chicano theory (Mexican American politicized identities), some of these college students identified Our Lady of Guadalupe with the Aztec goddess Tonantzin. It is likely that this association came through their college studies; in comparison to the other two cohorts in Castañeda-Liles's study, they were better educated and also English speaking. Imagery of Our Lady of Guadalupe, while playing upon traditional Catholic Christian images, also employs imagery from indigenous traditions. She is sometimes seen as a syncretic fusion which allowed the indigenous people to continue their devotion to their goddess on her sacred hill, but veiled as devotion for the Virgin Mary, which made it acceptable to the Spanish.[45] Arguably, the qualities of Tonantzin as the virgin mother of gods associated with a heavenly realm known as a "flower land" (shown in the out-of-season roses) were combined in devotion and imagery to the Virgin Mary of Catholicism. Regardless of the actuality of historical events, Our Lady of Guadalupe is certainly invoked as an indigenous symbol by Chicana groups. We should also note that some of the college students did not relate Our Lady of Guadalupe to Mary. For them, Mary was a white-skinned female distant from their experience, and so not the same as this saint whom they revered. This was not a factor for the other two cohorts. Finally, Our Lady of Guadalupe is also invoked in relation to the rights of immigrants among Mexican Americans, showing a new way that she is understood in the contemporary context.[46]

REFLECTIONS

A few questions will help us reflect on the issues:

1. Devotion to female saints/deities (etc.) is quite prominent in a number of traditions which are otherwise focused upon generally male figures (e.g., the goddess/bodhisattva Guanyin in East Asia; see box 2.9). What do you think might account for this as a feature of lived religion?

2. Our Lady of Guadalupe appears to be understood by many Mexican American women not just in relation to Catholic tradition but also in ways which go beyond the official teachings. In considering what she means, do you think we should pay more heed to official teachings or what we find in popular practice? Why?

3. In contemporary Chicano and mestizo theological speculation, and in historical context, Our Lady of Guadalupe is a figure that combines both Catholic and indigenous religious concepts and iconography. Notwithstanding her elite

following (Pope John Paul II [1920–2005] reportedly had a deep devotion to her), in what ways do you see her as a figure who appeals to marginal(ized) groups? In what ways do you think lived religion often develops in relation to groups that are in some ways separated from official/orthodox religious centers of power, and may offer points of resistance against elite traditions?

4. Is Our Lady of Guadalupe syncretic? What is meant by this? Does the image employ indigenous American and Catholic traits? Is she a figure who represents both Tonantzin and the Virgin Mary? Whose representation of this should we consider?

CASE STUDY 3B. THAI BUDDHISM AS LIVED RELIGION AND SYNCRETIC PRACTICE

Southeast Asian Buddhism, including Thai Buddhism, has often been termed "syncretic." Indeed, the day-to-day practice of Buddhism has been described as a syncretic system which includes even seemingly contradictory elements.[47] This was the context in which Melford Spiro distinguished elite and apotropaic Buddhism. However, this distinction is not always so clear-cut.

BASICS OF THAI BUDDHISM

Thai Buddhism follows Theravada tradition in emphasizing the perceived earliest texts, or Tripitaka. Theravada Buddhism emphasizes, in elite understandings, the role of monks as transmitters of the Buddha's teachings (*dharma*) and as the foundation of the community of Buddhism (*sangha*). Around 95 percent of Thai people identify as Buddhists. Their Buddhism follows the apotropaic model; nirvana may be seen as the goal for monks, but is not considered a goal for laypeople. Indeed, while monks are revered and held in high esteem, interactions with them are often not for teachings about elite Buddhist ideas, but for the purpose of attaining "merit" (*punya*), what we might term "beneficial *karma*" which will ensure a better reincarnation or other blessings. Moreover, this relationship is not just one way; monks recognize the interests of laypeople within this scheme of things. Indeed, most monks do not spend their time meditating and seeking awakening/nirvana. They are often involved in copying texts, maintaining monastery buildings, promoting education, or other matters.

PROTECTION AND ELITE BUDDHISM

Some may see "true" Buddhism as embodied in the elite practice, especially as based in the fourfold diagnosis of the Buddha (see box 3.7). However, the Tripitaka includes "protection spell" (*paritta*) texts. These refer to a variety of texts or phrases which provide various "protections": against seduction, for safe childbirth, or as general safekeeping charms.[48] Whether or not these protective verses go back to the Buddha, which is debated by scholars, they are embedded within the authoritative Buddhist texts. This provides a "scriptural," or institutional/elite, Buddhist rationale for what are often seen as the popular practices of "magical spells" for protection (see boxes 7.8 and 9.4).

SYNCRETIC ELEMENTS IN BUDDHISM

Thomas Kirsh split Thai religious practices into three distinct and separate levels or elements: Theravada Buddhism, folk Brahminism, and animism. The first refers to monastic and elite practices, and also the interaction of laypeople with monks. The second refers to the primary sets of devotion of ordinary people for specific needs or desires, often to deities typically understood as Hindu. Yet the people praying to them identify as Buddhist, not Hindu. Statues to these deities are also often found in Buddhist monasteries. These levels are not distinct, but are connected. The third is devotion to nature and local spirits, often termed "animism."[49] Throughout Thailand, in cities, towns, and the countryside, it is common to see small shrines to local deities or spirits, where people often leave food for animals and birds. Many Thais do not see a disconnect between the three levels. In ceremonies such as Buddhist funerals, it is common to leave

A Naga (snake deity) temple guardian figure, Chiang Mai, Thailand.

some portion of food offerings for animals, such as birds or other small creatures. In a way, this can be seen as consonant with elite Buddhist concepts that one should have compassion (*metta*) for all sentient creatures. However, such offerings probably also reflect both animistic practices and devotion to tutelary (guardian) spirits. The levels identified by Kirsh are not, as often supposed, distinct and discrete layers: they overlap and intersect.

BUDDHISM, ANIMISM, AND POPULAR SPIRIT MEDIUM CULTS

Indeed, within popular spirit medium cults (see box 3.8), which are sometimes contrasted with Buddhism, we also see a crossing over to Buddhism. Kitiarsa describes the shrine of one such cult which shows a definite hierarchy of deities/spirits/divinized figures in terms of how they are displayed (generally, the more senior, with larger statues, are placed higher on displays). She lists one example as follows (from senior to less senior):

Found in many parts of East and Southeast Asia, the spirit medium is a person who embodies various deities/spirits in special ceremonies. S/he (depending on the context they are often predominantly female or male) generally enters a trance in which the spirit may possess her/him, and then act in ways associated with that spirit as well as speaking on its behalf, often answering questions put by supplicants. Though sometimes found in temples, or temple ceremonies, they are often distinct from institutional religious structures.

- Lord Buddha as supreme deity
- magic monks/saints (famous, miracle-performing figures)
- Hindu gods/goddesses
- Chinese deities, for example, Guanyin (see box 2.9) and Mazu (a sea goddess)
- royal spirits
- local guardian and other tutelary spirits

As befits Thai religious sensibilities, the Buddha is given supreme place. So, is this a Buddhist practice? Or, perhaps, spirit mediums place their system in relation to Buddhism to give credence to their practices? For Kitiarsa, this should be spoken of as hybridity; she argues that we see here not simply a blending of spirit mediumship into Buddhism, but a very distinct set of local practices that draw from Buddhism but are not part of Buddhism. She argues it is not syncretic or popular Buddhism, but a different set of folk or local practices. Certainly, the lower-level deities are often prayed to, as they are seen as accessible. But, is it really clear that this is distinct and not part of Buddhism? And, if this is not, what about ordinary practices of Thai Buddhists praying to "Hindu" deities who are found in Buddhist temples? Do the presumptions arise from the data, or from what a WRP-inspired religious studies theory (including sociological and anthropological theory inspired by the same lineage) suggests—a theory that assumes we should find a clear distinction between elite and popular/folk and between different religious systems, with anything syncretic being inherently illegitimate?

REFLECTIONS

Some questions will help us think through issues raised by this case study:

I.   In a religious tradition known to you, can you think of any similar aspects of syncretic fusion? If so, how do you relate to or understand these? If not, do you think this affects how you understand and think about these practices when seen elsewhere?

2. Thinking back to the hybridity/syncretism theory, as represented by figures such as Bakhtin and Bhabha, do you see elements that help you think about the range of practices seen here?

3. If we do not assume that the elite, textual, and monastic Buddhist traditions are "correct" Buddhism, do we see the kind of syncretism found in ordinary practices to be equally a form of Buddhism? Or is it some other tradition? Does the fact that what are normally considered to be Hindu deities are found in Buddhist temples show that they have become part of Buddhism in this context?

.   .   .

QUESTIONS AND CONNECTING THOUGHTS

This chapter is intimately linked to chapter 1 in terms of helping us reconceptualize how to think about "religion." However, it also crosses over with discussions about material religion (chapter 9), colonialism and Orientalism (chapter 7), and gender (chapter 10), as all of these pick out neglected areas of thinking about religious practice and what religion may be. We should also note that a focus on lived religion does not mean that we ignore elite religion, or downplay it. Indeed, there are certainly those whose version of religion is the elite version, or some variation of that, and so it is their lived experience. Ignoring that would be equally one-sided. However, considering these complications helps us focus on things we might otherwise not see. There are also other relations to chapters beyond this, such as what counts as secular or religious (chapter 16). Some questions may help us think about these issues:

1. Does seeing such things as gardening, social work, or other "mundane" activities as religious reinforce the "hard deconstructivist" attack on the term "religion" as effectively meaningless? Or does it simply help us expand our conception of how "religion" may be usefully employed as an essentially contested concept (see chapter 1)?

2. To what extent do you think studying religion should balance between a focus on elite tradition and lived religion? Is either more significant in some situations, or more worthy of attention in certain contexts?

3. If all religions are syncretic, how and why does this entail us rethinking the borders, boundaries, and names of religions? When do such borders exist as fixed social realities (see box 1.9), and when are they more fluid and malleable membranes?

4. Is there a clear line between lived religion and elite practice? If not, how would you demarcate them? If yes, what is that line?

FURTHER READING

THEORY

Ammerman, Nancy Tatom. *Sacred Stories, Spiritual Tribes: Finding Religion in Everyday Life* (Oxford: Oxford University Press, 2013), 56–90.

Harvey, Graham. *Food, Sex and Strangers: Understanding Religion as Everyday Life* (Durham: Acumen, 2013).

Kitiarsa, Pattana. "Beyond Syncretism: Hybridization of Popular Religion in Contemporary Thailand," *Journal of Southeast Asian Studies* 36.3 (2005): 461–87.

Leopold, Anita, and Jeppe Jensen, eds. *Syncretism in Religion: A Reader* (New York: Routledge, 2004).

McGuire, Meredith. *Lived Religion* (Oxford: Oxford University Press, 2008).

Orsi, Robert. "Is the Study of Lived Religion Irrelevant to the World We Live in?" *Journal for the Scientific Study of Religion* 42.2 (2003): 169–74.

Orsi, Robert. *The Madonna of 115th Street: Faith and Community in Italian Harlem, 1880–1950*, 3rd ed. (New Haven: Yale University Press, 2010).

Young, Robert. *Colonial Desire: Hybridity in Theory, Culture and Race* (New York: Routledge, 1995).

CASE STUDY 3A. MEXICAN AMERICAN CATHOLICISM AND OUR LADY OF GUADALUPE

Burkhardt, Louise. "The Cult of the Virgin of Guadalupe in Mexico," in *South and Mesoamerican Native Spirituality: From the Cult of the Feathered Serpent to the Theology of Liberation*, ed. Gary Gossen and Miguel León-Portilla (London: SCM, 1993), 198–227.

Castañenda-Liles, María Del Socorro. *Our Lady of Everyday Life: La Virgen de Guadalupe and the Catholic Imagination of Mexican American Women* (Oxford: Oxford University Press, 2018), especially 146–66.

Lara, Irene. "Goddess of the Americas in the Decolonial Imaginary: Beyond the Virtuous Virgen/Pagan Puta Dichotomy," *Feminist Studies* 34.1/2 (2008): 99–127.

Rodriquez, Jeanette. *Our Lady of Guadalupe: Faith and Empowerment among Mexican-American Women* (Austin: University of Texas, 1994), 61–86.

CASE STUDY 3B. THAI BUDDHISM AS LIVED RELIGION AND SYNCRETIC PRACTICE

Crosby, Kate. *Theravada Buddhism: Continuity, Identity, and Diversity* (Chichester: Wiley-Blackwell, 2014).

Kitiarsa, Pattana. "Beyond Syncretism: Hybridization of Popular Religion in Contemporary Thailand," *Journal of Southeast Asian Studies* 36.3 (2005): 461–87.

Kitiarsa, Pattana. *Mediums, Monks, and Amulets* (Chiang Mai: Silkworm Books, 2012).

Swearer, Donald. *The Buddhist World of Southeast Asia* (Albany: State University of New York Press, 1995).

THEORIES, METHODOLOGIES, AND CRITICAL DEBATES

4

HISTORY

Historical Methodology and the Invention of Tradition

IN WHICH WE EXPLORE:

How historians (of religion) think and understand the world

The history of religion, including the invention of tradition

Case studies exploring the historical Jesus and the Christ of faith distinction, and the associations of the mythical Laozi with the birth of Daoism

INTRODUCTION

In many places, the academic study of religion is known as the history of religions. Arguably the most significant of all international scholarly organizations (in the field) is the International Association for the History of Religions (IAHR). However, the study of religion is not simply about the past. The primary focus of this book is the contemporary situation. Nevertheless, the history of religions is of vital importance for understanding the contemporary context:

- Religions have always changed and transformed. What any religion looks like now is not what it looked like at any previous point. This awareness helps avoid essentialized conceptions about what any religion is or should be.

- The way any religion operates now, in a specific location, depends on the how and why of its arrival and adaptation to a new situation. Historical context is therefore necessary to understand the present.

WAS THERE RELIGION IN THE PAST?

A well-known saying in historical studies is, "The past is a different country; they do things differently there." In previous periods, the things we term "religions" were not characterized in the exact way they are now. This means we cannot expect to neatly define a "religious" sphere. However, it is conceptually confused to suppose we must abandon the term: the ancient Greeks had no word for slavery, but the institution of slavery was widespread (see box 1.8). Likewise, many other words in modern English, including "politics," "philosophy," "culture," "economics," and "art," will not map exactly onto historical usages. This is a problem of all translation and historical study, not a unique problem with the term "religion" (see box 1.7); it applies to many "essentially contested concepts" (see chapter 1). Nevertheless, we cannot simply assume "religion" (or any term) means the same elsewhere as it does in the modern Western world.

- The skills and tools of interpreting past events apply equally to present-day contexts and situations.

These four key points should also be noted:

1. In some ways, the history of religions is often the point where a confessional understanding of a religion (the insider stance; see chapter 2) rubs up against the scholarly interpretation (the outsider stance). Many communities see themselves in a faithful lineage to imagined "original" teachings (see chapter 3).

2. Because of the nature of the history of religions methodology, we will spend comparatively longer on case studies to get a clear and strong sense of context.

3. The methods of historical research are not necessarily distinctive and overlap with other methods. Nevertheless, there are distinct theoretical issues.

4. As "religion" is a modern term from a particular context (see chapter 1), our concept of "religion" may not always fit neatly into historical contexts (see box 4.1).

We begin by asking how historians think about historical "facts." We then consider whether we can learn from history, looking at Chinese Confucian conceptions. Next, we address the growth of historical consciousness and methodology, and their association with the Renaissance and Enlightenment, relating this to various religious traditions and non-Western thought systems. We then explore Bruce Lincoln's method for reading historical religious texts. We will finish, as usual, by exploring two case studies.

John Lewis Gaddis takes issue with the time machine approach to history: the idea that you can go back and know firsthand the events of the past to get the "truth." For instance, as an example of a time machine approach, if one went back to Sarajevo to see Archduke Ferdinand being shot, would this help answer the question of whether this shooting led to the outbreak of WWI? This raises wider issues about how we come to know the past:

Selectivity:[1] As a hypothetical time traveler you would have access only to the unfolding of certain pieces of information in one place.

Simultaneity: A historian can be in more than one place at one time. They are "standing apart from the events they describe" and so "can understand and, more significantly, *compare* events."[2]

Seeds: Any narrative about history (what a historian narrates) begins somewhere. Therefore, the origins, the seeds that sowed the situation, may remain untold. So, we have what for Antonio Gramsci (1891–1937) is history as told only in "fragments." The back story about our supposed norms or starting point may remain unseen (like seeds in the ground).[3] The time traveler may not see what happened before she arrived.

Scale: The historian is able to focus on specifics (as the time traveler may be in a specific place), but also to transcend that to cover the macroscopic and not just the microscopic.[4]

We also need to be aware that all history is about interpretation. Indeed, much contemporary historical study is not necessarily concerned with asking whether certain events are true or not true. Rather, it is about the meaning and interpretation of these events, the narratives in which they are embedded, and what these tell us about the communities and traditions who pass stories down. This is not to suggest that facts are not important, and at least two things compel us to take them seriously:

Relativism is neither intellectually coherent nor useful as an academic tool (see introduction, chapter 9, and box 2.5).

Fake news is not the same as news. Facts matter.

Yet, in history, we often deal in probability rather than certainty. Narratives and histories may be passed by word of mouth (oral history) long before being written down as "recorded history." But this is not to say the latter is more reliable:

Oral histories can also pass on facts.

Written history was often composed by the "winners" (of battles) and literate elites. We must be cautious about what they recorded (or did not record).

BOX 4.2 **THE SCHOLAR AS "WANDERER" IN A SEA OF FOG**

Gaddis invokes a famous painting by Caspar David Friedrich (1774–1840), *The Wanderer above a Sea of Fog* (1818), in which we see a (young) man, his back to us, atop a craggy outcrop of rock looking into the distance, where we see occasional peaks, glimpses of trees and landscapes, but all blending with and immersed in the fog or clouds.[1] Whether one knows the painting or not, his image is clear. The historian is like the person: looking out at a scene where some things seem clear, but much is simply obscured. The viewer may choose to survey the whole, or focus on the specific and particular. However, we also need to look at the looker: who or what is the historian? What does she see? Why does she see in the way she does? This relates to issues in other chapters, but especially reflexivity (see chapter 2), an awareness of one's own prejudices and situatedness: to acknowledge that your culture, class, gender, race, nationality, position in time and space, and so on, affect what you see and how you see it (see chapters 3, 7, and 10).

---

1 Gaddis, *Landscape of History*, 129. The painting and a commentary on it can be found at www.artble.com/artists/caspar_david_friedrich/paintings/wanderer_above_the_sea_of_fog.

We must ask: what do we see or know (see box 4.2)?

TERMINOLOGY

If history is about interpretation, the question of what is "true" ("facts") can be difficult. Moreover, many different words are used, especially when discussing what are seen as religious narratives, each of which may give us different perspectives on the veracity of the events or stories relayed, for instance, terms such as "myth" or "legend." Here, it is useful to establish some benchmarks for employing these (see box 4.3).

HISTORIANS AND THE FUTURE?

Gaddis' invocation of *The Wanderer above a Sea of Fog* raises another question about historians: do they see the past or future?[5] Does the past inform us about potential patterns in human societies and behavior? We may be familiar with the adage "Those who do not know the past are condemned to repeat it." While not part of historical methodology, it raises questions. One aspect of good historical work is paying attention to particulars, noting the very distinct situation and context of what occurred. Nevertheless, Gaddis argues that comparison, including across time, is generally assumed as viable by the historian (see chapter 11). For instance, the rise of authoritarian regimes or dictators across time may be marked by similarities: nationalist populism, curtailing the rule of law, and rewriting or reinterpreting history. Who says history does not matter![6]

For Confucius (traditionally, 551–479 BCE) and subsequent Confucians, history was of fundamental significance. Historical narratives such as the Book of Documents (*shujing,* or Classic of History) and the Spring and Autumn Annals (*chunqiu*) were central to understanding both good ethical behavior and governance. Confucians held that we could learn from both the positive example of ancient Sage Kings and how events unfolded in times of turmoil.[7] Today, in East Asia, the study of history is considered more central to understanding contemporary politics, ethics, and public life than is typical in the West. How and why we study history is both geographically and historically contingent.

THE HISTORICAL-CRITICAL METHOD: ITS HISTORY AND PERSPECTIVES
ORIGIN STORIES

The Enlightenment was a period in European history from around the sixteenth to the eighteenth centuries when we see the birth of what we term modernity (see box 16.1). It saw the birth of modern science, and also the historical-critical method, when traditions and authorities started to be questioned more thoroughly through rational critique. It was made possible because of the growth of historical consciousness in the Renaissance (see box 4.4). At that time, people became aware that our ideas, concepts, and ways of life

WHAT IS THE RENAISSANCE?

The Renaissance, signifying "rebirth," is typically dated from ca, 1350/1400 to 1600/1650 and is often traced to Florence.[1] It looked back to Greece and Rome, and witnessed a flowering of science and the arts in Europe. The human became central to philosophy and thinking, signaled by the term "humanism"; notably, the early humanists were Christians.[2] Study of Greek, Hebrew, and other languages flourished, and this helped develop a new historical awareness that there had been differing viewpoints and cultural outlooks in human history.

While today associated with the development of "the West," tracing an imagined European lineage back to Greece, the Renaissance was multicultural and global.[3] The then far more advanced Islamic developments in science and philosophy provided the bedrock, hence the Renaissance's origins in Italian trading cities.[4] Indeed, the Greeks themselves had no sense of being "European," as we understand it; their cultural points and learning came from the great civilizations of Persia, Egypt, and India. Philosophy was seen to originate in India, Africa, or the Islamic world.[5]

---

1 See John Martin, ed., *The Renaissance World* (New York: Routledge, 2007).

2 See Jonathan Arnold, *The Great Humanists: An Introduction* (London: I. B. Tauris, 2011).

3 See Leah Clarke, "Globalisation Was Rife in the 16th Century—Clues from Renaissance Paintings," *Conversation* (10 May 2019), http://theconversation.com/globalisation-was-rife-in-the-16th-century-clues-from-renaissance-paintings-116087?utm_medium=email&utm_campaign=Latest%20from%20The%20Conversation%20for%20May%2013%202019%20-%201307412204&utm_content=Latest%20from%20The%20Conversation%20for%20May%2013%202019%20-%201307412204+CID_9b7d7c556f4cd05eaa38e4c7c9799034&utm_source=campaign_monitor_uk&utm_term=Globalisation%20was%20rife%20in%20othe%2016th%20century%20%20clues%20from%20Renaissance%20paintings.

4 See John Hobson, *The Eastern Origins of Western Civilisation* (Cambridge: Cambridge University Press, 2004), 173–83.

5 In the words of Roger Bacon (1214–1292): "Philosophy is drawn from the Muslims," cited in Aziz Atiya, *Crusade, Commerce, and Culture* (Bloomington: Indiana University Press, 1962), 220. See also Christopher Beckwith, *Warriors of the Cloisters: The Central Asian Origins of Science in the Medieval World* (Princeton: Princeton University Press, 2012), 147–49.

---

had shifted quite dramatically over time. It is hard to overemphasize this dramatic shift in understanding. From assuming that people of the past were more or less just like us, culturally speaking, people started to realize we had changed. Note that there is no clear division between the Renaissance and Enlightenment, but the intellectual shift turns from southern Europe and Italy (Renaissance) to northern Europe, especially Germany and Scotland (Enlightenment).

The historical-critical method of the Enlightenment was an outgrowth of this historical consciousness in practice. If we had changed and developed over time, then we could study these changes through historical documents and records. So, a critical eye was cast upon old texts.

The Hebrew Bible (Christian Old Testament) was first scrutinized, and later the New Testament. However, this challenge was not initially against Christianity per se.

THE BIBLE, JESUS, AND HISTORICAL CRITICISM

In 1774, Gotthold Ephraim Lessing (1729–1781) published *Concerning the Intention of Jesus and His Teaching*, including some passages from a work by Hermann Samuel Reimarus (1694–1768) under the title "Fragments." Reimarus's original work, *An Apology for the Rational Worshipper of God*, was not published during his lifetime because he was afraid of the reaction it would cause, as it challenged traditional Christian teachings on Jesus's divinity and teachings. Lessing argued we could find the real Jesus behind the mythic accretions in the Gospel stories. Reimarus argued that Jesus was an apocalyptic teacher (somebody who expected the end times to come) whose mission failed: Jesus had expected God to deliver the Jews from Roman rule, and so his last cry from the cross was one of despair. Further, Reimarus argued, Jesus's disciples invented the resurrection to hide their embarrassment at their teacher's death, created a "spiritualized" redemption (rather than a physical and political one), and innovated doctrinally.[1]

---

1 See Clinton Bennett, *In Search of Jesus* (London: Continuum, 2001), 95–98.

Questioning the Hebrew Bible was part of the Protestant Reformation (see box 9.3). Studying Hebrew made it clear that contemporary Jews used a different, shorter, Hebrew Bible (Tanakh).[8] For Protestants, this was evidence of alleged distortion of Christianity by the Catholics, though Catholics followed earlier Jewish precedent.[9] However, several high-profile cases made historical criticism suspect to many Jews and Christians. For instance, Baruch Spinoza (1632–1677) was exiled from the Jewish community in Amsterdam for suggesting that the first five books of the Hebrew Bible were not written by Moses.[10] While accepted scholarship today, it remains contentious for many Orthodox Jews. Of more significance to Christians were challenges to the New Testament and Jesus's supposed divine status (see box 4.5 and case study 4A).

RELIGIONS AND HISTORICAL CRITICISM

Despite the potential challenges, during the nineteenth century many mainstream Protestant Christian denominations accepted the basis of historical criticism, if not every conclusion. They accepted that the Bible was subject to historical development, that it was a human document, and that various facts had been distorted by human scribes. In the 1960s, the Catholic Christian church also accepted historical criticism. However, in the early twentieth century, Protestant Christian fundamentalism, especially in the United States, directly challenged this historical-critical approach, as many Christians continue to do (see chapter 15). The historical-critical approach has developed more closely alongside (Western) Christianity, which has given Christians longer to adjust to the critiques it raises. But for many religions, a historical-critical reading of their texts is not widely accepted. This raises a number of questions for scholars: Should they be concerned with how religious traditions interpret their work? Should they engage with members of religious traditions in this work?

THE INVENTION OF TRADITION

Danièle Hervieu-Léger argues that what distinguishes religion from other forms of life is submission to tradition (though this is debatable, as tradition is key in many social organizations). Many religious traditions trace themselves back via tradition—which means "that which is passed on"—to some original starting point, perhaps a revelation. Religion has, Hervieu-Léger argues, an "appeal to a line of witnesses" and can best be defined as an association to "a chain of memory."[11] We can note various examples:

- Christianity often appeals to what it terms an "apostolic succession" to show that current leaders and teachings can be linked back to the earliest Jesus movement (see box 4.11).
- Zen Buddhism, which arose in China around the fifth to sixth centuries CE, justified itself by appealing to a chain of patriarchs, notably the semi-legendary Bodhidharma (ca. 470–520 CE), leading back to the Buddha.[12]
- When Islamic scholars (*ulama*) codified the sayings of Muhammed (*hadith*), they sought chains of transmission, via what were deemed trustworthy lineages, to assess authenticity.[13]

Scholars have long noted that two significant factors apply to tradition. First, the only stable aspect of tradition is that it always changes. Tradition is not an unchanging and monolithic chain, but a set of ideas, texts, and practices that adapt over time. Second, traditions always begin somewhere, and what we think of as ancient traditions may have more recent beginnings. Historians, therefore, speak about the "invention of tradition,"[14] which also applies to "sacred tradition."[15] To note a few examples:

- The long black coats and curled locks of hair of Hasidic Judaism date back to their life in eastern Europe around the seventeenth and eighteenth centuries. Often seen as a defining characteristic of their Orthodox Judaism, this appearance is actually a relatively recent innovation in a claimed three-thousand-year lineage.[16]
- Today, many Evangelical Christians assert that Jesus, as God, suffered for humanity's sins. They often link this to Chalcedonian Orthodoxy, referring to the Council of Chalcedon (451 CE),which determined issues on the Trinity and Jesus's nature, a touchstone in orthodox belief for Protestant, Catholic,

and Orthodox Christians. However, the Council of Chalcedon, prior to other discussions, declared an anathema (excommunication) on anyone who believed that God suffered in Jesus's crucifixion.[17]

- Sunni Muslims typically aver that the Quran is not simply the specific revelation to Muhammad, but exists as the eternal revelation of God. This viewpoint developed in disputes around the ninth to tenth centuries.[18]

ORIENTALISM AND DECOLONIZING HISTORICAL RESEARCH

Some have asserted that historical-critical methods are an Orientalist assault on non-Western traditions. In brief (see chapter 7, especially box 7.3), Edward Said's Orientalist thesis posits that Western study of the Orient aims to assert power and control. Certainly, non-Western systems, such as Confucian notions of history, typically do not count as legitimate theory, but only as data for study. Indeed, nearly all Western academic theory, not just in the study of religion but across almost every discipline, is almost entirely Western-centric (and still predominantly white, male, and elite). The method we have laid out here is one determined by what is generally seen as a modern Western approach. A decolonial lens raises questions about how we regard such methodology. This question is simply raised here and left with individual readers as part of wider discussions in this book and beyond, where racist undertones in the history of religion lineage have been noted.[19] Indeed, as history may show that traditions have been invented, this may be seen to have a liberatory message for various oppressed groups. Once it becomes clear that certain ways of seeing the world are not "natural," but developed at particular times, often with certain narratives claiming to assert authority of one community/class/race/(etc.) over others, these may be challenged. The archaeological/genealogical method of figures such as Michel Foucault (1926–1984) is one source for such readings of history.

HOW TO READ A RELIGIOUS TEXT
BRUCE LINCOLN AND CRITICAL READING

One particular way of reading historical texts is exemplified by Bruce Lincoln's analysis of a small portion of a Hindu text called the Chandogya Upanishad.[20] This Upanishad outlines an argument that the priestly caste (*brahmin*) should be regarded as superior to that of the rulers and warriors (*kshatriya*) (see box 4.6).

However, Lincoln's choice of text is incidental to his methodology. The following two quotes outline key principles:

As a first principle, noncontroversial in itself (I hope), but far-reaching in its implications, let me advance the observation that, like all other texts, those that constitute themselves as religious are human products.

THE CASTE SYSTEM, THE CHANDOGYA UPANISHAD, AND HINDUISM

The caste system refers to the Indian social system whereby people are divided into one of four main castes (*varna*): priests (*brahmin*), warriors and rulers (*kshatriya*), merchants and craftspeople (*vaishya*), and workers and serfs (*shudra*). These four main castes were split into subcastes. Then, based upon family occupation, at least twenty thousand subgroups (*jati*) exist. Below all four castes come the so-called untouchables, or outcasts, today known as Dalits; "Dalit," which means "broken," is how they identify. The caste system is most associated with Hinduism as it is justified in key texts of that tradition, especially the Chandogya Upanishad, the Bhagavad Gita, the Brihadaranyaka Upanishad, and the Laws of Manu. However, it permeates Indian Christianity and Sikhism, both of which officially denounce caste. Caste was outlawed in 1950 under article 15 of the India Constitution, but remains rife in many places, especially affecting Dalits.[1] Arguably it became more widespread under British rule than it had been before due to codifications of a supposed Hindu legal/social system. In medieval India there was resistance to it from devotional (*bhakti*) traditions.[2] Notably, uncovering the history of how the caste system developed has led some Dalit thinkers to argue against those who have claimed it has always been a part of Indian/Hindu tradition, as it has a clear heritage and origin.

---

1 See Gavin Flood, *An Introduction to Hinduism* (Cambridge: Cambridge University Press, 1996), 58–61; and McKim Marriott, "Varna and Jati," in *The Hindu World*, ed. Sushil Mittal and Gene Thursby (New York: Routledge, 2004), 357–82.
2 This resistance arguably never attained long-lasting results. See Karen Pechilis, "Bhakti," in *The Bloomsbury Companion to Hindu Studies*, ed. Jessica Frazier (London: Bloomsbury, 2011), 107–22, 116–18; and Flood, *Introduction to Hinduism*, 135.

As with secular exercises in persuasion, we need to ask: Who is trying to persuade whom of what in this text? In what context is the attempt situated, and what are the consequences should it succeed?[21]

Let us spend a bit of time unpacking what Lincoln is saying here. The first quote aligns with historical-critical method, and so is (he hopes) uncontroversial. Some in religious traditions do not regard their texts as human products, but we speak here of a scholarly attitude.

We can evaluate the second principle a bit more. First, he says that religious texts are like secular texts (a problematic dichotomy [see chapter 16], but we know what he means). Moreover, they are acts of persuasion. That is to say, somebody has written the text because they have an argument to make, a story to tell, a narrative to propagate. These texts are embedded within human communities as acts of power. One group (the writer's) wants to impart a message to another group. So, Lincoln asks us to look at four questions (the first has two parts). Let us take our time with each to see the significance of them:

- Who is trying to persuade whom in this text? Most historical texts come from an elite group as most people were illiterate. But which group, and to whom is it addressed? In Lincoln's text, it is written by priests (*brahmins*) to the class of warriors and rulers/kings (*kshatriyas*).

- What are they trying to persuade them about? This means unpacking the argument of the text. This Upanishad argues that the highest group in the social hierarchy should be the priests. Anyone familiar with the standard taxonomy of the Hindu caste system (see box 4.6) will find this uncontroversial. But how did this come about?

- In what context is the attempt situated? This may require some knowledge of the textual history, or there may be clues in the text. For Lincoln's text, it is a situation of some social upheaval.

- What are the consequences should it succeed? This final question comes to the nub of the issue: Who benefits, and in what way? If the act of persuasion is successful, what is the outcome? Lincoln argues the result would be a changed social order, where the priestly caste must be deferred to (at least ideally).

Such a reading partakes in a hermeneutics of suspicion (see box 2.7) by not reading the text at face value. But, further, it focuses on the power dynamics and act of persuasion entailed, employing social constructionism to question the text (see chapter 5). It goes beyond a simple historical or phenomenological description to a critical analysis of the textual dynamics. It does not simply say about a text that "it teaches *x*, and says *y*" but asks of it, "why does it teach *x*?" and "who benefits from saying *y*?"

THE IMPERATIVE: "HOW TO READ"

For many scholars, Lincoln's method is *the* model. The very title of his work is itself an imperative: this is *how to read!* Indeed, I include it here as an exemplary model of how a religious text *may* be read. However, is it the only way?

Lincoln's question about power and persuasion fashions the hermeneutics of suspicion into a powerful tool to see the way that such texts seek to influence people. Indeed, it applies not just to historical texts, but contemporary manifestations of persuasion: from political speeches to media reports, from advertising to conversational tactics. However, it is a limited way of engaging the world. Indeed, advocates of such a position do not generally ask others to employ it on their own work. As such, we may ask: what happens if we read Lincoln's paper via his own methodology (see box 4.7)?

Bryan Van Norden questions certain ways of employing the hermeneutics of suspicion. He recounts, at a talk he gave, being heavily criticized for not critically engaging the agenda of the author he discussed. Norden had taken a typically philosophical stance, arguing that the author meant sincerely what was said, employing what he terms a "hermeneutics of faith." Norden argues that not every text is written to change a social context or undermine a political structure. Indeed, even if we grant some agenda, Norden argues for something very different: that sometimes we should seek a meaning in the text in the way it speaks to us at a more personal level.[22] We learn about, for instance, the human situation or ourselves, much as we do from reading great literature. Again, from a Confucian perspective, we can seek to learn what a historical text, or situation, may tell us today: to learn from the lessons of the past. Lincoln's method is one way to read a historical text, but not the only way, nor the only scholarly way of reading. Historical methodologies all have a particular history that shapes how they ask us to look at the world. This is not to dismiss them all as only relative, but to acknowledge that we need to understand where we stand and the agenda we bring to reading texts, thereby being open to other possible ways of reading and seeing the world.

.   .   .

CASE STUDY 4A. THE HISTORICAL JESUS AND THE CHRIST OF FAITH

One of the longest running scholarly debates is the distinction between the Jesus of history and the Christ of faith (see box 4.8). We cannot take on this whole debate, so we will look at one very short passage (Mark 1:1–8) and some key terminology.

BOX 4.8 **THE JESUS OF HISTORY AND CHRIST OF FAITH**

Since the publication of Herman Samuel Reimarus's (1694–1768) work in 1774 (see box 4.5), scholars have distinguished between Christian theological teaching about Jesus (Christology) and the historical evidence. This often contrasts a divine Jesus ("the Christ of faith") with a human teacher ("the Jesus of history"). From the historical development of Christology, and from what can be ascertained about the development and dating of the New Testament texts, scholars agree that Jesus could not have understood himself to be divine and the second person of the Trinity, as later doctrinal formulations teach.[1]

Mythical image of the baby Jesus with Mary, Berlin, Germany.

---

1 For social context, see Linda Woodhead, *An Introduction to Christianity* (Cambridge: Cambridge University Press, 2004), 45–51; for the theological debates, see Alister McGrath, *Historical Theology: An Introduction to the Christian Tradition* (Oxford: Blackwell, 1998), 61–72.

BACKGROUND 1: THE QUESTS FOR THE HISTORICAL JESUS

For over two hundred years, scholars have debated what, if anything, we can know about the historical Jesus. These debates are often split into four periods ("quests").[23] Note: These are numbered as either three or four quests because one period is sometimes seen as a "no quest" period:

First Quest (late eighteenth to early twentieth centuries): The disparity of the Christ of faith and the Jesus of history is noted. Attempts are made to peel away legends to find the "real Jesus" in the Gospel texts.

Second Quest ("No Quest") (early to mid-twentieth century): The failure of the first quest to find a "real Jesus" led many to believe it was impossible to distinguish between history and legend. The quest was dropped.

Third Quest (mid-twentieth century–1980s): On 20 October 1953, Ernst Käsemann (1906–1998) gave a lecture proposing that the first quest failed because the historical Jesus was the Christ of faith; theological teaching was asserted as history.

Fourth Quest (1980s–now): Acknowledging limitations in previous quests, scholars do not seek the "real Jesus" but argue we can credibly construct a historical figure. The main innovation is exploring the cultural, social, and political context, employing contemporary Jewish and Roman sources as well as archaeology. Scholars now try and understand Jesus as a figure of his place and time rather than trying to extract him from a book.

Mainstream scholarship does not seriously doubt that Jesus existed, which some populist intellectuals, dubbed the "mythicists," assert (see box 4.9).

BACKGROUND 2: READING A GOSPEL TEXT: MARK 1:1–8

We will focus on verses 1–8 of chapter 1 of the Gospel according to Mark (NIV):[24]

1 The beginning of the good news about Jesus the Messiah,[a] 2as it is written in Isaiah the prophet:
"I will send my messenger ahead of you, who will prepare your way"[c] —
3"a voice of one calling in the wilderness, 'Prepare the way for the Lord, make straight paths for him.'"[d]
4And so John the Baptist appeared in the wilderness, preaching a baptism of repentance for the forgiveness of sins. 5The whole Judean countryside and all the people of Jerusalem went out to him. Confessing their sins, they were baptized by him in the Jordan River. 6John wore clothing made of camel's hair, with a leather belt around his waist, and he ate locusts and wild honey. 7And this was his message: "After me comes the one more

THE MYTHICISTS: DID JESUS EXIST?

The "mythicist" argument that Jesus did not exist as a historical person has managed to enlist some seemingly credible spokespeople:

- Christopher Hitchens (1949–2011) was a highly respected public intellectual, but his arguments on Jesus lack scholarly merit as they are based on flimsy argument and a misunderstanding of historical evidence and methods.
- Richard Carrier has a PhD in classics and claims a "scientific" method. However, it may be argued that he has a suspect use of data and grossly misapplies Bayes' theorem (a theorem for assessing probability).[1]
- Richard Price was a theology professor at an Evangelical Christian university; he was never a credible academic scholar and his arguments are not robust.

Michael Ruse notes: "There is a highly vocal group of deniers of the existence of Jesus. But frankly, they come across like most conspiracy theorists, overpassionate in their cause, unwilling to compromise, and (a sure sign) very touchy when you question their credentials."[2] A more thoughtful mythicist, who suggests agnosticism may be appropriate, is Raphael Lataster, but even his work is not generally found to be convincing.

---

1 For a mathematical refutation of Carrier's use of Bayes' theorem, see https://irrco.wordpress .com/2012/09/08/a-mathematical-review-of-proving-history-by-richard-carrier/; and on his misrepresentation of issues, see Maurice Casey, *Jesus: Evidence and Argument or Mythicist Myths?* (London: Bloomsbury, 2014), 14–16, 230–31.
2 Michael Ruse, *Atheism: What Everyone Needs to Know* (Oxford: Oxford University Press, 2015), 134. See also Casey, *Jesus*.

powerful than I, the straps of whose sandals I am not worthy to stoop down and untie. [8]I baptize you with[e] water, but he will baptize you with[f] the Holy Spirit."

[*TEXTUAL notes*—a: Or *Jesus Christ. Messiah* (Hebrew) and *Christ* (Greek) both mean *Anointed One*. b: Some manuscripts do not have *the Son of God*. c: Mal 3:1. d: Isa: 40:3. e: Or *in*. f: Or *in*.]

Based on this excerpt, ask yourself the following questions:

What strikes you as the main claims?
　　Who do you think they are addressed to?
　　Who do you think they are aimed against?
What narratives does this text place itself in relation to?
　　What traditions or authorities are appealed to?
　　How does it relate itself to surrounding traditions?

Think through these questions before you carry on reading.

WHOSE GOSPELS? WHICH GOSPELS?

The names attached to the four Gospels are not indicative of authors, though John's Gospel is often held to come from the Johannine community (i.e., the disciples around John). Possibly someone named Luke, referred to in Paul's letters, is the author of both that Gospel and the Acts of the Apostles (both are generally held to have the same author). None was written with a name. Names were given later. However, the four Gospels in the Bible are almost certainly the oldest, and therefore the closet to the oral traditions of Jesus's direct disciples. The other Gospels we know of were written in the second century or later and show the thought of their period. Therefore, while instructive on early Christian developments, they are not pertinent to the historical Jesus. The one exception is the Gospel of Thomas, which holds early material, perhaps some of the earliest narratives we have, but was only finalized in the second century with much later material. Scholars debate how much weight should be given to it.[1]

---

1 Ehrman, *New Testament*, 217–36, 242–46.

CONTEXTUAL NOTES

It is important that we establish some Fourth Quest contextual notes.

Is This Text Reliable?

Scholars distinguish what they term the three synoptic Gospels—Matthew, Mark, and Luke—from the Gospel of John. "Synoptic," from Greek, means "to see together" and refers to overlaps and similarities in structure and content. Most scholars believe the synoptics were earlier: Mark (ca. 65–75 CE), Matthew and Luke (ca. 75–85 CE), John (ca. 85–100 CE). Importantly, most scholars see the synoptics as our best sources about the historical Jesus (see box 4.10).[25]

History or Storytelling?

It was normal for ancient writers to "make up" speeches. A good example is Jesus's trial before Pilate when no Gospel writer was present. This may strike us as dishonest, but it was how history was written then. Roman historians did the same, putting words into the mouths of emperors. But it means that the "presentation of Jesus in the New Testament is in fact itself a representation: it resembles a set of paintings more closely than it does a photograph."[26] Further, we know that the Gospels were altered over centuries until reaching more or less fixed forms.[27] Translations are also more or less accurate.

A Jewish Context?

Jesus was Jewish. So were his disciples. Recent studies have underlined how deeply Jewish Jesus's teachings were, and place him contextually as a Galilean rabbi in a

THE JESUS MOVEMENT

Referring to Jesus's early followers as part of the Jesus movement allows us to avoid the misleading lens of speaking of them as "Christians," which implies a separate religious identity. Jesus's early followers would not have understood themselves as "Christian": Jesus and all his disciples were Jewish. While the term "Christian" developed early, it was initially a Jewish term for followers of a Jewish messiah ("Christ" in Greek). A differentiated "Christian" tradition did not begin until very late in the first century CE at the earliest, and more likely in the second century. Until the Jewish rebellions of 66–73 CE and 132–135 CE, being Jewish was advantageous for Christians; it meant they belonged to a recognized *religio* (lineage tradition, see box 1.1) and had, as Jews, special exemption not to engage in the cult of the emperor. However, after these revolts, being Jewish became increasingly problematic socially. Further, with increasing distance from Jesus's first generation of disciples, the majority of converts and devotees were Gentiles (non-Jews), meaning that the Galilean rabbi Yeshua (Jesus in Aramaic, the language he spoke) became increasingly pictured in Greco-Roman and Gentile ways. However, a full separation did not occur until the fourth century, when Christianity became linked to imperial aspirations.[1]

---

1 On the separation of Christianity and Judaism, see Judith Lieu, *Neither Jew nor Greek? Constructing Early Christianity* (London: Bloomsbury, 2016), 31–49.

Hellenized Jewish world. Paul was also a deeply Jewish writer whose work makes most sense when read within the context of contemporary Jewish writing.[28] Various points stem from this awareness. One, the words and language used in the Gospels and other early "Christian" texts have to be understood within a Jewish framework, not later Christian interpretations. The Jesus movement (see box 4.11), and its rabbi, make more sense in this context.[29]

KEY POINTS

We will now interrogate the text through some key issues and phrases:

Good news: The opening phrase tells the reader that this is an important message for them. It is an attempt at persuasion.

Christ/Messiah: Literally, "the anointed one," this places Jesus in relation to Jewish tradition. It refers to many important figures, such as kings or prophets. Judaism in this period had a range of interpretations of who the Messiah might be, and also whether the Messiah was expected to appear. The idea of a warrior figure who would defeat the Romans was one of various interpretations.[30] Importantly, no Jewish interpretation sees the Messiah as a divine figure: a first-century CE Jewish lens gives "Messiah" a very different meaning from a "Christ of faith" lens.

Son of God: While not appearing in every early text, the phrase "Son of God" is often held to clearly signal Jesus's divinity in this Gospel. But, to Jewish ears, it does not.[31] We can note three distinct meanings. First, most commonly, every Jew of the time would have regarded themselves as a "son (or daughter) of God." Second, it signified some special relationship to God, like a king or prophet. This is probably the intended usage. No language in the synoptics (read in context) implies Jesus's divinity.[32] Only in the later Gospel of John, which arguably shows Greco-Roman influences, do Jewish writers put words into Jesus's mouth that close the gap between him and God. The notion of demi-gods, or god-men such as Hercules, was well known in Greco-Roman mythology.[33] Third, "son of God" possibly signified special creatures, such as giants or angels (still creatures, and not God). This was not common and is least likely.

Hebrew Scripture: It is suggested that prophecy is fulfilled, placing Jesus in a certain lineage. It may indicate the audience is expected to know the verses. Notably, we have very little or no evidence that many of the verses used by the Jesus movement to show that Jesus was the Messiah were used this way by earlier Jewish tradition. It seems largely to be an innovation to explain how, assuming a victorious warrior Messiah was envisaged, a "failed" Messiah could actually be the Messiah.

John the Baptist: There was probably contestation between John's and Jesus's disciples. We know that in the decades following Jesus's death, John retained a larger following. In this passage, John is framed as a "forerunner," a powerful prophet but only a messenger for Jesus, while John's baptism with water is discursively distinguished from Jesus's baptism with spirit.

We could ask further questions: is the reader already a Christian/member of the Jesus movement (box 4.11)? Do they know Isaiah/John the Baptist? Is the audience Jewish or Gentile (non-Jewish), or both? A further question is whether we are we reading this through the ideological assumptions of contemporary Jewish or later Christian theological eyes?

REFLECTIONS

Some questions will help draw various implications out of this case study:

1. Place yourself, imaginatively, in the situation of a contemporary Christian faced with the evidence that the earliest Gospels do not understand Jesus as divine, but simply as a human teacher. (Maybe research a wider range of literature first.)

How do you respond? Do you reinterpret your belief in the light of historical argument? Reject the historical arguments out of hand? Or find some way to mediate between these two?

NOTE: Some Christian scholars who work on the historical Jesus question have sought to reconcile this. For instance, Marcus Borg speaks of a pre-resurrection (pre-Easter) Jesus, and the experience of the post-resurrection (post-Easter) Christ.[34]

2. In what ways is Mark 1:1–8 an act of persuasion? To whom, of what, in what context, and with what consequences? Do not forget to focus on the first-century Jewish context.

3. What do you think are the differences of reading this text (or any other) through a historical lens, rather than a religious lens? What techniques of reading are most useful?

4. For some, historical methods allow a return to "origins," or the earliest teachings. This is suspect to some historians, who argue that myth and history are always too entangled (the earliest texts are written as part of a tradition). This also raises questions about interpretation. To what extent may any historical opinion simply be an opinion, or are some things factual? Is the traditional Christian reading of these texts simply another interpretation? Who decides?

CASE STUDY 4B. LAOZI, THE DAODEJING, AND THE ORIGINS OF DAOISM

We will look at ways that a historical narrative challenges a religious narrative. In this case we will explore the tradition of Daoism, and its mythical (see box 4.3) founder, Laozi.

THE LIVES OF LAOZI

Laozi is actually a title meaning something like "Old Master," and our knowledge of who this may be relies on Sima Qian (ca. 145–86 BCE). Sima attributed what became a significant Daoist text, the Daodejing, to the Old Master, and provided a biography. However, he admits that he does not know who the Old Master was, providing three biographies for potential candidates, although he says it could be somebody else. Despite his uncertainty, subsequent histories and Daoist tradition simply took the first biography, with various additions, as historical fact (see box 4.12).

WHAT DO WE KNOW?

Did Laozi exist? The three figures Sima discusses are probably historical figures; however, it is doubtful any relates to the mythical Old Master described. For instance, it is doubtful that any of them was an elder teacher and a contemporary of Confucius.

The standard story of Laozi goes along these lines. His personal name was Lao Dan, though as a deity he is often called Laojun. He was the chief archivist of the Zhou Dynasty (1046–256 BCE), but decided to leave China. As he was departing for the West, he was urged to write the Daodejing by a border guard. He is said to have been an elder contemporary of Confucius (traditionally, 551–479 BCE), and berated the latter for his misunderstanding. In later legends, it is said he became the Buddha, but taught only a simplified version of his ideas in the West (i.e., India). We are also told that he stayed in his mother's womb till he was eighty-one, emerging as a white-haired old man. In later Daoist traditions, he is regarded as a manifestation of the Dao.

Did Laozi (Old Master) write the Daodejing? We can say no. It was long accepted that the standard recension of the Daodejing (the version of the text passed on by tradition that most of us know as the Daodejing) was the original. However, archaeology has disproved this. No Daodejing goes back to when Laozi needed to live according to the legends. It first existed as sets of sayings which were only later codified into a standard text, probably at the Jixia Academy in the second century BCE. One scholar has suggested the early sayings may be a set of folk aphorisms from one region or village attributed to the wise elders, or old masters; lacking a plural noun form, *laozi* (in Chinese) could be singular or plural.[35] The standard recension only goes back to the second century CE. It is also significantly different from older versions in at least two ways:

Order: When the sayings were codified as a unified text, it became two parts: *dao* and *de. Dao* means "way," signifying here a transcendent unknowable reality, and contains the more cosmological and philosophical aspects. *De* means "virtue" and contains the primarily social and political teachings. The standard recension places the *dao* part first, stressing the "religious" and cosmological aspects which inform the *de* parts; hence *dao-de-jing* (classic). Earlier versions placed the *de* first (*de-dao-jing*), and it was seemingly primarily read as a book about statecraft and political management.

Anti-Confucian elements: These are not in earlier versions. They reflect a situation in the second century CE when Confucianism had already become the dominant state ideology. They do not reflect an ancient division between Daoist and Confucian traditions, which is also read into Sima's narrative of the Old Master's relation to Confucius.

In short, we have no access to any historical figure that we can relate to the alleged Laozi of legend. Moreover, the Daodejing is not a text with a single author. Rather, it is a composite book of sayings developed over time.

We can also rule Laozi out as the founder of Daoism. Scholars agree that no institutional form of Daoism (see box 4.13) existed until at least the second century CE, though the earliest institutionalized Daoists, the Celestial Masters, did claim visions of Laozi as part of their legitimacy. The association of Laozi with a supposed older school of Daoist philosophy, related to the Zhuangzi, is likewise not historical: the Daodejing does not go back to the dates needed. The relationship of the Daodejing to other early lineages or sources for what become Daoism is debated by scholars.[36]

REFLECTIONS

Some questions will help us reflect on the issues raised.

1. Many Daoists and Chinese scholars reject what they see as Orientalist Western scholarship, instead relying on traditional narratives. Indeed, the traditional narrative of Laozi is still taught in mainstream Chinese education. Do you think historians need to be mindful of applying a Western Enlightenment paradigm to critique other cultures?

2. In what ways do you see the traditional story of Laozi as a form of persuasion: toward whom, and what consequences follow if accepted?

3. Do you find the historical-critical method to be inherently antithetical to traditional beliefs or religious traditions? In what ways do you think "positive" usages could be made by religious communities of such readings?

   NOTE: Despite claims that the Daodejing is the central text of Daoism, it has often been secondary, even marginal, in some traditions. It was often looked to for inspirational philosophy rather than any central content: it taught neither spiritual cultivation nor ritual. A central thrust of Daoism has always been embodied practice rather than textual study.[37]

4. Does the historian have a duty to the religious communities she investigates? If so, what is that duty? How do you think historians who are members of a tradition should or will differ in how they approach these issues?

·   ·   ·

QUESTIONS AND CONNECTING THOUGHTS

This chapter intersects with others. The methods suggested are influenced by social constructionism (see chapter 5), as well as feminist and postcolonial theory (see chapters 10 and 7, respectively). We need also to consider what "religion" means in historical contexts (chapter 1). We also explore historical questions elsewhere, especially in some case studies (including 1B, 5A, 7A, 9B, 11A, 13A, and 17B). To help us think through issues raised here, we end with some questions for reflection:

1. How do you think history should be read? To illuminate how the present came to be? To provide a guide to the future? To reveal liberatory narratives to empower oppressed groups? Or, some other way, or a combination of various ways?

2. Is the historical method always going to be in conflict with traditional religious beliefs? Think of other examples (perhaps with further research). To what extent does the historical method undermine central tenets? In what ways do scholars who are also within that religion seek to reconcile or deal with these issues? Should this be of concern to the historian as scholar?

3. History has normally been written by elites, and its study is often of elite groups. To what extent does that mean the views of more marginalized groups, whether that is because of gender, race, class, or other causes, are not heard? How might this be rectified? Should this be a concern to the historian as scholar?

4. How and why do we study history? Can it help us determine the future? Does it help illuminate the present? Can we read texts for personal learning and knowledge? Can uncovering historical power plays be a source of liberatory narratives for oppressed groups? Should all of these methods, and others, be of concern to the historian as scholar?

5.   If all history is about interpretation, in the sea of fog, can we ever talk about facts? If not, is any interpretation as good as any other? What about claims that seem blatantly false or damaging? Are "religious authorities" equal to "secular scholars" in pronouncing interpretations in this case? Should this be a concern to the historian as scholar?

FURTHER READING

THEORY

Gaddis, John Lewis. *The Landscape of History: How Historians Map the Past* (Oxford: Oxford University Press, 2004).

Hammer, O., and R.D. Lewis, eds. *The Invention of Sacred Tradition* (Cambridge: Cambridge University Press, 2007).

Hervieu-Léger, Danièle. *Religion as a Chain of Memory* (Cambridge: Polity Press, 2000).

Lincoln, Bruce. "How to Read a Religious Text: Reflections on Some Passages of the Chāndogya Upanishad," *History of Religions* 46.2 (2006): 127–39.

Olson, Carl. *The Allure of Decadent Thinking: Religious Studies and the Challenge of Postmodernism* (Oxford: Oxford University Press, 2013), 109–16, 128–33.

Wolffe, John, and Ronald Hutton. "John Wolffe and Ronald Hutton on Historical Approaches," podcast, Religious Studies Project (2013), www.religiousstudiesproject.com /podcast/podcast-john-wolffe-and-ronald-hutton-on-historical-approaches/.

CASE STUDY 4A. THE HISTORICAL JESUS
AND THE CHRIST OF FAITH

Ehrman, Bart. *How Jesus Became God: The Exaltation of a Jewish Preacher from Galilee* (New York: HarperOne, 2014), 85–128.

Levine, Amy-Jill. *The Misunderstood Jew: The Church and the Scandal of the Jewish Jesus* (New York: HarperOne, 2006), 17–52.

Martin, Craig. *A Critical Introduction to the Study of Religion*, 2nd ed. (New York: Routledge, 2017), 140–41, 148–50.

Vermes, Geza. *Jesus the Jew: A Historian's Reading of the Gospel* (London: Collins, 1973).

Vermes, Geza. *The Changing Faces of Jesus* (London: Penguin, 2000), 237–80.

CASE STUDY 4B. LAOZI, THE DAODEJING,
AND THE ORIGINS OF DAOISM

Graham, A.C. "The Origins of the Legend of Lao Tan," in *Lao-tzu and the Tao-te-ching*, ed. Livia Kohn and Michael LaFargue (Albany: State University of New York Press, 1988), 23–40.

Kirkland, Russell. *Taoism: The Enduring Tradition* (London and New York: Routledge, 2004), 20–73.

Kohn, Livia. "The Lao-tzu Myth," in Kohn and LaFargue, *Lao-tzu*, 41–62.

Komjathy, Louis. *The Daoist Tradition: An Introduction* (London: Bloomsbury, 2013), 17–28.

Roth, Harold. *Original Tao: Inward Training (Nei-yeh) and the Foundations of Taoist Mysticism* (New York: Columbia University Press, 1999), 5–9.

5

POWER
Social Constructionism, Habitus, and Authority

IN WHICH WE EXPLORE:

Social constructionism and related critical methodologies and philosophies
The concepts of discourse and habitus, and issues related to power and legitimacy
Critiques of social constructionism and debates within the field
Case studies looking at mosques and minarets, and forms of individualist (New Age)
   spiritualities

INTRODUCTION

In this chapter, we look at a range of what can broadly be termed "critical" approaches to the study of religion, which include strands coming from such areas as

- social constructionism,
- deconstruction,
- poststructuralism,
- critical theory,
- the genealogical/archaeological/historicizing approach to concepts, and
- discourse analysis.

These draw from a range of linked, sometimes overlapping, but often distinct or even conflicting, schools of theory and particular theorists. Moreover, each can be understood in a range of ways. We will not explore the background and lineage of every school; rather, we are looking for the tools we gain from such approaches. These inform methodologies employed across this book, but here we take a closer look at some ideas. We will use social constructionism as a general catchall to name these approaches.

It would be useful to start by noting the kinds of positions, questions, and issues raised by such an approach:

- perceiving religious tradition as human products[1]
- a concern with questions of power and legitimacy
- seeing religious doctrines and practices as forms of discourse (see box 5.1)
- often, a focus on liberationist agendas, seeking for social justice or challenging colonialism (but critical scholarship can also support Western-centric, racist, or patriarchal standpoints)[2]

We begin by looking at how discourse makes our world appear "natural" to us, and a range of theorists who have helped us question this. Next, we deal specifically with social constructionism's relation to religious traditions. After that we address some potential criticisms of social constructionism, then explore our two case studies.

QUESTIONING OUR WORLD
SOCIETY: NATURAL OR CONSTRUCTED?

The world around us typically appears "natural" to us. The clothes people wear, the food we eat, the forms of greetings, and festivals are what—in many cases—we have grown up with, our parents grew up with, our grandparents grew up with, and so on. In today's increasingly globalized world, though, we may live in places or cities where rapid change has occurred, with diversity and change rather than homogeneity and tradition as the norm. However, even if we live in contexts quite different from previous generations, we tend to have a familiarity with the world around as "the way things are." This is well summed up by Craig Martin as follows:

> Societies, human relations, social artifacts, etc. do not simply exist; they are created by human languages, practices, habits, and so on. However, most of us take the world as it is presented to us for granted: we rarely stop to question how it got to be the way it did, or what social and historical conditions made our particular world possible. When we take the world for granted in this way, it becomes almost "natural" to us, and as such we cannot see the social world that produced it.[3]

Let us take an example: ask yourself what you ate for breakfast this morning. Is this what you normally eat? Is it what your family eats? Is it what most of your friends eat? Whatever it was, there is a good chance that it seemed a natural breakfast to you. However, it is very culturally and contextually specific:

US: breakfast cereal with milk (cow's), or some pastries (likely very sweet), accompanied by orange juice and/or coffee.

China: noodles or *baozi* (steamed savory buns), maybe with *youtiao* (fried dough sticks); savory rather than sweet and, traditionally, not including milk or orange juice.

UK: maybe a "full English" of eggs (fried, boiled, or scrambled), slices of bacon, sausages (probably pork), fried bread, fried tomatoes, baked beans, and maybe black pudding (a sausage composed of dried blood and animal fat), accompanied by strong black tea with milk.

For different people, at different times, and in different places, what seems natural differs dramatically. This is as true about religion as it is about breakfast. Equally, this context shapes what you think is "unnatural," or even "disgusting."

THE MASTERS OF SUSPICION

From around the late nineteenth century, a number of scholars in Europe started to ask critical questions about the way we see the world, and so what we think is normal and natural. Of course, it was not only Europeans who asked questions about the way the world is. Saying that the world need not be the way it is has always been part of human philosophizing and religionizing:

- Hebrew prophets (ca. 1000 BCE) wanted to reorder society to enfranchise the poor, outcasts, and those socially disadvantaged, including immigrants.

Some Christians today speak about God's "preferential option for the poor."[4]

- Socrates (470–399 BCE) developed Socratic questioning: asking what we really mean by concepts such as "justice," "truth," and "beauty."[5]
- Confucius (ca. 551–479 BCE) argued that there is a better way to organize society; for instance, that it was wrong to bury live servants in the tombs of their masters.[6]
- Monasticism sometimes offered a radical critique of the world, seeing poverty, simplicity, and interiority as the path toward human fulfillment.[7]

However, Paul Ricoeur (1913–2005) identified a particular lineage of scholars who questioned our world and the place of religion in it, whom he termed the "masters of suspicion" (see box 5.2).[8] Ricoeur also gave us the phrase "hermeneutics of suspicion" (see box 2.7), which for him characterized the approach of these figures: to critique, destabilize, and be critical in our approach to accepted forms of knowledge, power regimes, and ways of seeing the world.

Our ways of seeing the world, and the language we use about it, create very definite consequences in terms of how we behave and perceive the world. You may be familiar with a famous psychological experiment conducted among third-grade primary students. On the first day, blue-eyed children were praised; they were told that they were smarter, neater, and better, and they got encouragement from the teacher. Meanwhile, brown-eyed children were rebuked and ridiculed. Subsequently, this was reversed; the brown-eyed children were praised, and the blue-eyed children rebuked and ridiculed. The results showed two key things. First, on the days they were favored, students scored better on tests, while those ridiculed did worse. Second, they behaved differently: the group picked out as "superior" behaved in a mean-spirited way to the "inferior" group.[9] We may be shocked by the ethical issues in this research (it might not be possible to do it today), but we need to stop and think about the implications of this study and what it tells us. These findings are supported by other research, and so we can to some degree generalize beyond this case:

- Words, whether of praise or condemnation, affect how people perform in society.
- As a result of in-group bias (see chapter 6), we are mean-spirited to our out-groups.
- Assumptions of inferiority or superiority can be supported by language and discourse without being based in any "natural" difference.
- We change the world through how we speak about others.

Systems of social and cultural construction, and domination, often involve complicated intersections with various groups (see chapters 3, 7, and 10, and box 13.8), which may assert certain hierarchies as natural. For Antonio Gramsci (1890–1932), the motif

BOX 5.2 **THE MASTERS OF SUSPICION AND BEYOND**

According to Paul Ricoeur (1913–2005), three thinkers in particular challenged our typical ideas of the world, in particular, destabilizing the idea of religion as a natural part of the world. We can briefly note why they are significant for us.

Karl Marx (1818–1883) argued that the power of ideology and global capital keeps us captive within systems of thought. Marx described religion as the "opium of the people," suggesting that by promising a future life, it helped keep people suppressed despite their suffering and downtrodden status. But Marx was not entirely dismissive of religion, saying: "Religion is the sigh of the oppressed masses, the heart of a heartless world, and the soul of soulless conditions."[1] It gave a way for people to express their yearnings within the system and provided some comfort (like opium?). His central contribution for us was that systematic social structures serve to keep us within certain boundaries of thinking and acting.

Sigmund Freud (1856–1939) argued that we are often driven by the unconscious, and so are unaware of our true desires. Religion, Freud argued, was a form of neurosis fostering an infantile state of dependency upon a divine father figure. His central contribution for us was suggesting that our unconscious is a strong force driving our beliefs, thinking, and actions.

Friedrich Nietzsche (1844–1900) argued for what we might term the immoral origins of morality, or the untruthfulness of the origins of truth. In particular, Nietzsche contrasted Christian morality, which emphasizes humility and peace, with what he argued were older and more vibrant "pagan" traditions of warrior morality which saw bravery and strength as virtues. Society, for him, was weakened by Christianity. Nietzsche's central contribution for us was showing that our basis for morality could be otherwise, and that Christianity or religion was simply one source for this.[2]

These figures helped lay the basis for critical theory and social constructionism by suggesting that society is based upon contextual norms rather than universal ones. However, they were not alone, and some other significant figures should be mentioned:

Charles Darwin (1809–1882) justified a worldview which did not need a creator deity.[3] Hence religion's "natural" place in the world is displaced.

Michel Foucault (1926–1984) showed that today's seemingly "natural" concepts and systems have a history. While parts of Foucault's work are debatable (his historical surveys are often overgeneralized), his general thesis is arguably sound.[4]

---

1 Karl Marx, *Critique of Hegel's Philosophy of Right,* trans. Joseph O'Malley and Annette Jolin (Cambridge: Cambridge University Press, 1970), 131.

2 On the master/slave morality dichotomy, see Friedrich Nietzsche, *On the Genealogy of Morality,* ed. Keith Ansell-Pearson, trans. Carol Diethe (Cambridge: Cambridge University Press, 2007).

3 See Paul Hedges, *Towards Better Disagreement: Religion and Atheism in Dialogue* (London: Jessica Kingsley, 2017), 155.

4 See Anon, "Michel Foucault," *Social Theory Rewired* (Routledge, 2016),http://routledgesoc.com /profile/michel-foucault.

Jean-Francois Lyotard (1924–1998) asserted "postmodernism" (see box 2.5) meant all grand theories (metanarratives) are suspect, leaving us with only local and contextual theories.

Immanuel Kant (1724–1804): Some thinkers discussed here are often contrasted with a modern/Enlightenment tradition associated with Kant (see box 16.1). However, Kant asked people to question tradition,[5] advanced a hermeneutics of suspicion (see box 2.7), and argued that reason is contingent as our existing worldview shapes what else we come to know.[6]

Gayatri Chakravorty Spivak: We have traced a lineage through white, Western, elite, male thinkers. Spivak, among others, has shown that, especially in colonial contexts, the way knowledge and religion are constructed is neither "natural" nor universal (see chapters 3, 7, and 10, and box 7.6).[7]

---

5 Immanuel Kant, "What Is the Enlightenment" (1784), www.columbia.edu/acis/ets/CCREAD /etscc/kant.html.

6 Kant argued in the preface of the *Critique of Pure Reason* (1787) that while previous theories of knowledge had assumed that "our cognition must conform to the objects" (i.e., our understanding is based upon the reality of things external to us), we should ask whether "objects must conform to our knowledge" (i.e., things known fit into our existing theories and perceptions). See M. Rohlf, "Immanuel Kant," in *The Stanford Encyclopedia of Philosophy* (2016), https://plato.stanford.edu/entries/kant/. For Kant, the mind is no longer "a mirror" that simply pictures what is out there. Kant is arguably key to many later developments; see Béatrice Longuenesse, *Kant and the Capacity to Judge: Sensibility and Discursivity in the Transcendental Analytic of the Critique of Pure Reason* (Princeton: Princeton University Press, 1999), 239.

7 See Caroline Lee Schwenz, "Spivak, Gayatri Chakravorty," *ScholarBlogs@Emory* (2014), https:// scholarblogs.emory.edu/postcolonialstudies/2014/06/19/spivak-gayatri-chakravorty/.

---

of hegemony looks at how economic forces, and associated sociopolitical regimes, make certain ways of life seem natural; this was inspired by a Marxist critique of capitalism, but it can have a wider application. While, even from a non-Marxist lens, class is significant[10] as a feature of hegemonic social construction, especially when backed by political and economic dominance, but gender, racial, or other perspectives cannot be ignored in the intersectional construction of hegemonic domination. The theorist Pierre Bourdieu (1930–2002) used different rites of passage (see box 12.4) as examples:

· A rite marking the passage from childhood to manhood "tends to make the smallest, weakest, in short, the most effeminate man, separated by a difference in nature and essence from the most masculine woman . . . implying that he is a real man, which is not always immediately obvious."[11]

· Rituals in society can serve "to sanction and sanctify a particular state of things, an established order, in exactly the way that a constitution does in the legal and political sense of the term," whereby "an *investiture* (of a knight, Deputy, President . . .) consists of sanctioning and sanctifying a difference (pre-existent or not) by making it *known* and *recognized;* it consists of making it exist as a social difference, known and recognized as such by the agent invested and everyone else."[12]

Relating to social identity theory (chapter 6), we can only have certain roles because society says they exist: I cannot be a monarch in a republic, nor can I be a president in a monarchy; I cannot be a nun in Islam, nor can I be a jurisprudential expert (*ulama*, or Islamic legal scholar) in Buddhism. Furthermore, our society permits not only what we can be, but also what we think are the "natural" qualities of such roles—but how can it be "natural" when the particular history, tradition, and structure of our society are the only things which permit them to exist? Indeed, following Foucault's notion of the archaeology/genealogy of knowledge ("historicizing"), we can see how our ideas of such things as monks, nuns, priests, *ulama*, shamans, magicians, and scholars have shifted over time.

HABITUS

We have seen that society constructs our social world and its possibilities for our thinking. A useful concept for looking at this, which comes from Bourdieu, is habitus (see box 5.3):

> The conditionings associated with a particular class of conditions of existence produce *habitus,* systems of durable, transposable dispositions, **structured structures** predisposed to function as **structuring structures**, that is as principles which generate and **organize practices and representations** that can be objectively adapted to their outcomes without presupposing conscious aims at ends or an express mastery of the operations necessary in order to obtain them.[13]

Jonathan Z. Smith (1938–2017) expresses well why this is important for us: "The disciplined study of any subject is, among other things, an assault on self-evidence, on matters taken for granted."[14] In other words, we can explore how terms, concepts, practices, rituals, doctrines, or whatever it may be came about. Whatever may be the natural or taken-for-granted practices in one culture, in one period, for one tradition, will not be natural or taken for granted for another. This also includes academic constructions and explanations. This relates to who, or what, lays down the rules which we must obey. Notably, for Bourdieu, our living within the frame of habitus speaks about our competence in dealing with our social world.[15]

RELIGION AS SOCIAL CONSTRUCTION
AND STRUCTURING STRUCTURE
AUTHORITY AND POWER

In many contemporary societies, religions and religious leaders no longer have the influence which they once had (see chapter 16), but they remain deeply influential

HABITUS

To help think about habitus, we can relate it to two more common and related English words: "habit" and "habitat." A habitat, often used in biology, is the place we inhabit and so speaks about the world around us. But here, think beyond simply the natural world of trees, plants, and animals (though that is constructed as part of our habitus, or lived environment; see box 17.1) and think of the social and cultural world: the regulations and norms we live with, such as what we eat, drink, and wear, or how our society is structured into family units, work units, and political units. All this gives us **"structured structures"**: the norms of our society are supported by the surrounding culture. This in turn makes them **"structuring structures"** because they structure us. When you go out to buy breakfast, your culture determines what type of shop you go to and what type of food you buy. Whether you go to school from the age of five or seven is determined by the society you are in and its expectations. Does your school teach you Darwinian evolution, or intelligent design, or simply avoid this as too contentious? Do you (or your parents) want you to become an accountant, a doctor, a teacher, an anarchist, a farmer, a nun, or a social media influencer? Only in certain societies can you even aspire to some of these. You are structured by the structures of your society as to what is even possible for you to think or want. In other terms, the society we live in will **"organize practices and representations"** of what is possible, desirable, laudable, or undesirable for us. Class, gender, and race also affect what you believe you can do, or what you believe you can become. Our "habits," our natural forms of behavior and thinking, are shaped through this "habitat." This is habitus.

globally. This can include via direct or indirect political power (see chapter 18), in the individual influence on adherents' behavior and spending (see case study 5B, and boxes 3.4 and 16.9), or through cultural or moral influences on what we regard as norms in society. Forms of religious power can, moreover, be theorized in many ways. One of the most influential of these is Max Weber's (1864–1920) concept of charisma (see box 5.4).

TEXTUAL AUTHORITIES

In many traditions, certain texts have some binding authority. This may be interpreted as "scripture," but this term may not always clarify if we see it related to, for instance, "revelation" (see box 1.3 and chapter 11). However, a "revealed scripture" may not always be the ultimate authority. While mainstream Islamic understanding of the Quran sees it as the literal word of God, it is read through Muhammad's example (*sunnah*) and the interpretation of the community of scholars (see box 11.3). Therefore, a Muslim does not traditionally go to the Quran to see what it means for them. They will seek out a scholar (*ulama*) and get a legal opinion (*fatwa*). Importantly, these are normally only opinions and so are not binding. Muslims have been known to ask several

BOX 5.4 **CHARISMA AND CHARISMATIC LEADERS**

First conceptualized by Max Weber (1864–1920),[1] charisma is a form of moral and attractive force that particular individuals exhibit. This often comes from promising some change often linked to a "higher" power. It may be seen as revolutionary, because the charismatic leader may offer a radical new vision in society. Charisma may involve powerful and persuasive rhetoric, appeals to divine authority, or tapping into a particular zeitgeist. For Weber, it is particularly associated with religious founders. This could be the founder of a particular religious tradition or an innovator within a lineage. Charisma may become "routinized" or "institutionalized" with successors, appointed to or inheriting leadership, bearing some aspect of the charisma. With this, a religion may change from being revolutionary (associated with change) to being conservative (embedded within and supporting existing social structures), though these two are ideal types.[2] Notably, things which may be signs of leadership in one context may or may not be seen such ways in other cultures or at other times. Hence charismatic leadership will vary:

Fetullah Gulen: Founder of the Hizmet (literally, "service") movement, based in Turkish Sufi tradition. Gulen is an educational theorist and spiritual leader. Today, he lives in exile in the US and sees few guests, but through his writings and sermons he exercises a continuing influence.[3] His movement is controversial in some contexts.

Richard Dawkins: His "New Atheist" (see case study 8A) aggressive debating style and strong advocacy of the belief that science and religion are inevitably in conflict have been attractive forces. However, some of his views, especially on Twitter, have drawn derision even from staunch atheists, meaning his star has faded somewhat. Dawkins does not appeal to any divine force, but offers "revolutionary change" by appealing to the "higher forces" of "reason" and "science."

Pope Francis I: As the Pope, Francis represents an institutionalized charisma. Nevertheless, many have been drawn to, among other things, his perceived humility, openness to the poor and weak, acceptance of different sexual orientations, and outreach to atheists. Arguably, therefore, he has manifested his own charisma.

Your professor: As someone (presumably) holding a university teaching position, she or he is presumed to be knowledgeable and authoritative. Is there an institutionalized charisma inherent in her or his role? Does she or he also manifest charisma in any other ways?

---

1 Max Weber, "Discipline and Charisma," in *From Max Weber: Essays in Sociology*, ed. and trans. H. H. Gerth and C. Wright Mills (New York: Routledge, 2009): 262–65.

2 See Anon, "Ideal-Types," *Sociology Theory Unwired* (2016), http://routledgesoc.com/category/profile-tags/ideal-types.

3 See Christina Welch and Paul Hedges, "Charisma, Scriptures, Revelation, and Reason: Sources of Religious Authority," in *Controversies in Contemporary Religion*, ed. Paul Hedges, vol. 1 (Santa Barbara: Praeger, 2014): 57–80, 75; and Scott Fitzgerald, "Conceptualizing and Understanding the Gülen Movement," *Social Compass* 11 (2017): 1–10.

Traditionally, almost every religion has insisted that its texts need careful interpretation; hence priests or specialists have mediated textual interpretation to the community. The idea that the text has a "clear meaning" is a distinctly Protestant Christian dynamic. With this comes the idea that we should go to the text to return to the origins of religion, with each believer reading it to get the meaning directly for themselves. (A similar idea is found in certain Salafi forms of Islam, but this is also a modern innovation.) Reading texts in a literal, or straightforward, way is associated with what is typically termed "fundamentalist" or "literalist" traditions (see chapter 15). However, the idea of going to the text to read it directly is also promoted by liberals/progressives/modernists who may equally insist that we need to return to the "sources" rather than rely on tradition. This Protestant dynamic also informed modern scholarship, which presumed that the text was the "real" source of religion, making the study of religion text-centric (see chapter 1) and neglecting lived religion (see chapter 3). It also influences the very direct and literalist approach found among some atheist critics of religion who assume that they can directly get the "clear meaning" by reading the text and drawing out whatever they find there.[1] This tends to ignore the context a text was written in, as well as traditional forms of interpretation and understanding. Meaning is highly individualized: what a text means to me takes precedence over any scholarly assessment around such things as authorial intent, how it was understood in its early context, and nuanced interpretations.[2]

---

1 Mohammad Hassan Khalil, *Jihad, Radicalism, and the New Atheism* (Cambridge: Cambridge University Press, 2017), 168, 97–129, suggests that Sam Harris reads the Quran more literally and with less attention to context than Osama bin Laden (1957–2011).

2 On the problems of assuming an authorial voice or a clear meaning in texts, see Hans-Georg Gadamer, *Truth and Method*, trans. William Glen-Doepel, 2nd ed. (London: Sheed and Ward, 1979); and Stanley Fish, *Is There a Text in This Class? The Authority of Interpretive Communities* (Cambridge: Harvard University Press, 1982). On textual interpretation in the study of religion, see Garrett Green, "Hermeneutics," in *The Routledge Companion to the Study of Religion*, 2nd ed., ed. John Hinnells (New York: Routledge, 2010), 411–25.

scholars for several *fatwas* to get the one they want. Nevertheless, the consensus of scholars becomes authoritative for the community. This is very different from parts of Protestant Christianity. The Protestant Reformation (see box 9.3) sought to put translations of the Bible into the hands of laypeople as it was believed that no priest stood between the believer and God. Therefore, each individual should be free to read and interpret the Bible for themselves (see box 5.5). It also reversed centuries of tradition which held that learned priests and certain forms of interpretation were necessary to understand the Bible.[16]

To help consider the issues raised so far, we can look at Martin's seven principles of social constructionism, which concern how society constructs our social world:[17]

1. "Words are tools that humans use to delimit from the stuff of the world that is of interest to them." Example: "People of the Book" (*ahl al-kitab*) is an Arabic term to denote primarily Jews and Christians which has regulated how some Muslims relate to some non-Muslims (see box 13.2).

2. "The tools we use produce the world for us; if we used a different set of tools, we would have a different world." Example: spirituality (see box 5.6).

3. "The uses of words are variable." Example: Is a prophet a preacher of righteousness, a military leader, a critic of those in power, or somebody seeking to restore a former practice? Or, all of these and more?

4. "Variable uses are all we have—there are no intrinsically right or wrong uses of words, just different uses." Example: Depending on Buddhist usage, *sangha* may be the institution of monastics, or all Buddhists in four traditional categories (monks, nuns, laymen, laywomen).[18]

5. "Although the uses of words change, this does not mean anything is true—whether a claim is true depends on the agreed use of the words for a particular community." Example: *Dao* is the Chinese term meaning "the way," but there are many disputers of the way.[19]

6. "What we are as humans is a result or product of the concepts and practices in our societies." Example: Only in certain traditions can somebody be a priest, and then maybe only certain people (often men; see case study 10A).

7. "Social facts, although social, are nevertheless real facts—if only for the community that recognizes them as such." Example: Being born to the Hindu priestly (*brahmin*) caste traditionally gave someone a place in society very different from being born a Dalit (see box 4.6). While entirely constructed, social structures are a social reality (see box 1.9).

Society's discourse informs, indeed is part of, the structures that give words meaning, and determines what is and is not possible in our social worlds. This is as much true with those traditions and ways of life we term religions as any other arena. It also affects the way we give value to certain things, and not others: the former in sociological terms is often called a fetish (see box 5.7).

HANG ON A MINUTE: WHAT'S WRONG WITH SOCIAL CONSTRUCTIONISM?

As social constructionism and critical theory underlies much of this book, we should consider potential criticisms to understand problems with at least some scholarly employments.

SPIRITUALITY

In contemporary usage, "spirituality" is often contrasted with "religion." Religion connotes, in this sense, institutionalized traditions and adherence to specific creeds and dogmas. Spirituality, in this sense, is seen as individual, giving freedom to choose, and as based in alternative, or "New Age," beliefs associated with such things as yoga, mindfulness, the use of crystals for healing, or similar activities that one can tap into as and when one chooses. Many scholars object to this usage, for a variety of reasons:

· The term "spirituality" is based in traditional Christian forms of prayer and devotion; therefore some argue it is misemployed here.

· As religion is tricky to define (see chapter 1), the distinction of it as a reified object contrasted with spirituality is analytically weak.

· This usage rests upon a particular Western and contemporary lineage which neglects wider understandings of both terms.

We can recognize these critiques,[1] but for the purposes of utility we will employ "spirituality" in ways which fit the contemporary usage. This is because it reflects a standard form of contemporary English language usage, where we see trends toward rejecting institutional "religion" for an "individualized" "spirituality" (see case study 5B).[2] Nevertheless, we need to recognize it as a specific part of discourse, and not as a "natural" or an analytic term.

---

1 See Philip Sheldrake, *A Brief History of Spirituality* (Oxford: Blackwell, 2007), 1–4; Arthur Holder, "Introduction," in *The Blackwell Companion to Christian Spirituality*, ed. Arthur Holder (Oxford: Blackwell, 2005), 1–11, 1–5; and Anna King and Paul Hedges, "What Is Religion? Or, What Is It We Are Talking About?," in *Controversies in Contemporary Religion*, vol. 1, ed. Paul Hedges (Santa Barbara: Praeger, 2014), 1–30, 22–24.

2 See Linda Woodhead and Paul Heelas, *The Spiritual Revolution: Why Religion Is Giving Way to Spirituality* (Oxford: Blackwell, 2005).

THE DECOLONIAL QUESTION

Critical theory challenges accepted ways of seeing the world via a hermeneutics of suspicion (see box 2.7). However, this theory comes from a white, Western, and primarily middle-class and male lineage of scholarship which can support the continued dominance of that very lineage (which it in theory critiques).[20] Martin notes: "I'm still waiting for critical scholars to come to a widespread realization of this."[21] For instance, some critical scholarship seems to assume that "Hinduism" and "Buddhism" can only have been produced by Western "invention," as Asians could not develop complex, transnational conceptions themselves (see case study 7A). Again, figures such as Jacques Derrida (1930–2004), whose work draws from his situation as an Algerian Jew, are often assumed simply to be part of a lineage of critical scholarship from George W. F. Hegel (1770–1831)

In sociology, a fetish is an item given "excessive" value, or valorized beyond its immediate worth. The term has a lineage from European interaction with Africa, where a fetish referred to items used as "magical/religious" (see box 7.8) charms in African traditional practices. For Europeans, these items seemed valued, or imbued with presumed powers beyond their inherent nature. For Karl Marx (1818–1883), the term was applied to the way that, under capitalism, an item was given excessive economic value. Marx thought an item's value should relate to the labor of the craftsperson alongside basic costs. Sigmund Freud (1856–1939) related the fetish to sexual fascination. Jean Baudrillard (1929–2007) extended fetish theory, arguing that the value of objects reflects their use as objects of "social exchange" where value may relate to ostentation. A fetish is therefore valued because it has a role in a particular discourse or social form, which in the twenty-first century may include such things as the iPhone, Burberry clothing, Chanel no. 5, and so on. These products are given values far in excess of their basic parts and labor value. For Baudrillard, items have value as part of a "symbolic exchange," and it is the power of the discourse of the whole symbolic system which provides the value of the fetish.[1]

---

1 See Tim Dent, "Fetishism and the Social Value of Objects," *Sociological Review* 44.3 (1996): 495–516; and J. Lorand Matory, *The Fetish Revisited: Marx, Freud, and the Gods Black People Make* (Durham: Duke University Press, 2018).

onward and so to be in line with Orientalist and Western-centric theory, even though such figures critique this lineage.[22] Again, the dominance of "whiteness" in the theory of the study of religion, including in supposedly critical lineages, has been argued to be a continuing problem.[23]

NON-REALISM AND RELATIVISM

For some scholars, social construction, broadly construed, entails a radical non-realism, or relativism. These are related concepts, but not equivalent. We stress the former first (see box 5.8), and develop the latter below.

LIBERATION, ACTIVISM, AND THE STUDY OF RELIGION

Various strands of social constructionism and critical theory are based in forms of social critique/justice for liberatory ends. In religious studies, Martin avers that a concern with injustice and oppression animates his work.[24] However, many scholars of religion are wary of engaging in anything that may seem to be "advocacy," summed up in

BOX 5.8 **NON-REALISM AND CRITICAL REALISM**

Scholars unfortunately use terminology in varying ways, sometimes using different terms for very similar ideas (see introduction). Our definitions below are offered recognizing that none of these terms has a single definition, with various usages by differing scholars:[1]

Non-realism (sometimes anti-realism), in an "extreme" form, says there is no physical reality beyond that constructed by discourse. This is very problematic. More sophisticated versions hold that discourse means we do not directly access "reality" as it is, but only know and experience what is within our social and linguistic experience. Our "direct" experience is of a "conditioned" and "mind-dependent" "reality."[2]

Realism holds we encounter "reality" directly as it is, and our language directly describes "real" stuff.

Anti-representationalism, associated with Richard Rorty, claims to be a third way between realism and extreme non-realism. It asserts that "reality" exists but we can make no claims about it because we only know our discourse, not "reality" itself. However, it is little different from sophisticated non-realism, and when nuanced to address perceived problems has been argued to lead to critical realism.[3]

Critical realism mediates between "extreme" realist and non-realist poles. It accepts that "reality" (actual physical stuff) comes to us through socially constructed means and linguistic construction. However, it holds that "reality" affects us too strongly to be seen as merely a second-hand experience, as in Karen Barad's "agential realism" concept.[4] It aligns with this book's arguments.

Leading scholars of social constructionism such as Peter Berger and Sally Haslanger have explicitly repudiated non-realism,[5] while John Searle has argued that we can

---

1 See David Chalmers, "Ontological Anti-Realism," in *Metametaphysics: New Essays on the Foundations of Ontology,* ed. D. Manley, D. Chalmers, and R. Wasserman (Oxford: Oxford University Press, 2009): 77–129; Sven Rosenkranz, "Realism and Anti-Realism," *Oxford Bibliographies* (2015), https://www.oxfordbibliographies.com/view/document/obo-9780195396577/obo-9780195396577-0098.xml. See also Ernest Sosa, Jaegwon Kim, Jeremy Fantl, and Mathew McGrath, eds., *Epistemology: An Anthology,* 2nd ed. (Oxford: Blackwell, 2008), 3–72.

2 Martin likens discourse to a blueprint for a house—which in turn is made of "real" stuff, i.e., bricks and mortar—but which forms the basis of our experience (Craig Martin, personal email correspondence with author, 2018; and Craig Martin, peer review comments, 2019).

3 See Teemu Taira, "Assembling Our Toolboxes: A Response," *Implicit Religion* 20.4 (2017): 427–36, 430–31. Notably, defenses of Rorty have often moved toward a realist stance for justification; see, e.g., Jonathan Knowles, "Rortian Realism," *Metaphilosophy* 49.1–2 (2018): 90–114. This makes it more aligned with critical realism.

4 Karen Barad, *Meeting the Universe Halfway: Quantum Physics and the Entanglement of Matter and Meaning* (Durham: Duke University Press, 2007), 132–85.

5 Sally Haslanger, *Resisting Reality: Social Construction and Social Critique* (Oxford: Oxford University Press, 2012), 198–215, 154–55; and Peter Berger, *The Many Altars of Modernity: Toward a Paradigm for Religion in a Pluralist Age* (Berlin: De Gruyter, 2014), 11–12.

meaningfully resolve the apparent paradox that we make seemingly objective state-ments about subjective and socially constructed human systems.[6] The arguments in this book lead us to resist non-realist stances:

- Taking materiality and embodiment seriously (see chapter 9, especially boxes 9.2, 9.10, and 9.11) shows that it is not "discourse all the way down," as some non-realists claim.[7] Despite the claims of non-realism or anti-representationalism as a "third way," these stances remain locked in logocentrism (see box 9.1), wherein concepts are stressed over embodiment in ways reminiscent of traditional West-ern philosophy. It also fails to deal with the relationship of solid physical "reality" to "discourse." For instance, while the way a society views agriculture may be "discourse"—as a gift from the gods, a product of civilization, and so on—we cannot use "discourse" to make crops grow without water, or discursively turn a sandy, hot desert into a hospitable place to grow roses. Physical "reality" is the bedrock upon which "discourse" is built, not vice versa. It is not surprising that we find non-realist scholars, but not non-realist farmers.[8]

- Postcolonial, decolonial, and feminist standpoints (see chapters 7, 10, and 18) all counter the Western and male-centric worldview that "reality" or embodiment can be dismissed as secondary. Non-realism is embedded in a certain worldview. This is discussed more fully in other chapters.

---

6 John Searle, *Making the Social World: The Structure of Human Civilization* (Oxford: Oxford Univer-sity Press, 2010).

7 Often, when pressed, non-/anti-realists argue for something more like critical realism. For in-stance, they will say, having argued that "it is discourse all the way down," that this does not mean that everything is discourse. As such, they will admit that they do not, for instance, believe that discourse can change aspects of physical reality (discourse does not, in other words, go "all the way down" as it cannot create doors in walls or allow people to fly). Such a representation, they will say, is an unfair caricature or strawman. But what else is "discourse all the way down" meant to mean? Sophisticated non-realists steer clear of such stances but as they nuance their position, or address its weaknesses, it still typically seems to overlap with critical realism despite their disavowal of the latter (and their stereotyping of this stance as uncritical). Again, non-realists will often argue that social construction-ist or other theorists align with their views with such figures as Berger, Haslanger, and Barad all being called on for support, despite such figures often explicitly disavowing non-realist stances. Our socially and linguistically mediated conscious experience and thinking may be all discourse, but not everything is discourse.

8 Most biologists who seriously consider social constructionism argue that non-realism typically "grant[s] language and other forms of representation more power in determining our ontologies than they deserve"; Barad, *Meeting the Universe*, 133. See also Rebecca Jordan-Young, *Brain Storm* (Cam-bridge: Harvard University Press, 2010). Again, the neurologist Anil Seth denies that the fact that neu-rology tells us that conscious reality is constructed means that we do not directly run up against physi-cal reality in ways which are not mediated through perception (and so social-linguistic discourse); see Anil Seth, interview, "Anil Seth on Why Our Senses Are Fine-Tuned for Utility, not for 'Reality,'" *Aeon* (30 June 2020), https://aeon.co/videos/anil-seth-on-why-our-senses-are-fine-tuned-for-utility-not-for-reality?fbclid=IwAROrB_yjKgOkoFrgt3OS7CPeXK-crvsFXNoGaOkbWDRxKaLu9hu8nra8X6g.

Bruce Lincoln's highly influential "Theses on Method."[25] Meanwhile, Russell McCutcheon has argued that a concept such as justice cannot be employed by critical scholars, whose role should be only to expose the discourse of others as the term "justice" has no real meaning.[26] This tends to entail a "relativist" stance, though relativism is internally incoherent and often based in a naive "folk postmodernism" (see box 2.5).[27] Contrary to such stances, feminist and Black scholars, among others, have argued that scholarship should not be neutral (see chapters 7, 10, and 18).[28] For example:

- W. E. B. Du Bois (1868–1963) saw his work on the situation of Black people in the US as not simply outlining how discourse on blackness was constructed, but as seeking to change their situation.[29]
- Biko Agozino has studied why there are disproportionate numbers of Black women in prison in the UK, and has campaigned for changes.[30]
- Romila Thapar has very clear views resisting the discourse of right-wing Hindu nationalism, or Hindutva, as antithetical to Hindu or Indian values.[31]
- Catharine MacKinnon has argued that notions of objectivity are based on male-dominated ways of reasoning and affect the practice of law, which needs to change.[32]

Some may argue that these people are not "proper" scholars because they do not obey the rules that certain elite, white, Western, male professors think they should obey. However, it is precisely such hegemonic discourses that critical stances may help us dismantle—especially when, as Martin observed, many proponents of critical theory fail to recognize the bias of their own standpoints. This approach accords with recent arguments by Christopher Driscoll and Monica Miller, who see the use of critical theory as often a way to distance the white scholar's work from nonwhite (Black) traditions and methods.[33] Moreover, arguing that a scholar only interrogates other people's discourse suggests a naive assumption that the scholar is beyond politics and standpoints (see chapter 18).[34] But, often in the study of religion, the social justice aspects of critical theory are considered suspect and nonscholarly. Scholarship is never entirely neutral; nor is advocacy always scholarship. But to strictly demarcate between these fails to notice the political nature of all scholarship (see box 4.7 and chapter 18).

· · ·

CASE STUDY 5A. MOSQUES, MINARETS, AND POWER

The physical environment, as much as texts or leaders, forms part of the habitus of our lives. Whether it is temples, banks, shopping malls, or IKEA outlets, buildings shape the landscape (both physical and conceptual) and may tell us what is significant or valued in our societies (see chapter 17).[35]

Minarets dominate the skyline in Istanbul, Turkey.

THE ROLE OF THE MINARET

Despite being a visually noticeable aspect of a mosque, the minaret—like the dome—is technically not essential. Islamic tradition determined that a mosque (*masjid,* literally, "place of prostration") must have:

- a (large) prayer hall,
- a niche showing the direction to Mecca (*mihrab*), and
- facilities for ritual cleansing/washing (*wudhu*).

Minarets are not essential. In Muhammad's time, the call to prayer was often made from the roof of the mosque, particularly by the *muezzin* (person who issues the call for prayer) Bilal. But, especially in cities, a high minaret was useful for the call to prayer to be heard. Today, there is not normally a person physically on the minaret offering the call to prayer, with loudspeakers being common. Moreover, in many Muslim-majority countries, the call to prayer is no longer made from the minaret in any form. This is partly for reasons of noise pollution, but also for practicality. In modern cities, with traffic noise and numerous tall buildings, the call will not get far. Instead, the call for prayer is made on media such as TV or radio, though often also broadcast in the main prayer hall.

We could note various possible interpretations of the minaret. As one social interpretation, the minaret makes the mosque visible and signals its prominence in the community. Religiously, it could be a symbol of communal piety, and in reaching toward the heavens, it might be a symbol of humanity's quest for the transcendent (see box 1.10). In Foucauldian terms, it could be a symbol of surveillance and domination, where we are always seen and under the eye and control of God or the religious authorities (see chapter 17). In hegemonic analysis, it is a symbol of economic and political power, including the domination of the public space by religion.

MINARETS AND POWER

In Islamic history, the minaret developed in a particular trajectory associated with the early dynasties. After the four immediate successors to Muhammad (the Four Rightly Guided Caliphs), the leadership of the Islamic community fell to its first dynasty, the Umayyads (661–750). Based in Damascus, rather than Mecca and Medina, these new caliphs wanted to show their authority in those traditional centers of power. They built huge new minarets at what is termed the Prophet's Mosque in Medina, signifying their power over Muhammad's followers there. They also acted as a symbol of divine legitimation for their rule.

The following dynasty, the Abbasid caliphate (750–1258), under its third caliph, al-Mahdi (775–85), shortened the Medina minarets. Meanwhile, they heightened and made slenderer the minarets in Mecca, making a statement of their own power against the previous rulers. Such developments in Islam's two major cities and elsewhere continue to this day. For instance, much criticized by many Muslims globally, the current Saudi rulers have made dramatic changes in Mecca and Medina. Buildings reputedly from Muhammad's time have been demolished, and many older structures have been demolished or modernized. This is in line with Wahhabism,[36] which rejects veneration for anything apart from the Quran via Wahhabi interpretation. As well as stamping their own style and monuments on these sites, they are also stripping away what they regard as idolatrous attachment to tradition.

Some Muslims have criticized the opulence and scale of many Islamic buildings, and the lifestyle of some rulers, with "tall and ostentatious buildings" being seen as "incompatible" with the "Prophetic ideal of simplicity and moderation."[37] This started with the first dynasty, the Umayyads, and continues to today.

THE SWISS BAN

In 2009, a national referendum in Switzerland approved a ban on the construction of minarets in new mosque constructions. Importantly, building mosques was not banned, simply building minarets. In a traditionally Christian country, the site of minarets competing with churches' steeples on the skyline became an issue for some. Notably, for many Swiss, the bid to ban minarets was not taken very seriously. It was first raised as an issue in 2007, when many saw it as a fringe movement, and the referendum saw what many regarded as a very low turnout of just over 50 percent. Many, it seemed, simply thought it was not worthwhile voting as the ban would never pass. Nevertheless, with just over 57 percent of those who voted in favor, so representing about a quarter of the population, the campaign succeeded. This shocked many Swiss, who thought the result violated their tradition of tolerance. Moves in the courts to reverse it have failed because a minaret is not a necessity for a mosque, and so technically the ban does not prohibit freedom of religion (see chapter 16). To overturn an existing law requires a much higher percentage, so this has not been tried.

REFLECTIONS

Some questions will help us think through the issues raised in this case study:

1. Thinking from the perspective of a Muslim living in Switzerland, how do you think the minaret ban would shape your perception of Islam's position in Swiss society?

2. In what ways do buildings represent the authority or legitimacy of a religion, belief system, ideology, or tradition? How far does the minaret signify ownership of space, or make the tradition seem a "natural" part of the landscape of a city/region/country?

3. Is Islamic (or other religious) architecture primarily based on displays of power (bigger, taller, wider)? In what ways are different representations of a religion created through the sort of buildings it has, the sort of architecture or art displayed, and so on? Does this create a particular habitus in terms of how the religion is seen and understood? (Reading chapter 17 will provide further perspectives.)

CASE STUDY 5B. INDIVIDUAL (NEW AGE/ALTERNATIVE) SPIRITUALITY AS MODERNITY'S IDEOLOGY

Many people today contrast "religion," which they associate with hierarchical or institutionalized practices and traditions, with "spirituality" (see box 5.6). Hence the category of the SBNR, or "spiritual but not religious" (see box 2.8). Here, we focus on Craig Martin's argument that although individual spirituality is portrayed as inherently positive and freeing, it is connected to modern trends in consumerism and capitalism and so offers limited personal choice.

THE INDIVIDUAL, THE SPIRITUAL, AND BEING ALTERNATIVE

In an analysis of the relationship of religion to contemporary consumer culture, Martin argues that much contemporary individualized religion is deeply implicated in modes of capitalist and modern culture. Without entering into the details of his arguments,[38] here we can sketch the outlines of his position. Martin suggests that despite the claims of individuals to be following their own path, they are often swayed by hegemonic trends and fashions which shape what we perceive to be individual choice (see chapter, 6 on "individual" identities). Martin notes Georg Simmel's (1858–1918) work, wherein fashion is "tied to conformity and differentiation."[39] Also, drawing on Pierre Bourdieu (1930–2002), Martin argues that "ideologies become widely accepted, taken for granted, and sedimented as established wisdom—*doxa,* as Pierre Bourdieu puts it."[40] Martin continues:

> In this way capitalist infrastructures can have an explanatory priority over the superstructures that legitimate them. . . . [Therefore] . . . "individual religion," I will argue, is a specific strand of capitalist ideology, a strand that obscures the causes of "individual choice" while encouraging "individuals" to produce, consume, and accommodate themselves to the regnant mode of production.[41]

This is similar to the sociological concept of the fetish (see box 5.7). Within "alternative spiritualties," "New Age religion," the worldview of the "SBNR" (or however we term it), "doing your own thing," "searching for your own path," or "finding your own truth" may be valorized as the most valued symbolic goal. These motifs become fetishes.

SPIRITUALITY VERSUS RELIGION

A key part of the spirituality discourse is that it allows you to be free and express your own values, spiritual leanings, personality, truths, and so on. "Religion," by contrast, is seen as heavily regulated and oppressive, forcing you into certain traditional patterns. Tradition (as "religion"), here, is contrasted with the "freedom" of individual choice. This is certainly more typical of contemporary culture than, as far as we can tell, previous historical periods. Religious or spiritual traditions or practices, however conceptualized, have generally been tied into kinship, social, or national/regional/tribal networks which have expressed how those within that group variously practice, believe, and act. Martin correctly notes trajectories in contemporary individual spirituality back to the Christian Protestant Reformation which helped develop contemporary notions of individual autonomy (see box 9.3). However, focus on the individual's interior life are far older. Martin Luther (1483–1546) and Desiderius Erasmus (1466–1536) drew on late medieval devotion, which can be traced, in some form, at least as far back as Augustine of Hippo (354–430), while patterns of a somewhat individual interior religious practice can be observed comparatively and cross-culturally over centuries.[42] Nevertheless, until modern times, these have been tied into ways of understanding the self that are deeply social and communal. The modern contrast and conceptualization of "spirituality" as "individual" and something distinct from "religion" is related to trends and patterns in contemporary Western societies, though often drawing on older trends and concepts which are thought anew in this context.

Martin's argument accords with a somewhat similar critique of contemporary spirituality by Richard King and Jeremy Carrette,[43] who argue that modern capitalism has affected the way in which religions or spiritualities are expressed. They have become—especially in modern forms of "spirituality"—commodities in the capitalist marketplace. Spirituality is sold, gurus charge for their services, healing crystals can be bought in high-end shops for large sums, and alternative therapies have become fashionable lifestyle choices. Arguably, though, this misconstrues the way that religion has operated throughout history. It has always been part of the marketplace and essentially a commodity for sale (see box 3.4): pilgrimage sites grew rich on the "gifts" of pilgrims; priests, leaders, gurus, and monks requested "gifts" "to the deity" in return for teachings or services; religious leaders request "tithes" or other payments for community belonging or blessings (see box 16.9); and various goods, whether they be icons, relics, charms, blessed water, halal-certified mobile phones, or others have often been on sale. In today's IT-connected world, there are now options for this to be spread wider through advertising channels, TV evangelists' channels, or social media. The sale of religion and spirituality is, if anything, intensified rather than new. Nevertheless, the way in which certain blessings, good fortune, or services are made into fetishes can certainly be observed.

The core of Martin's argument is that "individual spirituality" is essentially a product which is marketized, packaged, and sold. While often portrayed as an alternative to modern consumerism, it is actually entirely within its grip. Indeed, because of the cost of many aspects, only those successful in the capitalist marketplace can afford many of the products of such spirituality, whether it be aura cleansing, spirituality massages in Bali, or Kabbalah water, to name only a few products that have been marketed as "spiritual."[44] This ties into the context where social media influencers may seek to assert their views against "experts" (here, traditional religious leaders).[45]

REFLECTIONS

The following set of questions should help think through some issues:

1. In what ways do you think that you may be influenced by the notion of individual spirituality? Where do you see it in your life or those of people you know?
2. In what ways is the concept of "spirituality" in contemporary discourse created in relation to modern ideas of individualism and consumerism? How far would you agree that it is a deeply commoditized concept?
3. What do you understand as the distinction between "religion" and "spirituality" in contemporary "New Age"/"SBNR" discourse? How is it framed to favor the concept of "spirituality" over "religion"? In particular, what would you see as the sources of authority which legitimize the discourse of "spirituality"?

·　　·　　·

QUESTIONS AND CONNECTING THOUGHTS

The methods of this chapter infuse the whole book, providing a critical lens to approach phenomena variously described as "religion" with a particular eye to the way discourse creates, determines, and shapes how we experience our world. This approach is sometimes quite explicit, as in in chapters 4 and 9. At other times, this may take a more background role. However, we have also explicitly raised problems that lurk within social constructionism. Non-realist readings are critiqued by mainstream social constructionism and postcolonial, feminist, and embodied perspectives (see chapters 7, 10, and 9, respectively). This criticism draws from both social justice and theoretical analysis. Like any tool or method, social constructionism may be used or developed in ways that detract from rather than increase understanding and intellectual coherence. Some questions will help us think through the issues:

1. What in your social world appears "natural" to yourself and your society (social group), but is simply a particular way of doing things? What constructs the habitus of your life?

2. Do you see the legacy of figures such as the masters of suspicion to be hostile to religion, or simply tools to explore various social phenomena?

3. What forms of authority do you see as most prevalent in a religious tradition you are familiar with, for example, charisma, textual authority, tradition/custom, and so on?

4. Is it "discourse all the way down"? Are there aspects of our social world which are not simply social/linguistic discourse? Do we know these apart from socially constructed linguistic forms? If so, is everything simply relative? (It is useful to answer this after reading chapter 9.)

FURTHER READING
THEORY

Berger, Peter, and Thomas Luckmann. *The Social Construction of Reality: A Treatise in the Sociology of Knowledge* (London: Penguin, 1966).

Bourdieu, Pierre. *Language and Symbolic Power,* ed. John Thompson, trans. Gino Raymond (Cambridge: Harvard University Press, 1993).

Haslanger, Sally. *Resisting Reality: Social Construction and Social Critique* (Oxford: Oxford University Press, 2013).

Lincoln, Bruce. *Discourse and the Construction of Reality: Comparative Studies of Myth, Ritual, and Classification* (Oxford: Oxford University Press, 1989), 131–41.

Martin, Craig. *A Critical Introduction to the Study of Religion,* 2nd ed. (New York: Routledge, 2017).

Ramey, Steven. "Introduction: Writing, Riting, and Righting in the Critical Study of Religion," in *Writing Religion: The Case for the Critical Study of Religion,* ed. Steven Ramey (Tuscaloosa: University of Alabama Press, 2015), 1–16.

CASE STUDY 5A. MOSQUES, MINARETS, AND POWER

Tayob, Abdulkader. *Islam: The Basics* (Oxford: Oneworld, 2003), 1–30.

Waines, David. *An Introduction to Islam,* 2nd ed. (Cambridge: Cambridge University Press, 2003), 196–201.

CASE STUDY 5B. INDIVIDUAL (NEW AGE/ALTERNATIVE) SPIRITUALITY AS MODERNITY'S IDEOLOGY

Arjana, Sophia Rose. *Buying Buddha, Selling Rumi: Orientalism and the Mystical Marketplace* (Oxford: Oneworld, 2020).

Carrette, Jeremy, and Richard King. *Selling Spirituality: The Silent Takeover of Religion* (New York: Routledge, 2004).

Martin, Craig. *Capitalizing Religion: Ideology and the Opiate of the Bourgeoisie* (London: Bloomsbury, 2014).

Martin, Craig. "Delimiting Religion," *Method and Theory in the Study of Religion* 21.2 (2009): 157–76.

6

IDENTITY
Social Identity Theory, In-Groups, Out-Groups, and Conflict

IN WHICH WE EXPLORE:

The importance of identity, including ideas of the self and narrative identity
Social identity theory as a tool for exploring religion
The role of identity in conflict and in-group and out-group identification
Case studies of the Indian Shiv Sena movement, and white Evangelical Christians in the US

INTRODUCTION

Who am I? Probably a question we have all asked ourselves at various times. Indeed, the question of identity is never far away. Whether I think about myself, my family, my team, my gang, my country, or my world, we are always thinking in terms of identities at different levels. But, as we will discuss, this is not simply about who "I am" or who "we are," but also who "you are" or who "they are." That is, our identity is often defined as much by what we are not, as what we are.

To start thinking about this, we will do a quick exercise. So, think about your own nation or country. What is it that defines national identity? This could be particular characteristics, or a national narrative, or even distinctive food or customs. Make the list now.

Your list might be an "insider" or an "outsider" list (see chapter 2), that is, your list might reflect ways that nationals of that country think about themselves, or it might have to do with things that other people associate with that country. For instance, if you identified things such as Buckingham Palace or guards dressed in red as British, these would typically be outsider motifs. You might also want to think about how other people might make their own lists. For instance:

- If you are a young person, how or why do you think your list would differ from that of an older person, or vice versa?

- If you are a long-established native of your country, how do you think a new immigrant, or someone from a second- or third-generation immigrant family would make their list, or vice versa?

- If you live in the capital of the country, or a major city, how do you think somebody from a rural area or a more peripheral part of the country would make their list, or vice versa?

- How might other aspects of your identity affect the way that you or others might make their lists (e.g., gender, ethnic or racial identity, sexuality, etc.)?

This exercise should help you see that identity is not always clear or straightforward, but often depends on a personal perspective or situation. Further, when asked to define yourself, you are likely to give different answers at different times. This is partly because we all have a range of identities. The way we behave with our families is different from the way we behave with friends or colleagues. Someone who is very straightlaced and respectable at work might be a rave-loving hedonist on the weekends! As a parent, sister, nurse, football fan, fountain pen collector, yoga practitioner, and student of religion one person will appear different to different people at different times. They may even engage in behaviors that some find inconsistent or arbitrary. We explore social identity theory, including some key concepts, and then in-groups and out-groups in relation to religious identities, before looking at identity and conflict. We end with our two case studies.

GETTING METHODOLOGICAL: THINKING THROUGH IDENTITY
SOCIAL IDENTITY THEORY

One problem with thinking about identity, as noted, is that it is used in many ways: self-identity, group identity, the roles we play, and our interactions are all often talked about by this one word. Indeed, as a couple of scholars have put it: "The language of 'identity' is ubiquitous in contemporary social science, cutting across psychoanalysis, psychology, political science, sociology, and history. The common usage of the term identity, however, belies the considerable variability in both its conceptual meaning and its theoretical role."[1] The authors here are right: identity is everywhere. The trouble with this, as they suggest, is that sometimes when we appear to be talking about the same thing, we are in fact talking about quite different things. It also means that the term gets bandied around as though it is being used with some theoretical precision when sometimes it is being only loosely and carelessly thrown into discussions. Sometimes people will say "it is about identity" as though that explains everything. But, without knowing how or why we are using the word, it really explains nothing. Therefore, we will seek to define quite clearly what we mean by identity, or rather some of the different ways we use the term. In particular, we will focus on what is often called social identity theory (SIT). This comes out of a tradition within social psychology, but we will also look at wider usages in sociology, psychology, linguistics, and elsewhere to help give a wider sense of its theoretical usage.

Henri Tajfel (1919–1982) defined "identity" in the following way: "that part of an individual's self-concept which derives from his knowledge of his membership in a social group (or groups) together with the value and emotional significance attached to that membership."[2] This short quote is quite rich in significance, and we can draw out what are seen to be the two significant parts of identity defined in it: (1) self in the group, and (2) the group to the self. Let us explain these a little more. The first one is fairly straightforward; it is basically our identity with a particular group. So, for example, somebody may say:

- "I am Indonesian."
- "I am a student of philosophy."
- "I am a tennis player."

Each of these identities places the person within a specific group. It is, referring to the quote, about her "knowledge of membership in a social group." The group to the self concerns the "value and emotional significance" that these hold for her. So, she might say:

- "I am proud to belong to a multiethnic and tolerant democracy."
- "I am a critical thinker who learns from the world's greatest minds."
- "My aim is to emulate my hero, Serena Williams."

Identity is therefore not just a "thing" which one has, but something with content that informs the way we relate to the world and others. As another example, someone might say, separating here the two parts of identity: "I am American" ... "and I am damn proud to be a citizen of the greatest country on earth."[3]

MY IDENTITY

An important issue can be drawn out from the discussion above: identity is not just individual. It cannot be. Our identity is always shaped in social, cultural, political, and religious contexts. This is important, and worth noting further, especially for anybody raised in the Western world. Over the last several hundred years, the West has increasingly focused on the individual as the center of identity and as the "true self." You are told to "be yourself," "be true to yourself," "do what you want," and to be "an individual."[4]

However, the very idea that you can be an individual relies upon a cultural world that tells you that this is an ideal, and that this is what you should do. As humans we learn through the process of socialization. This starts, generally, with our families, especially parents and siblings (though in many cases the wider family of grandparents and cousins may be an intimate part of our social world), and continues in school with our friends and teachers. Throughout our lives we are also beset by images from the media, corporate advertising, films, novels, internet pornography, strangers we meet in chance encounters, magazines, billboards, and so on. The idea that we can ever have an individual identity or just be ourselves is very much a fiction (see also case study 5B). Our sense of self is always formed in social and cultural contexts. Indeed, we need to be careful how we use such terms as "self," "role," and "identity" (see box 6.1).

CORE ASPECTS OF IDENTITY

Having set out some key aspects of what we mean by "identity," we need to clarify a few issues. First, any identity depends upon a cultural and social context. For instance, I cannot be a tribal chieftain in a modern Western democratic nation. Equally, I could not have been a president in a medieval feudal society. The roles simply do not exist. Indeed, our social situation also tells us a lot about what these roles mean. For instance, being a king within a feudal monarchy is different from being a king or queen in a modern constitutional monarchy. We can only ever have identities that are possible within specific social situations.

Second, identities are formed in relation to other identities. As noted, identity is often about who we are not. Our image of who the "other" is often informs our own identity more than we would think. Gender identities are a case in point (see chapter 10). A lot of research on neurology suggests that there are very few differences between men and women in certain ways. However, our societies can create quite stark differences. If we want to be male, for instance, we may believe that we need to be aggressive, dominant, and strong, which would be a way to differentiate our identity from a "female identity," meaning here passive, submissive, and weak. Importantly, these are not natural nor given identities, but ones embedded in social concepts which are taught to us by society (see chapter 5). Or we may see subjects like science and mathematics as being more "male" subjects (see box 6.2).

Third, identities are never singular, but always plural. We may have a sense of ourselves as being essentially "one person," while religious identities may assert a singular and monolithic sense of self as "Christian," "Sikh," "Muslim," and so on. However, our identities have many different components. For instance, a Christian may also be a female, a Nigerian, an accountant, and a Harry Potter fan. A Baha'i may be a male, a Mexican, a sociologist, and a Terry Pratchett fan. Nobody has only one identity. Some of these identities will overlap and interact in varied ways, even affecting the other identities we hold. For instance, in many countries being a female Buddhist in the Theravada

BOX 6.1 **SELF, ROLE, AND IDENTITY**

A distinction needs to be made between the concepts "self," "role," and "identity" (noting the last of these is the focus of SIT and this chapter).[1] The self refers to your own internal notion of what makes you an "I." It is therefore about how you relate to your roles or identities. "Role" refers to the various external "faces" that you put on (people may call these your "persona"). So, you may "play," or have, the role of a parent, child, rabbi, or layperson, and so on. This is very much about the way that you relate to, or are seen to relate to, others around you. Again, these are always social: even being an anarchist or a loner is a specific culturally formulated role that we take on.

Finally, identities have two types:

Internal: This is the interiorization of the beliefs, actions, and commitments associated with a particular role. While to some extent roles are generic, we each take these on and act them out in certain ways. This is really when it becomes significant in terms of a human being as a social actor.

External: This is who you are in relation to others, or your position in relation to others and their identities. So, as a brother, maybe your behavior changes when you are with your older brother or younger sister. As a nun you may be the senior or junior one—which may change depending on context, while you may defer to your senior in public but challenge them in private. The way roles get played out are not simply monolithic and static.

We may also note that some aspects of our roles or identity are self-description—those we claim—while others are ascription, those ascribed to us by others or society in ways beyond our control. However, we need to be aware that often self-description may be due to, or is largely due to, influences beyond ourselves; hence it is not a strict distinction (see case study 5B).

Identity is about the acting out, or manifesting, of self and roles. While many people use the term "identity" to refer to self and roles, we will distinguish them to be more precise. For our purposes, neither self nor role is a significant analytical category: only as manifested in identity do they become behavior we can study.

---

1 See Paul Hedges and Angela Coco, "Belonging, Behaving, Believing, Becoming: Religion and Identity," in *Controversies in Contemporary Religion*, ed. Paul Hedges, vol. 1 (Santa Barbara: Praeger), 163–90, 163–67.

tradition will mean that you cannot join the monastic community (*sangha*) because there is no order of nuns, whereas a male Buddhist can become a monk (see case study 10B). Likewise, an American Muslim would find it easier to convert to becoming an atheist than a Saudi Arabian Muslim. Similarly, being an Arsenal fan, a Manchester United fan, or a Chelsea fan will not make much difference to an English Methodist Christian identity. However, being male or female, bisexual or straight, a Sudanese immigrant, or a recent convert from Jainism might make a huge difference.

SCIENCE, MATHEMATICS, AND GENDER

Western societies tend to think of mathematics and science as "male subjects." Our image of a scientist is likely to be male. Boys are more often encouraged to pursue these subjects at school or university. There is even a perception that males are naturally more inclined, even better, at such subjects. Some studies suggest that males do perform better in mathematics than females in places such as the UK and US. What is not clear is the extent to which this is because, from a young age, females become socialized in ways that suggest they are not good at mathematics. They adopt an identity that is not that of a scientist or mathematician. Males, conversely, may take on an identity as a scientist or mathematician more easily. Some people suggest this is down to differences in the brain. However, in other countries, we see females performing equally or even outperforming males in mathematics.[1] This cannot be explained if we assume that the differences are innate in the brain. Indeed, contrary to popular presentations that there are male and female brains, contemporary neurology says all brains possess qualities that we may typically describe as both "male" and "female."

---

1 See Melanie Hargreaves, Matt Homer, and Bronwen Swinnerton, "A Comparison of Performance and Attitudes in Mathematics amongst the 'Gifted': Are Boys Better at Mathematics or Do They Just Think They Are?," *Assessment in Education: Principles, Policy and Practice* 15.1 (2008): 19–38; and Janet S. Hyde and Janet E. Mertz, "Gender, Culture and Mathematics," *Proceedings of the National Academy of the Sciences United States* 106.22 (2009): 8801–7.

Fourth, we do not have a fixed identity. We may speak instead of our identities as always in the process of becoming.[5] This, again, may seem counterintuitive as we often have a pretty sure and solid sense of who we are, or what it means to be a Lutheran, a Russian, a gaming fanatic, or whatever. However, we need to take into account a range of factors that affect this. One of these is the question of our identities as a narrative. That is to say, we tell stories about who we are, where we come from, and how we relate to the world around us.[6] These will change as we grow older, and will also depend on when and where we tell the story (see box 6.3).

Finally, we come to the issue of the intertextuality of our identities. This refers to the way that our identities, or narratives, relate to other parts of our identities or other narratives we have about ourselves. Suppose, for instance, a Canadian and a Mexican claim a Christian identity. We can ask how their nationality relates to their religious identity, as the narrative about this will affect the narrative of religious identity. Their Christian identity will also manifest differently in the way they relate to others, for instance, in meeting atheists, Hindus, Jews, or Zoroastrians. Denominational differences will also affect it; are they a Methodist or an Anglican (Episcopalian)? And then, what type of Methodist or Anglican? Again, this will interact with their other roles and identities—as a homosexual, as a Hispanic, as an aunt, and so on. Whatever the case,

NARRATIVE IDENTITIES

I, the author of this book, am a middle aged (though I like to think of myself as still quite young) British academic. I currently work in Singapore and lived in China for several years. My main research interests include interreligious relations, method and theory in the study of religion, and intercultural hermeneutics. This brief narrative will tell you a little bit about myself. However, it is far from the full story of the several decades I have lived on this Earth. What have I not told you about myself? Relationships, siblings, and children may be areas people ask about. What are my favorite foods, hobbies, sports, musical genres, films? (I am really bored by football [soccer]—something you may not expect from a British person!) Any time we think about who we are, we are selecting bits of our biography, and this relates to roles and contexts. For instance, I based the brief narrative identity given above on the fact that I am writing an academic book as I relate it. If you met me at a party, or a tennis match, or halfway up a mountain near Chiang Mai in Thailand, I would probably introduce myself in different ways. This is partly because I would be playing a different role, but also at those times other things might be at the forefront of my mind—and so my identity at those times would be more associated with other roles. I might even come across as rude or standoffish (not on purpose normally!), as I have aspects of an autistic personality (not uncommon in academics).[1] We forget some things, some memories suddenly come back to us, and we emphasize other things. This is all part of who we are at any time. The way we are as a person is never fixed, but is fluid and changing based on the stories we tell about ourselves. We also change our memories as we remember them in particular contexts.[2] One thing you might want to ask yourself is whether some narrative identities are truer than others, or whether some of them are false.

---

1 See Lorna Wing, *The Autistic Spectrum* (London: Robinson, 2001).
2 See Giuliana Mazzoni, "The 'Real You' Is a Myth—We Constantly Create False Memories to Achieve the Identity We Want," *Conversation* (19 September 2018), https://theconversation.com/the-real-you-is-a-myth-we-constantly-create-false-memories-to-achieve-the-identity-we-want-103253?utm_medium=email&utm_campaign=Latest%20from%20The%20Conversation%20for%20September%2020%202018%20-%20111639984&utm_content=Latest%20from%20The%20Conversation%20for%20September%2020%202018%20-%20111639984+CID_dfcf59db9119abbee94646cc7dcae3a6&utm_source=campaign_monitor_uk&utm_term=significantly%20influences%20what%20we%20remember.

the identity will not remain static but will always interact with other identities and the identities of others.

IN-GROUP AND OUT-GROUP IDENTITIES
SELF AND OTHER

Arguably, the most significant part of thinking about SIT and how our identities shape us is in terms of the in-group and out-group dynamic.[7] This comes back to the theme we have discussed of our identity always being created by who we are not. This is an inevitable part of being human, and no matter where we are it seems inevitable that we will always categorize our world and others in such ways. Even if I say I am the kind of person who does not categorize others, I have immediately put myself into the in-group of "people who do not categorize others" and therefore made an out-group of "people who do categorize others"!

Such in-group and out-group categorizations lead to identity formation in various ways. It can be between families, wider social groups, or nations. These are also not stable or fixed. So, for instance, if I have an in-group of soccer fans, and an out-group of non-soccer fans, this may well become a different in-group and out-group when I think about specific teams: Barcelona versus Real Madrid, for instance. I might also distinguish within the fans of my team between really committed fans, who follow the team to every game, and nominal fans. Such a distinction is certainly common in the way we perceive religious identities, of those within "my religion" versus those outside "my religion" (see chapters 2 and 13).

An important further aspect, analyzed well by the field of sociolinguistics, is the tendency to valorize my own group and put down the out-group. Our language is often set up this way, with a sense of "positive" or "negative" language. So, for instance, historically many cultures have defined themselves as "civilized" and their out-groups as "barbarians" or "primitive" (see chapter 7).[8] Likewise, we will associate what we see as positive traits as being those possessed by our in-group, and naturally we will see out-groups as having negative traits. This heightens the possibility to see the out-group as a threat, or in some way inherently harmful, to the interests and well-being of ourselves, our society, our culture, and so on. We need to consider some of the evidence around this to show how common it is.

IN-GROUPS AND OUT-GROUPS

First off, we need to state that there are no natural identities. As noted, we can only ever have identities that are possible in our society. Furthermore, all in-groups and out-groups are fluid, not fixed (see box 6.4).

Next, we need to consider research on in-group and out-group prejudice and stereotyping. This, we should note, is based upon many studies and shows quite consistent patterns (see chapter 5).[9] I will note some key features with examples.

Overstressing In-Group Similarities and Out-Group Differences
We tend to argue what we have in common with those in our in-group is more salient, and emphasize differences with anybody in an out-group. For instance, if Christians form one in-group with Buddhists as their out-group, the Christians might stress their belief in God as an important difference. However, this distinction may not be so straightforward (see box 6.5). This is not simply true of religion, but also social categories. Indeed,

BOX 6.4 **CREATING IN-GROUPS AND OUT-GROUPS**

Some identities may seem more stable or natural to us than others (see chapter 5). For instance, those based around race and ethnicity (see box 18.6) or perhaps religion and nationality seem like more stable identities. However, from a historical and social perspective none of these are fixed; rather, they are always "imagined" (see chapter 18). Our tendency to see some as fixed and stable is what Rogers Brubaker terms "groupism," the imagining of certain identities as being more real than they are.[1] But no nation has existed in its present form over history. The boundary and territory of every nation and state has changed; indeed, many countries have only existed for relatively short periods of time. Somebody living in parts of what are now the US would have been a subject of British rule in 1775, and somebody in present-day Singapore would have been so in 1959. Likewise, the way we mark distinctions of ethnicity or race have changed over time. What might appear to be somebody's identity based on skin color might be different if we look at DNA tests tracking the areas of the globe where their ancestors came from. So, for instance, somebody who appears to be "white" based on their skin color might have a DNA profile suggesting that they have a significant "Black African" ancestry.[2]

Our sense of in-group and out-group allegiances and affiliations are also permeable. For instance, within a social milieu infused with socialist or communist sensibilities, there may be a natural affinity between members of the working class that crosses racial or ethnic boundaries. So, somebody who identifies as, for instance, Chinese working class may relate to Black African working-class people as their comrades rather than relating to members of the Chinese upper classes. Notably, historical research in the US has shown that members of the Irish immigrant community were often servants. However, as a growing distinction between Black and white identities grew there, they became accepted as part of "white society." This was in part a move by slave owners and others to ensure that the combined and oppressed masses of immigrant African slaves and Irish indentured servants would not find common cause.[3]

---

1 See Rogers Brubaker, "Ethnicity without Groups," *Archives Européenes de Sociologie* 43.2 (2002): 163–89; Ien Ang, "Beyond Chinese Groupism: Chinese Australians between Assimilation, Multiculturalism and Diaspora," *Ethnic and Racial Studies* 37.7 (2014): 1184–96; and Andreas Wimmer, "Elementary Strategies of Ethnic Boundary Making," *Ethnic and Racial Studies* 31.6 (2008): 1025–55.

2 See Susan Svrluga, "To Bring a Divided Country Together, Start with a Little Spit," *Washington Post* (24 December 2016), www.washingtonpost.com/news/grade-point/wp/2016/12/24/to-bring-a-divided-country-together-start-with-a-little-spit/?utm_term=.d25oc5672c71; and Tara Bahrampour, "They Considered Themselves White, but DNA Tests Told a More Complex Story," *Washington Post* (6 February 2018), www.washingtonpost.com/local/social-issues/they-considered-themselves-white-but-dna-tests-told-a-more-complex-story/2018/02/06/16215d1a-e181-11e7-8679-a9728984779c_story.html?noredirect=on&utm_term=.52e0827658eb.

3 On the creation of such identities in the US, see Sean Harvey, "Ideas of Race in Early America," in *Oxford Research Encyclopaedias: American History* (2016), http://oxfordre.com/americanhistory/view/10.1093/acrefore/9780199329175.001.0001/acrefore-9780199329175-e-262.

BOX 6.5 **THE BUDDHA, FAITH, AND CHRISTIAN IDENTITY**

For many Pure Land Buddhists, the most significant aspect of their practice is faith in the saving power of Amida Buddha, who arguably functions as a "god" providing "salvation through grace" to his devotees (see box 14.7). Indeed, when Catholics first arrived in Japan, some of them reported that the devil had reached there before them and taught the "Lutheran heresy."[1] Scholars argue over the Lutheran-Pure Land Buddhist conceptual overlap, but regardless of this, the identity creation is significant. In these early encounters, Catholics identified their in-group against Buddhist and Lutherans as a combined out-group of believers in pure faith. Yet, today, Christians would typically stress the similarities of all Christians as believing in God as against Buddhists, who do not.

Amida Buddha flanked by bodhisattvas, BW Monastery, Singapore.

---

1 See Fritz Buri, "The Concept of Grace in Paul, Shinran, and Luther," *Eastern Buddhist* 9.2 (2004): 21–42; and Burnett Hillman Streeter, *The Buddha and the Christ* (London: Macmillan, 1932), 89–92, 103–10.

scholars may overstress similarities of their in-group and overemphasize (and stereotype) differences from out-groups (e.g., religious studies scholars vs. theologians, critical religion scholars vs. more traditional scholars).

Favoring Our In-Group

Studies where people are placed in two random groups (e.g., a blue group and a green group) show bias even when there is no other association with group members. In such studies, when asked to allocate resources, people—having been told they belong to one group—generally give more resources to their own group, even though these are random groups comprising people who have never met each other before. The influence of in-group and out-group dynamics on human interactions is very strong. We can probably think of examples where a particular religious community has argued it should be treated in a particular way or given preferential treatment. The question would be the extent to which this is shaped not by anything about religious bias per se, but simply in-group preference (see chapter 5).

Self-Stereotyping and Identifying with Other Members of Our In-group

If we are stressing a specific religious identity, and then asked to describe ourselves, we will typically give a narrative that relates to the features we see as characteristic of that religion. A Buddhist, for instance, might describe himself as compassionate, calm, and caring. A Christian might describe herself as devout, loving, and evangelistic. Such descriptions, we should note, can be very different from the way people would talk about themselves when asked to define themselves without their religious identity being foregrounded.

Using Universal Stereotypes

The use of universal stereotypes is perhaps the most problematic feature, because not only do we associate our in-group with positive characteristics (e.g., trustworthy, peaceful, loyal), we also give out-groups negative characteristics (e.g., aggressive, treacherous, etc.). This phenomenon is found often in making distinctions based on gender (see chapter 10) or in colonial contexts (see chapter 7, especially boxes 7.3 and 7.4). If asked what the typical characteristics of Muslims are, a Muslim might say peaceful, fashionable, and ethical. Conversely, particularly in the context of what is often termed Islamophobia (see box 15.5), a non-Muslim might say violent, traditional, and unkind. Such stereotypes ignore the vast diversity of human societies and human beings: Are Indonesian Muslims like Tunisian Muslims? Are Brazilian Muslims like Dutch Muslims?

Understanding In-Group Salient Features as More Unique and Distinctive Than They Are

Across a wide spectrum of religious traditions, the pattern of finding some form of trinitarian formula to talk about deity, or the transcendent (see box 1.10), is not uncommon. Christians have the Trinity (Father, Son, and Holy Spirit); the Hindu family of tradition has the Three Forms (*trimurti*, i.e., Vishnu as maintainer [of the universe], Shiva as destroyer, and Brahma as creator); and Mahayana Buddhism has the Three Bodies of the Buddha (*trikaya*) ("transcendental" [supreme and unmanifested], "supernatural" [celestial Buddhas], and earthly [the historical Buddha]).[10] While some scholars see conceptual similarities, other scholars and many Christian theologians stress differences. A Christian theologian might argue that the Trinity is not only different in substance (it says different things from the *trimurti* or *trikaya*), but also qualitatively and substantively different, that is, representing a wholly superior spiritual aspiration and conception.[11] The latter claim would not simply be analytic, but a distinctive identity claim to stress difference and superiority. Notably, such claims would also often overstress similarity, as in the first point above; that is, the Christian trinitarian notion would be seen as homogenous across Christian faith traditions, a view that overlooks the vast differences historically and theologically between various Christian understandings of the Trinity.[12]

IDENTITY SALIENCE

A final part of the picture in our brief description of SIT is the concept of identity salience. This is the chance of any particular identity, and the action(s) associated with it, being called upon in any specific situation. In different situations, we are more likely to choose specific roles and act these out as our embodied identity in different ways. A Catholic priest in a church might typically play the role of the ritual celebrant and so perform Mass at the appointed time. When representing his church at a gathering of community leaders, he would not, however, start performing Mass; being a ritual leader would not be a salient identity. When he visits his mother, his role as community leader will probably not be his enacted identity.

At different times, particular identities may take a primary role, and so our identity will be manifested in relation to that. This may involve a hierarchy of salience where, in any situation, specific identities may be more powerful than others, and so become those which we act upon.

IDENTITY AND CONFLICT
RELIGIOUS TRIBALIZATION

Jeannine Hill Fletcher argues that religious identities can have real consequences: "With the introduction of tribalization, we are pressed to see that the theological construction of religions as containers of identity is not merely an abstract problem but has material implications."[13]

By the notion of "container," she is referring to the problematic construction of religion as a single and static monolithic identity, which goes against what identity theory tells us. As discussed in chapters 1 and 3, the concept of religion is itself more fluid than we typically imagine. "Tribalization" refers to the kind of in-group and out-group dynamics we have discussed, where we each sit within our in-group identities and see ourselves as facing various others who may be against us. Indeed, many see religions as inherently leading to conflict (see especially chapter 15). However, conflict is not inevitable simply because of in-group and out-group dynamics.[14]

IDENTITY, VIOLENCE, AND THREAT PERCEPTION

The likelihood of some form of conflict grows when we see the out-group as being potentially hostile or some form of threat to us (see box 6.6).[15] This may not just be a direct physical threat—as when we are attacked in war, for example—but also as an existential threat to our culture, society, or way of life. We may also feel threatened when we fear a loss of our own identity (often some form of dilution of our boundaries) by another group. This is mainly the case where one single identity (e.g., a religious identity) has become predominant or highlighted. When our imagined identity becomes singular and static, we react negatively to anything which might challenge this sense of who we are and our central core identity. It is notable that a seemingly strong/stable, fixed/static, and singular identity—despite its monolithic certainty—is actually often an unstable and fragile conception, relating to Brubaker's notion of groupism (see box 6.4). It can also be the case where sharp dichotomies exist together, especially when imagined and idealized core identities are opposed as monolithic opposites; arguably this is found in Samuel Huntington's clash of civilizations thesis (see box 14.4).[16] This concerns a sense of polarized and stereotyped identities which are seen as clashing, in what may be termed a contestation of sacred values (see box 18.7).

Indeed, studies show that where plural identities exist, and we have a clear sense of these multiple identities, there is generally less chance of hostility and conflict. Some have suggested it is one reason why women often make good peacemakers, because they may share a common identity as women and mothers which makes them overcome otherwise polarized identities. To note one way such dynamics work, for many years while Catholic and Protestant Christians often stood in antagonism in Northern Ireland, a sense of being fellow citizens in other countries is a factor which means such antagonism does not develop, or has been resolved, between these groups elsewhere (see box 9.3). Notably, what became known as "the Troubles" was not originally a religious divide, but about political allegiances, with Catholics and Protestants historically on both sides of this divide; what is termed "religious violence" often involves a complex set of factors (see chapter 15, especially box 15.6). Various aspects of SIT and psychology are useful in understanding contexts such as Northern Ireland and the sectarian divisions along perceived religious lines which existed, and still linger, there.[17]

IDENTITY AND IN-GROUP OUT-GROUP THREAT PERCEPTION

Identities, by themselves, do not necessarily result in tension or conflict. Even sharply marked in-group and out-group differences need not always lead to hostility. Rather, specific identities can be set up and polarized in ways that promote clashes. Religious identities may lend themselves to this (like may other identities) in various ways:

- by becoming a primary or monolithic identity
- by assuming a sense of unquestionable "ultimacy"
- when, as a monolithic identity, it is challenged/undermined or perceived as under threat
- when another religion is largely unknown but stereotyped/portrayed negatively as an out-group
- when another religion is perceived as an existential threat to our own religion or way of life
- when another religion is portrayed negatively and its members feel threatened

In Fletcher's terms the threat comes not from a religious identity itself, but tribalization in some form.

KEY FEATURES OF IDENTITY

It would be useful to sum up and clarify some key aspects of SIT:

- We use "identity" to refer to the twin poles of internal and external manifestation of actions. Self and roles are often spoken of as identities but, unless acted out as an identity, give little analytical clarity.
- Identities are always plural, fluid, and changeable. They are based in the narratives we (as individuals and groups/communities) tell about ourselves. Importantly, these narratives are not simply verbal, but are also acted out as manifestations of identity.
- At times, we imagine our identities as static and monolithic. This is where we often see identities leading to conflict; a fixed or unchanging religious or national sense of identity will often resist change or other out-groups.
- The creation of in-group and out-group involves separation from others. While not inevitable, we cannot simply say this is arbitrary, either. Our society and culture will inform the kind of in-groups and out-groups we build.

- Conflict arising from in-group out-group dynamics is not inevitable in and of itself. It tends to occur where identities become polarized and/or monolithic.

. . .

CASE STUDY 6A. SHIV SENA, HINDU NATIONALISM, AND IDENTITY POLITICS

Identities, and in-group and out-group affiliation, are never fixed, but always plural and changing. Meanwhile, the way identity is formed through identity salience is significant. Particular cases can help elucidate this, especially if we trace the historical transformation of groups or movements that are embedded in strong forms of identity.

BAL THACKERAY AND SHIV SENA

Shiv Sena is a citizen advocacy group and political party founded in 1966 by Bal (Balasaheb Keshav) Thackeray (1926–2012). It is local to the Maharashtra State in India, especially Mumbai (formerly Bombay), and is particularly notorious for its association with Hindu nationalist politics and violence. A journalist by profession, Thackeray originally founded Shiv Sena as an organization to fight for Maharashtrian rights. Mumbai is India's financial and cultural center (the famous Bollywood film industry is located there), and so many Indians are drawn to the state. Appealing to the poor and disenfranchised, Thackeray argued for the rights of those indigenous to the state against newcomers. However, Shiv Sena found itself losing ground in the 1980s, and, to boost support, Thackeray changed focus, striking an alliance with the Bharatiya Janata Party (BJP) in 1984. Shiv Sena now embraced Hindutva ideology (see box 6.7) and Hindu nationalist politics.

CREATING HINDU NATIONALISM AND HINDUTVA IDEOLOGY

Indian nationalism was a response to Western, primarily British, colonialism. Prior to British colonization, India did not exist as a single entity, even under the Mughals (sixteenth to eighteenth centuries) or Emperor Ashoka (ca. 250 BCE). The conception of the nation-state is, in fact, relatively new, originating in European political thought in recent centuries (see chapter 18). In response to British rule, and in the context of the ascendancy of the nation-state, Indians developed their own nationalist movement. There was a secular strand associated with the Congress Party, founded in 1885 as the Indian National Congress. It saw India as a nation inclusive of all religions, with Jawaharlal Nehru (1847–1964) and Mohandas "Mahatma" Gandhi (1869–1948) as prominent leaders. There was also a Hindu nationalist strand. Not initially politically significant, it spawned later leaders and groups. Important figures include V. D. Savarkar (1883–1966), who

BOX 6.7 **SAVARKAR'S HINDUTVA AND ITS CONSEQUENCES**

"Hindutva" means something like "Hinduness" and has various connotations. It can be traced to the 1870s in Bengal, where, in its usage by figures such as Rabindranath Tagore (1861–1941), it was an inclusive term about Indian cultural identity, with non-Hindus such as the Catholic Christian convert Brahmabandhab Upadhyay (1861–1907) using the term. However, a new and exclusive meaning would be given to the term by V. D. Savarkar (1883–1966).

In 1923, Savarkar wrote a booklet (that went through a few editions and titles, including *What Is Hindutva?*) widely known as *Hindutva: Who Is a Hindu?*[1] It outlined a new exclusivist notion of Hindutva adopted by militant Hindu nationalism. He defined three central aspects:

- *Location:* The Hindu is somebody who lives in Hindustan (i.e., India).
- *Race:* The Hindus are people united by a "bond of common blood."
- *Culture:* The Hindu is somebody who regards India as a "holyland" or "fatherland."

According to Savarkar, all three are needed to make somebody a Hindu; this has four important consequences:

- First, it is not enough to reside in India, as perceived foreigners do not have "common blood."
- Second, some religious affiliations are included—Hindus, Sikhs, Jains, and Buddhists—as their sacred sites are located in (or around) India, making it their "holyland."
- Third, explicitly excluded are Muslims and Christians, as their "holyland" is outside of India.
- Fourth, consequently, some Indians, despite the "bond of common blood," are excluded.

A distinct and clear split is therefore made between the in-group and the out-group.

Many Hindutva ideologues claim Hindutva is not religiously exclusive, but tolerant. Certainly, for Savarkar, Hindutva was not about religious belief, as he was an atheist. So, it does not make claims about the truth or falsity of Christianity or Islam, or castigate different beliefs. Rather, the question about being native to India is key. In practice, though, tolerance and inclusion are not always manifested by Hindutva advocates. Muslims and Christians have been excluded and verbally and physically attacked.

---

1 V. D. Savarkar, *Hindutva: Who Is a Hindu?* 5th ed. (Bombay: M/s Bhave, 1969 [1923]), https://archive.org/stream/hindutva-vinayak-damodar-savarkar-pdf/hindutva-vd-savarkar_djvu.txt.

helped create contemporary discourse on Hindutva ideology (see box 6.7), and Pandit Mohan Malaviya (1861–1946), the first vice chancellor (head) of the Benares Hindu University, which was founded to promote Hindu and Sanskrit learning and culture. The two strands were not entirely distinct, and Malaviya was twice president of the Indian National Congress. Nevertheless, they represent different trajectories.

At independence, India became a secular democracy (see chapter 16), though one in which religion continued to be seen as a part of the ethos of the country, which Rajeev Bhargava and others claim makes it distinct from typical Western secular democracies.[18] In recent decades, though, the Hindu nationalist movement has become increasingly dominant, and the BJP has become the Congress Party's main challenger. It attained power as part of a coalition for a short time in the 1990s, but saw its most notable victory in the 2014 general election, when Narendra Modi won 286 of the 543 seats, making the BJP the first party since 1984 to have an overall majority. A majority increased in the 2019 general election.

BACKGROUND: AYODHYA, MILITANCY, AND RAMA

The BJP is associated with a number of other Hindu nationalist groups, some of which are often seen as more militant and associated with outbreaks of communal violence. One particularly violent incident is seen as having helped secure the path to the BJP's power and success: the Ayodhya incident of 1992 (see box 17.5). Ayodhya is believed by some to be the birthplace of the god Rama. Significantly, Rama is symbolic for the militant nationalists because he is a warrior god.[19]

In 1528, the Babri Masjid (mosque) was built there, on a site which allegedly was where the temple marking Rama's exact birthplace was located. Inciting anger, the BJP organized a mass pilgrimage to Ayodhya to rebuild the Rama Temple. The pilgrimage was part of a campaign that collected bricks and money and ended in December 1992 with approximately one hundred thousand volunteers from the BJP and other organizations arriving at the site. The police have been blamed for not stopping them, but given the size of the protest—which probably took the authorities by surprise—it was hard to stop what became the demolition of the mosque by this crowd. The site is now subject to legal disputes and government control. Importantly, after the demolition, the government of India undertook an archaeological excavation of the site to determine if the mosque actually was built on the site of an earlier Hindu temple. To date, the final report of the excavation has not been publicly released (see box 17.5).

SHIV SENA, HINDUTVA, AND IDENTITY

As noted, beginning in 1984, Thackeray threw in his lot behind the BJP, becoming also a notable Hindutva ideologue. Certainly, some key aspects of Thackeray's ideology and the identity of Shiv Sena members is worth noting. Hindutva seeks to defend Hinduism from both Muslims and the liberal secular elites who are seen to threaten it. It has opposed aspects of what has been seen as Western culture in India, for instance, opposing the celebration of Valentine's Day, with young couples being harassed for holding hands or kissing in public. It also opposes women wearing jeans. The language it uses is also quite militant, speaking of a "dharma war" (*dharayudh*), its members being warriors of the deity Shiva (*Sainiks*), and looking for street fights (*rada*). The tough street language he uses has been seen to spark communal tensions, with two of his papers, *Marmik* and *Saamna,* being seen as influential in inciting violence in the 1992–1993 Bombay riots.[20]

In terms of in-group and out-group dynamics, we see strong stereotyping, with Shiv Sena portrayed as the good guys because they support Hinduism/religion/duty (*dharma*). Meanwhile, opponents are portrayed as a hostile threat. This can be a moral threat, for instance, immoral Western culture that threatens Hindu women by making them engage in acts of public immorality (as they define it)—wearing jeans is seen as symbolic of this. Stereotyping of the in-group and out-group is at work with Western, secular, and liberal culture seen as immoral compared with the morality of Hindu culture. The perceived threat can also be physical, especially when it comes to Muslims; hence the justification for violence.[21] Here, the concept of identity salience is useful; if you are a member of Shiv Sena, you will see yourself as a Shiva warrior who is up for a street fight (in defense of *dharma*, of course). In times of tension this militant identity may therefore come to the fore.

REFLECTIONS

We can ask some questions about Shiv Sena, Hindutva, and identity:

1. From the perspective of a potential Shiv Sena supporter, what aspects of the narrative and identity of this party do you think would be most appealing and why?
2. Which aspects of identity theory do you find most useful for thinking about and understanding a group such as Shiv Sena?
3. Note key moments and issues in the way that the identity of Shiv Sena has been created and re-created.
4. The particular identity of Shiv Sena, and much Hindu nationalism, emphasizes violence and militancy, and so images like Rama and Shiva's warriors are invoked. This downplays irenic traditions within Hinduism, for example, nonviolence (*ahimsa*) as extolled by Gandhi. Other images of the gods are not brought to light; for instance, Shiva has many facets and his role as ascetic is not mentioned in creating this identity. Think about how and why such images may change the type of identity in terms of roles, salience, and so on.

CASE STUDY 6B. RACE, RELIGION, AND THE AMERICAN WHITE EVANGELICAL

Some see a toxic mixture when religion, race/ethnicity (see box 18.6), and politics/nationalism are combined (see chapter 18). Religion is often held as needing to be kept distinct from politics in secular nations (see chapter 16), though this association is not always perceived as "toxic"; for instance, religious involvement in politics can be pro-war or anti-war, pro–civil rights or anti–civil rights, and so on. Some see the contemporary relation of race, nationalism, and religion in the US as a dividing line between party boundaries within the country as a whole.

THE CHRISTIAN RIGHT IN THE US

The US is generally seen as a secular democracy, with a clear divide between religion and the state in terms of freedom of religion (see chapter 16). Nevertheless, religion is prominent in its politics; it has been argued that nobody can become president without a declared Christian affiliation, which is a social rather than a constitutional requirement. The Christian right, and its support for the Republican Party is, arguably, the clearest manifestation of this connection. Today, it has become largely a white Evangelical identity linking race, religion, and politics.

The Christian right originated in the 1970s, coming to prominence under President Jimmy Carter, but attaining its greatest influence during the tenure of Ronald Reagan, who served two terms as US president from 1981–1989. The main concern was the moral and economic decline of the country, seen as linked: because the United States had lost its religious roots, it was not prospering. While the Christian right declined after Reagan, it emerged as a significant force behind Donald Trump's election victory in 2016. An Evangelical alliance of pastors stood behind him, and he gained 81 per cent of the white Evangelical vote (helping him gain the presidential office, despite losing the popular vote). He also ran on a deeply nationalist ticket, popularizing the slogan "Make America Great Again" (ironically emblazoned on hats made in China), and promising jobs and economic revival. Alongside a strong nationalism, issues which have particularly motivated the religious right include abortion and LGBTQI issues.

IDENTITY, EVANGELICALISM, AND RACE

The legacy of what is known as Jim Crow, the segregation practiced in much of the US through the twentieth century, alongside lynching and racial discrimination more broadly, remains a stark factor affecting the US today. Studies have shown that rigid racial identities tend to be upheld by those who see themselves as politically traditionalist and those with exclusive sectarian religious identities. Nostalgia for an imagined 1950s America, when a white Protestant tradition was dominant, is another factor. Some argue that

President Trump spoke particularly to the demographic associated with these factors, and asserts an authoritarian aggression that appeals to them.[22] Yet, Evangelical Christian theological and ethical quandaries have also risen in relation to the right-wing nationalist triumphalism that often goes alongside this. Such quandaries have also emerged in the context of accepting Trump as a messianic figure.

Regarding Trump, there have been allegations of behavior which may seem un-Christian, especially the alleged dalliances with, assaults on, and groping of, women. Yet it appears many white Evangelical voters, both male and female, stood by him as representing Evangelical values despite his behavior as an individual; further, such behavior was sometimes dismissed by supporters as "fake news." Meanwhile, the macho aggressive posturing, and vaunting of wealth and power, is seen by some to also be in complete contradistinction to the teachings and life of Jesus.

Religion, politics, and race are deeply intertwined in this, and we may note some ways they have manifested. One involved the so-called birther issue, where former president Barack Obama's US citizenship was questioned. Meanwhile, racial group identities have been divided in voting. In 2017, in a tight race in the historically Republican state of Alabama, the highly conservative Republican favorite Roy Moore was beaten by the relatively unknown Democrat Doug Jones; Moore garnered 80 percent of the white Evangelical vote (62 percent of all white votes), and Jones received 95 per cent of the Black Evangelical vote (98 percent of all Black votes). Like Trump, Moore faced many accusations of improper behavior, but white Evangelicals more than any others stood by him, while Black Evangelicals strongly rejected him.

REFLECTIONS

Some questions will help bring these issues into focus for us:

1. From the perspective of a white American Evangelical, what do you think would be the main appeal of a candidate such as Donald Trump? Is it to make American great again? To ensure your religious-ethical values, such as anti-abortion and anti-LGBTQI, are enshrined in law? A nostalgic vision of a past when your white Protestant identity was the unchallenged mainstream? Also, how do you think a religious/Evangelical voter would balance support for a candidate whose personal behavior is seen as un-Christian if they uphold key religio-ethical tenets as policy?

2. Race is for some a defining issue here: some argue the vote for Trump, and others, is mainly about protecting a disappearing white culture. How far do you think the issue is about racial identity as opposed to a wider religious or political identity? Can these be separated? More broadly, while race (or ethnicity) is a very unstable form of identity, discuss the extent to which you think it plays a role in relation to politics and religion in other contexts you know.

3. Consider how identity salience plays into these issues: Is there a hierarchy of identities which take precedence? What aspects of an assumed identity are played out in any specific context?

.   .   .

QUESTIONS AND CONNECTING THOUGHTS

Identities are always specific, and therefore plural. Therefore, we cannot just speak about, for instance, a person's Buddhist identity. A person might be a female Hispanic Californian Zen Buddhist, or a male Chinese New Yorker Pure Land Buddhist. This relates to issues in other chapters, such as lived religion (chapter 3), colonialism and postcolonialism (chapter 7), space and place (chapter 17), and gender (chapter 10). Identities are also always political (see chapter 18). This, of course, applies not just to religious identities, but also scholarly ones: one person claims they practice critical religion, while another identifies as a phenomenologist, somebody else is called a sociologist of religion, while her colleague is a philosopher of religion. These identities will affect our behavior and thinking in studying, categorizing, and defining religion. They even help inform why we think that certain ways to define or study religion are better or worse than others. Some questions will be helpful for us to think through these issues:

1. What are your identities in relation to religion and its study? For instance, do you identify with a specific religion; with atheism; as spiritual but not religious; as someone who says the term makes no sense; as a sociologist, philosopher, anthropologist of religion? What are the implications of this for you as a student of religion?
2. Every religious tradition has in-groups and out-groups. To what extent does SIT help explain this? For instance, is hostility toward another group, or simply bias toward your own group, based on specific religious teachings, or human identity formation?
3. Our two case studies looked at specific countries and/or movements. Do you think you could apply SIT to a context that is more familiar to you to help analyze it? Or could you apply it to a context less familiar to you to help you understand it?

FURTHER READING
THEORY

Alarid, Michael. "Identity Theory and Social Identity Theory: Basics," video (2013), www.youtube.com/watch?v=YcRNQtvOCbc.

Brewer, Marilynn B. "Ingroup Identification and Intergroup Conflict," in *Social Identity, Intergroup Conflict and Conflict Reduction,* ed. Richard Ashmore, Lee Jussim, and David Wilder (Oxford: Oxford University Press, 2001), 17–41.

Hedges, Paul, and Angela Coco. "Belonging, Behaving, Believing, Becoming: Religion and Identity," in *Controversies in Contemporary Religion*, ed. Paul Hedges, vol. 1 (Santa Barbara: Praeger, 2014), 163–90.

Jenkins, Richard. *Social Identity*, 4th ed. (New York: Routledge, 2014).

McKeown, Shelley, Reeshma Haji, and Neil Ferguson, eds. *Understanding Peace and Conflict through Social Identity Theory: Contemporary Global Perspectives* (New York: Springer, 2016).

Stets, Jan E., and Peter Burke. "A Sociological Approach to Self and Identity," in *Handbook of Self and Identity*, 2nd ed., ed. Mark Leary and June Price Tangney (New York: Guilford Press, 2013), 128–52.

Stryker, Sheldon, and Burke, Peter J. "The Past, Present and Future of an Identity Theory," *Social Psychology Quarterly* 63.4 (2000): 284–97.

Tajfel, Henri. *Social Identity and Intergroup Relations* (Cambridge: Cambridge University Press, 1981).

CASE STUDY 6A. SHIV SENA, HINDU NATIONALISM, AND IDENTITY POLITICS

Jaffrelot, Christophe. "The Fate of Secularism," in *The BJP in Power: Indian Democracy and Religious Nationalism*, ed. Milan Vaishnav (Washington, DC: Carnegie Foundation, 2019), https://carnegieendowment.org/files/BJP_In_Power_final.pdf.

Katzenstein, Mary, Uday Mehta, and Usha Thakkar. "The Rebirth of Shiv Sena: The Symbiosis of Discursive and Organizational Power," *Journal of Asian Studies* 56.2 (1997): 371–90.

Lipner, Julius. "Hindu Fundamentalism," in *Fundamentalisms: Threats and Ideologies in the Modern World*, ed. James Dunn (London: I. B. Tauris, 2015), 93–116.

Riaz, Ali. "Religion as a Political Ideology in South Asia," in *The Politics of Religion in South and Southeast Asia*, ed. Ishtiaq Ahmed (New York: Routledge, 2011), 13–25.

Roy, Abhik. "Regenerating Masculinity in the Construction of Hindu Nationalist Identity: A Case Study of Shiv Sena," *Communication Studies* 57:2 (2006): 135–52.

Savarkar, V. D. *Essentials of Hindutva* (1923), https://archive.org/stream/hindutva-vinayak-damodar-savarkar-pdf/hindutva-vd-savarkar_djvu.txt.

CASE STUDY 6B. RACE, RELIGION, AND THE AMERICAN WHITE EVANGELICAL

Drake, Janine Giordano. "Race, Class, Religion, and American Citizenship," in *Oxford Research Encyclopedia of Religion* (Oxford: Oxford University Press, 2017), DOI: 10.1093/acrefore/9780199340378.013.489.

Gorski, Philip. "Conservative Protestantism in the United States: Toward a Comparative Historical Perspective," in *Evangelicals and Democracy in America*, vol. 1, ed. S. Brint and J. Schroedel (New York: Russell Sage, 2009), 74–114.

Hills, Darius. "Back to a White Future: White Religious Loss, Donald Trump, and the Problem of Belonging," *Black Theology* 16.1 (2018): 38–52.

Perry, Samuel, and Andrew Whitehead. "Christian Nationalism and White Racial Boundaries: Examining Whites' Opposition to Interracial Marriage," *Ethnic and Racial Studies* 38.10 (2015): 1671–89.

Pew Research Center. "White Evangelicals See Trump as Fighting for Their Beliefs, Though Many Have Mixed Feelings about His Personal Conduct," Pew Research Center (12 March 2020), www.pewforum.org/2020/03/12/white-evangelicals-see-trump-as-fighting-for-their-beliefs-though-many-have-mixed-feelings-about-his-personal-conduct/.

COLONIALISM
Postcolonialism, Orientalism, and Decolonization

IN WHICH WE EXPLORE:

The way that colonialism, imperialism, and postcolonial theory affect how we
understand religion

The concepts of Orientalism and decolonization in relation to the study of religion

The connection of race and religion

Case studies on the "invention" of Hinduism and the portrayal of various global
indigenous traditions as magic, superstition, and religion

INTRODUCTION: RELIGION, EMPIRES, AND CIVILIZATION
THE RISE OF THE WEST

How religion is viewed today is inseparable from the history of Western colonialism and
imperialism that has shaped the modern world. Yet, for much of history, Europe—
particularly northwestern Europe—was a marginal backwater. Civilization, globalization,
and progress were found elsewhere: China pioneered many inventions that made the
modern world possible; Central Asia was the heart of commerce and the exchange of
ideas; the Islamic empires across North Africa and the Middle East made staggering
advances in mathematics and science; and the older civilizational centers of Babylon,
Egypt, and the Indus Valley often remained areas of great significance.

A number of shifts changed the dynamic of world power:

- Spanish and Portuguese explorations to the "New World" of the Americas—made possible by the collapse of indigenous civilizations from diseases imported from Europe—brought gold and riches to Europe.[1]
- From the Renaissance period (see box 4.4), the scientific advances of the Islamic world were passed to Europe, though only in the late eighteenth to the nineteenth century did Western science and military technology surpass other regions.[2]
- A decline in Asian empires coincided with Europe's incursions, but before the nineteenth century, most European colonial ventures in Asia were small coastal trading outposts reliant on the goodwill of native rulers.[3]

These factors have meant that for about the last two hundred years European (mainly British, Dutch, French, and German) imperialism dominated the globe. The twentieth century saw the US dominate as the historical fortunes of countries waxed and waned.

This brief history encapsulates why it is impossible to think about religion apart from the history of colonialism and imperialism: the rise of European and American power has meant that Western cultural and scholarly conceptions have dominated the globe, with English language (see chapter 2) dominating discourse (see box 5.1). This includes how such terms as "religion" and "race" are understood and experienced.

RELIGION, CIVILIZATION, AND THE COLONIAL PROJECT

As Europeans "discovered" cultures distinct from their own, they defined aspects of these as "religion." This relates to the development of what is known as the world religions paradigm (WRP; see chapter 1 and box 2.1), solidified in the nineteenth century based on certain European Enlightenment (see box 16.1) and Protestant Christian presuppositions. Religion was held to be something having

- a central and original text,
- specific beliefs,
- certain forms of institution,
- distinct practices, and
- a deity (or deities).

In short, what was counted as "religion" or dismissed as "superstition" often depended on what looked familiar to Protestant missionaries and colonial administrators. There was often a racialized aspect to this, associated with "civilization." Under the WRP schema, what often passed as "objective study" of non-Christian religions was often simply Western Christian bias, used to show the superiority of Christian paradigms.[4]

Civilization was a key aspect. European colonizers (see box 7.1) often asserted that they were justified to take and occupy land if the indigenous inhabitants did not have "civilization." In the African context, because religion was associated with civilization, the denial of the term "religion" to indigenous customs supplied "evidence" to support land annexation to settlers.[5] Terms such as "savages," "primitive," "superstition," and "magic" played a role in dismissing indigenous religion (see boxes 7.8, 9.4, and 12.2). For many missionaries, the project of conversion was not simply one of replacing an existing religion with Christianity, but of bringing civilization. This could entail teaching indigenous inhabitants the customs, language, literature, and manners of the country from which the missionary came. These were presumed to epitomize the very perfection of "Christian civilization."[6] Religion was a part of the control, classification, and management of imperial systems. While sometimes missionaries and colonial regimes were distinct, and many missionaries resisted what they saw as unjust treatment of indigenous peoples by (secular) colonial authorities, there was nevertheless a close imbrication of the two.[7] The modern study of religion arises, more or less directly, out of the colonial and imperial context of the last couple of centuries.

In this chapter, having noted how colonialism and religion are linked, we next explore the concept of Orientalism before looking at postcolonial theory more widely. In this, we also look at the distinction between postcolonialism and decolonialization, drawing on Walter Mignolo. We then address the connection of race and religion before discussing how we might decolonize the curriculum. We end with our two case studies.

THE ORIENT AND ORIENTALISM
WHAT IS THE "ORIENT"?

The Orient and the Occident refer, respectively, to the East and the West. However, what do we mean by them? Often, we associate the Orient with Asia and the Occident with

BOX 7.2 **ISTANBUL AS ORIENT?**

Only one city straddles two continents: Istanbul. Its left/western side sits in Europe, while its right/eastern side sits in Asia. Between the two lies the Bosphorus. To many, Istanbul may stir images of the exotic, the Orient, and the mysterious. Yet, for centuries, it was (as Constantinople) the capital of the Roman Empire, often thought of as definitively European/Western. Emperor Constantine (ca. 272–337 CE) moved his capital here from Rome, which was in the more barbarous Western half of the empire, not the more civilized East. Moreover, a visitor today, crossing the Bosphorus by ferry looking to the eastern shore will see, in Asia, primarily a modern city full of blocks of apartments and factories. But looking West, to Europe, she will see a skyscape dominated by the minarets of mosques and the towers of the old Ottoman Tokapi Palace. Our vision of Asia/the Orient and Europe/the Occident are shaped by our perspectives, location in the world, and historical events. They are not simply factual representations of the world as it is.

Europe (and North America); however, this is inadequate (see box 7.2). For one thing, where do we place Africa and South America if we use this binary division? For another, Europe is a modern idea, and with it also the way we think of Asia. Indeed, both are vast and internally diverse. By Europe, as the "West," we typically mean northwestern Europe only, with southern and eastern Europeans being "othered" (see box 13.7).

EDWARD SAID AND ORIENTALISM

The concept Orientalism is linked to Edward Said (1935–2003), who argued a powerful thesis that Western interpretations of the East, primarily Islam and the Middle East, are always misinterpretations (see box 7.3).[8] Nevertheless, they create powerful falsehoods that shape our vision. This thesis has been extended by others to Asia and beyond.

Said's critique has been so influential that it has changed the way we think about the term "Orientalist": before, the term was used to denote a respected scholar; after, it was used as a derogatory term.

Said distinguished between two forms of Orientalism:

Latent Orientalism: our presuppositions in mental forms about the Orient

Manifest Orientalism: manifestations of Orientalist thinking, normally acted out in political, economic, and social arenas

For Said, as a result of latent Orientalism, we are prone to behaving in terms of manifest Orientalism. However, it is not a unique feature of Western or imperial thinking/ideology (see box 7.4).

BOX 7.3 **SAID'S ORIENTALIST THESIS**

Edward Said's main thesis can be concisely stated in three key points:

- European (American) study and fascination with the "Orient" is political. Drawing on Michel Foucault (1926–1984), Said asserts that all discourse (see box 5.1) aims to exert power over the other.
- "Orientalism" (the study and description of the "Orient") manufactures false constructions of the "Orient." Western scholarship is inherently ideological; hence wrong as it cannot truly understand that which it seeks to control and represent.
- Western identity is created in relation to the falsely construed "Orient." Said suggests that the "Orient" becomes a shadow side of the West, as though it only mirrors back one's own "darker" (itself, arguably, a racialized term) image. While the West is portrayed in a positive way (i.e., rational, democratic, advanced, etc.), the opposite is applied to the "Orient" (i.e., irrational, despotic, backward, etc.). Further, the Orient is construed as exotic. This binary is also gendered (see chapter 10, especially box 10.2), with the masculine/West valorized and the feminine/Oriental derided.

WHAT SAID HELPS US SEE

Said's analysis gives us a lens to see the imbrication of scholarly descriptions of religions and regimes of power. The connection of description and power was through both colonial systems of administration (for instance, in census data that counted members of particular religions, but also determined what those groups were), and missionary endeavor (you need to understand the other religion to overcome it). Moreover, dismissing indigenous categories as "superstition," "magic," or "primitive religion" (see boxes 7.8 and 12.2) created the notion of the "white man's burden," which sought to justify bringing civilization and religion to the "native."[9] Civilization, or whatever we see as progress (Christianity, democracy, science, human rights, etc.) is often defined by hegemonic Western discourses.

However, we also need to consider ways in which Said's thesis has been subject to critique. This is not to dismiss it, but will help us see the limits of any theory. No matter how helpful any theory has been, and insightful it remains, we must always be aware of its blind spots and areas in which more nuance is needed.

WHAT SAID DOESN'T HELP US SEE

Here we will look at various critics of Said's original thesis (and others who have extended the Orientalist thesis) in four main categories:

ORIENTALISM, OCCIDENTALISM, AND STEREOTYPES

What Said named in *Orientalism* is not a unique Western distortion, but normal human behavior:

- We have a propensity to stereotype, even demonize, our out-groups (see chapter 6).
- We use what we already know to understand new things, what Hans-Georg Gadamer (1900–2002) terms "prejudices," which for him are the basis of our own knowledge, and not in and of themselves distortions (see box 2.6).

Just as Said used the term "Orientalism" to name the way that Westerners distort the East, so there exists Occidentalism, whereby Easterners distort the West. Othering (see box 13.5) representations of those different from us as stereotyped out-groups (see chapter 6) is a standard feature of human knowing:[1]

- Al-Biruni (973–1048) is argued to have used "essentialization" to describe India long before Europeans arrived.[2]
- Kiri Paramore argues that China deploys notions of "religion" toward Xinjiang and Tibet that align with Western colonial representations once made against China.[3]

"Orientalism" is not a special form of modern European imperial ideology. Rather, we are talking about features of human classification. Therefore, perhaps, the question is not whether we distort others and create stereotypes in our understanding. Inevitably we do. But we can ask two questions:

- Do we seek to enact exclusion or to improve communication?
- Is every (mis)understanding/stereotype equally (in)valid? Elsewhere we argue against relativism (see introduction, box 2.5, and chapters 5 and 9).

---

1 For a wider discussion on prejudice, identity, and stereotypes, see Paul Hedges, *Religious Hatred: Prejudice, Islamophobia, and Antisemitism in Global Context* (London: Bloomsbury, 2021), chapter 1.
2 Wilhelm Halbfass, "Research and Reflection: Responses to my Respondents," in *Beyond Orientalism: The Work of Wilhelm Halbfass and Its Impact on Indian and Cross-Cultural Studies*, ed. Eli Franco and Karin Preisendaz (Amsterdam: Rodopi, 1997), 1–25, 14.
3 See Kiri Paramore, "Introduction," in *Religion and Orientalism in Asian Studies*, ed. Kiri Paramore (London: Bloomsbury, 2016), 1–12, 5.

Western agency: Said's thesis perceives the "West" as the only actor with agency, with the Orient (Muslims, Hindus, etc.) simply as receivers of a one-way flow of ideas and conceptions. The significance of non-Western participation in global movements is made invisible, and the impact of the Orient on the West is effectively dismissed.[10]

Constructed criteria: Talal Asad has suggested that the question is not whether Europe is guilty and others innocent. The West was not the only imperial power. Rather, we need to understand the historical construction of criteria

Buddhist and Hindu statues as museum exhibits. Collection of the Asian Civilisations Museum, Singapore.

which shapes the way we see the world. Richard King argues that Said fails both to see that the terms Orient/East and Occident/West are constructed and unstable, and to analyze their "hyper-reality" status, where the concepts become more real than the actual facts.[11]

Unhelpful binaries: Lisa Lowe has argued that focusing on the East-West binary and imperial/colonial power means we miss complex sets of relations including gender, race, class, nation, and sexuality. For instance, there are not simply colonizers and colonized, but power differentials within each group. Some of the "colonized" may be more influential than some "colonizers."[12]

Bad theory: Said and others often only cite scholars or administrators who were deeply bigoted, ignoring those who attempted more sympathetic and detailed studies. Not all Western scholars simply misinterpreted, and more accurate and less accurate (more/less biased) studies were conducted. The more accurate (Western and non-Western) scholarship can help identify the inaccuracies. Further, Said ignores the the degree to which "Western" thought was infused with "Eastern" ideas.[13]

THE RELIGIOUS AS EXOTIC EXHIBIT

One area related to these discussions is the way that religion is presented in both academia and the public sphere. From a Western perspective, not forgetting how recent waves of immigration have changed this in some areas, religions besides Christianity—and to some extent Judaism and regionally certain others—have often been seen as "exotic." They are seen to come from far away, to be unknown, and so are exoticized. They are perceived as something strange or different; their presence, in the form of "relics" exhibited in museum contexts, highlights their exoticism. This affects how the imagery or artifacts of another tradition are related to or understood.[14]

DEFINING POSTCOLONIALISM
POSTCOLONIALISM: GEOGRAPHICAL, CHRONOLOGICAL, OR METHODOLOGICAL?

Here, postcolonialism is an umbrella term under which we could place Said's Orientalism and decolonization (see box 7.5). Some definitions of it are inadequate:

- A geographical definition would refer only to scholarship from previously colonized groups (as a result of Western colonialism).
- A chronological definition would refer only to the period after (Western/ British) colonial rule.

Neither of these reflects the breadth of postcolonial scholarship, which includes the following foci:

Political: Postcolonial scholarship focuses upon giving voice and power to disempowered groups such as women or minorities (see box 7.6). It is often activist scholarship and does not claim simply to be "neutral" (i.e., to stand outside events) and to just observe the world (see chapters 5, 10, and 18). It shows that much traditional (Western) discourse, or academic practice, may mask certain voices.

Ongoing colonial agendas: First, just because direct colonial rule no longer exists, it does not mean that indirect or coercive force does not continue. Forms of knowledge production remain dominated by the West. Many non-Westerners also have, as Syed Hussein Alatas (1928–2007) posited, a "captive mind,"[15] remaining enthralled by the West, which they are afraid/unable to intellectually escape from. Economic inequality is maintained through trade agreements and unequal power on the global stage, often termed neocolonialism. Therefore, postcolonialism seeks to problematize conventional categories which are deployed by colonizing or oppressive forces. Second, just because the colonization of a perceived foreign power ends, this does not mean that freedom begins. The existence of unequal power relations within groups in that society means that essentially "colonial" forms of rule, representation, or oppression continue. Colonial-style power structures may be retained.

Multifaceted: Postcolonial scholarship stresses plurality and multiplicity, in terms of approaches taken, methods used (methodological polymorphism), and voices heard. It will pay attention to such things as music, art, and other ways of knowing or representing the world beyond elite literate traditions and cultures (see chapter 3).

We now survey some theories and central figures in postcolonial studies.

THE SUBALTERN

The Subaltern Studies Collective (SSC), a group of Indian scholars founded by Ranajit Guha, were concerned that conventional nationalist historiographies (methods of studying history) did not adequately represent non-elites. They felt that the way history was studied, collected, and told favored only certain groups. Therefore, they tried to highlight the condition of what is termed the subaltern (see box 7.6).

Importantly, the SSC saw their object of study not as the subaltern, but rather the systems of discourse that erase the subaltern. They studied neglected groups in order to overturn the methods, assumptions, and norms that keep subalterns oppressed and unable to be heard.

Notably, non-Western ways of seeing the world have become subaltern forms of knowledge. The current supremacy of the worldview developed (almost entirely by—or attributed almost entirely to—men) in (mainly) northwestern Europe, and latterly the US (and to a lesser degree some other "Western" nations) has come alongside coloniality, which entails the delegitimization of other worldviews, languages, theories of knowledge, and so on (see box 18.1). As such, indigenous forms of knowing, thinking, and perceiving have become only "data," with it being assumed that theory belongs to

WHO IS A SUBALTERN?

Ranajit Guha famously described the subaltern as "the demographic difference between the total Indian population and all of those whom we have described as 'elite.'"[1] In other words, the non-elites: those whose voices are silenced, ignored, not heard, or considered irrelevant. The term "subaltern" was coined by Antonio Gramsci (1891–1937) as a way to avoid using "proletariat" in the context of the censorship and surveillance of his political work. However, "subaltern" also has an advantage, as it can refer to those subordinated to regimes of power beyond class (the Marxist usage of "proletariat") to include such issues as gender, race, nationality, and so on (see box 10.9).[2] It refers to various non-elites in society, including women, the poor, the working class, people of color, LGBTQI, or other suppressed/oppressed groups. We can note some important issues:

- Subalterns are not homogenous nor without internal hierarchies. For instance, women may be of a lower status than males (see chapter 10).

- What was once a subaltern group may attain power, and others may lose it; "subaltern" is "a shifting signifier."[3]

- The lives or concept of the subaltern may be romanticized or seen in an overly positive light, as though switching power from the elites to the subalterns would resolve all problems. The subaltern may oppress others as much as any elite when the chance arises.

---

1 Ranajit Guha, *Subaltern Studies I: Writings on South Asian History and Society* (New Delhi: Oxford University Press, 1982), 8.

2 Notably, Marxism is not inherently critical of colonialism and imperialism. Karl Marx (1818–1883) suggested that British colonialism may have positive benefits, e.g., in the removal of the Indian caste system (see box 4.6).

3 King, *Orientalism and Religion*, 195.

a particular Western genealogy of thought, resulting in "epistemicide" (the killing of other forms of ways of knowing).[16] This relates to the captive mind discussed above, and various interests throughout this chapter and book as a whole. Nevertheless, it should be stressed that there is no pure Western worldview, for it has always learned from global voices, even if these are not acknowledged (see box 7.7 below).

SPIVAK, SUBALTERNS, AND STRATEGIC ESSENTIALISM

Gayatri Chakravorty Spivak recognizes that terms such as "Asian women" are problematic, as they both feed into colonial/Orientalist tropes and also essentialize diversity. What links an Iranian businesswoman and a farmer's wife from Tajikistan? However, she argues that using such terms, employed as "strategic essentialism," can disrupt the discourse of hegemonic forces. Categories can be named that need attention, becoming a base for political activism, which Spivak sees as key to postcolonial scholarship.

Spivak has also problematized the notion of the subaltern, especially by asking the question: "Can the Subaltern Speak?"[17] Her question is rhetorical, highlighting that the very essence of a subaltern is somebody whose voice is not heard in mainstream discourse. Yet, at the same time, she considers the ambivalence/tension with elite scholars (scholars are not subalterns) or activists supposing to speak for or represent the subaltern. How do we know whose voice is really heard? Spivak does not deny the need to work on their behalf, but stresses the need for awareness of how we speak for others. Further, as a subaltern has no voice, once a subaltern's voice becomes part of the discourse, they are arguably no longer a subaltern. Hence she problematizes how we envisage the subaltern.

BHABHA AND THIRD SPACE

Homi Bhabha has theorized hybridity as "Third Space," the creative place between two cultures when they meet (see box 3.3). Notably, for Bhabha, this Third Space "focuses on the problem of the ambivalence of cultural authority."[18] It shows that control is not absolute, for the colonized can subvert culture and meaning even when dominated politically or militarily.

Bhabha also notes that "postcolonial criticism bears witness to the unequal and uneven forces of cultural representation involved in the contest for political and social authority within the modern world order."[19] That is, even in a postcolonial period, we still see neocolonialism where Western modes of production in terms of cultural power, academic norms, and other forms of control (beyond continued economic control and military dominance) are ascendant. Brands such as Coca-Cola and McDonald's, Hollywood movies, and an obsession with skin whitening (to look "white" or erase "dark" skin tones[20]) still have major effects on parts of the world. Power, he tells us, is not just direct, but is also found in myths, fantasies, dreams, and obsessions.[21]

ALATAS AND IBN KHALDUN'S SOCIOLOGY OF ENSLAVEMENT

Syed Farid Alatas has argued that rather than being seen merely as data, the scholarly theories of the Muslim scholar Ibn Khaldun (1332–1406) can be a source for sociological theory. While Ernest Gellner (1925–1995) employed Ibn Khaldun to help theorize North African society, Alatas's more comprehensive study argues Ibn Khaldun's method can help inform the wider discipline.[22]

Ibn Khaldun's theory of state formation, in brief terms, sees a cycle whereby nomadic tribes are united by a charismatic leader who overthrows an existing and sedentary dynasty. These, in turn, become sedentary dynasties destined to be overthrown. Ibn Khaldun hypothesized advantages among nomadic groups, and weaknesses in sedentary societies, leading to this. Importantly, "group feeling" (*asabiyyah*) tended to be stronger in nomadic groups. In many sedentary societies an overreliance on law, especially in those societies favoring elite groups with a minority controlling the majority, could weaken the fortitude of the people as they grew more submissive and relied on regulations. Alatas notes that, while accurate, Ibn Khaldun did not foresee how this cycle would cease once the power of states or dynasties shifted from a tribal basis.[23] Ibn Khaldun saw the combination of religion and "group feeling" as particularly potent, and noted many examples of charismatic preachers (see box 5.4), often Sufis, who had been influential in uniting tribes.

Alatas further argues that Ibn Khaldun's theory of the development of luxury in sedentary societies can help conceptualize our enslavement to certain ways of life. Ibn Khaldun's analysis differs from, and adds to, modern sociological analysis. Existing theory links our enslavement to alienation in capitalist production (Karl Marx, 1818–1893) or the rationalization and institutionalization of modern society in terms of law, bureaucracy, and modern cities (Max Weber, 1864–1920).[24] Ibn Khaldun addresses the way that a dominant elite's sway can weaken group feeling. This is because we come to rely on laws and regulations which often support the elite minority's interests; hence we sublimate group feeling. Alatas uses Ibn Khaldun to give an example of theory coming from beyond Western sources which supplements Western theories.

RACE AND RELIGION

RACE AND RELIGION AS COLONIAL AND ORIENTALIST CATEGORIES

The age of European colonialism saw Europeans claiming a lineage of global supremacy in areas such as philosophy (see box 7.7), science,[25] and religion. In this, "race" played a role (see box 18.6). Religion was also sometimes invoked to justify what was termed "scientific racism," the notion that racial categories and hierarchies could be proven based upon supposedly scientific analysis, often backed with reference to biblical verses. Indeed, some have argued that "race" and "religion" are bound together.[26]

Foundational figures in the study of religion discussed "race." F. Max Müller's (1823–1900) so-called Aryan race theory (not to be confused with later Nazi Aryan race theory) was key to his ideas about the relationship between Indian and European languages and religion. However, as Tomoko Masuzawa makes clear, Müller rejected the notion that race was a scientific category, and his own work as a philologist countered notions about different human races because they did not match the linguistic families his work uncovered.[27] However, often based on an evolutionary or hierarchical conception, race and religion were conflated. In other words, some claimed that a connection of the "higher" race to "higher" or more "civilized" religion existed; conversely, the "lower" races were seen to have "primitive" religion. Hence, in the social context in which our modern notions of race and religion have developed, race and religion have often been

PHILOSOPHY AND RACE: IMAGINED LINEAGES

Before the eighteenth century, it was generally held that philosophy began in the Middle East, South Asia, or Africa.[1] After this period, a new genealogy of philosophy enthroned Greece as the source, with a claimed direct lineage through Europe. Philosophy became solely white and Western. This was the period when the concept of "race" coalesced in Western thought,[2] with a new confidence and belief in European dominance. The idea that certain "races," primarily "white," were superior to others, with the least esteemed often those termed "negros," or various "aboriginals," was key. This idea was expounded by such thinkers as David Hume (1711–1776) and Immanuel Kant (1724–1804). It became assumed that "philosophy" belonged only to Europe, and nonwhite thinkers were written out of its history.[3] Indeed, still today, it can be argued that whiteness is part of what constitutes theory.[4]

---

1 Peter Park, *Africa, Asia and the History of Philosophy: Racism in the Formation of the Philosophical Canon, 1780–1830* (Albany: State University of New York Press, 2013).

2 Though it arguably has early roots; see Geraldine Heng, *The Invention of Race in the European Middle Ages* (Cambridge: Cambridge University Press, 2018). However, modern Western racial theory seems to have roots in the Iberian Peninsula around the late fifteenth century and is tied into the development of racial and racialized religious prejudice; see Paul Hedges, *Religious Hatred: Prejudice, Islamophobia, and Antisemitism in Global Context* (London: Bloomsbury, 2021), chapter 5.

3 See Park, *Africa, Asia and the History*, xii–xiii, 92–95; and Bryan Van Norden, *Taking Back Philosophy: A Multicultural Manifesto* (New York: Columbia University Press, 2017). Kant asserted that the white race "contains all incentives and talents in itself," the "Hindus" finally "acquire culture in the highest degree, but only in the arts and not in the sciences. They never raise it up to abstract concepts," while the "Negro race . . . acquire[s] culture, but only a culture of slaves; that is, they allow themselves to be trained," Immanuel Kant, *Lectures on Anthropology* (Cambridge: Cambridge University Press, 2013 [1781–1782]), 301–3. Notably, in his final work, Kant seemed to repudiate these views; see Katrin Flikschuh and Lea Ypi, eds., *Kant and Colonialism: Historical and Critical Perspectives* (Oxford: Oxford University Press, 2014).

4 See Christopher Driscoll and Monica Miller, *Method as Identity: Manufacturing Distance in the Academic Study of Religion* (Lanham, MD: Lexington, 2019).

associated: "Historically and conceptually, there is no cordon sanitaire between history, culture, nationality, ethnicity, and race. Race is a motley crew, and that motley crew includes religion. Religion is constitutive of race."[28] Certainly, from around the sixteenth century in Spain, prejudice against Jews and Muslims (Antisemitism and Islamophobia) took on a racialized aspect that in some ways came to dominate over older religiously based forms of prejudice in Western discourse.[29]

The kind of hierarchy that relates race and religion is involved in a number of the binaries and oppositions that are explored elsewhere in this volume, for instance, between what counts as "religion" and what counts as "superstition," what are "acceptable" forms of religion and what are described as "primitive" forms of religion (see box 7.8). In the context of European colonialism, this often meant distinguishing between the religion of "white" people and the "superstition" of "black," "brown," "yellow," or other peoples, though some "whites" were seen to have "better" religions than other

BOX 7.8 **MAGIC, RELIGION, AND SUPERSTITION**

The term "religion" is often applied to traditions and practices of which we approve, while "cult" is reserved for those we do not approve of (see box 1.5). The modern concept of religion arose in English and European discourse in the period of colonial expansion and imperial dominance (see chapter 1). A distinction was also made between "religion" and "superstition." This was based upon a variety of criteria. One key criterion was that "religion" had to look like the mainly Protestant practices of the dominant northwestern European scholars and colonial officials. Those holding this view often condemned, therefore, not just non-Christian practices but also non-Protestant Christian practices such as Catholicism (see boxes 9.3 and 9.4). This distinction was also related to race, as it was assumed that "reason" and "civilization" were primarily the products of Europe (see box 7.7). Therefore, those who were of non-European, that is " nonwhite," races were deemed to be superstitious. This distinction also followed lines of class and gender: elite/male practices were "religion," whereas marginal/subaltern/female practices were "superstition" (see chapters 3 and 10). "Magic" was also often invoked as another term for things that failed to be classified as "religion" (see box 12.2). In colonial contexts, the employment of "superstition" or "magic" played a role in delegitimization (see case study 7B). It has became a tool taken up in many languages and systems of thought to delimit the boundaries of "correct" and "incorrect" practice. It affects not only perceived legitimacy but also legal rights (see chapter 16).

"whites." Religion and race have been related categories, with the former used as means to control or legitimize certain forms of belief, cultural practice, or behavior.

"WHITENESS," RACE, AND RELIGION

We can raise two further issues here. First, some current criticism of the term "religion," which even takes issue with (in part) its imbrication with colonial regimes of power, may serve to maintain the interests of white hegemonic elites, with whiteness referring to the fact that being "white" is often seen as both invisible but also a perceived norm, as well as being the position of power from which mainstream (i.e., white, but generally also Western, male, and middle class) scholarship and social norms come. Much critical theory and method in the study of religion, according to Monica Miller and Christopher Driscoll, reflect what are seen as the maintenance of distance between "white" and " nonwhite" ways of thinking, being, and doing.[30] Of course, who gets to count as "white" may vary in differing contexts.[31] Three concepts highlight this:

> *White savior:* Withholding the term "religion" helped permit colonial powers to
> deny that those colonized had "civilization" and legitimate rights (see case

study 7B and box 7.9). Today, some scholars say that having attained recognition as a "religion," and concomitant rights (see chapter 16), indigenous groups and others remain deluded. Without the scholar as "white savior," the "natives" (i.e., nonwhite non-Westerners) persist in ignorance (now thinking that they have "religion").

Agency: When "critical" scholarship argues that traditions such as "Hinduism" or "Buddhism" are solely the creation of Western scholarship (on the former, see case study 7A), the ideological assumption is that any complex system of ideas or transnational networks could not possibly be created by "Orientals." In the creation and understanding of the tradition they are assigned to (align themselves with), agency is denied to nonwhite, non-Western, peoples.

Essentialism: Religious traditions have been reshaped under the impact of modernity, including Western colonial and neocolonial power. However, traditions have constantly evolved under the impact of many dynamics (see chapter 4). To claim a religion never existed before Westerners came and "invented" it assumes an essentialist judgment: the "essence" of that tradition can be precisely defined, but only by white, Western scholarship.

Second, some critical scholarship devalues the work of scholars of color. A sharp distinction is often made between confessional theological and a religious studies approach (see chapter 2). Yet, in the American context, some scholars of what has been termed Black religious studies believe this distinction does not hold, with at least one scholar arguing that

> the best religious scholarship in the Black academy is, perforce, "believing scholarship," accepting all the risks that such a position entails. It could not be otherwise. The centuries-old struggle for Black humanity in a racist environment has not encouraged the development of dispassionate, armchair science of religion for preparing the leadership of the Black Church in North America.[32]

W. E. B. Du Bois's (1868–1963) work, which was intimately related to advocacy for Black people in society, would therefore not be regarded as scholarship but activism in some religious studies perspectives (see chapter 5). The fact that much postcolonial and decolonial scholarship assume that unjust and inequitable regimes of power creation need to be challenged runs antithetical to many established norms in the study of religion (see introduction and chapters 5, 10, and 18). Indeed, it has been argued that modernity may rest upon problematic bases in which race and religion are constituted in relation to discourses of secularism and rationality which lead to deep systemic problems, an issue raised by scholars such as Achille Mbembe, Walter Mignolo, and Sylvia Wynter (see also chapter 16).[33] A postcolonial lens alerts us to how scholarship is defined and performed under Western (often also elite, white, male) norms.

Students, and scholars, ask such questions as "Why is my curriculum so white?" "Why do all the theorists come from the Western world?" Even where nonwhite and/or non-Western scholars are included, scholarship from women, LGBTQI scholars, and other minority groups still often remains under- (or un-)represented. A heritage of white colonial leaders, including slave traders (though these were never only white or Western) have also long been memorialized in statues and others legacies at many universities.[34]

Notably, many of the scholars we have surveyed above, such as Mignolo, Said, Du Bois, Spivak, and Bhabha, all work within Western universities. Even those working outside the West, such as Alatas, remain in academic systems based on Western norms. But there is a historical myopia in this view:

- The world's oldest university-style institution was Nalanda, in India, a Buddhist foundation.
- The oldest continually operating university is in the Moroccan city of Fez, which traditionally taught an Islamic-based curriculum.
- Europe's oldest university was founded by Muslims (the first was Cordoba, but the oldest still in operation is Bologna).
- Later Christian/European universities copied Muslim examples.
- Modern secular universities evolved from these.
- Modern Western academic curricula and learning have been deeply influenced by learning from the Muslim-majority world which had absorbed Buddhist influences, and also has influences from China.[35]

One role of postcolonial scholarship can be to show the intellectual dependency of so-called Western science and reason on a global exchange of ideas.

Others have moved to expand the academic canon of accepted theorists, for instance, Alatas's work on Ibn Khaldun, while James Spickard has tried to introduce a non-Western sociology of religion which also draws from Ibn Khaldun, among others.[36] However, to simply mine the history of ideas for great figures—more likely than not male, because they were often the ones with access to literacy and chances for valorization—would risk ignoring contemporary non-Western and nonwhite thinkers. Above, we have suggested implications for Black religious studies, as have figures such as Miller. Throughout this book, contemporary non-Western scholarship is included as part of the discussion and analysis. This is not, though, to dismiss Western thinkers as "bad," but to see more widely. But more can certainly be done. You might ask what else can be done in your context to decolonize the curriculum. As Samir Amin (1931–2018) suggests, simply showing the Eurocentric focus of theory is not enough, without developing new ways of studying and exploring the world drawing from a wider range of sources and theories.[37] This may lead to what Chen Kuan-Hsing has termed a "deimperialization" of "knowledge production" that must "transcend the structural limitations" of traditional modes and centers of power.[38]

Finally, we may note that it is wrong to see decolonization as something to be attained, or a simple intellectual task. Rather, we need to speak of decolonizing, as it will surely be ongoing work. Indeed, much decolonization falls prey to problems such as Northerncentrism, where scholars of the "Global North" (often US-centric) cite each other and ignore those from the "Global South."[39] Steps may be taken, but there are many layers to what needs to be done. Indeed, due to the embedded nature of prejudice in human identity creation processes,[40] we will always need to decolonize whatever we have attained when it becomes the new established norm; this involves seeing decolonizing work as intersectional and multifaceted. Indeed, it involves not just decolonizing a curriculum but having a decolonizing mind-set.

·   ·   ·

CASE STUDY 7A. BEYOND "INVENTING" HINDUISM

Hinduism is often seen as the paradigmatic case of a "religion" solely "invented" by Western colonial and scholarly classification. It is argued that no such term or concept existed before the British and other Europeans arrived. We can call this the "invention hypothesis." However, recent scholarship suggests that the term "Hinduism," while an imposition, simply helps codify a self-recognized tradition. In postcolonial terms, these arguments raise many issues.

INVENTING A RELIGION

The term "Hinduism" morphed from a geographical marker for the area beyond the Indus River (Hindustan) to naming the culture and people of that region (Hindus), to classifying the religion of those people (Hinduism). Therefore, some argue that "Hinduism" is the result of (primarily British) colonial imposition.

Prior to Western colonialism, South Asia had many traditions (*dharma*) named after specific lineages of teachers, for example, Shankaradharma (followers of Shankara), Ramanujadharma (followers of Ramanuja), and Buddhadharma (followers of the Buddha). Meanwhile, worshippers of particular deities were named by those traditions, such as Shaivites (Shiva's devotees), Vaishnavas (Vishnu's devotees), and Shaktas (Goddess devotees), normally in specific schools such as Shaiva Siddhanta or Shri Vaishnavism. Some scholars assert lumping some of these under the common rubric "Hinduism" does conceptual violence to these discrete traditions. Therefore, properly, we should only speak of Shaivism, Vaishnavism, Shaktism, Buddhadharma, and so on.

The invention hypothesis posits that only in the eighteenth to nineteenth century was a "religion" named "Hinduism" created. Today, some argue that although "Hindus" claim the designation, it should be recognized as an identity shaped primarily, or only, by white Western (male) Orientalist scholars; Sanatana Dharma, a term preferred today by some Hindus as being "indigenous," is also a reactive term against Christianity and incorporates Western notions.[41]

HAS THE WEST SHAPED HINDUISM?

Before looking at arguments against the invention hypothesis, it is worth noting ways in which we can speak of Hinduism being shaped by Western colonial rule and classification, which include the following:

Non-dualism as essence: For generations, students of Hinduism have read in their textbooks that the central philosophy of Hinduism is non-dualism (Advaita Vedanta), which argues that the human soul and absolute reality are one and the same. However, the dualist (Dvaita Vedanta) school, which sees deity and the human as distinct, has been the majority opinion.[42] Non-dualism as an elite philosophical position was deemed significant by Western interpreters (see box 14.2).

Sati *as universal practice: Sati,* or "widow burning," was often picked out by early Western travelers to India to demonstrate the barbarity of Hinduism. However, prior to the British colonial period, *sati* appears to have been neither common nor universal. In what is modern-day Rajasthan, one of its few historical centers, the wives of the Rajputs (local nobles) who considered themselves elite warriors saw *sati* as a way for wives to show their own bravery. The constant repetition in Orientalist scholarship that this was a Hindu practice seems responsible for its exaltation today, by some nationalist Hindus, as a core Hindu practice standing in contradistinction to Western norms.

The centrality of the Vedas: Almost any textbook on Hinduism will say the central "scriptures" of Hinduism are the Vedas. However, written in Sanskrit, an ancient language, they were accessible only to literate elites. Central to aspects of temple worship and elite philosophical traditions, they were not the basis of lived religion (see chapter 3, see also box 14.2). The main schools of devotion to Shiva, Vishnu, and the Goddess have their own sectarian texts, called Puranas. The Puranas, the Epics (the Ramayana and Mahabharata), and many other texts were typically regarded as equal to the Vedas. But, under the influence of certain Hindu elites, Western writers vaunted what they understood as "revelation" (*shruti,* literally, "that which was heard"), which they took to be only the Vedas, seeing other texts as part of "tradition" (*shrmiti;* literally, "that which was preserved/handed down").

The interests of certain Hindu elites have shaped the Western, and modern, notion of Hinduism. It could almost be argued that Hinduism, in this sense, was not so much invented by Westerners but by elite Hindus keen to secure their own sectarian position.

Will Sweetman used to hold the invention hypothesis, but has recently spoken strongly against it. [43] Sweetman argues that what scholars came to conceptualize as a single religious system under the term "Hinduism" actually makes sense of various medieval precolonial structures of South Asian thought. Likewise, David Lorenzen states: "The claim that Hinduism was invented or constructed by European colonizers, mostly British, sometime after 1800 is false."[44] Lorenzen argues that what we call Hinduism attained its shape, in rivalry with Islam, in the period between 1200 and 1500, while Andrew Nicholson and Alexis Sanderson assert "Hinduism" was not simply reliant on Moghul colonialism.[45] According to Sanderson:

> By the end of the first millennium of the Christian era the consensus had indeed come to conceptualize a complex entity corresponding to Hinduism as opposed to Buddhism and Jainism, excluding only certain forms of antinomian Śākta-Śaiva observance that could not be reconciled with basic Vaidika values of ritual purity and the separation of castes.[46]

Sanderson argues that, for around the last thousand years, a "complex entity" that shared such things as Vedanta philosophy (in competing forms) and a common ritual system (based in tantric texts) existed across the traditions that worshipped Shiva, Vishnu, and the Goddess, and which recognized six orthodox schools of philosophy. Importantly, these were identified as "orthodox" (*astika*), as opposed to the "unorthodox" (*nastika*) philosophies of Buddhism and Jainism. This is, however, not to deny meeting points with the latter two; religious borders and diversity are defined variously (see chapter 13). Nevertheless, as "unorthodox" schools they were, at the very least, outside mainstream "Hinduism."

While the particular designation "Hinduism" is the result of colonial imposition, we see a coherence and unity before Western influences. This does not overturn how the meeting of particular elites and the Western imagination have shaped Hinduism today. However, all traditions change over time. Further, Sweetman argues that early Western scholars of Hinduism did not simply imagine these things from nowhere: they looked at indigenous classificatory systems. Indeed, if "Hinduism" made no sense in terms of indigenous concepts, Sweetman asks how it ever took root? One traditional answer is that the classification was part of a British divide-and-rule policy (a common form of colonial governance) in which Hindus, Muslims, Jains, Sikhs, and Buddhists were made to emphasize differences which were essentially created. There is some truth to such an accusation, yet it cannot explain everything. Nicholson's work shows that Hinduism was not so much "invented" as "unified" or "codified," and that we "should finally put to rest the notion that there was no conception of a specifically Hindu religious identity" before Western colonialism.[47] The once fashionable conception of "invention" now looks increasingly problematic.

REFLECTIONS

We can think through these issues in various ways:

1. From the perspective of a contemporary Hindu, how would you react to scholars asserting the right to decide whether or not your "religion" exists and who created it? How does it affect your perception of your tradition?
2. The naming of traditions is not simply an academic exercise. They have political consequences (see chapter 1 and case study 1A). Some militant right-wing Hindu nationalists have seized upon scholarship showing that "Hinduism" preceded the Moghuls and British as evidence of the ancient "essence" of their tradition. How should scholars respond to such (mis)use of their work? What responsibility do they have toward public understanding of their ideas?
3. Which aspects of postcolonial theory help us to explain and conceptualize the ways in which debates on the term "Hinduism" have taken place and evolved?
4. Do you think that (contemporary critical) Western scholarship takes agency away from indigenous and non-Western peoples? Does it assume that the Western world has "created," "discovered," and "invented" the world in ways which ignores voices from elsewhere?

CASE STUDY 7B. MAGIC, SUPERSTITION, AND RELIGION IN SOUTHEAST ASIA AND AFRICA

This case study explores the way that terms such as "magic," "religion," and "superstition" (see box 7.8) have been employed to give legitimacy, or take it away. This is related to questions around racial hierarchies, including in the North American context (see box 7.9). In this case study we provide two brief cameos of a Southeast Asian and an African context to help explicate the issues.

BACKGROUND, CAMEO 1: SPIRIT MEDIUM CULTS IN SOUTHEAST ASIA

Spirit medium cults in places such as Southeast Asia presume the medium is capable of being possessed by various deities or spirits. Often entering a trance state, the medium may act out or speak the wishes of the particular deity or spirit seen to be possessing them. Often based in small-scale local rituals, these have commonly been classified as "superstition" by colonial explorers, scholars of religion, and representatives of what are seen as the "major" "world religions." Generally, this is because their activities lack clear textual authority, priestly hierarchies, and also social prestige. In Vietnam, some spirit mediums are not open about their vocation, aware that the stigma of "superstition" may be applied to them.[48] However, the concept of superstition is not simple, with differentiation between spirit medium groups. Some spirit medium practitioners see their devotion as "Mother Goddess religion" and disparage those they see as focused on "lesser" spirits as "superstition."[49] Likewise, some groups whose teachings strongly emphasize morality suggest their tradition is "religion" but castigate other groups as "superstition."

BACKGROUND, CAMEO 2: AN AFRICAN ANCHOR

David Chidester has argued that, at times of conflict or tension in Southern Africa, indigenous groups were denied "religion," especially during early conquests. Later, however, when they were pacified or defeated, it was admitted that they had religion.[50] While Chidester's neat mapping of conflict and categorization oversimplifies,[51] he identifies the often-political motives for applying these terms. Here, we explore a specific case study, in which Chidester shows how the Xhosa tribe's attitudes toward an anchor they found on a beach were categorized.

In the early nineteenth century, a number of European explorers observed that particular respect was paid by the Xhosa to an anchor that had been washed up on a beach following a shipwreck. One of the kings had broken a piece off and died shortly thereafter. As such, it was regarded as an item with particular "magical" powers. Xhosa passing by the anchor would salute to pay their respects. For Europeans, this signaled that the Xhosa were "addicted to the grossest superstitions" and "believed in magic, charms, oaths, curses, prognostics, piles of stones, and an anchor."[52] It was reported that these people entirely lacked religion as well as civilization, and the anchor was found in a "country inhabited by the most barbarous and monstrous of the human species."[53] Chidester makes clear that as well as marking the barbarity of these people (conveniently overlooking what appears to be the kindness with which survivors of the wreck were treated), the denial of "religion" and insistence that these people only had "superstition" played into a set of oppositions and characterizations that not only diminished the Africans, but also was at times used to diminish Catholics (see box 9.3).

From the 1870s onward, though, some argued the anchor played a role in the "primitive religion" possessed by the Xhosa, sometimes termed as fetishism (here, the worship of particular objects which are seen to be imbued with a spirit; see box 5.7). Importantly, their "level" of religion was often seen as part of the evolution of humanity's religious life and was marked as a low or original stage, befitting "savages" and their "primitive" or " childlike" minds. It was held to show a mentality "found in colonized people abroad, but also among children, women, rural peasants, the working class, criminals, the insane and, following Lubbock, even animals in Europe."[54] Chidester also notes how later scholars, who supported apartheid in South Africa, denied religion to those this system decried as "primitive" and "not rational." Speaking specifically of the Bantu, Chidester notes: "Therefore, the relegation of eighty per cent of the population to thirteen per cent of the land could be justified in terms of the comparative findings of the modern study of religion."[55]

REFLECTIONS

A few questions will help us consider this case study:

1. Some members of Vietnamese spirit medium groups labeled their own practices as "religion," but dismissed other spirit medium groups as "superstitious." In these examples, which practices or groups would you designate with the label "religion" and which as "superstition"? Why?

2. Chidester notes that these categorizations were not only about "religious matters," but fitted into a wider set of categories that degraded certain people. By denying "religion," or full rationality, to colonized people, Catholics (who in turn leveled similar charges against Protestants), women, the working class, peasants, and so on, some groups are privileged in discourse while others are not. In what ways do

you think contemporary categories of "religion," "superstition," and "magic" are based in notions of hierarchies that favor specific groups at the expense of others?

3. Race, civilization, religion, legitimacy, and political control can be bound together in what gets classified as "religion" or "superstition," especially in colonial contexts. To what degree do you see these as being based upon imagined racial or other markers of identity?

.   .   .

QUESTIONS AND CONNECTING THOUGHTS

The issues raised in this chapter relate to the definition of religion and its creation (chapter 1), as well as other related concepts such as class (chapter 3), gender (chapter 10), and race (chapter 18). We have also addressed themes which are developed elsewhere, such as the distinction between "magic," "superstition," and related terms (see chapters 1, 9, and 12); syncretism and hybridity (chapter 3), and politics (chapter 18); and in-group out-group relations (chapter 6). The postcolonial context also relates to how dominant discourses are framed in many areas, for instance, religious diversity (chapter 13) and the secular (chapter 16). Elsewhere, we will see how colonial exploration and conquest was involved in the creation of certain realms of knowledge.

We conclude with a few questions to help reflect on themes in this chapter:

1. In what ways would you seek to decolonize your curriculum? Is this necessary? What more could this chapter (and book) have done in this regard? Or, if you think there is not a need to decolonize the curriculum, why is that?

2. Which theories or theorists of postcolonialism do you find most useful to help you think through the issues encountered and discussed throughout this chapter? Explain.

3. For some, religion's imbrication with theories of race and the colonial legacy is a compelling reason why it must be abandoned. But, if we abandon "religion," what about many other terms with a similar lineage/usage, which would include "culture," "philosophy," "civilization," "art," "science," and "history"? They have been used to exclude certain traditions or systems of thought. Must we abandon them all? Also, can we distinguish between words that may legitimately be kept and used (perhaps "scholarship," "history," "culture," and "politics," among others), as useful essentially contested concepts (see chapter 1), and those we may wish to abandon altogether, such as (presumably?) "savage," "Negro," "uncivilized," and so forth?

4. The way European colonizers stereotyped and classified others is, in terms of human dynamics, tied to ways in which previous colonizing powers have done so, or even the way any dominant forces labels others. Is there anything specific

about what Western colonization and neocolonialism has done—apart from being the latest (and, arguably, most globally dominant) regime of power?

5. How do we know whether our representation of any other group or individual is ever accurate or truthful? Can we adequately know the other, or must we accept a relativism in which every interpretation is equally untrue? (See introduction and chapters 1, 2, 5, and 9).

FURTHER READING

THEORY

Chen, Kuan-Hsing. *Asia as Method: Toward Deimperialization* (Durham: Duke University Press, 2010).

Clarke, J. J. *Oriental Enlightenment: The Encounter between Asian and Western Thought* (New York: Routledge, 1997).

Driscoll, Christopher, and Monica Miller. *Method as Identity: Manufacturing Distance in the Academic Study of Religion* (Lanham, MD: Lexington, 2019).

King, Richard. *Orientalism and Religion: Postcolonial Theory, India, and "The Mystic East"* (New York: Routledge, 1999), 187–218.

Maldonado-Torres, Nelson. "Religion, Modernity, and Coloniality," in *Religion, Theory, Critique: Classic and Contemporary Approaches and Methodologies,* ed. Richard King (New York: Columbia University Press, 2017), 447–54.

Mandair, Arvind. *Religion and the Specter of the West: Sikhism, India, Postcoloniality, and the Politics of Translation* (New York: Columbia University Press, 2009).

Mignolo, Walter. *The Darker Side of Western Modernity: Global Futures, Decolonial Options* (Durham: Duke University Press, 2011), 181–209.

Morny, Joy. "Revisiting Postcolonialism and Religion," *Journal for the Academic Study of Religion* 25.2 (2012): 102–22.

Spivak, Gayatri Chakravorty. "Can the Subaltern Speak?" in *Marxism and the Interpretation of Culture,* ed. Cary Nelson and Lawrence Grossberg (Basingstoke: Macmillan, 1988), 271–313.

Sugirtharajah, Sharada. *Imagining Hinduism: A Postcolonial Perspective* (London and New York: Routledge, 2003).

CASE STUDY 7A. BEYOND "INVENTING" HINDUISM

King, *Orientalism and Religion*, 96–117.

Nicholson, Andrew. *Unifying Hinduism: Philosophy and Identity in Indian Intellectual History* (New York: Columbia University Press, 2014).

Sweetman, Will. "Against Invention: A Richer History for 'Hinduism,'" RSP Podcast (19 February 2018), www.religiousstudiesproject.com/podcast/against-invention-a-richer-history-for-hinduism.

Antonio, Edward. "Indigenous African Traditions as Models for Theorizing Religion," in King, *Religion, Theory, Critique:* 147–54.

Chidester, David. "Anchoring Religion in the World: A Southern African History of Comparative Religion," *Religion* 26.2 (1996): 141–59.

Kendall, Laurel. "Gods, Gifts, Markets, and Superstition: Spirited Consumption from Korea to Vietnam," in *Engaging the Spirit World: Popular Beliefs and Practices in Modern Southeast Asia,* ed. Kirsten Endres and Andrea Lausner (New York: Berghahn Books, 2011), 103–20.

8

BRAINS
The Cognitive Science of Religion and Beyond

IN WHICH WE EXPLORE:

Key areas in the cognitive science of religion (CSR) and related fields such as
evolutionary anthropology

The question of whether religion is an evolutionary by-product

Issues in religious experience and neuroscience

Two case studies looking at the relationship/definition of religion and atheism,
and how religiosity may affect prosocial behavior

INTRODUCTION
ORIGINS AND BASICS

The way we think as human beings is clearly linked to a number of central areas discussed
in this book. For instance, how we can conceptualize notions such as religion, how we
create rituals, or act ethically? This raises questions for us about the structures of our
brains and the evolutionary pathways that have led us to behave as we do. The cognitive
science of religion (CSR) is a relatively new disciplinary field, beginning in the 1990s but
only developing strongly in the twenty-first century.

The CSR builds from cognitive science, which has a number of disciplinary bases,
including neuroscience, computer science, psycholinguistics, evolutionary biology,
and fields such as anthropology and philosophy. In this chapter, we address the CSR
and fields such as evolutionary theories of religion which are closely related.[1] Founda-

THE COGNITIVE REVOLUTION AND COGNITION

Sometimes termed the "cognitive revolution," the interdisciplinary study of cognitive science has radically overturned the previous behaviorist model. The behaviorist model assumed the human mind was a tabula rasa, or "blank slate," on which each culture created its own template.[1] We now know that the human mind is a complex set of interactions and systems, something resembling both computer hardware and software. The human mind is not therefore a tabula rasa onto which cultural ideas are imprinted. Rather, innate dispositions, behaviors, and even conceptions are inbuilt through our evolutionary, biological, and genetic blueprint that shape how we think and respond to the world around us. For instance, cognitive science indicates that written language could only develop because we had brains already programmed for certain forms of pattern recognition.[2] Cognitive science and the CSR explore human cognition as part of this. The term "cognition" has some technical usages, but—for our purposes—a relatively "unsophisticated" definition suffices: how minds come to envisage symbols and concepts, and then process this through perception and thought.[3] Importantly, the CSR is not inherently "reductionist," seeking to explain all religious processes or cultural formations as based in mind/brain/cognitive processes (though some advocates seem to do this); rather, it is interdisciplinary, employing diverse interpretations of the data to form a richer picture.[4]

---

1 See Steven Pinker, *The Blank Slate: The Modern Denial of Human Nature* (New York: Viking, 2002).

2 See Derek Hodgson, "How Did Reading and Writing Evolve? Neuroscience Gives a Clue," *Conversation* (4 March 2019), https://theconversation.com/how-did-reading-and-writing-evolve-neuroscience-gives-a-clue-112337.

3 This relies on the "unsophisticated" definition put forward by Aaron C. T. Smith, *Thinking about Religion: Extending the Cognitive Science of Religion* (Basingstoke: Palgrave Macmillan, 2014), 2.

4 See William McCorkle Jr. and Dimitris Xygalatas, "Introduction: Social Minds, Mental Cultures—Weaving Together Cognition and Culture in the Study of Religion," in *Mental Culture: Classical Social Theory and the Cognitive Science of Religion,* ed. Dimitris Xygalatas and William McCorkle Jr. (Durham: Acumen, 2013), 1–10, 5.

tional figures such as Pascal Boyer and Scott Atran[2] have argued that studying religion requires understanding the way that religious ideas become embedded in our minds, as well as how and why they develop and get passed on in evolutionary and neurological terms. These add important new explanations and concepts for helping us to understand and interpret the phenomena that we define as religious. Importantly, cognitive science has marked a huge shift in how we understand human nature, moving away from older behavioral models that saw the human mind as a blank slate (see box 8.1).

INSIGHTS AND CHANGES IN THE FIELD

Notably, while based in what may seem scientific data, not all aspects of the CSR have provided powerful tools for exploring religion. We should note the value it provides and point to areas where it has not been so fruitful. Two basic hypotheses have been as follows:

- Religious concepts appeal and stick in our minds because they are "minimally counterintuitive ideas" (MCI).[3]
- Religion is a by-product of standard evolutionary processes and cognitive functions.

An MCI is an idea which fits our basic categories but also breaks them in some way. For instance, a cow that talks would be an MCI, because it only breaks one thing we expect a cow to do. A flying cow that walked on two legs and talked would be a "maximally counterintuitive idea." However, while often assumed in the literature as an explanation for how religious ideas become embedded in our minds, there is little evidence that MCIs are more memorable than other ideas.[4] Also, there are many MCIs which are not "religious," so employing this as a reason for religion's persistence is problematic.[5] Indeed, within religions/cultural traditions, many ideas do not strike believers as being counterintuitive. When exploring which ideas get passed on, we need to look at cultural and social factors that determine social patterns rather than simply assuming some basic cognitive aspect of the mind is responsible. While the CSR has critiqued sociological and psychological explanations of religion for ignoring cognitive structures, suggesting the answer is only cognitive seems equally lopsided and inadequate.[6]

Arguing that religion is an evolutionary and cognitive by-product seems more fruitful. For instance, we have an inbuilt evolutionary propensity to imagine sentience, or creatures, even when they do not exist. A simple example is when we see a rustling movement and shadows in long grass. We are evolutionarily adapted to imagine that this might be a predator, for instance a tiger or some saber-toothed ancestor of that feline, which sees us as dinner. Those who were not very good at making the connection between rustling and shadows only needed to make one mistake and they did not survive. However, those who made many positive connections, even if some of these were false positives, would run away and therefore survive to reproduce and pass on their genes. Imagining things which are not there, in some circumstances, is arguably a positive evolutionary benefit. This may then extend to imagining that other creatures, even supernatural ones, are part of our landscape of experience. Notably, a jump could be made here to argue that religious ideas are nothing but evolutionary by-products. However, that something can be explained in certain ways does not show that that explanation is the sole and only cause. We address such debates further below.

In this chapter, we begin by noting what is often termed the "standard model" (SM) of the CSR (see box 8.2), areas where most authors concur on basic or key points. We then address some key issues, including religion's supposed origins, how the CSR defines "religion," whether religion is beneficial, and religious experiences. At various points, other scientific lenses or approaches beyond, but generally intersecting with, the CSR are drawn into the discussion. We end with two case studies.

BOX 8.2 **THE STANDARD MODEL OF THE COGNITIVE SCIENCE OF RELIGION**

According to leading cognitive science of religion (CSR) scholar Justin Barrett, the field "draws upon the cognitive sciences to explain how pan-cultural features of human minds, interacting with their natural and social environments, inform and constrain religious thought and action."[1] The basic tenets of CSR:

1. CSR scholars reject full-bodied cultural relativism. The evolution of *Homo sapiens* has resulted in species-level commonalities; everything is not determined in culturally/socially specific ways.

2. Likewise, some aspects of our worldviews and behavior will be precultural.

3. Our "mental tools" both inform and constrain what may be seen as our religious experience—as well as our wider culture, thought, and behavior.

4. CSR explores facets that can be found across individuals, looking for recurring patterns, ideas, practices, and so on.[2]

The term "standard model" (SM) comes from Pascal Boyer, and refers to key assumptions or working hypotheses in the CSR. Aaron Smith provides a summary of recent thought:[3]

1. What we term "religious" functions are to some extent "parasitic" upon neural or evolutionary functions which exist for other purposes.

2. Religious assumptions defy our ordinary experiences of the world.

3. We "naturally" intuit supernatural beings, and we make assumptions about what these "agents" want and feel based upon our own capacities to ascribe agency and emotion to others.

4. We are prepared to engage in costly ritual endeavors and activities related to supernatural agents and the social networks associated with them.

5. Innate moral reasoning and intuition may be tied in to what we attribute to supernatural agents.

While a common core, these hypotheses are being challenged within the field as it progresses. Nevertheless, they are part of the mainstream discussion.

---

1 Justin Barrett, "Cognitive Science of Religion: Looking Back, Looking Forward," *Journal for the Scientific Study of Religion* 50.2 (2011): 229–39, 230.

2 Barrett, "Cognitive Science of Religion," 231.

3 Smith, *Thinking about Religion*, 7–8. Smith provides seven propositions, which I synthesize into five. Others provide different overviews of the SM; see, e.g., Barrett and Trigg, "Cognitive and Evolutionary Studies of Religion," 4–7, who speak about "commitments."

IS RELIGION A BY-PRODUCT OF EVOLUTION?

AGENCY DETECTION

Do we have a propensity toward attributing agency to immaterial things? Stewart Guthrie has argued that both humans and animals tend to attribute agency as a strategic response. As noted in our tiger example above, this is not about irrational thinking so much as an essential survival instinct. The concept that many animals (including humans) create illusions as an evolved response to their environment means, for Guthrie, that "all of us inevitably think we see agents where, in reality, none exists."[7] Possibly, the best-known statement is Justin Barrett's concept of the hyperactive agent detection device (HADD).[8] According to this hypothesis, we are overactive in attributing agency to things, which for Barrett means not simply immaterial objects but also, potentially, events in our lives. Therefore, through what might be called a normal cognitive process, we come to religious beliefs. This is not, of course, to suggest that we are somehow innately religious, though one investigator, Deborah Kelemen, has suggested that around the age of five, children may be "intuitive theists," by which she means that they naturally attribute agency to many things around them in the world.[9] We discuss this further below.

Importantly, while the HADD has been a standard part of the CSR, recent work has questioned it, noting two problems: it is conceptually diffuse, and empirical data is lacking.[10] In short: "While the theory provides a convincing evolutionary explanation of how such a bias may have developed, it does a poor job at explaining how the perceptual system encompassing this bias actually operates."[11] Therefore, some scholars have suggested that "predictive processing" may provide a better model. This is a process which explains how the brain, with minimal effort, relays a reasonably accurate picture of our world to us, though one always relayed to us via our mind.[12] Importantly, this suggests that our experience of any "supernatural" entities may not simply be based upon a preexisting neural predilection, but is also heavily influenced by cultural factors that may lead us to expect to find certain types of agents. This is significant, as it suggests that religious conceptions may not be straightforwardly based upon cognitive structures. Rather, they are part of a complex interplay between these structures and our cultural expectations. It has also been suggested that attributing agency to events comes from having a theory of mind, that is, the socially necessary supposition that other people (which may extend to unseen entities) think and do things with purpose.[13] However, this still raises questions that need to be answered as to what mechanisms allow us to experience such features of experience.[14] One hypothesis behind HADD, that we are prone to perceive supernatural agents, is not itself undermined but arguably refined.

THE CONCEPTION OF RELIGION IN THE CSR

Arguably, the CSR overemphasizes the world religions paradigm (WRP; see chapter 1 and box 2.1).[15] In the WRP, predominantly (modern) Western and (Protestant) Christian

BOX 8.3 **ARE CAPITALISM AND MARKET FORCES RELIGIOUS?**

We normally assign modern economics to the sphere of secularism (see chapter 16), and thus consider it non-religious. However, we could argue that the way that "market forces" are described within capitalism as having agency is inherently "religious." Market forces are unseen powers that ensure the market balances itself, controls supply and demand, leads to competitiveness and innovation; trust in them will lead to our best possible future. In other words, an entirely immaterial conception, with no direct empirical evidence (nobody has ever seen a "market force," though selected human actions may be deemed to represent them), is posited as capable of influencing the world around us. While not seen as a "deity," or even possessing its own active will, it is in many ways indistinguishable from a supernatural force. Indeed, we are often told we must trust the economists—the "high priests" of capitalism—who assert that the mysterious movement of market forces means that things will all work out for the best (often in the face of empirical evidence to the contrary!).

norms are foregrounded, shaping what is assumed to be significant, what is studied, and how it is studied. For instance, a common indicator of religion in the CSR are supernatural agents.[16] This may not adequately address a range of traditions such as Confucianism, which, while having elements that seem clearly "religious" (e.g., sacrifices to Heaven/ *tian*), also has atheistic strands skeptical of supernatural beings and interventions (see box 8.7). Again, the CSR concern with cognition may highlight ideas and beliefs, ignoring embodied practices and ritual activity (see chapters 3, 9, and 12). The latter may also not always be accurately assessed, with some CSR scholarship describing ritual (wrongly) as "invariable" and "inflexible," although tradition and ritual are always changing (see chapter 4).[17] Therefore what gets studied as religion (or gets sidelined as "superstition" or "magic"; see boxes 7.8, 9.4, and 12.2) may not reflect all "religious practice," hence limiting the insights that can be gleaned.[18] The CSR may not capture as "religion" all relevant data. We could, for instance, ask: is capitalism a religion (see box 8.3)?

Problems with the term "religion" do not mean we should dismiss the whole enterprise of the CSR as ill-considered, and recent work is more alert to critical problems of definition. Further, the CSR itself provides arguments in the debate. Two key points may be noted:

· The CSR is suggestive that those areas we define as religious may be based in a common genetic heritage across the human race, and even in the wider animal kingdom. Against arguments that there is no common religious realm, the CSR may demonstrate commonality based in deep-seated evolutionary and biological drives, instinctual urges, and ways of experiencing which are prelinguistic and precultural and which relate to how we typically define those spheres identified as religious (see boxes 8.1 and 8.2). This also accords with thinkers such as Achille Mbembe, who has argued: "The deep structure of our world is the same everywhere . . . because we share in a common humanity." He has argued that critical theory should not be used to show difference, but to show similarity between groups.[19] It points to the way that an understanding of the CSR in these terms accords with critical theory (chapter 5) read through a decolonizing lens (chapter 7).

· The CSR aligns with contemporary critical scholarship in not seeing religion as a sui generis domain (see box 1.4), that is, one that is unique and self-contained.[20] It crosses over into a whole range of other cognitive functions. Cognitive science suggests we will not find specific religion "modules"[21] in the brain. We therefore expect those realms of life we term "religious" to cross over, in meaningful ways, with other aspects of human culture and society.

The CSR therefore does not settle the debate but is arguably supportive of a nuanced perspective on religion as an essentially contested concept (see chapter 1).

IS RELIGION NATURAL?

Is religion natural to humans? We need to be careful with our language here. Barrett and others suggest that religion is "natural" in the sense that it is an easily acquired habit of the mind (and body), while the processes leading to it do not require much cognitive attention. This is quite different from saying we are innately religious. We have cognitive processes that may easily lead to those sets of beliefs and habits we label religious (perhaps for some more than others). But there does not seem to be any sense, from the CSR, that religion is hardwired. Further, it appears to be an offshoot of other general features of our biological heritage.

A set of recent studies suggests that the capacities that lie behind human religiosity are the result of millions of years of development.[22] Various "building blocks" emerged, such that we cannot simply speak about the development of religion at one time or place. Rather, different elements and components came together, which leads us to see religiosity as linked to various capacities in the human being (and, in the view of some theorists, other animals as well). A further important question arises from this: does the CSR disprove God/religion by explaining how religion arose? (see box 8.4)

The capacity (potential) for religion may be within our minds. However, this does not make religion any more "natural" than, say, investment banking, ice hockey, or writing literature.[23] At the same time, it seems highly likely—maybe even inevitable?—being the type of creatures that we are, that something like religion would have developed.[24] Somewhat like warfare, religion is "natural" given what humans are, and is something we tend (inevitably) to engage in (all too frequently, some may suggest).[25]

BOX 8.4 **DOES THE COGNITIVE SCIENCE OF RELIGION DISPROVE GOD/RELIGION?**

Figures such as Pascal Boyer, Stephen Pinker, and Daniel Dennett seem to take the CSR as a route toward atheist arguments:[1] if we can explain how and why religion arises in the human mind, then "divine" or "supernatural" explanations are unnecessary. Indeed, some might say we know why people invoke religious explanations. In short, after being exposed to the CSR, should (rational) humans stop being religious? Many scholars, both in CSR and philosophy, suggest that such a jump is problematic.[2] Having theories as to how things may have developed is very different from showing this is how they did develop, and proving it is all that they are.

Indeed, a central argument in the CSR, the HADD (hyperactive agent detection device) hypothesis, is subject to considerable critique in terms of its failure to meet empirical criteria that would ground it: it may be a very good explanation of how something *might* have developed, but that does not make it true. Even if we did find out that we are prone to experience things which are not there, it does not show that everything we experience (physical or otherwise) is not there. Indeed, arguably, if religion is evolutionarily explainable, this may be a case for justifiable belief; many philosophers speak about epistemic justifiability (i.e., whether a belief can be justified as a belief). If a belief can be said to be reasonable and rational—there is a reason why we have it—then it may be a justified belief.[3] (Though a "justified"/"reasonable" belief is not, necessarily, a "true"/"correct" belief.) Neil Messer argues that because we see the CSR as "scientific," we often assume it is on surer ground than it is. He suggests that, at most, the CSR suggests grounds for epistemic unreliability or a general hermeneutics of suspicion (see box 2.7) in relation to religion. Moreover, as religion itself refers to a potentially broad array of phenomena, we will not likely find any single explanation or dis/proof.[4]

---

1 See Daniel Dennett, *Breaking the Spell: Religion as a Natural Phenomenon* (London: Penguin, 2006). On critiques of Dennett, see Messer, *Theological Neuroethics*, 21, 29.

2 See Hans van Eyghen, "Two Types of 'Explaining Away' arguments in the Cognitive Science of Religion," *Zygon: Journal of Religion and Science* 51.4 (2016): 966–82; and Kelly James Clark and Dani Rabinowitz, "Knowledge and the Objection to Religious Belief from Cognitive Science," in Trigg and Barrett, *Roots of Religion*, 113–26.

3 See Joshua Thurow, "Does Cognitive Science Show Belief in God to Be Irrational? The Epistemic Consequences of the Cognitive Science of Religion," *International Journal for the Philosophy of Religion* 74.1 (2013): 77–98; and Hans Van Eyghen, "Is Supernatural Belief Unreliably Formed," *International Journal for the Philosophy of Religion* (2018), https://doi.org/10.1007/s11153-018-9671-4.

4 See Aku Visala, "Explaining Religion at Different Levels: From Fundamentalism to Pluralism," in Trigg and Barrett, *Roots of Religion*, 55–74.

PURPORTED BENEFITS OF RELIGION
IS RELIGION AN EVOLUTIONARY PLUS?

David Sloan Wilson has perhaps most clearly developed arguments that religion may have adaptive value.[26] This, we should note, is entirely different from any argument as to the truth or falsity of religious claims. Wilson has two main arguments:

- Societies which have shared religious traditions and beliefs will probably be more cohesive,[27] and so be more likely to survive and reproduce.
- Because religions teach values such as altruism and self-sacrifice, it is likely that at least a few individuals within the group will model these virtues, sacrificing themselves for the group rather than seeking their self-interest, and this will likely have a beneficial effect on group survival.

It is difficult to see how exactly one would test such a hypothesis. One critique of Wilson's work is that although he developed his theory on the basis of a case study of Protestant Christian reformer John Calvin's (1509–1564) ideas, he only employed those ideas which fit his analysis, with much of Calvin's thought ignored.[28] Also, Wilson's theory relies upon a very generic sense of what religion is.

While not drawing on the CSR, we can see a comparable argument for survival of particular forms of one religion in Linda Woodhead's argument that one reason why what became the Catholic and Orthodox strands of Christianity in the early centuries CE eventually emerged victorious over their rivals (various groups often termed "Gnosticism") was a set of factors which included their willingness to align themselves with imperial power and their emphasis on the importance of family and procreation. In contrast, at least some other Christian traditions were primarily ascetic and held that human procreation should be restricted. These latter groups would have difficulty sustaining themselves over generations. Indeed, being ascetic and often critical of much of society, they would not be so likely to win imperial favor as good citizens.[29] Therefore, the success of certain groups is not linked to their being religious, as opposed to others who did not have religion. Rather, it is about the specific social mores a tradition embodies (religious or non-religious), and how those are utilized in a specific context. There is no inherent trait of religion per se that ensures its survival. This links back to our discussion of the often generic way that "religion" is defined in the CSR, while a more nuanced approach by religious studies scholars problematizes this, showing the need to not simply assume basic cognitive factors are at play, but wider cultural, social, and political factors as well (which the CSR is increasingly taking on board).

RELIGION AND MORAL BEHAVIOR

There are indications that belief in what is termed a "moralistic" deity, one who monitors people's behavior and enacts divine retribution for misdemeanors, may encourage more prosocial behavior.[30] Importantly, evolutionary studies also suggest that morality may not simply be based in our religious systems. Seeking to benefit the group may be based in evolutionary development. We, and other animals, may have mirror neurons, meaning that empathy is a built-in trait, or capacity.[31] Certainly, many of the most secular societies (see chapter 16) have strong indicators of morality (crime rates and indexes of corruption are low).[32] We are likely to see complex interactions between religion and morality (see case study 8B).

Another hypothesis in the CSR is that as human social complexity increased, especially as we moved from patterns of small-scale kinship groups in villages toward large-scale cities, where anonymity increased, we saw a development of what some term "high gods." High gods refer to deities who stress morality, are all-powerful creators, oversee values concerned with universal equality, and may judge and punish wrongdoing. This arguably promotes prosocial behavior, where we interact with people in the wider society in ways which promote the greater social good, including prosocial behavior toward those who cannot (or are not likely to) reciprocate our generosity/goodwill. In particular, it is hypothesized that, as we moved from foraging to agrarian societies, and developed more complex social structures, our conceptions of deity shifted away from local deities (whose concern would typically be with such things as ritual and taboos and/or functions such as resource conservation or agriculture) toward high gods.[33] Indeed, there are indications that believing that you are being watched—whether by some all-seeing deity figure or otherwise—may incline people to behave more honestly or not "steal," at least in certain situations. While this thesis is disputed, the majority of large-scale studies have tended to support it.[34]

Some have argued that evidence of an inbuilt moral sense undermines religion's claims that its texts and teaching encourage moral behavior. However, both Islamic and Catholic Christian traditions have argued for "natural law," especially in the thought of figures such as Thomas Aquinas (1225–1274) and Abu Hamid al-Ghazali (ca. 1056–1111), meaning that humans have an inherent moral sense. A similar claim in the Confucian context was also made by Mencius (372–289 BCE).[35]

As a final note, a number of studies suggest that people with some religious belief are often more psychologically stable and fulfilled in their lives.[36] What to make of such evidence is debated, including whether religion or simply communal association gives any purported benefits.[37] Religion's critics see it as a placebo, or a crutch, that makes facing the uncertainty of life easier. Such arguments go beyond the actual empirical data into issues of interpretation.

MYSTICAL AND RELIGIOUS EXPERIENCE IN THE MIND
STIMULATING THE BRAIN

One hypothesis is that certain parts of the brain are associated with what have been termed "mystical" or "peak" religious experiences (see box 8.5). These have been identified as existing

BOX 8.5 **MYSTICAL, PEAK, PSYCHOTIC, SPIRITUAL,
AND RELIGIOUS EXPERIENCES**

A range of terms get used to describe unusual human experiences, which have variously been attributed to religious impulses or mental health issues. These vary widely
and include

- feelings of exaltation,
- a sense of oneness with the world/universe,
- experiencing hallucinations/visions,
- sensing the presence of some force or power, and
- journeys into realms beyond this world.

How they get classified tends to depend upon the society and the specific context in
which they occur.[1] Some are actually quite common, such as hearing the voice, or sensing the presence, of a deceased partner or relative.[2] A cross-cultural (UK, Turkey, and
China) study shows that around 60 to 65 percent in each population has at some point

Statue representing the religious experience of a Christian saint as the wound of love, Saint
Gerolf Church, Drongen, Belgium.

---

1 See Craig Martin, "Experience," in *The Oxford Handbook of the Study of Religion,* ed. Steven Engler
and Michael Stausberg (Oxford: Oxford University Press, 2016), 525–40; and Paul Hedges, "Encounters
with Ultimacy? Autobiographical and Critical Perspectives in the Academic Study of Religion," *Open
Theology* 4: 355–72.
2 See Simon McCarthy-Jones, *Can't You Hear Them? The Science and Significance of Hearing Voices*
(London: Jessica Kingsley, 2017).

experienced something that may be described as mystical/religious/spiritual.[3] Some of what are often seen as "peak" experiences, that is, states of exaltation and visions (hallucinations) of the divine, have often been termed "mystical" experiences, whereas more "everyday" experiences are often referred to as simply "religious" or "spiritual" experiences. However, it is a somewhat arbitrary and unstable distinction.[4] While often seen as occurring "out of the blue," altered states of consciousness or brain states somewhat predictably arise from prayer, mediation, and and other religious disciplines, as well as from the use of certain intoxicants. The types of experiences and the paths to them are, though, quite diverse and arguably should not all be classed together.

---

3 Xinzhong Yao and Paul Badham, *Religious Experience in Contemporary China* (Cardiff: University of Wales Press, 2007); and Xinzhong Yao, "Religious Experience in Contemporary China," *Modern Believing* 47.2 (2006): 44–61; Cafer Yaran, "Religious Experience in Contemporary Turkey," *Modern Believing* 51.4 (2010): 45–68; and Paul Badham, "Religion in Britain and China: Similarities and Differences," *Modern Believing* 49.1 (2008): 50–58.

4 Those reporting religious experiences have, on the assumption that any religious experience is unusual, been deemed "religious virtuosi," a term coined by Max Weber (1864–1920), or as "mystics." But some experiences are quite common; see Schmidt, *Study of Religious Experience*. For classical and recent studies, see William James, *The Varieties of Religious Experience* (New York: Longmans, Green, 1902); Evelyn Underhill, *Mysticism: A Study in the Nature and Development of Spiritual Consciousness* (Grand Rapids, MI: Christian Classics Ethereal Library, n.d. [1911]), www.ccel.org/ccel/underhill/mysticism .pdf?membership_type=b108f8d8331236b8b61aa39bc6f86075c12d7e005; Richard Woods, *Understanding Mysticism* (London: Athlone Press, 1980); Ann Taves, *Religious Experience Reconsidered* (Princeton: Princeton University Press, 2009); and Richard King, "Mysticism and Spirituality," in *The Routledge Companion to the Study of Religion*, 2nd ed., ed. John Hinnells (New York: Routledge, 2010), 323–38.

in various parts of the brain.[38] Among the areas explored, some studies have focused on the relationship of psychotic experiences[39] and hallucinations with mystical experiences; others have focused on exploring brain waves in experienced meditators. Notably, a key finding concerning the former is that while certain common areas in the brain may seem to be stimulated, there are stark differences: "Psychotic hallucinations induce negative emotional and behavioral responses while mystical hallucinations lead to positive and adaptive outcomes," including "significantly lower levels of post-experience distress."[40]

Nevertheless, distinguishing psychotic and religious experiences is somewhat arbitrary. Michel Foucault (1926–1984) observed that, from around the eighteenth century, Western societies started to pathologize various conditions, witnessing a growth of psychiatric hospitals and the medicalization of madness, which before had been regarded differently.[41] Meanwhile, Georg Feuerstein (1947–2012) explored the concept of "holy fools," people who would probably today be classed as mentally ill, but whose experiences have sometimes been seen as inspiration from the divine.[42] In shamanic societies, those who experienced visions would often come under the training of a shaman who would lead them to explore their own inner world, even seeking what might seem a "psychotic breakdown" before seeking to rebuild and integrate them into society, but now in the exalted position of a shaman.[43]

Studies seeking to locate religion in the brain have found that what are labeled as religious thoughts, prayers, or experiences show little difference from mental or cognitive activity in general. However, some claim advanced scanning equipment and the use of seasoned meditation practitioners have shown interesting results. These studies have often focused particularly on Buddhist and some Christian meditation/prayer techniques and practitioners.

The work of Eugene d'Aquili (1940–1998) and Andrew Newberg is well known.[44] Their work has not been without its critics, especially as d'Aquili and Newberg suggested that neural evidence pointed to some common core experience, even a common divine source, behind all religions. They described their work as "neurotheology."[45] Armin Geertz has dismissed their work, noting that the "neuropsychology of religion has been plagued by sensationalist accounts published by scholars self-designated as 'neurotheologians.'"[46] In particular, Geertz notes that often such studies have tried to look for what is sometimes popularly termed the "god spot" in the brain; however, many parts of the brain are involved in religion and religious experiences (see box 8.6). Further, Uffe Schjoedt has argued that the kind of experimentation conducted by d'Aquili and Newberg shows a number of typical patterns of poor conduct found in the area. While not invalidating all aspects of their data, this certainly problematizes the kind of conclusions drawn from it.[47]

Careful experimental work and studies have also countered many other popular or high-profile experiments. One example is Michael Persinger's (1965–2018) "god-helmet." Persinger claimed this device (designed to stimulate certain neural areas with electricity) could induce "mystical experiences" in 80 percent of people who tried it. Attempts to replicate this by other researchers have failed, while the very low-level electrical currents Persinger used seem dubious to many researchers.[48]

THINKING ABOUT RELIGION AND ISSUES IN THE CSR

Five points can be highlighted from the CSR:

· Religion cannot be neatly mapped or explained in neurological or evolutionary terms. Rather, we see "the spread of certain religious elements as a dynamic process coevolving with escalating social complexity over time."[49]

· The CSR has often taken the WRP and empirical studies with Western Christians as a base (see chapter 7), but is now grappling with complexities beyond this.

· The CSR arguably supports a definition of religion as an essentially contested concept (see chapter 1), indicating species-level commonality arising through evolutionary and cognitive similarities, for instance our predisposition to making meaning and predicating "supernatural" "agents."

RELIGIOUS COGNITION AND THE "GOD-SPOT"

Understanding the way that religion is wired into the brain is currently a distant pros-pect. The full range of cognitive areas that seem to relate to what we term "religion" are not yet known. Certainly, there is no sign of a single area that relates to "religion" or "religious experience," popularly known as the "god-spot." As Dennett puts it: "Until we develop better *general* theories of cognitive architecture for the representa-tion of content in the brain, using neuroimaging to study religious belief is almost as hapless as using a voltmeter to study a chess-playing computer."[1]

Importantly, work in this area is indicating that far from there being a single com-mon religious experience or source, as d'Aquili and Newberg argued, or specific areas which could simply be stimulated to produce specific experiences, as Persinger argued, different types of what we may term "religious experiences" not only involve several different areas of the brain being stimulated, but also seem to indicate dif-ferent types of experience.[2] Further, how these relate to the wider cultural and social claims of religious traditions is still open to debate and needs further study.

1 Dennett, *Breaking the Spell*, 316. This quote also reflects the problematic notion that religion is primarily about beliefs.
2 See Schjoedt, "The Religious Brain"; and Messer, *Theological Neuroethics*, 23.

- While controversial, studies of "religious experience" indicate cross-tradition similarities. Notwithstanding different types of religious experience (see boxes 8.5 and 8.6)—something that occurs within traditions—we may posit meaningful cross-cultural correlations that make comparative investigations viable (see chapter 11).[50]
- Things we typically term "religion" are linked with generic cognitive functions and evolutionary developments. This suggests that any simple distinction of certain things as "religious" as opposed to what we may see as "non-religious" or atheist are problematic (see case study 8A).

.   .   .

CASE STUDY 8A. RELIGION, NON-RELIGION, AND ATHEISM

The distinction between atheists and the religious may seem a simple and natural one, but the borders are not always clear. The CSR can help us consider the differences.

ATHEISM AS THE DENIAL OF GOD

What we tend to know as atheism developed within the Western world in the period known as the Enlightenment (see box 16.1), when it became increasingly possible to challenge religious worldviews and authorities without fear of reprisal or death. There-fore, atheism has often defined itself against Christianity, but also against the other so-called Abrahamic religions (Judaism, Christianity, and Islam; see box 2.2). It is often seen as the antithesis of an all-powerful creator God: "a-theism." But, does this make Buddhists, who also deny this deity, atheists? Many Buddhists assert they are atheists. Yet many Buddhists affirm a belief in many deities. Traditionally, Buddhism did not deny the existence of deities; it disputed the existence of an all-powerful creator deity. Deities were, like humans and animals, beings caught up in the endless cycle of birth, death, and rebirth (*samsara*). Buddhism is sometimes called a non-theistic religion. Indeed, many Western atheists may not accept Buddhists, even if they deny deities, as being "real" atheists because they associate them as having "supernatural" beliefs in such things as rebirth guided by the law of cause and effect (*karma*) and the attainment of awakening/nirvana as a final end.

THE NEW ATHEISTS

From around the end of the twentieth century, a group of writers critical of religion earned the name the "New Atheists." The four figures, sometimes called the Four Horsemen of New Atheism, were Christopher Hitchens (1949–2011), Richard Dawkins, Daniel Den-nett, and Sam Harris. Others associated with this movement, which is marked by a strongly antagonistic polemic against religion as the root of all evil,[51] include Jerry Coyne, Stephen Fry, and Ayaan Hirsi Ali. We can note several central claims:

- Religion is inherently dangerous, if not outright evil and pernicious.
- Religious belief is irrational and primitive, akin to superstition (see boxes 7.8, 9.4, and 12.2).
- Science has disproved religion, studying science destroys religious belief, and the two spheres have constantly been at war.
- Evidence from cognitive science shows the origins of religion and disproves it.

In books, public lectures, television series, and other platforms the New Atheist voice was, for a while at least, the public face of atheism. It stoked a sense of stark division and contestation. However, the CSR, historical, and other scientific data contest the New Atheist attitude:

- Religion and science have not been continually warring worldviews—indeed, both religion and science are, to some degree, creations of the modern world as distinct spheres.[52] Many religious believers, including theologians, were often at the forefront of scientific advance and discovery.[53]
- One study shows that studying philosophy or the social sciences makes you far more likely to lose (Christian) religious belief than studying the natural sciences.[54] While data shows scientists in the US have lower levels of belief

than average in the population, data from Hong Kong shows the reverse.[55] Cultural factors seem significant.

- Religious belief appears to be a perfectly "natural," even "rational" way of being human looked at in an evolutionary and cognitive perspective. It is not clear-cut that this shows religion is false.
- Religion appears to give emotional and psychological benefits, and may make us more prosocial.

Matters are more complicated than suggesting that a set of complex human cultural traditions ("religion") can be neatly categorized as either simply wholly "good" or "bad."[56]

GLOBAL PATHWAYS TO ATHEISM

Understood broadly as denial of a supreme creator deity alongside other supernatural entities and repudiation of "superstition" and "magic," we can see atheism in many cultures over centuries, even millennia. We can name such figures as Democritus (460–370 BCE) or Giulio Cesare Vanini (1585–1619), but we can also see this in a wider global context (see box 8.7). When we consider a global context, it may seem less clear where and how atheists and non-atheists can be distinguished from each other.

NON-RELIGION

Globally, increasing numbers of people no longer identify as belonging to any religion. After the 2011 UK census, Dawkins congratulated Wales as being the most atheist region because it had many more people who claimed to belong to "no religion."[57] However, this confuses having no religious affiliation with being an atheist. Studies of those with no religion, the "nones" (see box 2.8), suggests a wide spectrum of worldviews within this group with many seemingly "religious." Often studied under the category of non-religion,[58] this group provides reasons to further consider the boundaries of religion.

REFLECTIONS

A number of questions may help us think through this issue in relation to the CSR:

1. Do you agree or disagree with the "New Atheist" argument that religion is inherently damaging, dangerous, and irrational? In what ways do scientific studies suggest it may be beneficial? Does the CSR show it may be rational to believe? How to balance the arguments?
2. Figures such as Dennett argue that the CSR shows how religion evolved, thus disproving its truth claims. Is this argument justified?
3. If "normal" human behavior and cognitive processes, such as seeing meaningful connections in events in our lives, is related both to what we term "religion" and

BOX 8.7 **ATHEISM IN GLOBAL PERSPECTIVE**

Atheism, broadly defined, has been found globally and throughout history. Here, we will note examples from China and India.

Confucianism: Confucius's (traditionally, 551–479 BCE) saying: "You have not yet learned to serve men, how to serve the spirits" (Analects XI:12), exemplifies for some an atheist inclination. However, Confucius seemed to have believed in "Heaven" (*tian*). While probably not a personal deity for Confucius, he likely envisaged "Heaven" as an impersonal transcendent (see box 1.10) reality. Nevertheless, Xunzi (310–215 BCE) almost certainly was atheist. Xunzi criticized those who believed that prayers for rain made it rain, stating it would have rained anyway. He also suggested that Confucianism's complex rituals were not directed to any divine reality, but simply regulated human behavior. Some later Confucians followed Xunzi's rationalist and materialist views, denying that sacrifices to Confucius and ancestors were "worship," but were simply paying homage to a great teacher and their dead forebears (see case study 1B).

Hinduism: By the medieval period there were six recognized "orthodox" (*astika*) schools of philosophy, which were opposed to the "unorthodox" (*nastika*) schools, including Buddhism and Jainism (see case study 7A).[1] The Sanskrit terms "orthodox" and "unorthodox" derive from a root term meaning "there is," indicating one who "believes" in deity/absolute reality (*Brahman*), against the arguably "atheist" Buddhist and Jain traditions which deny *Brahman*.[2] However, at least one of these orthodox schools, Samkhya, has been classed as "materialist." Its legendary founder, Kapila, has been claimed to be an atheist.[3] However, while Samkhya metaphysics sees all existence as essentially material (*prakriti*), it also argues for a form of "spirit" (*purusha*) which underlies our consciousness. Meanwhile, traditional Buddhism and Jainism would not typically be seen as atheist in contemporary terms. Perhaps the most thoroughgoing materialist, or atheist, classical philosophy in Indian thought is another "unorthodox" (*nastika*) tradition, the Charvaka school.[4]

---

1 See Gavin Flood, *An Introduction to Hinduism* (Cambridge: Cambridge University Press, 1996), 224–26.

2 See Paul Williams with Anthony Tribe and Alexander Wynne, *Buddhist Thought: A Complete Introduction to the Indian Tradition,* 2nd ed. (New York: Routledge, 2012), 1–29.

3 Bina Gupta, *An Introduction to Indian Philosophy: Perspectives on Reality, Knowledge and Freedom* (New York: Routledge, 2012), 130–43. Some Mimamsa philosophy arguments can even be seen as denying a God.

4 Gupta, *Introduction to Indian Philosophy,* 55–65.

to everyday processes of thought, how might we rethink the boundary of religion and non-religion in the light of the CSR?

4. Considering the CSR and global data on diverse religious beliefs, may we distinguish between what counts as being "religious" and what counts as being "atheist"? Is there any clear distinction?

CASE STUDY 8B. ANCESTORS, JESUS, AND PROSOCIAL BEHAVIOR IN FIJI

This case study explores issues relating to the notion that belief in "high gods"—those deities who stress morality, are all-powerful creators, oversee values concerned with universal equality, and judge and punish wrongdoing—may promote prosocial behavior. That is, such belief may work toward the benefit of wider "imagined communities" (see chapter 18), especially those whom we may never meet or from whom we expect no reciprocal benefits.

RELIGION AND SOCIETY IN YASAWA ISLAND, FIJI

Rita McNamara and Joseph Henrich have sought to explore the way that reflecting either on the Christian "Bible God" (*Kalou ni vola,* "God of the book") or local ancestors/ deities (Kalou-vu) affects prosocial behavior. This study took place on Yasawa Island, Fiji, where Christianity and local ancestor beliefs are blended. The inhabitants live in primarily small-scale village groups, marked by an extended range of kinship:

· immediate family,
· extended family (*itokatoka*),
· clan (*mataqali,* a lineage of several *itokatoka* united by a common male ancestor), and
· phratry (*yasuva,* or a collection of several clans linked by a common deified ancestor, or Kalou-vu).

Despite being mainly Methodist Christian (though recently adherence to the Pentecostal Christian Assemblies of God Church, AoG, is becoming more common), they combine their Christian faith with belief in and reverence for ancestors. This is common across Fiji. For converts to AoG churches, worship of Kalou-vu is forbidden as they are classified as *tevoro* ("demons"). Nevertheless, common rites which link back to these ancestral traditions still abound across both Methodist and AoG devotees.

JESUS VERSUS THE ANCESTORS?

The study involved testing whether, in simulated situations, when primed with either ideas concerning their Christian beliefs or beliefs about the ancestors, Fijians would be more prosocial to figures distant from their society, or whether they would favor themselves and their own local group. The project used a game where, unmonitored, participants could allocate resources based upon a game of chance. Thus, they could either follow the chance, or "cheat," cheating meaning that they allocated resources to a particular party (themselves or close kin). While the two scholars recognized limitations to their study, which requires further research, the overall result was that, with other factors being equal, when primed with thoughts of the Kalou-vu they would favor their own local kinship groups, and when primed with thoughts of the Christian deity they would counteract this bias with a broader prosocial sharing of resources with distant Fijians. Notably, a control primer based upon a common Fijian identity also showed results similar to that for priming with the Christian deity, though it is unclear how far this might be affected by Christian identity being deeply imbued in Fiji. Certainly, this one study is far from definitive, but it fits alongside a range of studies which are exploring the way that reflection on specific religious ideas may affect behavior.

REFLECTIONS

Some questions will help us reflect upon the issue:

1. To what extent do you think your own treatment of those close to you, or distant from you, is affected by your religious beliefs, or lack therefore? How would you seek to test this in yourself and others?
2. The CSR makes hypotheses about how and why our religious worldviews developed. Do you find the argument that different social arrangements—for example, small- versus large-scale, or agrarian, hunter-gather, industrial, postindustrial, feudal, capitalist, societies—will alter our notions of any deities or supernatural agents? Are certain conceptions of deity, or the absolute, more compelling in some contexts?
3. To what extent are (moral or social) values, if any, related to the differences found between priming with the ancestors and the Christian God? For instance, the term "more prosocial" implies that behavior of this kind is inherently "better." However, in some societies and ethical systems, favoring one's own group is considered a greater good. How should students of religion discuss such issues? Does the answer vary by cultural/geographical context?

· · ·

QUESTIONS AND CONNECTING THOUGHTS

The CSR has clear links with other discussions in this text, including the meaning of the term "religion" (chapter 1), reasons why religion and violence may be linked (chapter 15), the ways that humans have evolved as ritual animals (chapter 12), issues around gender and sexuality (chapter 10), and the possibility of comparative religion (chapter 11). We could certainly expand upon this list. Indeed, with the exponential growth of the CSR, this approach is likely to become an increasing factor in many areas of the study of religion. However, despite many potential benefits, there has been considerable resistance to engaging the CSR from some scholars of religion. This is related, partially, to territorial boundaries: the humanities, and certain social sciences, operate differently from the physical sciences and other social sciences. In particular, the emphasis upon hard, empirical data and quantifiable statistics is very different from the study of meaning and interpretation. The two, though, need not be antithetical. We may hypothesize that the CSR will need to become more deeply embedded in interpretative, critical, and more philosophical questions if its potential is to be reached.

Some questions will help us think further through the issues:

1. Considering your own academic and educational background, how inclined do you feel toward engaging the CSR as a disciplinary tool for understanding religion? Explain.

2. In some areas, such as the notion of HADD (hyperactive agent detection device), the CSR has hypothesized ways that it seems reasonable that certain religious responses may have evolved, but which have proven very difficult to prove empirically. Indeed, some parts of the hypothesis seem faulty. Of course, scientific method relies upon developing hypotheses which are tested and abandoned or improved with new evidence. In this case, it seems that the hypothesis is being modified or replaced with another way to explain the detection of "agents." How convinced are you by arguments that deities or spirits arise from such evolutionary mechanisms?

3. Do you find the CSR broadly supporting atheism, or not? Justify your answer with arguments.

4. Is religion "natural" for humans? What is meant by this, and why must we clearly define what we mean by "natural" when we ask this question?

FURTHER READING
THEORY

Andersen, Marc, Thies Pfeiffer, Sebastian Müller, and Uffe Schjoedt. "Agency Detection in Predictive Minds: A Virtual Reality Study," *Religion, Brain, and Behavior* 9.1 (2019): 52–64.

Boyer, Pascal. *Religion Explained: The Evolutionary Origins of Religious Thought* (New York: Basic Books, 2001).

Geertz, Armin. "Cognitive Science," in *The Oxford Handbook of the Study of Religion*, ed. Michael Stausberg and Steven Engler (Oxford: Oxford University Press, 2016), 97–110.

Ilkka, Pyysiäinen. "Religion and the Brain: Cognitive Science as a Basis for Theories of Religion," in *Religion, Theory, Critique: Classic and Contemporary Approaches and Methodologies,* ed. Richard King (New York: Columbia University Press, 2017), 229–36.

Sloane, Jason, and William McCorkle, eds. *The Cognitive Science of Religion: A Methodological Introduction to Key Empirical Studies* (London: Bloomsbury, 2019).

Trigg, Roger, and Justin Barrett, eds. *The Roots of Religion: Exploring the Cognitive Science of Religion* (New York: Routledge, 2016).

CASE STUDY 8A. RELIGION, NON-RELIGION, AND ATHEISM

Hedges, Paul. *Towards Better Disagreement: Religion and Atheism in Dialogue* (London: Jessica Kingsley, 2017), 14–35.

Lee, Lois. "Non-religion," in Stausberg and Engler, *Oxford Handbook*, 84–96.

Van Eyghen, Hans. *Arguing from Cognitive Science of Religion: Is Religious Belief Debunked?* (London: Bloomsbury, 2020).

van Eyghen, Hans. "Two Types of 'Explaining Away' arguments in the Cognitive Science of Religion," *Zygon: Journal of Religion and Science* 51.4 (2016): 966–82.

Wilson, David Sloan. "Why Richard Dawkins Is Wrong about Religion," in *The Edge of Reasons: Science and Religion in Modern Society*, ed. David Bentley (London: Continuum, 2008), 119–36.

CASE STUDY 8B. ANCESTORS, JESUS, AND PROSOCIAL
BEHAVIOR IN FIJI

McNamara, Rita Anne. "Which God Is Watching?," in Sloane and McCorkle, *Cognitive Science*, 41–54.

McNamara, Rita Anne, and Joseph Heinrich. "Jesus vs. the Ancestors: How Specific Religious Beliefs Shape Prosociality on Yasawa Island, Fiji," *Religion, Brain, and Behavior* 8.2 (2018): 185–204.

Purzycki, Benjamin, Joseph Henrich, Coren Apicella, Quentin D. Atkinson, Adam Baimel, Emma Cohen, Rita Anne McNamara, Aiyana K. Willard, Dimitris Xygalatas, and Ara Norenzayan. "The Evolution of Religion and Morality: A Synthesis of Ethnographic and Experimental Evidence from Eight Societies," *Religion, Brain and Behavior* 8.2 (2018): 101–32.

BODIES
Material Religion, Embodiment, and Materiality

IN WHICH WE EXPLORE:

The field of material religion and regimes of bodily discipline

The concepts of embodiment and materiality

How the material signifies what counts as religion, magic, or superstition

Case studies exploring perceived miracles related to material structures, and embodied practice and regimes of bodily discipline at a Christian shrine

INTRODUCTION

The material aspects of religion—such as buildings, actions, or clothing—may seem peripheral, or simply physical reflections of beliefs or spiritual experiences (see box 8.5). Globally and historically, many religions have downplayed the physical world, seeing it as dependent upon a "transcendent" power (see box 1.10) or as a bond that keeps us from contemplating "higher" matters. This can be seen as paradoxical, for spiritual aspirations are always embedded in material artifacts.[1] Moreover, insofar as we can study religion, all we have access to are the physical, or phenomenal (material, available to the senses), aspects:

· Doctrines or beliefs often exist as texts (bits of paper, papyrus, stone tablets, etc.).

· Oral teachings need an embodied person speaking to other embodied persons.

· Religion involves diverse material aspects such as rituals, buildings, and so on.

Hindu temple gate showing the spiritual represented in material form, Sri Mariamman Temple, Singapore.

Therefore, to study religion, however we envisage it, is to study material or embodied religion. Religion is embodied, emplaced, and enacted.[2]

This chapter is not focused solely on the physical stuff of material religion; seriously considering material religion forces us to acknowledge the centrality of human embodiment in our knowing and thinking. Western thought has often assumed that knowledge is first and foremost an intellectual and almost disembodied process (see box 9.1). However, the material turn, a recent focus on the significance of the material, suggests that our knowledge does not primarily begin in our minds, language, or social interactions. All these are dependent upon the realm of physicality, which forms the basis of subsequent human experiences and linguistic and social contemplation, notwithstanding that we only conceptualize the world through social and linguistic structures of thought.

Taking the material world seriously will lead to three important points, addressed sequentially in this chapter:

BOX 9.1 **IDEALISM, EMPIRICISM, AND LOGOCENTRISM**

Stretching back to what are often seen as the origins of philosophy in ancient Greece (though the ancient Greeks saw wisdom originating in Asia or Africa; see box 7.7), we see two poles exemplified in Plato (ca. 427–347 BCE) and Aristotle (384–322 BCE). They, respectively, represent the traditions of idealism and empiricism:

- An idealist worldview says that our understanding of anything first arises in the mind, and that pure ideas (such as mathematical formula like 2 + 2=4) are the only secure and certain form of knowledge. For Plato, our knowledge was grounded in a transcendent realm of "Ideas" or "Forms." For him, our bodies were a prison that ensnared us (see box 10.1).

- An empiricist worldview says that our understanding of anything always begins with sense experience of the world. We know 2 + 2=4 first as an experience, because we have two apples and then add two more apples. Ideas and thoughts are secondary, based on study of the world. Aristotle dismissed Plato's realm of "Forms" and argued that we can only know by examining the world around us.

However, Western philosophy in either camp has arguably been focused upon disembodied ideas and words.[1] This emphasis assumes that knowledge is primarily something in our minds that can be disassociated from our embodied self.[2] This can be expressed through the term "logocentrism": *logos* is Greek for "word" or "reason"; adding "-centrism" emphasizes seeing language/linguistic reasoning as central. However, focusing on language or reason (alone) as our source of knowledge is misleading. Emotions are central to how we think, while our physical experiences also shape our thoughts: tension, anger, or tiredness are all factors in how we respond to arguments, data, and ideas. Taking embodiment seriously reconfigures how we view human understanding and reason (see box 9.10).

Note: Logocentrism is associated with Jacques Derrida (1930–2004).[3] For Derrida, logocentrism stressed that Western philosophy gave priority to the spoken word over the written word. However, in our usage, Derrida's own thought remains logocentric because it still assumes the priority of language over embodied knowledge.

---

1 Arguably, this is true of many traditions; however, the so-called Western philosophical tradition has most influenced contemporary academic thought.

2 See Vásquez, *More Than Belief.*

3 "Logocentrism" was first used by Ludwig Klages (1872–1956). See Jack Reynolds, "Jacques Derrida (1930–2004)," in *Internet Encyclopedia of Philosophy* (n.d.), www.iep.utm.edu/derrida/; and Michael Harrison, "logocentrism," *Chicago School of Media Theory* (blog) (2018), https://lucian.uchicago.edu/blogs/mediatheory/keywords/logocentrism/.

1. Focusing upon material religion is not simply about thinking about material things (books, buildings, behavior, etc.) instead of immaterial things (beliefs, experiences, etc.). This chapter can be seen alongside chapters 1 and 3 in moving away from certain traditional notions of religion often termed the world religions paradigm (WRP) (see chapter 1 and box 2.1). Studying material religion is not just thinking about different things, but thinking differently about what we term "religion."

2. Our embodiment (see box 9.2) is not itself a neutral or natural given. It is regulated through social structures, what may be termed "regimes of knowledge." This includes the classification of bodies as gendered, raced, or otherwise ranked by systems of colonial, patriarchal, or other orders of control (see chapters 5, 7, and 10).

3. Taking embodiment seriously has important consequences for how we think about thinking. This includes how we conceptualize what we term "religions" and how we make sense of conflicting data and worldviews.

THEORIZING MATERIAL RELIGION
BEING EMBODIED

The material turn has meant that a number of scholars of religion stress embodied practice or materiality.[3] This shifts our focus to religion as performative, corporeal, and ephemeral: physical things do not last; they decay. It contrasts with the WRP, which regards religion as cognitive, disembodied, and an essence, and therefore being framed as eternal.

Here, we can reinforce an important point: this is not simply about changing the object of study, for example, from books and teachings to rituals and practices. Rather, it is about altering the nature of study: to religion *as* embodiment, that is, understanding how religion is first and foremost something enacted, not ideas later given some physical form (see box 9.2).

We must remember that embodiment has real consequences:

·   It is implicated in divisions based on gender or race (see, respectively, chapters 10 and 7).

·   It means that our world is not simply socially or linguistically constructed, but fundamentally underpinned by our being-in-the-world.

RITUAL: SYMBOL OR ACTION?

A significant aspect of material religion is ritual (see chapter 12). We can discuss ritual as a form of bodily practice, or what Marcel Mauss (1872–1950) termed "techniques of the body."[4] Mauss argued that specific bodily forms of practice are not simply physical but also social and psychological. The phrase draws attention to what we do (not just what

WHAT ARE EMBODIMENT AND BEING-IN-THE-WORLD?

Maurice Merleau-Ponty (1908–1961) stated the following about our situation as human beings: "Insofar as I have hands, feet, a body, I sustain around me intentions which are not dependent on my decisions and which affect my surroundings in a way that I do not choose."[1]

For Merleau-Ponty, it is not so much that we have beliefs, or make intellectual choices, that affects our being-in-the-world (see below). Rather, this happens in reverse. It is our situatedness as embodied creatures who have the state of being-in-the-world that determines what kinds of thoughts, beliefs, and ideas we can have, although the way our culture has conceptualized material things also affects how we see and understand them. In short, as thinking, acting, and social creatures we cannot escape the limitations and realities of our bodies, which bind us to life within a material world that affects who and what we are.

"Being-in-the-world" (from German, *Dasein*, literally, "being there") is employed here to refer to the way that we exist in an embodied and all-encompassing physical environment that is not simply of our choosing. The term was coined by the philosopher Martin Heidegger (1889–1976), but we employ it without taking on a specifically Heideggerian philosophy.[2] Our being-in-the-world is both social and cultural, yet also physical and embodied. We cannot exceed the limits of our embodiment, while this is also prescribed in various ways by our social conditioning. Heidegger spoke of it as "being thrown," meaning we are placed in a certain context in which we must exist.

---

1 Maurice Merleau-Ponty, *The Phenomenology of Perception* (New York: Routledge, 1962 [1948]), 440.
2 See Michael Wheeler, "Martin Heidegger," in *Stanford Encyclopedia of Philosophy* (2011), 2.2.3, available at: https://plato.stanford.edu/entries/heidegger/.

we think), but also notes how our actions are not separate from, but are implicated in, our self-presentation and our worldviews.[5]

Meredith McGuire argues that disputes between Protestants and Catholics in the sixteenth-century Christian Reformations (see box 9.3) had important ramifications for the conceptualization of rituals, which continue to today. For reformers such as Martin Luther (1483–1546), the Eucharist was simply symbolic. In Catholic theology, the doctrine of transubstantiation, or the "real presence," argued that the bread and wine "actually" become Jesus's body and blood, if not literally, then at least in their "essence" (see box 12.6). In other words, before the Reformation, a ritual was seen as a form of effective action; that is, a ritual enacted a particular effect upon the world. This understanding was portrayed by Protestants as "superstition." This, McGuire argues, was an aspect of the demarcation of medieval ways of seeing the world from modern ways of seeing the world. It helped distinguish between what was termed "magic" or "superstition" and what was termed "religion" (see box 9.4).[6]

THE CHRISTIAN REFORMATIONS AND THEIR CONSEQUENCES

Conventionally dated to 1517, based on actions attributed to Martin Luther (1483–1546), the Protestant Reformation was a wide movement across the fifteenth and sixteenth centuries which developed from medieval Catholic Christian thought and caused significant ruptures in what had gone before.[1] Moreover, the Protestant Reformation was not unified: Martin Luther and John Calvin (1509–1564), founded, respectively, Lutheranism and Calvinism/Presbyterianism; the Mennonites, Quakers, Amish, and others also emerged.[2] The Protestant Reformation also inspired a "Catholic Reformation," exemplified in the important Council of Trent (1545–1563, actually a series of councils or meetings).[3]

These Catholic-Protestant disputations have had ongoing implications for Western, and therefore global, thought. Arguably, Protestantism was associated with moves toward the modern nation-state, individualism, and the merchant-based capitalist economy; rather than being a cause, per se, it gave the rising middle classes and princes a role of leadership and identity that was religiously legitimated.[4] Further, the polemics that demarcated Protestants from Catholics became influential in defining religion today as it was mainly in northwestern European states and later North America, where Protestants were ascendant, that modern Western scholarship arose (see chapter 1). Whether thinkers were religious or not, the worldview of Protestantism permeated normative categories of thought.

---

1 See Eamon Duffy, *The Stripping of the Altars: Traditional Religion in England, 1400–1580*, 2nd ed. (New Haven: Yale University Press, 2005); and Diarmaid MacCulloch, *The Reformation: A History* (London: Penguin, 2005).

2 For a brief overview of some major Christian traditions, see Alister McGrath, *Christianity: An Introduction*, 3rd ed. (Chichester: Wiley, 2015), 199–219.

3 See Alister McGrath, *Historical Theology* (Oxford: Blackwell, 1998), 190–95.

4 See Linda Woodhead, *An Introduction to Christianity* (Cambridge: Cambridge University Press, 2004), 162–69.

The Protestant conceptualization of ritual has consequences for modern thinking. Religion has become conceptualized through the lens of symbols, doctrines, and concepts of the transcendent (see box 1.10). These take precedence over the embodied and material world. Three examples can help demonstrate how such theorizing hides the inherent materiality of religious practice:

Christian Eucharist: A ritual reenactment of Jesus's "last supper" with his disciples before his execution, the Eucharist links Christians with the wider body of "saints" (in this sense, all Christians living and dead) and seeks reconciliation with God. Those involved will variously sit, stand, or kneel (see case study 11B), with particular postures exemplifying attitudes of devotion. In Catholic traditions, you will also see the elevation of the host—where the

BOX 9.4 **THE MATERIAL DISTINCTION OF MAGIC, SUPERSTITION, RELIGION, AND SCIENCE**

The terms "religion," "magic," "superstition," and "science" are often taken to be quite distinct spheres (see boxes 7.8 and 12.2). Probably, when you hear them, you have a sense of what types of things would fit under each. For instance, where would you place the following?

· acupuncture and traditional Chinese medicine (TCM)

· alchemy

· animal sacrifice

· astrology

· astronomy

· Bible reading

· Buddhist meditation

· chemistry

· dowsing (for water)

· palm reading

· prophesies

    Possibly, you categorized things which seemed "inward" or "spiritual" as "religion"; specific "secular" disciplines as "science"; and things related to the material world which did not seem "scientific" as "superstition" or "magic." This marks a general trend in modern thought which draws from Protestantism (see box 9.3):

Religion: The Protestant emphasis on symbols, inner experience, and preaching dominate how we see religion. They are private and internal.

Modernity: "Secular" and "religious" spheres were separated as the modern period progressed. The former is public and physical; the latter private and interior (see chapter 16).

Science: Secular modernity demarcated a distinct sphere of (physical) science (a category that has been contested and created),[1] separate from religion.

Superstition/Magic: The point where the physical/secular meets religion became a site for labeling practices as "superstition," especially those not deemed "rational."

Non-Protestants: Catholic ritual became classed as superstition; likewise, any "religion" beyond Protestant Europe was characterized as "superstition," "magic," or "primitive" religion (see box 7.8).

---

1 See Peter Harrison, *The Territories of Science and Religion* (Chicago: University of Chicago Press, 2015).

bread that represents Jesus's body (the host) is held aloft—which is often seen as a "spiritual" highpoint. In some traditions, acts such as kissing texts, bowing at various points, and genuflection (a type of bow that involves going down on one knee to show deep respect) are also performed. Though the Eucharist is spoken of as spiritual feeding, participants engage bodily: to be devout, one performs acts of devotion (techniques of the body). Community aspects are often stressed, emphasizing being embodied among other bodies.

Buddhist Meditation: Generally seen as focused on the "inner" life of the practitioner, Buddhist meditation involves correct bodily positions as prescribed by Buddhist textual sources (see box 9.5).[7] An upright sitting position is common, while many basic meditations begin with a focus on the meditator's breath. She should first become aware of this: the breath as it comes in and out. Arguably, meditation purifies both mind and body, because in Buddhist anthropology (here meaning the conception of humanity) we are composed of what are termed the five "heaps/aggregates" (*skandhas*), which are both mental and physical, including consciousness, perception, and the body.[8] Bodily posture, breath, and awareness of one's body emphasize the embodied nature of Buddhist meditation.

Islamic Prayer (*salat*): For many Muslims, strict devotion involves praying five times a day, with precise injunctions of routinized bodily practice. In the Sunni tradition, the five prayers (*salat*) are performed as follows in a set number of cycles: standing, arms folded (often reciting verses from the Quran); bowing from the waist; standing; prostration; sitting; prostration. While it is when standing or sitting that more verbal prayers or textual verses are recited, it is in prostration "when one is closest to God, expressing utter selflessness, devotion and obedience," while the postures should "generate humility and self-awareness of one's own finitude in the presence of God."[9] Importantly, particularly on Fridays, the prayer should be communal, stressing embodied presence among others.[10] In Islamic prayer, the physical movements are what are seen to exemplify and even generate the mental/spiritual attitudes (see box 9.6).

THE SPIRITUAL AS PHYSICAL

Some may remain unconvinced that everything that we see, know, and think about as religious or spiritual is mediated through the body. We are generally culturally bred to believe that such matters are essentially about some "inner," "transcendent," or "spiritual" aspect. But, if people say they have met a "holy" person, any description will entail a physical quality (see box 9.7). Likewise, when people describe a "sacred place" (see chapter 17), they often say they see it in the landscape or building. Even feeling "inspired" by

BOX 9.5 **BUDDHIST SITTING**

The Discourse on the Applications of Mindfulness (Satipatthana Sutra), while stressing mental awareness, discusses bodily awareness, noting that "a monk gone to the forest . . . sits down cross-legged, holding his back erect, and establishes mindfulness in front of him."[1] The bodily posture seems integral because it is what awareness is based on. Seated, standing, lying, and walking postures are discussed in various texts.[2] In Japan, Zen master Dogen (1200–1253) wrote a text entitled "How Everyone Can Sit," describing meditation as primarily an activity of the body, hence accessible to all.[3] In Zen Buddhism, meditators may sit in the traditional Japanese kneeling (*seiza*) meditation position for hours at a time; meditation periods exceeding three hours are not uncommon. This can entail intense pain: try kneeling with your back straight for just one minute and you will probably start to feel considerable discomfort. Finding ways to be aware of, but not focused on, the pain is part of the discipline.

---

1 Satipatthana Sutra, cited in *Original Buddhist Sources: A Reader,* ed. Carl Olson (New Brunswick: Rutgers University Press, 2005, 69–77, 70 (see also 70–73).
2 See Shaw, *Buddhist Meditation,* 16–17; Shaw, *Introduction to Buddhist Meditation.*
3 Eihei Dogen, "Fukanzazengi: How Everyone Can Sit," trans. Yasuda Joshu Dainen and Anzan Hoshin (1986 [ca. 1227, revised ca. 1233 and 1242]), White Wind Zen Community, https://wwzc.org /dharma-text/fukanzazengi-how-everyone-can-sit.

BOX 9.6 **IS ISLAMIC PRAYER AND TRADITION A FORM OF SELF-CULTIVATION PRACTICE?**

Falun Gong is a Chinese form of self-cultivation practice (see case study 1A and box 1.11), and calling it a "religion" may lead us to neglect certain things. Likewise, describing Islam as a "religion" may lead us to neglect aspects of its physical practice, which includes traditions around physical health (i.e., eating dates and other food, and fasting practices), and embodied spiritual practice (i.e., prayer, pilgrimage, and fasting). The fast is a discipline of the body, but it is intended to discipline the "spirit" (inevitably intertwined with physical practice). Indeed, some Muslims point to recent studies suggesting that fasting has health benefits as a sign that God (in Arabic, Allah, literally, "the God") prescribed something good for the Muslim community.[1] Given the centrality of embodied practice to lived Islam (see chapter 3), does describing it as a self-cultivation practice rather than a religion help? (On comparison, see chapter 11.) This would make physical practices integral, instead of a WRP representation, which typically stresses doctrine.

---

1 Sartaj Ahmad, K. Goel, K. Maroof, P. Goel, M. Arif, M. Amir, and M. Abid, "Psycho-Social Behaviour and Health Benefits of Islamic Fasting during the Month of Ramadan," *Journal of Community Medicine and Health Education* 2.178 (2012): 1–4.

The Hebrew Bible recounts "divine" encounters affecting the body of the person. When Moses descended from the mountain after being given the Ten Commandments, he is described as "shining" (Ex. 34:29). The Israelite people at first cannot look directly at him. Here, an encounter with the divine enacts a physical transformation. In Orthodox Christianity some *staretz* (holy people/saints) have also been described as appearing to shine following particular religious experiences or as part of their closeness to deity.

In Buddhism, early texts describe a physical transformation of the Buddha after his experience of awakening/nirvana. Between Bodhgaya (where he was awakened) and Sarnath (where he delivered his first teaching), the Buddha met a spiritual seeker who stopped him and asked what he was (human or deity), because he was like no other human. At Sarnath, his old disciples initially shunned him (they believed he had renounced the path of a true ascetic), but they also *saw* he had changed and so sought his teaching.[1]

---

1 See Perry Schmidt-Leukel, *Understanding Buddhism* (Edinburgh: Dunedin Academic Press, 2006), 19–29.

reading a "sacred book" is a physical act: touching the text or seeing words. We come to know what is termed the "religious," "spiritual," or "transcendent" always and only through our embodied experiences.

FRAMING OUR WORLD

Drawing on the work of scholars Eric Goffman and Eric Gombrich,[11] Daniel Miller has approached materiality by focusing on the way we frame our world.[12] In particular, Gombrich spoke about the way that in an art gallery we typically see pictures in frames, but it is not the frame—the most omnipresent artifact—that we look at. Rather, the work of the frame is to be invisible. A good frame, one suitable for the picture, means that we typically do not notice it. Miller's argument is that much of the material framing of our world is like this: it is the obvious, the everyday, the mundane items which are essential to (what we may term) things-being-in-their-place (see box 12.3 on matter out of place) that we overlook. This insight is significant when we discuss material religion, because many everyday aspects of religion which are part of regular practice may be overlooked or unnoticed. But it is often these techniques of the body which help frame, or regulate, religious (or non-religious) lives, practice, beliefs, and behavior. They form a large part of our being-in-the-world. Framing, following Goffman, concerns the way that our world is shaped or constructed in ways we hardly notice: it is "framed" such that it appears "natural" to us (see chapter 5).[13]

GREEKS AND MODERNS

Bryan Turner states that "our bodies are regulated and administered for the benefit of the social order,"[14] often framed in ways we hardly notice (especially in our own culture; see chapter 5). Think about ways we behave at school or the office, or the etiquette for riding the train or bus, standing in queue at the supermarket checkout, or greeting people by bowing, shaking hands, rubbing noses, or high-fiving.

Much regulation, in Western forms of Christianity, follows from the logocentric perspective of Western thought (box 9.1). The body has been subjected to the spirit in various disciplines and regimes, with the material often seen as lower and needing to be made subject to our rational or spiritual self, something which is often gendered (see box 10.1). This has resulted in certain bodies being seen as more exalted or significant than other bodies.[15] This has prevailed under various representations of soul and body. Many early and medieval Christians saw these as intimately entwined,[16] but in the early modern period, following an interpretation of René Descartes (1596–1650), the mind and body were envisaged as distinct, referred to as "Cartesian dualism."[17]

Michel Foucault (1926–1984), especially in his work on madness and sexuality, argued there was an increased regimentation and disciplining of the body in modernity.[18] Starting from around the eighteenth century, the body becomes the object of precise calculations and measurements. Our bodies are today quantified in ways that have never happened before. Turner notes that Foucault offers a further insight from Mauss and Merleau-Ponty, who both focused on the individual as an actor, and lacked the historical and sociological lens that Foucault brings.[19] Mauss's "techniques ["disciplines," in Foucault's language] of the body" need supplementing by Foucault's recognition of the regulation of populations.[20] Embodiment, in other words, is both individual and social. Importantly, embodiment, while a constant in some ways (a body today is much like a body a hundred years ago), is also malleable and changing over time (how we think about our bodies today is not how our ancestors thought about them) and location. Turner argues we need to see how the personal and social factors combine.[21] Today, the body and religion are often framed as essentially private, as opposed to the realm of reason, which is part of the public secular arena (see chapter 16). However, the body is often publicly regimented, seen clearly in colonial contexts.

COLONIAL BODIES

In imperial regimes, bodies have been classified into various groups to be controlled and regulated. This has affected the conceptualization of the religion of the classified groups. From the early modern period and beyond (circa sixteenth to nineteenth centuries), an evolutionary scheme was used to classify races, cultures/civilizations, and religions.[22] This graded them into ranks from higher/more advanced to lower/less advanced. This disciplinary classification was often related to the bodies of those classified. Hence, it was held that "higher races" had higher religions and civilizations, while "savages" were without civilization and with degraded or no religions (see chapter 7 and box 18.6). Syed Hussein Alatas (1928–2007) has discussed what he describes as "the myth of the lazy native," with European colonialism creating racial classifications.[23] Indigenous groups were often originally seen as industrious and hardworking, but when no longer economically valued by colonizers they were deemed inherently "lazy." Aníbal Quijano (1928–2018) sees both race and gender as historically constructed terms that allowed exploitation and domination of non-European bodies.[24] In many colonial accounts, the bodies of non-Westerners were deemed "feminine," harking back to Plato (see box 10.1), and rendering them inferior to the "masculine" Western body (see chapters 7 and 10). Whether based upon such issues as race, class, gender, or other qualities, we see hierarchies of material bodies. Representations of corporeal nature and religious authority were often woven together. In the Cameroon Grassfields of the 1890s, conversion to Christianity could involve "young men and in particular young women . . . quite literally changing their bodies."[25] These colonial divisions are an embodiment of ideology: we do not simply divide the world into ideas, but into precise physical forms.

We should not see such classification as unique to Western colonialism. It reflects how all groups classify others (see chapter 6 and box 7.4). Especially where we do not understand the other's culture or language, their body is often "read" or "imagined" to gain understanding (see box 9.8). For instance, Japanese scholar Kato Hiroyuki (1836–1916), a committed materialist, argued that Christianity as practiced was "superstitious,"[26] while a group of Japanese visitors to the US in the early twentieth century were shocked that a very "modern" society was infused by displays of spiritualism and Pentecostal Christianity, which they likewise saw as "superstition." Nevertheless, today, Western colonial and neocolonial regimes of bodily classification remain most intensely potent.

REGIMES OF EMBODIMENT: SECULAR AND RELIGIOUS

We do not see all regimes of bodily discipline in negative terms. In contemporary Western societies, we tend to see the "secular" (see chapter 16) disciplines of athletics, healthy eating, and dieting or exercise to attain a "beach body" as positive endeavors (often mediated via advertising). These things are not themselves "good": representations of idealized bodies, especially excessively thin female models or uber-macho male models are linked to feelings of inadequacy and illnesses in the population, which often goes alongside fat-shaming.[27] There is also overlap between "secular" and "religious" disciplines of the body with such things as yoga, mindfulness,[28] Tai Chi, or acupuncture often labeled as "spirituality" (see boxes 5.6 and 2.8), though others may see them as "superstition" (see box 9.9). There may also be tensions. Religious discourse may valorize fasting over dieting, that is, periods of not eating or drinking for religious ends (see box 9.6). Indeed,

If you have ever been in a foreign country not knowing the language, you may have paid more attention to the bodies and actions of the local people (see chapter 2). We do this to gain a window into their world in lieu of linguistic understanding. British missionaries (and other explorers and colonial administrators) did this to understand Chinese religion.[1] Eric Reinders argues that, based on their own cultural conditioning, these Protestant Christian missionaries made—generally negative—assumptions about the religion and worldview of the Chinese:

· Performing a kowtow meant people were obsequious and servile.

· Using incense meant they were superstitious.

· Chinese religion was empty of meaning or sense.

· The Chinese were "inscrutable."

Many of these assumptions were based on the way that Protestants had negative attitudes toward Catholics (see boxes 9.3 and 9.4), which they simply read onto Chinese religion.[2] While often wrong, these assumptions established persistent stereotypes.

---

1 Eric Reinders, *Borrowed Gods and Foreign Bodies: Christian Missionaries Imagine Chinese Religion* (Berkeley: University of California Press, 2004).
2 In relation to Daoism, indigenous Confucian traditions abetted Western misinterpretations; see case study 4B.

disciplines of religion that cause pain or discomfort can be seen as extreme. Nevertheless, potentially harmful activities may be seen as positive when undertaken by sportspeople or performers to attain "peak performance." Our ideas of what forms of bodily discipline are "normal" vary considerably. Importantly, religious disciplines are often portrayed as positive forms of "training" or "discipline" that bestow benefits (rather than as punishment). Discipline/mortification of the self/soul/spirit is always a form of bodily practice.

EMBODIMENT, MATERIALITY, AND KNOWLEDGE
THINKING AS EMBODIED BEINGS

The material turn means that we cannot simply see concepts as based in immaterial thoughts: our thinking is embedded in embodiment. By emphasizing embodiment, we are not suggesting that it is a "given," a brute fact. Certainly, there are natural laws and brute facts of existence, but we experience them as being "thrown" into a certain cultural context which is part of our being-in the-world (see box 9.2). For instance, it is a natural and universal fact of embodiment that we age. Yet how we envisage such things as infancy, childhood, youth, middle age, and old age are cultural forms. Again, society gives significance to certain bodies, such as that of the monarch/ruler: touching, or in some places even seeing, the ruler may be taboo, or it may transfer (divine) blessings and power. We need to think how our socially constructed world and our physically given world relate.

Merleau-Ponty "showed that the consciousness of being, and of being in the world, comes through the body."[29] Our idea of self is related to our embodied sense of identity and other bodies. We think about things as being above us, behind us, and so on—we think as beings in space (see chapter 17). From a biological point of view, the body not only precedes language, in that it evolved first, but also forms a basis for our language. Contrary to the influential Sapir-Whorf thesis,[30] which suggests that everything we experience is a linguistic construct, we need to consider the material world as significant, including our evolutionary heritage (see chapter 8). As Ludwig Wittgenstein (1889–1951) once remarked, we cannot even describe the aroma of coffee.[31] Simply stated: we have many experiences we do not have words for. We can experience things without being able to name them. Indeed, many experiences are predominantly prelinguistic: pain is an example (if you have ever burned your hand on a hot pan or hit a nail into your finger—I hope you have not done either—you will know this). We are aware of certain experiences without some priority of naming. This is simple biology. The parts of the brain that experience and respond to these things are prelinguistic—they evolved earlier than the frontal temporal cortex, where linguistic skills sit. In slightly inaccurate but helpful terms: here is the reptilian part of our brain, rather than the mammalian or primate part of our brain.[32] This part of the brain goes back to our more primal urges, often expressed as the four *F*s: fight, flight, fornicate, fodder. Indeed, these bodily experiences overrule our normal rational mind and ways of thinking: have you ever tried studying when you are angry, afraid, horny, or hungry? My guess is that you find it difficult. We all do. Embodiment, as recent studies show, is far more dominant in our intellectual lives than we like to think. In a sense Plato was right: our body is a snare for our rational selves. In less pessimistic terms, Confucian anthropology stresses our embodiment as part of our natures.[33] This stress on embodiment does not deny the role of linguistic construction: when we think about specific experiences of pain—whether we regard it as beneficial or harmful, whether we go to a hospital or priest for treatment, and so on—it becomes social and linguistic. To stress only one aspect is lopsided,[34] and stressing only the construction of categories within discourse without considering their application and utilization is problematic.[35]

MATERIALITY, KNOWING, AND POWER

In terms of theorizing what materiality means, scholars influenced by the material turn have grappled with the issue of how we know. Various scholars have employed the term "materiality" (see box 9.10) to address the sense of the significance of our embodiment and the material world for thinking. In particular, they have challenged some common understandings of social constructionism (see chapter 5) seen in phrases such as "it is discourse all the way down." This suggests that we never encounter the physical world, only social or linguistic realities. Taking the material turn seriously, this book concurs with scholars such as Manuel Vásquez, who stress the importance of the material. This includes understanding that a decolonial approach takes us beyond the Western logocentric emphasis on the primacy of social and linguistic construction.[36]

Developing from the issue of decoloniality (see chapter 7), we can take a wider stance to include issues of gender (chapter 10) and class to note the significance of these in considering materiality and questions of power, in three consecutive points:

1. The material turn is not simply abstract philosophy, but accords with issues picked up by feminist and decolonial/postcolonial scholars. For those oppressed by various regimes of discourse, embodiment and regimes of disciplining bodies shape actuality. Experiencing our material limits is a very real fact. A Black body on a lynching tree is not (primarily) a social construct to other Black bodies.

2. The idea that we and our world is simply a social/linguistic construct is based upon a white, male, Western, middle- (or upper-) class normativity. It assumes that we can make ourselves anew, be infinitely adaptable, and

BOX 9.10 **MATERIALITY: BEYOND MATERIAL CULTURE**

Focusing on material culture may simply change what we study, but by the term "materiality" scholars such as Daniel Miller have argued we need to more radically think about how we understand. Material culture has often been used for the study of specific human-constructed objects and artifacts, but this has until recently been regarded as a focus upon somewhat vulgar or peripheral things, and not the "higher" pursuit of abstract ideas and social and linguistic concerns.[1] Maurice Merleau-Ponty (1908–1961) has been influential for theorizing the significance of the body and material things, while Miller has shown the significance of Pierre Bourdieu (1930–2002) and Bruno Latour in studying materiality. Bourdieu observed how people are educated into the normative expectations of their society (see chapter 5).[2] Miller notes this is always about physical regimes of embodiment. However, while social constructionism focuses upon the social and linguistic regimes that determine how we see things, materiality stresses that everything is embedded within physical domains (regimes of embodiment) that cannot be escaped. The physical forms the basis of our knowing and thinking: if our embodiment were otherwise, we would think/perceive the world in different ways.[3] Human values, cultures, and social forms only exist objectified in material forms or human performance.[4] In this sense, we can see social forms as only a specific form of a wider material culture. Latour has noted that much traditional Western theory tends to miss what we can term the agency of the nonhuman and material world.[5] Michael Rowlands has argued that taking theory such as that by Michel Foucault (1926–1984) and Marcel Mauss (1872–1950) seriously entails realizing that our self-realization is tied to material reality: we cannot simply have a socially constructed sense of freedom unless it is also physical and material.[6] Power is not embedded in simply controlling social and linguistic patterns—though this shapes how we see material realities; material conditions themselves inscribe and are inscribed in people, places, control of resources, and so on (see chapters 7 and 10). Understanding that social realities (see box 1.9) exist at the juxtaposition of both social construction and material facts is imperative. Materiality is not denying social constructionism, but realizing that it is embedded in systems of material embodiment that control and delimit our actions and understandings.

---

1 See Miller, "Materiality."

2 Pierre Bourdieu, *Outline of a Theory of Practice*, trans. Richard Nice (Cambridge: Cambridge University Press, 1977).

3 See Tim Ingold, "Materials against Materiality," *Archaeological Dialogues* 14.1 (2007): 1–16. Ingold's basic premise is the need to take physicality seriously; however, he argues that many theorists of materiality distance us from the material through an overload of abstract theory.

4 See Daniel Miller, "Why Some Things Matter," in *Material Cultures: Why Some Things Matter*, ed. Daniel Miller (London: University College London Press, 1988), 3–21.

5 For a short account, see Bruno Latour, "On Interobjectivity," *Mind, Culture and Activity* 3.4 (1996): 228–45.

6 See Rowlands, "A Materialist Approach."

have no natural limitations. This theory is not a neutral description, but comes from a stance of unreflexive privilege. Perhaps a Californian executive in the IT business can visualize the world this way, but not a female peasant farmer in Myanmar.

3. Therefore, any supposedly critical theory or social constructionism that does not include the material turn is liable not to be truly decolonial. In the words of Audre Lorde: "The master's tools will never dismantle the master's house."[37]

SCHOLARSHIP IN RELIGION, LOGOCENTRISM, AND BEYOND

Turner observes that talking about the body is not the same as partaking in the material turn and rejecting logocentrism. Turner suggests this applies to Foucault and Jean-Paul Sartre (1905–1980), both of whom talk about the importance of the body.[38] But they do not, like Merleau-Ponty, recognize that embodiment shapes how we know and experience. They valorize language over embodiment. David Morgan suggests that even critical scholars of religion are implicated in this:[39] the modern Protestant Christian sensibility is deeply embedded in scholarship.[40]

Some scholars of religion have taken materiality seriously. Based in comparative work on renewal in charismatic Catholic Christianity and the American Navajo tradition, Thomas Csordas combines embodiment theory alongside Bourdieu's concept of habitus (see box 5.3) to stress what he terms "the preobjective character of bodily being-in-the-world."[41] Csordas stresses embodiment's significance in wider social networks in ways that accord with Foucault's priorities. Vásquez has heavily theorized a new form of phenomenology, and his thinking accords in large part with arguments in this book.[42] Finally, Morgan argues that Charles Sanders Peirce's (1839–1914) semiotics allows us to rethink language as other than simply a set of arbitrary signifiers (see box 9.11) against some interpretations of social constructionism (see box 5.8).

.   .   .

CASE STUDY 9A. WEEPING GODS AND DRINKING STATUES

We look at two examples of "miracles"[43] mediated through the material, which are for others "superstition." Both have resonances with lived religion (chapter 3).

THE DRINKING GANESH STATUES

In 2008, first in India and then globally, reports started circulating that statues (*murti*) of certain Hindu deities, primarily Ganesh (the elephant-headed son of Shiva and Parvati), were drinking milk. Videos went viral and the global media covered the story.

BOX 9.11 **SIGNIFIERS, LANGUAGE, AND EMBODIMENT**

In contemporary linguistics and epistemology (theories of knowledge), it is recognized that there is no direct correlation between words and things. For instance, the word "rose" has no direct relation to a particular flower. Our words may be termed "empty signifiers," though in technical usage by Ernesto Laclau (1935–2014) this does not mean they are arbitrary.[1] They are "shifting signifiers" tied to a chain of meanings, implicated in regimes of power to exclude, for example, race or gender (see chapters 7 and 10), and negotiated in discourse. David Morgan also suggests the work of Charles Sanders Peirce (1839–1914) shows that not all language is arbitrary. Peirce argues we should move from semiology (which stresses language as textuality) toward semiotics (which can help add embodied elements).[2] While each word may be arbitrary, they fit into patterns of symbolic meaning. Indeed, some things may be said to make more sense as symbols. For instance, if a rock symbolizes stability, it is not entirely arbitrary, but is what Peirce terms an icon relating to what it represents. A bullet hole in glass is what Peirce terms an index that points to the bullet that was shot through it (we know something made the hole). But it is not a direct correspondence; perhaps we are mistaken; maybe an arrow made the hole. Nevertheless, Morgan argues that to suggest that every signifier is arbitrary does not do justice to our being-in-the-world as embodied creatures.

---

1 Ernesto Laclau, *On Populist Reason* (London: Verso, 2005).
2 Morgan, "Materiality," 274.

Within a week or so of the phenomenon starting, it died down. Sporadic outbreaks of this phenomenon have occurred both before and after this. For devotees, it was a "miracle."

In Hinduism, when a statue is enshrined at a temple, a ceremony invites the deity into the statue, enabling worship (*darshan,* "seeing" and "being seen" by the deity). While many Hindus are clear they do not worship the physical statue, but rather, the divine spirit represented, the statues are, for many, an actual locus of divine presence. It is in the physical statute that the divine is embodied and seen.

For skeptics, a variety of explanations were employed to explain this "superstitious" belief. In some of the videos (viewable online), it appeared that a bowl of milk placed to the mouth, or trunk, of the statue allowed much liquid to simply slip away (on white marble maybe not always so clear). Others suggested that quite a few of the statues were made of porous materials, and the milk or other liquids was absorbed. Certain examples seemed ambiguous enough for both skeptics and believers to claim that the other side failed to explain the evidence of people's eyes. Significantly, while we are discussing "facts," they are contested by people's perceptions and interpretations.

A WEEPING JESUS

In Mumbai (formerly Bombay), India, in 2012, a large statue of the crucified Jesus in the grounds of a church started to "weep." "Tears" were seen to come down the face of the statue and these were collected by eager devotees. The parish priest declared this "a miracle." The "tears" were collected and distributed. Some drank the "tears," and it was believed that miracles, especially healing, could result for those who came in contact with this "holy" liquid.

Others were not convinced that they were witnessing a miracle. Indeed, one Indian skeptic went to the church to investigate. What he discovered was a leak in some pipes above the statue, allowing liquid to seep down. Worryingly, his research discovered that it was not simply water but sewage. He therefore notified the church and others to warn them about the danger of consuming these "tears." He also asserted it was not a miracle. The response was not quite what he expected. Under India's blasphemy laws, he was charged with offending the religious sensibilities of the Christians. The skeptic had to flee India with the threat of legal action and jail hanging over him. What he considered as seeking a "scientific" explanation to dismiss this "superstition" ended with him accused under another category: "blasphemy." We should note that while the local priest recognized this as a miracle, the hierarchy of the church did not give it that designation.

REFLECTIONS

A series of questions will help us think about this situation:

1. As a Hindu or Christian devotee, who accepts these alleged miracles, how would you respond to suggestions that your religious beliefs were simply superstition? How would you frame them to assert their credibility?
2. Does the fact that such miracles cross into areas which can be explored scientifically make them readily open to accusations of superstition? Is it primarily their connection with physicality and the material that makes these examples seem superstitious to many?
3. These examples show the manifestation of religion in material form. Consider the regimes of knowledge that determine what physical forms counts as religion, superstition, magic, or science.

CASE STUDY 9B. EMBODIED PRACTICE AT A CHRISTIAN SHRINE

This case study considers architecture and pilgrimage. Our focus is not simply on these as physical structures, but the associated regimes of bodily discipline.

CHRISTIAN ARCHITECTURE AND THE GOTHIC

In nineteenth-century Britain, architects following Augustus Welby Northmore Pugin (1812–1852) valorized the Gothic style as the epitome of Christian architecture, leading to what is known as the Gothic Revival.[44] The Gothic style,[45] typical of medieval European church architecture, employs pointed arches, and is found in various styles. It probably developed from influences from Islamic Spain (Al-Andalusia) and from the earlier Romanesque style. The first Gothic cathedrals developed in France. The cathedrals of Notre Dame (literally "Our Lady," signifying dedication to Jesus's mother Mary) in Char- tres and Paris are classic examples.

Gothic was not simply an architectural style, but also a theological ideology. Com- pared to the older Romanesque style, Gothic cathedrals and churches were filled with light, and allowed (because their pillars could carry more weight) grand designs that soared to the sky. This was theorized in terms of a "theology of light," where the material world (directly) represented divine glory. In the new grand spaces, bathed with colored windows from stained glazing, the devotee should feel as though they were already in the "heavenly Jerusalem" (heaven envisaged as a city, specifically Jerusalem). The soaring ceilings and columns were also intended to overwhelm the visitor with their own insignificance. The scale of the building represented the might of deity. The very physicality of the building was meant to invoke a "religious" realization. Similarly, the length of the cathedral meant that the high altar (in the sanctuary, where the priest presided over the eucharist) was far away from the main body of the church (nave), where the general congregation stood. (Seating was not generally introduced until at least the sixteenth century or later.) The transcendent holiness and separateness of deity, as well as church authority, was emphasized. This was further signified by a (rood) screen, either of stone or wood, that separated the nave from both the priests (seated in the quire, an area beyond the rood screen but before the sanctuary) and the act of the Eucharist. Sometimes this would be hardly visible to the congregation. The Gothic cathedral was not, therefore, simply a pretty building design. It was an embodied regime of discipline in stone. Through their embodied interaction with the building, worshippers were expected to get a better sense of the religious realm, and their lowly position in relation to it.

PILGRIMAGE AND EXPERIENCING

Many of these medieval cathedrals became sites for pilgrimage. Among the most famous was Canterbury, in the South of England. Here, Archbishop Thomas Becket (ca. 1119– 1170) was killed by knights acting for (if not directly ordered by) King Henry II. Thomas was enshrined as a martyr (somebody killed for their faith). It was believed that martyrs were close to God and so their relics (bones and items associated with them) were seen as potent sites of divine blessing or miracles. Stories of miracles related to Becket's relics (his body, or especially popular was his blood sold in diluted form) made Canterbury a wealthy and popular shrine. However, the cathedral was not designed to receive these thousands of pilgrims, nor the devotion in the crypt where Becket's bones were first housed. Therefore, from the pilgrim donations, a large new shrine was built at the far east end of the cathedral, allowing pilgrims to enter through one door and exit via another—essentially, medieval crowd control. In the midst of this was the magnificent shrine to Becket, which over time became increasingly adorned with the gold, silver, and precious gems left by grateful recipients of believed miracles, or hopeful recipients of future miracles.[46] The design was intended to instill in devotees a sense of the prestige and power of the shrine, and to manage their bodily movements. Before the shrine, it would be expected that pilgrims would bow, kneel, or prostrate themselves to show their devotion. Moreover, ordinary pilgrims only had access to certain areas. Regimes of physical discipline are often associated with worldviews or ideologies (religious, cultural, or otherwise), and are given shape through the physical environment.

REFLECTIONS

Some questions will help us think through these issues:

1. In what ways does a building you are familiar with encourage certain regimes of physical discipline?
2. Merleau-Ponty suggested that the fact of our embodiment meant that "I sustain around me intentions which are not dependent on my decisions." What do you understand by this? How do you think interaction with the physical environment of a medieval Gothic cathedral (or comparable structure) creates "intentions" that go beyond your decisions? Is this partly determined by having a worldview that relates to the structure? Or, even if your worldview is different (or even contrary), might you still be impelled to behave or experience in some ways by the design?
3. The medieval Gothic cathedral was explicitly built to reflect a "heavenly Jerusalem." Is it possible to convey ideas of an afterlife or transcendent realm that is not physical? Are our perceptions of what is religious always and only mediated in embodied form?
4. To what extent do you think beliefs and ideas are embedded in the physical performances related to those beliefs? If somebody had a belief which had no (potential) embodied action associated with it, would it be meaningful? In what way?

·   ·   ·

QUESTIONS AND CONNECTING THOUGHTS

The themes of this chapter intersect with other chapters, such as lived religion, which is often embodied (chapter 3), concerns with the lived environment and geography (chapter 17), and ritual (chapter 12). We also see theoretical crossovers with feminist thinking, which often stresses embodiment (chapter 10); postcolonialism, which notes how certain bodies have been valued more than others (chapter 7); and social constructionism (chapter 5). In these terms, we also recognize the way that imaginaries of religion have stressed privatized and disembodied forms (chapters 1 and 16), which has real political consequences (chapter 18). Some questions will help us think through the issues raised:

1. Philosophical thought experiments often ask us to imagine that we are only "brains in vats," or similar. However, this arguably betrays an extremely logocentric conception of what we are, how we interact with other people, how we know, and how we experience the world. How central do you think embodiment is to who you are, what you know, and how you know it?

2. Would you agree that religion, and whatever we might consider spiritual/transcendent reality to be, is only encountered or represented through embodied form?

3. What do you see as the main differences in thinking about religion after the material turn compared to via the WRP?

4. Is the difference between religion, magic, superstition, and science only culturally based? In what ways may we be able to meaningfully employ these terms in any coherent academic sense?

FURTHER READING

THEORY

Chidester, David. *Religion: Material Dynamics* (Berkeley: University of California Press, 2018).

Meyer, Birgit and Dick Houtman. "Introduction: Material Religion—How Things Matter," in *Things: Religion and the Question of Materiality,* ed. Dick Houtman and Birgit Meyer (New York: Fordham University Press, 2012), 1–23.

Miller, Daniel. "Materiality: An Introduction," in *Materiality,* ed. Daniel Miller (Durham: Duke University Press, 2005), 1–50.

Morgan, David. *The Embodied Eye: Religious Visual Culture and the Social Life of Feeling* (Berkeley: University of California Press, 2012).

Narayanan, Vasudha, ed. *The Wiley Blackwell Companion to Religion and Materiality* (Chichester: Wiley, 2020).

Orsi, Robert. *Between Heaven and Earth: The Religious Worlds People Make and the Scholars Who Study Them* (Princeton: Princeton University Press, 2006).

Plate, S. Brent. "A History of Religion in 5½ Objects," video (2012), www.youtube.com /watch?v=RoQ1k9h9yB0.

Torre, Renée de la. "Religion and Embodiment: Religion and the (Latin American) Bodies That Practice It," in *Controversies in Contemporary Religion,* ed. Paul Hedges, vol. 1 (Santa Barbara: Praeger, 2014), 81–112.

Turner, Bryan. *The Body and Society,* 3rd ed. (London: Sage, 2008).

Vásquez, Manuel. *More Than Belief: A Materialist Theory of Religion* (Oxford: Oxford University Press, 2011).

CASE STUDY 9A. WEEPING GODS AND DRINKING STATUES

Anon. "Unexplained: Hindu Drinking Statues," video, Unexplained Web (2013), www.youtube.com/watch?v=KXrGCH8nCao.

CNN. "Man Leaves India after 'Debunking' Weeping Jesus," CNN (7 December 2012), www.youtube.com/watch?v=GaqIBpK62Yo.

Eck, Diana. *Darśan: Seeing the Divine Image in India,* 2nd ed. (New York: Columbia University Press, 1996), 3–31.

Mann, Richard. "Hinduism in the News: The Shifting Role of Religion and the Media in Canadian Public Life," *Canadine Journal of Communication* 40.1 (2015): 87–103.

Vidal, Dennis. "When the Gods Drink Milk! Empiricism and Belief in Contemporary Hinduism," *South Asian Research* 18.2 (1998): 149–71.

CASE STUDY 9B. EMBODIED PRACTICE AT A CHRISTIAN SHRINE

Blick, Sarah. "Canterbury Cathedral," in *Encyclopedia of Medieval Pilgrimage,* ed. Larissa Taylor, John Friedman, Kathy Gower, Thomas Izbicki, and Rita Tekippe (Leiden: Brill, 2010), 83–84.

Blick, Sarah. "Reconstructing the Shrine of St Thomas Becket, Canterbury Cathedral," *Konsthistorisk Tidskrift* 72.4 (2003): 256–86.

Bruce, Gordan. "Cathedrals and Theology of Light," video, Yale University, https://coursera.org/lecture/western-christianity-200-1650/cathedrals-and-theology-of-light-OoqFs.

Coleman, Simon, and Peter Collins. "The Shape of Faith or the Architectural Forms of the Religious Life," in *Materializing Religion: Expression, Performance and Ritual,* ed. Elisabeth Arweck and William Keenan (Aldershot: Ashgate, 2006), 32–44.

Hendrix, John. *Architecture as Cosmology: Lincoln Cathedral and English Gothic Architecture* (Bern: Peter Lang, 2011), 3–8.

Scott, Robert. *The Gothic Enterprise: A Guide to Understanding the Medieval Cathedral* (Berkley: University of California Press, 2011), 121–33, 147–70.

Suger (Abbot). "On What Was Done in his Administration," trans. David Burr, *Medieval Sourcebook, Fordham University* (1996), https://sourcebooks.fordham.edu/source/sugar.asp.

10

GENDER
Feminism, Sexuality, and Religion

IN WHICH WE EXPLORE:

The position of women and sexuality in a variety of religious traditions

What feminism(s) is (are), and its (their) role in the study of religion

The concept of gender constructionism

Case studies of Christian attitudes toward women priests, and controversies around the ordination of Theravada Buddhist nuns

INTRODUCTION

Feminism is an established disciplinary perspective that has changed the way we look at everything from art to politics, society to history. But what is it, and what does it mean for the study of religion? These are questions we will seek to explore. Before starting this chapter, we may consider that despite some advances in recent years, the academic study of religion still remains largely dominated by men, especially in professorial appointments.[1]

In this chapter, we will chart some historical trends and issues, focusing upon the Christian West and the legacy from Greek philosophy, which extolled the male and masculine, and denigrated the female and feminine. This is important to understand the wider context in which religion and gender has been experienced and theorized, including in colonial and postcolonial contexts. We then proceed to address issues in feminist theory and gender constructionism, before looking at some ways religious

BOX 10.1 **MALE AND FEMALE IN GREEK PHILOSOPHY**

In Plato's thought, men were creatures of the mind, rational and capable of searching for "spiritual truth" (Greek "philosophy" was thoroughly infused with concerns we would now term "religious"). The body, associated with the "female" characteristics of emotion and raw physicality, was seen as a prison for the mind. Further, Plato believed that women were a snare to the male and unsuited by temperament to the philosophical and rational life. Plato's thought was not atypical. Pythagoras's school, perhaps best seen as a "religious" group, saw a binary between male and female which somewhat mirrored Plato's thinking (notwithstanding that significant female mathematicians were members of his school). Aristotle, who helped form the foundations of medieval (and modern) science, saw women as misbegotten men.[1]

---

1 Nicholas Smith, "Plato and Aristotle on the Nature of Women," *Journal of the History of Philosophy* 21.4 (1983): 467–78.

traditions have been studied and engaged with by feminist scholars and introducing some theoretical perspectives. We conclude with two case studies.

THE CONSTRUCTION OF THE FEMALE
GREEKS AND CHRISTIANS

Why begin our study of gender in contemporary religion around two and a half thousand years ago in ancient Greece, a world and time very different from our own? The reason is that many of the tropes, or themes, found then have been transmitted to our context. For instance, Plato thought that the ideal of the philosophical life, to transcend the everyday reality of this world, was a quest reserved for men (see box 10.1).

Meanwhile, Christianity arose as a Jewish sect, and so drew heavily from the Hebrew Bible and Israelite tradition, but Judaism had for centuries been embedded in Greek culture. While predominantly patriarchal (from the Greek words *pater*, "father," and *arché*, "rule," i.e., "the rule of the father"), Judaism did not denigrate the female in the same way Plato had.[2] Indeed, the early Jesus movement (see box 4.11) seemed remarkably egalitarian compared to the surrounding culture (see case study 10A). Yet, as Christianity grew, it integrated more Greco-Roman thought, including Neoplatonism. This influenced early and medieval Christian writers and traditions:

- For early Christians, martyrs (those who died for their faith) were highly regarded, including Perpetua and Felicity (third century CE). However, narratives recounting their death say they became "honorary men," reflecting Platonic prejudice: in order to be spiritual, a woman must become male.[3]

- The Genesis account (Gen 3:1–6) of Eve persuading Adam to eat fruit (often represented as a pomegranate or an apple) from the tree of life, after being tempted by a snake, has led some Christian thinkers to blame women for humanity's troubles, or in Christian terminology, for "sin."[4] Tertullian (ca. 160–220 CE), who described women as "the devil's gateway," asserted that women should continually repent. Augustine of Hippo (ca. 354–430 CE) saw women, whom he saw as inherently tempting to men, as responsible for original sin (Augustine's theory that the fruit-eating incident meant that all humanity was immersed in sin from which they could not free themselves).[5]
- Some medieval Christian monks were forbidden from having physical contact with women, including their sisters and mothers, as women were seen as innately lustful and so might tempt men to turn away from spiritual contemplation. Still today, the famous Orthodox Christian monastic center in Greece at Mount Athos does not permit entry to women or female animals (e.g., donkeys).

Modern Western culture, at least partially, has inherited ancient Greek perceptions of women and men via Christianity. One modification, solidly established by the nineteenth century, was that women had become associated with purity and chastity,[6] while men were seen as the gender subject to sexual desire. But, while women needed to be protected from predatory males, they could be (and are still) blamed for rape or sexual assault if they had "tempted" men or failed to be "modest" in their behavior, dress, and so on.[7]

THE COLONIAL CONSTRUCTION OF THE FEMINIZED OTHER

Edward Said's (1935–2003) Orientalist thesis (see chapter 7, especially box 7.3) argued that Western scholarship portrays the Orient as "feminine," while the West is "masculine" (see box 10.2). This goes alongside a set of interlinked binaries, including the following:

Orient: feminine, emotional, despotic, backward

West: masculine, rational, democratic, advanced

However, it would be wrong to see representations of women as weak, emotional, and lacking rationality as being purely a product of the Greek legacy. Most human societies, at least for the last couple of thousand years, have been patriarchal. There are disputes as to whether archaeological finds of powerful mother goddess figurines in many places are indicative of the overthrow of a previous matriarchal culture.[8] Nevertheless, evidence suggests that women often held powerful positions (as leaders, scholars, priests, etc.) in many ancient societies. Women leaders have not been unknown in fairly recent times (and still today) in various global contexts, with, for instance, Malay female rulers being praised in the context of Islamic tradition and local custom, sometimes to the bewilder-ment of Westerners.[9]

SOUTH ASIA

Records suggest that women were priests and philosophers in the early Vedic period (ca. 1500–500 BCE), though later sidelined. The Laws of Manu declared that women must be obedient to, respectively, their father, husbands, and sons (see box 10.3). The early Buddhist tradition struggled with the question of whether women could be part of the monastic order (see case study 10B). This was around the time that women were being displaced from their more significant roles in life and thought.

This is not to say that women were not significant in later periods. In *bhakti* tra-ditions (devotional Hinduism), some women were leaders and "saints." In the Shri Vaishnava tradition of South India,[10] the foundational poet-saints of the sixth to ninth centuries, the Alvars, included twelve men and one woman. While far from gender balanced (but notably including lower-class men, including a Dalit—the untouchable caste), the Alvars represented what could be termed a liberatory movement against tradi-tions in which solely high-caste males could be religious leaders. Further, Vishnu and Shri are technically seen as coequal deities. Some also argue that the presence of power-ful female deities gives Hinduism feminist credibility (see box 10.4).

BOX 10.3 **THE LAWS OF MANU**

While some have argued that Asian traditions were less patriarchal than European society, the evidence on this is mixed. The Laws of Manu (Manusmriti) (ca. 200 BCE–200 CE) decreed that a woman should be subservient to

- her father as a daughter,
- her husband as a wife, and
- her sons as a widow.

Furthermore, it states: "Though destitute of virtue, or seeking pleasure elsewhere, or devoid of good qualities, a husband must be constantly worshipped as a god by a faithful wife" (Manu 5:154). It appears that women had greater equality in the early Vedic period (before ca. 500 BCE), but during the period of the writing of the Hindu law code literature (*dharmashastras*, ca. 500 BCE–200 CE), including the Laws of Manu, this changed. However, it is unclear how influential these texts were before British colonial rule.

BOX 10.4 **IS THE GODDESS A FEMINIST?**

Many have argued that because Hinduism contains strong female Goddesses, it has a natural feminist affinity, certainly in comparison to the Abrahamic (see box 2.2) monotheisms of Judaism, Christianity, and Islam.[1] In the Goddess (Shakta) traditions, the feminine aspect of deity is portrayed as supreme. Some goddesses are both powerful and ferocious:[2]

- Kali is sometimes portrayed dancing on the body of her lifeless husband, Shiva. Seemingly gruesome, this portrayal represents the Hindu concept that spiritual energy (*shakti*) is feminine, making male deities powerless (dead) without her.
- Durga manifested from the combined spiritual energy of all the gods when they were in despair after defeat by a buffalo demon. Using the weapons of Shiva and Vishnu, and mounted on her lion steed, she defeats the buffalo demon, demonstrating her supreme power.

However, all Goddess traditions were dominated by men. Indeed, idealized Goddesses arguably belittle actual women by being impossible role models. This argument is made of other significant female figures. For instance, the Virgin Mary as mother and virgin has a position no real woman can obtain. It has also been argued that the Buddhist Guanyin (see box 2.9) represents an impossibly idealized female

---

1 The title of this box is borrowed from Alf Hiltebeitel and Kathleen Erndl, eds., *Is the Goddess a Feminist? The Politics of South Asian Goddesses* (New York: New York University Press, 2000).

2 See Flood, *Introduction to Hinduism*, 174–97.

ideal, though she also allowed women to assume a role in lay (non-monastic) celibate orders, which was a potential route to escape unhappy marriages.[3] Moreover, some contemporary Indian feminists have taken the ferocious Goddesses as role models to resist sexism or harassment. For some, "playing Durga" in the workplace or public sphere becomes a legitimate and indigenous way to assert female authority.[4]

Kali dancing on the body of Shiva, representing the feminine Shakti as the animating divine power, author's collection.

---

3 See Paul Hedges, "The Identity of Guanyin: Religion, Convention, and Subversion," *Culture and Religion* 13.1 (2012): 91–106.

4 See Ann Grodzins Gold, "Gender," in *Studying Hinduism: Key Concepts and Methods*, ed. Sushil Mittal and Gene Thursby (London and New York: Routledge, 2008), 178–93.

CHINA

Traditional Chinese society placed women under men in the social and family hierarchy. This is often attributed to the mores of Confucian decorum. From about the eleventh century, neo-Confucianism was implicated in traditions such as foot-binding, in which high-class women had their feet broken and bound tightly with cloth from birth to stop their growth to attain what was seen as the ideal of small "lotus" feet. Many, though, would assert that this is not inherent in Confucianism, and some feminist theorists have seen common ground with Confucian virtue ethics.[11] We may also note that when Protestant Christian missionaries arrived, generally starting in the mid-nineteenth century, some supported foot-binding as part of Chinese culture, while others opposed it.

In contrast to Confucianism, Daoism is often portrayed as "feminist friendly," with three main arguments assembled. First, passages from the Daodejing seen to extol the soft, weak, and feminine over the hard, strong, and masculine (DDJ: 78) are invoked.[12] This is often linked to yin-yang theory, which sees a polarity of masculine and feminine, light and dark, arising and descending, and so on, which has also been argued as pointing to equality in Daoism. However, yin-yang theory is generically Chinese, not specifically Daoist. Second, Daoism has given women leadership roles: the early Celestial Masters school (from the second century CE) had female priests, though the highest leadership was male, and the later Quanzhen Daoist school (from the twelfth century) had female monastic lineages that were equal to the male-led schools, though by about the sixteenth century all had become subservient to male-led lineages. Third, some schools of Daoism, associated with internal alchemy (*neidan,* or "biospiritual cultivation"; see box 1.11), argued that women had a natural advantage over men in developing their spirituality. Assessing these three arguments, we can say that, overall, while Daoism has valorized women in ways not typical of many other religions, it could hardly be characterized as inherently feminist.[13]

CONTEMPORARY PAGANISMS

Contemporary Pagan, or neo-Pagan, movements have developed in Europe (and North America and Australasia), seeking to reclaim, or re-create ("invent") indigenous pre-Christian religious traditions. This includes such movements as Druid orders that look back to Celtic traditions arising from the nineteenth century, followers of Norse mythology, and Goddess[14] worshippers.[15] The latter have especially formulated themselves as feminist religious movements. In Glastonbury in the UK, a place strongly associated with such traditions, the Glastonbury Goddess Temple has for some time been part of the wider Pagan and New Age "spiritual" infrastructure of the town, with the nearby Glastonbury Tor sometimes framed as a sign of the Goddess in the landscape there (see box 17.2):

THE GODDESS is alive in Glastonbury, visible for all to see in the shapes of the sacred landscape.

She is soft as the rounded hills of Her body and sweet as the apple blossom that grows in Her orchards.

Here Her love enfolds us every day and Her voice is always near, carried on the wind, whispering through the mists of Avalon.

Her Mysteries are as deep as the Cauldron She stirs, taking us down into Her depths and lifting us up to Her heights.

She is our Source, our Inspiration and our Love.[16]

FEMINISM AND GENDER CONSTRUCTIONISM: DEVELOPMENTS AND THEORY
WAVES OF FEMINISM AND GENDER CONSTRUCTIONISM

For Mary Daly (1928–2010): "If God is male, then the male is God."[17] This provocative statement can be seen as a critique of both Christianity and structures that promote patriarchy in society. Importantly, while feminism is in many ways broadly secular (see chapter 16), it has grown in a Christian cultural context that has become the dominant global narrative, especially in terms of academic feminist theory.

Feminism and gender constructionism are often identified as having three "waves." These developed chronologically, but have subsequently coexisted as types, or styles, of feminism and gender constructionism. To briefly demarcate:

Feminism: concerned with the rights of women in society, especially domination by patriarchy (though wider oppression is recognized in later theory)

Gender Constructionism: looks at the way that society's notions of men and women and masculine and feminine are discursively created

We can briefly outline each wave, before noting some other points in depth.

First-Wave Feminism (Liberal Feminism)

First-wave feminism emphasizes the equality of men and women as rational beings, epitomized by a work like *A Vindication of the Rights of Women* (1792) by Mary Woll-stonecraft (1759–1797). In texts such as *The Women's Bible* (1895), by Elizabeth Cady Stanton (1815–1902), liberal feminism highlighted the fact that women are obscured in history and religious traditions.[18] The movement sought equal rights in terms of education, voting, and reproduction. Its key victory was voting rights, gained by the suffragette movements. Questions of enfranchisement and restrictions on entering politics were not just a matter for women, though, affecting non-Christians (in Europe, especially Jews[19]), the poor (property requirements for voting), and nonwhites (with inequality remaining for long periods in such places as South Africa and the US). Although not part of most first-wave feminist reflection, such issues found a voice in figures such as Sojourner Truth (ca. 1797–1883), who foreshadowed various critiques (see box 10.5).

Second-Wave Feminism and Gender Constructionism

Second-wave feminism is rooted in texts such as Simone de Beauvoir's (1908–1986) *The Second Sex* (1949) and the work of figures such as Judith Butler.[20] Beauvoir stated that one is "not born a woman, but becomes one," an idea developed by theorists such as Monique Wittig (1935–2003) and Butler. For instance, in society, boys are given toy soldiers, encouraged to play outside, and dressed in certain colors (blue, green, army fatigues, etc.), whereas girls are given dolls, encouraged to play at tea parties and cooking, and dressed in traditionally feminine colors, particularly pink.[21] Second-wave feminism argued that a toxic patriarchal culture imposed a domineering and violent masculine culture and aggressive politics. In Christian feminist theology, figures such as Daly rejected Christianity as inherently patriarchal and oppressive, whereas others, such as Rosemary Radford Ruether, believed patriarchy could be removed to reform Christianity.[22] Under the influence of second-wave feminism, legislation on reproductive rights became enshrined in law in many countries.[23] We address critiques below.

Third-Wave Feminism (Naturalist Feminism)

Third-wave feminism is partly a reaction against both the first and second waves, especially the way they construct the "male" and "female," and their denial of embodiment, which seems to dissolve all difference into sameness (see below). It rejects second-wave feminism's condemnation of men, which sometimes occurs in its vilification of patriarchy (not all men are the problem). It also problematizes the previous foci upon white Western women, heterosexual women, and only those women born as women, the last being a reason why some second-wave feminists, such as Germaine Greer, found themselves subsequently criticized.[24] Some now speak of a fourth wave around these issues.

SEX OR GENDER?

A common distinction:

"Sex": the biological issue of embodiment as male and female (broadly, genitalia).

"Gender": behavioral patterns that socially signify male and female.

However, even "sex" is not uncontroversial. A significant number of babies are born as intersex, with ambiguous genitalia.[1] Depending on how this sexual ambiguity is determined, the occurrence is from 1 in 4,500 to 1 in 50, but most sources suggest 1 in 1,500–2,000. They are normally given surgery to fit a single gender, though in many places this is now strongly discouraged. Further, some people born with one "sex" identify with the other "sex," sometimes undergoing surgical change. Such a situation is termed "transgender." Again, contemporary neuroscience argues that we cannot demarcate "male" and "female" brains.[2] Moreover, certain societies have also identified more than two gender types (see box 10.7). These issues complicate the assumption that there are simply two clear and distinct human sexes, and shows that our concepts are, at least partially, culturally determined.

---

1 Today the term "intersex" is preferred over the traditional term "hermaphroditic" (both female and male, from the Greek deities Hermes and Aphrodite, who comingled into one body); see Susannah Cornwall, *Sex and Uncertainty in the Body of Christ: Intersex Conditions and Christian Theology* (London: SCM Press, 2010).
2 See Rebecca Jordan-Young, *Brain Storm* (Cambridge: Harvard University Press, 2010).

CONSTRUCTING MEN, WOMEN, AND OTHER GENDERS

Since the rise of gender constructionism, some have argued that there is simply no difference between men and women, and the categories are solely created by society. Butler argues that gender is a performance (see chapter 12), with gender (our performance of masculine or feminine) preceding sex (being male or female in a "natural"/biological/bodily way; see box 10.6).[25] Most radically, some female (second-wave) feminists would assert that they have "no vagina" and so are not biologically women, because they see this as a socially constructed concept and not a physical actuality.

A significant third-wave critique of both liberal feminism and Butlerian gender constructionism is the denial of any difference between men and women; the former, because it argues they share common rationality; the latter, because it argues they are only distinguished by social conditioning. The vast majority (see box 10.6) do have differently sexed bodies. Even the most radical female gender constructionists who deny sex and state they have "no vagina" differ from males in that men cannot give birth. However, some women cannot give birth either, so even this is not an absolute signifier of sexual/gender difference.[26] On theoretical grounds, the notion that our embodiment is only linguistically constructed can be seen as returning to problematic Greek philosophical trends which deny embodiment: mind/language is often valorized over body/physicality (see chapter 9). Further, Daniel Boyarin has argued that constructing an androgyne sexless body plays into patriarchal cultural norms, as this supposed sexless being is based upon a "masculine" norm.[27] While critical scholars accept gender constructionism's notion that "male" and "female" genders are created by society, the more radical claim that no male or female sex exists is deeply problematic. Rather, with Luce Irigaray and others, we may wish to reverse the valorization of what is prized: why do we have cultural norms that see the qualities we call "masculine" as positive and the "feminine" ones as more negative?[28]

From considering the construction of male and female, a further issue arising is the dominance of heteronormativity, or heteropatriarchy. This refers to a worldview that enforces a sense of binary gender patterns, with heterosexual relationships and desire seen as normative and natural. This is often reinforced by religious traditions, alongside popular cultural forms such as Hollywood, Bollywood, and so on. In debates over the legality of same-sex marriage, it has often been Christian churches insisting that marriage is only between a man and a woman. Transgender, where someone wishes to change their gender assigned at birth, because they feel like somebody of the opposite gender, is also often opposed on religious grounds. Despite this, there are also some religious traditions which are seen to be supportive of such standpoints, and Christian theologians have drawn from areas such as the queer theory developed by figures such as Michel Foucault (1926–1984) (see box 10.7).

FEMINISM, RACE, AND INTERSECTIONALITY

Both first-wave and second-wave feminism focused on white, Western, middle-class women. This meant the concerns of only a small group of women (literate, financially resourced, and Western-centric) became defined as normative for all women. Many feminist scholars and activists have discussed the way that feminism is defined by "whiteness" and Western norms, including bell hooks,[29] Kum-Kum Bhavani and Margaret Coulson,[30] Chandra Mohanty,[31] and Audre Lorde (1934–1992).[32] Moreover, the way that male and female are constructed in different cultures varies,[33] while distinct regional or specific feminist movements have arisen to address other contexts:[34]

- Womanist theory relates to the experience of Black African women.
- Mestiza feminist theories speak to Latino and South and Central American women.
- Islamic feminism addresses the experience of women in Islam.
- Various Asian feminist theories also exist.

These often go hand in hand with, or relate to, particular theological trends, such as womanist theology or Muslima theology.[35] These changing patterns and wider context have affected how specific issues have been addressed (see box 10.8).

BOX 10.7 **THE QUEERNESS OF RELIGIOUS IDENTITIES**

Carter Heyward and Elizabeth Stuart have pioneered queer theology, arguing that the Bible and Christian tradition subvert fixed gender identities. For instance, in Hebrew texts, God's original creation, Adama, is intersex, later separated into Adam and Eve. In medieval art, Jesus was depicted producing milk from the wound in his side (where a spear pierced him at the crucifixion), playing with notions of a male body lactating. Meanwhile, in Hindu traditions, a third gender, the *hijra*, has long been recognized, though British colonizers saw them as so offensive that they were perceived as a danger to colonial rule.[1] Normally men who identify and dress as women, they live on the edges of society but are believed to have the power to both bless and curse, so are often welcomed at high-society weddings and birth ceremonies. In some versions of the Ramayana, when the Rama asked both women and men to follow him, the *hijras*, being neither, waited for fourteen years for Rama to return, earning them a certain prestige. Moreover, modern India legally recognizes them as a third gender, meaning sex-change surgery is available at government hospitals. Early Buddhist texts also record people changing sexes within one life. (Of course, in Buddhist thought, people also change sex between rebirths.) The Buddhist monastic regulations (Vinaya), while not allowing intersex people to enter the monastic *sangha* for fear of scandal (they were associated with prostitution and promiscuity), recognized they can attain awakening/nirvana. It has also been suggested that Guanyin (see box 2.9) subverts gender norms.[2]

---

1 See Jessica Hinchey, *Governing Gender and Sexuality in Colonial India: The Hijra, c. 1850–1900* (Cambridge: Cambridge University Press, 2019).

2 See Paul Hedges, "Guanyin and Identity: The Image of a Subversive Religious Icon," *Religion and Culture* 13.1 (2012): 91–106.

Oppression of women is often no longer seen as a single issue, but as linked to oppressions based on issues including geographical location, economic situation, class, race, and so on. Focusing on race, gender, and class, Kimberlé Crenshaw has coined the term "intersectionality."[36] This dovetails with Elisabeth Schüssler Fiorenza's use of the concept of kyriarchy to replace patriarchy by implying that oppression comes from many factors (see box 10.9). Alongside this, feminist theory now includes a focus on such things as hybridity in the construction and nature of identities and religious belonging (see chapter 3).[37] There has also been a recognition of the complexity of some traditions and issues which were typically disparaged by second-wave feminist thought (see box 10.8). This overview shows that feminism does not mean one single thing, and the various waves are not monolithic. Therefore, any dismissal of feminism needs to be aware that it may simply be rejecting one particular style of feminism that many other feminists also dismiss.

BOX 10.8 **IS THE HIJAB FEMINIST OR OPPRESSIVE?**

Much feminist thought has portrayed the hijab as inherently oppressive, although veiling and bodily covering in Islamic cultures is diverse.[1] Here, we employ "veiling" and "hijab" as generic terms. In traditional feminism, the hijab is seen as something which men force women to wear. It also serves to keep the female form "othered" in social terms: unlike the male form, the female body needs covering to be accepted in the public sphere.

Many Muslim feminists accept this critique, and see veiling as patriarchal and even misogynistic, noting that neither the Quran nor the sayings of Muhammed (*hadith*) stipulate it (see box 16.12):

- Quran 33:53 is often cited in support of veiling, but in fact speaks about the prophet's wives being behind a curtain when spoken to,[2] relating to the status of a leader's wives.[3]
- Quran 33:59 suggests that women should "cast their garments over their person" when traveling so they are "not molested," but this does not mean always veiling.

Moreover, Muhammad's wives held important public positions: Khadijah was a successful businesswoman, and Aishah led an army in battle. However, in all four mainstream law schools of Sunni Islam, the hijab is mandated by the scholars (*ulama*); therefore, it is arguably required by Islamic tradition (see box 11.3). Reading the Quran's injunction that women should cover their "bosom" (Q 24:30–32), alongside other verses and certain sayings of Muhammed, the scholars have argued that women should let their headgear extend onto their bosoms, which means covering their ears, neck, and chest (*aura*). Some Muslim feminists argue this reflects a patriarchal bias. Veiling was also never universal in Muslim cultures, being associated mainly with the Arabic world, where it was seemingly adopted from the Christian Byzantine Empire.

Recently, however, some Muslim feminists have argued that wearing hijab may be a feminist act:

- Some educated (young) women voluntarily veil as a statement of their own religiosity.
- It can be a statement against the perceived objectification of women in Western culture; rather than being judged merely as bodies, or expected to wear revealing clothes for the male gaze, the hijab gives freedom.
- It arguably represents a contextual feminism not based on the cultural norms of white, Western, middle-class women.

---

1 See Elizabeth Bucar, *Pious Fashion: How Muslim Women Dress* (Cambridge: Harvard University Press, 2017).

2 Susanne C. Monahan, William Mirola, and Michael Emerson, eds., *Sociology of Religion: A Reader*, 2nd ed. (New York: Routledge, 2016), 104.

3 Leila Ahmed, *Women and Gender in Islam* (New Haven: Yale University Press, 1992), 53–54.

This is not to suggest, as Muslim feminists aver, that the hijab is inherently feminist. When women are forced to wear it, especially "heavy" veiling (i.e., the *niqab* or *burqa*), it is often seen as oppressive. Conversely, being forced to remove the veil can be seen as repressive (see case study 16B). Casting the hijab as inherently feminist or anti-feminist negates female agency in adopting or rejecting it.

BOX 10.9 **KYRIARCHY**

"Kyriarchy" is a term coined by Elisabeth Schüssler Fiorenza to replace patriarchy. It comes from the Greek term for "lord/ruler," connoting the rule of a lord, stressing not just women's oppression but oppression based on ethnicity, class, economic status, or other factors.[1] As such it connects with notions such as intersectionality.

---

1 See Helene Egnell, *Other Voices: A Study of Christian Feminist Approaches to Religious Plurality East and West* (Uppsala: Studia Missionalia Svecana, 2006), 28; and Elisabeth Schüssler Fiorenza, *But She Said: Feminist Practices of Biblical Interpretation* (Boston: Beacon Press, 1992).

Another key concept is the "outsider within," developed by Patricia Hill Collins.[38] She discusses the place of African Americans in the US as a group who belong but do not have a full place within society. It can also be employed to discuss the position of women in religious traditions. For instance, in Catholic Christianity, women cannot become priests, while in many schools of Theravada Buddhism, the order of nuns (*bhikkunis*) no longer exists (see case studies 10A and 10B, respectively). Moreover, as Francis Beale noted, there is a "double jeopardy" in the case of women who happen to be both Black and female:[39] they are oppressed not only on account of gender but also on account of race. The intersection of such identities can lead to disproportionate disadvantages. For instance, Biko Agozino has noted that Black women are often cited as the typical drug couriers despite evidence showing this group is mostly male, and that there is a lack of clear statistics on the racial profile.[40] In religious contexts, those who are double minorities likewise face a double jeopardy in terms of not being recognized by their traditions.

AGAINST PATRIARCHAL SCHOLARSHIP

Feminist thinkers have challenged many norms of patriarchal scholarship, including forms of practices, and ways of thinking developed in traditional contexts. One key theory is standpoint epistemology.[41] This argues that our ways of knowing and understanding the world are embedded in the social and cultural position we hold. It aligns with what is often termed the Rashomon effect, which says that your particular place in the world affects what you (can) see and understand. The term comes from the film *Rashomon* (1950), by Akira Kurosawa (1910–1998), in which a crime story is told from the perspective of four different witnesses, and so we see the very different ways each understands what they see based upon their context and experience. So-called memory intrusions mean that we reconstruct our memories based upon cultural expectations.[42] This argument resonates with and informs issues addressed elsewhere in this book:

- the frequent sidelining of lived religion in favor of the teachings and traditions of elites (see chapter 3)
- whether scholarship should be activist and political (see chapters 5, 7, and 18)
- the desire for objectivity and neutrality, which is belied by the facts that we speak a certain language, meaning we express our ideas in culturally and socially conditioned terms; live at a certain junction in time when particular ideas are dominant; and come from differing geographical locations which, despite our globalized and interconnected world, means we are taught in different ways, have different life chances and opportunities, and will meet and know different people who affect what we think and how we think it (see introduction and chapters 2, 5, 7, and 18)

This is not to say that all feminist scholarship has an activist agenda, that activism is the same as scholarship, or that feminist theory does not believe in truth or objective facts. However, the scholarly work of unveiling histories of oppression is arguably a political act in itself. Some argue it necessitates action, making feminism inherently activist. Certainly, from many feminist standpoints, assuming a stance of disinterested so-called objectivity supports unequal power structures and fails to reflect standpoint epistemology, which shows our situatedness.[43] Yet some scholars believe anything that looks like an activist stance has no place in the academic study of religion, even arguing that feminism is an ideology, making it data for study, like a theological belief (see chapter 2), rather than a scholarly method.[44] What it means to engage in feminist studies of religion is therefore a contested topic.

APPLYING THEORIES TO RELIGIOUS TRADITIONS

HERSTORY

Women's voices have been ignored in the historical record, which "herstory" (not history/"his-story"), seeks to reclaim. For instance:

Recovering women's activities: In ancient Greece and elsewhere, priestesses seem to have been equally active as male priests but were ignored and sidelined both then and now.[45]

Recovering specific figures: Hildegard of Bingen (1098–1179), often identified as a "mystic" (see box 8.5),[46] was a major intellectual figure who corresponded with popes and wrote some of the most significant and beautiful medieval music of her time.[47] Hildegard's thought, like that of many other women of her period, was often based in visions.[48] This has sometimes been dismissed as not worthy of serious scholarly attention, with characterizations of women's religiosity as "emotional/irrational" (see box 10.1). However, women's writings, and forms of experience, represented a way of creatively making spaces in a patriarchal social order to enable them to engage with theological and philosophical ideas.

CHALLENGING THE "MALESTREAM"

"Malestream" concepts are those based in a patriarchal worldview but which are presented as universal. The term was coined by Fiorenza. For instance:

- Christian feminist theologians have critiqued the notion that humility or selflessness is a virtue. For the male, traditionally constructed as egotistical, proud, and arrogant, humility may be a virtue. But for women, traditionally taught to be passive, submissive, and subservient (especially to men), it may be a vice by further undermining their confidence. Therefore, building confidence and pride may be the virtue that women need.[49]
- Biblical scholars have looked at the role of goddesses in the Hebrew Bible, even noting their role as a consort of the Israelite deity Yahweh (i.e., the figure identified as God), challenging the tradition's (patriarchal) self-representation.
- Islamic feminist thinkers have questioned veiling as a tradition prescribed by patriarchal traditions (see box 10.8).

One issue we may raise here is to ask what the difference is between masculine/feminine ways of thinking or scholarship, as well as what actually marks something as feminist scholarship. To help clarify one way this is perceived, we can look at the way Jeannine Hill Fletcher distinguishes between style and content.[50] She suggests two forms of scholarship:

- *Masculine style:* argumentative and objective, where the disengaged expert is distanced from the subjects of research and discussion
- *Feminine style:* dialogic and open-ended, recognizing and valuing the way personal experience informs the research and data

And she suggest three types of content:

- *Traditional content:* focuses on male actors and includes masculine biases that take male experience and perspectives as the norm for "religion"
- *Female-focused content:* includes the experience of women in the religious tradition in recognition that gender impacts one's experience in a religious tradition

- *Feminist content:* includes a systematic analysis of the ways in which religious traditions function as structures of oppression

Fletcher's labeling of some forms of scholarship as "feminine" or "masculine" may reinforce gender stereotypes. It could even be disempowering to women if they are told their work is "masculine."[51] Nevertheless, it may usefully help us see ways in which feminist scholarship approaches issues and perspectives, and particularly how it highlights that simply including women in narratives may still not be seen as doing feminist scholarship.

ECOFEMINISM AND ACTIVISM

The term "ecofeminism" was coined by Françoise d'Eaubonne (1920–2005) in 1974, and refers to the intersection of feminist thought with ecology.[52] This has been developed by figures such as Ruether and Vandana Shiva, who has drawn from Hindu thought. Shiva has argued that the privatization of land and water is driven by Western corporate greed based in a patriarchal cultural worldview.[53] Others have noted that, in many cases, exploitation of resources with higher profit margins seem to have greater negative impacts on women, the poor, indigenous groups, nature, and water resources. One mestiza group, the Con-spirando Collective (roughly translated as "breathing together"), have reconceived Christian figures such as God, Eve, and Christ to be more gender inclusive and less prone to attitudes of exploitation, as well as developing rites invoking an ancient Sumerian queen as a resource for female empowerment.[54] As discussed, much contemporary feminism is not focused only on oppression of women, but this can remain a primary focus: "In examining patriarchy, feminist theories expose the structures, such as class, race, region, religion, sexuality, and nationality, that subordinate and oppress women."[55]

Feminist scholars also study oppressive/patriarchal social and political structures and women's resistance. One example is work done by Aihwa Ong on women working in a free-trade zone factory run by the Japanese in Malaysia.[56] To resist the lack of working rights, which included demands for submission both in working practices and sexual compliance with managers, the women complained of forest demons inhabiting the factory and harassing them. At first these complaints were dismissed by the management, but mass protests by the female workforce led to the former agreeing to exorcise the factory. This was a sign of their collective power in a situation where other means of protest were unavailable.

·   ·   ·

CASE STUDY 10A. PRIESTS, PAUL, AND REWRITING TEXTS

Christian opposition to women's priesthood is often predicated upon biblical texts denying the possibility. However, feminist and historical (see chapter 4) scrutiny of the texts undermine this.

Throughout the last fifteen hundred years, most Christian traditions have denied women the opportunity to become priests. Images from the Hebrew Bible associate priestesses with what are pejoratively termed "pagan" traditions, while biblical injunctions are invoked against the possibility of women priests. Most significant is perhaps the following passage from one of Paul's letters:

> As in all the churches of the saints, the women should keep silence in the churches. For they are not permitted to speak, but should be subordinate as even the law says. If there is anything they desire to know, let them ask their husbands at home. For it is shameful for a woman to speak in church. (1 Cor. 14:33b–35)

Taking Paul as a definitive authority, Christian leaders have argued that women cannot become priests. If they cannot even talk in churches, how can they lead worship?

WHAT DIDN'T PAUL SAY?

We may cite the wider passage from which the above verses are taken:

> Let two or three prophets speak, and let the others weigh what is said. If a revelation is made to another sitting by, let the first be silent. For you can all prophesy one by one, so that all may learn and be encouraged; and the spirits of prophets are subject to prophets. For God is a God of confusion but a God of peace. [*] What! Did the word of God originate with you, or are you the only ones it has reached? If anyone thinks that he is a prophet, or spiritual, he should acknowledge that what I am writing to you is a command of the Lord. If any one does not recognize this, he is not recognized. So, my brethren, earnestly desire to prophesy, and do not forbid speaking in tongues; but all things should be done decently and in order. (1 Cor. 14:29–33a, 36–40)

This passage (omitting verses 33b–35, marked by the asterisk) is a clear and coherent argument. This alone suggests the verses cited before should not be here. But, we have at least two other reasons to believe Paul did not write 33b–35. First, early versions of this text do not normally include verses 33b–35; it appears to have been inserted later, but over time became standard. Second, Paul's other (genuine) works suggests that far from being misogynistic, he was actually a protofeminist.

WHAT DID PAUL SAY?

We may note just a few passages from Paul as indicative. First, a snippet from Romans: "Greet Prisca [other translations use Priscilla] and Aquila, my fellow workers in Jesus Christ" (Rom. 16:3 RSV). Reading this today we might pass it without notice. But, in context, it is remarkable. In the whole of Greco-Roman classical literature there are only two known passages where a wife's name is placed before her husband's: this one, and one in which a Roman emperor's mother is honored.[57] Therefore, the prestige Paul gave to Priscilla (Aquila's wife) seems remarkable; as a Christian evangelist she is honored above her husband, a man. Elsewhere, Paul makes no gender distinctions, listing men and women together as "disciples" and "preachers" (see Philemon and Philippians 4:2–3).

CONTEMPORARY DISPUTES ON WOMEN PRIESTS AND TEXTUAL AUTHORITY

In contemporary debates, Paul's words, and other historical evidence, play an important role in the debates over women priests. In many mainstream Protestant Christian traditions (but not Catholic or Orthodox traditions), women can now become priests and bishops. This partly reflects changing gender roles in society. But, a reevaluation of biblical evidence is significant: Jesus seems to have regarded some female followers as significant parts of his movement, and Paul supported women priests.

However, opponents of women priests often argue contrarily. Certainly, most historical evidence concerns interpretation rather than clear fact (see chapter 4), although the majority of historians accept that women held roles equating to what we would today term "priests" in the early centuries of Christianity. Critics note that Paul only ever termed women as "deacons," a rank today below priest. But this hierarchy did not exist in Paul's day: "deacon" is a privileged title in Paul's work. Importantly, because the traditional stance (against women priests) is often seen as normative, many countries provide laws exempting Christian churches from gender equality legislation on employment.

REFLECTIONS

Some questions can help us draw out the issues from this case study:

1. Many Christians struggle with the suggestion that the accepted canon (authorized biblical text) has been tampered with. Despite clear evidence that Paul's letters were edited, most churches resist changes to the canon. From the stance of an advocate of women's priesthood, how would you view the continuing presence of texts which deny them this right in the Bible? Is the text honored by tradition and therefore sacrosanct despite being inauthentic?
2. The historical evidence points to a female-friendly attitude (by both Jesus and Paul) in the early Jesus movement (see box 4.11). Do you think Christianity is therefore inherently patriarchal, or not?
3. To what extent do you think that religious traditions should be allowed to be exempt from gender equality laws on employment? How does this relate to laws on freedom of religion (see chapter 16)?

CASE STUDY 10B. BUDDHIST FEMINISMS AND NUNS

We reflect upon some ways that Buddhist feminists have engaged their tradition.

FOUNDING THE FEMALE MONASTIC SANGHA

Initially the Buddhist monastic community (*sangha*) contained only monks. In due course, a fourfold order emerged: monks (*bhikkhu*), nuns (*bhikkuni*), laymen, and laywomen. This led to monastic-lay and male-female demarcations, signifying—in both cases—higher-lower statuses. Traditional records suggest founding the nuns order was contested. Initially the Buddha refused requests by women for ordination, even though his own mother wished to become a nun. These women went to the Buddha's close disciple Ananda, who queried the Buddha: can women attain awakening/nirvana? The Buddha replied in the affirmative. So, Ananda pushed: why refuse them the opportunity to become monastics? This account troubles Buddhist feminists because the Buddha is portrayed as resisting. Further, it is recorded that the Buddha argued the refusal was because if women were ordained the whole monastic community and his teachings (*dharma*) would disappear five hundred years earlier than they would have otherwise. Hence, for some, the nuns order has always been regarded as problematic. Notably, textual analysis and Buddhist feminist thought suggests much of this record was created later. He may have resisted at first, but almost certainly did not claim it would affect the monastic community and his teachings.

Further, it seems the Buddha insisted on eight extra rules for nuns, though currently Theravada nuns have 311 rules compared to 227 for monks. Some were to avoid scandal (so no gender mixing), but two are notable:

·   Nuns cannot ordain other nuns; this requires both monks and nuns.
·   Although seniority in the monastic order is normally based on time ordained, every nun was required to bow to any monk no matter the seniority level (i.e., a nun ordained for seventy years must bow to a monk ordained for only one hour).

NUNS IN THERAVADA BUDDHISM TODAY

By about the eleventh century, the nuns' order in Theravada Buddhism was in decline, and had disappeared by about the thirteenth century. It remained in Mahayana Buddhism. Moreover, nuns always had lower prestige:

·   Despite the Buddha's recorded assertion that women could attain awakening, this was denied by many later Buddhist traditions.
·   Laypeople often saw gifts to nuns giving less merit than gifts to monks.
·   Due to the prophesy of the teaching declining due to nuns, some saw their decline as beneficial.

Nevertheless, from at least the nineteenth century, women wishing to follow a monastic path in Theravada Buddhist–majority countries organized lay (non-monastic), female celibate communities. In the twentieth century, moves were made to ordain new nuns.

This renewal is deeply controversial, and many do not acknowledge these ordinations. One reason is that nuns ordaining nuns breaks the regulation that says both monks and nuns are needed. However, Mahayana monks have been involved in ordaining new Theravada nuns. Again, opponents argue this is illegitimate as they represent a different lineage, though supporters of nuns reply that the Mahayana lineage came originally from the same lineage.[58] Today, an increasing number of women from Theravada Buddhist backgrounds are seeking ordination as nuns, often through Taiwanese Mahayana lineages. This is sometimes part of Buddhist feminist movements. However, other feminists may object that it subjects women to inherently patriarchal traditions.

REFLECTIONS

The following questions will allow us to consider some issues raised here:

1. Using Patricia Hill Collins's notion of "outsiders within," how do you think the experience of being a woman in Theravada Buddhism, which does not allow female nuns, affects their experience within that religion? Are they "second-class citizens," especially those who aspire to the monastic life? Are they less of an insider (see chapter 2) in some way? Reflect on a situation in which you are an "outsider within" to help think through this.
2. Buddhists argue about whether founding the nuns order was protofeminist, being the first ever female monastic community, or whether it was deeply patriarchal, burdening them as second class. Consider the arguments on each side.
3. Is the reordination of women as Theravada Buddhist nuns a feminist movement? Consider different definitions of what feminism may or may not be.

· · ·

QUESTIONS AND CONNECTING THOUGHTS

Because women are part of religious traditions, we could suggest interactions with every chapter. But specific connections relate to perceptions of the female in colonial contexts (chapter 7); issues around embodiment (chapter 9); women's religious practices as lived religion being sidelined (chapter 3); the construction of gender and sexual identities in social identity theory (chapter 6), and social constructionism (chapter 5). We can discuss various issues raised:

1. Mary Daly said: "If God is male, then the male is God." What do you understand by this? Do you believe that men are exalted if traditions display predominantly masculine images of deity with male-only hierarchies?

2. Is taking a feminist stance in religious studies simply about highlighting women's roles in the traditions studied, or does it involve taking on specific methodological stances, or even an activist agenda for equality and justice?

3. How do you understand the intersectionality of women's rights with issues such as race and class? Do you think that women's rights issues can simply be looked at on their own, or must they be studied interconnectedly? Is the issue primarily kyriarchy rather than patriarchy?

4. Queer theory and gender construction has challenged the notion that there are only two sexes, or that gender roles are straightforward and "natural." What resonance does this find in religion? To what extent is it a challenge for and to religions?

5. With reference to a tradition you are familiar with, in what ways do you think women may be outsiders within? How do some people face issues of double jeopardy within religious traditions by being marginalized in more than one way?

FURTHER READING

THEORY

Anderson, Leona, and Pamela Dickey Young, eds., *Women and Religious Traditions,* 3rd ed. (Oxford: Oxford University Press, 2015).

Avishai, Orit. "Theorizing Gender from Religion Cases: Agency, Feminist Activism, and Masculinity," *Sociology of Religion* 77.3 (2016): 261–79.

Juschka, Darlene. "Feminism and Gender Theory," in *The Oxford Handbook of the Study of Religion,* ed. Michael Stausberg and Steven Engler (Oxford: Oxford University Press, 2016), 137–49.

Machado, Maria Das Dores Campos. "Sexuality and Religion: Homosexuality and Religious Values," in *Controversies in Contemporary Religion,* ed. Paul Hedges, vol. 2 (Santa Barbara: Praeger, 2014), 53–76.

Mohanty, Chandra. "Under Western Eyes: Feminist Scholarship and Colonial Discourses," *Feminist Review* 30 (1988): 65–88.

Swidler, Arlene. *Homosexuality and World Religions* (Valley Forge, PA: Trinity Press International, 1993).

Wheeler, Kayla. "Women in Religion: Does Gender Matter?," in Hedges, *Controversies in Contemporary Religion,* vol. 2, 1–21.

CASE STUDY 10A. PAUL, PRIESTS, AND REWRITING TEXTS

Furnish, Victor. *The Moral Teachings of Paul* (Nashville: Abingdon Press, 1979), 84–114.

Torjesen, Karen. "Reconstruction of Women's Early Christian History," in *Searching the Scriptures: A Feminist Introduction,* ed. Elisabeth Schüssler Fiorenza (London: SCM Press, 1993), 290–310.

Young, Frances. "Hermeneutical Questions: The Ordination of Women in the Light of Biblical and Patristic Typology," in *Women and Ordination in the Christian Churches: Interna-*

tional Perspectives, ed. Ian Jones, Janet Wootton, and Kirsty Thorpe (London: T. & T. Clark, 2008), 21–39.

Young, Pamela Dickey. "Women in Christianity," in *Women and Religious Traditions,* Anderson and Young, eds.

CASE STUDY 10B. BUDDHIST FEMINISMS

Cantwell, Cathy. *Buddhism: The Basics* (New York: Routledge, 2010), 129–39.

Crosby, Kate. *Theravada Buddhism: Continuity, Diversity, and Identity* (Chichester: Wiley-Blackwell, 2014), 218–37.

Falk, Monica. "Women in Between: Becoming Religious Persons in Thailand," in *Women's Buddhism, Buddhism's Women: Tradition, Revision, Renewal,* ed. Ellison Findly (Boston: Wisdom Publications, 2000), 37–57.

Neumaier, Eva K. "Women in the Buddhist Traditions," in Anderson and Young, *Women and Religious Traditions,* 75–106.

Wilson, Liz. "Buddhism and Gender," in *Buddhism in the Modern World,* ed. David McMahan (New York: Routledge, 2012), 257–72.

COMPARISON
Comparative and Contrastive Methodologies

IN WHICH WE EXPLORE:

Scholarly discourse supporting and criticizing comparative religion

Methodology and debates relating to comparative religion

Contemporary justifications for comparison in the wider academic discourse

Case studies exploring Hinduism and Judaism, and Zen Buddhist and Protestant Christian sitting practices

INTRODUCTION

Comparative religion was once the mainstay of the academic study of religion, but for some scholars the whole venture is now in doubt for, as Richard King tells us, "anxiety about generating cross-cultural claims has cast doubt upon the very possibility of a *comparative* study of religion."[1] Reasons for these doubts include the following:

- If religion itself is a disputed concept that is not found across cultures, then comparison may be argued to be illegitimate as what is compared are different areas of society, culture, and experience.

- Many of the "great comparativists" of the twentieth century employed questionable methods, for example, having an implicit theological agenda or subsuming specifics to generic symbolic frameworks.

- Acts of comparison may distort, especially when involving broad concepts or making sweeping claims across traditions.

Here, we will not explore the history of how comparative method lost its once central role.[2] However, we must address the doubts and criticisms to argue why we should include comparison in the scholar's toolbox. While we will focus primarily on methods and theories in good practice, it is necessary that we discuss critiques and doubts about comparison for at least two reasons:

- It is certainly possible (and easy) to do comparison badly, and the critical debates keep us alert as to what should be avoided.
- For comparison to be accepted as a viable method in the study of religion, we must address arguments against it, not just arguments in favor of it.

CRITICISMS OF COMPARATIVE RELIGION
SCHOLARLY TRENDS

In chapter 1, we argued that the category religion can still be meaningfully employed, despite the modern Western (Christian and colonial) perspective that informs the world religion paradigm (WRP) (see box 2.1). Moreover, many critics of comparative religion's legacy do not argue we should entirely abandon the practice. For instance, a scholar often seen as one of comparison's greatest critics, Jonathan Z. Smith (1938–2017), targeted bad comparison, not comparison per se,[3] though, arguably, he is too prescriptive in delimiting the possibility of comparison.

Comparison is a normative practice in many fields: we see studies of comparative politics, philosophy, philology, and poetry.[4] But, more deeply, it is one of the fundamental aspects of human understanding. As Jeppe Sinding Jensen has put it: "Comparison drives our intentionality and inference-systems."[5] As humans, we place new things in relation to things already known (see introduction and box 2.6). All attempts to explain or understand are infused with comparison. We say something is like something else; we discuss similarities or differences; and, even when contrasting, we play the game of comparison (x is not like y). To know means to compare. Perhaps consider whether you are comparing what you are reading here with other ideas you have previously read or heard.

POOR COMPARISON

However, comparison may be done badly. Poor comparison by major twentieth century scholars led J. Z. Smith to set strict and exacting limits on the practice. He argued that much comparison was a "magical act" of creating something new (see box 11.1). In part, he was correct. Comparison is inventive: we place two things together to see what we had not seen before. However, as Jensen states: "There really is 'no problem' (my favorite Caribbean ethno-theory) but then perhaps also less 'magic' and 'mystique.'"[6] Here, we

JONATHAN Z. SMITH'S TYPOLOGY OF COMPARISONS

In his essay "In Comparison a Magic Dwells," Jonathan Z. Smith (1938–2017) identifies three main forms of comparative method, each of which he claims are problematic.[1] They are the encyclopedic, the morphological, and the ethnographic. He also mentions a fourth, the evolutionary. Criticizing early scholars of religion such as James G. Frazer (1854–1941), whose book *The Golden Bough* (1890) collected myth and folklore across the world to identify patterns within them, Smith claims such comparative approaches are problematically about the memory of the scholar. Things sometimes ring a bell and get classed together, with few rules that define what should be remembered as significant. Hence comparison is often unsystematic and "magical."

Ethnographic comparison: This is based on a traveler's impressions, and is not systematic. It is primarily idiosyncratic.

Encyclopedic comparison: A topical arrangement is made under classes which the scholar decides on. But rarely, Smith claims, does the scholar explain where these categories come from, nor are they properly compared or explained.

Morphological comparison: This is said to be about archetypes and binaries, such as "representative/aberrant" or "progressive/degraded," made to rank or rate aspects of a tradition. Such comparison, Smith suggests, normally relies upon moments of special "insight" or an "intuitive leap."

Evolutionary comparison: This is about the dynamics of change and adaptation over time. However, he says he knows of no satisfactory example.

---

1 J. Z. Smith, "In Comparison a Magic Dwells," in Patton and Ray, *A Magic Still Dwells*, 23–44.

will employ J. Z. Smith's term "magic" to speak about what seem to be illicit comparisons that lack analytic rigor. However, with Jensen, we oppose a strong interpretation of "magic" which would suggest all comparison is impossible, as if it were only ever "conjuring up" false similarities. Rather, it is something quite "natural."

AVOIDING "MAGIC" IN COMPARISON
KEY METHODOLOGICAL GUIDES

J. Z. Smith quotes a phrase from one of Plato's later dialogues: "A cautious man should above all be on his guard against resemblances; they are a very slippery sort of thing."[7] This is certainly true. Those who have learned a foreign language will probably have come across what are sometimes termed "false friends": words which look like a word in your own language, but have subtly different or even utterly different meanings. When we come to comparison, we also need to be aware of such problems. Here, we can usefully think about how some introductions to religion are structured around the WRP, such that each religion is introduced under a range of broadly similar categories—founders, scriptures, priesthood, rituals, doctrines, and so on. This may lead to the sense that each religion is of a broadly similar type with easily comparable elements that relate to each other in very straightforward ways. But this can be "magic," the conjuring up of seeming similarities where they do not exist. We will explore the category "scripture" to show typical problems.

ON NOT COMPARING SCRIPTURES

Most of those traditions we call religions have significant texts, which might be mapped onto a list like this:

- Buddhism: Tripitaka
- Christianity: Bible
- Confucianism: Classics
- Daoism: Daodejing
- Hinduism: Vedas
- Islam: Quran
- Judaism: Tanakh
- Sikhism: Guru Granth Sahib

However, any comparison based on this would probably hide more than it reveals. In *What is Scripture?*,[8] Wilfred Cantwell Smith argues that "scripture" is a common category and for comparison we only need extend it beyond Christianity. While insightful in various ways, W. C. Smith's text fails to grasp key facets of difference, including:

- the meaning of "scripture,"
- differing significances and interpretations, and
- the texts in context.

More issues could be raised, but these three serve our purposes. First, the English term "scripture" comes from Greek (via Latin) meaning "the writings." In the Christian New Testament, it referred to what became the Christian Old Testament (Hebrew Bible), and later became used for the entire Christian Bible in the sense of the inspired or authoritative books.[9] For some, this is reason to dismiss it, arguing that a Christian word speaks only to that tradition; this, however, commits the etymological fallacy (see box 11.2).

However, the Christian usage gives rise to a valid criticism: not all the books that W. C. Smith says we can call "scripture" are (seen as) "inspired" or "divine revelation." Seen this way, "scripture" is misleading: the Confucian Classics are seen as human texts coming from what we may term "wise sages"; the Buddhist Tripitaka is believed to be the teachings of the Buddha rather than divine revelation.[10]

BOX 11.2 **THE ETYMOLOGICAL FALLACY**

A philosophical term for confusing a term's origins (its etymology) with its meaning by either:

- assuming a word can only ever have the meaning originally ascribed to it, or
- arguing because a word comes from one place or tradition, that it can only ever be meaningfully used of that place or tradition.

All words come from somewhere and have a history, they evolve in meaning and usage over time. However, from a scholarly standpoint, we need to be aware of how a word is used differently in varying contexts. A good example is a Darwinian catchphrase: "survival of the fittest." In modern English, we associate "fit" with being physically strong, well-toned, and so on, and hence assume that it means that the strongest and most powerful will win. However, in nineteenth century English, as Darwin used it, "fit" most commonly meant "appropriate" or "suitable" (i.e., is it a good fit). Therefore, it suggests not the strongest physically but those best adapted would survive. Yet, we do not say that "fit" is used incorrectly today because the meaning has changed.

Would replacing "scripture" with a more "neutral" term such as "classics" or "significant texts" help? Probably not, for we would still find ourselves in a veritable comparative minefield. Such an endeavor might involve assuming that words meaningful to us are universally applicable (see box 11.5, below). Further, which texts are significant (the "classics")? Is it only certain presumed "original" texts from "founders"? We would find many texts not fitting this criterion, while it does not address the diverse traditions around these texts.

Second, let us therefore look at the significance and interpretation of the texts. We must remember that texts are not always what is most important. Arguably, Islam is the tradition that gives its text the greatest significance. As Sunni Islam developed, it became normative to regard the Quran as the Word of God, and untranslatable from Arabic because this is how it was delivered verbatim from God as a coeternal truth. However, Muslims have not traditionally gone directly to the Quran (see box 11.3). While many fundamentalist (see chapter 15) Protestant Christians speak of the Bible as inerrant and believe they can understand it directly, for Catholics and many other Christians the Bible is only one pillar; equally important, or for some more so, is tradition. Oral teachings and tradition may have equal or more authority than the text itself.[11] The Protestant idea of *sola scriptura,* "by scripture alone," which implied that anyone could come to and know God's revelation simply by reading the Bible for themselves only developed in the sixteenth century. Indeed, historically, it is an unusual concept (see box 5.5).

The idea that you need a community to interpret texts has a resonance beyond comparison.[12] While the common (modern Western) assumption is that if you want to know

BOX 11.3 **QURAN, *HADITH,* AND INTERPRETATION**

Although the Quran is revelation for Islam, Muslims interpret it through the lens of the sayings of Muhammad (*hadith*). These are sometimes spoken of as a second layer of Islamic "scripture." Moreover, in terms of application, Islamic tradition asserts that *hadith* are secondary to the consensus of the scholars (*ulama*), as Muhammad is quoted as saying his community would never go astray. There is even a *hadith* which says that in the future some people will ask what the Quran says and base their understanding on that, however, we are told that such people are actually outside of Islam! Therefore while, as revelation, the Quran is supreme, followed by the *hadith*, in traditional Islamic interpretation the Quran does not take precedence. Only through the example of Muhammad and then subsequent scholars have Muslims traditionally interpreted what the Quran means.[1]

1 See Jonathan Brown, *Misquoting Muhammad: The Challenge and Choices of Interpreting the Prophet's Legacy* (Oxford: Oneworld, 2014), especially 17–18.

what a religion teaches you should go and read its texts, a "straightforward," or literal, reading will not reveal how it is understood and interpreted, nor what it meant when written centuries earlier.[13] Besides, even the most literalist readers do not read everything literally (see chapter 15).

Third, we address the texts in context. Texts have meanings in relation to other texts and the wider tradition. The theological significance of the Bible for Christians and the Quran for Muslims is an example (see box 11.4). The actual significance of texts, their role, and interpretive strategies as part of the wider tradition are also important:

- The Buddhist tradition was originally an oral one because it was believed that written teachings were inferior to the passing of tradition by word of mouth.

- In Daoism, initiation into any lineage relies on master-to-disciple transmission; the texts were often considered too obscure to simply read and understand. Indeed, the Daodejing, while often taken as the "original" and "foundational" text, was for many Daoist traditions relatively insignificant as it told you neither how to develop spiritual practices nor how to perform rituals.[14]

- Standard textbook introductions to Hinduism will tell you that the Vedas are the central texts. However, written in Sanskrit, they were, and remain, inaccessible and largely irrelevant to most Hindus. People are more familiar with the two epics (the Ramayana and Mahabharata) and the specific devotional texts (Puranas) of their own tradition. Moreover, the three most significant deities of contemporary Hindu devotion (Vishnu, Shiva, and the Goddess) are either peripheral or absent in the Vedas.[15]

BOX 11.4 **SHOULD WE COMPARE THE QURAN TO THE BIBLE OR JESUS?**

It is a commonplace that Islam and Christianity are textual traditions ("religions of the book"). The Quran and the Bible are fundamental for each tradition. Yet a direct comparison is problematic. From about the eleventh century, in Sunni Islam, the Quran was accepted to be not only a verbatim record of the Revelation, via Gabriel, from God (see box 13.11), understood to have been received by Muhammad, but moreover literally the Word of God as not simply the words spoken to Muhammad at that time, but something co-eternal with God (in this box, capitals denote the exalted status of these concepts in their specific tradition).[1] In other words, the Quran was not just contextual as something made known to Muhammad at a specific time and place, but a fundamental Truth that is everlasting and unchangeable (though in Islamic interpretation of the Quran, some verses are superseded by others, termed "abrogation"). Meanwhile, what became orthodox Christian reflection on Jesus (Christology) defined him as the Word of God: co-eternal with the Father, part of the tripartite deity (Trinity), and God's Revelation in human form.[2] Therefore, it has been argued that comparison should be between the Quran and Jesus:[3] both are the co-eternal Word of God and the Revelation of the divine on Earth. Notably, within mainstream Christian thought, terming the Bible the "word of god" may be said to be honorific as it records Jesus as Revelation; some theologians even argue that certain Protestant language about the Bible being "Revelation" and the "Word of God" borders on heresy (false teaching) because it makes pieces of paper equal to the Incarnation/Revelation of God, that is, Jesus. The distinction is theological, but significant for the careful scholar of religion because it points to the contextual understanding of these texts within their tradition.

---

1 See Michael Cook, *The Koran: A Very Short Introduction* (Oxford: Oxford University Press, 2000), 109–15.

2 See McGrath, *Historical Theology*, 61–69.

3 See Paul Hedges, "The Contemporary Context of Muslim-Christian Dialogue," in *Contemporary Muslim-Christian Encounters: Developments, Diversity, Dialogues*, ed. Paul Hedges (London: Bloomsbury, 2015): 17–32, 26. Stephen Prothero extends the analogy, suggesting that Muhammad is like the Virgin Mary who births the Word of God, and he suggests reading the Quran is like the Christian Eucharist in being "how you incorporate the divine into your body"; see Stephen Prothero, *God Is Not One: The Eight Rival Religions That Run the World* (New York: HarperOne, 2010), 39.

Our discussion so far shows that the category of "scripture" or "significant texts" tells us little about the meaning, readership, usage, or nature of the texts described.

OUR NORMS ARE NOT UNIVERSAL

Implicit in what we have said above is the danger of applying our terms as universal models for comparison. Every word or phrase is embedded in a cultural and social milieu that grounds it. However, even critical scholars sometimes seem to assume that the words of their own culture have a universal applicability (see box 11.5). Of course, this is not to say that we can never use words derived from English, or even Christian, contexts for comparison. We all stand within particular places and so must talk from our context. Robert Campany ably dismisses what he (ironically) terms the "essentially theological" nature of (secular) scholarly arguments about the permissibility of only using "local terms" (i.e., those derived from the place or time studied). Campany argues that this assumes an "Immaculate Cultural Other" before which we can only be silent.[16] For instance, in the contemporary context, if we decry the use of English terms/concepts, we could not talk (in English, or with words derived from English contexts) about French politics, Japanese economic policies, or Malaysian elections. Rather, in scholarly terms, we need to be aware that we are using terms that speak to our concerns, yet may provide insights beyond our context (see box 1.8). Indeed, one would need to fully study and understand another culture (on its own terms, and in its own language) before it would be possible to say that such terms have no comparative utility.

ON NOT BEING ILLUMINATED

In contradistinction to J. Z. Smith, Arvind Sharma argues that those occasions when memory suggests a link are significant.[17] Speaking of "reciprocal illumination" Sharma says we gain meaningful personal insights. As an example, he tells us how his understanding of divine providence based on a story from Hinduism was extended when he read a passage from the *Zhuangzi*, despite it coming from a nontheistic tradition.[18] We are no doubt all familiar with sudden "breakthrough moments" to a new understanding triggered by a similarity or likeness. Sharma says these are "truths" which deepen our understanding. We may feel Sharma's model is common sense. However, let us stick with J. Z. Smith a little longer, to see why, at a scholarly level, this "illumination" is "magical."

If some things seem meaningful to us, this may be existentially valuable. However, is it illuminating in any analytical or scholarly way? I will give an example (recalled from memory and slightly adapted) of part of a conversation I witnessed:

A: So which bits of these texts are the scriptures?

B: They are all scriptures.

A: But some parts must be revelation, and others commentary on that revelation?

B: Er, no, they are all writings by our founder and successors.

A: Then the writings by the founder are the scriptures, and the other bits interpret that.

B: No, they're all part of our scriptures.

A: But some parts you said are about religion, and others deal with other topics. So those first parts are the revelation, and the others must be interpretation on applying the religion.

B: We don't make that distinction.

DID THE POPE DELIVER A HOMILY OR A PEP TALK?

Russell McCutcheon has argued that a talk by Pope Benedict XVI should not be spoken of by scholars as a homily.[1] This, he argues, is a native/theological/insider term, and so has no analytic validity (on "insider," see chapter 2). However, saying the Pope's "pep talk," McCutcheon argues, has analytic comparative validity. McCutcheon argues we must dismiss terms with "religious" baggage, though he does not develop a rationale for the corollary, which is to replace them with "secular" terms (see chapter 16). This raises an analytic question about how far our cultural milieu affects what we believe are meaningful terms for comparison. McCutcheon seems to argue a term from his own cultural milieu (contemporary American popular culture) is analytic and can carry weight across cultural divides, whereas other terms (from other cultural realms) cannot. Later in the talk, he argues that if an Indian came and tried to describe him in terms of "caste," this would be invalid; perhaps he does not see himself this way, but class divisions—often determined by birth (in the US context often therefore racial)—are deeply inbuilt in Western societies. What inherently makes "pep talk" a "good" term and "caste" a "bad" term is not explained beyond what makes sense to McCutcheon.[2] One might argue that "class" is more universal and "caste" more specific, but this reflects a sense of Western concepts/theory as universal. However, the very terms we choose will inevitably shape what it is we see, and taking only our own culture's terms limits our vision. This is not to suggest that McCutcheon sees his culture as better than others, or that he thinks American cultural terms have a universal validity. Nevertheless, the way his argument is structured fits into a pattern whereby Western cultural terms are prioritized over those from elsewhere (see box 11.7, and chapter 7).

---

1 See Russell McCutcheon, "Religion before 'Religion,' or the Persistence of Imagining Religion," lecture at the Leibniz University, Hanover, Germany (7 February 2011), www.youtube.com/watch?v=Cxk7_-7PxEw; and William Arnal and Russell McCutcheon, *The Sacred Is the Profane: The Political Nature of "Religion"* (Oxford: Oxford University Press, 2012), ix–x. It is notable that McCutcheon is a well-known critic of the term "religion," arguing it has no meaningful content, yet can seemingly readily identify things which are "religious" and so seemingly has a fixed notion of what "religion" is.

2 Kathryn McClymond was told (by another scholar) that "*dharma*" (an Indian term typically denoting something like "duty") only makes sense in relation to Hinduism, while English terms such as "law" are universal; meaning, she argues, that we "'other' non-Christian, non-Western (and non-English based) traditions," Kathryn McClymond, "Comparison as Conversation and Craft," *Religions* 9.39 (2018): 1–9, 3.

In this conversation, A came from a religion where his "scripture" has two clear parts: the "revelation" and the "interpretation." Therefore, he asked B how her scriptures made sense in his terms. B's tradition, however, did not make such a distinction; she framed all the writings as "scripture." Now, it may have been existentially helpful for A to try and think about other people's texts in ways which were like his. But, to B, the insights that A was trying to make violated her sense of her texts. Nevertheless, I am pretty sure that A walked away from the conversation feeling that he now understood B's texts better because he had worked out which bits were revelation and which bits were interpretation or commentary. This one example is, of course, far from an argument that all such forms of understanding are flawed or distorting. However, our meaningful insights or "illuminations" may not be scholarly or accurate. This, we may suggest, is what J. Z. Smith means by comparison being "magical"; something that is conjured with little analytic value, despite resonating personally.

However, while comparison may be badly done, it is not illicit. King tells us that there is "a vitally important role for the comparative study of religion in the modern academy."[19]

GETTING DOWN TO COMPARATIVE AND CONTRASTIVE ACTS
DIFFERENCE AND METHODOLOGICAL MANIPULATION

So far, we have not said why this chapter (and this section) goes by the double terminology of "comparative" and "contrastive." Hopefully the reason will become clear here. Any act of comparison only helps so far; in it we gain but we also lose. The endeavor calls for both comparison and contrast (see box 11.6). This is key for J. Z. Smith, who states: "Comparison requires the acceptance of difference as the grounds of it being interesting, and a methodological manipulation of that difference to achieve some stated cognitive end."[20] Methodological manipulation means we do not simply put two things next to each other and expect to be illuminated. Rather, we need to actively engage this difference to clarify some end. Of course, we may at times discover something other than what we expected. We can even contend, contra J. Z. Smith, that at times the discovery of some similarity may be just as "interesting." But, on the whole, it is only because of difference that comparison, and contrast, helps us see what we had not seen before.

TYPES OF COMPARISON

We should briefly discuss what types of comparison are advocated here. We have mentioned J. Z. Smith's taxonomy of four types of comparison. However, Oliver Freiberger notes these are designed primarily "to reveal the deficiencies of past scholarship,"[21] so are not neutral descriptions. Moreover, J. Z. Smith's pejorative usage of "magic" seems to make comparison almost illegitimate and ignores its very ordinariness; yet as Jensen told us, it is "no problem." Various other typologies of comparison have also been advanced;[22] however, each has its own agenda and favors certain forms of practice over others. Perhaps, the most useful is J. Z. Smith's twofold use of homology and analogy, adapted from the biological sciences:[23]

- "Homology" refers to biological descent and implies a direct connection; hence two things can be compared because of their related lineage.

- "Analogy" is about similar functions or shared traits, though lacking common descent.
- An example of a homologue is wings in two bird species, and an analogue is wings in birds compared to insects.

The former relates to J. Z. Smith's evolutionary category in his taxonomy. However, as Campany argues, in many contexts we are more likely to be looking at analogies, and so will expect both differences and similarities.[24] Beyond this, we will not posit any type of comparison as either inherently licit or illicit;[25] even a much-vaunted criticism, that only small-scale, localized comparison is permissible and grand-scale whole-tradition comparison is always illegitimate, does not stand critical scrutiny (see case study 11A).[26] Rather, with J. Z. Smith, our focus is how to do "methodological manipulation" for "stated cognitive ends."

COMPARING AND CONTRASTING: TWO GUIDING RULES

One of the twentieth century's most significant works of comparative religion was Mircea Eliade's (1907–1986) *Patterns in Comparative Religion*.[27] *Patterns* classified the myths and narratives of various religions into categories and subcategories, including "The Sky and Sky Gods," "The Moon and Its Mystique," "The Earth, Woman, and Fertility," and "Sacred Places: Temple, Palace, 'Centre of the World.'" Eliade's work has been heavily critiqued, particularly for being theological and for collapsing specifics into his unifying criteria. One image he expounded on at length was the *axis mundi*, or center of the world, which was exemplified, he believed, in various stories of cosmic trees or central mountains.[28] Critics argue that Eliade exaggerated the significance of marginal myths to make them seem like universal patterns of religion while also distorting elements of various stories to fit a common predetermined narrative that he believed all *axis mundi* images should exhibit. Of course, this does not mean that he never pointed to any common elements. But he stressed similarity at the expense of difference. His method was simply comparative and not contrastive. A first methodological rule is to remain aware of the dangers of seeing, or making, patterns which do not exist: the magical conjuring act.

The concepts of lived religion (chapter 3) and material religion (chapter 9) stress that religion is not so much about doctrine as it is about practice and habits, as well as physical regimes. This is not to deny, especially in some situations, that doctrine is an essential aspect, especially for defining barriers and lineages within elite traditions. Yet, even within one "religion," we see many doctrinal differences. It is therefore difficult to know what should be made of any doctrinal similarities (and differences) across religions. Moreover, doctrines mean little if divorced from how they are lived out in practice. Indeed, Gavin Flood states: "Arguably, it is in practices, rather than in doctrines, that we find a deeper commonality to religions."[29] How beliefs or traditions get lived out, and operate within the human social world, is therefore perhaps the place to look. We may relate this to social identity theory (chapter 6), where the "self" (our personal sense of who we are) is not analytically useful, while "identity" (enacted social behavior) is useful. The abstract or internal remains less useful unless we can identify it with aspects of social reality, such as form, function, structure, and meaning, as Jensen argues.[30] That is to say, it is not simply that we can only compare actions or behavior (material aspects); we can also compare words and ideas, but only as they become part of a shared social structure. A second methodological rule, therefore, is to focus on practices and social structures rather than doctrines.

COMPARING AND CONTRASTING: CATEGORIES FOR THINKING

Flood has studied ascetic, what are often termed "mystical" (see box 8.5), traditions, and argues for common forms of behavior and expression across religions. For instance, he has shown the significance of ritual expression and also common motifs of ascent and descent.[31] Importantly, Flood stresses context, not just looking for similarity but also difference. Indeed, while we argued a category such as "scripture" fails as a comparative model, it can be useful if we take a comparative and contrastive method. If we subsume one tradition to categories from another, then we will likely distort the former. However, would it be impermissible to look perhaps at the Confucian Classics and ask in what senses they are not like the scripture of Christianity? Or, contrarily, take the notion of the "classic" in its Confucian sense, *jing,* and ask, how does this apply to the Christian biblical texts? Such a tool may help provoke us into thinking about:

- what we do see, and do not see; and
- what we do understand, and do not understand.

None of this suggests any essential classification of either as "scripture" or "classic." The key point is that some categories come from a deep investigation into particular areas of traditions (as in Flood's example) or may be more ad hoc investigative methods, as in the example of "scripture" and "classic." Comparative and contrastive categories need not carry the weight of universal themes that marked Eliade's work. There are also fairly universal experiences across cultures; death is an example. While conceptualized differently, without too much overgeneralization, most religious traditions have invested resources in theorizing what happens, how humans should respond, and appropriate practices.[32] The death rites of, for instance, Sunni Islam and Theravada Buddhism in contemporary Thailand, or Humanism and Methodist Christianity in the UK, could be examples where comparison might be legitimately employed. The aim might be to see how particular communities respond or how death is managed within and across families whose identities are informed by different religious or cultural traditions.

Another example might be what we can broadly term "sacred space"—temples, churches, gurdwaras, synagogues, or sacred groves. We would not wish to suggest that the terms "sacred" (see box 18.7), or even "space," mean the same thing in each case; our focus would be on human meaning making in geographical spaces (see chapter 17). However, within a comparative and contrastive perspective, our aim would not be to inscribe a single meaning onto such places, but rather to understand the differences. Indeed, we could also explore "secular" (see chapter 16) spaces with "sacred" significance, such as civic or war memorials, including the Lincoln Memorial in Washington, DC, or the Cenotaph in London. Our access is always and only to the social and cultural worlds of expression: "We never compare the things 'in themselves,' only the stories about them."[33]

GROUNDING COMPARISON THEORETICALLY

While we have discussed some rules for responsible comparison, we must also consider the theoretical possibility. As King told us, there is "anxiety about generating cross-cultural claims" because some question the very possibility of cross-cultural understanding and communication. To answer such critics, Flood has developed arguments that combine hermeneutical phenomenology, the cognitive science of religion, and social cognition. Here, we combine these with social constructionism and linguistic philosophy to ground comparative methodology.[34]

For Flood, hermeneutical phenomenology is "the enterprise of explaining and understanding what shows itself as always mediated through signs, texts and histories."[35] This allows an orientation toward seeking an understanding of human practices in history "because all human beings perform cultural practices" which "allows me to understand the cultural practices of others as well as my own."[36] It is only because we already know certain things that we can understand anything else, so our preconceptions form the basis of everything else that we come to know; this is another way of stating that all knowledge is inherently comparative. It invokes Hans-Georg Gadamer's (1900–2002) reimagining of "prejudice" as positive: that our existing concepts ("prejudices") are what make new knowledge possible (see introduction and box 2.6). This brief statement glosses over the technicalities of the arguments.[37] In brief, we can investigate human social interaction (whether we term it cultural, religious, or otherwise) since we partake within shared human systems.[38]

One criticism (associated also with Gadamer's use of prejudice) is that comparison means reading the other in terms of ourselves; that is, Western scholars have traditionally used Protestant Christian lenses (see chapter 1). While it is inevitable that our preconceptions ("prejudices") inform new knowledge we encounter, critical perspectives alert us to the power differentials inherent within this. Regimes of power will shape what we know and possibly the hermeneutical lens through which we see. Our opening of horizons (see introduction)[39] may be shaped by dominant modes of knowing, meaning a reflexive attitude is needed (see box 2.7).

Contemporary linguistic philosophy, Jensen argues, also leads us to expect that comparison should be possible (see also introduction). Despite differences across cultures, a common substructure of language exists which must relate as a human endeavor of meaning making. Replying to J. Z. Smith's comment that comparison is magical, Jensen states that "my (somewhat insolent) reply is 'why magic?,'" because comparison is actually a natural human activity.[40] Jensen points out that "interpretative differences" do not make meta-languages (comparative terms) "epistemically incommensurable or mutually untranslatable."[41] Further, "linguistic meaning is public, inter-subjective, and translatable and therefore it is not just 'meaning for someone.'"[42] That is, meanings expressed in language become the common property of our social and cultural worlds and so may be related to other such linguistically expressed meanings. Jensen contrasts his work to that of Rudolf Otto (1869–1937), who was looking for private experiences and "ineffable" experience; Jensen notes that no such private individual language can exist. Meaning must be found in social practice and communication.[43]

Beyond the philosophical arguments, Flood notes the "sociobiological inheritance" that is "common to human beings."[44] Against outdated assumptions that human

COMPARISON, CONTRAST, AND DECOLONIAL METHODOLOGIES

Terms such as "religion" have been employed or withheld based upon regimes of power, especially in colonial contexts, to give legitimacy or deny legitimacy to certain traditions, cultures, or practices (see chapter 7, especially boxes 7.8 and 7.9). Likewise, comparison and contrast have acted to sanction or give priority to certain traditions. Indeed, assuming that terms from the Christian tradition such as "scripture" or "theology" form natural markers for comparative work emphasizes Christianity as a supposed norm. However, equally, scholars who wish to delegitimize comparison often have their own agendas as to what is or is not given value or authority. Scholarship itself is a deeply political practice (see chapter 18). Much critical scholarship is embedded in structures of white, male, Western scholarship (see chapters 5, 7, and 10). We should also not assume that comparative scholarship is inherently colonial in nature because, first, refusing comparison can be a way to deny validity to certain realms of thought and ways of thinking, and second, as noted above, comparison is a basic part of human understanding and not a specific Orientalist methodology (see box 7.4).

societies carry more dissimilarity than similarity, current psychological, neurological, and anthropological investigations suggest a deep species-level commonality.[45] It goes beyond this chapter to lay out the deep, inbuilt evolutionary aspects behind behavioral responses (see chapter 8). But, as one example, altruistic responses seem common among both young human children and apes, showing deep-rooted behavior.[46] A number of scholars have taken up these concepts as justifications for comparison.[47]

Yet, hermeneutical, scientific, or linguistic perspectives do not mean we can simply read easily across traditions. From the standpoint of critical social constructionism (see chapter 5), all human discourse may be forms of power over the other. A hermeneutics of suspicion (see box 2.7) toward discourses of power should inform our practice. This will include issues and power dynamics related to such things as gender, class, race, and colonialism (see, variously, chapters 3, 7, 10, and 18), where comparative methodologies have not always been innocent (see box 11.7).[48]

In summation, while some scholars have suggested that human cultures are particular and cannot be compared, this runs counter to current thinking in philosophical, social scientific, and scientific disciplines. Patterns of human language and our evolutionary and biological heritage mean that we should be able to meaningfully interpret patterns of behavior across cultures. This includes religious expression. Further, as our methodological discussions suggested, our focus should be on practice rather than doctrine (see chapters 3 and 12).

·   ·   ·

CASE STUDY 11A. COMPARING HINDUISM AND JUDAISM

This first case study does not primarily engage in a comparative act. Rather, it seeks to show how categories for comparison and contrast have been drawn on the macro scale that may hinder or help understanding, or shape the power dynamics and perception of different traditions.

TRADITIONAL CATEGORIZATIONS: ASSERTED AND CONTESTED

Scholars have noted that Hinduism and Judaism have often been seen as, in certain ways, polar opposites:

- Hinduism is seen to be polytheistic and rich in symbolism (iconocentric).
- Judaism is seen to be monotheistic and averse to images (iconoclastic).

Within the WRP (see box 2.1), though, they have been put into similar niches as:

- "ethnic religions" (i.e., they belong, primarily at least, to one specific people and/or geographical context), and
- nonmissionary religions (they do not seek converts).

All of these portrayals, while having some semblance to aspects (even mainstream ones) of each tradition, are nevertheless inaccurate when taken as monolithic, or essentialist, statements. Let us note a few issues:

- They perpetuate a stereotype of the traditions. Many Hindus would see their tradition as monotheistic, not polytheistic (the many gods may be seen as manifestations of the One God/dess), and Judaism has welcomed or even sought converts in some historical contexts.
- Despite old assumptions that the two traditions are historically isolated cultural forms, we know that long and quite deep interactions have taken place over two thousand years or more. Jewish traders regularly traveled to, and even lived and settled in, India during the Roman period when a strong trade route existed, while Indian holymen (*sadhus*) were also known across the Roman Empire.
- Interesting and solid comparative scholarship has highlighted ways these traditions challenge some older expectations about what religions are.

We will explore some of this in the following section.

COMPARATIVE PATTERNS IN HINDUISM AND JUDAISM

Barbara Holdrege observes that the notion of religion that arose in nineteenth-century Europe from Protestant Christian norms (i.e., the WRP) saw religion as characterized by four things which she sees challenged by these traditions.[49] The WRP paradigm, Holdrege argues, sees religion:

- as emphasizing sacred and profane as distinct, and the sacred as separate from culture;
- as defined by belief, with ritual, practice, and law as secondary;
- as emphasizing the individual over the community; and
- as universalizing, which means that mission is normative.

In contrast, she says an analysis of Hinduism and Judaism:

- gives alternative models of religion as cultural and communal;
- gives priority to practice, law, and ritual; and
- ties tradition to ethnicity and culture, with blood descent as central.

This would give us a different model of "religion." Moreover, Holdrege argues both traditions are

> *ethno-cultural systems* concerned with issues of family, ethnic and cultural integrity, blood lineages, and the inter-generational transmission of traditions; *elite textual communities* . . .; *religions of orthopraxy* characterized by hereditary priesthoods and sacrificial traditions, comprehensive legal systems, complex dietary laws, and elaborate regulations concerning purity and impurity . . . [; underlying] these shared characteristics is *embodiment* . . . of ethno-cultural identity tied to a specific people, language, and land.[50]

Holdrege and others argue that far from being distinct, these traditions have much in common. Indeed, she highlights aspects of religious traditions which may be hidden if the WRP is the norm. Certainly, much comparative religion builds from primarily Christian-inspired categories. Therefore, models from other traditions, in this case Hinduism and Judaism, are important. Thus we may find meaningful comparison where we might not expect it. However, we should not see this as unproblematic, and while fascinating and insightful, we can note certain things about Holdrege's analysis:

- While contesting the opposition of these traditions, some versions of the WRP suggest the same similarities, meaning Holdrege's work accords with what some see as stereotypes. This does not necessarily show she is right or wrong. However, different ways of seeing show different results.
- We should not universalize her way of seeing religion. While embodiment and material religion are important, we cannot neglect other facets of traditions, like beliefs. Notably, Holdrege does not suggest this.
- The analysis picks significant and mainstream parts of each tradition but may downplay or lose other aspects.

Some questions may help us think through these issues:

1. What some have dismissed as antiquated stereotypes are (at least partially) reinforced by excellent contemporary scholarship as meaningful statements (i.e., that Hinduism and Judaism are focused on ethnic identities). Think about how you would respond to accusations of stereotyping and representation in this or other situations. When is something a false stereotype and when is it a fair representation of mainstream ideas?

2. In comparison, macro-level analysis (tradition to tradition) will inevitably erase distinctions and particularities. For instance, while many (even most) Jewish and Hindu traditions do not seek converts, even discouraging them, there have been times when proselytizing activity has been encouraged by some groups within each tradition. Do you think macro-level comparison can be useful to give general impressions, or should we stick only to micro-level and localized comparison?

3. In this case study, we have spoken mainly about comparing rather than contrasting. What areas of contrast do you see, or do you know about (maybe with further research) between these two traditions? Do you think comparing (noting similarities) or contrasting (noting differences) proves more insightful in understanding the relations of Hinduism and Judaism? Explain with examples.

CASE STUDY 11B. A COMPARISON OF ZEN BUDDHIST AND PROTESTANT CHRISTIAN SITTING PRACTICES

This case study asks what happens when we take concepts from one tradition and attempt to look back on a tradition familiar to us. (Here, an assumption is that the majority of readers come from contexts where a Protestant, or other Christian, identity is more dominant than a Zen, or other Buddhist, identity.) This new lens may be shaped to see certain things and perhaps represents the lens of certain elites (in terms of gender, race, class, etc.). Further, the attempt to move to this position is a difficult one; we cannot wholly see with another's eyes. Nevertheless, the possibility of such an endeavor remains.

ZEN BUDDHIST SITTING

"Zen" (Chinese: Ch'an) is the Japanese word for Buddhist meditation (Sanskrit: *dhyana*), meaning Zen Buddhism is "the meditation school." The main form of meditation is *zazen*, literally, "seated meditation." The practitioner assumes the Japanese kneeling posture, *seiza*. With back straight and eyes narrowed, but not closed, she simply sits. In other traditions the cross-legged "lotus" posture may be used. It is often done communally, but can be done alone. But even communally, each meditates in their own practice. In basic meditation, the breath is "followed": just observing the breath coming in and

Pews in a chapel, as a site for Christian sitting practices, St. David's University College chapel, Lampeter, UK.

out. Thoughts are observed, at least their arising and passing. The practitioner does not let herself focus on them, and if she does, she returns to following the breath. The aim is not control of the mind—to control it involves fighting or effort, which would be counterproductive. Rather, one is just *in the sitting*: observing, or being aware, of the sensations in the body. It can be very painful for beginners, and even for experienced practitioners when done over many hours. The breath, the arising of thoughts in the mind, the noises of birds, wind, cars, or whatever it may be beyond the meditator, are simply what one is aware of, without concentrating on any. One particularly "follows" the breath, being aware of it coming in and going out. Through it all, one simply sits.

PROTESTANT RITUALS OF SITTING

Despite variations, the most dominant Protestant practice of sitting is probably the Sunday Eucharist service. This is found in Anglican (Episcopalian), Lutheran, Methodist, and other traditions; regionally, and within traditions, the performance can vary widely (for one form, see case study 12B).

In general, sitting plays a large part. Typically, on pews (or chairs), the devotees sit in ranks facing the communion table or altar. It is a communal activity with group responses, and seen as congregational. There is no determined sitting posture, though uniformity will often be seen. Significantly, though, sitting does not form part of the practice itself. Moreover, it is interspersed with times of standing and kneeling, and sometimes walking about in more or less ritualized forms. Indeed, when the devotee is sitting, the focus is not on the breath or the mind, but more often listening, whether to the words of scripture, the service, or sermon. Indeed, for Protestants, kneeling, as opposed to sitting, may be more like *zazen* (seated meditation). It is common in quite a few traditions for the words "Let us pray," or similar, to be accompanied by a requirement or expectation to kneel. While sitting is normally done with eyes open, in kneeling eyes will often be closed and the worshipper should focus on prayers and the deity.

EAST ASIAN DEVOTIONAL POSTURES

Generally, these Christian ritualized sets of postures do not so much resemble sitting (*zazen*) as they resemble other forms of devotion. Typically, when one enters a Buddhist (or Chinese) temple compound, the devotee will light several (often three) incense sticks and perform a series of standing bows, often facing the four directions, before placing them in a holder. After that, she will kneel and prostrate herself (kow-tow) before a specific statue, perhaps repeating this in various temple courtyards. Here, the devotee may also say prayers (normally silently), and the attention is not on the breath, but on devotion or requests to a deity/Buddha (in East Asia, this will most commonly be to the Bodhisattva Guanyin; see box 2.9). While often done alongside others, especially in large or busy temples, it is ultimately the act of an individual, though prayers are often made for others, and families will go to the temple together.

COMPARATIVE THOUGHTS

We have seen that Protestant "sitting" is very different from *zazen*. If Zen is taken as a norm, we might say that Protestants do not sit/pray/meditate (notwithstanding many Christians who practice forms of Buddhist meditation).[51] The predominant practice of meditation/*zazen* from the Zen Buddhist tradition does not easily map onto the predominant Protestant practices of "worship" or "prayer."

Even if we look at other forms of Buddhist/Chinese devotion, we still see something quite distinct. Focusing on Chinese usage, the terms used to describe the typical practices of laypeople include either the practice/action (e.g. "bowing [to the Buddha]" [*laifo*], or the intention (e.g., "seeking blessings/happiness/good fortune" [*qiufu*]). The Chinese term that many equate with "prayer" (*qidao*) has a sense of wishing or hoping (for good fortune). Many Christians use a term that means something like "addressing God" or more literally "pray tell" (*daogao*), while Muslims employ a term denoting ritual action (*libai*). Another often used Buddhist term is "reciting scriptures" (*nianjing*). These terms show different expectations in various traditions. These terms or concepts, like *zazen*, may usefully inform thinking about what is often broadly termed prayer, worship, or meditation. While we may often, generically, say that forms of prayer or meditation are common across religions (using Western or Christian language), this example shows that it does not give much analytic rigor. Here, the contrastive aspect (i.e., understanding the differences) seems important.

Consider the following questions:

1. If Protestants do not engage in seated meditation (*zazen*), does this mean they do not "pray" or "meditate"? What happens if a Christian does practice Zen meditation?
2. Consider (with research) the different terms used for activities we may associate with prayer (e.g., meditation, worship, veneration, paying devotion) in a tradition you are familiar with. What are their meanings and implications? Compare them to the (native) terms of another tradition. What is lost, or revealed, by translating the terms (i.e., saying that Christians, Muslims, Buddhists, Sikhs, etc., all pray)?
3. What other comparisons and contrasts would you draw between *zazen* practice and Christian prayer/worship? Or Buddhist seeking blessings (*qiufu*) and Christian prayer/worship?

·   ·   ·

QUESTIONS AND CONNECTING THOUGHTS

This chapter connects to various other chapters. For instance, to do comparison we need some sense of what "religion" means (chapters 1, 3, 9). Meanwhile, questions about power, gender, and politics arise (see chapters 5, 10, and 18, respectively). In particular, some have alleged that comparative religion has been complicit with colonial agendas (chapter 7), or has simply drawn a false sense of similarity. While correct, this does not delegitimize comparison:

- Comparison is a part of human meaning making and reasoning; we cannot simply set it aside.
- While comparison was part of colonial domination, so was writing books and sailing ships; it is conceptually confused to dismiss all of these as inherently colonial.
- Despite past malpractice, current philosophical and scientific arguments suggest comparison can make sense of our world.

Some questions can help us think through various issues:

1. Comparative religion is laden with issues of power and representation of the other: Whose categories? Who decides what is compared? Who does the comparison? Do you think that comparative religion is too imbricated with these issues to ever be a viable discipline?
2. A key question raised in comparative study is whether we can actually understand across religious and cultural worlds. Discuss what you see as the arguments for or against acts of comparison and contrast in such a perspective (see also chapter 2).

3. Do you think that comparison (showing similarities) or contrast (showing differences) is more likely to be fruitful in the work of comparative religion? In our two case studies, one focused on comparison and the other on contrast; which did you find more illuminating and why?

FURTHER READING

THEORY

Doniger, Wendy. "Post-Modern and -Colonial -Structural Comparisons," in *A Magic Still Dwells: Comparative Religion in the Postmodern Age*, ed. Kimberley Patton and Benjamin Ray (Berkeley: University of California Press, 2000), 63–74.

Flood, Gavin. "Religious Practice and the Nature of the Human," in Schmidt-Leukel and Nehring, *Interreligious Comparisons*, 130–41.

Jensen, Jeppe Sinding. "Why Magic? It's Just Comparison," *Method and Theory in the Study of Religion* 16.1 (2004): 45–60.

Patton, Kimberley. "Juggling Torches: Why We Still Need Comparative Religion," in Patton and Ray, *Magic Still Dwells*, 153–71.

Schmidt-Leukel, Perry, and Andreas Nehring, eds. *Interreligious Comparisons in Religious Studies and Theology: Comparison Revisited* (London: Bloomsbury, 2016).

Smith, Jonathan Z. "In Comparison a Magic Dwells," in Patton and Ray, *Magic Still Dwells*, 23–44.

CASE STUDY 11A. COMPARING HINDUISM AND JUDAISM

Brill, Alan. *Rabbi on the Ganges: A Jewish-Hindu Encounter* (Lanham, MD: Lexington Books, 2019).

Goshen-Gottstein, Alon. *The Jewish Encounter with Hinduism* (Basingstoke: Palgrave Macmillan, 2016).

Holdrege, Barbara. "Hindu-Jewish Encounters," in *The Wiley-Blackwell Companion to Inter-Religious Dialogue*, ed. Catherine Cornille (Chichester: Wiley-Blackwell, 2013), 410–37.

Holdrege, Barbara. "What's Beyond the Post? Comparative Analysis as a Critical Method," in Patton and Ray, *Magic Still Dwells*, 77–91.

Theodor, Ithamar, and Yudit Kornberg Greenberg, eds. *Dharma and Halacha: Comparative Studies in Hindu-Jewish Philosophy and Religion* (Lanham, MD: Lexington Books, 2018).

CASE STUDY 11B. A COMPARISON OF ZEN BUDDHISM AND PROTESTANT CHRISTIAN SITTING PRACTICES

Blée, Fabrice. "Can Christians Engage in Non-Christian Practices? Eastern Meditations and Contemplative Prayer," in *Controversies in Contemporary Religion*, ed. Paul Hedges, vol. 3 (Santa Barbara: Praeger, 2014), 277–304.

Braak, André van der. "The Practice of Zazen as Ritual Performance," in *Ritual Participation and Interreligious Dialogue: Boundaries, Transgressions and Innovations*, ed. Marianne Moyaert and Joris Geldhof (London and New York: Bloomsbury, 2015), 156–65.

Dogen, Eihai. "Fukanzazangi: How Everyone Can Sit," trans. Yasuda Joshu Dainen and Anzan Hoshin (1227), wwzc.org/dharma-text/fukanzazengi-how-everyone-can-sit.

Harvey, Peter, *An Introduction to Buddhism*, 2nd ed. (Cambridge: Cambridge University Press, 2013), 237–44, 361–64.

King, Ursula. "A Response to Reflections on Buddhist and Christian Religious Practices," *Buddhist-Christian Studies* 22 (2002): 105–12.

McGrath, Alister. *Christianity: An Introduction*, 3rd ed. (Chichester: Wiley, 2015), 226–29, 234–36.

12

RITUAL
Ritualization, Myth, and Performance

IN WHICH WE EXPLORE:

Theories of ritual and the concepts of ritualization and performativity

The relationship of myth and ritual

Case studies comparing the Zen Buddhist tea ceremony with the Anglican (Episcopalian) Christian Eucharist, and exploring Buddhist ordination

INTRODUCTION

For many theorists, ritual has been a defining feature of those areas we call "religion."[1] However, ritual is not unique to religious traditions. Think back on what you did this morning, maybe something like this:

· You switched off your alarm and rolled over.

· You went to the bathroom and brushed your teeth.

· You went downstairs and got out a bowl and a spoon.

· You poured cereal and milk into the bowl and then lifted your spoon and began eating.

If this is your daily pattern (or something like it), then you could be said to be engaging in ritual. You may object that this is simply a routine. But what is the difference between a ritual and a routine? Indeed, you will see many examples of such ritual or routine:

- In parliaments or senates, there are set procedures, particular orders for actions, set forms of words, and so on.
- When an athlete performs a certain action (e.g., a baseball pitcher before pitching, a snooker player before striking the ball, a tennis player before serving), it may be a set part of her performance.

All of this may be spoken of as ritual or routine. However, by ritual we often signify some special meaning to the actions, differentiating it from routine. However, this is certainly not tied only to areas we would commonly designate as "religious." State openings of parliament are often termed rituals. Again, a sports player often believes their routinized actions bring them good luck. What significance do you attach to your morning ritual, especially if something is missed? You may not believe it brings you luck or is necessary, but you may feel the day has not started right if something is missed. What about the act, in US schools, of the pledge of allegiance to the flag (see case study 18B)? The barrier between ritual and routine is thin and ill-defined, much like barriers between religious and non-religious arenas (see chapters 1, 3, 8, 16, and 18).

In contemporary scholarly usage, ritual does not signify some area of behavior linked to "supernatural" or "religious" intent; we would struggle mightily to find a definition that is applied only in this way (see box 12.1). Indeed, ritual studies is a distinct field, developed by Ronald Grimes amongst others, that intersects with areas such as theatre studies, religious studies, sociology, media studies, and linguistics.

Today, ritual is a prominent part of the study of religion, with some seeing ritual behavior as more significant than doctrine or belief (see chapters 3 and 9). However, for reasons we explore below, it was often sidelined or ignored by scholars of religion, being the preserve of anthropology or sociology. In this chapter, we begin by looking at some of the traditional theory on ritual studies, including areas such as functionalism, violence, purity, and liminality. Next, we look at the Protestant-inspired prejudice that often led to ritual being sidelined and discuss ritual's relationship to myth and belief. We then address performance studies and performativity. We conclude with two case studies.

SOME CLASSICAL RITUAL THEORY
FUNCTIONALIST THEORIES

Early academic attempts to categorize ritual provide a backdrop for contemporary theories, which often counter what are seen as previous misjudgments. Nevertheless, parts of classical ritual theory remain insightful. One key aspect was functionalism; functionalist theories tried to explain religion/ritual by the role it played in human societies or cultures. These theories can be split, for our purposes, into three camps: psychological, social, and structural.

A typical psychological functionalist was Bronislaw Malinowski (1884–1942). He believed that we needed a holistic (big picture) study of society to see how every part functioned in relation to the others. In an important study of Melanesian culture in the Trobriand Islands,[2] Malinowski argued that ritual was a psychological tool to help us cope with life's uncertainties. He argued that "magic," "science," and "religion" coexisted by serving different functions, with magic and religion being the sources of ritual (see box 9.4). Meanwhile, Émile Durkheim (1858–1917) was a social functionalist. For him, ritual primarily concerned cohesion within the community, so serving a social function.[3] He suggested religious rituals gave an experience that seemed to go beyond the social group and enabled them to relate to each other via a perceived higher power. Certainly, some rituals, especially those involving "high-cost" (physically demanding) participation, seem to enhance social cohesion of participants and community

BOX 12.2 **SCIENCE, MAGIC, AND RELIGION**

Sociology developed from the thought of the European Enlightenment (see box 16.1), which often saw society progressing from a more "primitive" and "superstitious" form to a "rational" and "secular" worldview (see chapter 16). This is exemplified in the evolutionary model argued for by Émile Durkheim (1858–1917), who saw an inevitable linear progression from magic to science:

· Magic is primitive science that seeks to manipulate the world.

· Religion adds more sophisticated systems to explain magic.

· Science is the culmination of this progression through rational thought.

Durkheim suggested that modern societies would need to create new rituals to replace those of religion for social bonding. Other thinkers have not seen the difference as linear, with Bronislaw Malinowksi (1884–1942) suggesting the three could coexist:

· Science was about understanding how the world worked, and so was practical.

· Magic represented attempts to produce direct results (e.g., rituals for rain), serving a psychological role to temper frustrations over a lack of control of the environment, and so was also practical.

· Religion served existential needs, such as the fear of death.

The distinctions of Malinowski and Durkheim between religion and magic (and science) are not very tenable (see boxes 7.8 and 9.4).[1] While it would be naive to suggest that the natural sciences are simply another worldview, directly comparable to "religion" or "magic," a sharp distinction between these categories is less stable than we might imagine. What we today call "science" was not labeled this way in the past, and has origins in areas we would label philosophy, theology, or religion.[2]

---

1 There are arguments that "magic" can be disentangled from the negative connotations that have accrued around it and be rehabilitated, or else that it marks a fairly clear realm of practice in the ancient world; see, respectively, Daniel Dubuisson, *Religion and Magic in Western Culture* (Leiden: Brill, 2016); and Lindsay Watson, *Magic in Ancient Greece and Rome* (London: Bloomsbury, 2019). However, the various ways in which "magic" may be defined, especially as delineated from "religion" (our main concern here) prove problematic. For instance, if magic is seen to be concerned with such realms as health, wealth, and good harvests, we also see prayers and intercessions for such things within those areas we define as "religion." Again, the notion of specific ritual forms which produce clear effects or where certain incantations will deliver certain results also crosses over into a host of spheres we might delineate as "religious," such as wording formulas including the Christian practice invoking the "Father, Son, and Holy Spirit" (and also Hindu, Buddhist, and Jewish use of mantras or sacred words), or with ritualized Daoist (or Christian and other traditions) practices of exorcism. Even in Mediterranean antiquity, "magic" was often used as a derogatory term for other people's rituals, but crossed the borders into what we would see as "religion" in terms of ritual practice and theories of effect (see box 9.4), see Naomi Janowitz, *Magic in the Roman World: Pagans, Jews and Christians* (New York: Routledge, 2002); and Naomi Janowitz, *Icons of Power: Ritual Practices in Late Antiquity* (University Park: Pennsylvania State University Press, 2002). For an overall study of the term "magic," see Randall Styers, *Making Magic: Religion, Magic, and Science in the Modern World* (Oxford: Oxford University Press, 2004).

2 See Peter Harrison, *The Domains of Science and Religion* (Chicago: Chicago University Press, 2015); and Paul Hedges, *Towards Better Disagreement: Religion and Atheism in Dialogue* (London: Jessica Kingsley, 2017), 137–43, and 154–55.

Ritual enactment at a Confucian ancestral shrine, Andong, South Korea.

members as spectators.[4] While Malinowski believed that religion, magic, and science could coexist, Durkheim saw a linear evolutionary model (see box 12.2).

An example of a structural functionalist is Lucien Lévy-Bruhl (1857–1939). He saw preliterate people as irrational, stuck in a mind-set dominated by supernatural thinking. Ritual, he believed, related to this worldview and had no purpose; rather, it took structure from symbols, myths, and an irrational worldview.

Other scholars might classify functionalist definitions of ritual differently, but these three categories help us to see three distinct ways in which ritual is approached:

1. as a psychological and existential experience and practice;
2. as a social and communal experience and practice;
3. as a mythic worldview expressing experience and practice.

These arguments have been heavily criticized, often for their dismissive attitude of non-Europeans (see chapter 7), as well as their arbitrary definitions of science, magic/superstition, and religion. A. R. Radcliffe-Brown (1881–1955) challenged Malinowski by arguing that rituals have a role in creating our fears. Radcliffe-Brown and others argued that rituals do not necessarily resolve or subdue our fears of the unknown/untamed so much as create systems that reinforce our sense of the precariousness of our existence, perhaps through systems which posit the need to appease various supernatural agents. A wider criticism was found in figures such as Clifford Geertz (1926–2006), who argued for "a more dynamic form of functionalist theory" which does not simply demarcate ritual in clear-cut ways.[5] Functionalism as a whole has been criticized for seeking to determine, in definite ways, what a ritual is or does, and how it ties into specific benefits for an individual and/or society. Different people, or parts of society, may relate to rituals in varying ways. Further, while Geertz's "more dynamic" system may seek to integrate various functions it also, perhaps, does not relate to the wider ways in which ritual may function.

RITUAL AND BOUNDARIES

Durkheim's view of ritual as creating internal social bonding neglects that in-group identities often rely on the exclusion of out-groups (see chapter 6). Further, what about rituals that are performed alone? Or groups that demarcate themselves from the wider society? Mary Douglas (1921–2007) suggested that rituals have a role in dictating how we demarcate the world, especially in terms of purity and impurity (see box 12.3). As acts of demarcation, rituals may show us what is important to us, and what is not; what is pure, and what is impure, as well as who we are and who we are not. Douglas's view of rituals as boundary-creating has been persistent and influential in many ways.

RITES OF PASSAGE AND LIMINALITY

A rite of passage is a ritual in which one passes from one stage of life to another (see box 12.4). We speak here about moving from one status to another. This is important because, for many, rituals have real power (see chapters 3 and 9, and boxes 9.3, 9.4, and 12.6). For instance, without the correct ritual (public display), one may not be recognized by one's community as married—which can have real effects on one's status in many societies, and even in many modern nation-states (tax breaks can accrue to those married). Again, in traditional Hindu death rites, the correct performance is not simply for display or to make the mourners feel better, but is necessary to ensure the spirit of the deceased becomes an ancestor.[6]

Theorizing rites of passage is most closely associated with Victor Turner (1920–1983), who extended the ideas of Arnold Van Gennep (1873–1957).[7] Van Gennep distinguished between two principal types of rites:

· rituals of individual transition, where one passes from one state to another, for example, death, marriage, ordination, coming of age
· rituals marking the passage of time, especially between periods, for example, seasonal rites such as autumn/harvest rites, new year festivals

RITUAL, DANGER, AND PURITY

Anthropologist Mary Douglas (1921–2007) spoke about rituals as forms of symbolic communication which could enact change. She termed this "magic" (see box 9.4). This is related to the concepts of purity and impurity.[1] The latter, considered taboo, demarcates what was permissible and impermissible within a society. She spoke of the impure as "matter out of place," referring to things that are where they should not be. In a ritual context, impurity is something which could render a ritual impure/ineffective. Matter out of place could refer to things which are seen to be physically "unclean," for example, feces or other such waste products. Douglas employed the phrase "dirt is matter out of place"—earth in a field is "soil," but on your plate it is "dirt." Certain people or things can also be symbolized as somehow "impure." Examples might include a menstruating woman (in a number of cultures blood, especially menstrual blood, signifies impurity),[2] or an inauspicious sign (e.g., black cats). Impurity, therefore, lurks as a danger within the world. While focusing upon certain indigenous tribes, Douglas's work has also had wider usage. In contemporary society, some may suggest that the gentrification of cities makes homeless people into "dirt" as "matter out of place." In a religious context, pork may be food to most Christians, but is "matter out of place" on the plates of most Muslims or Jews. Douglas's classification of "pure" and "impure" relates to the demarcation of our world in social constructionism (see chapter 5), and the identity construction of the out-group (see chapter 6), including religious differences (see chapter 13). Alternatively, rituals can also serve as a means to restore purity.

---

1 Mary Douglas, *Purity and Danger: An Analysis of the Concepts of Pollution and Taboo* (London: Routledge and Kegan Paul, 1966).

2 See William E. Phipps, "The Menstrual Taboo in the Judeo-Christian Tradition," *Journal of Religion and Health* 19.4 (1980): 298–303; M. Guterman, P. Mehta, and M. Gibbs, "Menstrual Taboos among Major Religions," *Internet Journal of World Health and Societal Politics* 5.2 (2007), http://ispub.com /IJWH/5/2/8213; and Alan Cole, *Mothers and Sons in Chinese Buddhism* (Stanford: Stanford University Press, 1998), 197–217.

In addition to this, Van Gennep also noted a threefold structure of rites of passage:

· rites of separation: initial state
· rites of transition: liminal period
· rites of incorporation: final state

In other words, a rite of passage would have a first step in which the person (or people) undergoing it would be separated from their previous life stage (rites of separation). They would then undergo various rites designed to enact change (rites of transition). It was this midway point, the liminal period, that Turner particularly focused on (see box 12.5). Finally, rites would take place to reincorporate the person(s) back into society or into their new stage of life. These stages could be marked in various ways, such as position in relation to other people, special clothing, particular words, or specific acts. A traditional/modern Western Christian church wedding ceremony can serve as an example:

Rites of separation: The bride wears a wedding dress, which marks an act of separation from single people. She is not meant to see her intended during this time, which signals a peculiar stage of life. In church, her father takes her up the aisle to stand beside her intended, marking a separation from one family group and integration into another.

Rites of transition: During the words of the service, the couple stand separated from the rest of their tribes before the priest at the altar. Before the final "I do," the couple make promises to each other, before God, and the tribes, marking their movement from being single people to married people. This is a time of flux and transition.

Rites of incorporation: In the final part of the ceremony, the priest often utters the words: "I now pronounce you man and wife." The transition from single to couple is now complete, so they have a new place within society. The couple will walk back down the aisle between the two tribes and so are physically part of this group again. During the wedding feast they eat with both tribes, marking the reintegration back into society as a married couple.

RITUAL VIOLENCE, TRANSFORMATION, AND SACRIFICE

We offer a first definition of sacrifice: *giving up (offering to the deity) something of value.* René Girard (1923–2015) explored the notion of the hero as criminal/innocent victim who

BOX 12.5 **LIMINALITY**

Liminality is a stage of transition, when one passes from one way of life, or way of being, to another.[1] The term comes from the Latin *limen,* or door lintel, signifying passing over. It may seem transitory and insignificant, but Victor Turner (1920–1983) argues it is the very heart of ritual. He termed it a time "betwixt and between,"[2] neither in nor out of the world because there is no fixed status. In a wedding rite, one is neither fully single nor fully married between the initial separation, for example, putting on a wedding dress, and the final pronouncement and return to the family. For Turner, this is a delicate time of transition and change. He blends what we have termed structuralist, social, and psychological analysis:

· Particular structural mythic words and acts are performed: Unless a society believes and has a "myth" of weddings—not all societies see marriage in the same way—then one cannot get married. It is thus part of a structure integral to the rites and myths.

· A separation and reintegration in social terms is performed: From single to married, and a change, in many cases, occurs from belonging to one family to now belonging to another family.

· An awareness and existential experience of being different.

It is also a potential time of chaos and disorder, because until the ritual is finished there is uncertainty: What will happen? How will one feel? What will the outcome be? Imagine a wedding in which either the bride or groom does not say "I do." Being "jilted" at the altar still carries a lot of social stigma in contemporary society. One has started to enter a new stage and emerged without that being finished. Notably, while often quite a short stage, the liminal state could also be longer. In pilgrimage, where journeys could be days, weeks, or even months, the pilgrim is in a liminal state: outside their normal life and routine and not yet returned.

In a related usage, some speak of particular places as liminal, signifying that they stand as a crossing point between postulated realms (often this world and [an]other "spiritual" world[s]). This can be seen as a "thin place," where the distance between realms is more permeable, and may be down to location or else dependent upon particular times, rituals, or seasons which mark or create such crossing places (see chapter 17).

---

1 See Hazel Andrews and Les Roberts, "Liminality," in *International Encyclopedia of the Social and Behavioral Sciences,* 2nd ed., ed. James Wright (Kidlington: Elsevier Science, 2015), 131–37.
2 Victor Turner, *The Forest of Symbols: Aspects of Ndembu Ritual* (Ithaca: Cornell University Press: 1967), 93–111.

is killed as a scapegoat to ritually purge a community's perceived "sins" (see box 15.3).[8] While some theorists stress sacrifice as a largely positive or purifying ritual, Girard brought attention to the enacted violence. Girard posited that animal sacrifice was primarily to assuage some form of guilt. It acted as a way to avoid murder, because the animal stood in for the person who might otherwise be killed because they are blamed for whatever has been suffered or is seen to have gone wrong in society. For Girard, it concerned a primal lust for blood which had to be satisfied. Girard's theories came from contemplation of Greek myth and ancient Jewish and Christian texts. The myth of Oedipus is key, but also the replacing of Abraham's son Isaac with a ram (Gen. 22:1–19) as a sacrifice,[9] and Jesus's sacrificial death. It is therefore hard to universalize his concepts, including the wider social or personal sense of guilt and sin. Nevertheless, Girard usefully raises the issue that enacted violence may be part of the ritual process.

Antagonistic aspects of sacrifice have also been explored, with many scholars focusing on animal sacrifice. They may be done to appease aggrieved ancestors or to transfer rights of leadership between an old tribal leader and his virile son.[10] However, Kathryn McClymond points out that many sacrifices are not animal-based, but include vegetative matter or liquids. Moreover, rituals with animal sacrifice are typically complex and contain many elements.[11] Therefore, focusing on violent or blood-sacrificial elements is a very limited picture. One critique of some early theory is its fixation on areas which seem "outlandish," "exotic," or "grotesque."

A second definition of sacrifice is *the transformation of one thing into another*. This is not necessarily distinct from, but may complement, our first definition. However, seeing sacrifice as giving up something of value is only a partial understanding. An example is Pierre Bourdieu's (1930–2002) concept of "misrecognition." He studied the Kabyle people of Algeria, for whom harvesting a crop is tantamount to killing the field. It is seen as murder of what has been brought to fecundity through the ground and hard work. Bourdieu observes that the very last grain, seen to contain the spirit of the field, is given special treatment. This sacrificial ritual can be seen as transforming murder into "an acceptable sacrifice."[12] Bourdieu sees this as "enacted misrecognition." The Kabyle collectively deceive themselves, refusing to acknowledge the crime of murder because of this ritual act. In becoming the sacrifice, it is transformed. Transformation is also seen in other sacrifices: physical food becomes heavenly food; donations of money or food to monastics/holy people become blessings; burned paper money becomes bribes in the afterlife. Violence is not the (sole) focus, or mechanism, of ritual or sacrifice.

THE POWER OF RITUAL? SYMBOL OR ENACTMENT

THE PROTESTANT IMAGINATION

We will now address why many dismiss ritual as shallow or just show. This concerns the historical dominance of Protestant over Catholic Christianity in the intellectual milieu of modern northwestern Europe (see box 9.3). Protestant critique of Catholicism involved

THE CHRISTIAN EUCHARIST AS RITUAL ACT

The Eucharist is the ritual reenactment of Jesus's Last Supper (generally understood by Christians as the Jewish Passover meal he shared with his disciples before being executed by the Romans).[1] In the Catholic doctrine of transubstantiation, the bread and wine (Jesus is believed to have asked his disciples to remember him through these elements) are spoken of as *actually* becoming Jesus's flesh and blood.[2] Therefore, the Eucharistic ritual enacts change: it has power. In Christian Protestant theology, however, the Eucharist is seen as symbolic (see box 9.3). Protestant denominations have varying stances; in the Lutheran tradition the bread and wine are simply symbols acting as a reminder of Jesus's perceived self-sacrifice. The ritual itself changes nothing; it is just an activity where the participants think about or remember things. It has no power.[3] This represents a shift from embodied practices (a physical act of ritual as active agent) to a cognitive activity (remembering as the primary work of ritual). This relates to the way that ritual became associated with "magic" or "superstition" (see chapter 9, especially box 9.4).

---

1 Some contemporary scholarship argues it was not a Passover meal. Following John's Gospel, it appears to be too early chronologically, with the symbolic association being made by early Christians. Either way, the meal was very different from the contemporary Seder.

2 This does not mean literally, though it was often understood that way in medieval times. Technically it relates to debates on "substance" and "accidents" in medieval adaptations of Aristotelian philosophy; see Marilyn McCord Adams, *Some Later Medieval Theories of the Eucharist* (Oxford: Oxford University Press, 2010), 179–96.

3 On these debates, see Alister McGrath, *Historical Theology* (Oxford: Blackwell, 1998), 195–200.

a return to the assumed "pure origins" of Christianity in the biblical sources (see chapter 4). Catholics were accused of inventing traditions, and this was often especially situated in terms of the priestly hierarchy and ritual activity, often termed "priestcraft." For Protestant critics, ritual was associated with superstition and was contrasted with Protestantism's emphasis upon doctrine and the word as the basis of true Christianity (see box 12.6).[13] This entailed a shift from the material and performative to the abstract and linguistic as what properly constituted religion (see chapters 1, 3, and 9).

In the 1980s, building from Michel Foucault's (1926–1984) genealogical exploration of the history of ideas,[14] Talal Asad, Catherine Bell (1953–2008), and Jonathan Z. Smith (1938–2017) started to question the Protestant-inspired understanding of ritual. Ritual, these scholars noted, was often sidelined in studying religion. Instead anthropology, originally the study of perceived "primitive" peoples, paid attention to ritual. Asad argued that in the modern world ritual was removed from its medieval monastic context, where it was part of "a rule of life" (following traditional Christian monastic terminology)[15] or what Giorgio Agamben would term a "form of life."[16] That is to say, a pattern which would itself shape us and become part of our whole way of being. In the Protestant imaginary, ritual was separated from other areas of life, and its power to transform us was hidden or ignored. The Protestant attitude affected scholarly stances:

- Rituals were seen as symbols at best. They had no actual power to transform things. They were seen as superstitious and shallow.
- It was assumed that rituals were merely acts mechanically followed out without any deep effect on the people carrying them out. They were seen as a secondary to myth or doctrine.
- Rituals were seen as signs of a primitive or oppressive worldview, and therefore routinely ignored.

The challenge by scholarship led to the performative turn discussed below. But, first, we briefly survey debates on myth[17] and ritual.

MYTH AND RITUAL

Robert Segal notes: "Some theorists consider belief the heart of religion, others ritual."[18] In contrast to the Protestant-inspired emphasis upon texts, doctrines, and beliefs, some contemporary scholars have dismissed these as secondary and stressed ritual as being almost entirely foundational for religion.[19] It was the biblical scholar William Robertson Smith (1846–1894) who first prioritized ritual over the then dominant alternative theory. Either emphasis, though, is likely to take us astray.

Functionalist theories have been applied to myth as much as ritual. Edward Burnett Tylor (1832–1917) saw myth as a form of primitive science, for example, the theory that volcanoes or earthquakes are caused by invisible spirits. Others argued they are about social bonding. Claude Lévi-Strauss (1908–2009) saw them as a form of classification that divides (structures) the world, though still acting as primitive science.[20] Many theorists, such as James G. Frazer (1854–1941), whose *Golden Bough* still enjoys popular influence,[21] created theories of myth-ritual. Ritual is either seen as dependent upon myth, that is, a particular myth (belief) is acted out in ritual, or ritual is seen as prior to myth (belief), and so it creates or reinforces certain worldviews which become expressed as myth (belief). Either theory, taken as a generalized universal, is inadequate. Not all myths and rituals are directly related. Today, most theorists see the myth-ritual hypothesis as largely redundant. Whether this is warranted is debatable, as there are links in at least some cases.

Finally, Frits Staal theorized the "meaninglessness of ritual" based on studies of the Vedic ritual system.[22] For Staal, ritual was entirely separate from any cognitive structure. It was done for its own sake. His reading of Vedic rituals is not uncontested, and like other theories often assumes a universal norm based upon a particular case study. Nevertheless, he prefigures some later theory, breaking an assumption that we should see ritual as communication, that is, trying to say something or explicate an idea. The entire purpose and function of ritual may be embedded within the ritual itself.

PERFORMANCE AND RITUAL
PERFORMANCE AS RITUAL

The term "performance" is one which we typically associate with the theater, movies, and acting. We might ask, "What did you think of Daisy Ridley's performance in *Star Wars: The Force Awakens*?"; or, "Did you see the performance of *The Mouse Trap* at the theater last night?" Theorizing performance in ritual studies certainly comes from theater studies, but also through linguistic anthropology. In linguistics, "competence" is the technical ability to express oneself in a given language, and "performance" is the actual patterns and utterances in speech. Likewise, ritual competence is whether the priest/ritual leader knows the precise actions and words needed, while ritual performance is the form, nature, and experience of any specific ceremony. "Performativity," meanwhile, refers to both intended and unintended aspects of any specific performance, or what the audience takes away. The so-called performative turn involves a shift in emphasis from specific rites, often associated with acting out particular structures and symbols, to seeing ritual as having performative power. This links to the Foucauldian turn of scholars such as Asad, noted above. The ritual does not just stand in for something else, but has its own integrity. Aspects of this had appeared in some early theory: Bourdieu had spoken of ritual as "performative magic," focusing on the significance of embodiment and its power to effect change (see chapter 9); effective performance was vital for Durkheim's theory that ritual builds social cohesion; and Staal discussed it as having its own integrity. In performance theory, what is done is being stressed: "Not much about ritual is incontrovertible, but that rituals are composed of actions is not open to doubt."[23]

Describing religious ritual[24] as performance may seem counterintuitive. For instance, the Christian Eucharist is spoken of as having a celebrant, not an actor, a congregation, not an audience. Nevertheless, most ritual has an element of public display. Indeed, spectacle, persuasion, and showmanship are parts of much of what is typically classed as religious ritual. Anybody who has attended a Christian Pentecostal mega-church (sometimes defined as those with congregations in excess of two thousand) will have been struck by the use of lights, music, impassioned oratory, stage management, and other elements to create something of a "show" (see box 16.9). It is not only in such highly professional and slick venues, which often consciously mimic a stage show, that we see "theatrical" performance. The more traditional rites of, for instance, the Greek Orthodox Church involve actions, words, music, and incense, all combining to create a certain effect upon those present.[25] Indeed, the aesthetic experience may be a key component in some ritual (see case study 12A).[26]

Despite crossover, some theorists do distinguish between ritual and theatrical performance. Erika Fischer-Lichte argues that ritual is somehow transformative, while theatrical performance is not.[27] However, Richard Schechner's work destabilizes even this distinction. While he believes that the modern entertainment industry (theater, cinema, etc.) has a "fourth wall" between performers and the audience, meaning it is simply entertainment, with no other message, he argues that many traditional forms of drama were indistinguishable from ritual. They were meant to be transformative of society and the participants, both audience and performers.[28] Indeed, some contemporary theater and other art forms aim for such transformation. A rigid distinction between theatrical performance and ritual as performance is therefore problematic. Indeed, the theatrical performance in cinematic media such as *Star Wars* has become a source of religious inspiration for some in the founding of Jedi Temples.[29]

PERFORMANCE THEORY: SPEECH ACTS

John L. Austin's (1911–1960) theory of the "speech act" stressed language as "doing."[30] This opposed traditional philosophy of language, which often stressed the propositional truth of statements, and so echoes developments begun by Ludwig Wittgenstein (1889–1951). For instance, logical positivist philosophy emphasized only grammatical coherence and correspondence to actuality. For logical positivists, if I say "It is raining," only two questions can be asked: is it linguistically coherent, and is there actually precipitation? For Austin, we must look at the context: why do I say this, to whom, and in what situation? Perhaps my statement "It is raining" means "Let's not go for a walk," or has some other actual effect, such as stopping you from going outside. Austin gave a threefold typology of speech acts:

Illocutionary acts: the meaning intended and the actual semantic construction that enacts it

Locutionary acts: the utterance itself.

Perlocutionary acts: the actual effect, regardless of intention

Austin was concerned with the effect of language, and he introduced the term "felicity" to denote this. This stressed the social context. For instance, if a judge sentences a prisoner to jail, saying "I sentence you to five years in jail," it is of little meaning to ask: "is it true?" Rather, Austin says, we can ask of the statement: "is it effective?" This depends on context:

- the judge making this statement in a particular location and time (in a court in session);
- the judge acting in her official capacity (as opposed to speaking in a personal capacity); and
- the judge making this statement in the right cultural setting (a Dutch judge cannot do this in Argentina).

Relating this to Austin's threefold typology, we can see this:

Illocutionary act: The judge wants to sentence a prisoner (meaning intended), which depends upon the context of being in court, acting officially, and following procedure (semantic constructions, both in language and context).

Locutionary act: The judge utters the statement—"I sentence you to five years in jail" (the utterance itself).

Perlocutionary act: The prisoner is taken away by the police/prison officers to jail (actual effect).

Speech acts resemble rituals in various ways: there is often a context, prescribed wording, and a set of actions which make them effective. For instance, a Christian priest eating bread and wine in a restaurant will not be performing the Eucharist (despite breaking bread and drinking wine).

PERFORMANCE THEORY: RITUALIZED ACTION

Key in Austin's language theory is embodiment and social context, rather than simply words and meanings. This is a key emphasis in theories of performance, which draw from Austin, John Searle,[31] theater, opera, dance, music, and communication media, including news and sports. These areas, like ritual, have an element of performance. Erving Goffman (1922–1982) has also been influential through his concern with the way that we present the self in everyday life, especially in the "face-to-face" encounters with other people.[32] In ritual theory this has been developed by Catherine Bell, who introduced the concept of ritualization (see box 12.7).

PERFORMANCE THEORY: PERSUASION

Schechner worked with Turner, who had spoken of ritual as a "social drama," emphasizing the continuum between theater, or drama, and ritual activities. All such activities often entail attempts to persuade, influence, or affect the audience; even if contemporary drama is primarily entertainment, actors need to persuade the audience that their performance is compelling. This idea of performance affecting the audience goes back to Aristotle's (384–322 BCE) *Poetics*, where he argued dramatic performances could give some form of emotional release or expression.[33] Notably, Aristotle's term "catharsis," which means "purification" or "purgation" in Greek, did not intend that dramatic performances actually give us a ritual purification (transformation). Rather, his term was a metaphor, expressing feelings of tragic pleasure in watching the dramatic tragedies of his time. Hence, for Aristotle, theater was about entertainment, and so could be distinguished from ritual in a way analogous to the usage we noted in Fischer-Lichte's work. Nevertheless, we again see the key notion that performance is an act of persuasion in some form. In classical theory, we can see this when Ibn Sina (980–1037) places his discussion of Aristotle's *Poetics* under the heading of "logic" in the *Cure* (*al-Shifa*, also *Book of Healing*, or *Healing*) but discusses how art affects us differently from logical argument, hence showing that persuasion can combine various elements.[34]

RITUALIZATION

Catherine Bell (1953–2008) gave us the term "ritualization" to speak about the way that forms of behavior are patterned for us by ritual action and social expectation.[1] While Erving Goffman (1922–1982) focused on such things as greetings, handshakes, and pleasantries, Bell extended this to ritual behavior more widely. Bell notes: "Ritualization is first and foremost a strategy for the construction of certain types of power relationships effective within particular social organizations."[2] We can see a direct link here to theories around social construction and particularly Pierre Bourdieu's (1930–2002) theory of habitus (see box 5.3). Bell's work also challenged the traditional hierarchies/dichotomies of thought-action/mind-body. That is to say, she addressed the question of whether belief/myth is prior to ritual/action. She argued that ritualized action shapes what we think and shapes how we act. We do not see a hierarchy, but understand the imbricated nature of ritualized performance as both thought and action. This accords with arguments recognizing both the linguistic/social construction of reality and embodiment/materiality as basic to our understanding of the world (see chapters 5 and 9).

---

1 Bell did not see her work in ritual theory as coterminous with performance theory. She believed the two, while mutually insightful, were distinct. See Ronald Grimes, "Performance," in Kreinath et al., *Theorizing Rituals*, 379–94, 392.
2 Catherine Bell, *Ritual Theory, Ritual Practice* (Oxford: Oxford University Press, 1992), 197.

PERFORMATIVITY: PERFORMING A ROLE

Though theorized by Austin and others, performativity is often associated with Judith Butler's work on gender construction. She argues that our being male or female is based upon our performance of the norms that society associates with these identities (see chapter 10). Performativity, in her terms, particularly focuses on acts—spoken or physical—which have real effects in creating our world. Performativity differs from performance, which is simply the doing of things. This is seen in what she terms "performatives," which are "inserted in a citational chain, and that means that the temporal conditions for making the speech act precede and exceed the momentary occasion of its enunciation."[35] That is to say, they become part of the framing of our world as discourse. This is seen, Butler argues, in gender because as we perform it shapes the way that we are seen, but also exceeds any moment in which we perform by being tied into a wider discourse in society which is both shaping us and being shaped by us.[36] Likewise ritual, by being repeated and reperformed, often with demarcated forms of discourse, is a performative. Butler also suggested that performativity could be subversive, for we could perform otherwise than society expects us, or a ritual could be enacted against an established norm; this, however, is seen as something which is not easy and which may reinforce the norms or simply fail to be understood.[37]

This notion of action is key in contemporary theory. As noted above, Asad theorized that from medieval to modern times ritual had moved from being part of a form of life which enthused our being, to being seen as only a set of mechanical actions. Contemporary ritual theory stresses, in the work of Bell and others, the embodied activity. We move from studying ritual (as particular acts) to ritualization (where the ritual itself is the performative power). Stanley Tambiah noted three ways to speak of a ritual as performative:[38]

1. In Austin's sense of being a speech act, it is a statement that is effective in some sense.
2. By it being an act of theater, it is a staged performance.
3. It has a "duplex structure," meaning that it enacts a certain myth (a worldview or cosmological schema), but also gives a sense of legitimacy to certain social hierarchies.

To end this section, we can pick up on this through a quote by Grimes: "Because performativity depends on dissimulation, it is dangerous and must be rendered transparent and questionable."[39] That is, Grimes claims that performance, by seeking to be something other than it is, may be deceptive. Two points follow for us. First, as in Tambiah's third point, it legitimates social hierarchies, and we must be aware of this. Second, just as early theorists were found wanting by later theory, performativity does not give us a final view on ritual, and we should be critical of our own perspectives: scholarship is, arguably, a type of performance and so may equally be prone to dissimulation; hence we should be reflexive of our own practice (see chapter 2).

· · ·

CASE STUDY 12A. THE ZEN TEA CEREMONY AND PROTESTANT EUCHARIST AS PERFORMANCE AND RITUAL

The English terms "ritual," "rite," and "ceremony" signify various forms of routinized behavior, but may not relate to native terms in other traditions. While Japanese contains a number of terms that can be translated as "ritual," they do not directly correlate.[40] However, our focus here is not terminology, though the question of how whatever we see as ritual, art, or something else so designated is raised. We focus on two distinct rituals as performance and aesthetic acts.

THE ZEN TEA CEREMONY

The Japanese Zen tea ceremony developed around the sixteenth century. Partly in reaction to opulent tea parties at court, it stressed simplicity and minimalism. Basically, a host provides tea for guests; however, the ceremony is imbued with many layers. There are many variations of the ritual, and here we will follow an influential form associated with the tea master Sen no Rikyu (1522–1591).

The teahouse is set within a specifically designed garden. The garden is intended to provide a set of impressions to the guest as they wind their way along the path to the teahouse. This is not a time for conversation, but rather for contemplation of the beauty of the garden, more specifically, with a sense of transitoriness in nature, for the beauty will pass. On reaching the teahouse, guests remove their shoes and enter through doors that are small enough that they must bow down to enter. This is to emphasize humility, but it also means that large items such as swords will be left outside. The host will prepare the tea in a strictly ritualized pattern, which includes washing the tea leaves (never tea bags!) and the cups. Often the utensils, which include a brush for cleaning, the cups, and teapot, among other pieces, may include an antique item. Guests should show their knowledge and appreciation by remarking on its aesthetic quality. Rikyu was known for the *wabi* aesthetic of rustic simplicity, even crudeness, and today, in line with Japanese aesthetics, pieces may include a crack, which stresses both the transitoriness of life and the beauty of the item—a flaw is held to help enhance other facets.[41] Conversation should not be free, but follow strict patterns. Besides commenting on the utensils, this may include complimenting the host's performance, the exquisite layout of the garden, or the quality of the tea. Notably, the room itself may be bare with only a low table upon which the tea set is placed. Poetry may be recited, often created for the occasion, and should reflect the specifics of the event, for example the garden layout or tea set.

Importantly, this strict and circumscribed ritual is not to limit the freedom of participants but to help keep their mind free of distraction and to focus on simplicity, the transitoriness of existence, humility, and other virtues. The whole ceremony and context is specifically designed to reflect a Zen worldview.

THE HIGH CHURCH ANGLICAN/EPISCOPALIAN EUCHARIST

The exact performance of a Christian Eucharist varies geographically, chronologically, and by tradition. Here we outline an Anglican (Episcopalian) "high church" (emphasis on ritualized traditions) approach.

Presuming a churchgoing family, they will attend the church together. The congregation will arrive, often chatting to acquaintances before sitting in long pews set out in rows facing the altar at the east end of the building. Regulars will probably have one place they always sit, despite there being no reserved seating. The building itself is from the Victorian era (nineteenth century) and built in a faux medieval Gothic style (see case study 9B). Pictures and statues of saints in medieval style can be found. The priest, in ceremonial robes, will enter following a procession led by a person carrying a cross, two candle bearers, a thurifer (incense carrier), and the choir, with the organ playing. The hymns will be traditional with words and music written a hundred or more years earlier. (Note: only some parts of the service are mentioned here.) After an introduction, a confession of sins will take place, when the participants kneel, before the reading of various biblical passages. Almost all parts of the service are generic from week to week, but specific weekly passages of the Bible are prescribed. This will typically involve an Old Testament reading, a New Testament reading (not from a Gospel); a psalm, which may be sung (psalms are ancient Israelite ritual hymns), culminating with a Gospel reading. The Gospel book will be processed to the center of the church, flanked by candles, and will be wafted with incense before being read. After this, a statement of faith, the Nicene Creed, is recited, which is based upon wording agreed at councils during the fifth century CE. All attendees stand and face east for this. Hymns will be sung between various parts of the service. The service now proceeds toward its climax in the ritual blessing of the bread and wine, which symbolize Jesus's body and blood (see box 12.6). The priest will recite various prescribed words, and the congregation will follow with set responses. Every participant, if a fully initiated Christian, can receive some of the bread and wine. After the distribution of bread and wine is completed, a final blessing is given, and then the priest leaves in procession. Typically, the priest stands at the door of the church to chat with and say good-bye to the leaving members. Tea and coffee may be served at the back of the church or in an adjacent hall as an act of community fellowship. The whole service is enthused with ritualized Christian symbols, with the final part emphasizing (in theory at least) the community aspects of tradition.

RITUAL, ART, AND PERFORMANCE

In the two examples, the forms of behavior and attitudes expected of participants are very different. But similarities include precise and scripted, or at least circumscribed, words and actions: specific speech acts. Further, a ritual expert with ritual competence would lead. Distinct worldviews underlie each ritual, leading to expectations of what should be thought or experienced. There are also aesthetic elements of each ritual, with some form of dramatic element or show. Yet both may be said to be ritual, rather than theater, in terms of having some transformative significance.

REFLECTIONS

The following questions can help tease out some of these issues:

1. The two rituals described are very different. Which ritual appeals more to your aesthetic or other sensibilities? Why? How significant is the aesthetic element to a ritual?
2. Consider and explain the role of performance, either as linguistic speech act or dramatic performative staging, in each ritual.
3. How far can either be said to be performative, and how does this relate to it being a dramatic/performative/artistic experience?

4. What other aspects of ritual theory are most useful in discussing and describing these two sets of rituals? In particular, consider the ways in which each event does something very different with reference to myth-ritual theory.

CASE STUDY 12B. BUDDHIST ORDINATION RITES

We explore a Buddhist rite of passage, in this case marking entry and progression in the religious life. We will discuss ordination as it applies to a Buddhist monk (different rules apply to nuns; see case study 10B). Our description will be of typical Theravada rites, but similar rules apply in Mahayana Buddhism. There are two levels of ordination:

-   "Lower" ordination, or "going forth": In this level of ordination, the initiate becomes a novice (*shramana*) and follows the ten precepts (an extended code of Buddhist morality[42]). Admission to this level occurs from seven years of age onward.
-   "Higher" ordination, or "admission": The initiate becomes a monk (*bhikkhu*), following full monastic regulations (Vinaya) of the 227 precepts. Admission is from nineteen years of age (traditionally measured from conception, so often stated as twenty years old).

ASPECTS OF RITUAL

In both ordinations, some similar rules are in place:

-   Five properly ordained monks must be present to conduct the ceremony.
-   The ordination area is often marked off with sacred boundary stones.
-   Sometimes a triple altar (tiered stage) is constructed.
-   The initiate's head is shaved.
-   Initiates begin by wearing everyday clothes and receive new monastic robes which are donned during the ceremony.
-   An alms bowl is received.
-   Scriptures are recited, especially those on the Buddha's founding of the monastic community (*sangha*) and his "going forth" from his home to seek awakening/nirvana.

The ordination ceremony is often a festival, with the families and local community celebrating the entry of the new novices or monks into what is considered a noble profession. For laypeople, supporting the ceremony gains "merit" (*punya*), or good *karma*, which is believed to assist in obtaining a better rebirth.

Neither form of ordination is irreversible, though returning to lay life is more common for novices, since this level can function as a period of testing to see if full ordination is suitable. This is also variable by location: some stigma attaches to ex-monks in Sri Lanka, but in Thailand it is common for people to enter and leave the monastic order.

REFLECTIONS

Some questions can help us relate Buddhist ordination to ritual theory:

1. What similarities do you see to rites of passage you are familiar with? What are the differences, and how do you think this may affect your perception of this ceremony?

2. In what ways can the ordination ceremony be described as a rite of passage? Which aspects link to rites of separation and reintegration, as well as a liminal stage?

3. From a social functionalist perspective, the ordination of monastics provides a time for the lay community and monks to integrate and bond. The laypeople will typically pay for the robes, the ceremony, and give gifts of money and/or food to the monastery (*dana*). Meanwhile, the laypeople will receive blessings and have opportunities for merit (*punya*) collection. The relationship of the two groups will be reinforced. In what other ways do you think ritual theory can be applied to the ordination ceremony?

4. Catherine Bell's notion of ritualization would stress the way that social hierarchies and power relations are enacted in the ceremony. What ways do you think this ritual shows domination and power relations?

·   ·   ·

QUESTIONS AND CONNECTING THOUGHTS

There are many places at which ritual theory crosses over into other areas. For instance, like "religion" (chapter 1), "ritual" is embedded in a particular Western and Christian heritage, which has often determined how it is theorized (see chapter 7). It plays a key part in lived religion (chapter 3) and material religion (chapter 9). Social constructionism cites many of the same theorists (chapter 5). Ritual demarcates the pure and impure, which relates to how we create identities (chapter 6). Women are often excluded from many ritual practices (chapter 10). Ritual or performance also appears in various case studies (e.g., case studies 1B, 9A, 11B, 17A, 18B). This does not fully explore the range of issues engaged. We will conclude with some questions to think through the issues:

1. Consider how you engage in ritual within a realm of your life. Perhaps at home or at work? Are your lectures, seminars, and classes ritual(ized) events?

2. Do you consider ritual to just be for show, or does it actually have some power? Does this depend on the particular ritual? Consider what it means for a ritual to be performative.

3. Mary Douglas's notion of "matter out of place" applies beyond ritual. Consider ways in which your society (in either religious or non-religious terms) demarcates barriers and distinctions between "pure" and "impure." How is this policed? Are there ways in which ritual allows something to cross this barrier?

4. What do you understand by liminality? Give an example of a liminal event, time, person, or stage. Does it relate to Van Gennep's three types of rites (separation, transition, integration)?

5. Think about a major (religious, state, etc.) ritual and analyze it in terms of performance theory and speech acts. What is done, where, by whom, with what intent, and what effect? You may ask in what senses it is a performance to persuade, and what types of speech structures give it power.

FURTHER READING

THEORY

Asad, Talal. *Genealogy of Religion: Discipline and Reasons of Power in Christianity and Islam* (Baltimore: John Hopkins University Press, 2009).

Bell, Catherine. "Ritual," in *The Blackwell Companion to the Study of Religion*, ed. Robert Segal (Chichester: Wiley-Blackwell, 2009), 397–412.

Brunotte, Ulrike. "Classic Ritual Theories," in *Religion, Theory, Critique: Classic and Contemporary Approaches and Methodologies*, ed. Richard King (New York: Columbia University Press, 2017), 351–65.

Grimes, Ronald. *The Craft of Ritual Studies* (Oxford: Oxford University Press, 2014).

Grimes, Ronald. "Performance," in *Theorizing Rituals: Issues, Topics, Approaches, Concepts*, ed. Jens Kreinath, Jan Snoek, and Michael Stausberg (Leiden: Brill, 2008), 379–94.

McClymond, Kathryn. *Beyond Sacred Violence* (Baltimore: John Hopkins University Press, 2008).

Michaels, Axel, and William S. Sax. "Performance," in *The Oxford Handbook of the Study of Religion*, ed. Michael Stausberg and Steven Engler (Oxford: Oxford University Press, 2016), 304–15.

Segal, Robert. "Myth and Ritual," in *The Routledge Companion to the Study of Religion*, 2nd ed., ed. John Hinnells (New York: Routledge, 2010), 372–96.

Smith, Jonathan Z. *To Take Place: Toward Theory in Ritual* (Chicago: Chicago University Press, 1987).

Stewart, Pamela, and Andrew Strathern. *Ritual: Key Concepts in Religion* (London: Bloomsbury, 2014).

Tambiah, Stanley. "A Performative Approach to Ritual: Radcliffe-Brown Lecture," *Proceedings of the British Academy* 65 (1979): 113–69.

CASE STUDY 12A. THE ZEN BUDDHIST TEA CEREMONY
AND PROTESTANT CHRISTIAN EUCHARIST AS PERFORMANCE
AND RITUAL

Begin Japanology. "Documentary: Japanese Tea Ceremony," *Begin Japanology* (2017), www.youtube.com/watch?v=gx59Y8VFseo.

Castro, Lucas. "Tea Cerimony [*sic*] Explained," YouTube.com (2010), www.youtube.com /watch?v=K6_KC3OuZek.

Chryssides, George. *Christianity Today: An Introduction* (London: Continuum, 2010), 10–11, 123–26.

McGrath, Alister. *Christianity: An Introduction,* 3rd ed. (Chichester: Wiley-Blackwell, 2015), 116–17, 334–36.

Smart History. "William Butterfield, All Saints, Margaret Street," Khan Academy (2012), www.youtube.com/watch?v=OMEDRrGpybY.

Trinity Church. "Sunday 11: 15 am Holy Eucharist," Trinity Church Wall Street (2017), www.trinitywallstreet.org/video/sunday-1115am-holy-eucharist-50.

Williams, Ron, and James Boyd. "Aesthetics," in Kreinath et al., *Theorizing Rituals,* 285–305.

Wilson, Daniel. "The Japanese Tea Ceremony and Pancultural Definitions of Art," *Journal of Aesthetics and Art Criticism* 76.1 (2018): 33–44.

CASE STUDY 12B. BUDDHIST ORDINATION RITES

Crosby, Kate. *Theravada Buddhism: Continuity, Diversity, and Identity* (Chichester: Wiley-Blackwell, 2014), 197–210.

Gombrich, Richard. *Theravada Buddhism: A Social History from Ancient Benares to Modern Colombo* (New York: Routledge, 2006), 107–18.

Import Food. "Buddhist Monk Ordination Ceremony," YouTube.com (2011), www .youtube.com/watch?v=M7c3LMnx5ig.

Lamb, Christopher. "Rites of Passage," in *Buddhism,* ed. Peter Harvey (London: Continuum, 2001), 151–80.

Swearer, Donald. *The Buddhist World of Southeast Asia* (Albany: State University of New York Press, 1995), 36–42.

RELIGIOUS DIVERSITY AND SOCIETY

13

DIVERSITY
Religious Borders, Identities, and Discourses

IN WHICH WE EXPLORE

The notion of diversity in relation to the problem of defining "religion"

Religious diversity in global contexts and relating to identity

The typology of exclusivism-inclusivism-pluralism as a descriptive marker

Case studies on the discourse of Al-Andalusia, and Catholic Christian theology
of religions in Asian and European contexts

INTRODUCTION

Do you regard religious diversity as a new phenomenon? It probably depends where you come from. Many argue that the contemporary world has unprecedented levels of religious diversity. However, religious diversity has been the norm in many cultures throughout history. Across Asia, Buddhists, Christians, Daoists, Hindus, Jains, Muslims, Sikhs, Zoroastrians, and others have rubbed shoulders for centuries. However, North Americans, Western Europeans, Australians, and others often speak of religious diversity as new.[1]

We begin by looking at how diversity has been understood in differing global contexts, focusing on Western, Chinese, and Islamic perspectives. We also address how scholars think about these issues. Next, we present the typology of exclusivism-inclusivism-pluralism as sets of descriptive markers which can demarcate both theological and social stances toward diversity, before we address some issues for thinking about diversity, including identity theory (see also chapter 6) and supersessionism. We end, as ever, with our two case studies.

UNDERSTANDING RELIGIOUS DIVERSITY

THE "DIVERSITY OF DIVERSITY"?

If religion is an "essentially contested concept" (see especially chapter 1), global contexts of diversity can help us reflect on the porous and permeable boundaries of any religion. Particular historical and cultural lenses inform our ways of conceiving religious boundaries and classifications. Indeed, the modern, Western notion of diversity as "new" does not prevail in most of the world, and involves a certain myopia in forgetting the diversity of Europe and beyond.[2]

RELIGIOUS DIVERSITY IN THE CHINESE CONTEXT

Traditional Chinese religion is typically divided into three main strands, but we may add a fourth:[3] Confucianism, Daoism, Buddhism, and folk religion. The Western naming of these traditions, while shaping what each entails, is not solely about Western "creation," but builds upon indigenous categories (see chapter 7, especially case study 7A).[4] However, understanding them as separate religions within the world religions paradigm (WRP; see chapter 1 and box 2.1), misconstrues the Chinese context (see box 13.1). One notable aspect of the Chinese religious ecology is the concept of the "three traditions" (*sanjiao*), where each tradition was sometimes seen as providing for different areas of life: Confucianism regulated public morality; Buddhism dealt with the afterlife; Daoism concerned biospiritual cultivation (on this concept see box 1.11).[5] Fierce polemics occurred between the traditions, sometimes conceived in exclusive ways, yet this was far from the sole model.[6]

TRADITIONAL ISLAMIC CONCEPTIONS OF RELIGIOUS DIVERSITY

Islam has used the notion of the "People of the Book" (*ahl al-kitab*), among others, to make sense of religious diversity. The Quran distinguishes at least five traditions: polytheism, Islam, Judaism, Christianity, and Sabianism. The last three, classed as "People of the Book" (see box 13.2), are distinguished from polytheists, who seem to be regarded as having an illegitimate form of practice and belief: they do not believe in one God and do not follow the teachings of a recognized prophet. In Islamic law (*shariah*) the People of the Book were deemed "protected people" (*dhimmi*), meaning if they lived under Muslim rule they would be protected and allowed to follow their own customs and practices.[7] This distinguished them from "infidels" (*kafir*, also "unbelievers"), which variously indicated those not protected.[8]

As the empires that embraced Islam spread, they encountered Zoroastrianism, Hinduism, Buddhism, and other traditions. At least some Muslim jurists (*ulama*) argued

STRATEGIC RELIGIOUS PARTICIPATION IN CHINESE RELIGIOSITY

In traditional Chinese society there was not normally any barrier that prevented people from partaking in, or making use of, the resources of Buddhism, Confucianism, Daoism, and folk religion.[1] People participated in, or made use of, traditions as needed rather than explicitly "identifying" with one, or any, religion. This is termed strategic religious participation (SRP). While each was a distinct tradition (at least after around 1000 CE, when neo-Confucianism arose, but in certain ways before then too), they were not perceived as distinct and bounded territories along the lines of the WRP model. Meanwhile, there were shared cosmological assumptions: a shared religious landscape (SRL). The assumption was of essential compatibility. Monks, priests, and nuns were initiated into specific Buddhist or Daoist lineages, while Confucian literati, at least from the rise of neo-Confucianism, would identify with that in contradistinction to Buddhism and Daoism. Nevertheless, people saw no issue in seeking strategic participation in the different traditions, at both grassroots and elite levels. For instance: Buddhists were seen as experts in funerals and were approached for these services; Celestial Master Daoists were seen as the exorcists par excellence and so would be hired for this; Daoist priests were, and still are, sent to study under a Buddhist master if the latter is seen as having a particular expertise, while Quanzhen Daoism explicitly included elements from various traditions.[2] Such border crossing of traditions may appear similar to what scholars sometimes call multiple religious identity (MRI; see case study 2B), but it is distinct.[3]

---

1 See Paul Hedges, "Multiple Religious Belonging after Religion: Theorising Strategic Religious Participation in a Shared Religious Landscape as a Chinese Model," *Open Theology* 3.1 (2017): 48–72.

2 Paul Hedges, "Why Are There Many Gods?: Religious Diversity and Its Challenges," in *Controversies in Contemporary Religion*, ed. Paul Hedges, vol. 1 (Santa Barbara: Praeger, 2014), 191–218, 198.

3 See Hedges, "Multiple Religious Belonging," 56–59.

that they should be recognized as "People of the Book"; that is, they had significant texts which could be attributed to a prophet—the Quran indicated a prophet was sent to every people.[9] Islam, therefore, had its own theory of religious diversity distinct from the WRP model. However, in modern times, Islam tends to denote a fixed tradition different from the other religions of Christianity, Hinduism, Sikhism, and so on.

MEDIEVAL EUROPEAN CHRISTIANS AND DIVERSITY

For medieval European[10] Christians, the world was perceived as mono-religious. All that existed was (Catholic) Christianity and various heresies: Jews had failed to recognize their Messiah, making them "failed Christians"; Muhammad, according to a widespread tradition, was a cardinal who set up his own heresy after he failed to become Pope; and the Orthodox, Cathars, and other Christians were seen as schismatic heretics. Few Pagans still existed, and so there was essentially no concept of religious diversity. The diversity encountered with colonialism was, therefore, a shock.[11]

A TYPOLOGY FOR CLASSIFYING APPROACHES TO DIVERSITY

The typology of approaches termed exclusivisms-inclusivisms-pluralisms (sometimes a fourth is added: particularities[12]) was developed by Alan Race[13] to describe Christian theological attitudes toward non-Christian religions. Meanwhile, Diana Eck used the terms to speak primarily about social attitudes toward religious diversity (see box 13.3).[14] Both were originally used in somewhat theological ways, and by those who supported a pluralist stance. However, arguably, they can function as simple descriptive markers, as employed here.[15] This also raises the question as to whether scholars should take a stance on how we approach diversity (see box 13.4).

EXCLUSIVISMS, INCLUSIVISMS, AND PLURALISMS AS DESCRIPTIVE MARKERS

We begin by setting the terms out as both theological and social markers. (For the former, this will be primarily in relation to the Christian context in which they were developed.) As theological markers they can help us think about how different religions conceptualize

The terms "religious diversity" and "pluralism" are often used interchangeably to talk about contexts of religious multiplicity. However, herein, we will employ "diversity" simply as a descriptive marker of such multiplicity. "Pluralism" will be reserved for attitudes (social or theological) toward religious diversity which see it as a positive virtue or embrace it in various ways.

Are scholars simply neutral and impartial observers of religious diversity? Or can they take a position on the issues? This relates to questions raised elsewhere (see chapters 2, 5, 7, 10, and 18). Oddbjørn Leirvik has noted that scholars are involved in the networks of power that create our social discourse (see box 5.1),[1] while Lori Beaman has argued, quoting Kenneth Gergen, that "the aim of research would not be to illuminate what is but to create what is to become."[2] That is to say, scholarship and the study of religion is not simply saying what is out there (and what it says, why it says it, and whose agenda is supported by it), but also arguing for better ways of being in the world. Many scholars of religion, however, see this as a theological, or activist, approach rather than as a religious studies approach.

1 Oddbjörn Leirvik, *Interreligious Studies: A Relational Approach to Religious Activism and the Study of Religion* (London: Bloomsbury, 2014), 11–12.
2 Lori Beaman, *Deep Equality in an Era of Religious Diversity* (Oxford: Oxford University Press, 2017), 194, quoting Kenneth Gergen.

religious diversity (though arguably they could also be markers of how atheists assess religious diversity[16]). As social markers, they help conceptualize attitudes in the public sphere in relation to diversity (this can apply equally to ethnic/racial diversity as much as religious diversity).

Exclusivisms (theological): One religion (tradition, belief, revelation, etc.) possesses the whole truth, and therefore other religions must be false. The exclusivist does not necessarily insist that others will go to hell. Nevertheless, the basic dynamic is that one's own tradition, or that part of the tradition one belongs to, is the source of all truth, light, and knowledge. Therefore, others are necessarily in error.

Exclusivisms (social): A socially exclusivist attitude is antagonistic to religious/cultural/ethnic diversity, which sees it as, perhaps, diluting or threatening the purity of one's own culture/country/tradition/race.[17] It resists learning from the Other (see box 13.5).

Exclusivism was typical of Christian Protestant missionaries in the nineteenth century,
and is still prevalent among many.[18] It would be wrong, though, to assume that exclusivism is "taught" by the Bible (see box 13.10). In general terms, most religions represent
this dynamic at certain times.[19]

> *Inclusivisms (theological):* Race described inclusivism as "a dialectical yes and
> no."[20] Inclusivists accept some truth in other religions, yet insist their own
> tradition contains the fullness of truth. Inclusivists can veer toward a more
> exclusivist stance, seeing other religions as partial reflections of their own,
> but at most only leading toward it. As such, salvation is not achievable
> through other religions: conversion is needed. Other inclusivists assert other
> religions could be the route to salvation, but this is actually attained through
> the truths explicated in their own religion.[21]

> *Inclusivisms (social):* Social inclusivism involves a tolerance (see box 13.6) of
> difference as perhaps a pragmatic but not desirable necessity of life. The
> inclusivist may recognize some value in diversity, but she may not always
> welcome it or see other cultures and traditions as equal to her own.

Christian inclusivists appeal to many biblical passages and notable Christian theologians
such as Irenaeus of Lyons (ca. 120/140–200/203 CE), Justin Martin(100–165), Origen
(ca. 183–253/254), Augustine of Hippo (354–430), Pope Gregory the Great (ca. 540–604),
Thomas Aquinas (1225–1274), and Charles Wesley (1707–1788).[22] Most mainstream
Christian denominations today hold an inclusivist position. Arguably, it has been very

It is sometimes suggested that social harmony between religions requires toleration of one another's views. However, others suggest that toleration is not enough.[1] The origins of the term "toleration" go back to medieval pharmacy. Toleration was the amount of a poisonous substance (sometimes administered for medical purposes) a body could accept before dying. To tolerate something means to accept it, even if we do not like it. As such, many suggest that we need to move beyond toleration to what are seen as the virtues of acceptance or appreciation. However, for some, toleration of the Other (see box 13.5) is already a big step.

1 See, e.g., Perry Schmidt-Leukel, *Transformation by Integration: How Inter-Faith Encounter Changes Christianity* (London: SCM, 2009); and Mia Kimmons, "'Tolerance' Is Not Enough," *Asha Leader* 22.8 (2017), 8–9, https://leader.pubs.asha.org/doi/10.1044/leader.FMP.22082017.8.

common across religions, encapsulating mainstream Islamic approaches,[23] and is also found in Hinduism and Buddhism.[24]

Pluralisms (theological): Potentially, many religions may be equal sources of revelation and divine knowledge. Pluralism does not entail admitting that every possible claimed religion or practice is equally effective or revealed; there may be false or inadequate forms of religion or spirituality. However, for the pluralist, there are reasons for claiming that one's own religion/tradition alone is not necessarily and absolutely the only unique and perfect form of knowing of the divine/transcendent.[25]

Pluralisms (social): In social terms, pluralists embrace and rejoice in the social, religious, and cultural diversity around us. Diversity is seen as a source for potential growth and learning. The kaleidoscope of diversity is seen as being, if recognized as such, a benefit for all.[26]

A directly stated Christian pluralist position arose only in the twentieth century. Nevertheless, Christian pluralists claim support from the Bible and its theological tradition. Others term it a "post-Christian" stance,[27] so it is useful to see why Christian theologians may argue for it (see box 13.7). Pluralism has never been normative in other traditions, though certain Hindu texts are read to support it, while many Daoists today (and perhaps also historically) argue that as the Dao is always multiple there can never only be one true expression of it; hence many religious paths must be valid.[28]

THE TYPOLOGY BEYOND CHRISTIANITY

Some have suggested that the terms fit quite well onto many religions, representing these patterns of:

BOX 13.7 **CHRISTIAN PLURALIST JUSTIFICATIONS
IN THE BIBLE AND TRADITION**

That the Persian king Cyrus, who was a Zoroastrian, is described as God's regent on Earth and the Messiah (Is. 45:1)—the title associated with Jesus (see case study 4A)—is argued by pluralists to show that God does not see religious affiliation as significant. Likewise, in the New Testament, several people are said to be acceptable to God by their good actions and trust in the divine, not in Jesus or his actions.[1] Some pluralist theologians have further argued that God's universal love suggests a universal access is offered, while others mention their experience of meeting people of other religions who seem to have just as deep a life of prayer and are as filled with compassion as any Christian.[2]

---

1 See Hedges, *Controversies in Interreligious Dialogue*, 137–43.
2 See John Hick, *An Autobiography* (Oxford: Oneworld, 2005). On Hick's pluralism, see Hedges, *Controversies in Interreligious Dialogue*, 113–15.

Exclusion/exclusivisms: We alone are right; all others are wrong.

Inclusion/inclusivisms: We are completely right, but others have partial truths.

Openness/pluralisms: There are potentially many equally true paths.

For instance, Mohammed Hassan Khalil uses the three terms, but with a particular nuance, in relation to Islam:

> "Exclusivists" maintain that only their particular tradition or interpretation is salvific and that adherents of all other beliefs will be punished in hell. "Inclusivists" similarly affirm that theirs is the path of heaven but hold that sincere outsiders who could not have recognized it as such will be saved. "Pluralists" assert that, regardless of the circumstances, there are several religious traditions or interpretations that are equally effective salvifically.[29]

Khalil argues the inclusivist stance is the dominant one in Islam, even among many thinkers often seen as "conservative," such as Ibn Taymiyyah (1263–1328), who emphasized a literal reading of the Quran and the supreme authority of early traditions, where he found inclusivist teachings, as well as Abu Hamid al-Ghazali (ca. 1056–1111) and Shah Wali Allah (ca. 1703–1762).[30] Arguably, even if the typology can be readily applied to Islam, it does not show its applicability to all traditions. Guy Stroumsa has argued for a certain common ground in the development of Christianity, Judaism, and Islam in late antiquity (roughly first century to eighth century CE),[31] suggesting that any commonalities here may be due to shared histories.

Abraham Vélez de Cea has argued that the typology must be modified in application to Buddhism, though Kristin Kiblinger has more readily applied the typology in that context.[32] For our purposes, Cea argues three main points:

1. We should focus on the concept of "openness." For him the exclusivisms-inclusivisms-pluralisms typology is a continuum of degrees of openness.

2. We should make a distinction between "two types of openness: openness in practice and openness in theory."[33]

3. We have to see that each religion values different things. For Christianity, "God, grace, truth, goodness, love, justice, and so on"; for Buddhism, nirvana, the figure of the Buddha, the tradition (*sasana*), the teaching (*dharma*), and so on.

Cea's argument may shift the way we see the focus of exclusivisms-inclusivisms-pluralisms, especially in "theological" terms (though this term does not apply so readily to Buddhism). It shifts from a focus on salvation—the Christian conception—to other factors. Further, there have been two main approaches in applying the typology: one associated with Perry Schmidt-Leukel, which argues the typological terms are distinct options that logically classify every possible stance in relation to truth and falsity, and salvific options; and the other associated with Paul Hedges, which sees them as fluid heuristic signifiers that overlap but usefully provide what Max Weber would term "ideal types."[34] Here we favor the latter, which allows us to see the value of Cea's suggestion that it must be modified to perceive what Buddhists value as most significant.[35]

GRAPPLING WITH DIVERSITY AND IDENTITY
TONES AND TENDENCIES

While the typology helps demarcate stances/worldviews which tend broadly to be exclusivist, inclusivist, or pluralist, particular thinkers may be more or less "open" to the Other. John Nicol Farquhar (1861–1929), whose book *The Crown of Hinduism*[36] is often seen to epitomize inclusivism, argued that a Hindu who properly understands her own religion will be led to Christianity. His title indicates that Christianity is the final "crown" or fulfillment of Hinduism; indeed, this theological stance was often termed "fulfillment theology."[37] Farquhar argued that doctrines such as the Hindu notion of the *avatar*, instances where deities were seen to manifest in physical form, were anticipations or intimations toward the Christian doctrine of the incarnation, that is, the teaching that Jesus was deity manifest in human form. As such, Farquhar, a Christian evangelical missionary, saw many good elements in Hinduism, and the general thrust of that religion as leading toward his own. However, Farquhar saw deep deficiencies in Hinduism as a system, meaning there is no natural progression to Christianity. Rather, he argued, that Hinduism "must die" in order to become Christianity.[38] In this way, despite having inclusivist arguments, the tendency—or we may say tone—of Farquhar's argument was toward an exclusivist stance. Indeed, stated theological types may differ from a wider range of attitudes and behaviors, which may be worked out in how ideas are expressed or lived out.[39] As such, we need to think about how we create our identities in relation to in-groups and out-groups (see chapter 6).

RELIGIOUS BORDERS AND IDENTITIES: IN-GROUPS AND OUT-GROUPS

The perceived boundaries between religious traditions are not, and never have been, stable. It is useful to understand this in relation to social identity theory. While more fully elaborated in chapter 6, we note some aspects here.

First, everybody's identities are multiple, and often overlapping. Attitudes toward any specific religious (or non-religious) Other (see box 13.5) often depends upon factors outside the religious tradition. This also may affect whether we perceive the Other in positive or negative terms. Everybody tends to have more positive attitudes and behavior toward those we perceive to be part of our in-group, rather than those imagined as the out-group. Therefore, when religious identities get heightened, especially in times of potential conflictual encounter, we tend to support our own religion more (or identify more with a non-religious identity) and have more negative views toward out-groups. Further, these identities, as multiple, exist in relation to other identities, none of which are stable. We may therefore speak of these relationships of identities in terms of a "shifting third" (see box 13.8).

Identifying strongly with our in-group can lead toward what is termed "deindividuation," meaning you are more likely to act in a way appropriate to the norms of the group and identify more with the group than you would otherwise[40] by taking on salient behaviors in relation to that group. Importantly, this is not always against religious coexistence, as our religious identities, as much as any other identities, are "imagined." If a group stresses the unity of their identity as all "religious people," then the in-group and out-group identities will be quite different than in situations where, for instance, strong lines are drawn between Muslims, Christians, and Jews. But it must be remembered that identity is primarily constructed in relation to the Other, often by defining ourselves against what we are not (see chapter 6). Stuart Hall usefully reflects on this, which he notes is always a "process": "Identity emerges as a kind of unsettled space, or an unresolved question in that space, between a number of intersecting discourses . . . Identity is not a fixed point but an ambivalent point. Identity is also the relationship of the Other to oneself."[41] (Note: Another use of deindividuation is where the Other is deprived of their identity as an individual and treated generically as part of an out-group. This is often linked to the Other being dehumanized, which is related to othering [see boxes 13.5 and 15.9]).[42]

THE SHIFTING THIRD

Let us think about the relationship of two groups, for instance, Christian and Muslims. These groups do not exist in a vacuum. These identities exist in relation to other identities and concepts, two of which in the Christian-Muslim relationship today are Judaism and secularism. However, the third identity (in this case, Judaism or secularism) is not stable, so we may speak of it as a "shifting third";[1] moreover, "third" is not simply a numerical signifier as there may be multiple others involved in the relationship. The term "shifting third" is intended primarily to denote that when we think about the relationship between any two groups, we need to recognize that the relationship does not occur in a vacuum but always, and only, in relation to external factors which are not monolithic and stable: they shift. For instance: secularism may at times be seen as favoring Christianity more than Islam (see case study 16A); elsewhere, some Christians may see a minority such as Muslims being favored over them by a secular polity; at other times, Muslims and Christians may see themselves in a beleaguered alliance against a secular world (see chapter 16). Again, depending on the historical period and context, Judaism may be seen as more closely allied to Christians or Muslims. The "shifting third" helps us think about situations where two identities meet, as it is always in relation to at least one other which itself is not static nor stable.

1 See Paul Hedges, "The Contemporary Context of Muslim-Christian Dialogue," in *Contemporary Muslim-Christian Encounters: Developments, Diversity and Dialogues*, ed. Paul Hedges (London: Bloomsbury, 2015), 17–31, 27–29.

We can speak of a "common in-group identity."[43] Again, depending upon the context, what is seen as the salient behavior of specific religious identities will vary widely (see box 13.9). How this manifests as behavior will depend on whether the religious identity is seen as evangelistic and proselytizing, aggressive and domineering, peaceful, concerned only with one's own inner spiritual life and personal devotion, and so on.

This question of identity is important in understanding why, in particular situations, very different attitudes toward those perceived as the religious "Other" are found in different religions. In Christianity, and most religions, strands we can identify as pluralist, inclusivist, and exclusivist exist. In Christian terms, these claims often relate to interpretations of the Bible. However, we can see very different—competing—interpretations of the same text. Therefore, the readings may be said to come from assumed identities, rather than from the text itself (see box 13.10). As Hall has noted, all identities exist within discourses of power, in this case as competing interpretations of authoritative sources.[44]

A final issue is the intergroup sensitivity effect.[45] This concerns the way that we will more readily allow criticism from those we perceive as part of our own in-group, rather than criticism from an out-group. Much religious polemic and debate may relate to how

FOOTBALL (SOCCER) AND RELIGIOUS IDENTITIES

At the 2018 FIFA World Cup in Russia, many were amazed by the actions of Japanese and Senegalese football fans. At the end of their matches, these fans, as a group, tidied and picked up litter in the stands where they had been sitting.[1] They were left as spotless as when they first arrived. In contrast, after other teams had played, their fans generally left the stadium in a mess, with drink cups and food wrappings left everywhere. The way that Japanese and Senegalese football fans interpreted their identity was quite distinct. Simplistic claims that "religious people," "football fans," "atheists," or any other group all behaves in a certain way is to misunderstand human identity formation and the culturally specific behavior associated with those identities.

---

1 Adam Withnall, "World Cup 2018: Senegal and Japan Fans Praised for Cleaning Up Stadium after Match," *Independent* (20 June 2018), www.independent.co.uk/sport/football/world-cup/world-cup-2018-senegal-japan-fans-clean-stadium-russia-football-a8407341.html.

EXCLUSIVIST, INCLUSIVIST, AND PLURALIST READINGS OF JOHN'S GOSPEL

In John 14:6, Jesus is seen to say, "I am the Way, the Truth, and the Life, nobody comes to the Father but by me" (RSV). For exclusivists, this is generally taken as conclusive evidence that if Jesus is the only "way," then any other paths must be false. For inclusivists, however, it is often asserted that the text should be read in the wider context of the Gospel. Here, they refer to the opening lines, often termed the Prologue (John 1:1–18). This asserts that Jesus as the logos (literally "the Word")[1] is the source of all creation and is "the true light that enlightens every man [*sic*]" (John 1:9, RSV). This, from an inclusivist lens, shows that Jesus's presence is inherent in all people, and so when they exhibit "light" (good thoughts, words, deeds, etc.), they are responding to Jesus. A Christian pluralist, meanwhile, might argue that while Jesus points to the Father, this is not the only route to absolute reality: the Buddha, Prophet Muhammad, and others all point to divine reality by different names or paths. Saying Jesus points to the Father does not dismiss their truths. Likewise, pluralists might say, the prologue speaks in Christian terms about the common divine presence, but other traditions say this in their own way. Importantly, various interpretations can exist within each stance.

---

1 See Cheetham, "Inclusivisms," 66–68.

Religious diversity in symbols, author's collection.

we perceive the way the Other talks about us. Even if framed as constructive criticism, we tend to react negatively. This may also affect the way that we frame our religious identities. A further point concerns the fact that in times of tension, or perceived conflict, we become much less accepting even of internal in-group criticism. That is to say, we "hunker down" and take on a "siege" mentality in which we cannot accept any criticism. Our identities become less open to considering alternatives, dissent, or reflection. Often, this may be actualized in relation to specific symbols.

SUPERSESSIONISM

"Supersessionism" traditionally refers to the Christian belief that Judaism is fulfilled, or superseded, by Christianity, but in general usage can refer to the belief that one religion supersedes (fulfills) another. This means that one religion is seen to fully meet, make obsolete, or explain the religious values or functions of another religion. This has been a remarkably common way in which religious traditions have made sense of other religions:

- Christianity traditionally claimed it provided the final version (fulfillment of prophecy and culmination via Jesus as Messiah) of Judaism.[46] Islam makes a similar claim in relation to both Judaism and Christianity: Muhammad was the "seal of the prophets" and provided the definitive (and incorruptible) revelation.[47]

- Mahayana (literally, "greater vehicle") Buddhism claimed to be the "greater" teaching compared to the lesser teachings of Theravada Buddhism (traditionally, Mahayana referred to this school as Hinayana, "lesser vehicle"). Its claim was that in using only the Tripitaka, the Theravada did not access the full range of the Buddha's teachings found in the Mahayana scriptural texts.[48]

- Baha'i tradition asserts that their teachers, the Baha'u'llah and the Bab, are the latest in a long series of prophets who have appeared on Earth. Their teachings take the best of all previous prophets/religions and update them for the current world age.[49]

Supersessionism makes an identity claim of superiority. However, it does not necessarily say that every other religion is wrong, a claim often erroneously made by some atheist spokespeople: atheism is only a step more atheist than every other religion, as all religions say every other religion is wrong apart from theirs, or deny every other deity apart from their own; therefore, atheism only believes in one less religion/deity than any other religion.[50] Supersessionist thinking, which has been mainstream in many religions, does not always make this claim. Rather, it is often asserted (in inclusivist fashion) that another religion only has it partly right, or has some distant relationship to deity; for Buddhists, the "deity" question is thought about quite differently (see boxes 6.4 and 14.6).

·　　　·　　　·

CASE STUDY 13A. THE MEMORY OF AL-ANDALUSIA

In contemporary contexts of diversity, many refer to historical periods as exemplars or paradigms for engaging the present. Sometimes this is from an exclusivist stance, to argue that intolerance or exclusion have been normative. What are seen as more positive or irenic contexts are also looked back to, yet, to what extent, was toleration (see box 13.6) and coexistence exemplified in Al-Andalusia (medieval Islamic Spain)?

THE GOLDEN AGE HYPOTHESIS

Described by Maria Rosa Menocal (1953–2010) as the "ornament of the world,"[51] Al-Andalusia is seen as an Islamic golden age, in at least three ways:

- exemplary tolerance and interreligious coexistence
- the flowering of science and exchange of ideas across religious borders
- the flowering of culture and intercultural art across religious borders

Compared to much of the rest of "Europe,"[52] the flourishing of art, science, culture, music, and literature in Al-Andalusia was exemplary. This was, in large part, due to its connection to the more advanced civilizational complex of the Middle East. In Cordoba, both streetlights and sewer systems were found in the tenth century, something not found elsewhere in Europe until the nineteenth century. However, it is very much the question of interreligious coexistence that concerns us.

This period has been termed *"conviviencia,"* meaning "living together," connoting a time of tolerance and harmonious coexistence:

> The term *convivencia,* or living together, is often used to describe the coexistence of these three religious communities [Islam, Judaism, Christianity] in Islamic Spain. . . . [It] has come to represent the romanticized vision of a uniquely tolerant and symbiotic pluralism . . . especially attractive to those striving to improve interreligious relations.[53]

It is certainly true that Jewish, Christian, and Islamic scholars worked side by side on many projects. The chief ministers of many of the caliphs (leaders of the Islamic dynasties) were drawn from the ranks of Jewish and Christian subjects. Meanwhile, the great Jewish thinker Moses Maimonides (1135–1204) was born in Cordoba and flourished there;[54] Maimonides eventually had to leave because the situation soured, but found a new refuge in Muslim-controlled Cairo.

THE WARFARE HYPOTHESIS

Others hold a bleaker view, seeing *convivencia* as nothing but "myth":

> The best rulers of al-Andalus were autocrats who through brute force kept the peace in the face of religious, dynastic, racial, and other divisions.
> . . . Al-Mansur (d. 1002) . . . burned heretical books and terrorized Catholics, sacking Zaragoza . . . and Santiago de Compostela. In 985 he burned down Barcelona, enslaving all those he did not kill.[55]

Darío Fernández-Morera has attacked the conventional standpoint, suggesting it was a time of violence little different—perhaps even worse—than the rest of the medieval period. Certainly, violence and warfare erupted periodically, and rulers would use harsh punishments on their enemies. Further, far from literally *convivencia* ("living together"), many towns and cities were segregated. Again, it is argued that as the Iberian Peninsula was taken over by what is seen as an Islamic invasion, which was only stopped by stern resistance at the Battle of Poitier (19 September 1356), religious violence (see chapter 15) was the norm. Against evidence of Christian and Jewish ministers, it is suggested that accommodation was often born out of cunning rather than any sense of interreligious bonhomie. It meant that the minority Jews and Christians were loyal to the ruler, while no other Muslims could develop a power base. Moreover, sending Christian bishops as ambassadors to Christian nations was simply good statesmanship.

A final argument comes from the Spanish memory of a Christian reconquest in 1492, and the valorization of Christian knights such as the Spanish national hero El Cid (1048–1099). It is argued that this points to a Christian longing for freedom.

NEITHER THIS NOR THAT

Menocal's writings have been accused of highlighting positive encounters while ignoring the negatives; Fernández-Morera is accused of the inverse.[56] We can, rather than merely seeking some middle path, note elements of truth in both accounts:

- As in any medieval society, life was often brutal. Periods of warfare and dynastic change were nasty. For much of the period, Al-Andalusia saw competing cities, states, and dynasties with internecine conflict as the norm.

- Under the Islamic "protected people" (*dhimmi*) system, Jews and Christians were often given freedom to worship and conduct their own community affairs. This was in sharp contrast to the period after 1492. After the "Christian reconquest," Muslims and Jews faced forcible conversion, death, or exile. The situation of minorities in Al-Andalusia was generally better under Islamic than Christian rule.

- There were very different situations depending upon which Islamic dynasty was in control. It was better for religious minorities living under the Umayyad Dynasty (661–750 CE, the first Islamic dynasty to rule) than under some of the later Islamic dynasties, and in periods of conflict.

- The flourishing of arts and scholarship, especially among Jewish scholars, is symptomatic of relative freedom and opportunity. That Christian bishops were sent as ambassadors, while no doubt good policy, showed sufficient freedoms and the potential for high position, indicating some tolerance at the least.

- Alongside mutual learning and flourishing of arts and sciences, there was discontent. The existence of the famous martyrs of Cordoba—Christians who willingly insulted the Prophet Muhammad, to be killed as martyrs— shows dissatisfaction.[57] However, they acted against the wishes of the bishop and other Christian community leaders. It was also something the caliph sought to avoid. It does not show systematic oppression and discontent.

- Finally, that Spain's hero is remembered by his Arabic name, El Cid ("the Lord"), is telling. In the final battles that saw Islamic rule end, and throughout the period of Islamic rule, Christians fought other Christians, Muslims fought other Muslims, and both Christians and Muslims fought other Christians and Muslims. The later narrative of a "Christian reconquest" is a myth (see box 4.3), propagated very deliberately by the new rulers, Isabella and Ferdinand. These joint rulers of Granada needed this myth to secure their rule over other claimants. Indeed, El Cid was actually a mercenary who fought for both Christian and Muslim armies. We may also note that the original "Islamic invasion" was actually most likely a response to a request for help by Jews and Christians who were being persecuted by other Christians. The Muslim armies[58] fought alongside Jews and Christians to help end Christian oppression.

THE MEMORY OF AL-ANDALUSIA

While Al-Andalusia was certainly not an interreligious haven, it was not until the late eighteenth century at the earliest, or in many cases the nineteenth century (or even the twentieth) that Jewish minorities were given equivalent freedoms and protections in the Western (Christian/secular) world.[59] However, key to our interests is the question of how Al-Andalusia is remembered today. In part this relates to the question: does Al-Andalusia demonstrate a model in which Islam can be seen as representing an ideal of interreligious harmony? Religious minorities were certainly generally better protected in premodernity under Islamic rather than Christian rule. However, the "protected person" (*dhimmi*) status is a far cry from contemporary expectations of religious freedom (see chapter 16); Jews, Christians, and sometimes others needed to pay the "protection tax" (*jizya*) in return for partial autonomy—though this did exempt them from military service, with the caliph being responsible for their security. Also, notably, Islamic practices inspired the basis of contemporary discourses on freedom of religion (see box 16.11).

REFLECTIONS

These questions may help us think through some issues arising from this example:

1. If you had to debate an advocate for Al-Andalusia as an interfaith haven, what stance would you take? Would you largely agree that it was better than many comparable places, or try and demonstrate the many problems that existed there?
2. To what extent do you think Al-Andalusia provides a contemporary role model for interreligious coexistence between religions? Discuss examples you know of from other contexts/traditions where historical coexistence may provide a model for the contemporary context. How effective are such narratives?
3. Memories, or representations, of Al-Andalusia are often remarkably polarized: from haven to hell. What purpose do you think is served by these representations? Are such claims always political, or can we more accurately represent the situation?
4. Do you see identity as being key to the way that different people may remember situations like Al-Andalusia in different ways? Explain with examples.

CASE STUDY 13B. DOMINUS IESUS AND CATHOLIC CHRISTIANITY IN ASIA

Between 1962 and 1965, the Catholic Christian tradition held a major church council, the Second Vatican Council (Vatican II). This radically reformulated its approaches to society, other Christian traditions, non-Christian religions, and liturgy.[60] A church council's teachings are considered definitive and unalterable.

"OUTSIDE THE CHURCH THERE IS NO SALVATION" TO NOSTRA AETATE

Catholic Christian theology had shown both exclusivist and inclusivist trends. The latter is exemplified by such figures as Justin Martyr, Augustine of Hippo, and Thomas Aquinas. The former is apparent in a phrase that became standardized as church teaching: "*Extra ecclessiam nulla sallus*" ("Outside the church there is no salvation"). However, with Vatican II, Catholic teaching became securely inclusivist, as seen in documents from it such as Nostra Aetate, which states:

> The Catholic Church rejects nothing that is true and holy in these religions. She regards with sincere reverence those ways of conduct and of life, those precepts and teachings which, though differing in many aspects from the ones she holds and sets forth, nonetheless often reflect a ray of that Truth which enlightens all men.[61]

Kinship was affirmed, in particular, with both Judaism and Islam, with the document noting a shared heritage and worship of the same God (see box 13.11).

In practical terms, the Catholic tradition changed from seeing other religions as primarily to be approached through mission, to being partners in dialogue (see chapter 14). After Vatican II, the Secretariat for Non-Christian Religions was set up, which became known in 1964 as the Pontifical Council for Interreligious Dialogue (PCID), a separate department within the Vatican (the Catholic headquarters in Rome, Italy) under the jurisdiction of a cardinal.

DOMINUS IESUS AND ASIAN CHRISTIAN THEOLOGY

Vatican II recognized that religions such as Hinduism and Buddhism contained a "ray of . . . Truth." Asian Christians had long been engaged in dialogue and exchange with these traditions and sought to work out what they saw as the implications of Vatican II in terms of their ongoing experience of living alongside them. However, some church leaders in Europe (and elsewhere) believed that some in Asia (and elsewhere) were stretching the teachings of Vatican II beyond the proper limits. Among these was Cardinal Ratzinger (later Pope Benedict XVI), who headed the powerful Congregation for the Doctrine of the Faith (CDF, which oversees "orthodox" teaching). As cardinal prefect (head) of the CDF, Ratzinger issued the document Dominus Iesus to "clarify" the teachings of Vatican II and prescribe limits. It could not reverse the teachings of Vatican II, but offered an interpretation which could be considered authoritative.[62] Dominus Iesus declared: "If it is true that the followers of other religions can receive divine grace, it is also certain that *objectively speaking* they are in a gravely deficient situation in comparison with those who, in the Church, have the fullness of the means of salvation."[63]

Ratzinger pursued many theologians, especially pluralists, and many lost their teaching positions in Catholic universities. Some saw Dominus Iesus aimed at, among others, Jacques Dupuis (1923–2004), who had worked for many years in Asia. Dupuis saw his writings as simply a working through of the teachings of Vatican II.[64] His supporters believe he was ruthlessly persecuted, leading to his untimely death.[65] However, Ratzinger and conservative theologians saw his work as straying beyond church teachings.

Areas where theologians believed Vatican II allowed them to venture include

- employing "tools" from other religions, such as Christians practicing Buddhist meditation;[66]
- seeking to learn and incorporate insights from non-Christian religious traditions;[67] and
- acknowledging the mixed identities of Christians whose cultural background was infused by Asian religious thought.[68]

These, arguably, push at the edges of what is permissible, but such theological exploration is legitimate in the tradition. Questions of imagined "orthodoxy" are beyond the scope of this book. What is of significance is the way that the theological markers were deployed.

Jeannine Hill Fletcher has noted that while representing an inclusivist theological stance (mandated by Vatican II), Dominus Iesus had a tone that was distinctively exclusivist: "when the Congregation for the Doctrine of the Faith issued the document Dominus Iesus, the argument was not exclusivistic, but the tone of the document often tended to be."[69]

REFLECTIONS

Some questions will help us reflect on this:

1. The instances of religious diversity in Asia (mainly south and east) are often seen as a reason why Catholics there are frequently seen as more open to dialogue and theological exchange than those in the more mono-religious European context. How do you think contexts and identities affect views of the religious Other? How does your context affect your views?

2. Does it make sense to suggest that Christians, Muslims, and Jews affirm the same deity based upon the heritage and linguistic issues held to point that way? How does this claim differ as a theological proposition and a descriptive scholarly analytic proposition?

3. Given the quotations provided here, and any other background research you have done, how would you characterize the differences between the texts of Nostra Aetate and Dominus Iesus? Are there differences? Does the tone of theological statements matter? For example, Fletcher notes Dominus Iesus has an inclusivist theology but an exclusivist tone. What is conveyed by this differing language/tone?

4. How would you assess the factors behind Christians affirming exclusivist, inclusivist, or pluralist theological positions? What do you think may underlie claims to these theological identities?

·   ·   ·

QUESTIONS AND CONNECTING THOUGHTS

Discussing religious diversity entails some sense of determining how the term "religion" operates (chapter 1). Connections to some other chapters have been mentioned, but we can draw out some further ones: how religious traditions have conceptualized diversity will impact any potential dialogue (chapter 14); these questions have often been the concern of elite patriarchal traditions (see chapters 3 and 10); diversity is not just about doctrine but involves debates and competition over space (see chapters 9 and 17), with the "secular" sphere (chapter 16), in politics (chapter 18), and sometimes in violent forms (chapter 15). Some questions will help us reflect on these issues:

1. Would you classify yourself as an exclusivist, inclusivist, or pluralist? Is this a question that scholars should ask? Is being aware of your preference here important

for being reflexive in your approach to study (recognizing and acknowledging your own biases; see chapter 2)? It is also important to consider if these terms are only religious markers. Can atheists be classified by these terms too?

2. To what extent can we speak about religious diversity as a general concept when the very notion of "religion" is contextually embedded and contingent?

3. If a scholar argues that promoting pluralism is a societal good (perhaps as a social stance rather than a theological one), or the "best" mode for religious interaction, is this a betrayal of scholarly neutrality and impartiality? Consider that economists, sociologists, political scientists, and so on, will normally see it as part of their scholarly role to argue for "better" or "preferable" social goals or stances. Is this different for scholars of religion? Why? (See the related debates in chapters 5, 7, 10, 16, and 18.)

FURTHER READING

THEORY

Cheetham, David. "Religion and the Religious Other," in *Understanding Interreligious Relations*, ed. David Cheetham, Douglas Pratt, and David Thomas (Oxford: Oxford University Press, 2013), 15–36.

Eck, Diana. *Encountering God: A Spiritual Journey from Bozeman to Benares* (Boston: Beacon Press, 1993), 166–99.

Halafoff, Anna, and Paul Hedges. "Globalisation and Multifaith Societies," *Studies in Interreligious Dialogue* 25.2 (2015): 135–61.

Hedges, Paul. "Interreligious Engagement and Identity Theory: Assessing the Theology of Religions Typology as a Model for Dialogue and Encounter," *Journal for the Academic Study of Religion* 27.2 (2014): 198–221.

Markham, Ian. "A Religious Studies Approach to Questions about Religious Diversity," in *The Oxford Handbook of Religious Diversity*, ed. Chad Meister (Oxford: Oxford University Press, 2014), 21–28.

Marty, Martin. "Historical Reflections on Religious Diversity," in Meister, *Oxford Handbook*, 9–20.

CASE STUDY 13A. THE MEMORY OF AL-ANDALUSIA

Cohen, Mark. "The Golden Age of Jewish-Muslim Relations: Myth and Reality," in *A History of Jewish-Muslim Relations: From the Origins to the Present Day*, ed. Abdelwahab Meddeb and Benjamin Stora (Princeton: Princeton University Press, 2013), 28–38.

Deen Show. "When Islam and Muslims Ruled Jews and Christians Left Christian Persecution to Live with Muslims?," *The Deen Show* (2013), www.youtube.com/watch?v=bdNDns0p47E.

Delgado, Mariano. "From Acceptance to Religious Freedom: Considerations for *Convivencia* in Medieval Spain and Multireligious Coexistence Today," in *Contested Spaces, Common Ground: Space and Power structures in Contemporary Multireligious Societies*, ed. Ulrich Winkler, Lidia Rodríguez Fernández, and Oddbjørn Leirvik (Leiden: E. J. Brill, 2017), 225–40.

Fernández-Morera, Darío. "The Myth of the Andalusian Paradise." *The Intercollegiate Review* (Fall 2006): 23–31, www.mmisi.org/ir/41_02/fernandez-morera.pdf.

Pearce, Sarah. Review of *The Myth of the Andalusian Paradise: Muslims, Christians, and Jews under Islamic Rule in Medieval Spain,* by Darío Fernández-Morera (2017), https://wp.nyu.edu/sjpearce/2017/03/17/paradise-lost/.

Said, Imam Ghazali. "The Heritage of Al-Andalus and the Formation of Spanish History and Identity," *International Journal of History and Cultural Studies* 3.1 (2017): 63–76.

CASE STUDY 13B. DOMINUS IESUS AND CATHOLIC CHRISTIANITY IN ASIA

Chia, Edmund Kee-Fook. *World Christianity Meets World Religions: A Summa on Interfaith Dialogue* (Collegeville, MN: Liturgical Press Academic, 2018), 57–9, 111–19, 139–48, 179–85, 187–89.

Phan, Peter. *Being Religious Interreligiously: Asian Perspectives on Interfaith Dialogue* (Maryknoll, NY: Orbis, 2004): 85–101.

USCCB Committee on Doctrine. "Clarifications Required by the Book Being Religious Interreligiously: Asian Perspectives on Interfaith Dialogue by Reverend Peter C. Phan," United States Conference of Catholic Bishops (2007), www.usccb.org/about/doctrine/publications/upload/statement-on-being-religious-interreligiously.pdf.

Vatican. Nostra Aetate (1965), www.vatican.va/archive/hist_councils/ii_vatican_council/documents/vat-ii_decl_19651028_nostra-aetate_en.html.

Vatican. Dominus Iesus (2000), www.vatican.va/roman_curia/congregations/cfaith/documents/rc_con_cfaith_doc_20000806_dominus-Iesuss_en.html.

DIALOGUE

Interreligious Discourse and Critique

IN WHICH WE EXPLORE:

The discourse and contexts of interreligious dialogue

Typologies and criticisms of interreligious dialogue

Case studies of Muslim and Christian women in dialogue, and Buddhist-Christian dialogue

INTRODUCTION

I really need to start this chapter with a clear statement about what it is doing, because in the academic study of religion there is a great fear that the "neutral," "impartial," and "objective" study of religion may become "infected" by non-neutral, non-impartial, and non-objective people who want to promote interreligious/interfaith (see box 14.1) understanding and dialogue. However, this is a study of religion approach to interreligious dialogue (IRD). That is to say, our aim here is to analyze and explore the history, agendas, and discourse that exists and surrounds IRD. This is not to say IRD is a bad thing. Personally, I actually think it is (sometimes, but not always) quite a good thing if people get together and understand each other better—certainly if the alternative is fighting, insulting, or demonizing each other based on stereotypes and misinformation. However, this is not a "how-to" chapter on IRD, but a critical perspective on its practice and discourse.

INTERRELIGIOUS OR INTERFAITH? WHICH WORDS TO USE?

As far as this chapter is concerned, the terms "interreligious" and "interfaith" are essentially interchangeable. Distinctions are sometimes made:

Interreligious stresses the involvement of traditions, that is, "religions," whereas interfaith stresses individual people, that is, it concerns "their faith."

Interfaith excludes people without "religion" because atheists don't have faith, and so interreligious is more inclusive.

However, you can find different definitions:

Interreligious excludes people without religion, so interfaith is more inclusive.

Interfaith invokes faith traditions as specific lineages, whereas religion is about people's personal beliefs and commitments.

Perhaps the major difference is that "interreligious" tends to be more common in North America, and interfaith is more common in the UK. Here, I am using "interreligious." I also use the phrase "multifaith movement," as this is often found. Further, some distinguish between "multifaith," signifying "many religions," and "interreligious/interfaith" as indicating a dialogic interaction. The terminology is variously deployed. What is used here is not meant to be indicative of *the* correct usage.

In the light of what we have said above, when we see a quote such as the following: "We can only see into each other's souls if we take the trouble—and sometimes the risk—to visit each other,"[1] we will ask:

·   What assumptions lie behind such a claim?
·   What interests are promoted by such discourse?
·   What agendas are not part of such thoughts?

We certainly do not see it as a normative statement about the aims of this chapter, nor of IRD as a whole.

Notably, critical analysis of IRD is often part of the work of academics who actually do dialogue, because understanding the problems can help you do IRD better. As such, the world is not split between dialogue folk, who promote and cheer for dialogue, and critical scholars, who point out its potential problems and agendas. Indeed, a lot of the best criticism actually comes from people who do IRD, because they do not (so often) rely on stereotypes of what they think IRD is about.

We begin with the history of the multifaith movement and explore some classifications of IRD. We will then turn to some practices and rationales for IRD, as well as the way that some have defined what is needed for its practice, in particular, Catherine Cornille. We then explore a range of critiques and possible problems that arise within the practice of IRD. As always, we end with two case studies.

PARLIAMENTS AND RELIGIONS

According to most scholars, the multifaith movement can be dated quite precisely to 1893.[2] In that year, the World's Parliament of Religions (WPoR) was held in Chicago as part of the cultural events surrounding a larger world trade fair. In terms of institutional dialogue this can be seen as a starting point. However, two of its leading lights were Christian clergymen who believed that bringing representatives of all religions (actually just a select few) together would allow it to be seen that, objectively, Christianity was the superior religion.[3] The radical (at that time) move of having representatives meet together on an equal footing, with equal time, and without overt apologetics or attempts at conversion (at least in theory), was not therefore simply a move toward a liberal equitable stance where every religion was given equal respect.

The plan to showcase Christianity's believed inherent superiority did not transpire as planned. It may even be said to have somewhat backfired. Among the most popular speakers at the event were a handsome young Hindu named Vivekananda (1863–1902) and Buddhists representing the Zen and Theravada schools. Their messages resonated with the audience and received press attention, helping make both Hinduism and Buddhism better known in the West, including opportunities for lecture tours and missionary activity to promote both Buddhism and Hinduism (see box 14.2). In this period of European colonialism (see chapter 7), combined with intensive Western Christian missionary activity, the chance to have what were seen as leaders from "Asian religions" taking missions to the West was symbolically very important.

Anna Halafoff has shown that the 1893 WPoR was inspirational to many, but the multifaith movement only grew dramatically after World War II.[4] Of the pre-WWII interfaith groups, only the World Congress of Faiths (WCF) remains, founded in 1936 by the rather idiosyncratic Francis Younghusband (1863–1942).[5] The oldest still extant national interfaith organization is almost certainly the Inter-Religious Organisation of Singapore (IRO), set up in 1949 (it was the IRO of Singapore and Johor Bahru until 1961) in what was then British Malaya.[6]

In terms of landmark events, despite some moves for another parliament, it was not until the hundredth anniversary of the first Chicago event that another global world "parliament" was held (see box 14.3). These are now recurring events among a vast plethora of interfaith conferences, organizations, and activities globally.

THE CHRISTIAN IMPETUS TO DIALOGUE

Despite a growth in IRD since WWII, often linked to multiculturalism following immigration in Western societies,[7] IRD tended to remain something of a fringe interest. It became somewhat mainstreamed within the major Christian traditions, both Catholic and those within the World Council of Churches (WCC, a global organization which

VIVEKANANDA, HINDU MISSIONS TO THE WEST, AND HINDU PLURALISM

Vivekananda's (1863–1902) opening words at the World's Parliament of Religions (WPoR), "Dear sisters and brothers of America," earned him immediate respect. His speech, which suggested respect and equality among all religions, also resonated. Feted in the press, he was able to give lecture tours in both the United States and Europe, and set up what is now the Vedanta Society in New York in 1894 as the first of several branches of his Ramakrishna Mission outside India. He promoted Hinduism as a religion which embraced all religions as equal, often touted as "theological" pluralism (see chapter 13). However, the basis for this should be noted.

Vivekananda advocated "non-dualism" (Advaita Vedanta), the teaching that the absolute (Brahman/transcendent) is one with the human soul/spirit (hence non-dual). Vivekananda used this to formulate his own theory on the unity of all religions, based on his teacher, Ramakrishna (1836–1886). While Vivekananda accepted that every religion represented some truth about the divine, he saw a clear hierarchy: teachings about personal deities expressed a lower truth. Vivekananda believed the absolute transcended any personal dimension, and so union with the divine was a form of merger of the self into the impersonal oneness of absolute reality (*advaita*). His "Hindu pluralism" had clear higher and lower forms of religion and is best seen as inclusivism (see chapter 13).

As one of the first to actively bring Hinduism as a missionary religion to the West, Vivekananda also helped shape how it was perceived. His non-dual teachings, which may sound like what you have been taught about Hinduism, contrast with what most Hindus throughout history have believed (on speaking of Hinduism, see case study 7A). Most Hindus follow the devotional path (*bhakti*) and dualism (Dvaita Vedanta), where divine reality is seen as a personal deity, and the human soul is not merged with the absolute. However, figures like Vivekananda, as well as many Western interpreters of Hinduism, have favored the elite philosophical speculations of non-dualism as the "true" or "highest" Hinduism.[1]

---

1 See R. W. Neufeldt, "The Response of the Ramakrishna Mission," in *Modern Indian Responses to Religious Pluralism*, ed. Harold Coward (Albany: State University of New York Press, 1987), 65–84; and Stephen Gregg, *Swami Vivekananda and Non-Hindu Traditions* (London: Routledge, 2019). On Advaita Vedanta, see Richard King, *Orientalism and Religion: Postcolonial Theory, India and "The Mystic East"* (New York: Routledge, 1999), 118–42.

---

contains all mainstream Protestant and Orthodox traditions), in the final decades of the twentieth century.[8] This was often due to urging by the churches of the "Global South," for whom religious diversity was not a fringe matter, or simply a result of new immigration, but often a day-to-day reality of life, and had been for centuries.

The first move entailed major statements made at the Second Vatican Council (1962–1965), a landmark event for the Catholic Church in which it set out to bring itself into

THE PARLIAMENT(S) OF THE WORLD'S RELIGIONS (POWR)

To commemorate the 1893 World Parliament of Religions (WPoR), a 1993 Parliament of the World's Religions (PoWR—note the name change) was held in Chicago. It brought together many notable dignitaries and leaders of religious traditions, including Tibetan Buddhism's public figurehead, the Dalai Lama, and the Catholic archbishop of Chicago, Cardinal Joseph Bernardin. Catholics had participated in the 1893 event, though in 1895 the then Pope, Leo XIII, had forbade Catholics from being involved in what he termed "future promiscuous conventions." But the best part of a hundred years is a long time in religious history, and globally Catholics have been world leaders among Christians in promoting and pushing forward dialogue (see case study 13B).[1]

Hans Küng promoted his well-known Global Ethic (see box 14.5), while the 1993 PoWR was followed by parliaments in Cape Town, South Africa (1999); Barcelona, Spain (2004); Melbourne, Australia (2009); Salt Lake City, US (2015) (a planned 2014 event in Brussels had failed to materialize); and Toronto, Canada (2018).[2] Feted by some as the leading interfaith event, the parliaments are for others more of a circus of self-congratulation or an expensive self-promotion event for various leaders who see themselves as involved in multifaith work and interreligious dialogue.

Certain groups that were excluded or sidelined in 1893 have been included, even becoming significant. Indigenous American groups, absent in 1893, were present in 1993, while indigenous Australian Aborigine traditions were prominent in Melbourne in 2009. Only a handful of women were at the 1893 gathering, but have become more prominent as speakers. Representation of people of color, as well as a wider global representation, is also notable, while Pagans, goddess worshippers, animists, and others who were not part of the 1893 event are also often present.

---

1 See Clare Amos, "Vatican and World Council of Churches Initiatives: Weaving Interreligious Threads on Ecumenical Looms," in *Contemporary Muslim-Christian Encounters: Developments, Diversity and Dialogues*, ed. Paul Hedges (London: Bloomsbury Academic, 2015), 185–200.

2 At the time of writing, a venue is being sought for 2021, though, given the outbreak of Covid-19 in 2020 and upheavals from that, it is likely not to be held again until at least 2022.

---

alignment with the modern world (see case study 13B). In the post-WWII context, this included acknowledging that Christian teachings over almost two millennia had laid the groundwork for Antisemitism that allowed the Holocaust (Shoah) to happen.[9] The Shoah saw the deaths of around six million Jews in Europe by the Nazis, many in the gas chambers of the "death camps" set up for Hitler's "Final Solution."[10] The moves to acknowledge Judaism as Christianity's "older sibling," with its own covenant with God, also opened a door to thinking about Christianity's relationship to Islam, which also claimed to worship the God of Abraham (see box 13.11; see also box 2.2). Once a kinship with Muslims was acknowledged, the question of other religions also became an issue.

The net result was a move within Catholicism from approaching other religions primarily as opponents to be converted into being partners for dialogue. In practical terms it led to the setting up of what is now known as the Pontifical Council for Interreligious Dialogue (PCID).[11]

The moves by Catholics emboldened the WCC, which, led especially by the churches of the Global South, initiated their own body for dealing with IRD. In the WCC's case this is a subdivision of the wider department dealing with mission and evangelism. Though dialogue is seen as an activity with its own integrity and so not part of mission per se, Christians often walk a careful tightrope between acknowledging dialogue as a discrete activity and admitting that it holds a relationship to the perceived necessity of proclamation of the Gospel, that is, missionary activity.[12]

This discussion of Christianity is important: globally, Christians have been the prime instigators of dialogue, in part due to finances and Western intellectual capital (see chapter 7). However, this Christian and Western basis gives rise to a range of potential critiques:

- Non-Christians (itself a problematic term, putting together a great diversity of groups) sometimes perceive IRD as a continuation of Christian missionary activity under a new, subtler, guise.

- Christian agendas may shape the way dialogue is both performed and the topics under discussion, that is, certain theological questions being foregrounded.

- It is often perceived as a Western and liberal venture, which shapes what is seen as normative for dialogue and who is represented. This criticism is sometimes voiced by some non-Western Christians as well as non-Christian critics. This relates to wider debates in postcolonialism and decolonization (see chapter 7).

9/11 AND THE MOVE FROM THE PERIPHERY TO THE CENTER

By the late twentieth century, IRD had an institutional presence in mainstream Christianity globally, though often fairly marginal or sidelined in practice.[13] Events in the early twenty-first century would change that, and one in particular would be a defining moment, not just for IRD but in much of global consciousness. This was the terrorist attack, planned by Al-Qaeda under Osama bin Laden (1957–2011), on the World Trade Center in New York on 11 September 2001 (9/11). Two full passenger planes were flown into the twin towers, causing an inferno and the collapse of the buildings.[14] The attack showed for some a clear fault line between what was perceived as different civilizational worlds: the Christian West and the Muslim-majority world (see box 14.4). It also emphasized the connections of religion to violence and politics (see chapters 15 and 18, respectively).

BOX 14.4 **THE CLASH OF CIVILIZATIONS THESIS**

In the twenty-first century, many associate religion with violence, and as contrary to whatever they imagine "Western values" to be. This critique of religion is often leveled especially against Islam (see chapter 15). Many Muslims proclaim that theirs is the "religion of peace," and compatible with democracy, freedom, and human rights. An inevitable confrontation between the West, often portrayed as Christian (or Judeo-Christian), and the Muslim-majority world, was theorized by Samuel Huntington under the terminology of a "clash of civilizations."[1] This suggests future fault lines lie between major civilizational blocs, with three main ones being Western, Islamic, and Confucian. However, Huntington's thesis, and similar arguments by others, seem flawed:

- The assumption is that religions or cultures are monolithic and unchanging worldviews. In fact, every religion and culture has changed and shifted over time.
- The fault lines are not natural sites of enmity. In many places, these cultures have overlapped and lived peacefully together.
- Huntington's claim that "Islam has bloody borders"[2] references conflicts across diverse centuries in places where Islam has been present, something which could equally be said of Christianity. Indeed, quite a few of the "bloody borders" invoked have Western/Christian/colonial contexts.
- Suggestions that Islam is at war with the West can be met with a response that it is, if anything, a war of self-defense. Many Muslims have perceived the War on Terror as primarily a Western cover to continue its "crusade" against Islam; this term, used by some Western advocates for the war, harks back to medieval wars, which some Muslims still perceive—not always without cause—as part of ongoing Christian-centric aggression against them.[3]

Further, many situations of civilizational dialogue and exchange could be equally posited:

- The world's largest Muslim-majority country is not in the Middle East; it is Indonesia, an area which has seen centuries of relative religious harmony and peace compared to the rest of the world.[4]

---

1 Samuel Huntington, "The Clash of Civilizations?," *Foreign Affairs*, 72.3 (1993): 22–49.

2 Huntington, "Clash of Civilizations?," 35. One wonders, though, what this could mean. For a start, how can a historically contingent system of beliefs and practices have borders?

3 See Peter Waldman and Hugh Pope, "'Crusade' Reference Reinforces Fears War on Terrorism Is against Muslims," *Wall Street Journal* (21 September, 2001), www.wsj.com/articles /SB1001020294332922160. Huntington's clash of civilizations concept has also been seen as tied in to an Islamophobic agenda (see box 15.4); see Todd Green, *The Fear of Islam: An Introduction to Islamophobia in the West*, 2nd ed. (Minneapolis: Fortress Press, 2019).

4 See M. Ricklefs, *A History of Modern Indonesia since C. 1300*, 2nd ed. (Stanford: Stanford University Press, 1993); and Barbara Andaya, "Islam and Christianity in Southeast Asia, 1600–1700," *ISEAS Working Papers* no. 3 (Singapore: Institute of South East Asian Studies, 2016). Though current dynamics there are increasingly exclusive, see Charlotte Setijadi, "Ahok's Downfall and the Rise of Islamist Populism in Indonesia," *ISEAS Perspectives* 38 (2017), www.iseas.edu.sg/images/pdf/ISEAS_Perspective_2017_38.pdf. On the way that indigenous perspectives can be part of dialogue and peace-building there, though, see Lailatul Fitriyah, "Interstitial Theology and Interreligious Reconciliation in Post-War Maluku: The Work of Elifas Maspaitella and Jacklevyn Manuputty," *Interreligious Relations* 11 (2019), www.rsis.edu.sg/wp-content/uploads/2020/01/IRR-Issue-11-December-2019.pdf.

- When European thinkers started to theorize religious toleration and how to live alongside religious difference, philosophers such as John Locke (1632–1704) looked to the Islamic Ottoman Empire as an exemplar of harmonious religious diversity. The genesis of Western theories of religious toleration is based on an Islamic model (see box 16.11).

  Suggestions of an eternal clash between these worlds of thought, and a lack of possibility for areas of agreement or mutual learning, are simply historically wrong. Of course, Islamic culture has often been tied to a political agenda which dates back to Muhammad's role as both religious and political leader of the nascent Islamic community (see box 16.2). As such, we would expect to see some overlap between political conquests and religious warfare. However, this has equally been true, at many times, of Christianity, which is often tied to state power, interests, and national identities (see chapters 15 and 18).

In the context of 9/11 and other events, Patrice Brodeur has argued that IRD became noticed by "traditional centres of power."[15] To name the elephant in the room, for many politicians and others, there was a desire to reach out to Muslims, and IRD became one way to do this. Since 9/11, there has been an exponential growth in the number of organizations committed to IRD, while the growth of information technology has also allowed for global networking. Moreover, IRD is no longer simply a fringe interest within religious communities, but a matter seen as related to such issues as social cohesion, security, counterterrorism, and conflict resolution. This is not to say that these were not interests of the multifaith movement before then, but IRD has been allowed space within more mainstream discussions.[16] In short, IRD has become a political tool which politicians and others have sought to employ for the purpose of governance. This raises questions about whether the activity has changed as a result of these pressures. Indeed, we can note some examples of where IRD has become related to politics and politicians:

- The Tony Blair Faith Foundation (TBFF, a foundation set up by the former British prime minister and bearing his name) is an example of political interest in this domain. It works nationally (UK) and internationally for harmony, understanding, and social action in religiously diverse communities (IRD is not its only aim).
- In the US, the Interfaith Youth Core and its cofounder, Eboo Patel, have worked closely alongside government, with Patel being an adviser to President Barack Obama.[17]
- The IRO in Singapore, while an NGO, has often worked in tandem with the government, and is seen by many people as the IRD wing of government.[18]

Dialogue represented by many religions in one statue, St. Virgil Conference Centre, Salzburg, Austria.

- It can be argued that within contemporary multicultural and secular nation-states (see chapter 16), interreligious dialogue and engagement has become the acceptable form of manifesting religion.[19]
- Promoting IRD became related to policy; for example, in the UK, a document was produced by the Ministry for Communities and Local Government entitled "Side-by-Side and Face-to-Face" (2008).[20]

Approaching IRD today is therefore not simply about studying the way that religious traditions have sought to relate to each other, but also understanding the political agendas for which IRD may be harnessed by various actors, including NGOs and governments. Given this, Oddbjørn Leirvik has categorized what he terms:

- "spiritual" dialogues—those where the motivation is primarily personal, religious, or faith based; and
- "necessary" dialogues—those where the motivation is based on social, political, or peace-building concerns.[21]

Of course, any dialogue may have aspects of each, but Leirvik's typology provides one way to categorize certain types of activity.

IRD has been used to describe a range of different types of activity. However, most discussions follow a fourfold typology first defined by Eric Sharpe (1933–2000) in the 1970s, though with names given by the PCID (Sharpe's terminology in parenthesis):

- The dialogue of theological exchange (discursive dialogue)—what you might typically envisage as dialogue, where groups of "experts" (religious professionals or academics) discuss doctrines and ideas. It may be engaged by "non-experts" but is often assumed to need some form of education in the tradition.

- The dialogue of action (secular dialogue)—working together for common social goals, for example, environmental activism, poverty relief, or other ethical or social concerns.

- The dialogue of religious experience (interior dialogue)—coming together either to share or engage together in activities related to prayer, meditation, or contemplation.

- The dialogue of life (human dialogue)—where people of different religions interact together in "everyday" life, for instance, being coworkers or being in interfaith marriages.[22]

The term "dialogue" in this typology covers a very wide range of activities. Some of them are more intentional and seek understanding, or perhaps common words or statements across religions. Others may not be intentional, or may simply involve doing an activity together, rather than any exploration of another religion. It is debatable whether the term "dialogue" correctly describes these activities. The term itself refers to *dia-logos,* two Greek terms meaning respectively "across" (*dia*) and "reason" (*logos*). It is seen to mean "reasoning across worlds of religious difference."[23] Certainly, some dialogue theorists (religious and non-religious) seem to see "dialogue" as some particular, or special, form of human interaction about truth and meaning.

Working with the typological broadness, we see people involved in IRD for very diverse reasons, which include the following:

Multiculturalism and social cohesion: Being in a religiously diverse situation may lead you to seek to understand and find ways to live alongside your neighbor. This may involve seeking to repair divided community relations split along religious lines.[24]

Conflict (resolution): In places such as the Balkans in eastern Europe and Ambon in Indonesia, ethnic conflicts were partly framed as religious conflicts (see chapters 15 and 18), meaning IRD became an important part of learning to live peacefully afterward.[25]

Mission: In seeking to convert others, missionaries often seek to understand the
thought world of those they wish to convert, but sometimes this process leads
to greater appreciation and then dialogue.[26]

Practical activism: Based on perceived common concerns with people of
other religions, or those of no religion, alliances or shared projects arise.
Sometimes the issues are what are often termed "progressive," for example,
for women's rights or ecology, but Pope Benedict XVI sought to create an
interfaith anti-LGBTQI alliance. Such activities often reflect what some see as
shared ethical common ground (see box 14.5).[27]

Any critique or analysis of IRD therefore has to consider what type of activity is undertaken and the motives behind it. Indeed, the way that discourse on IRD is framed often
depends upon the particular agenda of the organization(s) involved as well as the intended
purpose. Such activities may align with governmental agendas, though some interfaith
campaigns may also seek to oppose particular government agendas. We may also ask
how these align with Leirvik's twofold categorization as "spiritual" or "necessary" dialogues.

CRITIQUES AND CRITICISMS OF THE IRD MOVEMENT

GENERAL CRITIQUES OF IRD

Russell McCutcheon has accused promotors of IRD of being liberals who seek alliances
with like-minded liberals for broadly progressive purposes and sideline those who do not
fit their agenda.[28] While true of some, this criticism certainly does not apply to Pope
Benedict's seeking an anti-LGBTQI interfaith alliance. Again, in places such as Ambon,
the credibility of interreligious peace-building work after the 1999–2002 civil conflicts
relied upon those involved being respected by the community as "traditional" leaders.
However, McCutcheon's criticism rings true in places: there is often criticism of perceived
"liberals" seeking dialogue who are distanced from perceived "conservatives." But, in
organizations such as the Catholic Church, which is in many ways deeply traditional, IRD
is institutionally validated. As such, McCutcheon's is at most only a partial critique of
some forms and types of dialogue.

Another criticism is that dialogue favors males and traditional elites. Ursula King
spoke of feminism as "a missing dimension of dialogue."[29] Many dialogues operate on
what is termed a "representative" model, that is, each religion sends leaders who speak
for the religion, and as leadership is often reserved for males (see chapter 10), women
are underrepresented. Moreover, because of hierarchical representation, lived religion
(see chapter 3) is neglected, with official or institutional forms represented as normative.
Therefore, IRD can reinforce the world religions paradigm (WRP; see chapter 1 and box
2.1). In events such as the WPoR and the PoWR, religions can be seen as sets of equivalent and equal traditions which stand as closed boxes of identity (see chapters 2, 3, 6, and

Most commonly associated with Hans Küng, the Global Ethic project asserts that behind every religious or cultural ethical system lies a set of core values. This is sometimes related to what is termed the Golden Rule: treat others as you wish to be treated ("positive" expression), or do not do to others what you do not want them to do to you ("negative" expression, sometimes called the "silver rule").[1] As brought to the 1993 PoWR, Küng's Global Ethic had four main items, each beginning with "Commitment to a culture of":

- nonviolence and respect for life
- solidarity and a just economic order
- tolerance and a life of truthfulness
- equal rights and partnership between men and women[2]

While voted on at the parliament, it is notable that it received far from a full endorsement. Moreover, even advocates of dialogue have criticized its aims in various ways. Related to Küng's proposals, and other versions of a Global Ethic, criticisms include the following:[3]

Empty statements: The phrases are almost meaningless. For instance, while almost everybody believes in " nonviolence," for some this means pacifism but for others it includes self-defense. It is sometimes asserted the commitments are made so generic that they lose any meaningful content, and it is the specifics which are contested.

Colonial: The Global Ethic favors Western and Christian ethical guidelines and is far from truly global. While Küng had global discussions before writing the Global Ethic, this is a general perception which is not without some merit.

Ineffective: People are inspired not by bland statements which are seen as "thin" ethical statements, but only by the "thick," more contextual ethics of their traditions.

---

1 This can be understood in very diverse ways; see Jacob Neusner and Bruce Chilton, *The Golden Rule: Ethics of Reciprocity in World Religions* (London: Continuum, 2009).

2 Hans Küng and Karl-Josef Kuschel, eds., *A Global Ethic: The Declaration of the Parliament of the World's Religions* (London: SCM, 1993). A fifth commitment to ecology and the Earth is often now included.

3 See Paul Hedges, "Concerns about the Global Ethic: A Sympathetic Critique and Suggestions for a New Direction," *Studies in Interreligious Dialogue* 18.1 (2008): 1–16; and Marianne Moyaert, *Response to the Religious Other: Ricoeur and the Fragility of Interreligious Encounters* (Lanham, MD: Lexington Books, 2014), 63–92.

box 13.1).[30] Borders between religions can be reinforced, or even created. In the Nepalese context, where people have traditionally practiced both Hindu and Buddhist traditions without any clear sense of belonging to one or the other, advocates of IRD have sought to create clear identities between Hindus and Buddhists to initiate IRD. However, Mark Owen has noted that this has created division and tensions which did not exist before.[31] IRD may add to social disharmony rather than alleviating it.

Even in situations where more clearly defined distinctions between religions already exist, it is not always clear how IRD can be utilized as a tool of social cohesion. From the perspective of notions of deliberative democracy as developed by scholars such as Jürgen Habermas, it has been argued that the dynamics of religious traditions can make attempts to create social cohesion problematic.[32] Meanwhile, Swamy Muthuray has observed how some elites promoting dialogue have ignored the practices of dialogue and existing social networks across borders that exist in communities.[33] While Muthuray spoke about the Indian context, a disconnect between "elite" dialogue practitioners and actual communities and their ways of social interaction may be a wider issue. Some involved in dialogue may seek to exclude others, which may be, as noted above, exclusion based on gender, class, intrareligious rivalry, or other factors. These are often intrareligious disputes rather than interreligious ones. Such issues include (with some representative examples) the following:

> *Intrareligious exclusion:* Sunni Muslims may object to Shia or Ahmadiyya Muslims being invited, or Catholic and Protestant Christians may object to the inclusion of Jehovah's Witnesses.[34]
>
> *Rivalries:* Differing Buddhist and Hindu groups may not agree who represents their religion, or disputes over prominence may appear when no clear hierarchy exists.
>
> *Unacceptable traditions:* Pagans and Wiccans may simply not be welcomed.
>
> *The non-religious:* Some IRD groups exclude atheists, agnostics, and humanists, but others include them, arguing for "interworldview dialogue."[35]
>
> *Inequality of representatives:* While some traditions have a trained professional leadership, often theologically versed in their tradition, this may not apply to all traditions in all locations, with for instance Islam often being represented by the prayer leader (*imam*), who may have no deep knowledge of the tradition.[36]

Another criticism is that advocates of IRD may assume false or superficial similarities as the basis for common agreement (see box 14.5). Another area that can be contentious is arguments that everyone in IRD believes in the same deity (see box 14.6).

This list of potential criticisms is far from comprehensive, but raises many frequently aired issues.

CORNILLE'S "CONDITIONS":
DIALOGUE AND WESTERN CHRISTIAN NORMS

Because of the hegemony of Christian and Western intellectual traditions in the creation and maintenance of IRD, the presuppositions underlying these traditions may become defining norms. To explore this, we will examine an influential set of conditions for IRD

BOX 14.6 **"WELL, AT LEAST WE ALL BELIEVE IN ONE GOD"**

A number of dialogue events involve claims that everybody present believes in the same God. This may be a matter of common agreement, with many mainstream Christians, Jews, and Muslims agreeing that they all worship the same deity (see box 13.11). Even many Hindus, especially from devotional and monotheistic strands of the traditions, may concur. However, it leaves many Buddhists sidelined. Many forms of Buddhism are distinctly non-theistic, by which we mean rejecting a supreme creator deity. Any deity which may exist would, for them, be another creature within the cycle of rebirth, needing to attain awakening/nirvana as much as any human. The aims and rationale of many religions may be quite distinct.[1] Despite this, many IRD organizations continue to recycle this platitude at meetings and even in official statements.

1 See Stephen Prothero, *God Is Not One: The Eight Rival Religions That Run the World* (New York: HarperOne, 2010).

developed by Catherine Cornille.[37] In her conditions, Cornille seems to assume the dialogue of theological exchange as normative, with dialogue being concerned with truth and authentic communication across cultural and religious worlds.[38] The five conditions are as follows:

Humility: For Cornille, humility is a universal religious virtue. However, she sees it here as an epistemological attitude (how we know). It signifies that, as humans, our knowledge is limited, so she asks believers to be aware that they may be in error regarding their religious ideas (not that the religion is wrong, but that individual humans lack full knowledge). This, she says, is not a natural stance for religions, and so requires a shift in perspective. Cornille is clear that it does not entail relativism.

Commitment: One must stand firmly and fully committed within a specific religion. She sees this as being "accountable": you speak from somewhere. Contrasting dialogue and mission, she asserts people must be witnesses to what they see as the truth of their religion. As such, anybody without a fixed religion cannot be a dialogue partner. She also sees a tradition as the basis for "discernment" (a term used in Christian theological language for assessing truth) to assess what is valuable in somebody else's religion, which may then be brought back to the "home tradition."

Interconnection: One must believe that a meaningful link between religions exists; not just cooperation, but an intrinsic connection despite fundamental borders to be crossed between distinct religious traditions.

Empathy: Cornille notes contestation over the possibility for genuinely "getting inside" the worldview of others (see chapter 2), but she holds we can cross over into the world of another. However, such crossing over is about understanding and has, for her, clear limits; ritual participation in other religious rites is impermissible, as is devotion to other deities.

Hospitality: For Cornille, hospitality is the "sole sufficient condition" (a technical philosophical term, basically meaning "all that is needed"). She argues it is a virtue in many traditions. It is for her the basis that allows somebody to journey "hospitably" from the home tradition to another tradition, to discern the values in the Other (see box 13.5 on this usage), and then return home. For instance, she says someone can ask how the ethics of another tradition relate to what is truly virtuous in their own tradition (what she terms "maximal" or "positive" norms), or whether they find aspects unjust (judged against "minimal" or "negative" norms). She says no judgment should be made in advance, and the criteria should develop in dialogue with growing understanding of the Other.

There may be various ways to analyze Cornille's conditions. Here, we take a post-colonial lens (see chapter 7), asking whether a particular Western (Catholic) Christian position underlies them. Are they a universal set of conditions for anyone entering dialogue, or a set of Western and (Catholic—Cornille's home tradition) Christian presuppositions about dialogue? We will assess them from the perspective of the Chinese religious landscape:

Humility: Arguably, humility, or something comparable, is common to many religions. The Daodejing prizes the lowly and not the exalted (DDJ: 39). While many Daoists hold that because the Dao always has many, even infinite, forms, truth must always be multiple and plural (see chapter 13). As such, against Cornille's suggestion that such epistemological humility is unnatural, it may seem normative from such a starting point. (Daoists in practice have often defended their "absolute truth" as much as many others, so this just represents a different way to frame the issue.)

Commitment: In China, people have tended to utilize or participate in the rites of different religions when useful: one may consult a Daoist exorcist, undertake Buddhist funeral rites, rely on Confucian ethics, and so on. Standing committed within only one tradition has not been the usual practice. This has been spoken of as strategic religious participation (SRP; see box 13.1).[39]

Interconnection: A corollary of strategic religious participation is that different religions can be engaged because a fairly common set of ideas, or a worldview, underlies them: a shared religious landscape (see box 13.1). This is certainly not to suggest that each religion says the same things or is identical. If this were the case, there would be no rationale in engaging each for different purposes. However, it radically undercuts Cornille's notion that we see distinct religious worldviews which may nevertheless be crossed.

Empathy: The condition of empathy resonates well with a Chinese religious standpoint: we can get inside another person's viewpoint. However, traditionally, engaging in any rites as well as worshipping a variety of deities would be utterly permissible (see box 13.1 and case study 1B).

Hospitality: Cornille draws upon a biblical virtue which comes from the background of a desert culture: one offers food, water, and shelter to travelers because one never knows when one will need the same.[40] Notions of reciprocity are common in Chinese worldviews; however, they are also distinct. In the Analects, Confucius says: "'To learn and then review what one has learned, how pleasant! To have friends coming in from afar, how delightful! Not being ruffled when a man finds himself unappreciated, what a gentleman!" (A 1:1). These words are believed to have been uttered after Confucius found his advice not accepted by various princes, and so this was how he greeted students who came to learn from him when he settled down. While traditionally related to offering hospitality to guests, it carries somewhat different overtones from the biblical perspectives. Its specific reference is to friends, not strangers, for instance, while it also stresses a teacher greeting students, whereas in biblical notions of hospitality one may expect to learn from the stranger rather than them coming to learn from you. Of course, it is not the only phrase or perspective that could be drawn on, but raises the issue that a Confucian attitude of "hospitality" will be different from a Western Christian one.

Readers are invited based on their own knowledge of Chinese, or other, perspectives to raise further critiques. This is not to suggest that Cornille's conditions were raised in bad faith, or to deny that many from China or elsewhere might find them appealing. Rather, it highlights how a Western Christian (Catholic) lens and the world religions paradigm (WRP) may lead to specific perspectives on IRD.

.   .   .

CASE STUDY 14A. CHRISTIAN AND MUSLIM WOMEN READING SCRIPTURES

Anne Hege Grung's studies of Muslim and Christian women who meet and read their scriptures together raises questions for us: about the dynamics of Muslim and Christian encounters, the place of women in IRD, and the role of forms of scriptural reading practices as a dialogical activity.

The women Grung studied came from a variety of religious, geographic, and cultural backgrounds. All described themselves as feminists. They included, among others, a Norwegian-Pakistani Sunni Muslim, a Norwegian-Iranian Shia Muslim, a Norwegian-African Lutheran with a Catholic upbringing, and a Norwegian Lutheran. They had come together for some time to share and read scriptures. As Grung puts it: "They had all been shaped through struggling with the same question: how to be a feminist and stay within the framework of the tradition?"[41]

The women modeled a storytelling approach. Rather than representative dialogue (where each person speaks for their tradition), the dynamic is to share individual journeys in a tradition. The storytelling model is more typical of women's dialogue,[42] but it is not useful to stereotype some approaches as feminine or masculine, or to downplay women's roles in representative dialogue.[43]

WOMEN AND DIALOGUE

As Grung notes, sometimes women are sidelined from dialogue because male leaders in a tradition which allows female leadership may not select women to dialogue with those who do not have female leadership for fear of offending them (though it is not clear that this has ever offended anyone). In relation to Islam and Christianity in particular, both are often portrayed as quite deeply patriarchal traditions which hold to traditional "family values." In many cases, both limit female leadership. Nevertheless, there are those who argue that, in their contexts, both Jesus and Muhammad were far more progressive in their treatment of women than the surrounding society.[44] Moreover, women on each side may feel that they have been marginalized or sidelined, if not discriminated against, within their own tradition. These are issues that can be brought to the dialogue table. However, they are often avoided, because dialogue partners may seek for areas of agreement that are seen as uncontentious. Female participants may also feel that their perspectives as women may not be fully respected. Further, these can be issues which each tradition feels are best discussed internally rather than airing their "dirty laundry" in public.

Grung argues that gender can never be completely removed nor ignored, for no matter what other differences arise, every participant in dialogue shares one thing in common: they are gendered. Therefore, whether discussed or not, gender is arguably always at the table of dialogue.

FEMINISTS ENGAGING SCRIPTURE IN DIALOGUE

The women engaged their scriptures in ways that were typical of their tradition. Interreligious learning took place in seeing how the other engaged their own texts. For the Muslim feminists, the Quran was seen as direct and literal revelation, so it could not be criticized. Hence, passages seen as problematic for feminists were addressed through finding interpretations or traditions to mitigate them. For example, one passage in the Quran allows men to beat their wives (Q 4:34). A feminist interpretation notes that Muhammed is said to have never beaten his own wives, and since following the traditions (Sunnah) of Muhammed is an ideal for Muslims (see box 11.3), it should not be done. Contrarily, some of the Christian feminists were ready to criticize parts of the biblical text. Some pointed to what they saw as the difference between the way that Jesus and Paul treated women, arguing Jesus should be the model. The Christian women were generally not ready to criticize Jesus or disregard what he said, but they felt that other parts of the text could be criticized. Those inspired by historical-critical approaches to the Bible (see case study 4A) were also ready to suggest that the genuine parts of Paul's letters were not negative, and that actually it was later additions to the text that were the problem (see case study 10B). This demonstrates a way each side learned about the other's approach to their respective texts, pointing to ways that an interfaith feminist conversation can increase understanding about the Other (see box 13.7 on this usage).

REFLECTION

Some questions will help us think through issues raised:

1. From the perspective of one of the women involved in these dialogues, what primary insights do you think you might gain about the other religion? Would it alter your views of what a feminist stance may be? (You may wish to consult chapter 10.)
2. Do you see the fact that women are often sidelined from dialogue events to be a significant criticism of IRD as a practice? Or does it reflect wider patterns in society and religious traditions rather than being an issue of IRD itself?
3. Do you think the position of women in different traditions should be a theme brought to the fore and discussed in IRD? Is it so fundamental an issue that it must be raised? Or is it a sensitive topic that is likely to make those involved defensive and so best raised within traditions as an internal issue?
4. In what way do you think other perspectives or groups are, or may be, excluded from IRD because of the dynamics of such encounters and the religious traditions involved?

CASE STUDY 14B. BUDDHIST-CHRISTIAN DIALOGUE: HISTORY AND DISCOURSE

A truism is that dialogue is always between people. Although it is common to see phrases such as the "Buddhist-Christian" dialogue, religions or systems of thought cannot dialogue. Actual encounters and acts of dialogue must involve specific human beings in specific contexts.

Analyzing dialogue involves human interaction with various dynamics: friendship between dialogue partners, situations of inequality and power dynamics, the colonial or postcolonial context of where and how they meet, and so on:

- In Asia, today's dialogues often occur in places where Christian missionaries came alongside European colonialism in what many still perceive as the twofold attack from the cross and the sword (see chapter 7).[45]
- For Western Buddhist converts, there may have been a conscious rejection of Christianity.
- The variety of Buddhism or Christianity involved (e.g., Theravada or Mahayana, Catholic or Protestant) affects perceptions.
- Prevalent theological attitudes (see chapter 13) will affect how an encounter is framed.

It is therefore impossible to make generalizations about Buddhist-Christian dialogue, or the specific encounters of individual Buddhists with individual Christians.

SOME HISTORICAL CAMEOS

There are many contexts of encounter and it is impossible to be exhaustive, so some brief cameos may be used here (see box 14.7).

FRIENDSHIP AND POWER

In the case of Martin Luther King Jr., a context of civil rights and anti-war sentiments led to a range of friendships across both racial and religious divides. Indeed, for others, friendship often forms part of interfaith understanding. The Dalai Lama in some of his writings has expressed how his understanding of Christianity grew from encounters with specific individuals.[46] These friendships or human encounters may shape how people come to appreciate how the virtues of another religion are lived out, or how they come to understand and appreciate the teachings or practice of another religion. Of course, meetings and personal encounters do not always lead to positive attitudes and dialogue.[47] Our first two historical cameos showed where meeting the religious Other led to negative views, with particular colonial dynamics shaping these encounters.

FRAMING DIFFERENCES

Theological or cultural worldviews also frame encounters. When Catholic missionaries saw Pure Land Buddhism as being false—akin to Lutheranism in a time of strong antagonism between Catholics and Protestants (see box 9.3)—they assumed that finding

BOX 14.7 **CONTEXTS OF BUDDHIST-CHRISTIAN ENCOUNTER**

Sometimes Christians and Buddhists meet in situations of hostility and sometimes in more irenic contexts. We give two brief cameos of each:

- When Portuguese Catholic missionaries arrived in Japan in the sixteenth century, some were shocked by Pure Land Buddhism. Pure Land Buddhists revere Amida Buddha, who was believed to have created a "Pure Land" where those who sincerely call upon him can be reborn. Rebirth there means that one is assured of attaining awakening/nirvana, though in popular devotion it is more like a paradise. Interpreting this as a form of "salvation" based purely on "faith"/"grace" (in Christian theological terms), the Portuguese Catholics argued that the devil had implanted Lutheranism (i.e., Protestant theology) before they arrived to thwart conversion to Catholic Christianity (see box 6.5).

- In the sixteenth century, Buddhists in Sri Lanka welcomed Christians to their temples, and would freely listen to Christian preaching and attend church. However, met with aggressive proselytization, with no gesture toward mutual ritual attendance, this attitude changed over time. In the late nineteenth century, Buddhists engaged in polemical debates with Christian preachers to argue for the "truth" of their tradition, and told Buddhist laypeople not to attend churches.[1]

- Today, in Japan and the West, many Christians learn *zazen* (seated Zen meditation). Some argue it is a tool for prayer and contemplation that can bring them closer to God. Many Zen monks/priests are happy to teach Christians without any expectation the latter will become Buddhists. Some Christians have had their experience of *satori* (the "realization" or "awakening" experience of Zen) recognized by their teachers, even becoming Zen teachers/masters themselves (see case study 2B; see also case study 11B).

- Martin Luther King Jr. (1929–1968) developed a deep mutual friendship and respect with Thich Nhat Hanh, a Zen Buddhist monk from Vietnam. King was already inspired by interreligious interaction, learning particularly from Mohandas (Mahatma) Gandhi (1869–1948) and Abraham Joshua Heschel (1907–1972). Nhat Hanh came to the United States in the context of the Vietnam War and witnessed many hate-filled anti-war protests. He argued that to be peace-makers, people must first "be peace" themselves,[2] practicing meditation to "purify" themselves. The idea of personally exemplifying peace was influential on King, and has influenced subsequent Christian activists and peace advocates.[3]

---

1 See Elizabeth Harris, "Exclusivism, Inclusivism, Pluralism: A Spatial Analysis," in Harris et al., *Twenty-First Century*, 57–75.

2 Thich Nhat Hanh, *Being Peace* (Berkeley: Parallax Press, 1987).

3 See Darrell Fasching, Dell Dechant, and David M. Lantigua, *Comparative Religious Ethics: A Narrative Approach to Global Ethics*, 2nd ed. (Chichester: Wiley-Blackwell, 2011), 4–9, 181–99, 257–59, 286–94.

the demonic in other religious traditions was normal. Catholics today expect that some light and truth can be found in other religions (see case study 13B). Today, teachings on Amida may therefore be framed as common ground around savior figures (see box 6.5). We could frame this in the terminology of exclusivism (my religion is true, others are false) and inclusivism (my religion is true, but others are partially true), respectively (see chapter 13). While exclusivist views do not stop dialogue, they may limit what forms of dialogue are possible, and would probably result in rejection of models such as Cornille's "conditions." Cornille's stance would typically be framed as inclusivist. This would play alongside personal encounters: exclusivist Christians may have Buddhist friends, but believing the latter are going to hell may wish to convert them; elsewhere friendships have led to people radically altering their views of another religious tradition.[48]

REFLECTIONS

The following questions will help think through these issues:

1.   Consider the extent to which you think friendship may be a factor in developing dialogue. How can it be a tool in increasing understanding between people? Does it always lead to mutual agreement and understanding? What are your experiences of this, if any?
2.   The Sri Lankan context shows different views on the possibility of sharing religious or ritual spaces. To what extent do you think the possibility of sharing ritual spaces is indicative of a willingness to engage in dialogue?
3.   The colonial legacy, and Christian and Western dominance related to this, has affected Buddhist-Christian dialogue in many places. To what extent do you think actual or perceived power differentials between religions, and their association with colonial power or oppression, affects the possibility and basis for dialogue? (See chapter 7 for issues around colonialism.)

.   .   .

QUESTIONS AND CONNECTING THOUGHTS

Connections between this chapter and others include issues of gender (chapter 10), the problematic "world religions paradigm" (see chapters 1, 3, and box 2.1), violence and peace-building (chapter 15), politics (chapter 18), and colonialism and postcolonialism (chapter 7), among others. Some aspects of these are further raised in the questions below:

1.   Some scholars of religion would see IRD as something a scholar cannot do (as a scholar at least, which would not of course stop them engaging in it in other contexts, perhaps as a concerned citizen). Do you think such a distinction can be viably maintained? See arguments that we all come with agendas and that no pure "neutral" academic space exists (especially chapters 2, 5, 7, 10, and 18). Or,

do you think academics should be involved, perhaps to give a more balanced and scholarly approach to IRD?

2. To what extent are Catherine Cornille's "conditions for dialogue" simply Western Christian norms not applicable elsewhere? Or is there enough commonality for them to be seen as a basis for other traditions too?

3. IRD is employed to describe many types of quite distinct activity. Do you think all of these should be called "dialogue"? Or, does the term "dialogue" only refer to certain types of encounter or exchange?

4. Many major dialogue events occur in Western nations or with money from significant Western organizations, or in association with the West. Does this mean that IRD is inherently implicated as a form of neocolonialism (see chapter 7), where Western norms dictate how different religious worlds meet and are expected to communicate? Do you think IRD would be conceived differently in non-Western contexts?

FURTHER READING
THEORY

Buber, Martin. *Between Man and Man* (New York: Routledge, 2007 [1947]), 1–45.

Cornille, Catherine. "Conditions for Inter-Religious Dialogue," in *The Wiley-Blackwell Companion to Inter-Religious Dialogue,* ed. Catherine Cornille (Chichester: Wiley-Blackwell, 2013), 20–33.

Halafoff, Anna. *The Multifaith Movement: Global Risks and Cosmopolitan Solutions* (New York: Springer, 2013).

Hedges, Paul. *Controversies in Interreligious Dialogue and the Theology of Religions* (London: SCM, 2010), 94–108.

McCutcheon, Russell. "The Category of 'Religion' and the Politics of Tolerance," in *Defining Religion: Investigating the Boundaries between the Sacred and the Secular,* ed. Arthur Greil and David Bromley (Amsterdam: JAI, 2002), 139–62.

Moyaert, Marianne. "Interreligious Dialogue," in *Understanding Interreligious Relations,* ed. David Cheetham, Douglas Pratt, and David Thomas (Oxford: Oxford University Press, 2013), 193–217.

Swamy, Muthuray. *The Problem with Interreligious Dialogue: Plurality, Conflict and Elitism in Hindu-Christian-Muslim Relations* (London: Bloomsbury, 2016).

CASE STUDY 14A. CHRISTIAN AND MUSLIM WOMEN READING SCRIPTURES

Grung, Anne Hege. "Gender and Muslim-Christian Dialogue," in *Contemporary Muslim-Christian Encounters: Developments, Diversity and Dialogues,* ed. Paul Hedges (London: Bloomsbury, 2015), 67–82.

Grung, Anne Hege. *Gender Justice in Muslim Christian Readings: Christian and Muslim Women in Norway Making Meaning of Texts from the Bible, the Koran, and the Hadith* (Oslo: Unipub, 2011).

Speelman, Gé. "Claiming Space for Women: Women Reading Scriptures in Critical Dialogue," in *Contested Spaces, Common Ground: Space and Power structures in Contemporary Multireligious Societies,* ed. Ulrich Winkler, Lidia Rodríguez Fernández, and Oddbjørn Leirvik (Leiden: E. J. Brill, 2017), 176–89.

CASE STUDY 14B. BUDDHIST-CHRISTIAN DIALOGUE: HISTORY AND DISCOURSE

Gyatso, Tenzin., *Towards the True Kinship of Faiths: How the World's Religions Can Come Together* (London: Abacus, 2010), 57–66.

Harris, Elizabeth. "Exclusivism, Inclusivism, Pluralism: A Spatial Analysis," in *Twenty-First Century Theologies of Religions: Retrospective and Future Prospects,* ed. Elizabeth Harris, Paul Hedges, and Shanthikumar Hettiarachchi (Leiden: Brill, 2017), 57–75.

Harris, Elizabeth. "Buddhism," in *Christian Approaches to Other Faiths,* ed. Paul Hedges and Alan Race (London: SCM, 2008), 234–54.

Lai, Whalen, and Michael von Bruck. *Christianity and Buddhism: A Multi-Cultural History of Their Dialogue* (Maryknoll, NY: Orbis, 2000).

15

VIOLENCE
Fundamentalism, Extremism, and Radicalization

IN WHICH WE EXPLORE

Definitions, origins, and conceptions of fundamentalism(s)

Theories of religious violence, warfare, and conflict

The concept of "radicalization" and connections of "fundamentalism"/"extremism" to violence

Case studies exploring the perceived connection of Islam to terrorism, and the relationship of Buddhism to violence

INTRODUCTION

The term "fundamentalism" may fill our minds with images: banner-waving anti-LGBTQI activists; gun-toting bearded militants; hellfire preachers; mobs of saffron-robed monks. Possibly, depending on your worldview and perspective, any or all of these images may have come to you.

However, before going any further, we must note several serious caveats:

- We deal with fundamentalism and violence together, but this does not mean that these are (necessarily) linked. Rather, we are dealing with how we imagine these concepts.

- We use the term "fundamentalism," but this chapter concerns the discourse (see box 5.1) around it rather than its "correct" meaning.

- In popular usage, "fundamentalism" is generally pejorative. As such, it is debatable whether scholarly employment can avoid this negative association.

We start off by discussing how the term "fundamentalism" arose and is now used. We will then move on to discuss potential links of groups often termed fundamentalist to violence and militancy. Next, we will address some links of religion to violence and theories around this, including "radicalization." We conclude with two case studies.

WHAT IS FUNDAMENTALISM?
THE FIRST FUNDAMENTALISTS

The term "fundamentalism" has a clear origin. Between 1910 and 1915, around three million booklets in a series entitled "The Fundamentals: A Testimony of Truth" were freely distributed in the UK and US. They set out what the authors saw as "the fundamentals" (i.e., core tenets) of Christianity. In the original series, these were belief in

- biblical inerrancy (it is infallible),
- direct creation ex nihilo (literally, "out of nothing"),
- miracles (i.e., those in the Bible),
- the virgin birth (of Jesus),
- crucifixion and bodily resurrection,
- substitution atonement (a specific theological view of how Jesus saves), and
- the imminent return of Jesus.

In 1920, an American Baptist named Curtis Lee Laws (1868–1946) became the first person known to explicitly call himself a fundamentalist, while Baptists in the southern US became the first fundamentalists as a group. In this original usage, a fundamentalist is someone who adheres to what they understand as the basic tenets, the fundamentals, of their religion. However, presumably everyone adheres to what they see as the fundamentals of their tradition. So, what marks this out as distinct?

Notably, while the term was first claimed by insiders (see chapter 2) as a badge of honor, it soon became used pejoratively (see box 15.1).

FUNDAMENTALISM'S GENESIS

The fundamentalist trajectory was a reaction to modernity, especially liberal (sometimes modernist) Christian theology.[1] Liberal Christian traditions seek to integrate the findings of modern science and historical-critical methods into the interpretation of the Bible and understanding of tradition (see chapter 4). As a modern movement, fundamentalism is often linked to the following:

SCOPES, CREATIONISM, AND FUNDAMENTALISM AS DEROGATORY

Shortly after the term "fundamentalism" was adopted by certain Protestant Christians in the United States, a legal dispute made it headline news. Reading biblical texts literally in English suggests God created the world in six days (the Hebrew term translated as "day" is more ambiguous), leading some Protestants to deny scientific accounts of evolution. Creationism (today, often reframed as intelligent design) refers to the belief that God created the universe and all species in six days, generally believed to be around five thousand years ago. In the 1920s, states across the US had leeway to determine whether they would teach evolution, creationism, or both. Teaching evolution was banned in Tennessee by the Butler Act. Defying this law, teacher John Thomas Scopes (1900–1970) was brought to trial in 1925 in the town of Dayton. In a carefully managed trial, broadcast across the nation, Scopes and his lawyers succeeded in making the fundamentalist creationists look stupid and ignorant. Although Scopes lost the case (he had breached the law, but was acquitted on a technicality on appeal), the so-called Scopes Monkey Trial helped make "fundamentalism" a derogatory term. Still claimed by some Southern Baptists, and those they influence, many "fundamentalist" Christians today prefer such terms as "Conservative Evangelical" or "Bible-believing Christian."[1]

---

1 See Edward Larson, *The Creation-Evolution Debate: Historical Perspectives* (Athens: University of Georgia Press, 2008).

Literalism: Acceptance of the claimed literal truth of the text. However, this is itself a form of interpretation: you decide how to read the text. Also, nobody reads everything literally; for example, when Jesus is described as "the true vine" or "the lamb of God," Christian literalists do not read this literally.

Traditionalism: Acceptance of beliefs or traditions handed down by tradition, not modern interpretations, although tradition always changes (see chapter 4).

Conservativism: Acceptance of "old-fashioned values" (similar to traditionalism).

Furthermore, we can note three points:

1. Today's fundamentalism may not be very "traditional": modern literalist interpretation is distinct,[2] the fixations are modern/contemporary issues,[3] and Christian beliefs have changed (see chapter 4).

2. While each term above is distinct, they are often used interchangeably.

3. Some aspects of fundamentalism are not necessarily modern: literal interpretations of texts have been propounded before, and the Fundamentalism Project's (see below) characteristics are not all new.

Today, "fundamentalism" can refer to a wide range of movements and traditions, but generally pejoratively. If a media headline uses "fundamentalism,"[4] it often implies "extremism" (see below). Even in scholarly usage, we see at least four problems with generalizing the term:

Derogatory: While aiming for neutrality, scholars use it only for extreme, not mainstream, groups. Therefore, it connotes problematic traditions.

Context: Beyond its original context (Christian literalism), it arguably becomes too generic. Yet suggesting a word only has meaning in its own context is problematic (see box 11.2).

Homogenizing: As a generic term, it potentially erases specific differences to emphasize only selected similarities (see chapter 11).

Linguistic hegemony: "Fundamentalism" is tied to English-language usage, so utilizes the particular dynamics of one language and certain geographical locations. Somewhat comparable terms in other languages would mean we envisage the phenomena differently (see chapters 2 and 7).[5]

The Fundamentalism Project, a five-year global study,[6] set out nine characteristics of fundamentalism:

Reactivity to the marginalization of religion: Fundamentalism is a reaction against secularization (see chapter 16) as religion becomes less significant in society.

Selectivity: Only certain aspects of a tradition are taken as the fundamentals.

Moral dualism: The world is seen in black-and-white terms.

Absolutism and inerrancy: Interpretations are seen as true and unquestionable.

Millennialism and messianism: The end of the world and a savior figure are expected.

Elect membership: Fundamentalism assumes full membership, or none at all.

Sharp boundaries: Truth and falsehood, saints and sinners, and so on, are clearly defined, with no gray areas.

Authoritarian organization: Leaders cannot be questioned.

Behavioral requirements: To be a member, specific forms of practice are required.

Typically added to this list by others are the following:

Inherently political: Its ideas should be implemented in society, or it wants to effect change.

Tendency to violence: Even if not promoting violence, its clear boundaries and harsh worldview mean that violence against what is outside, that is, "evil," is readily justifiable (see chapter 6).

Totalism: Fundamentalism explains not just areas about morals or the afterlife,
but everything about the world, how to live, and how to run society.

Scholars who support this definition typically suggest that not all factors are needed, with groups showing the majority of these being deemed fundamentalist.[7] However, other scholars are wary of a generic definition.[8] Beyond these issues, a concern is whether we are talking about a modern phenomenon or a trend found in various traditions historically. For instance, authoritarianism, moral dualism, literalism, totalism, violence, and claims of inerrancy are not new. As such, while a contemporary tradition labeled "fundamentalism" is not the same as a tradition found in the past—every religious tradition responds to its contemporary context (consciously or not)—this does not show that many dynamics of "fundamentalism" are only modern. Perhaps only the reaction to secularism and against historical-critical/liberal trends are the new parts of any fundamentalism today. The (re) establishment of certainty in fundamentalisms could be seen as symptomatic of human reactions to societal changes or perceived threats more broadly in terms of identity (see chapters 6 and 13), and a reaction against a wider malaise of perceived uncertainty.

The last point also helps explain why, given the lists of fundamentalist traits alongside typical portrayals, people join a "fundamentalist" tradition. Here, Linda Woodhead's distinction of the frontstage and backstage of fundamentalism is insightful.[9] The frontstage is what others see, often claims about aggression and authoritarianism. The backstage is the experience of those within it, where the focus is often upon the security of families, communities, and certainties that many find in such traditions. As with any phenomenon, a fundamentalist tradition is never only one-sided.

FUNDAMENTALISM, EXTREMISM, AND VIOLENCE

Many commentators (both academic and popular) associate fundamentalist-style groups or ideologies with violence. However, we also see other terms often employed to denote this link, for example, "extremist" or "militant." Often fundamentalism and extremism are used interchangeably: but do they mean the same thing? Or, rather, do we think they mean the same thing? Any association depends on how we define "fundamentalism." Indeed, some terms associated with fundamentalism do not so readily invoke connotations of violence, such as "literalism," "conservativism," or "traditionalism." Our question is therefore best stated not as whether "fundamentalism" leads to violence, but how any author employs the term. It may be used with more or less analytic clarity in any situation. Therefore, it may hide differences or potentially help give comparative insights (see chapter 11). Douglas Pratt has suggested that a continuum of approaches exists between those traditions which may simply be conservative at one end with those more likely to enact violence at another, but with no necessary link or progression. However, the authoritarianism and moral certainty of fundamentalism, Pratt suggests, lay the groundwork for what came to be the justification for violence toward outsiders.[10]

THE AMBIVALENCE OF THE SACRED

For many, the conjunction of the terms "religion" and "violence" may seem oxymoronic: true religion, we are often told, is not violent. Others see religion and violence as inextricably and intimately bound together. In either case we may quite legitimately ask what we imagine "real" religion to be (see chapter 1).

The phrase the "ambivalence of the sacred" was coined by Scott Appleby,[11] who argued that we see resources for both peace and violence in many religious traditions. In any tradition, we may find teachings and resources that speak about peace, fraternal love, and being good neighbors, but we also find justifications for violence, hatred, and warfare. Notably, the justifications for violence cannot simply be said to reside in what we might term "fringe" or "extremist" wings. Mainstream justifications for violence exist in almost every tradition:

- Catholic Christian crusades to the "Holy Land" were supported by popes and saints, including Bernard of Clairvaux (ca. 1090–1153), who saw killing Muslims as a Christian duty.[12]
- Mainstream Buddhist traditions have endorsed war and violence (see case study 15B).[13]

Claims that violence is an aberration need to deal with the ubiquity of mainstream endorsements of violence. Of course, these traditions also have teachings of peace and nonviolence,[14] with resources for overcoming demonization of the other and peacebuilding:[15] hence the ambivalence.

COSMIC WARS

Mark Juergensmeyer has suggested that religious conflicts may seem intractable because they become "cosmic wars":[16] battles between good and evil, truth and falsehood, saints and sinners. However, it does not take religion to raise the stakes;[17] nationalist narratives can be riven with exclusion, and we naturally vilify our out-groups (see chapter 6). Regardless of whether religious narratives are involved, it can become hard to seek resolution when "the enemy" denies our most "sacred" values (see box 18.7). Atrocities may be justified in the name of the sacred: once demonized, the enemy becomes less than human (see box 15.9).

MIMETIC VIOLENCE

The theory of mimesis, associated with René Girard (1923–2015), concerns imitation.[18] Philosophers since at least the time of Plato have noted that humans mimic each other. However, Girard employs the concept of mimesis to emphasize certain points beyond simple imitation:

A fierce Buddhist temple guardian, typically understood to chase away evil, Kong Meng San Phor Kark See Monastery, Singapore.

BOX 15.2 **THE SCAPEGOAT**

In Israelite tradition, a scapegoat was a sacrifice made by the community on the Day of Atonement. Unlike a normal sacrifice, it was made on the altar of the Jerusalem temple and was what is termed a "sin offering." It consisted of two male goats; one was slaughtered in the temple, but the other was taken into the wilderness. Here it was offered to Azazel, a demon of the desert, or wilderness, and according to the Mishnah (oral teachings later recorded as texts) was thrown over a precipice. The notion is that this animal carried the offenses of the community and so marked a means of restoration. For Girard, the scapegoat represented a form of social release. The violence of mimetic desire, felt between the sacrificers, was met with a lesser, small-scale, act of violence. This common act of violence against an innocent victim allowed a renewed social bond between the sacrificers. Girard argued this renewal of social bonds should be unconscious, so the sacrificers simply see themselves sharing in a joint endeavor, rather than rationalizing their action as killing an innocent life to assuage their own conflict.

- Mimesis typically refers to "negative" behavior rather than "positive" behavior: we imitate both what we think is laudable in others and what we think is negative.
- Mimesis may not be conscious, but rather, an instinctive response.
- Mimesis is often about shared (internal) goals, or mimetic desire.
- Shared (mimetic) desire becomes conflictual when parties compete for the same thing(s).
- Therefore, mimetic desire causes escalating social competition, even violence, in a cycle of desire to gain ascendancy or control.

Important to Girard's theory is the notion of the scapegoat, an innocent sacrificial victim on whom the growing inherent violence of mimetic desire is played out (see box 15.2).

Following Sigmund Freud (1856–1939), Girard understands all religious violence as symbolic. It arises in relation to sacrifice as a form of primal violence, based on two points. First, religious violence arises from the inherently conflictual elements of religious teaching, symbolism, and sacrifice; second, it is from sacrifice that all forms of violence inflicted in the name of religion arise. Girard's notion of the primacy of sacrifice is deeply contested (see chapter 12). Juergensmeyer believes that warfare is a more primal instinct, arguing that sacrifice probably arises from hunting or warfare rather than vice versa.[19] For Juergensmeyer, sacrifice is only one way in which human instincts for violence become embodied in traditions.

While challenged, Girard's theory has been extremely influential and the concept of mimesis and mimetic desire remain useful, with enemies often escalating tensions and rhetoric to mirror, or "outperform," their opponents (see boxes 15.3 and 15.4).

BOX 15.3 **REACTIVE CO-RADICALIZATION**

A number of scholars have theorized that violence on one side evokes a similar response on the other side. In Girardian terms, we are talking about a mimetic cycle of violence. Douglas Pratt uses the term "reactive co-radicalization" to refer to the ways that violence by those enacting terrorism in the name of Islam (see case study 15A) elicits violent responses from far-right Islamophobic (see box 15.4) actors, which prompts further discourse and acts of violence on the other side.[1]

---

1 Douglas Pratt, "Islamophobia as Reactive Co-radicalization," *Islam and Christian-Muslim Relations* 26.2 (2015): 205–18; and Douglas Pratt, *Religion and Extremism: Rejecting Diversity* (London: Bloomsbury, 2017).

BOX 15.4 **ISLAMOPHOBIA: IS IT A THING?**

I have friends on two sides of a debate:

- those who think that Islamophobia names a serious issue, concerning the irrational hatred and fear of Muslims, and
- those who think it does not exist, or object that their "legitimate concerns" about Islam are branded as an illness or delusion (a "phobia").

So, is Islamophobia real? Short answer: yes. Fear of Muslims committing terrorism is way out of proportion to the threat (see case study 15A).[1] Indeed, those most at risk from terrorist attacks are in fact Muslims. Globally, and in the West, Muslims (and others wrongly seen as Muslims[2]) get attacked on the street, insulted in public places, spat at on public transport, or generally subjected to suspicion.[3] Whatever we want to call it, even if we might debate the terminology, Islamophobia is real.

---

1 See John Mueller, *Overblown: How Politicians and the Terrorism Industry Inflate National Security Threats, and Why We Believe Them* (New York: Free Press, 2006).

2 Moni Basu, "Sikhs under Attack," CNN (14 September 2016), https://edition.cnn.com/2016/09/14/us/sikh-hate-crimes-list/index.html, provides a good timeline/overview.

3 See Todd Green, *The Fear of Islam: An Introduction to Islamophobia in the West* (Minneapolis: Fortress Press, 2015). Notably, Islamophobia has sometimes gone hand-in-hand with *Antisemitism;*; see Sipco Vellenga, "Anti-Semitism and Islamophobia in the Netherlands: Concepts, Developments, and Backdrops," *Journal of Contemporary Religion* 33.2 (2018): 175–92; and James Renton and Ben Gidley, eds., *Antisemitism and Islamophobia in Europe: A Shared Story?* (Basingstoke: Palgrave-Macmillan, 2017). See also Paul Hedges, *Religious Hatred: Prejudice, Islamophobia, and Antisemitism in Global Context* (London: Bloomsbury, 2021).

LEGITIMATING VIOLENCE

We have seen a number of theories of "religious violence" so far, but we should ask what is meant when we hear that term (see box 15.5). For some, religious violence is based in foundational texts. Rarely is this framed as justifying direct aggression. For instance, Sikhism's warrior traditions, especially the Khalsa, are often justified as protection for the oppressed.[20] However, parts of the Hebrew Bible and the New Testament, possibly the most blood-soaked and horrific texts in both quantity and quality of any of the world's largest religious traditions, have been termed "the dark side of the Bible" and seemingly give God-given instructions for genocide.[21] While some contrast the "peaceful" New Testament with the "violent" Hebrew Bible, the Book of Revelations in the former is full of images of war and violence, and Jesus's teachings are not simply irenic:

> Do not think that I have come to bring peace on earth; I have not come to bring peace, but a sword. For I have come to set a man against his father, and a daughter against her mother, and a daughter-in-law against her mother-in-law; and a man's foes will be those of his own household. (Mark 10:34–36, RSV)

We can also find injunctions for warfare in Hinduism and Islam (see case study 15A). For Hinduism, while Mohandas K. (known as "Mahatma") Gandhi (1869–1948) is famous for reading the Bhagavad Gita as a pacifist manifesto, it is read more easily (and traditionally) as a justification as to why a warrior (*kshatriya*) should fight and kill as a manifestation of his duty (*dharma*).[22]

These injunctions of religious violence do not readily fit modern sensibilities in at least two ways:

- Religion is generally seen as peaceful, perhaps concerned with interreligious dialogue, rather than as contestation (see chapter 14).
- Religion is generally seen as private and not concerned with the public, secular, space (see chapter 16).

However, historically, the religious realms of life have been so thoroughly imbricated into the social, cultural, and political fabric as to be indistinguishable (see chapters 3, 16, and 18). Connections between national, ethnic, or local identities and religion may essentially be inseparable (see case studies 6A, 6B, 15B, and 18A). Indeed, it is through "religious" texts that many social, cultural, legal, and political dictates were enshrined. Religious traditions and texts have often determined who is allowed to kill whom. Émile Durkheim (1858–1917) believed that a natural tension existed between religion and the modern nation-state because one central function of each is to determine the legitimate use of violence (see box 18.4).

However the enemy is defined, against whom violence is justified, it involves interpretation and identity creation (see chapter 6). For instance, Juergensmeyer explored the "Christian identity" ideology of certain white groups in the US,[23] particularly noting Robert Matthews, who led a splinter group of the Aryan Nations called "The Order." Referring to Blacks and Hispanics as "mudpeople," Matthews wanted to kill them alongside "race traitors" (whites who supported them) and Jews in "a racial and religious Armageddon."[24] For others, "Western/liberal secularism" (see chapter 16), which is seen to belittle the centrality of God, may be what their religious (traditional cultural) way of life needs to be defended against.[25]

THE JUST WAR TRADITION AND LIMITS ON VIOLENCE

Religious traditions have often put limits on violence and its implementation. The Christian "just war" concept is one example. However, we could arguably see "just war" as a legitimate comparative category (see chapter 11) found in many traditions (see box 15.6).

PATHWAYS TO TERRORISM AND "RADICALIZATION"
TERRORISM AND RELIGION: SOME KEY CONCEPTS

Today, terrorism often conjures an association with religion. However, its first modern usage was acts of state terror, especially the French Revolution's "Reign of Terror" (1793–1794). Only in the late nineteenth century did it become associated with nongovernmental political violence.[26] Let us consider some definitional ideas:

TYPES OF JUST WARS

Religious traditions often mandated who could, and could not, fight or declare war, what level of violence was permissible, who or what should be protected in warfare, and so on.

- *Christianity:* Augustine of Hippo (ca. 354–430) and Thomas Aquinas (ca. 1225–1274) helped determine *jus ad bellum* and *jus in bello* (roughly, "justice for war," and "justice in war") to determine who could declare war, when and why, and then what conduct would be permissible during war.[1]
- *Hinduism:* Warfare was the preserve of the warrior caste (*kshatriya*). Therefore, noncombatants should not be harmed or involved. Indeed, one medieval visitor to India recounted being amazed that, with a battle raging in the land alongside his, a farmer was able to calmly plough his land because it was not his duty (*dharma*) to fight.
- *Islam:* Islamic law (*shariah*) regulated military combat (see box 15.10), dictating that groups such as women, children, monks, and priests were considered inviolate and so should not be harmed (unless they directly attacked you first). Meanwhile, it was forbidden to damage people's means of livelihood or food sources (see also case study 15A).

---

1 See Gregory Reichberg, *Religion, War, and Ethics: A Sourcebook* (Cambridge: Cambridge University Press, 2014).

- The international system tends to see governments as legitimate agents of violence: they go to war; therefore, nongovernmental actors commit terrorist acts.
- Political motive separates terrorism from criminal activity; the latter is generally for financial gain.
- Terrorists, rather than freedom fighters, target civilian as opposed to military (or governmental) targets.
- A political or ideological motive will distinguish terrorism from murder.
- The motivation must be to instill terror via acts of shock and horror.

The above definitional concepts, like all definitions, are inadequate. For instance, many acts in war may be designed to instill terror in the civilian population. For instance, near the end of WWII the British prime minister Winston Churchill (1874–1965) ordered the fire-bombing of civilian areas in the German city of Dresden.[27] Against military resistance (the British Royal Air Force did not see it as a legitimate target), Churchill argued the Germans must be made to feel they had lost. Was this state terrorism, or a war crime? Likewise, in media reporting, some killings for political ends are labeled as terrorism, others as murders; religious affiliation and racial identity both seem to be factors involved in this. Regardless, we should note that few terrorists would tend to see themselves as "terrorists," if by this we mean people inflicting unjustified killing on innocent civilians. Rather, whether state or non-state actors, those involved see their violence as in some way legitimate or proportionate.

While we often see violence committed by those we label "religious terrorists" as distinct, it stems clearly from nineteenth-century European anarchists, who are recognized as the first of four waves of terrorism:[28]

- anarchism: 1880s–1900s
- anti-colonialism: 1930s–1950s
- New Left: 1960s–1970s
- religion: 1990s–today

It should be noted that right-wing terrorism is not seen to have a particular period and is also seen to be somewhat ideologically distinct (e.g., fascists [1920–1930s], to Anders Breivik's attacks in Norway [2011], to the Christchurch mosque attack [2019]).[29]

Anarchists justified attacks upon civilians by arguing that there are no "innocent bourgeoisie" (capitalist middle class) when they threw bombs into crowded cafés. The tactics, methods, and ideological underpinnings of today's religious terrorism, from civilian attacks to suicide bombings, do not emerge from religious texts but from previous secular terror organizations.[30]

WHAT IS WRONG WITH RADICALIZATION?

Since 2006, the term "radicalization" has been used to "explain" certain forms of terrorism.[31] However, in analytic terms, it is deeply problematic.[32] For politicians, or the media, being "radicalized" seems a catchall category to explain why

- a seemingly ordinary person ends up blowing themselves up at, for instance, a pop concert;
- people travel overseas to fight for militant neo-Islamic jihadist organizations in places such as Afghanistan, Syria, Iraq, or the Philippines; or
- somebody buys into far-right extremism and kills an elected politician or Muslims praying in a mosque.

But radicalization hides a range of motives and degrees of association, and minimizes the responsibility of politicians. While many scholars in the field agree the term is problematic, they employ it because it is widely recognized (people broadly know what you are talking about) and serves as a shorthand for a range of more complicated issues. However, it hides a lot of issues, including the following:

Ideology or friendship: Evidence from interviews with past and current members of terrorist networks show that only some are ideologically committed. Marc Sageman speaks about the "bunch of guys" factor—that people belong to close networks of friends, and often loyalty and group belonging is key.[33]

Socialization: Social actors (family, friends, peer group, etc.) influence an individual to adopt a worldview; it is how we all learn about the world. Some are socialized into a worldview we see as "radical." It is not a special process.

Sympathy: Some surveys suggest that quite a few Muslims may be sympathetic to aspects of the worldview of groups such as ISIS (often Daesh) or Al-Qaeda.[34] However, few share its militant interpretation of Islam or endorse terrorism. The sympathy may come from their opposition to corrupt regimes in the Middle East, while others may feel some sympathy for creating a caliphate but oppose violence.

Whether it be terrorism from the far right, far left, or religion, a "radical" worldview does not capture an important jump: why do some people who accept the same worldview commit acts of violence while others do not? Even if one has vilified one's enemies and justified violence, it may still be hard to kill a person. Consider a thought experiment: Under what circumstances would you kill another human being? We often see terrorists or suicide bombers as "fanatics" for their willingness to kill. However, history (and psychology/biology) suggests that most humans are willing to kill. When your country goes to war, will you kill "the enemy"? If somebody attacks your family, would you kill in self-defense? Very few people, when pushed, are fully committed pacifists.

PATHWAYS TO VIOLENCE: IS IT ABOUT ISLAM?

To name the elephant in the room, when we speak about religion and terrorism, probably Islam first comes to mind. Therefore, we will focus on this. However, we find violence, even terrorism, in other religious traditions (see case study 15B).[35] To study Islam and violence, we need to consider two terms: militant neo-Islamic jihadism (see box 15.7) and jihad (see box 15.8). While some ideologies growing out of Islam support various forms of terrorism, they often violate mainstream Islamic strictures.

Some key issues about pathways to terrorism or "radicalization" can be noted:

- The vast majority of terrorists do not come from a religious background, but have a background in petty crime or gangs.[36] ISIS's own analysis on recruits in its heyday showed that most had not read the Quran; a significant number did not know how to pray (*salat*); and, knowledge of Islamic jurisprudence (*shariah*) was exceptionally rare.
- There is no single pathway into "radicalization."[37]
- Social networks cause "radicalization," with self-radicalization being rare.[38]

MILITANT NEO-ISLAMIC JIHADISM

Here, we use the phrase "militant neo-Islamic jihadism" to name ideologies that endorse terrorism in the name of Islam. We can break down each word:[1]

- *Militant* connotes a militarized ideology that believes in violence.
- *Neo-Islamic* is used because it is based on a distinctly modern reading of Islam.
- *Jihadism* indicates the employment of jihad (see box 15.9) as "holy war."

This phrase helps in three ways:

- Most Muslims cannot identify the acts of terrorists with Islam because it relies on a specific (modern) interpretation that does not resonate with mainstream traditions.[2]
- Many terrorist tactics defy established rules of Islamic law (*shariah*) about how to conduct a "just war" (see box 15.6).
- We cannot divorce it from Islam, because we find many who accept it, genuinely believing that they are following Islam. However, terrorist ideologues are probably aware they draw heavily from secular terrorist ideologies.

---

1 See Paul Hedges, "Radicalisation: Examining a Concept, Its Use and Abuse," *Counter Terrorist Trends and Analyses* 9.10 (2017): 12–18.

2 See Mohammad Hassan Khalil, *Jihad, Radicalism, and the New Atheism* (Cambridge: Cambridge University Press, 2017).

JIHAD: BEYOND WAR

Contrary to claims that it means "holy war," jihad is more literally translated as "striving" or "struggle." This striving is moral, physical, and spiritual. Notably, a saying (*hadith*) of Muhammed reports that war/physical struggle is the "lesser jihad," while moral and spiritual striving is the "greater jihad." Indeed, claims that military jihad is mandated in the Quran are inaccurate. In the Quran, the Arabic words *harb* (warfare) and *qital* (fighting) are used, with jihad related to combat only once in the text. It is therefore not surprising that many Muslims say the term does not connote war; moral and spiritual striving is the "greater" striving; war is a "lesser" striving. Nevertheless, "jihad" is widely used for warfare in later Islamic tradition, among other meanings. We can distinguish "jihad" from contemporary ideologies of "jihadism" (see box 15.7).[1]

---

1 See Reuven Firestone, *Jihad: The Origin of Holy War in Islam* (Oxford: Oxford University Press, 2002); and "What Is Jihadism?" *BBC News* (11 December 2014), www.bbc.com/news/world-middle-east-30411519.

BOX 15.9 **MORAL DISENGAGEMENT AND HUMANIZATION**

Albert Bandura refers to the ways that humans distance themselves from others (and/or consequences) so they can cause harm to another as "moral disengagement."[1] He notes: "People do not usually engage in harmful conduct until they have justified, to themselves, the morality of their actions."[2] Much of this behavior is "normal," he holds, especially among boys as they get older ("normal" here does not necessarily mean "natural," but socialized behavior); notably, the mistreatment of women by some men is indicative of moral disengagement. Factors in moral disengagement include the following:

Moral justification: We claim our violent actions are good, that is, self-defense or "holy war," and so on.

Euphemistic labeling: We use terms that hide the harm we cause, for example, "collateral damage" rather than "killing civilians."

Advantageous comparison: We say that the harm we did is better than alternatives; for example, atrocities committed in the Vietnam War (1954–1975) were seen as "saving" them from communism.

Displacement of responsibility: We remove our own guilt by, for example, saying we were just carrying out orders.

Diffusion of responsibility: When a task is shared between many, no single person feels responsible; one person buys the bomb parts, another assembles the bomb, another plants it, and so on. Nobody takes on the whole.

Disregard or distortion of consequences: We find ways to minimize (in our minds) the harm caused, or tell ourselves it was not so bad.

Attribution of blame: We say that the victims "brought it on themselves," so we are blameless.

Dehumanization: We call those being killed or harmed "vermin," and so on.

These factors are common to human experience (see chapter 6), and not some special aspects of "radicalization." We see them in the manufacture and marketing of cigarettes, the launching of suicide bombs, telling "white lies," or bullying in the playground. The extent to which they are engaged in is important. However, Bandura argues they normally get weighed against a "power of humanization." This is a counterforce, which can sometimes be stronger, that humanizes the other.

---

1 Albert Bandura, *Social Foundations of Thought and Action: A Social Cognitive Theory* (Englewood Cliffs, NJ: Prentice-Hall, 1986).

2 Albert Bandura, "Selective Moral Disengagement in the Exercise of Moral Agency," *Journal of Moral Education* 31.2 (2002): 101–19, 103.

- The pathway to kill another human relates to moral disengagement (see box 15.9), not Islam.
- Relative poverty, perceptions of oppression, or the narrative of not belonging in society are factors in recruitment into militant neo-Islamic jihadism.
- Terrorists are not typically "crazed fanatics." They often operate in consistent and rational ways according to the worldview into which they are socialized. This is important for countering radical extremism (CVE) work.[39]
- While the rationale is not generally Islam per se, it becomes part of a legitimating ideology. Therefore, any integrated countermessage needs to consider religion.

·　　·　　·

CASE STUDY 15A. THE INVENTION OF ISLAMIC TERRORISM

Today, Islam is associated more than any other religion with terrorism. You may have heard this (false) adage: "While not all Muslims are terrorists, all terrorists are Muslims." However, this is far from accurate. Surveys by law enforcement agencies show that, even since 9/11, the threat of right-wing white supremacist terrorism in the United States far outweighs that from militant neo-Islamic jihadism.[40] So where does the image come from?

A SCENE

On Friday 13 November 2015, concertgoers in central Paris were at the Bataclan Theatre in central Paris enjoying the music of the Eagles of Death Metal. A night out, like many others, in a city of culture and art. At 21:40, a black Volkswagen Polo pulled up outside and three men entered the building. Heavily armed and wearing suicide vests, they soon created carnage, killing ninety people and critically injuring many more. A senior officer from the anti-crime branch was the first police officer on the scene and shot at one gunman, who blew himself up. The other two gunmen barricaded themselves upstairs with hostages as, at 22:15, officers from the BRI (Brigades de Recherche et d'Intervention), heavily armed specialists in hostage situations, arrived and made their way through the building. Determining that the kidnappers wanted to kill their hostages in front of the media, at 00:18 the officers stormed the room and shot one attacker, while the second attacker blew himself up. The police had advanced behind a shield which was hit by twenty-seven bullets in the fray. It was one of six coordinated gun and bomb attacks that occurred in Paris that night, all starting within around half an hour of each other.[41]

The three Bataclan attackers have been identified as Omar Ismail Mostefai, twenty-nine, Samy Animour, twenty-eight, and Foued Mohamed-Aggad, twenty-three. All of North African descent, they were known to the police and had been on watch or terror lists. Mostefai had a background in petty crime, but had since become a baker, played soccer with his coworkers, and was reported to be a very pleasant young man. Like many of the others involved that night, he had grown up in poor and relatively deprived suburbs (*banlieue*) around Paris, or Brussels, and was part of the immigrant subclass. They suffer from high rates of unemployment and discrimination.

The attackers told their hostages that they should blame France's president, François Hollande, for their plight: for involvement in killing Muslims in the Middle East. All the attackers that night, and the suspected mastermind behind the attacks, a man named Abdelhamid Abaaoud, a Belgian who was killed in a police raid in the Paris suburb of Saint-Denis a few days later, pledged allegiance to ISIS/Daesh. Their attack was therefore linked to militant neo-Islamist jihadism (see box 15.7). But, like many attacks, it is one that most Muslims find almost incomprehensible.

HISTORICAL AND BACKGROUND CONTEXTS

Fear of Islam has existed in Europe for over a thousand years (see boxes 14.4 and 15.4). Under Muhammed's successors, the united tribes of Arabia became a dynamic fighting force, soon taking Jerusalem and sweeping across North Africa and into the Iberian Peninsula. Iberian raiders almost reached Paris, and the Ottomans would only be stopped at the gates of Vienna, having taken Byzantium (modern day Istanbul) in 1453. The borders of empires became perceived as battle lines between Islam and Christianity. However, this is a selective historical memory:

- For centuries, Christians in the Middle East lived in relative peace.[42]
- While far from peaceful, medieval Al-Andalusia under Muslim rule was often exceptionally tolerant given the surrounding European context (see case study 13A).
- Christian monarchs Henry VIII (1491–1547) and Elizabeth I (1533–1603) of England allied with the Muslim Ottoman sultans against the Christian monarchs of France and Spain.
- Where Islam was not allied to imperial power, it traveled peacefully with traders and missionaries. For instance, Indonesia (the country with the largest Muslim population) largely lacks the civilizational clashes that mark Europe's memory.[43]

To imagine Islam as a threatening presence, or in one scholar's terms, surrounded by "bloody borders,"[44] is simply inaccurate.

TERROR AND THE TEXT

Critics of Islam often state that the Quran endorses killing, arguing that a good (following the fundamentals) Muslim must support violence;[45] therefore, peaceful Muslims are not

The following is a verse which many allege shows the violence inherent in the Quran:

> And when the sacred months have passed, then kill the polytheists wherever you find them and capture them and besiege them and sit in wait for them at every place of ambush. But if they should repent, establish prayer, and give zakat, let them [go] on their way. Indeed, Allah is Forgiving and Merciful. (Q. 9:5)

Due to its context, this passage is understood as a "war verse," that is, guidelines for practice within an ongoing conflict. Muslims have asked whether it has a general application to all polytheists, or just the specific ones being fought here. Most influential Islamic jurists (*ulama*) suggested the latter. Further, for Muslims, any text should be read only in the light of the traditions (*sunnah*) of Muhammad. Muhammad is held never to have declared an offensive war, only fighting in self-defense. Therefore, notwithstanding that some rulers have employed verses such as this to justify offensive warfare, Islamic tradition decrees it should not be read this way (see box 11.3). Finally, once declared, any warfare must be fought within the context of Muhammad's example and Islamic law (see box 15.6). Critics of Islam who cherry-pick selected verses often read in overly literal (see box 5.5) ways,[1] and typically exemplify Orientalist stereotypes (see chapter 7, especially box 7.3).

---

1 See Khalil, *Jihad*.

following their religion very well. Leaving aside confusions about how religions work (see especially chapter 3), this is inaccurate. On purely proportionate terms, the Christian Bible (both parts) contains more texts condoning and inciting violence than the Quran does.[46] The verses which suggest violence often have very particular contexts that are considered essential in traditional Islamic scholarship (see box 15.10). Moreover, Islam does not traditionally see jihad as "holy war" (see box 15.8), while suicide attacks (especially on civilians) and killing of civilians have never been part of Islam (see box 15.6).[47]

MUSLIM RESPONSES

When attacks associated with Islam occur, many are quick to ask why Muslims do not condemn these attacks; it may surprise us to know that numerous national and international Muslim groups and scholars have roundly condemned these attacks and stood in solidarity with the survivors.[48] Such things are often not newsworthy in the eyes of many mainstream media outlets.[49] This lack of knowledge has contributed to a rise in Islamophobia (see box 15.4). Muslims generally do not believe that such atrocities can be committed in their name.[50]

For many scholars, militant neo-Islamic jihadism (see box 15.7) is, like fundamentalism in Christianity, a reaction to modernity. It draws from the ideological and practical concepts of terrorism as political violence. Indeed, virtually every militant neo-Islamic jihadist organization today can, in some way, be traced back to the insurgents funded by the US and trained by the CIA in Afghanistan in the 1980s to resist the Russian occupation.[51] There is an important intellectual link to a Salafi movement of the eighteenth century associated with Muhammad ibn Abd al-Wahhab (1703–1791), known as Wahhabism, whose thought today underpins Saudi Arabian Islam. There are also roots in various anti-colonial contexts, and other modern Islamic religious teachers.[52] However, many Salafis are peaceful and politically quietest.[53] Even Wahhabism does not, in and of itself, advocate today's militant neo-Islamic jihadism,[54] although their very exclusionary thinking can underpin stark in-group and out-group identities (see chapter 6).[55]

REFLECTIONS

Some questions will help us reflect on the points raised:

1. From the perspective of a young Muslim in a country such as France, who might have been a concertgoer at the Bataclan concert in Paris, how would you respond to criticism by peers that this attack represents your religion?
2. What pathways to terrorism do you think may have inspired the Bataclan gunmen? How might moral disengagement, or other factors, be involved in this?
3. To what extent, do you think, is viewing Islam as inherently aggressive, violent, or threatening part of a history of imperial encounters? What aspects of Islamic tradition suggest that accounts that portray Islam this way are wrong? Conversely, what aspects might support such a view?
4. Would you classify militant neo-Islamic jihadism as a form of fundamentalism? Why, or why not?

CASE STUDY 15B. BUDDHISM AND VIOLENCE

Buddhism may evoke images of serene monks in meditation, smiling Buddha statues, and the concept of non-harm (*ahimsa*). However, Buddhism has been used to justify warfare, aggression, and violence.

A SCENE

In Sri Lanka, a saffron-robed monk stands before a crowd of people telling them that the teachings (*dharma*) and tradition (*sasana*) of Buddhism are under threat. He asserts that for 2,300 years only in this one nation has pure Theravada Buddhism been preserved,

THE BUDDHIST RULER AND JUSTIFIED VIOLENCE

Buddhist tradition sees King Ashoka (ca. 304–232 BCE) as a Buddhist ruler, celebrating him as an ideal monarch, a *chakravartin*. The *chakravartin* is a ruler who upholds Buddhist principles and defends the tradition. Therefore *ahimsa*, non-harm, is seen to characterize his rule. Nevertheless, Ashoka did not disband his army or law enforcement, which would often involve torture and execution. Such violence and killing was seen as justified, framed within the remit of the work of a compassionate ruler for the greater benefit. However, while tradition tells us that after gaining his empire Ashoka was so shocked by the death it entailed that he turned his back on violence, it seems he later slaughtered eighteen thousand Jains, among other "atrocities." Likewise, Buddhist rulers through history have been responsible for many wars, often endorsed and justified by monks.[1]

---

1 See Jerryson, *If You Meet the Buddha*, 30, 55–60.

but today the Sinhalese language (that of the majority, mainly Buddhist, population) and its traditions are fragile and at risk. The threat is aggression—if not violence, then at least proselytization—from Islam and Christianity. While Buddhism advocates non-harm (*ahimsa*), there is a need to defend Buddhism. The following day, a mob of Sinhalese Buddhists storm into a Muslim part of town, abuse and insult Muslims, and set fire to shops. This is later justified as a defensive assault by the Buddhists to forestall attacks by those who sought to destroy Buddhism.[56]

FROM THE DHARMA TO DESTRUCTION

In terms of scriptural injunctions and doctrinal standards, Buddhism appears utterly opposed to violence. Causing harm to others (*himsa*) is fundamentally countered by the principle of *ahimsa*, often translated as " nonviolence," though many scholars prefer "non-harm" as it encompasses much more. Killing another human being is one of the "grave crimes" that, according to the monastic regulations (Vinaya), sees a monk or nun expelled from the monastic community (*sangha*). Killing any sentient being (animal) is also discouraged; Buddhists have discouraged people from being butchers or fishers to avoid causing harm. However, the Buddhist tradition also contains rationales for violence and even killing.[57] These go back to the earliest days of the tradition. Buddhism received support from local rulers and developed a role for them (see box 15.11).

In early South Asian thought, the use of violence and even torture by kings was often conceived of as not being a form of harm. Rather, it was seen as a necessary, even beneficial, part of society. Moreover, while texts suggest that monks should avoid soldiers, and decree that soldiers in service to the state cannot become monks, this is not necessarily because such violent occupations were antithetical to monasticism. Rather, arguably, it was to show that Buddhism was not seeking to subvert the rule of law by inducing soldiers to become monks. Throughout history, Buddhism has made special provision for soldiers and monarchs, suggesting that intention is central to causing harm. While killing in anger will result in rebirths in hell or as an animal, it is said to be possible to kill and commit violence for compassionate reasons, detached from murderous thoughts. While promoting an ideal of *ahimsa,* Buddhism has nevertheless created a set of exceptions, or justifications, for certain acts of violence and killing.

BUDDHISM BETRAYED?

Scholars disagree as to whether violence can ever be justified in Buddhism:

- Stanley Tambiah (1929–2014) argues that justifications of violence are always a betrayal of Buddhism.[58]
- Tessa Bartholomeusz (1958–2001) argues that Buddhism has a "just war" tradition, although she sees it as problematic in relation to *ahimsa.*[59]
- Michael Jerryson argues that the right to commit violence and kill is built into scriptural injunctions, while fundamental traditional tenets support it.[60]

A significant dichotomy of opinion exists, which we can address in four points:

Just war: To defend Buddhism (*dharma/sasana*), many Buddhists hold that violence can be justified. Sayings attributed to the Buddha suggest that a defensive war is permissible. Moreover, some noncanonical texts suggest that enemies of Buddhism may be less than human (like beasts/animals, or even demonic), and therefore killing them is not a grave offense.

Ahimsa: For some, the principle of ahimsa is so fundamental that violence is never justified. Texts or teachings which suggest otherwise are seen as the faulty development of tradition.

Lay/monastic: There is a distinction between the pragmatic needs of laypeople in society, who may sometimes need to fight a "just/defensive" war, and the ideals expected of monks.

Nationalism: Buddhism is often linked to a national and an ethnic identity (see chapter 18). From the late nineteenth century in Sri Lanka, figures such as Anagarika Dhammapala (1864–1933) developed an ideology that connected Sinhalese ethnicity, Theravada Buddhism, and Sri Lankan nationalism. This is often tied to contemporary justifications for violence to protect Buddhism as an ethno-religio-national identity.[61]

Notably, some Buddhists who believe that Buddhists may fight in certain situations find the rhetoric and behavior of many contemporary figures who advocate Buddhist violence against

Muslims/Hindus/Christians unacceptable. They would describe them as militant/funda-mentalist/extremist/ultranationalist Buddhists.[62] It is not necessarily an either/or case: one might support the possibility of Buddhist violence, but say not all violence is justified.

REFLECTIONS

Some questions will help us think through the issues here:

1. From your understanding of Buddhism, is violence in defense of Buddhism justifiable or a betrayal of Buddhism?
2. Many of the debates revolve around the interpretation of texts, as well as balancing what are seen as fundamental principles against specific teachings. In relation to Buddhism, or other traditions you know of, how would you seek to understand the claims made on either side? How are "just war" traditions or self-defense legitimated?
3. Some rhetoric from contemporary Buddhist militants/fundamentalists/ultranationalists suggest that the very existence of Buddhism itself is at stake. How would you relate this to theories of religious violence?

.   .   .

QUESTIONS AND CONNECTING THOUGHTS

Connections in this chapter have been noted to identity and our natural vilification of out-groups (chapter 6), religion's relationship to politics (chapter 18), and secularism (chapter 16). However, the way we envisage religion is also significant (chapters 1, 3), especially in the way we imagine it through Orientalist lenses (chapter 7). We address some questions to help think through the issues:

1. Based on a tradition you are familiar with, do you think it justifies violence? In what circumstances? What different viewpoints exist on this?
2. Do you think the term "fundamentalism" is a useful scholarly and academic category? If so, in what ways? If not, can we speak meaningfully about potentially comparable traditions in varying contexts?
3. How would you define and employ a range of other terms, such as "extremist," "militant," "literalist," "traditionalist," "conservative," "radical," and so on? Do these have a general usage, or are they only meaningful in context?
4. Is it problematic to associate religion with violence or develop a general theory of religious violence?
5. Why do we more readily associate some religions with violence (Islam, to name the elephant in the room), and others with peace (e.g., Buddhism and Hinduism). All have, historically and today, justified both violent "extremism" and irenic pacifism. Is any religion more prone to either trend? Why?

6. What insights have you gained into violent terrorism, its motivations, justifications, and the pathways that lead to it? How important do you think the religious/Islamic factor is in militant neo-Islamic jihadism? Should we call it "Islamic" in any sense? Does failing to do so hide a key motivation for many actors?

FURTHER READING

THEORY

Dunn, James, ed. *Fundamentalisms: Threats and Ideologies in the Modern World* (London: I. B. Tauris, 2015).

Hedges, Paul. "Radicalisation: Examining a Concept, Its Use and Abuse," *Counter Terrorist Trends and Analyses* 9.10 (2017): 12–18.

Juergensmeyer, Mark. *Terror in the Mind of God: The Global Rise of Religious Violence*, 4th ed. (Berkeley: University of California Press, 2017).

Krogt, Christopher van der. "The Rise of Fundamentalisms," in *Controversies in Contemporary Religion*, ed. Paul Hedges (Santa Barbara: Praeger, 2014), vol. 3, 1–38.

Munson, Henry. "Fundamentalism," in *The Routledge Companion to the Study of Religion*, 2nd. ed., ed. John Hinnells (New York: Routledge, 2010), 354–71.

Neumann, Peter. *Radicalized: New Jihadists and the Threat to the West* (London: I. B. Tauris, 2016).

Reichberg, Gregory. *Religion, War, and Ethics: A Sourcebook* (Cambridge: Cambridge University Press, 2014).

Savage, Sara. "Head and Heart in Preventing Religious Radicalization," in *Head and Heart: Perspectives from Religion and Psychology*, ed. F. Watts and G. Dumbreck (West Conshohocken, PA: Templeton Press, 2013), 157–94.

CASE STUDY 15A. THE INVENTION OF ISLAMIC TERRORISM

Ali, Mohamed bin. *The Roots of Religious Extremism: Understanding the Salafi Doctrine of Al-Wala' wal Bara'* (London: Imperial College Press, 2015).

Hussain, Ed. "Islamic Fundamentalism," in Dunn, *Fundamentalisms*, 69–78.

Mohamed, Khalil Hassan. *Jihad, Radicalism, and the New Atheism* (Cambridge: Cambridge University Press, 2017).

Ruthven, Malise. *A Fury for God: The Islamist Attack on America* (London: Granta, 2002), 44–71.

CASE STUDY 15B. BUDDHISM AND VIOLENCE

Aljunied, Syed Mohammed Ad'ha. "Politics and Religion in Contemporary Burma: Buddhist Monks as Opposition," *Yonsei GSIS Journal of International Studies* 2.1 (2010): 37–50.

Deegalle, Mahinda, ed. *Buddhism, Conflict and Violence in Modern Sri Lanka* (New York: Routledge, 2006).

Fernando, Jude Lal. "Buddhism, Nationalism, and Violence in Asia," in Hedges, *Controversies in Contemporary Religion,* vol. 3, 61–90, 61–76.

Jerryson, Michael. *If You Meet the Buddha on the Road: Buddhism, Politics, and Violence* (Oxford: Oxford University Press, 2018).

Liow, Joseph Chinyong. *Religion and Nationalism in Southeast Asia* (Cambridge: Cambridge University Press, 2016), 105–10.

Pradeep, Anuruddha, "The Political Dimension of Buddhism in Sri Lanka," in *Buddhism in Asia: Revival and Reinvention,* ed. Nayanjot Lahiri and Upinder Singh (Singapore: Institute of South East Asia Studies, 2016), 261–89.

Walton, Matthew, and Susan Heyward. *Contesting Buddhist Narratives: Democratization, Nationalism, and Communal Violence in Myanmar* (Honolulu: East-West Centre, 2014).

16

SECULARISM
Secularization, Human Rights, and Religion

IN WHICH WE EXPLORE

Conceptions of the secular, secularism, and secularization

The co-creation of the secular and the religious

The secularization thesis and disputes around multiple modernities

The connection of religion and human rights

Case studies exploring the burkini ban in France, and Singapore's common space

INTRODUCTION

Secularism, for many of us, is a taken-for-granted—even "natural"—part of our world. We may have the notion that religion and the secular form a dichotomous pairing of our world as quite distinct, even opposite, spheres of life:

Secular: Public and political, the realm of the sciences and economics. It governs the public sphere, in which all citizens interact and live together.

Religious: Private and personal, the realm of religion, belief, and personal morality. It is not part of, and should generally be kept apart from, the public sphere.

In many countries we see a legal and constitutional framework which demarcates this. Countries as diverse as France, India, Singapore, Turkey, and the US either have constitutions which say they are secular or understand themselves to be secular. However, what it means to be "secular" is contested in governmental, legal, and scholarly terms. The notion of the religious and the secular as two distinct spheres is a modern concept with a particular history and trajectory; neither has "a natural domain or function."[1] We will explore this as we begin by looking at the origins and meanings of the term "secular," before proceeding to discuss secularism and secularization as ideology and process, with particular attention on the secularization thesis and its critics. We then address how freedom of religion and secularism are bound together in human rights. As always, we end with our two case studies.

FRAMING THE SECULAR

ORIGINS OF THE SECULAR

In Latin, "secular" means "of this age," and in medieval Europe referred to priests who lived among the laity ("in the world"), as opposed to those in monastic institutions, the "religious." This distinction of clergy was challenged in northwestern Europe by the Protestant Christian Reformation in the sixteenth century (see box 9.3). But it was during the European Enlightenment (see box 16.1) that secularism took on the meanings we know today. Notably, given global ideas flooding into Europe at this time, contrary to perceptions of it as simply being a European idea, global ideas, especially those from China, influenced Western conceptions of what the secular should be.[2]

Two important contexts for this new secular vision were France and the US,[3] which established two key secular principles:

> *Freedom from religion:* The state is not dominated by any religious institution. This relates to the French equivalent term *laïcité*, which from the French Revolution (1789) has referred to the separation of the institutions of the Catholic Christian Church from the institutions of the state.

> *Freedom of religion:* There is freedom to follow a variety of different religious (and non-religious) options. This relates to the First Amendment (to the US Constitution): "Congress shall make no law respecting an establishment of religion, or prohibiting the free exercise thereof."

These two are generally seen as the foundational cornerstones of a secular political system. Tariq Modood argues for a third principle, as countries such as the UK, Sweden, and Germany have or until recently had—in varying forms—an established church, but are understood as (paradigmatically) secular. However, arguably these European examples simply show that establishment can be in line with *freedom of* and *freedom from* religion. So, no third principle is established.[4] Globally, secularism has many permutations, as discussed below (see also box 18.3).

BOX 16.1 **THE EUROPEAN ENLIGHTENMENT**

Associated with the birth of modernity, the Enlightenment was a period when tradition was dramatically questioned.[1] Variously dated from around the sixteenth to the eighteenth centuries, or sometimes more narrowly from ca. 1720 to 1780, it was a period of change and transformation in many areas:

Scientific: Via the so-called Baconian method (named after Francis Bacon, 1561–1626), discoveries and theories were freely shared and discussed instead of being kept secret. New public scientific organizations such the Royal Society in London (1660) were formed, and learning from across the globe was brought to Europe.

Political: Feudal countries gave way to modern nation-states, with the notion of citizenship and the emerging concept of human rights altering perceptions of the individual's relationship to social and political structures.

Social: Mercantilism led to a rising middle class which challenged the power of the older feudal/landed upper classes. With new wealth, and increasing free time, a new literate and intellectual class developed.

Philosophical: No longer was philosophy "a handmaiden to religion" (i.e., existing to justify religious belief), but became an independent critical discipline. Thinkers questioned established orders in politics and religion.

Religious: Connections of religious to political orders were cut, and religious authorities—texts, clergy, and tradition—faced radical challenges. It was possible to express ideas such as atheism and deism without fear of oppression.

Three important notes:

1. The Enlightenment was not a single movement: it contained contradictory trends and continues to have various interpretations.

2. The transition between the Renaissance (see box 4.4) and the Enlightenment can be variously understood, but is partly about a shift from intellectual life being centered in southern Europe, especially Italy, to northwestern Europe, especially Germany, Britain, and the Low Countries.

3. Although often portrayed today as "Western," for those living through the Enlightenment such an idea was hardly conceivable. The Muslim-majority Ottoman Empire remained superior in scientific advances such as astronomy through much of this period; until the nineteenth century, the Indian subcontinent was technically superior in steel smelting; and China was seen, in many ways, as an intellectually superior civilization. However, from the late eighteenth and into the nineteenth century, European military and economic power increased, so the global debt of ideas was forgotten, and a narrative of the rise of the West from ancient Greece to the Enlightenment was constructed (see chapter 7, especially box 7.7).[2]

---

1 See Kieron O'Hara, *The Enlightenment* (Oxford: Oneworld, 2010); and Dorinda Outram, *The Enlightenment,* 3rd ed. (Cambridge: Cambridge University Press, 2013).

2 See John Hobson, *The Eastern Origins of Western Civilization* (Cambridge: Cambridge University Press, 2004); David Lyons, *The House of Wisdom: How the Arabs Transformed Western Civilization* (London: Bloomsbury, 2010); Jürgen Osterhammel, *Unfabling the East* (Princeton: Princeton University Press, 2018); and Paul Hedges, *Towards Better Disagreement: Religion and Atheism in Dialogue* (London: Jessica Kingsley, 2017), 138–44.

BOX 16.2 **WAS THERE A SECULAR BEFORE THE SECULAR?**

While modern conceptions of the secular arose in a mainly Western, Protestant, Enlightenment context, we can see intimations of such a division previously:

Medieval and early modern Europe: Monarchs ruled by "the divine right of kings": the political order was God's order. This was challenged in the English Civil War (1642–1651), with Parliament claiming its rights against the monarch; but it was also framed as a Protestant rebellion against a monarch inclined to Catholicism; hence it was not simply "secular."

Imperial China: The emperor ruled by the "Mandate of Heaven" (*tianming*) and was the "son of heaven," who could intercede with "heaven" (*tian*). This was mandated by Confucian teaching, but Confucian thought also contained "protosecular" elements denying a supernatural realm (see box 8.7, and case study 1B).[1]

Traditional Islamic thought: Muhammad manifested both religious and political authority, something claimed by some caliphs (in Arabic, "successor"). Moreover, Islamic religious law (*shariah*) includes laws on divorce, inheritance, and other matters typically classed as "secular." However, Islamic religious scholars (*ulama*) disputed the caliph's standing as a religious leader. It was they who interpreted *shariah,* insisting that the caliph's sphere was simply the temporal: he dictated governance in military and economic terms. After Muhammad, many Islamic scholars argued that nobody was both a religious and secular leader.[2]

Importantly, we can also ask a corollary question: was there "religion" before "religion"? In many societies, what we call religion was so tightly bound up with the whole of social life, cultural production, politics, and other spheres that designating only some aspect as "religion" does conceptual violence if we seek to separate it out as a distinct realm (see box 7.9). In this sense, the realms of the "secular" and the "religious" may be mutually codependent. This must be recognized, but it is also conceptually confused to suggest that terms cannot be used to help clarify matters of analytic interest in contexts where they do not, as it were, naturally arise, but the purpose of such usage must be recognized (see chapters 1 and 11, especially boxes 1.8 and 11.5).

---

1 See Herbert Fingarette, *Confucius: The Secular as Sacred* (Long Grove, IL: Waveland Press, 1972).
2 See Abdullah Saeed, "Secularism, State Neutrality, and Islam," in *The Oxford Handbook of Secularism,* ed. Phil Zuckerman and John Shook (Oxford: Oxford University Press, 2017), 188–200; and Mohamed Alami Musa, "Islam and Secularism in Singapore: Between Embrace and Belief," *Interreligious Relations* 3 (2019), www.rsis.edu.sg/rsis-publication/srp/interreligious-relations-irr-issue-3-islam-and-secularism-in-singapore-between-embracement-and-belief/#.Xs6OehNKg3g.

What we count as being religious or secular only arose because of a precise cultural and political context. It owes much to a particular Protestant vision of the world and the transition to modernity.

First, let us take a step back and ask: how were the religious and secular, as we term them today, framed before this period? The simple answer is that they were deeply intertwined. Arguably, before modernity, demarcating the religious and secular as two distinct realms is meaningless, although it was foreshadowed (see box 16.2).

Protestantism did not inevitably split the religious and secular. Under John Calvin (1509–1564), Geneva became a theocratic city-state, but a division was made between the church and magistrates which fed into the later logic of secular-religious divisions. Important dynamics occurring in the modern period included the following:

Republics and democracies: People became citizens equal under the law, relating to the state rather than being subjects beholden to the monarch-church nexus.

Centralized states: Governments provided education and health services, marginalizing the religious realm.

Mercantilism: Commerce grew and broke links to guilds, the medieval trade associations often tied to Catholic traditions.

Industrialization: The workplace and economic activity were further separated from traditional religious associations.

The changing religious and political landscape of northwestern Europe and North America meant that what was seen as "religious" (related to Protestant conceptions; see boxes 9.3 and 9.4) became seen as "private" and "individual" compared to the state's "public" realm.[5]

However, many Protestants do not believe that their religion is only private. It also affects how they do business, relate to their neighbors and colleagues, and who they vote for. Likewise, in many supposedly secular countries we see religion and politics tightly bound together. If you are thinking this: absolutely right! The world never works according to neat theories or binary patterns. Humans are messy, chaotic, and complicated creatures who do not obey the rules. We should therefore demarcate between several strands:

· theories of secularism versus the practice of secularism
· national, political, and legal conceptions of secularism versus the lived realities of doing secularism

- the theories and principles of political elites versus the theories and principles of the majority population (see chapter 3)

This is not to say that secularism is only theory. It is enshrined in constitutions and legal frameworks, and often operates as a background concept for whole populations. It is a social reality (see box 1.9). Nonetheless, the UK and the US, often seen as "typical" Western secular nation-states, illustrate some dynamics of the practice:

US: Strict separation of church and state means it is secular. But Christianity is commonly invoked by politicians (see case study 6B).

UK: Often seen as secular, the UK is actually a Christian state: (a) the monarch is head of church and state; (b) the Church of England is the established church (in England); (c) Anglican bishops sit by right in the House of Lords (upper chamber); and (d) Christian prayers open daily business in the House of Commons (lower chamber). But mainstream politicians have traditionally been wary of invoking religion.[6]

THEORIES OF SECULARISM AND SECULARIZATION: WESTERN AND BEYOND
CLASSIFICATIONS: SECULAR/SECULARISM/SECULARIZATION

Secularism is not simply a political system; it has social, legal, political, and philosophical levels. It may refer to

- distancing/removal of religious institutions/services from society or governance,
- decline in religious participation/believing, or
- an ideological stance that religion should not play a determinative role in public life.

Analytically, we can distinguish between three related terms (see box 16.3). However, different authors may use them in various ways.

We may note four further useful conceptualizations. First, from Rowan Williams:[7]

Procedural secularism: The public square should be neutral, so that no religion is preferred or given favor. The voices of specific commitments of religion/belief are allowed to be heard and are part of the discourse, but may not dominate or override other voices. This is seen as a "neutral" public sphere model.

Programmatic secularism: The public square should be emptied of religion. For value-free neutrality, religion should not be part of the public space. Specific

Secular: The public realm, seen as the jurisdiction of the modern nation-state and hence distinguished from the "religious." A practical outworking of secularism/secularization in society.

Secularism: An ideological proposition about what should be secular and the process of secularization.

Secularization: A process whereby things (e.g., health care, education, taxation, etc.) are moved to (secular) governmental control, and religious discourse on public and policy spheres is limited.

BOX 16.4 **GROTIUS: "AS IF THERE WERE NO GOD"**

"As if there were no God" (Latin: *etsi Deus non daretur*, literally, "as if God were not given") may sound like a very recent anti-religious way to propagate secularism; however, they are the words of Hugo Grotius (1583–1645). His concern was to find common ground for international legal injunctions between, primarily, Protestant and Catholic nation-states.[1] His answer was not to rely upon sectarian positions. Law would, following Grotius, act "as if there were no God." But Grotius did not believe that deity should be ignored: religion should affect how we think and behave. His principle remains a key part of how secular states operate at a legal or institutional level. It relates to Williams's procedural secularism.

---

1 See Peter Berger, *The Many Altars of Modernity: Toward a Paradigm for Religion in a Pluralist Age* (Berlin: De Gruyter, 2014), 52–53.

commitments of religious belief or belonging in public spaces should be made invisible. This is often seen as an "anti-religious" model.

Second, Hugo Grotius (1583–1645) asserted that we can operate, in the public sphere, as if there were no deity (see box 16.4).

Third, Karel Dobbelaere's "levels of secularization":[8]

Macro: society/institutional/governmental (national); concerns governance and the role of the state

Meso: organizational/practical (social); concerns society and the interaction of people

Micro: individual (personal); concerns the person, in terms of their private life and how they interact with the other levels

The commercial city center towers over even the largest temples, Singapore.

Processes of secularization take place at many levels which will interact and affect each other in various ways. How people understand it (micro-level) affects the daily workings (meso-level) and can influence policy (macro-level), while governmental/legal injunctions (macro-level) affect individuals (micro-level) and society (meso-level).

Finally, Silvio Ferrari argues that (Western) secularism favors certain kinds of religion. Modern(ized) Protestant forms, which are privatized and internal, are prioritized in secular spaces over forms which express themselves in ritual or public displays. In Ferrari's terms, the internal form (*forum internum*) is favored over the external form (*forum externum*).[9]

Each theory stresses a different point, but they may all be seen as working together.

THE SECULARIZATION THESIS

The secularization thesis is succinctly stated as follows: "In due course the sacred shall disappear altogether except, possibly, in the private realm."[10] It was embedded in sociology by Auguste Comte (1798–1857), who strongly opposed the dominance of Catholicism in French society, and by Émile Durkheim (1858–1917) and Max Weber (1864–1920). We can summarize the rationale behind the secularization thesis as follows:[11]

Increasing education: With greater knowledge, people will become less religious.

Increasing plurality: With globalization, our options are increased, destabilizing our local traditions.

Increasing scientific knowledge: Our understanding of the world means that we will no longer need religion to explain what we do not know.

Many of the theorists came from Europe and took that continent as a model. Declining belief and belonging there was assumed to be the natural outcome of modernity.[12] Even the United States, which is more religious, saw decline in urban areas, especially in the big coastal cities, often seen as most "modern." Data from Japan, which was taken to be very modern, was also read as indicating that religion was declining (see box 16.7 below).

CRITICS OF THE CLASSICAL SECULARIZATION THESIS

Grace Davie, José Casanova, and Peter Berger have been influential in rethinking secularization paradigms (see box 16.5).[13] Berger was perhaps the late twentieth century's most well-known proponent of the secularization thesis, but has now stated: "The world today is as furiously religious as it ever was."[14] Berger suggests, though, that aspects of the secularization thesis remain pertinent. Increasing diversity, he suggests, makes us aware of the contingency and negotiable status of our own culture and religion. Therefore, modernity, as globalization and diversity, does undermine religion to some degree. Berger sees this as related to modern turns to fundamentalism, which he sees as a fortification of belief in the face of uncertainty (see chapter 15).

According to Davie, secularization reached its heyday in the 1970s. This was in part due to the influence of anti-religious Communist-inspired regimes in the USSR (now Russia) and the People's Republic of China, which seemed to have decimated religion; however, religion is now resurgent.[15]

Feminist scholars also challenged the secularization thesis for being centered on male religious activity. Lived religion, especially women's practices, have not disappeared in the same ways (see chapters 3 and 10).

BEYOND EUROPE AND THE WEST

Critics also argue that evidence beyond Europe provides strong reasons to question the secularization thesis. Contrary to the European model, many speak of multiple modernities (see box 16.6).

In considering alternatives to Europe's pathway and the variety of different ways in which what we might say modernity is emerging, five particular dynamics are significant:

Perspectives: Is the experience of (northwestern) Europe inevitable globally, or contingent on specific local factors? Davie argues that theory is about

EXPLAINING RELIGIOUS CHANGE IN SECULAR SOCIETIES

Believing without belonging: Refers to the fact that while (in the UK/western European context) few people attend religious services or have institutional belonging, there are still indications that there are higher levels of belief, both orthodox and less so.[1]

Vicarious religion: Significant sections of some populations seem to appreciate that religious professionals and the actively faithful still continue the society's mainstream religious rites, and do this on behalf of (vicariously) the majority who do not attend. Furthermore, religious rituals are appreciated at significant times, such as periods of national mourning.[2]

Religion is changing: While traditional forms of institutional belonging and attendance are declining, people are engaging in other forms of "spiritual" practice (boxes 2.8 and 5.6), such as yoga, Tai Chi, and so on.[3]

---

1 Davie, *Religion in Britain since 1945.*

2 See Grace Davie, "Vicarious Religion: A Methodological Challenge," in *Everyday Religion: Observing Modern Religious Lives,* ed. Nancy Ammermann (Oxford: Oxford University Press, 2006), 21–35; and Steve Bruce and David Voas, "Vicarious Religion: An Examination and Critique," *Contemporary Religion* 25.2 (2010): 243–59.

3 See Linda Woodhead and Paul Heelas, *The Spiritual Revolution: Why Religion Is Giving Way to Spirituality* (Oxford: Blackwell, 2005). Many scholars were highly critical of the evidence presented in this book, but it remains the best-known example of this thesis.

EUROPEAN EXCEPTIONALISM AND MULTIPLE MODERNITIES

The decline of religion in Europe, which provided the basis for the secularization thesis, simply did not occur elsewhere. The US has largely remained more staunchly religious (Christian) than Europe.[1] But modern and secular nations in Asia have not become irreligious: India, Japan, Singapore, South Korea, Taiwan, Turkey, and other countries have remained resolutely religious. As such, assuming that the European process of modernization is a norm seems erroneous. We therefore need to see the problem of *European exceptionalism:* the secularization thesis, like much sociological theory, was based on the assumption of a European norm (see chapter 7).[2] One possible theory that arises from this is *multiple modernities:* the progress toward modernity and secularism may look very different in places other than Europe.[3]

---

1 The religious demographics in the US have also been changing rapidly in recent years, arguably in ways which mirror Europe, but it still remains more Christian and with only a fairly minimal atheist or agnostic presence; see Robert P. Jones, "America's Changing Religious Landscape," interview with Benjamin Marcus, Religious Studies Project, podcast (18 February 2019), www.religiousstudiesproject.com/podcast/americas-changing-religious-landscape/.

2 See Syed Farid Alatas, "Academic Dependency and the Global Division of Labour in the Social Sciences," *Current Sociology* 5.1 (2003): 599–613.

3 See Christian Smith and Brandon Vaidyanathan, "Multiple Modernities and Religion," in *The Oxford Handbook of Religious Diversity,* ed. Chad Meister (Oxford: Oxford University Press, 2011), 250–65; and S. N. Eisenstadt, "Multiple Modernities," *Daedalus* 129.1 (2000): 1–29.

describing what happens based on the empirical evidence, so talking about modernity will look different elsewhere.[16]

Cultural context: Do particular cultures/civilizations provide a bedrock which changes how modernity/secularism (assuming we still use these terms) manifests? Will there be distinct Confucian modernities, Islamic secularisms, and so on, in contrast to European/Protestant secularism?

Decolonial narratives: A number of scholars have argued that the creation of the conception of the secular, and with it religion, is tied up with racial classifications and the privileging of white (male, elite) normative discourses (see chapter 7). Vincent Lloyd argues that "the stories of secularism and racism are entwined."[17] This is explored by Sylvia Wynter, who sees "Man" becoming the central focus in secularism, away from a God-ordained order, allowing the conflux of such things as racialized identities and white supremacist thinking to be placed center stage in how the secular is envisaged. As such, narratives of white versus nonwhite, religion versus superstition, and a supposed rational and non-religious identity to be posited against the non-rational, primitive, nonwhite becomes, it is argued, part of the basis of secular thinking (see chapters 5, 7, and 18).[18]

Unmasking normative assumptions: Conventional theory has tended to argue from nineteenth-century European assumptions to a universal model. This may be a distinctly Orientalist approach (see box 7.3).

WRP (world religions paradigm): European, modern, and Protestant assumptions shape what is counted as religion, but religion is often done differently elsewhere. Japan is a good example (see box 16.7).

Scholars beyond the Western corpus also give us new perspectives. Benoy Kumar Sarkar (1887–1949) emphasized the need to rethink the borders of what we might consider religious or secular in relation to Hindu and Indian thought.[19] Sarkar stressed the material, secular, and rational aspects of Hindu and Indian traditions, which disrupts what we might see as their typically conceived boundaries (see also boxes 8.7 and 14.2). More recently, Rajeev Bhargava has argued that India provides a different model of secularism from that found in the West, with secularism being "religion-friendly."[20] In Indonesia, Nurcholish Madjid (1939–2005) employed the terminology of the secular in a particular way in relation to Islam, and theorized an Islamic secularization (see box 16.8).

The perceived reemergence of religion on the global stage also challenges the secularization thesis; we say "perceived" because, arguably, religion never went away (see chapter 18). However, in some countries which were staunchly secular in different ways, religion is increasingly a part of political discussion. This includes the US (see case study 6B), India (see case study 6A), and Turkey, which in 1928, under Mustafa Ataturk (1881–1938), removed the 1924 Constitution's declaration that "Islam is the religion of

BOX 16.7 **HOW RELIGIOUS ARE THE JAPANESE?**

Depending upon the statistics one looks at, Japan may appear to be one of the least religious countries in the world, with only a few people claiming religious belonging; or it may seem to be one of the most religious, with most people having allegiance—on average—to 2.8 religions. This statistic makes a lot more sense in relation to East Asian modes of religiosity (see chapter 1 and case studies 2B, 12B, and box 13.1) than in relation to classical Western theory on religion. In Japan, questions such as "are you a Buddhist?" typically imply "are you a Buddhist priest/monk?" As such, direct questions of this type elicit few affirmative responses, with mainly Christians and some members of new religious movements claiming "belonging."[1] However, if we explore family connections to a temple, attendance at New Year's festivals at shrines, or other forms of behavior, we can see Japanese people "doing" a lot of "religion." Opinions range as to what this signifies, but too many observers seek to fit East Asian patterns of religiosity into Western (Christian/scholarly) normative patterns.

---

1 On Japan's vast panoply of new religious movements (NRMs), see Nobutaka Inoue, "New Religious Movements in Global Context," in *Controversies in Contemporary Religion*, ed. Paul Hedges, vol. 3 (Santa Barbara: Praeger), 223–248.

BOX 16.8 **NURCHOLISH MADJID AND ISLAMIC SECULARIZATION**

Nurcholish Madjid (1939–2005) believed that secularization was a generally positive development. He said it should be welcomed by Muslims to help them distinguish between what was temporal (of this world) and what was transcendent (related to God/Allah).[1] He distinguished this from secularism, seeing the latter as a more ideological agenda which he opposed (like Williams's programmatic secularism). Madjid had two main concerns:

Cultural: To separate what he saw as properly belonging to Islam from "tradition."[2]

Political: Summed up in his phrase "Islam, Yes. Islamic Party, No."[3]

He was part of contentious debates as to the degree to which secularism/secularization was compatible with Islam. For Madjid and others, even from the time of Muhammad, the role of Prophet and the role of head of state were separate, whereas others saw them as integrated (see box 16.2). How a secular theory may grow out of Islam, and what it would look like, are contested. Importantly, such debates have occurred in many places and contexts.[4]

---

1 See Bahtiar Effendy, *Islam and the State in Indonesia* (Singapore: Institute of Southeast Asian Studies, 2003), 71–75.

2 See Luthfi Assyaukanie, *Islam and the Secular State in Indonesia* (Singapore: Institute of Southeast Asian Studies, 2009), 146–47.

3 Assyaukanje, *Islam and the Secular State,* 148.

4 See Saeed, "Secularism, State Neutrality, and Islam"; and Musa, "Islam and Secularism in Singapore."

the State." Both the 1937 and 1982 constitutions explicitly declared Turkey to be secular (*laïcité*), but the country has seen an Islamic political force emerge under President Recep Erdogan.[21]

THE SECULARIZATION THESIS: DEFENDED AND ASSESSED

The perceived "failure" of the secularization thesis is by no means universally accepted. Steve Bruce and others offer various defenses:[22]

Religion weakened: Even if not dead, religion's role in society is severely weakened within the secular/modern nation. It is no longer significant.

Slow decline: In 1851, 50 percent of the UK population attended church, but in 2015 only 8 percent attended church. While the decline is slower elsewhere, there is no reason to suppose this decline will reverse, or will not occur elsewhere.

From religion to spirituality: Spirituality is simply quasi-religion, that is, things such as yoga or a pick'n'mix approach without real commitment are seen as superficial and commercialized life-style choices, not religion.

The last throes of dying faith: The "return" of religion is a resurgence in the face of secularism, and can be interpreted as a sign of weakness.

Contexts: In more industrialized and developed areas we see a more secular society, but where it is more agrarian it is not (yet?) so secular. Contrary data are insignificant marginal exceptions. The secularization process is ongoing.

Critics and defenders of the secularization thesis often interpret the same data in different ways (or chose specific data to support key arguments). Two examples sum this up:

What is measured: In many places (but not all), institutional religion is declining, while the "nones" and the "spiritual but not religious" (SBNR; see box 2.8) are increasing. These people may engage in a variety of practices termed "spirituality" (see box 5.6) rather than engaging with institutions. Globally and historically, occasional engagement with institutions has not been unusual (see chapters 1, 3, and box 13.1). Is this therefore obviously "superficial" or unimportant?

Experiences: A long-term survey in the UK, from the mid-twentieth century to today, has found a similar number of people report what are broadly termed "spiritual" experiences (see box 8.5). Comparative surveys in both Turkey (hypothesized as more religious than the UK) and China (hypothesized as less religious than the UK) showed similar rates of reported experiences to those in the UK.[23] This may indicate that human "religiousness" (or at least one indicator of that) is not dependent upon secularization's advance (see also chapter 8).

We may conclude that, at the very least, the secularization hypothesis needs serious modification. That we will see worldwide declines matching Europe's falling religious attendance and adherence remains hypothetical. Equally, though, the multiple modernities hypothesis, while showing that modernity is happening differently, does not show that religion will persist elsewhere in the long term. Certainly, even many staunchly secular thinkers may profess an interest in "religion" or religious ideas and what they may contribute to our ways of seeing the world, which some have seen as part of a "post-secular" world.[24] We should nevertheless be wary of the primarily European and North American theory and data that dominates the debates.

FOUR TRENDS

If religion's place in society is changing in the modern world(s), secularization may be only one trend. Jayeel Serrano Cornelio speaks of four different trends:[25]

Secularization: As discussed, a decline of religion's significance and role in society.

Sacralization: Religion returns in various ways, with people perhaps once appearing only nominally committed showing more vocal commitment, whether in society or politics; religion is still (in some places increasingly) an important actor in society, providing health care or social services; activism is increasingly based on religious identities.

Detraditionalization: Traditional sources of authority are declining, often replaced by the internet (e.g., online preachers); self-authority becomes prominent;[26] religion is often commercialized (but see box 3.4) or becomes a spectacle; religion becomes action (social work or virtuous deeds), so there is no need for traditional rituals.

Universalization: Religion/spirituality is seen to be about the "ethic of humanity," doing good for all via common/shared moral values, or is about "everyday religion" (our day-to-day activities, rather than attendance, beliefs, rituals, etc.).

These are not all necessarily seen in the same place, and can be at times conflicting or overlapping trends. The rise of the so-called megachurch is indicative of aspects of these (see box 16.9).

Contemporary forms of religiosity can never simply be a "return" to the premodern. Tradition is rethought and re-expressed, or selectively kept (see chapters 4 and 15). Nevertheless, in our context, some scholars suggest that whereas secular modernity gave us disenchantment, we are today witnessing a reenchantment of the world (see box 16.10).

BOX 16.9 **THE MEGACHURCH AS DETRADITIONALIZATION, SACRALIZATION, AND "SECULARIZED" RELIGIOSITY**

Jayeel Serrano Cornelio suggests megachurches exemplify detraditionalization. They often involve spectacle (stage management, pop music, and performance) and provide "dogma without theology" (simplified and inspirational rather than intellectual preaching, often alongside literalist biblical interpretation; see chapter 15 and box 5.5). In many megachurches, what is termed the Prosperity Gospel is taught: a belief that God gives riches to those favored.[1] However, the growth of such churches, often in seemingly secular venues such as concert halls or convention centers, also seems to speak to a sacralization of the world, as they preach a " premodern" belief in miracles and healings. They also often bring a strong commitment to proclaiming their faith in public spaces, with a focus on proselytization. As such, while in some ways providing what may seem to be secular entertainment and a slimmed-down set of beliefs, the megachurch also pushes back against secularism.

---

1 See Catherine Gomes and Jonathan Tan, "Christianity as the Sixth Aspirational 'C,'" in *Money and Moralities in Contemporary Asia*, ed. L. Hoang and C. Aliipio (Amsterdam: Amsterdam University Press, 2020), 213–40; and Vicky Baker, "The Preachers Getting Rich from Poor Americans," *BBC* (29 May 2019), www.bbc.com/news/stories-47675301.

BOX 16.10 **DISENCHANTMENT AND REENCHANTMENT?**

Many early sociologists saw religion, magic, and superstition (see boxes 7.8, 9.4, and 12.2) as losing their grip on the modern world. This was termed "disenchantment," a term coined by Max Weber (1864–1920) in a 1918 lecture (in the German form, *entzauberung*). As the European Enlightenment (see box 16.1), industrialization, and secularization unfolded, it was felt that a more rational world free from "primitive" impulses would appear. However, in many places, it is clear that religion, magic, and superstition have not vanished. Some argue that in the contemporary world, or postmodernity (see box 2.5), they have returned as valid worldviews. This is reenchantment, but whether the world was ever disenchanted is debatable.[1]

---

1 See Philip Taylor, "Modernity and Re-enchantment in Post-Revolutionary Vietnam," in *Modernity and Re-enchantment: Religion in Post-Revolutionary Vietnam*, ed. Philip Taylor (Singapore: Institute of Southeast Asian Studies, 2007), 1–56, 2–4, 49–53.

We have reviewed what Scandinavians might call a smorgasbord of theory. Not all of it fits neatly together into one grand theory, and some bits are downright contradictory. However, it is natural that different contexts and disciplines will give us varying perspectives. We should not expect theory to be a neat package of ideas that explains everything and smooths out the edges. Rather, at best, it gives us gloves to grasp those rough edges.

We can, however, note some key points:

- Secular/ism/ization refers to a range of different things: processes, ideologies, spheres of life, and has many regional variations.
- There is no agreement among scholars on the processes and ideologies.
- Secularism is never simply neutral toward religion, but typically favors a privatized and internal form (*forum internum*) over an external form (*forum externum*).
- This is not simply theory, but has very real political and legal implications and consequences.
- The way that secularism is understood in any nation-state changes and develops over time.
- The relationship of religion and the secular is always contested and created, with no natural distinction between them. Arguably, they are co-created and need each other as an opposite to be capable of recognition.

HUMAN RIGHTS, SECULARISM, AND FREEDOM OF RELIGION
SECULARISM AND RELIGION IN PUBLIC LIFE: RIGHTS DISCOURSE

As secularization developed, a corresponding concern in Western societies was the growing discourse on human rights, including freedom of religion (see box 16.11). This included the rights of individuals to be free from coercion from religions favored by the state, but also to have no religion, and to exercise their other rights as citizens. Inevitably, some rights bump up against other rights. Human rights are essential to considering contemporary religion, because they underlie the legal social reality (see box 1.9) of religious practice in secular contexts.

The right to freedom of religion is enshrined in the 1948 Universal Declaration on Human Rights (UDHR), article 18:

Everyone has the right to freedom of thought, conscience and religion; this right includes freedom to change his religion or belief, and freedom, either alone or in community with others and in public or private, to manifest his religion or belief in teaching, practice, worship and observance.

Here, the standard rights to freedom of religion are laid out:

- freedom to change or retain belief,
- freedom from coercion, and
- freedom of practice (to manifest religion or belief).

"Freedom of religion and belief" entails not just religious belief, but other beliefs, such as atheism, humanism, and other worldviews and ideologies. Further, a wider range of documents clearly state what is protected, both in public and private spheres, including freedom to:[27]

- worship,
- celebrate holidays,
- follow prescribed diets,

- wear specified clothing,
- carry out life-cycle rituals,
- build seminaries,
- have schools, and
- distribute texts and publications for proselytization.

Examples of this institutionalized in law include the following:

- In the UK, Sikhs from the Khalsa tradition, who are required to wear turbans, do not need to wear a motorcycle helmet when riding a motorbike.[28]
- In the European Union, employers are called to do all they reasonably can to ensure that employees who celebrate particular religious festivals can take those days off work.
- In China, Christians of various denominations have seminaries and can print and distribute bibles, many of which are exported.

Whether these jurisdictions fulfill all parts of the rights framework may be matters of dispute.

A final key principle is the protection of minorities. A majority tradition (in interreligious or intrareligious contexts) cannot enforce its own precepts or practice on others.[29] There may be situations where not every minority can be accommodated for practical reasons. For instance, if a country provides for chaplains in hospitals, prisons, and the armed forces, it may not be required to supply a chaplain for every single strand of each religion. However, people's rights should not be unnecessarily infringed simply because they are a minority. Moreover, insofar as the contemporary multicultural and secular state favors certain types of external forms of religion (*forum externum*), arguably it can privilege interreligious dialogue as acceptable religious behavior (see chapter 14).[30]

LIMITS ON THE FREEDOM OF RELIGION

While human rights are generally seen as sacrosanct (see box 18.7), there are cases where certain rights may be held in abeyance. With respect to freedom of religion, this is set out in the International Convention on Civil and Political Rights (ICCPR), article 18(3):

> Freedom to manifest one's religion or beliefs may be subject only to such limitations as are prescribed by law and are necessary to protect public safety, order, health, or morals or the fundamental rights and freedoms of others.

Generally, this right is not seen as controversial. If somebody claimed that their religion required them to sacrifice babies to their deity or cause grievous physical harm to others, then standard laws would be applied to curtail these practices.[31] However, in many cases, religious groups have had long legal battles to obtain rights to perform practices which are generally illegal. For instance, some indigenous American Indian tribes, including Indian Christian churches, take a hallucinogenic substance called peyote as part of their rituals, while Rastafarians smoke cannabis as part of their worship. These have been allowed in some jurisdictions, but still remain illegal in others.[32] In addition, it is generally accepted that because of the particular customs or traditions of certain countries, the way that human rights are put into effect will have some cultural variations. The Organization for Security and Cooperation in Europe refers to this as the "margin of appreciation," noting that states may have laws and policies "that may differ . . . with regard to different histories and cultures. . . . This . . . should be respected . . . [but] it should not be interpreted with a degree of latitude that would permit the undermining of the substance of human rights values."[33] This is a matter of interpretation, rather than hard-and-fast rules.

It is unusual for freedom of religion to come into legal or political conflict over matters of belief. Rather, the issues become what is termed the right to manifest beliefs. To return to Ferrari's distinction: just as secularism favors an internal form (*forum internum*) over an external form (*forum externum*), so too does human rights discourse.

. . .

CASE STUDY 16A. *LAÏCITÉ* AND THE BURKINI BAN

In 2016, what might seem like a minor matter of discussion—what women may or may not wear on certain French beaches—became headline news around the world. Centered around an item of swimwear that covers the full body (except feet, hands, and face), known as the "burkini," the topic shot to prominence in the public imagination when the burkini was banned in the French resort of Cannes. It can be discussed from many angles: modest/pious fashion;[34] identity battles fought over women's bodies (see chapters 6 and 10);[35] Islamophobia (see box 15.4); or Orientalism (see chapter 7). Here, our focus is secularism and human rights.

THE BURKINI AND VEILING

The term "burkini" comes from combining *burqa* (also *burkha*) and "bikini." It allows women who believe that full body veiling is Islamically required (see box 16.12) to go to the beach appropriately dressed.[36] A number of non-Muslim women also wear the burkini, often for protection from UV rays.

"ISLAMIC EXTREMISM"

At its height, the burkini ban covered around thirty towns and cities, mainly in the South of France. It was initially supported by local courts, but the Supreme Court in France

BOX 16.12 **VEILING (HIJAB) IN ISLAM**

Historically, the practice of female veiling (hijab) was probably adapted by Arabic Muslims under the influence of the (Christian) Byzantine Empire. The Quran enjoins both men and women to dress modestly, cast down their glances, and guard their private parts, but does not mandate veiling (see box 10.8); but injunctions to modesty have more often been applied to women than men (see chapter 10). Evidence suggests it was not common in the early Islamic community, and was probably a minority practice historically, but has now become widespread. At least one saying of Muhammad (*hadith*) suggests it was not mandated in early Islam:

> When the son of a prominent companion of the Prophet asked his [Muhammad's] wife Aisha bint Talha to veil her face, she answered, "Since the Almighty hath put on me the stamp of beauty, it is my wish that the public should view the beauty and thereby recognized His grace unto them. On no account, therefore, will I veil myself."[1]

However, as all four major Sunni Muslim law schools prescribe hijab as mandatory, it can be seen as required (see box 11.3, but see also box 10.8). In various parts of the Islamic world, the requirement is understood differently.

---

1 Lynn Reese, *Women in the Muslim World: Personalities and Perspectives from the Past* (Berkeley: Women in World History Curriculum, 1998).

rejected the ban. The context of a state of emergency across France, following a number of terrorist attacks carried out by militant neo-Islamist jihadis (see box 15.7), should be noted.[37] For some, therefore, the ban was partly about public order, with the burkini described as a costume of Islamic extremism. Nevertheless, some denied the ban was specifically targeted at Islam. The deputy mayor of Nice, when asked by the press whether a nun could go to the beach wearing her habit (religious clothing, often including a headscarf), replied that they could not.[38] Even after the Supreme Court rulings, some politicians insisted that burkinis should still be prohibited, but the legal ruling prevailed.

LAÏCITÉ AND FRENCH CULTURE

Another issue was whether the burkini was compatible with French culture. This raised a set of overlapping but distinct issues. Some suggested that veiling is an "enslavement of women" and thus contrary to claimed French values of gender equality and feminism. Indeed, the right for a woman to bare her breasts was raised by the French prime minister Manuel Valls. Ironically, it was on the same beaches that the actress Brigitte Bardot

wore an iconic bikini considered too risqué by some. In 1953, this was considered a provocative act against public morals. A number of French towns banned the bikini—but
not Cannes or other beaches along the Riviera—as did Spain and some other (Catholic-
majority) countries. Pope Pius XII had declared the bikini "sinful" in 1951. However, in
the public imagination, this memory represents French openness to undressing.

Mirroring this, some French politicians called the burkini a "provocation."[39] However, this was not because it contradicts Catholic values, but a modern, strict interpretation of *laïcité*.[40] In recent years, *laïcité* has taken on a more ideological form, beyond the
separation of the church and state, with many holding that religion should not be visible
in the public sphere. Therefore, not just the burkini, but Islamic veiling—especially
full-face veils—are seen as an affront to the neutrality of the public sphere. However,
France is not "religiously empty," and the Catholic heritage still colors the public sphere.

HUMAN RIGHTS AND RELIGIOUS FREEDOMS

The Supreme Court declared the ban illegal rather than the burkini. Banning religiously
required clothing violates the freedom to manifest one's religion. While France sees itself
as a strong upholder of human rights, some politicians seemed ready at first to defy the
Supreme Court, and opinion polls suggested the majority of French people supported
the ban. Notably, in France and elsewhere in Europe, bans on a full-face veil have been
upheld, although there are arguments that this violates human rights principles.[41]

REFLECTIONS

Some questions will help to consider the issues raised:

1. How do you react to the concept of the burkini ban? Place yourself in one (or
   both) of the following positions: (a) a Muslim woman who considers that full-
   body veiling is a religious requirement, and (b) a French secularist who sees the
   beaches as a place of cultural significance where people should undress.
2. What differences do you see between the burkini ban and the ban on the full-face
   veil in terms of freedom of religion? Why do you think a court could overturn the
   first but keep the second? In what ways are they (legally) distinct?
3. Do you think that the French burkini ban could plausibly be argued to fall within
   a "margin of appreciation" because of the culture of bikini wearing in the South
   of France (from the 1950s) and its notions of feminism as allowing women to
   undress publicly? (See chapter 10, especially box 10.8.) To what extent can such a
   margin of appreciation alter basic freedoms?
4. In contemporary understandings, *laïcité* is often seen to signify the emptying
   of the public sphere of religious symbols, commitments, and values. Do you see

this as inherently antagonistic to freedom of religion? Is it inherently hostile to religion? Do you think that religious symbols should be limited in secular public spaces? To what extent? Also, to what extent does *laïcité* oppose certain religions/forms of religion, but may accommodate/tolerate other religions/forms of religion?

CASE STUDY 16B. SINGAPORE'S COMMON SPACE

Article 15 of Singapore's Constitution declares it to be a secular and democratic state. However, what does "secular" mean in this context? Singapore's Constitution provides freedom of religion; however, Singapore is a signatory to very few human rights conventions. Indeed, particularly in the 1990s, it was a strong advocate of what was termed "Asian values" as an alternative to human rights, arguing that the latter represented Western cultural values and the former described a set of (mainly East) Asian cultural values.[42] Like many countries, it has debates on how and where religion may manifest in the public sphere, or common space, as it is termed in Singapore.

SINGAPORE'S RELIGIOUSLY FRIENDLY SECULARISM

Singapore's leaders are clear that it promotes what might be termed a religious-friendly version of secularism. This is often portrayed as an Asian model, contrasted with a "Western model" that is seen to constrain religion. Despite conspicuous consumerism, religion is often heavily promoted in Singapore's common space:

- Politicians often speak of religion promoting moral values.
- Religious sites feature highly in promotion of the island state.
- Religious leaders have a place in many civic events. Politicians, while not stating their own religious stance, are often seen at temples, gurdwaras, churches, mosques, and other places of worship.

Further, in promoting interreligious dialogue as a tool for social cohesion, the government is often actively involved both directly and indirectly (see chapter 14).

MANAGING DIVERSITY AND RELIGION

However, Singapore's close management of religious affairs has been characterized as violating freedom of religion or being hostile to religion. On international indices of freedom of religion, Singapore tends to rate alongside oppressive regimes.[43] Singapore carefully manages and directs religious activity. The Maintenance of Religious Harmony Act (1990) stipulates that religious actors, when acting in such capacities, cannot voice political opinions, while derogatory words offending the sentiment of any religious community are proscribed. This includes banning aggressive proselytization, which might entail denigrating another religion.

Another factor is that most religious buildings are built on land which has only thirty-year leases. No site for religious usage can be built on land not designated for this purpose. This means that when plots become available, many groups are often bidding for the same plot, limiting availability for smaller or less well-funded groups. Moreover, because, after thirty years, many plots so designated have become important commercial land, they are no longer available for religious usage, and so religious groups are often pushed out of certain areas. Nevertheless, the government seeks to ensure that religious sites are as near as possible to dwellings in regulating land usage. Notably, a few historical religious sites (where land is held in perpetuity) and mosques are exempt from this process; for mosques, under laws governing the Malay-Muslim minority, there is guaranteed land (see case study 18A).

RELIGIOUSLY FRIENDLY OR CIRCUMSCRIBING RELIGION?

Kenneth Dean has suggested that far from being friendly to religion, the regulation of space means that Singapore's secular model is inherently, though not visibly, hostile to religion. While openly and ostensibly religion friendly, the actual practice, in his view, belies this. Religion is always being pushed to the margins. Certainly, out of necessity, some Chinese temples are now sharing the same spaces, with some temples disappearing entirely. The prioritizing of commercial interests in allocating land, which may be seen as typically secular (pragmatic), effectively marginalizes religion.

REFLECTIONS

Some questions allow us to consider this issue:

1. In your own experience, or context, would you say that the secular system is inherently a force that marginalizes religion? What model(s) of secularism/ization operate?
2. Despite the claim of many secular states that they make no laws regulating religion, every single government does this: tax breaks apply to certain traditions (often those officially recognized as "religions"); some traditions are banned (for what are seen as illegal activities); and certain practices may or may not be possible in public places. What do you think should be the limits of secular government regulation on religious spaces or traditions? To what extent are your views based upon your own cultural context?
3. Religious life and traditions are given much public prominence in Singapore, and most traditions are allowed to operate fully and openly. However, because

it prohibits what is termed "aggressive" evangelism (though low-key attempts to convert others are allowed), it is often seen as oppressive of religious rights.[44] With further research, how would you characterize Singapore's stance? Is it primarily religion friendly or hostile to religion? Does it depend upon which religion?

.   .   .

QUESTIONS AND CONNECTING THOUGHTS

The domains of the "religious" and the "secular" interrelate, and discourse on them, especially on human rights, affects the legal and political status of religion in society. Interconnections with issues in this book include the wider relationship of religion and politics (chapter 18); post/colonial contexts (chapter 7); the rights of men and women (chapter 10); what we think religion is (chapter 1); and the way that secular spaces frame dialogue between religions (chapter 14). Some questions will allow us to think through key issues:

1. Discuss what you understand secularism to be in your context. Do different people understand it differently? What type(s) of discourse on secularism exist? What resistance to it exists?
2. Is secularism an outgrowth of a specific religious worldview? If so, what would Buddhist, Confucian, and Islamic secularisms look like? Do we see multiple modernities?
3. What effects do such things as industrialization/postindustrialization and the rise of scientific worldviews have on secular societies and ways of seeing the world? Do they contribute to the ways we can act "as if there were no God"?
4. Is the secularization thesis still viable? If so, does it need modification? If not, what should replace it?

FURTHER READING
THEORY

Berger, Peter. *The Many Altars of Modernity: Toward a Paradigm for Religion in a Pluralist Age* (Berlin: de Gruyter, 2014).

Berger, Peter. "Peter Berger on the Failure of the Secularization Hypothesis," video, The Veritas Forum (2016), www.youtube.com/watch?v=62zSU-U9GGE, 00:00–18:00.

Bhargava, Rajeev, ed. *Secularism and Its Critics* (New Delhi: Oxford University Press, 2005).

Casanova, José. "Rethinking Secularization: A Global Comparative Perspective," *Hedgehog Review* 8 (2006): 7–22.

Copson, Andrew. *Secularism: Politics, Religion, and Freedom* (Oxford: Oxford University Press, 2017).

Cornelio, Jayeel. "Is Religion Dying? Secularization and Other Trends in the World Today," in *Controversies in Contemporary Religion*, ed. Paul Hedges, vol. 1 (Santa Barbara: Praeger, 2014), 219–46.

Davie, Grace. *Religion in Britain since 1945: Believing without Belonging* (Oxford: Blackwell, 1994).

Ghanea, Nazila, and Farrah Ahmed. "Religion and Human Rights: Conflicts and Connections," in Hedges, *Controversies in Contemporary Religion*, vol. 2, 77–100.

Taylor, Charles. *A Secular Age* (Cambridge: Oxford University Press, 2007).

Triandafyllidou, Anna, and Tariq Modood, eds. *The Problem of Religious Diversity: European Challenges, Asian Approaches* (Edinburgh: Edinburgh University Press, 2017).

Zuckermann, Phil, and John Shook, eds. *The Oxford Handbook of Secularism* (Oxford: Oxford University Press, 2017).

CASE STUDY 16A. *LAÏCITÉ* AND THE BURKINI BAN

Baubérot, Jean. "The Evolution of Secularism in France: Between Two Civil Religions," in *Comparative Secularisms in a Global Age*, ed. Linell Cady and Elizabeth Hurd (Basingstoke: Palgrave-Macmillan, 2010), 57–68.

Fuggle, Sophie. "Brigitte Bardot vs. the Burkini," *Foreign* Policy (23 August 2016), http://foreignpolicy.com/2016/08/23/brigitte-bardot-vs-the-burkini-france-burqini-ban/.

Hedges, Paul. "Fashion, Feminism or Freedom: Dissecting France's Ban on Burkini," *RSIS Commentary* 219 (2016), www.rsis.edu.sg/wp-content/uploads/2016/08/CO16219.pdf.

CASE STUDY 16B. SINGAPORE'S COMMON SPACE

Dean, Kenneth. "Parallel Universes: Chinese Temple Networks in Singapore, or, What Is Missing in the Singapore Model?," in *Handbook of Religion and the Asian City*, ed. Peter van der Veer (Berkeley: University of California Press, 2015), 273–95.

Dean, Kenneth, and Peter van der Veer, eds. *The Secular in South, East, and Southeast Asia* (Cham: Palgrave Macmillan, 2019).

Hedges, Paul, and Mohamed Imran Mohamed Taib. "The Interfaith Movement in Singapore: Precarious Toleration and Embedded Autonomy," in *The Interfaith Movement*, ed. John Fahy and Jan-Jonathan Bock (New York: Routledge, 2019), 139–56.

Musa, Mohamed Alami. "Engaging Religion with Pragmatism: The Singapore State's Management of Social Issues and Religious Tensions in the 1980s," RSIS Working Paper 305 (2017), www.rsis.edu.sg/rsis-publication/srp/wp305-engaging-religion-with-pragmatism-the-singapore-states-management-of-social-issues-and-religious-tensions-in-the-1980s/#.XsiNDhNKg3g.

17

GEOGRAPHY

Place, the Lived Environment, and Environmentalism

IN WHICH WE EXPLORE

Themes in the geography of religion, including the discourse of sacred sites
   and religious environmentalism

Theories of space, place, location, and the lived environment

Religious conflict and disputes related to place

Case studies of Buddhist environmentalism in Thailand, and Protestant Christian
   constructions of the "Holy Land"

INTRODUCTION

Everything we do as human beings is in a specific place. Where we eat, sleep, or pray
happens somewhere. Location is important. We also attach specific significance to certain
places: where we had our first kiss; memories of a summer holiday; places where we feel
safe; or areas considered sacred, or special, in some way. This chapter will deal with questions included within the field of the geography of religion, including notions of space
and place, conflict over specific locations, and environmentalism. The themes center
around what we will term the "lived environment" (see box 17.1).

We begin by thinking through the production of notions of space, place, and location
before moving into issues around the contestation over physical and symbolic places,
including how these may exclude some people. After that, we address the relationship
of religion to environmentalism, before concluding with our two case studies.

WHAT IS GEOGRAPHY, THE GEOGRAPHY OF RELIGION, AND THE "LIVED ENVIRONMENT"?

Many of us may remember geography from school in terms of maps, lists of capital cities, population statistics, or the physical terrain of mountains, fields, and rivers. Geography, as an academic field, means much more than this, sometimes split between "physical geography" and "social geography." Here, we focus more particularly on the latter, which concerns the ways that people live within the world, shape their environment, and construct perceptions of the world around them. The geography of religion, therefore, is about more than simply where we find members of different religions, but the way that religion shapes our experience of the world. This interaction between people and the physical world, and its construction in discourse (see box 5.1), is termed here the "lived environment." This does not simply refer to the world around us, but the world as it exists because we relate to it as we do. As humans, we name and emphasize certain things in the world as significant to us. Moreover, we are creatures who can change and shape the world around us. We live in an environment that is shaped by us, as much as it shapes us, and is seen by us through our living in it (see chapters 5 and 9).

LOOKING AT RELIGION THROUGH GEOGRAPHY AND SPACE

THINKING SPATIALLY

Geographers or not, we think about the world around us in spatial ways. If you think about the marks you got for your most recent essays, you might consider whether they were "higher" or "lower" than previous marks. We may want to be at the "center" of our social circle rather than somebody on the "margins." Meanwhile, societies have divisions between "upper," "middle," and "lower" classes. Using spatial metaphors and concepts is a taken-for-granted aspect of the way we speak and think about the world. It should be clear here that we are talking about more than simply physical space, but what Yi-Fu Tuan labels "mythic space."[1] Space is both material and metaphorical, solid and symbolic: shrines, temples, and churches have often been built on the tops of hills or in caves (see box 17.2).

It is often asserted that particular sites have an inherently sacred quality, the meaning of which can vary (see boxes 17.3 and 18.7). We also see contestation around how to make sense of any particular location. Different people, traditions, and cultures have seen the sacred and demonic in the same space, landscape, or temple. Our interest is then in what might be termed "the production of space,"[2] or how we come to think about certain spaces as variously "sacred," "secular," "interreligious," or otherwise.

Doreen Massey tells us: "The spatial is socially constituted. 'Space' is created out of the vast intricacies, the incredible complexities, of the interlocking and the

HILLS AND CAVES

Glastonbury Tor is a low hill near Somerset in the UK,[1] but stands out in the flat surrounding landscape, much of which used to be marshland or sea. Atop it stands a tower, all that remains of a church to St. Michael. It is likely that it was a sacred site long before this church was built, with legends associating it with Joseph of Arimathea, who is said to have brought the so-called Holy Grail from Jesus's Last Supper, while pre-Christian indigenous worship may well have occurred there. Today, it is considered sacred by contemporary Pagans, and has a special association with the Goddess, who is said to be embodied in the very landscape itself. It is not only high places that are associated with sacred sites. Caves have also had a long association with religious traditions. In Daoist traditions in China, many caves hold a special association. In particular, they are places where it is easier to seek harmony and balance with *qi*, the latent pyschospiritual matter which everything is believed to be composed of (see box 1.11).[2]

Glastonbury Tor, Somerset, UK.

---

1 See Marion Bowman, "Drawn to Glastonbury," in *Pilgrimage in Popular Culture*, ed. Ian Reader and Tony Walter (Basingstoke: Macmillan 1993), 29–62; and Paul Hedges, "Remembering and the Creation of (Sacred) Place: Glastonbury, (Anglican) Christian Theology, and Identity (in Post-Modernity)," *Journal of Implicit Religion* 17.3 (2014): 297–320.
2 See James Miller, *Daoism: A Short Introduction* (Oxford: Oneworld, 2003), 47–48, 148–50.

BOX 17.3 **SACRED/HOLY AS MARKER OF PLACE**

"Religious" buildings may be set apart, or made "holy/sacred/special" in some way;[1] the Hebrew term *qadosh*, meaning "to be set apart," is the etymological root of "holy/sacred." In sociological terms, the "sacred" may signify the most significant values of a culture (see box 18.7), which are not necessarily "religious." In Japan, many sites which are seen as particularly striking, as well as many streams, rivers, rocks, and other landscape phenomena, are seen to be sites of *kami*, which refers to spirits or spiritual energy.[2] In the Western Romantic tradition, such striking feelings inspired by landscapes could be seen to have some links with the qualities known as the sublime and the beautiful. These were seen as two qualities of landscapes: either thrilling, majestic, and unnerving (the sublime), or simply wonderful and lovely to behold (the beautiful). The notion of place as "sacred" always lies within the realms of human discourse. Here, we employ it to denote ways in which various societies demarcate certain places as having a distinct value, which may variously mean:

- liminal areas (see box 12.5) where the border between the human world and the world of deities (or other worlds) may be seen as permeable
- areas which are strong loci of some form of divine or transcendent power (see box 1.10)
- places which have particular memories or resonances that make them communally significant
- sites which are set apart (made "holy") for some particular, often spiritual-religious, function

This list is not intended as comprehensive, but notes some ways in which a particular place may be designated as sacred. It relates to the general sociological usage (box 18.7) of the highest values of a culture, but here denotes places designated as having special significance, meaning, or value. We will make use of "holy" occasionally if it fits the traditional meaning of "set apart" (from other parts of life).

---

1 Even critics of the term "religion" concede that temples and post offices are clearly distinguishable; see Paul Hedges, "Discourse on the Invention of Discourse: Why We Need the Terminology of 'Religion' and 'Religions,'" *Journal of Religious History* 38.1 (2014): 132–48, 147.

2 See "Kami," *BBC Religion* (2009), www.bbc.co.uk/religion/religions/shinto/beliefs/kami_1.shtml.

non-interlocking, and the network of relations at every scale from the local to the global."[3] Henri Lefebvre (1901–1991) spoke of social space in similar ways, noting that our activity takes place in locations which are given significant meaning through human interactions. The point is that we do not simply receive space as a given; rather, locations are known to us by our relationship to our society, culture, and the context we live in.

SYNCHRONIC AND DIACHRONIC ANALYSIS

"Synchronic" and "diachronic," terms which come from linguistics, are useful as lenses to think about spatial analysis:

> *Diachronic analysis:* historical analysis, looking at the development and history of something through time
>
> *Synchronic analysis:* looking at a particular moment in time, usually the present, in terms of the layers/meanings which are inscribed within something

Both Lefebvre and Michel de Certeau (1925–1986) focused on the synchronic; Kim Knott sums it up well:

> Synchronous spaces contain the past within them. An English cathedral may, for example, be situated on an early pre-Christian or Christian site, and may contain within its fabric many phases of building. Its texts, whether monumental, memorial, or manuscript, may add other historical traces, as do its ritual and spatial traditions. Both de Certeau and Lefebvre remark on this, the former writing of "stratified places," the latter of an "etymology of locations."[4]

You may be able to think of examples: for instance, a medieval European cathedral such as Lincoln in the UK, or historical temples in Asia such as the Temple of Confucius in Qufu, China. In such places, a myriad of historical layers exist in one place. Viewing them, the many layers of history piled up together, allows a synchronous experience or analysis. We may also employ a synchronous analysis of contemporary sites (see box 17.4).

Conversely, diachronic analysis explores the chronological development of the different layers, showing what has happened at different times and the conflicting narratives this may unveil. Both forms of analysis explore important and different facets, but in a contemporary context, synchronic analysis exposes the social interaction and the layers of connection that may be present in our experience of such sites.

Importantly, what these analyses of space give us is the understanding "that 'nothing is inherently sacred,' and that the presence of religion in space is a result of human agency."[5] It is a particular tradition, or human way of looking at particular places, that may make them seem significant, holy, or sacred (see boxes 17.3 and 18.7).

SPACE AND PLACE

Some writers distinguish "space" and "place," with the former referring to the generic and extended sense of distance we experience in everyday life. "Space" refers to the buildings and landscape around us. A "place" needs to have specific connotations and associations. That is to say, place is somewhere where narratives, memories, rituals, or enactments have occurred which give it significance.[6] This can be linked to Lefebvre's threefold categorization of how space is experienced. He speaks of "representations of space," "spaces of representation," and "spatial practice." However, we will rename them here somewhat:

Hegemonic space (representations of space): We live in a world which is already given to us by certain dominant authorities. These include spaces created for us in modern society by planners and architects, and for Lefebvre this involves ideology and power. It is the world as created for us by powerful interest groups. We can further relate Lefebvre's ideas to the French anthropologist Marc Augé's concept of "non-place," that is, areas such as airports, hotels, supermarkets, and shopping centers (as well as sitting before a TV or computer screen), which are very much universalized and impersonal.[7] This relates to "space" as used above.

Places of representation (spaces of representation): We live and interact with the space around us, by which we give symbolic value to locations. They become "place" to us. This might be about the way that minority, or subaltern (oppressed/non-elite; see box 7.6), groups seek to find place against a hegemonic cultural force that determines space. For Lefebvre, this often involved specific sites of meaning, such as graveyards, which need not necessarily be "religious" as we would commonly understand that term.

Spatial practice: The way we behave in space and place involves both the forms of practice and life that we go through in our everyday lives and behavior that gives meaning to space as place for us, or contests dominant expectations. However, we can never simply create our own practices that inscribe meaning onto the places we inhabit and dwell in a vacuum. Society and custom dictate the ways in which we relate to the world around us. As Lefebvre put it, social space "can in no way be compared to a blank page" upon which we find a particular message because it is "if anything, 'overinscribed'" in ways which may be like "a rough draft" and where we find "multifarious and over-lapping instructions."[8]

This threefold categorization is not meant to be discrete, but shows three conceptualizations which often overlap. We turn now to questions of contestation and dispute over sites that are variously deemed sacred, religious, secular, or holy.

CONTESTATION AND DISPUTE

Disputes and contestations—in discourse or as physical violence—over space occur for a variety of reasons, in part because of the nature of human societies. The examples below are far from comprehensive in terms of the issues that might arise.[9]

CLAIMED OWNERSHIP

Claimed ownership occurs when two or more branches of a particular religious tradition, or two or more religious traditions, claim rights to possess a particular place or location. Jerusalem is a richly contested site, and here just some notes are offered.[10] For many Jews, the Wailing Wall is believed to be the only remnant of the site of the original Jerusalem Temple that they were commanded to build by God. Today, the temple site is occupied by the Al-Aqsa Mosque complex, including the Dome of the Rock shrine. Claimed by certain Islamic and Jewish groups, the temple site is a flash point for protests. Jerusalem also sees Christian claims on parts of the city. Another example is the Ayodhya Mosque site in India (see box 17.5).

SACRED OR SECULAR

Conflicts can occur when a right to land is contested between a religious group and a non-religious/secular (on the latter term, see chapter 16) group, such as a government, or if something like an archaeological excavation takes place on land considered sacred.

The so-called Dakota Access Pipeline across the United States of America has seen a significant dispute between whether a particular area is sacred or secular. The pipeline cuts across areas that some of the Native American tribes believe to be liminal sites, places where the divine and human realms meet (see box 12.5). From this perspective, changing or tampering with them is considered sacrilegious.[11] Contrarily, if the land is simply understood as belonging to the government, or has been requisitioned, then it may be perceived as only being a secular space, though this does not address the environmental impact of the project. The situation of the Hagia Sophia in Istanbul is another example (see box 17.6).

BOX 17.5 **THE AYODHYA MOSQUE INCIDENT**

On 6 December 1992, a large crowd of militant Hindu activists breached police lines and demolished the Babri Masjid (mosque) in Ayodhya, India. Hindu militants claimed that the mosque, which was built in the sixteenth century and was no longer in active use, was built not just on the site of a temple of the Hindu deity Rama, but on the actual site of Rama's birth.[1] The incident can be placed in a long-standing contestation between Muslims and Hindus in South Asia that goes back at least as far as the Moghul Dynasties in the sixteenth century.

Disputes around this site began in the mid-nineteenth century, with a violent incident in 1853. This led to the British colonial administration placing a fence to separate Islamic (inner courtyard) and Hindu (outer courtyard) areas of worship. In 1949, shortly after independence, the Indian government declared the area disputed and closed and locked the premises. However, the 1980s saw an upsurge in momentum, with the Bharatiya Janata Party (BJP) taking up the issue, and their related activist arm, the Vishwa Hindu Parishad (VHP), laying the foundation of a Rama temple just outside the site in 1989. The BJP became the ruling party in the local state of Uttar Pradesh in 1991, and instigated a yearlong pilgrimage to rebuild the Rama temple. This effort began with collecting bricks and donations and ended with supporters flocking to Ayodhya, and the mosque's destruction. When deadly riots followed, killing over two thousand people across India, the central government started a commission of enquiry.

In 2002, to mark the tenth anniversary, the VHP reaffirmed its conviction to rebuild the temple, and further riots killed over a thousand people. The High Court intervened, ordering the Archaeological Survey of India to start an excavation to uncover the truth of what lay beneath the ruin. This began in 2003. An initial study suggested a temple may have lain under the ruins, but the full survey has never been released. However, it still remains unclear whether any temple, supposing there is one, is a Rama temple, and then whether it marked Rama's alleged birthplace.

Court cases have been launched against some of those involved in the 1992 destruction. Further, a 2010 Allahabad High Court ruling that the land be split into three parts (two to be given to different Hindu groups, and a third to a Muslim one) was challenged by the Supreme Court (India's highest judicial body), which overturned that ruling and maintained there was no current ownership. In March 2017, the Supreme Court declared the case to be "sensitive" and asked stakeholders to settle it out of court. However, disputes continued in court, with the Indian Supreme Court ruling in November 2019 that a Hindu temple could be built on the site, but with land being given to Muslims in a prominent place in the city for a mosque. The ruling both acknowledges a long-standing Hindu claim on the site, seen to outweigh the Muslim claim, but also the illegality of the destruction of the mosque. Subsequent legal challenges are possible.[2]

---

1 The history and context of the site is much disputed; see Gyanendra Pandey, *Routine Violence: Nations, Fragments, Histories* (Stanford: Stanford University Press, 2006), 68–102.

2 See Isha Dueby, "Ayodhya Land Ruling Has Thrust History into the Centre of Indian Politics—What This Means for the Future," *Conversation* (11 December 2019), https://theconversation.com/ayodhya-land-ruling-has-thrust-history-into-the-centre-of-indian-politics-what-this-means-for-the-future-127970; Kong and Woods, *Religion and Space*, 23–24; Anon., "Chronology of the Ayodhya Case," *Hindu* (27 September 2018—updated subsequently), www.thehindu.com/news/national/chronology-of-ayodhya-case/article25060329.ece; and Shereen Ratnagar, "Archaeology at the Heart of a Political Confrontation," *Current Anthropology* 45.2 (2004): 239–49.

BOX 17.6 **THE HAGIA SOPHIA MUSEUM**

As the grandest church in Christendom, the Hagia Sophia (Sacred Wisdom, or Ayaso-fia) Cathedral in Constantinople (now Istanbul) was reputed to be a marvel. However, when the city fell to the Ottoman Dynasty in 1453, who were to rule until 1922, it was converted into a mosque. Following Ottoman rule, Mustafa Kemal Ataturk (1881–1938) was keen to secularize Turkey. In 1935, Ataturk turned the mosque into the Hagia Sophia Museum. This was in part because the site was always contested. Many Greek Orthodox Christians believe the site should be returned to them. Meanwhile, today, many Turkish Muslims interpret a saying from Muhammad (*hadith*), generally considered trustworthy, that Constantinople would become an Islamic city, as a prophecy that with the conquest of Sultan Mehmet II Hagia Sophia should have become a mosque.[1] Ataturk's decision to make it into a secular museum was therefore a way to break with these contestations and declare it a neutral/secular site.

Much of the mosaic work that adorned the cathedral still remains, with tradition suggesting that when the Turkic conquerors arrived, they were so overwhelmed by its beauty that they could not bear to deface the site, despite Islamic prohibitions against certain forms of human representation in art. For centuries, it was covered in white plaster. Today, Islamic calligraphy and mosque features sit alongside mosaics of the Virgin Mary and baby Jesus.

Nevertheless, its status as a museum was often contested. Some Christians wished to see it restored as a church, while some Muslims wanted it to once again become a mosque. Moves toward this, and the eventual rededication of it as a mosque, occurred under the auspices of Turkish president Recep Erdogan. Despite its then secular status, quranic recitations took place inside the museum during Ramadan in 2015, and Erdogan himself recited verses from the Quran there in 2018. These acts were met with strong rebukes from the Greek government, amid fear this could be a stepping stone to reinstating it as a mosque. While the Turkish Supreme Court had previously rejected claims to hold prayers there and for it to become a mosque, a decision on 10 July 2020 declared that the change in status from mosque to museum had itself been illegal. With support by Erdogan, despite serious international opposition, it reopened as a mosque on July 24 that year.[2]

---

1 The *hadith* in question which reads "Verily you shall conquer Constantinople. What a wonderful leader will he be, and what a wonderful army will that army be!" has traditionally been considered to be referring to the apocalypse, that is, to be about the end of time. This is seen as a prophecy that after European Christians fight with Muslims against the Antichrist, the former then betray the latter but are defeated. It does not occur in the most authentic hadith collections, though some *hadith* in these do speak about the end-times conquest of Constantinople, which provides the traditional context (see https://sunnah.com/search?q=constantinople). It is a modern interpretation that it refers to the Ottoman conquest.

2 See Paul Hedges, "Hagia Sophia as Mosque or Museum: Religion in a Post-Secular World," *RSIS Commentary* CO20142 (2020), https://www.rsis.edu.sg/wp-content/uploads/2020/07/CO20142.pdf; Inside Story, "Will Hagia Sophia become a mosque again?," *Al Jazeera* (2 July 2020), https://www.aljazeera.com/programmes/insidestory/2020/07/hagia-sophia-mosque-200702172554721.html; and Berkley Forum, "Hagia Sophia: From Mosque to Museum" Berkley Centre (17 July 2020), https://berkleycenter.georgetown.edu/posts/hagia-sophia-from-museum-to-mosque. See also on wider issues,

The contestation over the building concerns not just its history, as both a Christian and an Islamic place of worship, but also its one-time status as an explicitly secular museum that showcased Istanbul's cultural heritage and the (sacred) artwork of the building. Its secular status was seen as an affront by those who wished to reinstate it as a religious site.

Ceren Katipoğlu and Çağla Caner-Yüksel, "Hagia Sophia 'Museum': A Humanist Project of the Turkish Republic," in *Constructing Cultural Identity, Representing Social Power*, eds. Cânâ Bilsel, Kim Esmark, Niyazi Kžzžlyürek, Ólafur Rastrick (Pisa: Plus-Pisa University Press, 2010): 205–225, and Eve Avdoulos, "Istanbul's Hagia Sophia: Challenges of managing sacred places," in *Personas y comunidades: Actas del Segundo Congreso Internacional de Buenas Prácticas en Patrimonio Mundial (Proceedings of the II Internacional Conference on Best Practices in World Heritage, People and Communities)*, ed. Universidad Complutense de Mad (Madrid: Universidad Complutense de Madrid, 2015): 180–203.

SYMBOLS AND FOCAL POINTS

Some spaces may become symbols and focal points when certain forms of building or specific locations become flash points because of what they represent. An example of a symbolic flash point would be the 2009 referendum in Switzerland banning the building of minarets. It should be noted that many in Switzerland considered the vote for the ban to be an extremist action with no chance of success. As a result, few people went to vote and, therefore, were surprised when this ban came into force. Nevertheless, it exemplifies the way that, for those who supported the ban, the site of minarets competing with the towers of Christian churches was seen to be emblematic of a changing religious landscape in their country, what some Islamophobic (see box 15.5) actors might term a "takeover" by Islam (see case study 5A).

CHANGING USAGE OR UNDERSTANDING

Sometimes one part of a religious tradition decides to repurpose, rebuild, or refashion a building in some way, or changes its understanding of the nature of that space. For example, in 2017, the Novena Catholic Church (Church of St. Alphonsus) in Singapore was reopened after a three-year renovation. The former building, from the 1950s, had been quite idiosyncratic, built in an eclectic modern style but with neoclassical features and an unusual triple dome at the front. The new church is an elaborate Gothic building with a vaulted roof, harking back to medieval Europe (see case study 9B). This has raised questions, not just on the cost of building in this fashion, but also on the appropriateness of building in a European style in contemporary Asia and whether it suggests an ongoing colonial memorialization, even a "captive mind," with European architectural styles used instead of Asian ones (see chapter 7).

REGULATION OF PRACTICE

Sometimes a restriction, either regulated or perceived, inhibits what may be done within a specific location. One issue that has arisen in a number of countries is the right of Muslims to use the minaret of mosques to issue the call to prayer. In particular, the use of loudspeakers has been curtailed. This has occurred in countries such as Germany, the UK, and the US. But the same restriction also exists in the Muslim-majority country of Pakistan, which sees itself as an Islamic nation-state. The issue is often one of noise pollution, and it is debatable whether it is essential to Islamic practice. In any case, various compromise solutions exist, for example, using radio to broadcast the call to prayer, or broadcasting it just within the mosque building (see case study 5A). Either way, the use of space, in its broadest sense, is restricted in terms of what can and cannot be practiced on the basis of certain legislation or regulations.

FACTORS IN IDENTITY AND CONFLICT

Given the significance of place to human beings, either individually or collectively, it is not surprising that such issues can arouse deep-seated sentiments relating to identities and values (see chapter 6), including identity disputes around the borders of traditions (see chapter 13). Hence, contestation may even lead to violence (see chapter 15). Moreover, because the disputes may be based in differing narratives about the meaning and significance of the sites in question, it can be hard to find common ground and to distinguish a basis for negotiation. To further understand conflicts over religious space, a range of factors may be considered, including the following:

- Is the conflict about ownership of the space, or autonomy to carry out activity within a space (or both)?
- Does it concern interreligious or intrareligious disagreement, or disagreement with a secular force?
- Is the scale local, national, or global?
- Has it erupted into violence, or not?
- Can it be mitigated or resolved, or is this not possible in this context?[12]

SPACE, CONTROL, AND EXCLUSION
THE PANOPTICON AND SPATIAL CONTROL

A famous image discussed by Michel Foucault (1926–1984) is the panopticon, which was a building suggested by Jeremy Bentham (1748–1832). Its design is for prisons and allows for a minimum amount of effort and maximum amount of surveillance.[13] The design is circular with a ring of open rooms in an outer circumference all facing inward to a central tower. This is the watchtower, and because the rooms on the outer ring are open, they are always accessible to view by anybody in the watchtower. In principle, constant, twenty-four-hour surveillance of every action, waking or sleeping, of the cell occupants is possible. Whether eating, defecating, or washing, nothing is private. The violation of personal space is total. As Foucault suggested, a guard need not be watching all the time, because the inmates will in fact self-regulate, knowing that surveillance can be occurring at any time. The potential to be seen, and therefore punished, always exists. While the panopticon represents an extreme example, it makes a good example of the way that space can be used to control and disempower a certain group, and to create codes of practice and behavior. A panopticon-style oversight can be found without spatial arrangements through the regulation/censorship of viewpoints, or when consensus seeking outweighs critical questioning.[14]

The power to control space is used in marketing. For instance, in the layout of supermarkets, goods which generate higher revenue in any category are often placed on shelves around eye level because that is where we are likely to look. Meanwhile, many supermarkets have a door on the right because some studies show that, at least in the US, people have a tendency to do their shopping counterclockwise, and hence the position of the door entices people further into the store. The use of space to elicit certain behaviors or attitudes is not novel. In one English cathedral, a way to control unruly schoolchildren from other European countries was to burn incense, as the smell of this instantly suggested that this was a sacred site and so decreed a certain decorum. Meanwhile, the design of some medieval cathedrals was partly to direct the flow of pilgrims, while the sense of height, space, and lighting was intended to awe those entering and present an image of a heavenly Jerusalem (see case study 9B).

EXCLUSION, BELONGING, AND SPATIAL IDENTITY

The control and manipulation of space also carries connotations of who is or is not included. The Swiss referendum banning the building of minarets may be seen as a blatant attempt to preserve a visible symbol of spatial identity of a skyline marked by "Christian church towers" by excluding perceived alien spatial identity markers—the "Islamic minaret" (see case study 5A). It is certainly not the only instance in which building regulations or the built environment signals exclusion of certain groups from public space, or the inclusion of other groups. Indeed, in many traditional societies, the sites of religious worship or devotion would often be—except for the spaces of rulers (castles, palaces, etc.)—what we might call exceptional, because they are:

· the only places extensively decorated by skilled artisans, for example, the carvings of Hindu temples in India;
· built of stone rather than wood, for example, churches in the European landscape;

- decorated and built with expensive materials, whether this be precious metals, stones, or woods, for example, the Golden Temple of Sikhism in Amritsar; or
- designed according to some specific formula or style which marked them apart as holy (see box 17.3), for example, the torii gates of Shinto shrines.

Meanwhile, exclusion may operate in various ways at such sites to control access or as a display of power, authority, or significance. For instance, in South India, the inner courts of many Hindu temples are only accessible to the three higher castes (see box 4.6), such that members of the lower caste or outcastes (Dalits), including foreigners, are not allowed to enter. Again, in the now destroyed Jewish Temple in Jerusalem, only the priests had access to the inner sanctum of the Holy of Holies. In traditional China, women when menstruating were not allowed access to temples (see chapter 10), an issue which was often self-regulated (harking back to our discussion of the panopticon). As such, in various ways, certain groups (women, lower castes, those from other religions or places, etc.) may find themselves excluded. Indeed, even if not physically excluded or barred, a predominant spatial identity of some places may mark ownership and thereby provide a social exclusion to certain groups.

Buildings may also signal belonging. The Hindu BAPS Swaminarayan Temple that opened in South London in 1995 was, at the time, the largest traditional stone-built Hindu temple outside of India.[15] Despite having a longstanding community center and temple area, this new building was partly to show that the originally immigrant community from South Asia now regarded themselves as established permanently in the UK and as belonging there. Such temple building beyond traditional homelands also relates to the complexities of diasporic communities, as is also the case with the Oshwal Jain Temple in outer London.[16]

RELIGION AND ENVIRONMENTALISM

It should come as no surprise to anyone who has read this far in this book that we simply cannot meaningfully ask the question as to whether religion and environmentalism are a natural match. What do we mean by religion? What form of which religious traditions are we discussing? Indeed, what exactly do we mean by environmentalism (see box 17.7)? Nevertheless, we often see blanket statements which argue either that religion is inherently pro- or anti-environmentalist, or that a specific tradition can be spoken of this way. This is often assumed of contemporary Pagan traditions, but it is not always the case.[17] The issue is often connected with the way that any specific tradition envisages its relationship to the world and therefore to a wider community. It may also mark a position about the relationship to the natural world, to science, to the built environment, and humanity's place within these, as well as relationships to other animals, other-than-human-persons, and the Earth as an ecosystem.[18]

Environmentalism is not a single philosophy or movement, but one which has changed over time, and varies in differing contexts. Broadly, it concerns the protection of our environment (the planet Earth). However, it may involve such diverse things as:

· seeking to protect pristine environments,

· developing sustainable farming in human-created environments,

· protecting animals and their habitats, and

· caring for the whole earth ecosystem.

Some distinguish between "shallow environmentalism," which is primarily focused on human benefits, and "deep environmentalism," which is concerned with all forms of life. Both forms are associated with a range of social and political activist movements.

IS RELIGION ENVIRONMENTALLY FRIENDLY?

It is fair to say that religious traditions have had no connection to what we would call today environmental concerns or ecological issues until recently. In part, this is because the concern is very much a new one in human history. As a species, we are just realizing that we can by our behavior wreak untold harm and change on the environment and our planet. Therefore, when environmental activists or religious spokespeople talk about the environmental messages found in scriptures and traditional teachings, it is applying a modern lens to texts that were talking about other concerns (see box 17.8).

However, is it correct to say that no religion can be environmentalist? Inherent in the arguments throughout this book has been the notion that all religions change and adapt over time (see chapter 4). Indeed, texts and traditions are always (and only can be) read within the contemporary context. Therefore, just as it could be argued that monasticism was not part of Christianity until about the fourth century CE but became part of that tradition,[19] so environmentalism may not have been part of any religion until the twentieth century or even the twenty-first, but it may become part of any religion in its evolving development. To argue that modern concerns cannot be part of any religion is simply a logical fallacy based on an essentialist notion of what religions are or should be. Religious traditions are reenvisaged in ways that speak to environmental concerns (see case study 17A).

DOMINION OR STEWARDSHIP?

Christianity has been the dominant religion in the West, where the development of science and technology have reached their current apogee.[20] It is in this context that environmentalism has arisen. Partly for this reason, some have argued that the way humanity has treated and destroyed the natural world is linked to the Christian worldview that has permeated the thinking of the modern world even in supposedly secular ways of thinking.[21] Often this is seen to have its roots in the creation narrative of Genesis, where man is given mastery over the world and other species. The traditional, and still widely used, English-language translation from 1611 known as the Authorized Version (or King James Bible) speaks of "dominion":

> And God said, Let us make man in our own image, after our likeness: and let them have dominion over the fish of the sea, and over the fowl of the air, and over the cattle, and over all the earth, and over every creeping thing that creepeth upon the earth. (Gen 1:26)

Some argue that the exploitation of resources and other creatures, with the world and animals instrumentalized as things for human usage, is the direct result of the ideological foundation of a Christian/biblical worldview which has been inherited by the Western world in its secular forms. Whether we can extrapolate directly from texts to the way that people behave is open to question (see chapter 3). Certainly, it is not the only way that Christianity has been seen to relate to these concerns.[22]

Despite the argument that Christianity is inherently anti-ecological—often contrasted with the supposed environmental credentials of Eastern or indigenous religions—it is clear that many Christians do have ecological concerns, and see these as based within their tradition. One rationale is to look at Genesis 1:26 in the original Hebrew. The word translated as "dominion" is more literally "stewardship." Therefore, rather than seeing humans as having mastery of creation to use as they wish (dominion), Christians may interpret the text as urging humans to protect the environment as a God-given duty of stewardship. Today, many Christians see their tradition as having strong environmental resources, a good example being the encyclical Laudito Si', issued by Pope Francis on climate change.[23]

Religious teachings are not only brought to bear in ways that seek to combat climate change and deal with the environmental crisis, but can also be rallied against such an agenda. In American Evangelical teachings that deny climate change, it is often understood that as creation comes from God it would be impossible for humans to dramatically change it.[24] Therefore, the Bible is used to deny scientific evidence. The way religious texts or traditions are used is a form of discourse that shapes the lived environment with which we interact (see chapters 5 and 9).

·　　·　　·

CASE STUDY 17A. TREES AS MONKS?

Imagine walking into a forest in Southeast Asia and seeing trees wrapped with the saffron robes of Buddhist monks. What would you think? Why would they be there? Is this art? A festival? Or something else? Here, we will focus on one way that Buddhism has related to environmental concerns.

TREES IN ROBES

In 1990, various Buddhist monks started to "ordain" trees. In northern Thailand, the monk Phrakru Pitak was greatly distressed by deforestation, through both legal and illegal logging operations. Given the reverence with which monks are held in that part of the world, the act of ordaining trees as monks by giving them saffron robes was a way to protect them. One of the village leaders, Suay Sisom, describes it this way:

> A tree wrapped by a robe represents a monk; if someone dares to cut it off, the demerit would equal that of killing a monk, and finally the destruction of the tree would lead to the end of his or her own life. . . . Since the trees have been ordained, no one has cut them or made charcoal in the forest.[25]

Importantly, the trees are not actually ordained. As things regarded as nonsentient in Buddhist ontology, trees could not keep the 227 precepts required by the monastic regulations (Vinaya). Nevertheless, as the quote from the village headman indicates, the act of ritual enrobement gives the trees a status that makes them efficaciously act as if they were monks: none dares harm them or touch the robes. This was observed by the ethnographer Susan Darlington, who recorded Pitak's work from 1990 and stated in 2006: "The forest was still lush, green, and cooler than the surrounding areas. . . . In contrast, the land surrounding the consecrated forest was denuded of trees."[26]

ECO MONKS, RITUALS, AND FARMING

From around the 1980s, monks have been engaged in activism and campaigning for the environment in Thailand, and are known as Eco Monks. Pitak had been preaching for some time about the problem of cutting down trees and degrading the environment, but he found that while villagers came to him for religious merit-making activities, they ignored his preaching and continued damaging the environment. To make his teachings effective, he sought to "preach" through spatial action rather than simply words or scriptural injunctions.

The action of ordaining trees, which involves a ritualized wrapping of a robe around the largest tree in a particular area of forest to sacralize the forest as a whole, is not done in isolation. Rather, it is part of a set of activities which involves education, training, and the promotion of new activities. The ceremonial action is only a very tiny proportion in terms of time and effort, about a day and a half, among months of other work. Nevertheless, it is understood by the monks and those involved to be central.

The ritual is a modification of a tradition whereby new robes are given to monks (see case study 12B), often with other gifts of money or food that would support their lives. In one case, it involved the gifting of twelve thousand saplings alongside the robes which are placed on the tree.

> These new trees were carefully chosen; they were species, such as fruit trees, that were profitable without having to be cut down. Having been sanctified and given [back] by the monks further protected them, as the villagers would see cutting them as a form of religious demerit (*baap*).[27]

The ritual therefore provides a dual role in helping promote more sustainable farming and agricultural practices, as well as giving religiously grounded reasons that make destruction of the forest unviable.

In this context, environmentalism is about maintaining sustainable livelihoods. It counters ways in which villagers have been complicit in destroying the environment, their own well-being, and their livelihood by working with loggers and planting commercial cash crops that led to degradation of the soil.[28]

One lens through which to look at this is our version of Lefebvre's threefold categorization:

Hegemonic space: For the villagers, the forest was originally perceived through the lens of commercial and business interests. It was seen as a commodity to be exploited for economic gain no matter the cost. Hegemonic external power interests (often economic) dictated the relationship to space.

Places of representation: Eco Monks such as Pitak offered a counternarrative by sacralizing, or reenchanting (see box 16.10), the forest. They showed the villagers how it could become differently perceived by them in agricultural terms.

Spatial practice: This differed under the two perspectives. Under the lens of hegemonic space, the villagers cut down trees and planted unsustainable crops that threatened their own existence and livelihood as instilled habits of practice, while also going to see Pitak as their form of religious merit-making practice unrelated to their other activities. Under the lens of places of representation, the villagers changed their forms of behavior. Pitak also instilled a more effective spatial practice for himself: from preaching to ritual "ordination," agricultural education and training, and promoting environmental concerns.

RELIGIOUS, POLITICAL, OR ENVIRONMENTAL?

Tree ordinations, while explicitly Buddhist, are also an environmental activity and political action. In the Thai context, monks are generally understood as concerned only with people's religious welfare. Indeed, some monks have been accused of being communist for resisting commercial activities. Nevertheless, Buddhist monks have framed tree ordination within their Buddhist religious duties in various ways:

- A traditional role of monks is to reduce suffering (*dukkha* ["suffering" is used here, but it is not always the best translation of *dukkha*; see box 3.7]) and harm (*himsa*). As environmental degradation and pollution harm people and other sentient beings, reducing these activities reduces harm.
- Buddhist teaching sees craving/desire (*trishna*) as a key source of human suffering (*dukkha*), keeping the mind captive to cycles of reincarnation (see box 3.7).[29] Therefore, resistance to activities associated with greed and desire (those driven by consumerism and commercial profit) is consistent with Buddhist teaching.
- As the government has taken over areas of life that were once the preserve of monks, such as education, health care, and so on, monks have found new ways to keep engaged with laypeople. For instance, the blessing of Buddha

statues is on the rise. Such social activism arguably extends, in relation to contemporary concerns, the relief of suffering and engagement in moral issues that has always been part of the monastic role.

Notably, Darlington commented on a sign that had been nailed to the tree prior to the ordination ceremony which read: "To destroy the forest is to destroy life." However, the word translated as "life" is *chaat*, which carries several connotations in Thai language and culture. It can also signify (re)birth (referencing Buddhist teachings on reincarnation and *karma*) and the nation. Let us consider the levels on which the sign can be read:

Ecological/environmental statement: Destroying the forest destroys life, meaning both trees and human life which depends on the environment, evoking self-interest even if not environmental awareness.

Karmic demerit: From a Buddhist perspective, karmic demerit would accrue from harming trees, which are now sacralized, having become in some ways like a monk, thus evoking religious concerns.

It destroys the whole country: In Thai thought, Buddhism, nation, and king are seen as three related pillars in national identity, so evoking nationalist sentiment.

A call to the nation as a whole to preserve the forest: It may be seen as a sensitive political criticism that the government is not doing enough to preserve the environment.[30]

The sign nailed to the tree might not seem powerful, like Pitak's original sermons. However, in the context of the ceremony and wider activism, it has a powerful resonance in the local context.

REFLECTION

Some questions will help us think this through:

1. If you were a monk or a layperson involved in the work of the Eco Monks, how do you think you might respond to charges that this was a "political" (and therefore illegitimate) activity, rather than a "religious" (and therefore legitimate) activity?
2. In what ways do you see the environmental activism described here as being a continuation, though in innovative ways, of traditional Buddhist practice? Or is it a new development within Buddhism? Does the environmental concern emanate from Buddhist resources and traditions? Or is it inserted into Buddhism?
3. How should we think about the entangled mesh of religious, social, political, and environmental aspects? Are they distinct, or impossible to separate?
4. In what ways does the theory of Lefebvre, or other spatial theory, help you think through the issues in this case study?

Within one tradition, there may be disputes as to which locations are sacred, or even whether any place has sacred status (see boxes 17.3 and 18.7).

THE HOLY LAND

The area where Jesus lived and walked, in modern-day Israel/Palestine, is significant in the Christian imagination as the Holy Land. However, there is not—and never has been—just one way of thinking about this part of the world. Many early Christian thinkers denied it had particular significance; if God was everywhere, then how could the Holy Spirit be more abundantly found there than anywhere else? Jerome (ca. 342–419) suggested it was significant on two grounds:

· We could understand Jesus's life better by traveling around the places mentioned in the Bible.
· Being in those places could evoke a strong emotional quickening of faith.

However, the most significant driver for the holiness of the Holy Land was the alleged discovery of the "true cross" (on which Jesus was crucified) by Empress Helena (ca. 246–330). She was mother to the emperor Constantine (ca. 272–337), who issued the Edict of Toleration (313 CE) stopping persecution of Christians in the Roman Empire. The alleged discovery of this relic, alongside the building of a grand new church, the Holy Sepulchre, started a strong impetus toward pilgrimage to the Holy Land, and toward seeing it as exceptionally spiritually potent.

In medieval Christian thought, certain sites became seen as places where divine power was more accessible and in which miracles were therefore more possible (see case study 9B).[31] Chief among these was the Holy Land, and specifically Jerusalem. And, within Jerusalem itself, the Church of the Holy Sepulchre. The Protestant Reformation of the sixteenth century (see box 9.3), however, challenged many aspects of church teaching that Reformation thinkers believed had developed after the time of the writing of the Bible and Jesus's apostles. Belief in the efficacious spiritual power of relics, saints, and sacred sites was part and parcel of what was rejected (see box 9.4).

CONTESTING SACRED PLACE

Nevertheless, the Holy Land still played a powerful part in the Protestant spiritual imaginary. Images of the New Jerusalem as the heavenly realm, reflection on Golgotha as the site of Jesus's crucifixion, and reference to places such as Nazareth and Bethlehem as part of Jesus's life story are all significant.[32] Indeed, we may reflect on different meanings of a term such as "sacred space." From a Christian standpoint,

- is an area "sacred" because it is a liminal realm (see box 12.5) or "holy" in some way (see box 17.3), where God may be encountered more readily; or
- is it simply a place associated with historical memories and/or mythological narratives?

GOLGOTHA

One example of a contestation is over the site of the Holy Sepulchre. This is already variously contested with ownership of the church shared mainly by various Orthodox Church denominations. There is also a Catholic Christian area, and the Coptic Orthodox Christian tradition has their space on the roof, but with a route down into a reservoir under the church where it is said the "true cross" was found. Moreover, the keys to the door of the church have for centuries been entrusted to a Muslim family, as the only more-or-less "neutral" or trusted custodian. Given the role that tradition played in identifying and sanctifying this site, some Protestants have recognized it as the site of Jesus's death, while others have not.[33] In the nineteenth century, a rock face outside Jerusalem's old city wall was claimed by some to be Golgotha, which means literally "the place of the skull," on account of its claimed resemblance to a skull. It has today become a place of pilgrimage for some Protestants, while an ancient tomb nearby has even been claimed as the actual tomb of Jesus.[34] It is included in certain Protestant pilgrimage/tour routes.

Regardless of the historical veracity of the claims by the various parties, we see here a contested landscape. Indeed, archaeological or historical investigations are unlikely to sway devotees of either site, given their embeddedness within tradition and socially constituted patterns of meaning. Both sites are also synchronous spaces where layers of history and meaning are piled up and "overinscribed." This is especially the case for the site of the Holy Sepulchre, where many churches have been built over the centuries. Recent renovations of the central shrine, which some believe surround the slab upon which Jesus was laid, have revealed a succession of shrines from different periods.[35] Moreover, the ritual enactments of the different denominations, each claiming partial ownership, all further complicate the site. This is compounded by different readings of scriptural texts, which in turn authorize different understandings of the locations. The rejection of certain sites by different traditions adds to the complexity.

REFLECTIONS

1. How would you explain why a site is meaningful to you/your tradition (religious or otherwise, i.e., national/ethnic, etc.) to somebody (from a tradition) that rejects it or does not understand it? What justifications arise? For instance, is it seen as inherently "sacred/holy," associated with a historical event, and so on?

2. Do you think diachronic or synchronic analysis is most useful to explain the significance of sacred sites? Explain with reference to the Holy Sepulchre or another site you are familiar with.

3. Jerome argued that coming to particular sites could strengthen people's faith due to the emotional bonds. Would this make a site sacred? What might this mean in relation to different traditions or usages?

4. What types of conflict do you see in disputes over the Holy Land and the Holy Sepulchre?

.   .   .

QUESTIONS AND CONNECTING THOUGHTS

Issues concerning the geography of religion and the lived environment have clear overlaps with areas such as material religion and embodiment (chapter 9) and lived religion (chapter 3), as all deal with the social reality (see box 1.9) of religion as practiced in the world. The approach here is inspired by social constructionism in the geography of religion (see chapter 5).[36] Contestation needs to be considered alongside questions of identity (chapter 6), as well as religion's connection to violence (chapter 15) and politics (chapter 18). It can also entail interreligious difference (chapter 13), and raise not just questions of contestation but also dialogue (chapter 14). Indeed, as we have seen, to discuss many of the issues, such as whether the disputes are inherently "religious" or not, we must consider the contentious term "religion" and its construction in human discourse (chapter 1), alongside the contested construction of the "secular" (chapter 16). Some questions will help us think through the issues raised:

1. In what ways do you create place and enact spatial practices? This could be in religious terms, academic study, or other areas of your life.

2. Do you see religions as fundamentally concerned with environmental concerns (see box 17.7)? To what extent must, or should, religions adapt to this issue? Relating to themes raised in other chapters (see especially chapters 5, 7, 10, and 18), should scholars merely study this? Or, can a scholar have an activist role in addressing climate change and environmental concerns?

3. What aspects of theory do you find most useful in thinking through the issues raised?

4. What do you understand by the term the "lived environment"? How would you classify the relationship of this concept to other themes in this chapter or book?

FURTHER READING
THEORY

Knott, Kim. *The Location of Religions: A Spatial Analysis* (New York: Routledge, 2005).
Kong, Lily, and Orlando Woods. *Religion and Space: Competition, Conflict and Violence in the Contemporary World* (London: Bloomsbury, 2016).

Lefebvre, Henri. *The Production of Space* (Oxford: Blackwell, 1991).

Miller, James. "Is Religion Environmentally Friendly: Connecting Religion and Ecology," in *Controversies in Contemporary Religion,* ed. Paul Hedges, vol. 2 (Santa Barbara: Praeger, 2014), 153–76.

Ronan, Marisa. "Religion and the Environment: Twenty-First Century American Evangelicalism and the Anthropocene," *Humanities* 6.92 (2017): 1–15.

Tucker, Mary Evelyn, and John Grim. "The Movement of Religion and Ecology: Emerging Field and Dynamic Force," in *Routledge Handbook of Religion and Ecology,* ed. Willis Jenkins, Mary Evelyn Tucker, and John Grim (New York: Routledge, 2017), 3–12.

CASE STUDY 17A. TREES AS MONKS?

Blum, M. L. "The Transcendentalist Ghost in EcoBuddhism," in *TransBuddhism: Transmission, Translation, and Transformation,* ed. Jay Garfield, Abraham Zablocki, and Nalini Bhushan (Amherst: University of Massachusetts Press, 2009), 209–38.

Darlington, Susan M. "The Ordination of a Tree: The Buddhist Ecology Movement in Thailand," *Ethnology* 37.1 (1998): 1–15.

Darlington, Susan M. *The Ordination of a Tree* (Albany: State University of New York Press, 2012).

Ives, Christopher. "Buddhism," in Jenkins et al., *Routledge Handbook of Religion,* 43–51.

Tannenbaum, N. "Protest, Tree Ordination, and the Changing Context of Political Religion," *Ethnology* 39.2 (2000): 109–27.

CASE STUDY 17B. PROTESTANT CHRISTIAN UNDERSTANDINGS OF THE "HOLY LAND"

Bajc, Vida. "Creating Ritual through Narrative, Place and Performance in Evangelical Protestant Pilgrimage in the Holy Land," *Mobilities* 2.3 (2007): 395–412.

Coleman, Simon. "A Tale of Two Centres? Representing Palestine to the British in the Nineteenth Century," *Mobilities* 2.3 (2007): 331–45.

Coleman, Simon, and John Elsner. *Pilgrimage: Past and Present in the World Religions* (London: British Museum Press, 1995), 78–103.

Galor, Katharina. *Finding Jerusalem: Archaeology between Science and Ideology* (Oakland: University of California Press, 2017), 132–45.

Tomlin, Graham. "Protestants and Pilgrimage," in *Explorations in a Christian Theology of Pilgrimage,* ed. Craig Bartholomew and Fred Hughes (Aldershot: Ashgate, 2004), 110–25.

POLITICS

Governance, the Colonial Wound, and the Sacred

IN WHICH WE EXPLORE:

The relationship of religion to politics and governance, including ethno-religious nationalisms

The concepts of the colonial wound, colonial difference, and the sacred

The political nature and contestation of scholarship

Case studies of the Malay-Muslim identity in Singapore, and the issue of saluting the flag for Jehovah's Witnesses in the United States.

INTRODUCTION

This is positioned as the last chapter of this book, though it could easily have been the first. If you have read your way through this book, you will no doubt have realized that religion is always, everywhere, and inherently political. That is small *p* "political": concerning human interactions in society related to power; not big *P* party political systems, although it can be involved in that too.

We start by looking at the inevitably political nature of scholarship through an exploration of the ongoing impacts on the study of religion of a particular European colonial context. Next, we consider ways that religion is intertwined with regimes of power and national political structures. We then highlight the connection of religion and ethnicity in nationalism. The concept of the "sacred" is then explored as a sociological term, to show how the highest values of nations and cultures can become a site of contestation. The politics of scholarship is revisited before we deal with our case studies.

THE POLITICS OF STUDYING RELIGION TODAY
THE POLITICAL ORIGINS OF THE STUDY OF RELIGION

The contemporary understanding and study of religion developed during the sixteenth to the twentieth centuries (see chapter 1) under the impact of European colonialism (see chapter 7):

- Studying religion was often done by Christian missionaries and colonial administrators (though these two groups could be in conflict).
- The first chairs of Sanskrit in European universities were often to study Hindu texts for missionary purposes, and foundational figures in the field often declared that proselytizing was a direct purpose of understanding other religions.[1]

We must not, however, overstate this. Studying other religions sometimes resulted in a growing appreciation and understanding that challenged European and Christian norms and values.[2] Understanding the "West" as always the hegemonic actor against a passive "East" is neither historically viable nor a useful analytic act (see box 7.4).

One aspect of this construction of religion in the colonial context is the relationship to racial categories (see box 18.6). The notion of race arose in the sixteenth century and became solidified in the eighteenth to nineteenth.[3] Tomoko Masuzawa has shown how attempts to categorize religions were often related to evolutionary perspectives and, explicitly or implicitly, interlinked racial theories.[4] Racial categories (see chapter 7), gender (see chapter 10), and class (see chapter 3) were factors creating "religion" in modern discourse (see box 5.1).

Walter Mignolo helps us see connections between the work of Partha Chatterjee and his concept of "colonial difference," Frantz Fanon (1925–1961) and his concept "the wretched of the earth,"[5] and Gloria Anzaldúa's (1942–2004) conception of the "colonial wound" (on the first and last, see box 18.1).[6] Combining Fanon's "wretched of the earth," which speaks of the lowest and most oppressed even among other oppressed groups, with Chatterjee's colonial difference and Anzaldúa's "colonial wound," Mignolo describes the matrix:

> So it is the colonial subaltern [see box 7.6] that carries on its shoulders the global colonial difference, the racialized colonial wound. They are what Frantz Fanon identified as "les damnés de la terre" ("the wretched of the earth"). What is the colonial difference and the colonial wound? To put it simply, it is the authority and legitimacy of Euro-centred epistemology, from the left to the right, assuming or explicitly declaring the inferiority of non-Christian, colored skin, of those not born speaking modern European languages or who were born speaking a surrogate version of a European language, like in British India, Spanish America, the French Caribbean, etc.[7]

BOX 18.1 **COLONIAL DIFFERENCE AND THE COLONIAL WOUND**

The Indian historian Partha Chatterjee noted that, in ruling India, the British saw their own understandings as being a universal template which could be applied anywhere, despite clear contextual origins. Thus, it was necessary for India to be trained and taught to think like the British. Chatterjee suggested that this was a general rule applied by colonial rulers everywhere, which he termed "the rule of the colonial difference."[1] As a principle, the colonial difference refers to the fact that the colonized are forced to accept ideas, concepts, and ways of thinking which are not their own but which are the dominant paradigms they must fit into. There is always a difference. This can be linked to Gloria Anzaldúa's (1942–2004) notion of the colonial wound.[2] This speaks about the cultural trauma of those who are colonized and so always have to live within a world where their language, culture, and ways of life are subservient/inferior to the dominant modes of knowledge, speaking, and power production. Chatterjee speaks about the process of creating the difference that colonialism brings about, and Anzaldúa speaks about the effects of it upon the colonized. Colonialism (see box 7.1), here, refers not simply to direct invasion by one country of another, but forms of domination that may be cultural, political, economic, or social, especially in relation to minority or oppressed groups (see box 7.5).

---

1 Partha Chatterjee, *The Nation and Its Fragments: Colonial and Postcolonial Histories* (Princeton: Princeton University Press, 1993).
2 Gloria Anzaldúa, *Borderland/La Frontera: The New Mestiza* (San Francisco: Aunt Lute, 1987).

There is a lot to unpack here, so let us pick out some key points to show how this relates to the study of religion:

- The study of religion, how it is studied, and what gets studied, is always a political choice determined by the matrix of modernity, colonialism, and the triad of race, gender, and class.
- The language of study is predominantly English. This determines, in part, who has access to and produces the texts. It also affects how we conceive of many concepts (see chapter 2).
- The contemporary notion of religion and what counts as religion has been determined partly by the factors noted above, but also by various elites, both Western and non-Western (see boxes 4.13 and 14.2).
- Eurocentric paradigms are still dominant, but over the last hundred years have been competing with American colonial and neocolonial power in the production of theory and discourse (see box 16.6).

- Colonial difference means that there is an imbalance of power and theoretical influence. Even when non-Western scholars are included, they need to play by Western rules. They continue to be inflicted by the colonial wound.
- This does not mean that there is a great debt of "Western guilt" or that "Western theory" is inherently bad. However, we need to acknowledge that certain dynamics have shaped the current global discourse in academia (see introduction).[8]

It has been useful to start this chapter off by covering this to avoid the notion that we can simply study such things as religion and politics as neutral and descriptive categories. Both categories have a history and are written into regimes of power and influence. Scholars do not simply study other people's discourse, nor are they above the political realm, but are part of it.

RELIGION AND POLITICS

LINKING

Some readers may think we have now reached the "meat" of the chapter as we look at the imbrication of religion with national and regional politics, especially ethno-nationalisms. However, the situation today exists because of the history of colonialism and domination of society by certain groups; it is not the "natural" order of things (see chapter 5).

THE INESCAPABLE ASSOCIATION

A significant date marking scholarly and political awareness of religion's significance to geopolitics was the 1979 Iranian Revolution, when a US-backed dictatorship was toppled by the public revolt that founded the Islamic Republic.[9] To note two brief examples:

- In MENA (Middle East and North Africa), events like the Arab Spring (2010–2012, a popular uprising against often secular dictatorships or repressive regimes) saw religious groups rise to power—though the final outcome is very mixed.[10]
- In the US, the Christian right has influenced the Republican Party since the 1970s (see case study 6B).

This gives a taste of some global associations of religion and politics today. Religion has been called the missing dimension of international relations,[11] with former US secretary of state John Kerry stating: "if I went back to college today, I think I would probably major in comparative religion, because that's how integrated it is in everything that we are working on and deciding and thinking about in life today."[12]

Let us briefly note some of the types of associations between religion and politics:

Religious leaders as politicians: Religious leadership is seen in hybrid theocracies such as Iran[13] and a perceived secular democracy such as the UK, where Church of England bishops sit by right in the upper house of Parliament (see chapter 16).

Ethical issues and religious lobbying: Religious groups or interreligious coalitions have lobbied against such things as abortion and LGBTQI rights, or for undertaking (or opposing) action on climate change (see chapters 14 and 17).

Religious support for/against candidates, parties, policies: In the US, white Evangelicals have backed many Republicans (see case study 6B); in Indonesia, some ultra-conservative Muslim groups rallied against a non-Muslim governor known as Ahok.[14]

Religious laws and policies: In Singapore, state law mandates Islamic law *(shariah)* for Muslim family law (see case study 18A); in many countries, blasphemy laws govern forms of speech.

Relations of religion to ethnicity, nationalism, identity: Buddhist identity in parts of Southeast Asia is tied to a growing nationalist discourse against Muslims;[15] religio-ethnic identities were part of conflicts in the former Yugoslavia in Europe.[16]

These examples, far from comprehensive, identify some of the main ways in which religion may be tied into, or related to, national, regional, or party-political processes.

RELIGION AS POLITICAL CONSTRUCTION

"Religion" is always constructed in specific contexts, often relating to particular political and legal schemas (see chapter 1). However, nation-states and political theorists typically speak as if a clear conception of religion existed. Some examples of the variability of its meaning include the following:

- While freedom of religion, as a human right, is embodied in the constitutions of most modern nation-states (see chapter 16), what counts as a religion varies (see case study 1A and box 7.8). Some countries have lists of recognized religions, so anything not on that list is not a religion, and therefore is not protected.

- Some traditions may be labeled as "cults," "superstitions," or otherwise to enable persecution, oppression, or for delegitimization (see boxes 1.5, 7.9, and 9.4). If something is not legitimately seen as a religion, it is denied a certain status in society.

- In most secular states, religion and politics are separated; however, what this means in theory and practice varies considerably (see chapter 16 and box 18.3).

SOME THEORISTS

The status of religion in the political structure has been discussed by such figures as Thomas Hobbes (1588–1679) and John Locke (1632–1704) (see box 18.2), and more recently by John Rawls (1921–2002) and Jürgen Habermas. Habermas has argued for the need for common public deliberation on how society and politics are run to take place in the public sphere, a third realm between government and private spheres.[17] While his early work debarred religion from this debate, Habermas's later work sees it as a necessary voice because people must bring their deepest commitments and values to the table. John Rawls,[18] who argued that government and the legal system should be based around fairness (because stripped of all other distinctions, everyone would want a system ensuring equality for all), concurs that religion could be one of many components informing people's ideas but has no privileged status.

These four theorists represent more-or-less consecutive trends from the early modern period to today:

- God seen as the very basis of human government
- God seen as underlying the system but to one side
- religion as sidelined from governance
- religion as a voice in the debate, but only as one perspective among others

Today, some secularists argue that religion should have no place in political debates or the public sphere. Nevertheless, that the vast majority of the world's population is religious means that this will influence their beliefs, ethics, and affiliations. Whether one believes religion should have a voice in the public and political sphere is arguably immaterial to a practical theory of how to regulate it.

This survey of ideas returns us to the notion of colonial difference and the colonial wound (box 18.1). Our four key theorists are all speaking primarily from a Christian/ Western/European context (American systems are derived from this). Their ideas have, nevertheless, had global reach through colonial and neocolonial domination of politics, economics, and ideas. But is what they say merely one provincial and localized stance? We leave this question open for reflection, though note that scholars outside this sphere have and still do contribute to these debates (see chapter 16 and box 7.7); when only the perspectives of limited (white, male) lineages and canons are considered, we may be led to ask with Hamid Dabashi, "can non-Europeans think?"[19]

SOME MODELS AND ISSUES FOR RELIGION AND POLITICS IN DIVERSE SOCIETIES

Challenges to the heritage of the "Christian" "Western" world have included the following:

Multiculturalism: Recent decades have seen increased religious and ethnic diversity across the Western world; this is not always new, but previously diversity was often marginalized or hidden.[20] The stance from which theorization arises has therefore changed.

Globalization:[21] Immigration, related to the previous point, is one factor, but globalization means much more, including the interconnectedness of the world in terms of IT, transport, and accessibility. Almost any part of the world and its images, activities, and current affairs can now be in our homes (or even our pockets) instantaneously. It is also potentially accessible to us in terms of transport and connections. However, we speak from a privileged situation. This ready accessibility to IT and transport is not a reality for many in the Global South or Two Thirds World. Wealth inequality is a factor, but also simply the ability to obtain a visa to travel.

The non-Western (and diverse) world: Theorizing about the world from Europe or North America is problematic (see box 18.1 and chapters 7 and 16). To speak of religious diversity as new or unprecedented ignores the normative daily experience over centuries in Africa and Asia (see chapter 13). We must realize that many parts of the world experience differently from the way we do—whoever we may be, and wherever we may be.

Globalization has made us increasingly aware that the way we practice whatever religion or non-religion we adhere to is not the only way of doing it.[22] Moreover, situations in other parts of the world may affect not only how we perceive or practice our own form(s) of belief, practice, or tradition, but also how we understand the way it relates to other people. The rising perception of religion's impact is exacerbated by globalization in a matrix woven by modernity and colonial legacies.[23]

Majority-minority dynamics are also an issue where one particular religious, or non-religious, system is dominant.[24] Majority groups may be favored by the state or may be more socially accepted. This leads to questions about how minority groups are treated: is there equality in legal provisions, in social treatment, or in other areas (see chapter 16 and case studies 1A, 16A, 18A, and 18B)? This may particularly affect atheists or those who do not profess a religious identity. The relationship of religious and non-religious groups in society varies greatly, with the potential for hostility or persecution often related to majority-minority dynamics and restrictions on religious practice.[25] The specific religious-secular relationship constitutes an aspect of this (see box 18.3).

NATIONALISM, RELIGION, AND THE IMAGINED NATION-STATE

The political theorist David Brown has theorized three types of nationalism:[26]

- *Civic nationalisms:* Citizens are linked to a particular nation-state via broadly secular principles and a common social contract.
- *Ethnocultural nationalisms:* The nation-state is identified with a particular ethnic identity; religious (often ethno-religious) nationalism is a subset.
- *Multicultural nationalisms:* A diverse set of ethnicities, or cultural groups, are seen as inherent to the makeup of the nation and none is favored.

All these forms of nationalism are modern. Secularism (see chapter 16) and the concept of the nation-state arose within Western political thought and practice only in the last few centuries.[27] It is distinct from the traditional country, which sometimes had no clear boundaries. Rather, centers of power (capitals, seats of powerful rulers, etc.) exerted an influence around them, while people's allegiance was often to their locality, or local ruler, rather than the country (this is often still true). This has been termed the "galactic polity."[28]

In almost all historical contexts, the political was linked to religious belief or tradition. As such, we could not distinguish between religion and politics as two distinct realms (see box 16.2). With their modern separation, various potential tensions follow, including the question of justified violence (see box 18.4).

Benedict Anderson's (1936–2015) notion of "imagined communities"[29] raises two key issues. First, no matter what country we live in, it is not possible to know everybody. Our sense of belonging to a common national community is "imagined," because it is not a "natural" association of people we know. If we feel outrage at a member of our nation being killed by an attacker from elsewhere, our sense of outrage is based on this imagined community, for we do not know that person. Indeed, beyond familial and small village communities, almost every community we inhabit is to some extent

BOX 18.3 **SECULARISM AND RELIGION IN RELATION TO POLITICS**

Relationships between nation-states and religions vary greatly depending on inter-pretations of secularism, or if secularism is rejected. Theoretical models and practice may differ, so we offer here a rough guide rather than a strict analysis of distinct types (see chapter 16):

Secularism as persecution: A secular state is hostile to religion, for example, China during the Cultural Revolution (1966–1976).[1]

Public secularism: Neutrality means the public sphere should have no overt display of religion, for example, France's contemporary practice of *laïcité* (see case study 16A).

Secularism as separation: Religious and governmental realms are distinct, where neither interferes with the other, for example, the US barrier between church and state (but see case studies 6B and 18B, and chapter 16).

Secularism as friendly: The state machine favors no religion, but religion is an impor-tant part of social and cultural life, for example, Singapore's "religious friendly" secularism (but see case studies 16B and 18A).

Secular-inclined establishment: Despite an established religion, the operation of the state is predominantly secular, for example, in the UK, where the monarch is head of both state and the established religion (see chapter 16).[2]

Secular-religious fusion: Religion is built into the constitution, but many religions are recognized, for example, Indonesia, whose Pancasila ("five principles") system protects six recognized religions.[3]

Religious privilege: Despite freedom of religion, special privileges for one means others are disadvantaged, for example, some Malaysian states today.[4]

Theocratic privilege: One religion is established, curbing all other religious and non-religious rights, for example, Saudi Arabia today.[5]

---

1 See James Miller, *Chinese Religions in Contemporary Society* (Santa Barbara: ABC-CLIO, 2006), 37–38, 62, 182.
2 See Paul Weller, *Religious Diversity in the UK: Contours and Issues* (London: Continuum, 2008), 52–53; and Tariq Modood, *Essays on Secularism and Multiculturalism* (London: Rowman and Littlefield, 2019).
3 See Liow, *Religion and Nationalism*, 185, 191–93.
4 See Liow, *Religion and Nationalism*, 135–74.
5 See Muhammad Al-Atawneh, "Is Saudi Arabia a Theocracy? Religion and Governance in Contem-porary Saudi Arabia," *Middle Eastern Studies* 45.5 (2009): 721–37.

imagined. Importantly, it is not that communities are not "real"; they may have very real ties and bonds as social realities (see box 1.9): we vote, go to war, and defend our nations and other communities as much as more personal or "natural" ones. However, they are imagined in the sense noted here, as we lack those close physical and personal bonds. This applies also to transnational religious identities, such as the Islamic notion of the community of believers (*ummah*).

Second, the borders of every country have evolved over decades, centuries, or millennia. There are no "natural" borders of any country. Even seemingly natural borders such as mountain ranges or rivers, or the fact of being an island, do not necessarily equate to borders. Borders are imagined:

US: once belonging to indigenous tribes, later European colonies; California and Texas were formerly parts of other countries

China: different borders in the Han Dynasty (ca. 200 BCE–200 CE), the Ming Dynasty (1368–1644), and today

UK: currently England, Wales, Scotland, and Northern Ireland, with wider territories like Gibraltar and the Falkland Islands; in medieval times, parts of today's France was ruled by monarchs of England; Queen Victoria was also the "Empress of India"

Singapore: in 1962, part of British Malaya; in 1963, part of Malaysia; in 1965, an independent city-state

Historical accident has created every nation; therefore, national identity is imagined. Indeed, even within one nation, or one village, or one family, disputes mean some groups are part of "my social group" and others are "the enemies" or "outsiders" (see chapter 6). None of our communities are natural; they are only ever imagined. This can be related to Charles Taylor's conception of "social imaginaries," which refers to "the deeper normative notions that underlie . . . expectations" of our social existence.[30]

Moreover, in secular nations we sometimes see a fusing of the imagery of the state with what might be termed "religious" associations, sometimes termed "civil religion" (see box 18.5).

CIVIL RELIGION

Associated with Robert Bellah (1927–2013),[1] "civil religion" refers to ways in which a state's secular system are imbued with religious qualities. It is sometimes referred to as "quasi-religious" and is seen to be a cohesive force, drawing from the work of Émile Durkheim (1858–1917). The first use of the term "civil religion" is probably in Jean-Jacques Rousseau's (1712–1778) *The Social Contract* (1762), which spoke of common religious beliefs shared by the community (see box 18.2). In its varied uses, civil religion broadly refers to common aspects of national belief that provide a unifying bond and give a sacred (see box 18.7) underpinning to national life.

IN THIS TEMPLE
AS IN THE HEARTS OF THE PEOPLE
FOR WHOM HE SAVED THE UNION
THE MEMORY OF ABRAHAM LINCOLN
IS ENSHRINED FOREVER

Temple to Abraham Lincoln, a site of American civil religion, Washington DC.

1 Robert Bellah, "Civil Religion in America," *Daedalus* 96.1 (1967): 1–27.

RELIGION, ETHNICITY, AND NATIONALISM

In Brown's second type of nationalism, religion can be linked to ethnic identities with distinct political connotations. This linkage of ethnicity, religion, and nation is not found only in countries with a religious or ethnic constitution but in those with secular systems too:

> *Germany:* A secular nation-state where Chancellor Angela Merkel stated that multiculturalism had failed. For some Germans, even if not churchgoing,

Germany is envisaged as part of Christian Europe (Christendom). Some link this to a white Christian identity.[31]

India: Rising Hindu religio-ethno-nationalism and its Hindutva ideology (see box 6.7) has challenged the secular nation-state (see case study 6A and chapter 16).

Malaysia: The Constitution gave a certain priority to the *bumiputera,* "or sons of the soil," meaning the indigenous peoples. Recent decades have seen this politicized as Malay-Muslim ethno-religious-nationalism via an association of Islam with "Malayness" and nationhood (see also case study 18A).[32]

Turkey: Mustapha Ataturk's (1881–1938) secularist vision has been challenged by the Islamic political nationalism of President Recep Erdogan (see also box 17.6).[33]

How religion is imagined to be connected to ethnicity and nationalism varies. While some have posited that religion is a unique problem exacerbating national conflicts, this seems untenable. Secular nationalist ideologies, as witnessed in the twentieth century, are quite capable of inducing atrocities and justifying war and genocide. Religion is not needed for humanity's inhumanity to its fellow creatures.[34] Whether religion magnifies such problems may be explored, but not asserted as fact (see chapter 15).

Importantly, many contemporary religio-political conflicts have origins within colonial or neocolonial political landscapes. To help secure its popularity, the then virtually unknown Islamic State of Iraq and Syria (ISIS)[35] made a symbolic act in one of its first videos. This act was the destruction of a wall of sand in the desert which marked the so-called Sykes-Picot line, a border arbitrarily drawn on a map across the desert between Iraq and Syria effectively creating new nation-states. This border has been much resented in part due to the way that British and French colonial officials in distant lands carved up the world. But it was also an unstable border dividing ethnic and cultural groups and leading to ongoing friction. This is not to justify any actions of ISIS, but simply to point to one of many examples of how conflicts were seeded by colonial powers.[36] In relation to the colonial difference and the colonial wound (see box 18.1), European colonial rule often demarcated (or created) racial or ethnic groups and divisions (see box 18.6). These could become the basis for later conflict or tension, and gave rise to (or exacerbated) various racial prejudices and stereotypes.[37] Likewise, the Eurocentric nature of theory that underpins the model of the nation-state itself often does not resonate well in local contexts.

THE SACRED: RELIGIOUS, SECULAR, POLITICAL
DEFINING THE SACRED

For some scholars the sacred is an illegitimate arena of study, if by this we mean some transcendent reality beyond our phenomenal world (see box 1.10). Immanuel Kant's

WHAT IS RACE/ETHNICITY?

The creation of theories of race developed in European thought around the sixteenth century, coterminous with the rise of colonialism.[1] By the nineteenth century, these often became associated with evolutionary theories and a ranking system of races that placed the "white races" at the highest level or most advanced, down through various ranks or grades to the lowest. Often Australian Aboriginals or Black Africans occupied this position. Indeed, "scientific racism" was seen to justify this.[2] However, as science has advanced, it has become clear that there is no basis for distinguishing different humans on the basis of racial categories. We share the same DNA, and the primary difference is melatonin in skin pigmentation. More recently, therefore, "ethnicity" has become a preferred term, which often refers to a cross between "racial" (skin color-ation), linguistic, cultural, and geographical signifiers. However, "ethnicity" is itself a slippery and nebulous term. Ethnicities can be described differently. People may change ethnicities or be recognized as belonging to different ethnic groups (see case study 18A). In employing these terms, we are not pointing to "natural" differentia-tions. Nevertheless, both race and ethnic markers are "social realities" (see box 1.9): people identify with them, oppress others based on their perception of them, and so on.[3] From a scholarly standpoint, we must be aware that neither has any scientific or analytic reference point beyond their existence in human discourse (see box 5.1). Furthermore, the imagined markers of racial/ethnic groups become racialized. That is to say, the markers become filled with particular content, often negative stereo-types as part of the creation of prejudice against those groups, leading to enacted discrimination.[4]

---

1 A medieval origin has been suggested; see Geraldine Heng, *The Invention of Race in the European Middle Ages* (Cambridge: Cambridge University Press, 2018). But the influential modes of racialized imaginaries today are those associated with Western modernity; see Hedges, *Religious Hatred*, and Bethencourt, *Racism*.

2 See Elazar Barkan, *The Retreat of Scientific Racism: Changing Concepts of Race in Britain and America between the World Wars* (Cambridge: Cambridge University Press, 1992).

3 As the scholar and anti-racism activist Ibram Kendi notes: "I still identify as Black. Not because I believe Blackness, or race, is a meaningful scientific category but because our societies, our policies, our ideas, our histories, and our cultures have rendered race and made it matter"; Ibram Kendi, *How to Be an Antiracist* (London: The Bodley Head, 2019), 37.

4 On racialization, see Nasar Meer, "Racialization and Religion: Race, Culture and Difference in the Study of Antisemitism and Islamophobia," *Ethnic and Racial Studies* 36.3 (2013): 385–98. On the connections of prejudice to racialized religious identities, see Hedges, *Religious Hatred*, chapters 1 and 5. For a clear account of the ascription of race in a colonial context, see Alatas, *Myth of the Lazy Native*.

(1724–1804) distinction between the phenomenal, our physical and social world, and the noumenal, metaphysical and divine realms, is widely followed:[38] the former can be known in human terms, whereas the latter is beyond human knowledge. However, Gordon Lynch suggests a cultural-sociological reconceptualization of the sacred to refer to the funda-mental values of any culture or society (see box 18.7).[39]

BOX 18.7 **THE SACRED AS SOCIOLOGICAL AND HUMAN CONSTRUCTION**

Gordon Lynch states that "the sacred is not generated by society, as Durkheim suggested, but rather the sacred constructs the idea of human society as a meaningful, moral collective."[1] In other words, the sacred is part of the social construction that creates the norms of our worldview (see chapter 5). It is part of the ideology of our imagined communities and what binds them together. Importantly, Lynch makes a distinction between seeing the sacred as some form of absolute and "*what people take to be* absolute realities."[2] He notes:

> Rather than thinking about the sacred as an ontological phenomenon that transcends signification, the cultural sociological approach understands sacrality as a particular form of cultural signification in which symbols, objects, sentiments, and practices are experienced as expressions of a normative, absolute reality.[3]

The values taken by a society as sacred are not necessarily what we may term "religious," but whatever operates as an absolute marker of truth or values: democracy, freedom of speech, liberty, and so on.

Lynch tells us to avoid the absolute dichotomy that Émile Durkheim (1858–1917) posited between the sacred and the profane as binary opposites. While society may create clear binaries of its sacred from that which it rejects, they may not exist as "natural" opposites, or as "pure" and "impure" (see box 12.3). Nevertheless, the "profane is the particular representation of evil constructed in relation to a specific sacred form."[4] Importantly, Lynch notes that while, in vernacular usage, we may associate "the sacred" with that which is good or pure, it can itself be a cause of harm or suffering, even "evil."[5] This is because societies, or the people within them, often violently protect or maintain their own "sacred" against the "sacred" of others. The sacred exists as much in "secular" societies as in "religious" ones, and both secular and religious forms can justify hostility against those who infringe upon their conceptions of the sacred.

---

1 Lynch, *Sacred*, 133.
2 Lynch, *Sacred*, 15, italics in original.
3 Lynch, *Sacred*, 15.
4 Lynch, *Sacred*, 134.
5 Lynch, *Sacred*, 136.

SECULAR SACREDS

Lynch gives us an example of the construction of sacred values in the atheist state context of the Soviet Union:

> Sacred symbolism was attached not simply to the revolution as a historical event or abstract principle, but to individuals who embodied its sacred essence. Lenin's early death in 1924 led to the establishment of an "Immortalization Commission," the outcomes of

which took material form in both the mummification of Lenin's body and its perpetual display in the mausoleum in Red Square.[40]

Meanwhile, Aida Arosoaie argues that part of the dispute between Western secular nation-states and a group such as ISIS can be portrayed as a conflict of opposing views of the sacred. In the former, the public sphere, freedom of speech, democracy, and other values are sacred and must be defended, so justifying the employment of violence in their defense.[41]

THE SACRED AND RELIGIOUS ETHNO-NATIONALISMS

The concept of the sacred can be applied to associations of ethno-religious nationalism. We can see this in modern Sri Lanka, where a different twist is given to traditional Buddhist concepts:

> My brave, brilliant soldier son
> Leaving [home] to defend the motherland
> The act of merit is enough
> To reach Nirvana in a future birth . . .
> Country, religion, race are my triple gems . . .
> The sangha is ever ready
> At the front
> If the race is threatened.[42]

The poem goes back to the civil war (1983–2009) between (minority) ethnic Tamil Hindus and (majority) ethnic Sinhala Buddhists. To inspire Sinhala Buddhists to fight, this poem suggests that the path to awakening/nirvana is guaranteed through being a soldier who defends the "motherland," rather than meditating and becoming a monk. More than this, the traditional Buddhist invocation of the Three Gems (*triratna*), which invokes the Buddha, his teachings (*dharma*), and the community of monks and nuns (*sangha*) as the basis of Buddhist life is replaced by another threefold invocation: country, religion, and race. In Sinhala Buddhist nationalism, these are the sacred foundations. Other Sri Lankan Buddhists reject this conflation of Buddhism with nationalism and militarism (see case study 15B).

SCHOLARSHIP AS POLITICAL

Earlier, we raised the topic of the study of the colonial origins of religion. Today, scholars can choose to teach a decolonial curriculum, including voices from beyond the (white, male, elitist) West, or to remain within the established academic "canon" (see chapter 7).[43] This emphasizes the inherently political nature of all scholarship.

Scholars tend to belong to various lineages of scholarship, which we may even call "tribal affiliations." In the study of religion these include critical religion, phenomenology, feminist studies in religion, postcolonialism, sociology of religion, interreligious studies, and so on. Where and how scholars place themselves in these boxes, and how they relate to those they see in other boxes, is a political question.

If we imagine that scholarship is always, necessarily, or only the pursuit of truth or better understanding, we forget that this is bound up with the choices people make, or that are forced upon them. The countries they study in (or are able to study in), the scholarly schools they are tutored in, and individual connections with particular people are all part of any scholar's journey as she learns her craft. As a student, even reading this book is to some extent political because it engages with arguments and debates within society and the scholarly community. Meanwhile, particular lineages of modern and contemporary thought, brought into possibility by colonial and postcolonial contexts, also play into this. The production of knowledge is at least partly about power: some scholars will tell you that you must follow their methods and their methods alone; some will have political allegiances to scholarly tribes or political parties; others will focus upon colonial, feminist, LGBTQI, racial, or other power interests. Within all this, scholars should locate themselves; be wary of the scholar who seeks to expose the agendas of others without stating where they come from. Or those who hide their own personal story or commitments—it can be a claim of scholarly neutrality, but that does not exist.[44] Everybody stands somewhere (see introduction and chapters 2, 5, and 9). Striving for objectivity, impartiality, and neutrality is not the same as being above the fray in some pure scholarly realm of criticality (see also chapters 7, 10, and 14).

·　　·　　·

CASE STUDY 18A. ETHNICITY AND RELIGION: THE SINGAPOREAN MALAY-MUSLIM IDENTITY

Religion and ethnicity are, in many places, coterminous identities. This is often conflated with particular political and national identities. Here, we explore the Malay-Muslim identity in Singapore.

COLONIALISM AND SINGAPORE'S "RACES"

British Malaya was sharply demarcated by ethnic identities which were part of the British colonial divide-and-rule policy. In Singapore, a southern island of this region, the city center was separated in ways which still exist in location names today—China Town, Little India, and Arab Street. But the division was never absolute, so while Little India is home to Hindu temples, Arab Street is dominated by the Sultan Mosque, and China Town houses Chinese temples, we see crossovers. Today in China Town, on one street you can readily encounter a mosque, a Hindu temple, and a Buddhist temple in quick succession.

Nevertheless, contemporary Singapore retains a legacy of this division. Inscribed into every citizen's identity card is their "racial" ("race" is the official term) identity under the so-called CMIO categorization: Chinese, Malay, Indian, Other.

STEREOTYPES, FLUIDITY, AND RELIGION

Clear stereotypes mark each "race" (the official term) in the minds of the others:

- Chinese, the majority, are industrious and hardworking.
- Indians are smelly and drinkers.
- Malays are ignorant and poorly educated.
- The Other category primarily stands for Eurasians, of mixed Asian and European ancestry, who are lazy.

However, there has been an increase in interracial marriage over the years,[45] and therefore these seemingly fixed and impervious boundaries are increasingly hazy.

These "racial" identities often signify religious identity. Most Indians are Hindus, though significant numbers are Christian, Muslim, and Sikh. Most Chinese follow Chinese religions (Buddhism, Daoism, and Chinese folk religion), though an increasing number identify with no religion or Christianity, and there are a very few Chinese Muslims. Most Eurasians are Christians. However, for the Malays, there is a remarkably high correspondence with Islam: over 98 percent. Indeed, converting out of Islam would effectively make somebody, in the eyes of most of the community, no longer a Malay.

Early colonial records show that before the British arrived, the native inhabitants, which has some relation to those now termed Malays, belonged to a variety of religious traditions, including Buddhism, though Islam was the majority tradition. The creation of fixed racial markers under British rule was accompanied by imagined stereotypes for each group[46] and religious demarcation.

THE MALAY-MUSLIM COMMUNITY

The background of Malay-Muslims is notable. When Singapore joined Malaysia in 1963, it was an anomaly as a Chinese-majority state.[47] In 1965, when Singapore separated as a nation-state, special protections were put in place for the Malay-Muslim population, which generally suffered from greater educational and economic hardship than the wider society, to ensure they were not disadvantaged in the Chinese-majority country, including the following:

- enactment of the Administration of Muslim Law Act (AMLA), establishing a Syariah (*shariah*/Islamic law) Court for Muslim family law
- establishment of the Ministry for Muslim Affairs
- establishment of the Islamic Religious Council (MUIS) as a statutory body to oversee the needs of the community.[48]

The term "Malay-Muslim identity" signifies that being Muslim and being Malay are, for many, virtually identical. To be recognized as ethnically Malay more or less means to be a Muslim, speak Malay, and follow Malay customs. While there is a distinct Indian Muslim community, many Indians who are Muslims (while marked as "I" on their identity cards) are effectively considered Malay if they speak Malay and follow Malay customs. Indeed, it may even be possible to be "white" and Malay.

CONTESTATION AND CONFLICT

Part of Singapore's founding mythology is that interethnic and interreligious conflict will inevitably erupt unless the relationships between the communities are carefully managed.[49] This mythology involves retelling the narratives of two events dating to just before Singapore's foundations: the 1960 Maria Hertogh riots and the 1964 race riots. The latter developed from clashes between Malay and Chinese youths during a parade for the Prophet Muhammad's birthday, with several days of unrest during which shophouses were burned and many were killed. However, we focus on the former.

Maria was a Dutch girl who was separated from her parents when the Japanese invaded during WWII. She was looked after by the family's Malay maid. After the war, the courts rejected a case by the birth parents for her return, finding that she now regarded herself as part of her adopted family, had converted to Islam, and was accepted by the Malay-Muslim community. However, shortly afterward, the adopted mother had Maria married to a Muslim man under Islamic customary law, and the birth parents sought legal custody to "protect" their young daughter. While the courts deliberated, Maria was kept in a convent. This inflamed the Malay-Muslim community, who thought she was being deliberately converted to Catholic Christianity, especially when newspapers showed what seemed to be Maria kneeling before the Virgin Mary. When the courts declared the marriage illegal—it had not followed civil law but customary practice—and returned Maria to her birth parents, riots broke out. The Malay-Muslim community was offended not just by what they saw as the British siding with the Dutch, but also the alleged forced conversion and the perceived insult to Islam in having the marriage annulled. There were also attacks on members of the Eurasian community, who were seen as linked to the Western and Christian powers. Importantly, it shows that someone who was white could be regarded as a Malay.

REFLECTIONS

Some questions will help us consider the issues raised:

1. Do you see your race or ethnic identity as linked to your religious or non-religious identity? If you do not see them as linked, why is this?
2. What do you see as the key relations of religion and ethnicity with specific reference to the Malay-Muslim identity? Why might the Malay identity be tied to a

specific religious identity in a way that is not the case for Chinese and Indians, for example?

3. The effects of British colonial rule are still evident in the Singaporean CMIO distinctions. To what extent do you think the current ethno-religious demarcation is a result of Western influence and categorization? You may discuss in relation to other religious or ethnic identities you are familiar with.

4. To what extent do you think such ethno-religious identities may be claimed from within the community, rather than being externally imposed (at least in current contexts)? What advantages may there be, or what factors may exist that reinforce a separate sense of Malay-Muslim identity over and against other identities? You may consider this question in your own context for a community which links ethnicity and religion.

CASE STUDY 18B. SALUTING THE FLAG:
THE CASE OF JEHOVAH'S WITNESSES IN THE UNITED STATES

There can be situations when a nation's sacred symbols conflict in some way with the deep-seated convictions of a religious community: a clash of the sacred.

THE FLAG AS SACRED IN AMERICAN LIFE

For many Americans, the most prominent symbol of their nation is the "The Stars and Stripes" or "Old Glory," two names for their national flag. It is arguably a sacred (see box 18.7) symbol of US patriotism as "elements of civil religion are clearly evident in flag protection campaigns; for instance, legislation created to guard the flag—a *venerated* object—from *desecration* is laden with religious-like legal language."[50] Importantly, the two terms italicized in this quote reflect the precise legal language found in US law. Meanwhile, customary usage highlights the flag's sacred status:

· It should not be allowed to touch the ground.
· There is a special angular pattern for folding it.
· Old flags should (ironically perhaps) be disposed of by burning

Since the nineteenth century, laws have existed to protect the flag from various "misuses" ranging from commercial appropriation to political dissent. This was particularly the case in times of war. Many of these laws have been overturned by the courts. Perhaps the most notable case is Texas v. Johnson, when the US Supreme Court ruled on 21 June 1989 that Gregory L. "Joey" Johnson could not be held guilty of desecrating the flag by burning it. Citing the protection of free speech under the First Amendment, it was the opinion of the Court that "we do not consecrate the flag by punishing its desecration, for in doing so we dilute the freedom that this cherished emblem represents."[51]

The US is normally classified as a secular country with a strong separation of church and state (see chapter 16 and box 18.3). However, in practice, religion is deeply interwoven into American civic life, culture, and politics:

- Presidents and others invoke the blessing "God bless America."
- "In God We Trust" is emblazoned on the currency.
- The religious right often supports Republican candidates (see case study 6B).

Further, Robert Bellah theorized American civil religion, wherein a secular form of religiosity permeates patriotism and national life (see box 18.5). Therefore, while we can describe the flag as a "secular sacred" symbol, it is not clearly demarcated from more overtly "religious" notions about American exceptionalism, the belief that the United States has a unique and special place within the world which is often seen to be ordained by God as a mission.[52]

JEHOVAH'S WITNESSES

The Jehovah's Witnesses (JWs) can be traced back to Charles Taze Russell (1852–1916) as one of several organizations evolving from his "Watch Tower Bible and Tract Society." On Russell's death, Joseph Franklin Rutherford (1869–1942) became the most significant figure in the power struggles for control of the movement, founding the JWs as a distinct tradition. They have been controversial in many countries on a number of counts:

Pacifism: By refusing to fight or enlist for national service, they have faced persecution.

Proselytization: The JWs are dedicated evangelists seeking new members, and their door-to-door campaigns have gained them some notoriety.

Christianity: JWs claim to be Christian, but most Christian traditions deny they are. This is mainly because they reject such doctrines as the Trinity, Jesus's full divinity, and eternal damnation.

JWS AND THE FLAG

Compulsory flag saluting was enforced by law in American schools from the 1930s to the 1940s. This was anathema for JWs. As their website today explains: "Jehovah's Witnesses believe that bowing down to a flag or saluting it, often in conjunction with an anthem, is a religious act that ascribes salvation, not to God, but to the State or to its leaders (Isaiah 43:11; 1 Corinthians 10:14; 1 John 5:21)."[53]

After a US Supreme Court decision upheld these laws in 1940, about fifteen hundred JWs were attacked by vigilante mobs, while around two thousand JW children were expelled from schools. To note one example:

In one of hundreds of incidents of vigilante justice, a group of American Legionnaires and local police in Richwood, West Virginia in 1940 forced a group of Jehovah's Witnesses to swallow large amounts of castor oil, roped them together, and paraded them around in front of a large crowd. To conclude the spectacle, the Witnesses were banished from the town and their cars vandalized.[54]

In 1942, the law on flag salutation was deemed by the Civil Rights Office of the US Department of Justice to be behind "an uninterrupted record of violence and persecution of the Witnesses" in which "devout religious people were being assaulted for their refusal to pledge allegiance to it."[55] Flag veneration, linked to American civil religion, was in these terms deemed a violation of freedom of religion (see chapter 16), contravening the US principles of "one nation under God" and equality for all before the law. In 1943, in West Virginia State Board of Education v. Barnette, the US Supreme Court overturned its 1940 ruling, holding that flag saluting should not be compulsory.

REFLECTIONS

Some questions will help us think through the issues raised:

1. What do you regard as your country's most sacred symbols or principles? How do you/your society "venerate" these, or not? Do they conflict with the religious standpoint of any groups?
2. Do you see the US flag as a secular patriotic sacred symbol, or a reflection of religious patriotism? Can we readily draw a line between these two?
3. JWs do not see their refusal to salute the flag (they will not sing national anthems, recite patriotic pledges, or vote in political elections) as anti-American or un-American. For them, it simply reflects a biblical worldview. Discuss the issues you see raised when a deep religious conviction runs counter to a national sacred symbol. You may want to consult discussions in chapters 1 and 16 on human rights.

.   .   .

QUESTIONS AND CONNECTING THOUGHTS

The theme of this chapter could be summed up by saying that all scholarship and all religion (or categorizations of religion) are inherently political. What gets to count as religion, and why, is determined by particular interest groups, which relates to definitions of religion, postcolonialism and race, gender, and class, among other issues (see, respectively, chapters 1, 7, 10, and 3). Theoretical overlaps occur with social constructionism, constructions of identity, and secularism (see, respectively, chapters 5, 6, and 16). Many other issues are also political in nature, including dialogue and diversity, religious violence, and space and place (see, respectively, chapters 13, 14, 15, and 17).

Our discussion about the political nature of scholarship has resonances throughout this book. The reader is asked to analyze the author's own standpoint and positioning in debates. Indeed, also, to question their own. Some questions arise from this:

1. The possibility of studying religion as an academic subject, and how you are allowed to study it, will be affected by a variety of factors: the nation you live/ study in, the identity of the institution you study in (religious or secular), and the colonial and political legacy that has determined what religion means in your context. What is the effect on what you study and how it is studied?
2. If all scholarship is political, is there a place for seeking truth and better understanding? Are they compatible? Or, is scholarship simply powerplay among scholars to advance their own views at the expense of others?
3. To what extent do you think the notions of colonial difference and the colonial wound help explain the way that discourse on religion is determined and prescribed by a legacy of Western colonial and neocolonial dominance in academic and cultural thought?
4. Is religion an inherently political concept?

FURTHER READING

THEORY

Haynes, Jeffrey, ed. *Routledge Handbook of Religion and Politics* (New York: Routledge, 2010).

Liow, Joseph Chinyong. *Religion and Nationalism in Southeast Asia* (Cambridge: Cambridge University Press, 2016).

Maddox, Marion. "Religion and Politics," in *Controversies in Contemporary Religion*, ed. Paul Hedges, vol. 2 (Santa Barbara: Praeger, 2014), 265–92.

Mignolo, Walter. *The Darker Side of Western Modernity: Global Futures, Decolonial Options* (Durham: Duke University Press, 2011).

Pace, Enzo. "Religion, Nationalism, and International Relations," in Hedges, *Controversies in Contemporary Religion*, vol. 2, 241–63.

Seiwert, Hubert. "Politics," in *The Oxford Handbook of the Study of Religion*, ed. Michael Stausberg and Steven Engler (Oxford: Oxford University Press, 2016), 430–49.

CASE STUDY 18A. ETHNICITY AND RELIGION:
THE SINGAPOREAN MALAY-MUSLIM IDENTITY

Alatas, Syed Hussein. *The Myth of the Lazy Native: A Study of the Image of the Malays, Filipinos and Javanese from the 16th to the 20th Century and Its Function in the Ideology of Colonial Capitalism* (New York: Routledge, 2010 [1977]), 35–51.

Chew, Peter. "Racism in Singapore: A Review and Recommendations for Future Research," *Journal of Pacific Rim Psychology* 12 (2018): 1–8.

Chua, B.H. *Taking Group Rights Seriously: Multiracialism in Singapore*, Asia Research Centre Working Paper 124 (2005), https://researchrepository.murdoch.edu.au/id/eprint/57256/1/wp124.pdf.

Goh, Daniel. "Diversity and Nation-Building in Singapore," Global Centre for Pluralism (2017), www.pluralism.ca/wp-content/uploads/2017/10/Singapore_DGoh_Complete_Case_EN.pdf.

Hirschman, C. "The Making of Race in Colonial Malaya: Political Economy and Racial Ideology," *Sociological Forum* 1.2 (1986): 330–61.

CASE STUDY 18B. SALUTING THE FLAG: THE CASE OF JEHOVAH'S WITNESSES IN THE US

Anon. "Flag Salute, Voting, and Civilian Service," Watchtower Online Library (n.d.), https//wol.jw.org/en/wol/d/r1/1p-e/1102008085.

Cunningham, Lillian. "Episode 16 of the Constitutional Podcast: 'The First Amendment'" (podcast), *Washington Post* (2018), https://www.washingtonpost.com/news/on-leadership/wp/2018/01/29/episode-16-of-the-constitutional-podcast-the-first-amendment/.

Martin, Leisa A. "Examining the Pledge of Allegiance," *Social Studies* 99.3 (2008): 127–31.

Morgan, David. *The Sacred Gaze: Religious Visual Culture in Theory and Practice* (Berkeley: University of California Press, 2005), 230–40.

Welch, Michael, and Jennifer Bryan. "Flag Desecration in American Culture: Offenses against Civil Religion and a Consecrated Symbol of Nationalism," *Crime, Law and Social Change* 26 (1997): 77–93.

GLOSSARY

This glossary includes technical and foreign terms, places, traditions, deities, mythical heroes, and so on. (Some postulated deity figures also appear in the Who's Who section if they relate to an identifiable historical figure.) There are, when useful, references to boxes (especially those that give extended definitions), chapters, and case studies. Some technical terms are discussed in more depth here, but generally these are very brief glosses; readers should seek specialized sources for details.

Foreign terms generally appear in their original language. For instance, if you look up non-dualism it will direct you to *advaita*. This is because many English translations do not convey the full meaning and may even distort the original.

ABRAHAM Mythical patriarch claimed by Jews, Christians, and Muslims. Cannot be identified with any historical figure, though his story may be based on a distantly remembered tribal chieftain or a composite of several figures. His role is understood differently in each religion.

ABRAHAMIC Denoting the claimed shared patriarchal lineage of Judaism, Christianity, and Islam to the mythical patriarch Abraham. See box 2.2.

ACTOR (SOCIAL) Individuals participating in society—you, me, and everyone. May refer to groups.

ADVAITA (ADVAITA VEDANTA) Hindu teaching that humans and the divine/transcendent share the same essence. Translated as "non-dualism." Tradition: Advaita Vedanta. See box 14.2.

AGENCY Having the power to enact change or control discourse.

AHL AL-KITAB Arabic: "People of the Book." In Islam, denotes Christians, Jews, and others. See box 13.2.

AHMADIYYA (ISLAM) Nineteenth-century Islamic tradition claiming Mirza Ghulam Ahmad (1835–1908) was the messiah. Many Muslims say they are heretics, or not Muslims.

AKAN Ghanaian meta-ethnic cultural group.

AL-AQSA MOSQUE Mosque complex where the Jerusalem Temple was situated.

ALLAH Arabic: "The God." Used by Muslims and Arabic-speaking Christians and Jews. See box 13.11.

ALMSGIVING See *dana* (Buddhism); *zakat* (Islam).

AL-QAEDA Loosely affiliated terrorist movement.

AMERICAN EXCEPTIONALISM Belief that God has given the US a particular global destiny and role.

ANATHEMA Christian decree of excommunication (expulsion from the church).

ANGLICANISM (EPISCOPALIANISM) Protestant Christian traditions stemming from the Church of England. Claims to be both Catholic and Reformed. Episcopalianism in the US.

ANIMISM Systems which see the natural world as infused with spirits.

ANTHROPOLOGY Academic study of human societies. Traditionally, but no longer, for societies deemed "primitive." Also, theories of humanity, for example, Buddhist anthropology, and so on.

ANTI-REALISM See non-realism.

ANTI-REPRESENTATIONALISM Theory that we only have access to reality through social discourse. See box 5.8.

ANTISEMITISM Coined in the nineteenth century for prejudice against Jewish people and tradition. Can be religious, racial, and political. Roots in the New Testament and Christian tradition. Transformed in the modern period to be more racialized. See chapter 14.

APOCALYPTIC To do with the end of the world in cosmological schemes.

APOCRYPHA Section in Protestant Christian Bibles. Books in the Catholic Old Testament not found in the sixteenth-century Jewish Hebrew Bible.

APOSTLE/APOSTOLIC Direct followers of Jesus. Lineage from them is asserted by some Christians as a source of authority.

APOTROPAIC Signifying the power to avert evil/bad luck or provide blessings such as wealth, childbirth, and so on. Used of religious practices not concerned with "salvific/transcendent" foci.

ARAB SPRING Prodemocracy protests in the Middle East ca. 2010–2012.

ARCHAEOLOGY OF KNOWLEDGE See genealogy of knowledge.

ASABIYYAH Arabic meaning "group feeling." Theorized by Ibn Khaldun for the strong connections of nomadic tribes, typically lost in settled civilizations.

ASHRAM Hindu religious or spiritual community. Used of some Christian monastic centers in India.

ASTIKA Hindu philosophies considered orthodox.

ATONEMENT (SUBSTITUTION) Christian theological speculation on how humanity becomes reconciled with God. Substitution atonement refers to a number of theories which suggest that mankind had to pay a "debt" because of sin and Jesus acted as the "ransom" which paid that debt. Two substitution theories are that (1) God was righteously angry with humanity and a "sin offering" was needed to appease God's wrath, and only Jesus as a pure "sacrificial lamb" could offer this; and (2) due to sin, humanity belonged to Satan (the devil), who had to be paid for its release, and he accepted Jesus as the debt payment, thus releasing humanity from its captivity due to sin. However, as Jesus was also fully God (in the doctrine of the Trinity), the devil could not hold Jesus and so was tricked.

AURA Area that Muslim women should keep covered according to Islamic legal prescriptions (*shariah*). See box 10.8.

AVATAR In Hinduism, manifestations of Vishnu in physical form, including Krishna and Rama. Said to be sent in times of evil/disorder.

AWAKENING See nirvana.

AXIAL AGE Largely discredited theory that a major religious change occurred from ca. 500 BCE–0 CE.

AXIS MUNDI Symbolic center of the world.

AYODHYA Indian city believed by many Hindus to be Rama's birthplace.

AZAZEL In Israelite tradition, a demon of the wilderness or desert.

BABRI MASJID (MOSQUE) Sixteenth-century mosque in Ayodhya, India. Destroyed in 1992. See box 17.5.

BAHA'I Nineteenth-century offshoot of Islam in Iran. Now, generally seen as a separate religion. Claims its teachings are the latest revelation, superseding previous religions. Persecuted as heretics in Iran and some other countries.

BAYES' THEOREM Theorem to assess probability developed by the English clergyman Thomas Bayes (1701–1776). Widely used today for probability. Difficult to apply, except as a general principle, for historical events.

BCE/CE See CE.

BEHAVIORIST MODEL Proposal that human nature is entirely created by culture.

BEING-IN-THE-WORLD Our situatedness as embodied, and socially determined, creatures which prescribes what kinds of thoughts, beliefs, and ideas we can have. See box 9.2.

BETWIXT AND BETWEEN Indicating a liminal state. See box 12.5.

BHAGAVAD GITA Literally, "Song of the Lord." Part of the Mahabharata, focusing on Krishna. Krishna tells Arjuna that as a warrior (*kshatriya*), it is Arjuna's duty to fight and kill. Read by Mohandas (Mahatma) Gandhi as a pacifist manifesto. Dated ca. 200 BCE to 200 CE.

BHAKTI Hindu devotional traditions.

BHARATIYA JANATA PARTY (BJP) Indian political party that expounds Hindu nationalism.

BHIKKHU Buddhist monk.

BHIKKUNI Buddhist nun.

BIBLE Literally, "the books." Jewish (Hebrew Bible) and Christian (Hebrew Bible/Old Testament and New Testament) canonical texts. The number and order of books is contested. See chapter 4.

BLANK SLATE Tabula rasa, literally, "scrubbed tablet." Often denoting human nature as having no characteristics except those given by culture and language.

BODH GAYA Site in present-day India where the Buddha probably attained awakening/ nirvana.

BODHISATTVA In Mahayana Buddhism, someone who compassionately renounces their final entry to awakening until all sentient beings are saved. May be already awakened. In Theravada Buddhism, the term denotes the Buddha before his awakening.

BOLLYWOOD Indian film industry in Mumbai (formerly Bombay).

BRAHMIN Priestly class in Indian caste system. See box 4.6.

BUDDHA Buddha is a title meaning "Awakened One." Generally associated with the historical founder of Buddhism, it is a title that can be applied to a number of awakened beings. The number of Buddhas in Mahayana Buddhism is extensive.

BUDDHA-NATURE In Mahayana Buddhism, inherent awakened nature of all beings.

BUMIPUTERA Literally, "sons of the soil." In parts of Southeast Asia, denotes indigenous groups, especially tribal people. Today, claimed in Malaysia by Malays to assert their priority over others.

BURKINI Bathing costume that covers the hair and the body except feet, face, and hands. Seen to be compatible with Islamic traditions of veiling (hijab). See case study 16A.

BURQA (ALSO BURKA) Form of veiling in Islamic tradition that involves covering the whole body in a large loose gown. See box 16.12.

BYZANTINE EMPIRE Name used for successor of the Roman Empire based in Byzantium (also Constantinople, later Istanbul), and claimed to be the Christian Roman Empire. Orthodox Christian tradition.

CALIPH Arabic: "successor." In Islamic tradition a political ruler. Rules a caliphate which is an Islamic claim to be the successor of Muhammad and to be defender of Islam's holy sites (primarily Mecca and Medina, also Jerusalem). See box 16.2.

CANON Literally, "rule/measure." Used for a collection of texts holding special authority. From Christian usage for the Bible, but used for any collection of texts with perceived authority.

CAPTIVE MIND Theory that formerly colonized peoples remain intellectually in thrall to the thought system of the colonizers.

CARTESIAN DUALISM Seeing mind and soul as distinct parts.

CARVAKA Indian unorthodox (nastika) school of philosophy. Materialist/atheist.

CASTE Indian social system. See box 4.6.

CATEGORIES (CATEGORIZATION) The social and psychological processes by which we divide the world to make it manageable. Some categories may be more analytically useful, others less so. In-group bias may affect our perception of this. See groups.

CATHARSIS Emotional release or pleasure attained through watching drama. See chapter 12.

CATHOLIC CHRISTIANITY The largest Christian tradition, headed by the Pope of Rome. Catholic means "universal" and is claimed by many churches.

CE (COMMON ERA) Non-Christian-centric dating terminology. Stands for "Common Era." BCE (Before the Common Era) and CE replace, respectively, BC ("Before Christ") and AD (Anno Domini, an acronym of the Latin "In the year of our Lord").

CELESTIAL MASTERS DAOISM Earliest known Daoist school. Founded second century CE. Today's Zhengyi Dao school claims a doubtful direct lineage descent from the earliest Celestial Masters.

CHAKRAVARTIN Ideal Buddhist ruler. See box 15.11.

CHARISMA A form of moral and attractive force that particular individuals exhibit. See box 5.4.

CHICANA Mexican American politicized identities.

CHRISTENDOM Physical area and historical perception of Europe as a Christian sphere.

CIVIL RELIGION A state's secular system intertwined with religious qualities. See box 18.5.

COGNITION Mental processes of understanding. See box 8.1.

COLLATERAL DAMAGE Euphemistic way of talking about unintended damage/harm in military campaigns. Mostly killing civilians.

COLONIAL DIFFERENCE The concept that the colonized are forced to accept ideas, concepts, and ways of thinking which are not their own but which are the dominant paradigms they must fit into. See box 18.1.

COLONIAL WOUND The cultural trauma of those who are colonized and so always have to live within a world where their language, culture, and ways of life are subservient/inferior to the dominant modes of knowledge, speaking, and power production. See box 18.1.

COLONIALISM The act of settling of colonies or settlements in other territories for the political, economic, or military benefit of the colonizer. See box 7.1.

COLONIALITY A theory of "salvation" justifying colonialism. See box 7.1.

CONFESSIONAL Here, indicating a theological/belief-based standpoint, as differentiated from a nonconfessional religious studies approach.

CONFUCIANISM See *rujiao*.

CONSERVATISM A commitment to tradition. See chapter 15.

CONSTANTINOPLE City (re)founded by Emperor Constantine as the capital of the Roman Empire. Founded by the Greeks in the seventh century BCE as Byzantium, this name was also used for the city in later times until the Ottoman conquest in 1453, when it was typically referred to as Istanbul, but it was still officially named Constantinople until 1930.

COSMIC WAR An imagined conflict between metaphysical forces in religion-related violence. See chapter 15.

CRITICAL REALISM Mediates between "extreme" realist and non-realist poles, accepting that "reality" (actual physical stuff) comes to us through socially constructed means and linguistic construction, but also that "reality" affects us too strongly to be seen as merely a second-hand experience. See box 5.8.

CRITICAL RELIGION Religious studies approach that draws on critical theory.

CRITICAL THEORY A range of recent theoretical approaches that question accepted norms. Often has a political or justice-based agenda stemming from its critical reading of social norms. See box 0.1.

CRUSADE Various European military incursions, mostly to capture the "Holy Land." Also, expeditions against heretical Christians, and one in particular which targeted Byzantium for financial gain. Circa eleventh century to fifteenth century. The term is applied anachronistically, and such ventures were termed in such ways as a "holy pilgrimage" in their own day.

CSR (COGNITIVE SCIENCE OF RELIGION) Study of religious origins and behavior through cognition and evolution. See chapter 8.

CULT Often used pejoratively to denote a religion the user has delegitimized. See box 1.5.

CULTURAL MARXISM A rhetorical term used by extreme right-wing pundits to dismiss critics and ideas they wish to demean. It is without any coherent analytic or intellectual value and conflates many schools of thought, thinkers, and ideas into a convenient bogeyman.

CULTURAL REVOLUTION Period of social, cultural, and political upheaval in Chinese history (1966–1976). Sought to destroy old/feudal forms of life and habits. Known as the Great Cultural Revolution in China.

DALIT Literally, "broken." Those below the Hindu caste system, or "outcasts." See box 4.6.

DANA In Buddhism, almsgiving, often a way for laypeople to gain merit (*punya*).

DAO Chinese: "way" or "path." May denote a transcendent reality and/or the path to following it. Used in Daoism, but common across many traditions.

DAODEJING (ALSO TAOTECHING, OR LAOZI) Text attributed to the mythical Laozi. See case study 4B.

DAOISM (DAOJIAO) Chinese religious tradition with many schools, often falsely portrayed as split between *daojiao* ("religion") and *daojia* ("philosophy"). See box 4.13.

DARSHAN In Hinduism, seeing and being seen by a deity. Often translated as "worship."

DECOLONIZATION Process intended to remove Western-centric bias. See box 7.5.

DECONSTRUCTION Herein, approaches that broadly seek to show the socially constructed nature of other concepts by "deconstructing" the terms we use. It stresses the internal tensions in terms and worldviews, such that they are inherently unstable and not fixed, as well as stressing that no meaning is final as terms always change meaning as contexts alter.

DEEN Arabic term with multiple meanings, including "custom," "usage," "direction," "judgment," and "retribution." Often poorly translated as "religion." See chapter 1.

DEISM Belief that a deity created the universe but does not actively intervene.

DEITY Posited transcendent being.

DEMERIT See *papa*.

DETRADITIONALIZATION Typically denoting religion as commercialized and simplified. See chapter 16.

DEVOTIONAL TRIANGLE The movement of passing tradition across generations that relates both to human-to-human encounters (horizontal, and forming the bottom edge of the triangle), and a divine-human encounter (vertical, and with the two bottom corners of the triangle intersecting with the top corner). See box 3.6.

DHARMA Sanskrit term used variously: in Hinduism, various meanings but primarily "duty"; in Buddhism, teachings of the Buddha. Often poorly translated as "religion."

DHIMMI In Islam, denotes Christians, Jews, and others. Varies by tradition, location, and period. They pay a "poll tax" (*jizya*), theoretically equal to Islamic alms (*zakat*), granting exemption from military service, protection by the Islamic polity, and freedom to worship and follow their own laws and traditions. See chapter 13.

DIACHRONIC (ANALYSIS) Layers of construction and meaning over time. See chapter 17.

DISCOURSE (ANALYSIS) Discourse refers to the ways in which knowledge is constituted in society/culture, which is determined by social norms and practices as well as the power relations which inhere between different groups. Discourse analysis asks who determines what counts as knowledge, what forms of life are valorized or permitted, and what are the historical and social processes, imbricated with regimes of power, that have allowed certain discourses to be dominant in any society, period, or culture. Some forms of discourse analysis focus on numerical instances of particular key terms and note their prevalence within texts (written or spoken), while other forms focus more on the way terms are employed in context. See box 5.1.

DIVERSITY Describing the fact of many religions in a society; distinguished from pluralism as an attitude to diversity. See box 13.3.

DOME OF THE ROCK Shrine inside the Al-Aqsa Mosque complex. Contains the rock where Muhammad allegedly landed on his night journey to Jerusalem. In some Jewish and Islamic traditions, the center point of the beginning of creation.

DUALISM See *dvaita*.

DUKKHA In Buddhism, "transitoriness." Often translated as "suffering." See box 3.7.

DURGA A "ferocious" Hindu deity. Either a consort of Shiva or the Goddess.

DVAITA (DVAITA VEDANTA) Hindu teaching that humans and deity are distinct. See box 14.2.

ECO MONK Monks involved in environmental activism. See case study 17A.

EIDETIC VISION In phenomenology, seeing things as a whole, not superficially or partially. See box 2.3.

EIGHTFOLD PATH Systematization of the Buddha's fourth teaching (in the Four Noble Truths) into eight parts under three sections: (1) Proper View/Wisdom—Right Belief, Right Thought; (2) Proper Conduct/Virtue—Right Speech, Right Conduct, Right Livelihood; (3) Proper Practice/Meditation—Right Endeavour, Right Mindfulness, Right Meditation.

EMBODIED PRACTICE An activity that involves our physical selves. See chapter 9.

EMBODIMENT Having bodies, which affects our way of being and knowing. See box 9.2.

EMIC-ETIC To understand/explain something in the terms of a tradition (emic) or using external terms (etic). Both are "outsider" stances. See chapter 2.

EMPIRICISM Positing knowledge as based in experience. See box 9.1.

EMPTY SIGNIFIER Typically used to mean a term with no fixed meaning. As used by Ernesto Laclau, it relates to Ferdinand de Saussure's "master signifier," which is the central controlling symbol in a system. By changing "master" to "empty," Laclau emphasized that it was contingent and not stable. Nevertheless, it operates in a set way, or range of ways, within any system, though it is negotiable. Relates to the "shifting signifier," coined by Claude Lévi-Strauss and used by Stuart Hall, denoting terms used in regimes of power in order to exclude. It is necessary to balance the claims of arbitrariness of usage with embeddedness in chains of meaning and negotiability, though the terms may have—as "shifting signifiers"—no "natural" referent point. See box 9.11.

ENCYCLICAL Catholic Christian teaching document issued by the Vatican/Pope which is not binding/unalterable.

ENLIGHTENMENT (BUDDHIST) See nirvana.

ENLIGHTENMENT (EUROPEAN) A period when tradition was dramatically questioned; roughly sixteenth to the eighteenth centuries, or sometimes more narrowly from ca. 1720 to 1780, it was a period of change and transformation in many areas. Seen as the beginnings of (Western) modernity. See box 16.1.

ENVIRONMENTALISM Broadly, environmentalism concerns the protection of our environment (the planet Earth); not a single philosophy or movement, but one which has changed over time, and varies in differing contexts. See box 17.7.

EPIC (HINDU) The Mahabharata and Ramayana. The two best-known and loved texts of Hinduism. Known through songs, storytelling, performances, and now film and television.

EPISTEMIC JUSTIFIABILITY Philosophical term for whether a belief can be justified.

EPISTEMOLOGY Theories of knowledge.

EPOCHÉ In phenomenology, the act of suspension of one's own judgment. See box 2.3.

ESSENTIALISM Treating something as if it had a solid unchanging core (an "essence").

ESSENTIALLY CONTESTED CONCEPTS Words or terms which cannot be adequately or finally defined, but which remain meaningful and useful. See chapter 1.

ETHNICITY Posits group characteristics in terms of "racial" (skin coloration), linguistic, cultural, and geographical signifiers, but is a slippery and nebulous term. Ethnicities can be described differently. See box 18.6.

ETYMOLOGICAL FALLACY A philosophical term for confusing a term's origins (its etymology) with its meaning. See box 11.2.

ETYMOLOGY The origins and history of words and their meanings.

EUCHARIST A Christian rite that commemorates the Last Supper, in which bread and wine are ritually consumed. See box 12.6 and case study 12A.

EUROPEAN EXCEPTIONALISM Assuming that European theories and trends are the basis for understanding the whole world.

EVANGELICALISM (EVANGELICAL) Movements in Protestant Christianity dating roughly from the seventeenth century that stressed emotive worship, personal commitment, and mission.

EXCLUSIVISM Theological: asserting only one religion possesses truth. Social: denying the value of diversity. See chapter 13.

EXCOMMUNICATION Christian decree of expulsion from the church.

FAKE NEWS Media stories which are knowingly untrue but spread to create distrust, confusion, and disinformation. Or, an "alternative truth."

FALUN GONG Chinese tradition of self-cultivation. See case study 1A.

FEMINISM Various movements for the political, economic, and social equality of women. See chapter 10.

FETISH Object given undue or excessive value. See box 5.7.

FILIAL PIETY In Chinese (and East Asian) thought, the duty a child owes to their parent. See case study 1B.

FIVE PILLARS Set of beliefs/practices typically seen as definitive of Islamic identity and tradition: recitation of *shahadah* (Islamic profession of faith in God and Muhammad as God's messenger), *salat* (five daily prayers), *zakat* (almsgiving), *sawm* (fasting during Ramadan), and *hajj* (pilgrimage to Mecca).

FORM OF LIFE A way of life in which we conform to certain rules/disciplines for some transformation or pattern of living.

FOUR NOBLE TRUTHS Seen as the basic teachings of the Buddha: *dukkha*—life and the world are transitory; *trishna*—our craving/desire for this transitoriness causes suffering; *nirvana*—"awakening" to the knowledge that there is a state beyond the cycle of suffering (*samsara*) entailed by the first two and reincarnation, and the way out of this cycle via the eightfold path. See box 3.7.

FRAME THEORY (FRAMING) The way that concepts are discursively placed to normalize them. See chapter 9.

FREEDOM FIGHTER Someone engaged in violent resistance movements for political ends. Discursively distinguished from terrorism.

FUNDAMENTALISM Variously defined, but most basically a movement asserting perceived core tenets (fundamentals). See chapter 15.

GENDER Behavioral patterns prescribed for males and females (and other recognized genders). See box 10.6.

GENDER CONSTRUCTIONISM Theories on the discourse of male and female. See chapter 10.

GENEALOGY OF KNOWLEDGE Terminology from Michel Foucault which refers to the investigation of the origins of terms and concepts to show that they determine our means of knowing and classifications. In this, it is methodologically similar to his archaeology of knowledge. However, genealogy is variously distinguished: showing how knowledge and power justify and distinguish between "true" or "false"; as the work of emancipation from regimes of knowledge; stressing the contingent nature of the knowledge uncovered. These terms are not mutually exclusive. Some use "archaeology of knowledge" in these ways.

GENUFLECTION A type of bow that involves going down on one knee.

GEOGRAPHY Academic field concerning human meaning making in the world. See box 17.1.

GLOBAL ETHIC Posited common core of morality across religions. See box 14.5.

GLOBALIZATION Variously defined, but signifying the interconnectedness of our world in terms of IT, travel, and so on.

GOD/DESS Signifies a posited non-supreme deity (with lowercase "g"). See Allah, Goddess.

GODDESS In Hinduism, with Shiva and Vishnu, one of the three most revered deities. The supreme deity. See box 10.4. Also, the/a deity of certain Pagan traditions.

GOD-SPOT Falsely posited singular part of the brain responsible for religious thoughts or experiences. See box 8.6.

GOLDEN RULE Rule of ethical conduct mandating that you treat others as you wish to be treated. See box 14.5.

GOTHIC Style of medieval European (church) architecture. Typical of medieval European church architecture; employs pointed arches and is found in various styles. See case study 9B.

GRACE Christian theological term for the free remission of sins by deity. Used sometimes, analogously, for similar systems in, for instance, Pure Land Buddhism and some Hindu *bhakti* traditions.

GROUPS (GROUPISM) A postulated collective composed of various members seen as having similar characteristics. To see these as natural, monolithic, or fixed—especially such things as racial, national, or religious groups—is to adhere to what Rogers Brubaker terms "groupism," or the false ascription of permanence to socially constructed categories. Nevertheless, many groups have a strong social reality.

GUANYIN Most revered figure in East Asian religiosity. See box 2.9.

GURU Sanksrit: roughly "one who provides light." Spiritual-religious teacher in South Asian, mainly Hindu, traditions.

GURU GRANTH SAHIB Collection of Sikh sacred writings. Contains writings from Hindu, Islamic, and Sikh figures.

HABITUS Conditioning from society's structures. See box 5.3.

HADITH Sayings attributed to Muhammad.

HAGIA SOPHIA Literally, "Holy Wisdom." Greatest church of Constantinople (Byzantium/Istanbul), originally built under Emperor Constantine. Converted into a mosque (1452) by the Ottoman Dynasty. A museum from 1935 until 2020. See box 17.6.

HALAKHA Body of Jewish legal thought.

HASIDIC JUDAISM Form of Orthodox Judaism that arose in the eighteenth century. Members are often marked out by distinctive clothes and hairstyles.

HEAVEN Variously posited afterlife realm. For Confucian usage, see *tian*.

HEBREW BIBLE Synonym for the Tanakh, or Old Testament. Emphasizes it is a Jewish text. Jews and Christians have differing versions. See chapter 4.

HEGEMONIC/HEGEMONY Generally, leadership or dominance by one group, state, or ideology, which, following Antonio Gramsci, concerns the economic and political domination that makes certain forms of life or systems of thought appear natural.

HENOTHEISM Systems with a superior deity among a host of other deities.

HERETIC Literally (from Greek *hairesis*), "to choose." Denotes "schismatic," somebody who breaks away, and/or "false believers." Developed in Christianity, but used generally of those with erroneous beliefs or in breakaway sects.

HERMAPHRODITE Both female and male. Today, "intersex" is preferred.

HERMENEUTICS Theories of interpretation. Originally denoted primarily Christian biblical interpretation, but also used for legal theory, and today all forms of textual interpretation. In philosophical hermeneutics, used for human interpretation in texts, speech, art, and so on.

HERMENEUTICS OF SUSPICION Questioning norms and accepted beliefs. See box 2.7.

HERMENEUTICS (PHILOSOPHICAL) See philosophical hermeneutics.

HETERONORMATIVITY Heterosexual relationships are seen as normative and natural.

HIGH GODS Within the CSR, high gods are deities that emphasize morality. See chapter 8.

HIJAB Veil or headscarf worn by some Muslim women. See boxes 10.8 and 16.12.

HIJRA In Indian tradition, a third gender. See box 10.7. In Islam, the migration of Muhammad and his followers from Mecca to the city that became known as Medina.

HINDUTVA Sanskrit: "Hinduness." Now, a term of Hindu nationalist discourse. See box 6.7.

HISTORIOGRAPHY Methods of studying history.

HOLY See *qadosh*.

HOLY LAND Christian term for area around today's Israel/Palestine, primarily areas associated with Jesus's life. See case study 17B.

HOLY SEPULCHRE Christian shrine, traditionally believed to be the site where Adam died and where Jesus was crucified and buried. See case study 17B.

HOMILY A religious talk.

HUANG-LAO A Chinese school (early centuries BCE) of self-cultivation practices (see box 1.11). Named after the mythical Yellow Emperor (Huangdi) and Laozi. Its connection to Daoism is debated. See case study 4B.

HUMANISM/HUMANIST Originally Christian scholars who used Greco-Roman resources and emphasized human knowledge. Typically, today, a specific atheist tradition.

HYBRIDITY A mixture of two (or more) entities or derived from two (or more) sources. See chapter 3.

HYPERACTIVE AGENT DETECTION DEVICE (HADD) Theory in the CSR that supposes humans are overactive in attributing agency to things. See chapter 8.

ICONOCENTRIC Traditions focused on images/symbols.

ICONOCLASTIC Critique of the use of images/symbols.

IDEAL TYPE In sociology, a concept which helps envisage particular forms of society/behavior, and so on. However, they are abstractions and may not appear so clearly or distinctly in real life.

IDEALISM Seeing the mind as the basis of all knowledge. See box 9.1.

IDENTITY External: enacted identity, playing out roles; internal: how we associate our self with our roles. See box 6.1.

IDENTITY SALIENCE Actions associated with particular roles or identities. See chapter 6.

IMAGINED A social perception rather than a natural state of affairs, although it may be a social reality.

IMAGINED COMMUNITIES A sense of belonging to a group (nation or otherwise) that is an imagined, instead of a natural, association. See chapter 18.

IMPERIALISM Policy of one territory ruling another. See box 7.1.

INCLUSIVISM Theological: many religions contain elements of truth, but only one contains the fullness of truth. Social: accepting diversity pragmatically, but not fully welcoming it. See chapter 13.

INDIGENOUS RELIGIONS Religious traditions of Indigenous Americans, Australian Aborigines, and so on.

INDULGENCES In Catholic Christianity, indulgences permit announcing remission of sins for performing a particular penance. In medieval devotion, typically understood/sold as remission of sins for those in Purgatory, with price indicating sin remission.

IN-GROUP A group with which we identify. See chapter 6.

INSIDER-OUTSIDER A devotee's standpoint (insider) or a non-devotee's (often scholarly) standpoint (outsider). See chapter 2.

INTERDISCIPLINARY Scholarly work that combines methods or aspects of various disciplines/methods/theories in one project or approach.

INTERRELIGIOUS DIALOGUE (IRD) Ill-defined term for diverse exchanges between different religions. See chapter 14.

INTERRELIGIOUS STUDIES (ALSO, INTERFAITH STUDIES) A multidisciplinary or interdisciplinary approach to the study of religion that stresses, and studies, the dynamic interaction between traditions. See introduction.

INTERSECTIONALITY Idea that that oppression is often not one-dimensional but can include factors relating to gender, race, and class.

INTERSEX Individuals born with reproductive anatomy that does not fit typical definitions of male or female bodies.

INTERWORLDVIEW DIALOGUE Interreligious dialogue that includes atheists, agnostics, and so on.

INTRARELIGIOUS DIALOGUE Dialogue within a single religion. See chapter 14.

ISIS Also IS, ISIL, Daesh. Terrorist group which sought to create a caliphate in Iraq and Syria. ISIS stands for the Islamic State in Iraq and Syria. Globally, most Muslim scholars have contested, even refuted: (a) their claims to be Islamic; (b) the legitimacy of the proclaimed caliphate; and, (c) their ideological underpinnings, especially as they exemplify militant neo-Islamic jihadism.

ISLAM Arabic: "submission" (to the will of God). See box 13.2.

ISLAM Denoting a distinct religion.

ISLAMOPHOBIA Prejudice against Muslims. See box 15.4.

ISRAELITE (TRADITIONS) Hebrew traditions before ca. 500 BCE. Scholars dispute whether Judaism applies before either ca. fifth century BCE or first century CE.

ISRAEL/PALESTINE Used to denote the area that encompasses both the modern-day State of Israel and the Palestinian territories. Seen by Christians as the "Holy Land" and by many Jews as the territory promised them by their deity in the Hebrew Bible (though the exact extent and area of this land is debated).

ISTANBUL See Constantinople.

JAINISM Religious tradition founded around the sixth century BCE by a figure known as Mahavira in South Asia. Probably slightly predates Buddhism.

JATI Subdivisions by family occupation in Indian caste system, for example, as weavers, leatherworkers, and so on. See box 4.6.

JEHOVAH'S WITNESSES American nineteenth-century offshoot of Christianity. Many Christians do not regard them as being Christian. See case study 18B.

JERUSALEM City in present-day Israel/Palestine. Sacred to Jews, Muslims, and Christians, among others. Site of the Jerusalem Temple, Christian Holy Sepulchre, and Al-Aqsa Mosque.

JERUSALEM TEMPLE Temple to Israelite deity Yahweh. First temple was destroyed by the Babylonians ca. sixth century BCE, rebuilt about fifty years later. Second temple was destroyed by the Romans in 70 CE. Many Jews believe it will be rbuilt by the Messiah. Currently, site is occupied by the Al-Aqsa Mosque. The Wailing/Western Wall is the only remnant of the second temple.

JESUIT A Catholic Christian order of missionaries and educators.

JESUS CHRIST In Christian theology (Christology), the Jewish rabbi known as Jesus of Nazareth as second person of the Trinity and deity, who became "incarnate" as a human. The transformation of Jesus into a postulated deity occurred over several centuries, and debates between differing sects as to his status, and how somebody could be both God and man, led to vociferous debates. Differing views on this existed from at least the second century CE and continue today. In the early centuries, and since the sixteenth century, some Christians rejected deified notions of the human Jesus; however, what has become mainstream Christianity has typically sought to refute these and alternative views of his explaining his deity status as heretical. See box 4.8 and case study 4A.

JIAO Chinese term meaning "tradition" or "lineage." *Jia,* meaning "family," is sometimes employed.

JIHAD Arabic, literally "striving/struggle." Often mistranslated as "holy war." See box 15.8.

JIZYA Arabic: often rendered as "poll tax." Some dispute this translation as it was not a tax per head. However, it is the standard English term. See *dhimmi.*

JUDAISM Traditions developing from the Hebrew Bible through the Mishnah, Talmud, and other sources. Often demarcated historically as Israelite religion (before ca. 500 BCE), Second Temple Judaism (ca. 500 BCE to 100 CE), and Rabbinic Judaism (ca. 100 CE to today). Each has various subdivisions and is not monolithic.

JUDEO-CHRISTIAN Used of an imagined shared common heritage, but problematic as it ignores the shared heritage with Islam (sometimes purposefully) and typically means reading Judaism in Christian terms.

JUS AD BELLUM Latin: "justice for war." Justifications for war. See box 15.6.

JUS IN BELLO Latin: "justice in war." Acts permissible in conducting warfare. See box 15.6.

JUST WAR Traditions stipulating legitimate reasons for, and conduct in, war. See box 15.6.

KALI "Ferocious" Hindu Goddess. Consort of Shiva or Goddess. See box 10.4.

KAMI Japanese: "spirits" in nature; transcendent deities; "special" humans; distinct or "sacred" quality. See box 17.3.

KARMA In Buddhism and Hinduism, the law of cause and effect, associated with reincarnation.

KOW-TOW Anglicized form of Chinese for "bowing the head." A kneeling position where the head is lowered to the floor, with hands by or before the head. Used to show respect to the emperor, high officials, one's parents, deities.

KRISHNA Hindu deity. Avatar of Vishnu. Revered in tales of his youth as a mischievous child and young cowherd. Devotion founded in the Bhagavad Gita.

KSHATRIYA Warrior; one of four classes in the Indian caste system. See box 4.6.

KYRIARCHY System of domination, oppression, and submission. See box 10.9.

LAÏCITÉ French concept of secularism. See chapter 16.

LANGUAGE GAME Idea that words are embedded within a particular set of usages (a "game"), which differs from other usages (other "games").

LAOZI Deity seen as one of the three manifestation of the Dao in Daoist traditions, and associated with the legendary rendering of the story of a probable historical figure. Also, sometimes used as a name for the Daodejing due to its mythic attribution to Laozi. See box 4.12.

LAST SUPPER Jesus's final meal with his disciples before his death. See box 12.6.

LAWS OF MANU (*MANUSHMRITI*) Text of Hindu "law code" (*dharmashastra*) literature. Lays out prescriptions for rituals, how a Hindu should live, the place of men and women, and caste distinctions. See box 10.3.

LAYPERSON In a religious tradition, a person who is not professional or ordained (e.g., not a priest, nun, etc.).

LEGEND Narrative told as a fact, but widely believed to be false. See box 4.3.

LGBTQI Acronym for lesbian, gay, bisexual, transgender, queer, and intersex.

LIBERAL FEMINISM First-wave feminism. Movements from around the European Enlightenment citing intellectual equality of men and women as a reason for equality. Sought voting rights for women (see chapter 10).

LIBERAL THEOLOGY Movement in Christianity from eighteenth century onward that consciously adapts to the modern world/knowledge.

LIBERATION THEOLOGY Christian theology originating in Latin America that argued for "God's preferential option for the poor." Found now beyond Christianity, and with various liberatory agendas (e.g., queer theology, Black theology, feminist theology, etc.).

LIBERATORY (LIBERATION) Denotes a desire/movement for freedom from some form of oppression/captivity. "Liberation" is also often used in English for various forms of "salvation" in religious traditions, especially referring to Buddhism and Hinduism.

LIMINAL(ITY) Stage of transition, flux, and uncertainty. Or a crossing point, from the Latin *limen* (door lintel). See box 12.5.

LINGUISTIC TURN Recognition that language is not simply a direct referent to objects in the world, but is culturally embedded and shapes our experience. Often associated with Ludwig Wittgenstein, but arguably develops from ideas first posited by Immanuel Kant.

LITERALISM Interpretative method of reading a text as if literally true. However, literalists are often selective about which parts they read as literal. See chapter 15.

LIVED ENVIRONMENT Referring to the human, natural, and built world as socially constructed. See box 17.1.

LIVED RELIGION Practice and behavior that distinguishes the experience of people from prescribed or elite tradition. See chapter 3.

LOGICAL POSITIVISM European philosophical school of the early twentieth century. Focused on securing the foundations of linguistic meaning and epistemology.

LOGOCENTRIC Here, language as the main form of knowing. See box 9.1.

LOGOS From Greek: "word" or "reasoning." Used in Christianity to denote Jesus as the "Word of God."

LUTHERANISM Protestant Christian traditions claiming direct descent from Martin Luther.

MACRO-LEVEL Here, denoting governmental level.

MAGIC Use of perceived "primitive" actions and worldviews. Often distinguished from science and religion. See boxes 7.8, 9.4, and 12.2.

MAGISTERIUM The teaching authority of Catholic Christianity based in the Pope and church hierarchy.

MAHABHARATA One of two Hindu epics. The world's longest poem, includes the Bhagavad Gita.

MAHAYANA BUDDHISM Traditions of China, Japan, Korea, Tibet, Vietnam, and so on. Uses the Tripitaka and Mahayana scriptures. Includes Zen, Vajrayana, and Pure Land schools. Largest Buddhist tradition.

MALESTREAM Ideas or traditions developed from the male standpoint. See chapter 10.

MANDATE OF HEAVEN See *tianming*.

MATERIAL CULTURE Physical artifacts created by humans as part of culture. See chapter 9.

MATERIALITY Stance that takes human embodiment as key to human understanding. See box 9.10.

MATERIAL TURN Movement in academic thought that sees our embodied nature and the material world as integral to our thinking and knowing. Draws from such thinkers as Maurice Merleau-Ponty and Pierre Bourdieu. See chapter 9.

MATRIARCHAL System wherein females hold power.

MCI (MINIMALLY COUNTERINTUITIVE IDEA) Ideas that resemble natural human ideas but differ in a small way. See chapter 8.

MECCA Capital city of modern-day Saudi Arabia. Center of early Islam. City of pilgrimage for Muslims as one of the Five Pillars. Became the direction of Muslim prayer; the direction was originally toward Jerusalem.

MEDINA City in modern-day Saudi Arabia. The "Prophet's City." Where Muhammad fled with the nascent Islamic community from Mecca in the *hijra*, ruling as invited leader among the warring factions.

MEGACHURCH A church (generally modern Evangelical or Pentecostal in form) that has a weekly attendance of over two thousand.

MERIT See *punya*.

MESO-LEVEL Here, denoting societal level.

MESSIAH (MESSIANIC) Hebrew term meaning "anointed" (with oil), signifying Israelite kings, prophets, and those favored by God. In Greek, "Christ." Judaism, Christianity, and Islam adapted the Zoroastrianism apocalyptic savior figure as a messianic motif. See box 3.2 and case study 4A. Used broadly in relation to traditions which envisage a future "savior" figure.

MESTIZA Feminine form of mestizo.

MESTIZO Originally a Spanish term for people of mixed European and Native American ancestry. Used to refer to much of the population in Mexico and Latin America and their culture.

METHODISM Protestant Christian traditions that branched out from Anglicanism in the eighteenth century. Founded by John Wesley.

METHODOLOGICAL AGNOSTICISM Avoiding judgments of truth or falsity. See box 2.4.

METHODOLOGICAL ATHEISM Stance which assumes religious traditions are false in terms of any transcendent claims. May seek to undermine or explain religion away.

METHODOLOGICAL POLYMORPHISM The use of many methods to obtain differing angles on a complex phenomenon. See introduction.

METTA Buddhist term equating closely to "compassion."

MICRO-LEVEL Here, denoting the individual level.

MILLET (SYSTEM) Ottoman system (though only codified as a system from about the eighteenth century) whereby religious/cultural minorities had their own courts for personal law (*millet* is a term for this system, and referring to each group). Equating to the wider Islamic *dhimmi* system. However, some *millets* also gave military service as part of this, contrary to the *dhimmi* system.

MIMESIS Imitation. See chapter 15.

MIMETIC DESIRE Desire for what another has. See chapter 15.

MINARET Tower in a mosque for the prayer call.

MINISTRY OF RITES Chinese medieval department of government in charge of religious affairs. Founded in the Tang Dynasty (ca. 618–907 CE).

MIRACLE An event transcending the laws of nature. See case study 9A.

MIRROR NEURONS Facets of the brain that allow us to perceive emotional states in others and feel them. Found in humans and at least some other animals.

MISHNAH Texts derived from Jewish oral traditions. Known as oral Torah.

MODERNITY Period from about the sixteenth century until today during which modern European thought and systems developed.

MONOLITHIC Single, massive, unchanging.

MONOTHEISM Belief in only one God.

MORAL DISENGAGEMENT Emotionally distancing to be able to cause harm to another. See box 15.9.

MORTIFICATION To subdue one's bodily desires.

MUEZZIN In Islam, person who issues the call for prayer.

MUGHAL (DYNASTY) Islamic dynasty that ruled much of northern South Asia from about the sixteenth to mid-eighteenth century. Afterward, splintered into smaller dynastic traditions. Incorporated into British India mid-nineteenth century. Of Turkic-Mongolian origins.

MULTIDISCIPLINARY Scholarly approach that brings a number of different fields/disciplines/approaches together, but each remains discrete in what it does, potentially providing diverse insights.

MULTIPLE MODERNITIES Theory that modernization happens in different ways in various sociocultural contexts. See box 16.6.

MULTIPLE RELIGIOUS IDENTITIES (BELONGING) (MRI) Identifying with (belonging to) more than one religion. See case study 2B.

MURTI In Hinduism, statue of a deity which becomes a locus for the presence of the deity, and hence *darshan* (worship) can take place through it. Generally, Hindus assert that they do not worship statues, but that it becomes a site in which the presence of the deity is potent/imbued/present. Traditionally, in temples, *murtis* are treated as the living presence of the deity, being washed, offered food, and sent to sleep at night.

MYSTIC(AL) Typically used to imply special forms of religious experience. See box 8.5

MYTH In early sociology, a "primitive" form of science or belief; more technically, a narrative that claims authority. See box 4.3.

NARRATIVE IDENTITY The stories we tell about who we are. See box 6.3.

NASTIKA "Unorthodox schools" in Hindu philosophy, primarily Buddhism and Jainism.

NATION-STATE Modern form of political division. See chapter 18.

NATURAL Disputed term. Used here to denote something seen as having an inherent quality, not a human social construction. See chapter 5.

NATURALIST FEMINISM Also known as third-wave feminism; partly a reaction against both the first and second waves, especially the way they construct the "male" and "female," and their denial of embodiment, which seems to dissolve all difference into sameness. See chapter 10.

NEIDAN Chinese term for "internal alchemy," or forms of Daoist bodily/spiritual self-cultivation. See box 1.11.

NEOCOLONIALISM Forms of domination (economic, cultural, etc.) that occur without direct (military/political) colonization.

NEO-CONFUCIANISM Form of Confucianism (*rujiao*) developing around 1000 CE. Drew
from Buddhism and Daoism.

NEOPLATONISM School of Plato's followers from around the second century BCE to ca.
1200 CE. Termed Neoplatonism, as not following Plato directly, based on a reading of
only certain texts.

NEUROTHEOLOGY Scientific study of the brain, but seeks religious/theological
explanations. See chapter 8.

NEW AGE (MOVEMENT) Late twentieth-century onward religious phenomenon that
asserted personal authority and realization over traditional religion. Associated with
practices such as yoga, meditation, and using crystals. Term denotes belief that we
are entering a new "spiritual" age, often dubbed the "Age of Aquarius." Today, often
superseded by the terms spiritual but not religious (SBNR), "nones," or the rubric
"mind, body, spirit." Denotes various groups and practices.

NEW ATHEISM Contemporary atheist movement, marked by strong polemics. See case
study 8A.

NEW TESTAMENT Christian term for the books it added to its canon beyond the Hebrew
Bible.

NIRVANA In Buddhism, the highest attainment; typically makes one a Buddha. Literally:
"awakened." Archaically: "enlightenment."

NOMINAL BELIEVER/PRACTITIONER Used for members of a religious community who
show relatively minimal attachment to that tradition, perhaps in terms of attendance or
other markers of commitment. Sometimes used theologically to denote "inauthentic,"
such that "true" or "committed" believers/practitioners are distinguished; however,
this is a normative/theological claim which makes presuppositions about what an
"authentic" and "inauthentic" form of that religion is.

NON-DUALISM See *advaita*.

NON-REALISM Claim that we only know the world through linguistic and social
interpretation, and therefore have no direct access (in any way) to it. See box 5.8.

NONES Those identifying with no religion. See box 2.8.

NON-RELIGION Traditions, worldviews, or systems that are not typically classed as
"religious" but intersect with the concept "religion" in various ways (e.g., nones, SBNR,
and also atheisms).

NORMATIVE Perceived standard, or norms, of a society, culture, or religion. Also used,
philosophically, to make claims about what should be the case, as in the phrase a
"normative claim."

OCCIDENT Synonym for the West.

OCCIDENTALISM Prejudice in which the West is stereotyped. See box 7.4.

OLD TESTAMENT Christian term for the Hebrew Bible.

ORDINATION Rite of passage in which a person takes on a religious role (e.g., as a nun,
monk, priest, bishop, etc.).

ORIENT Synonym for the East.

ORIENTALISM Stereotyped and political representations of the East. See box 7.3.

ORIGINAL SIN Developed by Augustine of Hippo based on his misreading of Paul's notion
of "sin" and the Adam and Eve story in Genesis. It implied that humans had an innate

moral failing to inevitably stray against God's will and were therefore rightly under God's judgment. It influenced Catholic and Protestant Christianity, the latter especially through Martin Luther's reading of Paul through Augustine.

ORTHODOX "Correct" beliefs. See also *astika*.

ORTHODOX CHRISTIANITY Churches of Greece, Russia, Ukraine, Asia Minor, and eastern Europe. See themselves as directly following the early church. Generally, saw Catholic Christians as schismatics from Middle Ages until the late twentieth century.

ORTHODOX JUDAISM Nineteenth-century term to denote adherence to what is seen as traditional beliefs and practices of Rabbinic Judaism.

OTHER-THAN-HUMAN-PERSONS Often used of animist beliefs that various nonhuman entities should be regarded with respect as "persons" (e.g., animals, ancestors, stones, the sun).

OTTOMAN (EMPIRE) Turkic tribal dynasty that converted to Islam during its conquests. Claimed the caliphate in 1362. Captured Byzantium (Constantinople/Istanbul) in 1453. Lasted 1299–1924.

OUR LADY OF GUADALUPE Claimed vision of the Virgin Mary in present-day Mexico that unites Catholic devotion with aspects of indigenous religiosity. See case study 3A.

OUT-GROUP Group with which we do not identify. See chapter 6.

PAGAN Originally used by Christians to refer to non-Christians and non-Jews. Today, claimed by traditions which are nature based and/or claiming derivation from pre-Christian religious resources.

PALI (CANON) See Tripitaka.

PANCASILA Literally "five principles," basis of Indonesia's Constitution, which stipulates freedom for six recognized religions (Islam, Confucianism, Buddhism, Hinduism, Protestantism, Catholicism).

PAPA In Buddhism, "demerit" or negative *karma;* the opposite of "merit" (*punya*).

PARITTA Writings in the Tripitaka which contain "magical spells." See case study 3B.

PARTICULARITIES Theological stance asserting the superiority of one's own tradition and the noncomparability of religions.

PATRIARCHAL System wherein males hold power.

PENTECOSTAL Christian tradition that believes the Holy Spirit allows people to "speak in tongues" (glossolalia). Often denotes emotive styles of worship. Developed from Evangelicalism in the early twentieth century in the US, but now global. Fastest growing Christian tradition.

PEOPLE OF THE BOOK See *ahl al-kitab.*

PERFORMANCE Variously: act of presenting something to an audience; to follow, or create, social expectations or roles to establish an identity. See chapter 12.

PERFORMATIVE To not simply do something, but to enact a social norm or challenge one by what one does.

PERFORMATIVE TURN Academic shift from seeing actions as secondary to belief to stressing how they establish belief and norms. See chapter 12.

PERFORMATIVITY Often, intended or unintended aspect of a specific act or ritual. See chapter 12.

PHENOMENOLOGY Methodology to study phenomena. See box 2.3.

PHILOSOPHICAL HERMENEUTICS School of philosophy concerned with human meaning making and interpretation. See boxes 0.2 and 2.6.

PLACE Areas within space to which we attach particular meaning or significance. See chapter 17.

PLURALISM Theological: many religions may be potentially true; social: valuing and embracing diversity. See chapter 13.

POLYTHEISM Systems that assert multiple deities.

POPE From Latin and Greek, literally, "father." Normally signifying the head of Catholic Christianity, the Bishop of Rome. However, there are popes in other Christian traditions.

POPULIST A political ideology aimed at appeasing the masses.

POSITIVISM Theory of knowledge (epistemology) suggesting that we can gain accurate and reliable knowledge of the world. Contrasted with relativism.

POSTCOLONIALISM Theoretical perspectives relating to the effects and aftermath of colonialism. See box 7.5.

POSTMODERNISM A widely defined set of worldviews and styles which in philosophy and the social sciences is characterized by suspicion of grand narratives of explanation associated with modernity/Enlightenment paradigms. See box 2.5.

POST-SECULAR Arguments that (1) religion persists in modern, secular contexts when secularization theory has posited it should have disappeared and must be accounted for with new theory, or (2) with the reemergence of religion after the secular age we have entered a new post-secular age. Arguably, at least some post-secular theory fails to understand the co-creation of both "secular" and "religion" as discursive binaries, positing them as essential and natural aspects of the world as discrete spheres.

POSTSTRUCTURALISM A variety of viewpoints associated with such scholars as Jacques Derrida, Michel Foucault, and Roland Barthes (sometimes also defined as a structuralist) which see the world as primarily socially and linguistically constructed.

POWER Ability to get others to behave, believe, or value things in the way the one exerting power wishes. It may be imposed by such things as force (physical/military), stricture (legal/expertise), custom (tradition/expectation), or society (norms/values). It may be directly coercive or subtle and indirect. It may be personal or collective. It may be perceived as coming from an authority (though authority and power could be distinguished, in that an authority figure or authoritative institution may not be able to exert power) or from within. Politicians, academics, celebrities, gangsters, family, activists, businesses, media, and others may be sources of power, or may lack power in some circumstances. See chapter 5.

PREJUDICE In philosophical hermeneutics, our preknowledge that determines how we know other things. For Hans-Georg Gadamer, not pejorative (see box 2.6). Also refers to systems of negative attitudes and ideas which are held (stereotypes) that result in discrimination (action based on prejudice).

PRIESTCRAFT Pejorative Protestant Christian term to dismiss the ritual activity of Catholic Christians. Extended to polemic against other religions too. Considered archaic.

PRODUCTION OF SPACE After Henri Lefebvre, the way that humans create and imbue the world around us with meaning. See chapter 9.

PROSOCIAL Behavior that promotes a greater societal common good. See chapter 8.

PROSPERITY GOSPEL Modern Christian teaching which says God blesses those favored with wealth. Often entails devotees being encouraged/coerced to make monetary contributions to churches/pastors to receive this favor. Often makes great wealth for the pastors/churches which teach it. No proven data that it works for the devotees/donators. See boxes 3.4 and 16.9.

PROTECTED PEOPLE See *dhimmi*.

PROTESTANT CHRISTIANITY Traditions of Western Christianity that broke away from Catholic Christianity in the sixteenth-century reformations. They stress the Bible and personal faith more than tradition.

PUBLIC SPHERE Realm between the governmental/national and private/family/individual of common civic life.

PUNYA "Merit" from "good actions." Understood as positive *karma* for beneficial reincarnations and/or to obtain material blessings.

PURANAS Hindu devotional texts to specific deities.

PURE LAND School of Mahayana Buddhism that focuses on devotion to Amida Buddha. Largest single tradition. Pure Lands are realms created by particular Buddhas wherein awakening is readily attained and which are accessed by devotion to the specific Buddha who created it. In popular devotion, it is portrayed as a heavenly paradise. See box 14.7.

PURGATORY Posited "intermediate state" between heaven and hell in Catholic Christian thought. A place where those not yet good enough for heaven are purified. Traditionally seen as a place of torment.

QADOSH Hebrew: "set apart." Often translated as "holy" or "sacred"; the latter from the Latin *sacer,* "to sanctify" or "make holy." See box 17.3.

QI In Chinese cosmology, the psychospiritual matter of which everything is composed (see box 1.11). Literally translated as "breath/air," but connotes far more.

QUANZHEN DAOISM Daoist monastic lineage that developed in the twelfth century.

QUEER THEOLOGY School of Christian theology derived from LGBTQI issues, queer theory, and liberation theology.

QIGONG Chinese traditions of slow movement for health and spiritual cultivation.

QURAN The scriptural text of Islam, traditionally held to be God's word directly revealed/dictated to Muhammad.

RABBI Often translated as "teacher" or "Lord." Perhaps better translated as "master," as this signifies accepting the authoritative teaching or words of the speaker.

RABBINIC JUDAISM Judaism as formulated under the teachers (rabbis) in the first and second centuries CE to exist in a situation of exile and without the Temple in Jerusalem.

RACE Postulated category of human differences not founded in science which overlaps with ethnicity. See box 18.6.

RACIALIZATION To ascribe specific qualities to particular "races" as generic features of all members of that "race" or group, generally as a form of prejudice. Also, to ascribe the nature of "race" (as an imagined group) to something.

RADICALIZATION Denotes socialization to violent worldviews. Considered a problematic term. See chapter 15.

RAMA Hindu deity. Incarnation (avatar) of Vishnu and exemplar of "duty" (*dharma*). Some devotees believe that Rama is a historical Indian king, but he cannot credibly be identified with any historical personage or even period.

RAMAYANA Hindu epic which tells the story of Rama.

RASHOMON EFFECT A single event that is described from a myriad of perspectives.

RASTAFARIANISM Afro-centric religious movement prominent in Jamaica, with influences from Christianity and other sources.

REDUCTIONIST(ISM) Analysis that reduces ideas to presumed fundamental basis.

REFLEXIVITY (REFLEXIVE TURN) Awareness of our own preconceptions in analysis and understanding. See box 2.7.

REFORMATIONS (CHRISTIAN) The period and movements in which Protestant Christianities split from Catholic Christianity. "The Reformation" is traditionally used to mean the Protestant reform movement, while "reformations" speaks of this in the context of a wider network of reforming activities, including those in the Catholic tradition. See box 9.3.

REINCARNATION Belief that humans (and other creatures) are reborn many times.

RELATIVISM Belief that there is no single truth (or that we can never know any truth). See chapters 5 and 9.

RELIC Item associated with holy people/saints. May be a body part or associated item. May have some sacred quality; some are believed to grant miracles.

RELIGION An "empty signifier"; areas of culture relating to transcendence; an essentially contested concept that can be usefully but carefully employed in relation to the social reality referenced in point 2.

RELIGIOUS STUDIES The academic and nonconfessional/secular study of religion. Various names exist for the discipline. Arguably implicated in regimes of colonial power and whiteness. See chapters 5, 7, and 18.

RENAISSANCE Period of cultural and intellectual renewal in Europe (roughly 1350 to 1650). See box 4.4.

REVELATION Literally, "to make known." In Christian usage, a message/text/truth from a deity to humanity. Arguably has some utility in non-Christian contexts, but the connotations are often different.

RITE OF PASSAGE Ritual to pass from one life stage to another. See box 12.4.

RITUAL Set of actions often differentiated from everyday routine. See box 12.1.

RITUALIZATION Act of making meaning. See box 12.7.

ROLE Socially determined form; the various external "faces" that you put on (people may call these your "persona"). So, you may "play," or have, the role of a parent, child, rabbi, or layperson, and so on. See box 6.1.

ROMANTICISM (ROMANTIC MOVEMENT) Largely late eighteenth- and nineteenth-century artistic and intellectual movement that rebelled against what was perceived as the overly rational stress of the European Enlightenment. It stressed feeling and intuition.

RUJIAO Literally, tradition(s) (*jiao*) of the scholars (*ru*). Associated with Confucius. Confucianism is considered an inaccurate name, as Confucius was a key synthesizer and textual editor, not a founder. Some contemporary scholars argue for "Ruism."

SABIANISM A religion mentioned in the Quran but unidentified by scholars. Classed as *ahl al-kitab* (People of the Book).

SACRALIZATION A return to religion, or reversal of secularization. See chapter 16.

SACRED That which is revered or most significant within society or particular subgroups in a society. See box 18.7.

SACRIFICE An act of giving something (to a deity) or an act of transformation. See chapter 12.

SADHU Hindu holy man or ascetic.

SALAFISM (SALAFI) Modern form of Islamic traditionalism. Salafis seek to follow the example of Muhammad and his earliest followers.

SALAT Islamic prayer. One of Islam's Five Pillars. See box 9.6.

SALIENCE (SALIENT BEHAVIOR) In social identity theory, the likelihood of particular behaviors being invoked in any given situation. See chapter 6.

SALVATION (SAVIOR/SALVIFIC) In Christianity, release from sin.

SAMKHYA Indian philosophical tradition, sometimes seen as materialist.

SAMSARA In Hindu and Buddhist thought, cycle of birth, death, and reincarnation.

SANATANA DHARMA Sanskrit: roughly, "eternal teaching." Many Hindus claim it as an indigenous term for Hinduism, but primarily a nineteenth-century term to match Hinduism.

SANT (TRADITION) North Indian devotional (bhakti) tradition. From about the fifteenth to sixteenth century. Drew from, primarily, Hindu bhakti and Sufi Muslim elements. The background of Sikhism.

SAPIR-WHORF THESIS Theory that language determines all aspects of human understanding.

SATI Indian practice of widows self-immolating on their husband's funeral pyre. See chapters 7 and 10.

SAVAGES Derogatory term for those not considered civilized.

SCAPEGOAT Innocent sacrificial victim symbolically killed. See box 15.2.

SCIENCE Denotes rational and systematic study of the natural world. Often discursively contrasted with religion and magic. See boxes 9.4 and 12.2.

SCRIPTURE Latin for "the writings"; used for the Christian Bible. Often problematically used for the "sacred" texts of many traditions. See box 1.3 and chapter 11.

SECOND TEMPLE JUDAISM Judaism of ca. 500 BCE to first century CE. Name signifies use of the second temple; the first was destroyed by the Persians (sixth century BCE), and the second by the Romans (70 CE).

SECULAR Nonreligious spheres of life. See chapter 16.

SECULAR DIALOGUE A type of interreligious dialogue based on action that aims at social goals such as social activism or ethical concerns.

SECULARISM Ideological stance concerning secularization. See chapter 16.

SECULARIZATION A process or movement toward being secular. See chapter 16.

SELF Your sense of who you are. See box 6.1.

SELF-CULTIVATION (PRACTICES/TECHNIQUES) Forms of Chinese bodily and spiritual purification. See box 1.11.

SEMIOLOGY/SEMIOTICS The study of symbol systems. See box 9.11.

SENTIENT BEINGS In Buddhism, term for animals, cosmologically posited creatures such as beings in hell and deities, and humans as fellow creatures subject to successive reincarnation (samsara). Hence should not be willfully harmed.

SEX Biological issue of embodiment as, typically, male or female. See box 10.6.

SHAIVITE Follower of Hindu deity Shiva.

SHAIVISM Traditions following Shiva in Hinduism.

SHAKTA Follower of the Hindu Goddess.

SHAKTI In Hinduism, divine power. Feminine and relates to the Goddess.

SHAKTISM Traditions of the Goddess in Hinduism.

SHAMANISM (SHAMAN) Narrowly, the religious practices of indigenous Siberian tribes, especially the Tungu. Broadly, traditions in which a skilled practitioner (shaman) has otherworldly/out-of-body journeys to transcendent/spiritual realms and/or interactions with spirits, for such purposes as healing, wisdom, community guidance, and protection from supernatural attacks. In broad usage, encompasses traditions from North America, Siberia, China, and beyond.

SHARIAH Islamic religio-juridical traditions. Not a law code; more a set of principles and legal opinions (*fatwas*). There are four mainstream Sunni Islamic schools of interpretation.

SHIA ISLAM Second largest tradition within Islam. Sees leadership as only coming from the bloodline of Muhammad via Ali. The name signifies "the partisans of Ali." Differences with Sunnis are more political than theological.

SHIFTING SIGNIFIER Typically used to mean a term with no fixed meaning, where words are tied to a chain of meanings, implicated in regimes of power to exclude, for example, people of certain races or gender. See empty signifier.

SHIFTING THIRD Another party/agent in a relationship between two groups that affects their relationship. See box 13.8.

SHIVA With Vishnu and the Goddess, one of the three most revered Hindu deities. Shiva is understood as the great ascetic.

SHMRITI See *shruti* and *shmriti*.

SHRAMANA Buddhist novice monk.

SHRI Hindu Goddess and consort of Vishnu.

SHRI VAISHNAVISM Vaishnavite tradition of southern India, in which the major deities are Shri and Vishnu as co-consorts/deity.

SHRUTI AND *SHMRITI* Sanskrit, literally: "that which was heard" and "that which was passed down." Hindu terms, the former generally signifying the Vedas, that is, "revelation." However, in any specific Hindu tradition more texts are typically counted, or regarded, as *shruti*, especially the epics and puranas. *Shmriti*, while believed to be "revelation," is distinguished because it was "passed down" before being written, and so is not considered direct revelation.

SIKHISM Religious tradition founded by Guru Nanak in sixteenth-century northern India. Understands Hinduism and Islam as worshipping the same deity. Accepts holy figures and texts from each tradition. Developed from the Sant tradition.

SIN From Greek, *hamartia:* "missing the mark." Typically refers to human moral wrongdoing. After Augustine of Hippo, an innate propensity to wrongdoing, termed "original sin," which marks us indelibly sinful. Sins were sometimes delineated into types (e.g. "pride," "lust," "avarice," etc., or as more or less heinous). Christian conceptions depart from biblical notions. In Paul's letters, *hamartia* was "missing the mark" (as in archery), that is, more a specific failure to perfection/duty than an innate moral defect. In Hebrew, related terms often signify purity or offense rather than moral defect.

SIN OFFERING A form of sacrifice in Israelite tradition that offers an "innocent" victim. See box 15.2 and atonement.

SKANDHAS In Buddhism, five factors (or "heaps"/"aggregates") that constitute a sentient being's mental and physical existence: form/body, sensations/feelings, perceptions, mental formation, and consciousness/awareness.

SOCIAL CONSTRUCTIONISM Theory that understands knowledge as socially and linguistically constructed (see chapter 5).

SOCIAL CONTRACT Rules, norms, and regulations which bind people together in society. See box 18.2.

SOCIAL FUNCTIONALISM Understanding of society or social features as fulfilling certain functions.

SOCIAL IDENTITY THEORY (SIT) Theory of individual and group identity, with a focus on the importance of the group. See chapters 6 and 13.

SOCIAL IMAGINARY Collective imagination, or worldview, of a society concerning values and norms. Not seen coherently or clearly laid; more of an ethos and background coloring than a set of distinct principles.

SOCIALIZATION Processes in which social actors influence/form an individual's worldview.

SOCIAL JUSTICE WARRIOR (SJW) Term often pejoratively employed to dismiss those concerned with social justice, personal and cultural dignity, and human rights. Often conflated by extreme right-wing pundits with cultural Marxism and other bogeymen of their imagining.

SOCIAL REALITY A human social construction, but one with real consequences. See box 1.9.

SPACE The extension of the world that appears before us. See chapter 17.

SPACES (PLACES) OF REPRESENTATION After Henri Lefebvre, the world as presented to us by hegemonic forces. See chapter 17.

SPATIAL PRACTICE The way we live in the world around us through habits or deliberate practices. See chapter 17.

SPEECH ACT (THEORY) Looks at language as "doing" something, instead of simply saying or telling. See chapter 12.

SPIRITUAL Denotes something that is seen as relating to a "religious" or "transcendent" realm. What gets to count as "spiritual" is culturally and contextually dependent. A problematic term, and so should be used with caution, but sometimes a convenient placeholder.

SPIRITUAL BUT NOT RELIGIOUS (SBNR) People who do not identify with any religion but still identify as spiritual. See box 2.8.

SPIRITUALITY In popular usage, "inner" aspects of religiosity, contrasted with religion. See box 5.6. Sometimes used, here, in a generic sense for many forms of the practice of religiosity. A problematic term, and so should be used with caution, but sometimes a convenient placeholder.

STANDARD MODEL (SM) Key working hypotheses in the cognitive science of religion. See box 8.2.

STANDPOINT EPISTEMOLOGY Recognition that perspective and background affect our knowledge and understanding.

STRATEGIC RELIGIOUS PARTICIPATION Engaging with religious traditions for specific purposes, especially in the Chinese cultural world. See box 13.1.

SUBALTERN Those who are not elites; those whose voices are silenced, ignored, not heard, or considered irrelevant. See box 7.6.

SUBLIME In European Romanticism, a quality of landscapes that is thrilling, majestic, and unnerving; contrasted with the beautiful.

SUFFERING See *dukkha*.

SUFFRAGETTE MOVEMENTS Movements for women to vote in public elections.

SUFISM Traditional Islamic ascetic and devotional practices, sometimes seeking direct experiences of God. Also, traditional devotional and social fraternities.

SUI GENERIS Latin: "of its own kind." See box 1.4.

SUNNAH In Islam, traditions of Muhammad encompassing his sayings (*hadith*) and behavior.

SUNNI (ISLAM) Largest school of Islam, comprising around 80 percent of all Muslims.

SUPERSESSIONISM Stance that one religion supersedes/fulfills/replaces another (see chapter 13).

SUPERSTITION Used pejoratively to refer to what are considered supernatural beliefs. See boxes 7.8, 9.4, and 12.2.

SUPREME ULTIMATE See *taiji*.

SYNCHRONIC (ANALYSIS) Layers of meaning observed at one time/point. See diachronic. See chapter 17.

SYNCRETISM Blending of two or more religious systems into a new one. See chapter 3.

TABOO Something that is prohibited by social or cultural customs. See box 12.3.

TAI CHI (CHUAN) (ALSO *TAIJIQUAN*) Chinese form of martial art and/or bodily health regime, related to self-cultivation.

TAIJI Chinese, literally "supreme ultimate." Referring to the absolute principle (*li*) of some Neo-Confucian and Daoist cosmological thought.

TAMIL TIGERS Sri Lankan Tamil ethnic military group founded in 1976. Variously termed terrorists or freedom fighters. Fought for a separate Tamil state in Sri Lanka in a civil war that lasted, on and off, from 1983 to 2009.

TANAKH Hebrew term for the Hebrew Bible, denoting the Torah (first five books), historical books, and books of prophets. Arranged differently from the Christian Old Testament.

TANTRA Hindu ritual texts that form basis for temple worship, first written in about the sixth to eighth century CE. Also, roughly, a philosophy in both Buddhism and Hinduism which posits that conventional notions of purity and impurity must be overcome. Very few tantric traditions literally partake in violation of conventions.

TERRORISM The use of violence to pursue political goals by instilling terror in civilian populations. See chapter 15.

THEOLOGY Greek: "God" (*theos*) plus "words/talk/language" (*logos*). Used in relation to debates about deity and transcendence in Christianity. Sometimes used, broadly, to denote related disputes in other traditions. An inadequate term as other traditions do not, typically, do "theology" in a Christian sense. Also, may refer to the discipline of the study of religion, traditionally Christianity, in universities. It may sometimes take a confessional form (following the teachings of a particular form of Christianity), or as academic theology, the study of those traditions. The distinction of academic and confessional theology is often porous or transgressed. Academic theology overlaps, also, with religious studies.

THERAVADA BUDDHISM Traditions of Sri Lanka, Myanmar, and Thailand. Sees itself as the original form of Buddhism, in contrast to Mahayana Buddhism. Relies on the Tripitaka.

THREE GEMS/REFUGES See *triratna*.

THROWN(NESS) We have been placed in a certain context in which we must exist. See box 9.2.

TIAN Chinese: "heaven/sky." In Confucian/Chinese thought, a transcendent principle. Often impersonal, but a personal deity in ancient China.

TIANMING Chinese: "Mandate of Heaven." Theory that the will of *tian* decrees the current ruler should govern. *Tianming* could also be withdrawn, traditionally indicated by natural disasters such as floods, famines, and so on. Mencius argued that overthrowing an emperor who had lost the *tianming* was legitimate, but Confucian tradition often justified suppression of any dissent via this concept.

TONANTZIN Aztec goddess who was a virgin mother of gods, and on whose sacred hill it is believed that Our Lady of Guadalupe appeared in a vision.

TRADITION Literally, "that which is passed on." Refers to the passing of practices, beliefs, and lineages over time.

TRADITIONALISM Accepting tradition rather than adaptation to modernity. See chapter 15.

TRANSCENDENT (TRANSCENDENCE) Here, denoting that which signifies concepts/beings/spheres that go beyond the phenomenal/physical world. Traditions which relate to this connote what are commonly termed "religions." Not clearly demarcated from Marxism, capitalism, or other systems which posit nonphysical realities. See boxes 1.10 and 8.3.

TRANSGENDER A person whose birth sex does not correspond with their gender identity. See chapter 10.

TRANSITORINESS See *dukkha*.

TRIKAYA Literally, "three bodies." In Mahayana Buddhism, the manifestation of Buddhas as supreme body (unembodied Buddha-nature), celestial body (heavenly manifestation), and transformation body (human being).

TRIMURTI Literally, "three forms." In Hinduism, belief that Brahma is creator of the universe, Shiva its destroyer, and Vishnu its preserver. Very few Hindus see these as a central "trinity" of deities, but they can represent manifestations of one deity in three forms.

TRINITY In Christian theology, the teaching that God is Father, Son, and Holy Spirit. For Christians, understood as monotheism.

TRIPITAKA Literally, "three baskets." The Buddhist canon of sermons of the Buddha (Sutra), philosophy (Abhidharma), and monastic regulation (Vinaya). Sometimes known as the Pali canon after the language it was first written in.

TRIRATNA Literally, "three gems," but often "three refuges." In Buddhism, the invocation of the Buddha, his teachings (*dharma*), and the community of monks and nuns (*sangha*). Used in initiations to become a Buddhist and monastic ordination, with a threefold repetition in which the aspirant states, "I take refuge in . . ."

TRUTH Big *T* "Truth" concerns whether something is really correct in an absolute sense. Small *t* "truth" concerns whether something is meaningfully correct within the bounds of potential human knowledge.

TUNGU Siberian tribe.

TUTELARY SPIRIT Spirits or deities who are guardians/patrons of a particular location, clan, profession, and so on.

ULAMA Islamic religio-juridical scholars, or jurists.

UNIVERSALIZATION Here, religion/spirituality interlaced with day-to-day activities and seen as common practices across religions. See chapter 16.

UPANISHAD Philosophical Hindu texts, included in the Vedas and written ca. 800–400 BCE.

VAISHNAVA Follower of the Hindu deity Vishnu.

VAISHNAVISM Traditions of Vishnu in Hinduism.

VEDA Sanskrit texts often seen as foundational for Hinduism. There are four principle Vedas, each with various sections. Written ca. 1500–400 BCE.

VEDANTA Literally, "the end of the Vedas." Schools of Hindu philosophy.

VERSTEHEN German, meaning "understanding or reliving another's experience." See chapter 2.

VINAYA Buddhist monastic regulations; part of the Tripitaka.

VIRGIN MARY Jesus's mother posited as mother and virgin; often related to devotion in Christian traditions.

VISHNU With Shiva and the Goddess, one of the three most revered Hindu deities. Vishnu is the single most revered deity, often as one his of incarnations (avatars), especially Krishna or Rama.

VISHWA HINDU PARISHAD (VHP) Activist Hindu nationalist group, linked to the Bharatiya Janata Party. Associated with numerous alleged violent attacks on Muslims and other minorities in India.

WABI Principle in Japanese aesthetics stressing simplicity and rusticity, often joined with the concept of *sabi,* denoting transitoriness, and linked with Zen in what is termed *wabi-sabi* aesthetics. See case study 12B.

WAHHABISM A form of Salafism (the term they would self-identify by) stemming from Mohammad Ibn Abd-al-Wahhab. Today, the official form of Islam in Saudi Arabia.

WAILING WALL (WESTERN WALL) Last standing remnant of the second Jerusalem Temple. It was the base wall of the mount on which the temple was built.

WAY See *dao.*

WHITENESS Describes the experiences and norms associated in contemporary society with being perceived as being white. See chapter 7.

WHITE SAVIOR Notion that non-white/non-Westerners are ignorant/oppressed without white/Western "savior" figures to free them. See chapter 7.

WOMANIST Black feminist perspectives.

WORLD RELIGIONS PARADIGM (WRP) Way of thinking about and classifying religions employing mainly modern, Western, Protestant Christian conceptions. See chapter 1 and box 2.1.

WORLD WAR II (WWII) Global conflict that lasted from 1939 to 1945 (World War I lasted from 1914 to 1918, officially 1914 to 1919). Often differently dated by Americans as they joined both wars late. These wars, which devastated Europe, marked the move from European, particularly British, to American global hegemony.

XHOSA Southern African indigenous tribe.

XIEJIAO Chinese, meaning "erroneous/heterodox tradition." Sometimes officially translated as "evil cult." See box 1.5.

YIN-YANG (THEORY) Chinese cosmological theory positing the coexistence of two related polarities: "dark" yin and "light" yang. In differing systems, sometimes yin or yang is more powerful, but they are predominantly seen as equal and replacing each other in cycles. Yin is associated with the feminine and earth, yang with the masculine and heaven/sky (*tian*). Often associated with Daoism, but found across many Chinese schools of thought.

YOGA (YOGA) One of six orthodox (*astika*) schools of Hindu philosophy. Today, often known as a form of bodily health practice which derives from various South Asian traditions of spiritual discipline, but codified in various ways as modern yoga postural practices.

ZAKAT Arabic: "almsgiving." In Islam, a tithe from Muslims to a community coffer which is intended to support the poor and destitute. One of the Five Pillars of Islam.

ZAZEN Japanese: "seated meditation." See case study 11B.

ZEN Japanese: "meditation" (Chinese: Ch'an). School of Mahayana Buddhism that focuses on meditation.

ZHUANGZI Philosophical book attributed to a Chinese thinker of the same name from the fifth century BCE. Parts of the book are generally seen as going back to that date, but late sections are certainly later, and it was finalized probably in the early centuries CE when it became associated with a mythical Daoist school of philosophy.

ZOROASTRIANISM Religion founded by Zoroaster. Possibly the first monotheistic tradition. Later accepted a dualist system in which the good deity was matched by an (almost) equally strong evil deity. Associated with Persia.

WHO'S WHO

Rather than disrupt the flow of the book by introducing people in the text, brief biographies are given here. This list does not include every thinker cited, but key theorists and some lesser known or up-and-coming thinkers are highlighted. It also includes religious leaders and a number of historical and contemporary figures of interest. Those generally seen as legendary (see box 4.3) or who are primarily posited as deity figures, appear in the glossary; some appear in both lists depending on their differing roles. Some of the country designations are anachronistic but are used to give a sense of where figures came from. The term "influential" is used for modern and contemporary scholars of religion who are often seen as being widely cited and known for their work beyond their immediate field of expertise. Terms such as "important" or "foundational" are sometimes used of historical figures, but other significant figures are only briefly noted if generally widely known.

ABHISHTIKANANDA See Henri Le Saux.

ABRAHAM Mythical patriarch for Jews, Christians, and Muslims. See glossary.

ASMA AFSARUDDIN American scholar of Islam.

GIORGIO AGAMBEN Italian philosopher. Known for his *Homo Sacer* project.

(ONWU) BIKO AGOZINO African American scholar of law and decolonization.

SYED FARID ALATAS Singaporean sociologist and postcolonial theorist.

SYED HUSSEIN ALATAS (1928–2007) Malaysian sociologist who theorized the "captive mind."

AL-BIRUNI (973–1048) Persian Muslim scholar and explorer.

ABU HAMID AL-GHAZALI (CA. 1056–1111) Arabic philosopher and jurist. Generally
   regarded as the most important Sunni thinker. He was critical of some speculative

Islamic philosophers and is often seen as curtailing the influence of Greek philosophy in later Islamic thought. Also, a Sufi.

THOMAS AQUINAS (1225–1274) Italian Catholic Christian saint. Posthumously became the most important thinker of that tradition, but considered suspect during his life.

AYAAN HIRSI ALI Somali-Dutch-American activist and feminist anti-Islamic populist writer.

SAMIR AMIN (1931–2018) Egyptian-French economist and political scientist.

BENEDICT ANDERSON (1936–2015) British and American political scientist and historian. Known for his notion of imagined communities.

GLORIA EVANGELINA ANZALDÚA (1942–2004) Mexican American cultural theorist who developed the concept of the colonial wound.

SCOTT APPLEBY American scholar of religious violence. Best known for *The Ambivalence of the Sacred*.

ARISTOTLE (384–322 BCE) Athenian philosopher who is foundational for modern philosophy. A student of Plato.

TALAL ASAD American cultural anthropologist, born in Saudi Arabia and educated in the UK. A postcolonial scholar.

ASHOKA (CA. 304–232 BCE) South Asian king who united most of modern India in his Mauryan Dynasty empire. Often believed to have become a Buddhist, and seen by many as the model *chakravartin*, or Buddhist monarch.

MUSTAFA KEMAL ATATURK (1881–1938) Turkish "father of the nation" and secularist politician. Key in the transition from Turkey as center of the Ottoman Dynasty into a modern secular nation-state.

AUGUSTINE (OF HIPPO) (CA. 354–430) Important North African Christian theologian and saint. Known for his theory of original sin.

J. L. AUSTIN (1911–1960) British linguistic philosopher. Helped develop performance theory.

FRANCIS BACON (1561–1621) British scientist credited with the Baconian method as the basis of modern scientific method.

ROGER BACON (1214–1292) A British Franciscan friar who advanced science by emphasis on empirical observation. He was the first Westerner to accurately describe how to make gunpowder.

JUSTIN BARRETT American experimental psychologist. Known for his work in the cognitive science of religion.

TESSA BARTHOLOMEUSZ (1958–2001) Sri Lankan scholar of religion, gender, and identity.

LORI BEAMAN Canadian scholar of religious diversity and social change.

SIMONE DE BEAUVOIR (1908–1986) French existential philosopher, known for *The Second Sex*.

CATHERINE BELL (1953–2008) American religious studies scholar, noted for her work on ritual.

ROBERT BELLAH (1927–2013) American sociologist renowned for his notion of civil religion.

JEREMY BENTHAM (1748–1832) British philosopher and political theorist.

PETER BERGER British sociologist renowned for his work on the secularization theory and social constructionism.

BERNARD OF CLAIRVAUX (CA. 1090–1153) French Catholic Christian saint, given the title the "Doctor of Love" for his "love mysticism" (speaking of the soul's longing for God as being like a lover). Significant propagandist for the crusades.

HOMI BHABHA Indian Parsi (Zoroastrian) postcolonial scholar.

RAJEEV BHARGAVA Indian political scientist and scholar of secularism.

KUM-KUM BHAVANI American sociologist and feminist scholar.

BILAL IBN RABAH (CA. 580–640) Abyssinian Muslim *muezzin* noted for his loud and melodious voice. Often held to be an early Black African Muslim freed from slavery.

BODHIDHARMA (TRADITIONALLY 483–540 CE) Central Asian semi-legendary Zen patriarch. Seen as the founder of Zen (Chan) Buddhism in China.

DAVID BOHM (1917–1992) British physicist and theorist of dialogue.

PIERRE BOURDIEU (1930–2002) French sociologist, anthropologist, and philosopher, particularly known for his concept of habitus.

MARCUS BORG American biblical and historical Jesus scholar.

PASCAL BOYER French American cognitive anthropologist.

PATRICE BRODEUR Canadian scholar of Islam and interreligious studies.

MARTIN BUBER (1878–1965) Austrian-Israeli Jewish philosopher, known for *I and Thou*.

BUDDHA (CA. SIXTH CENTURY BCE) Nepalese, conventionally named Siddhartha Gautama. Founder of Buddhism. Buddha is a title meaning "awakened one." While the figure known as the Buddha almost certainly existed, little if anything can be known with certainty about his life or teachings.

JUDITH BUTLER American scholar. Key thinker in gender theory. Described gender as performative.

JOHN CALVIN (1509–1604) Swiss Protestant leader. Inspired the Calvinist, or Presbyterian, tradition.

MARÍA DEL SOCORRO CASTAÑENDA-LILES Spanish American scholar of religion.

MICHEL DE CERTEAU (1925–1986) French Jesuit philosopher and sociologist.

PARTHA CHATTERJEE Indian postcolonial historian. Theorized colonial difference.

CHEN KUAN-HSING Taiwanese scholar of cultural studies.

DAVID CHIDESTER South African scholar of religion.

CICERO (106–43 BCE) Roman statesman and scholar.

PATRICIA HILL COLLINS American scholar, with interests in race, class, and gender.

AUGUSTE COMTE (1798–1857) French sociologist. Important in theorizing the secularization thesis.

CONFUCIUS (TRADITIONALLY 551–479 BCE) (Kongzi) Chinese philosopher. Synthesizer of the *ru* (scholar's) tradition (i.e., Confucianism).

CONSTANTINE (CA. 272–337) Serbian-born Roman emperor. Issued the Edict of Toleration (313) legalizing Christianity in the Roman Empire. Often claimed as a Christian convert, but possibly utilized Christianity for political advantage while remaining an adherent of his patron Apollo.

JAYEEL SERRANO CORNELIO Filipino sociologist of religion.

KIMBERLÉ CRENSHAW American scholar of law and critical race theory. Noted for the concept of intersectionality.

HAMID DABASHI Iranian scholar.

MARY DALY (1928–2010) American Christian feminist theologian, later a radical lesbian feminist. Famously stated that "if God is male, then the male is God."

SUSAN DARLINGTON American anthropologist.

GRACE DAVIE British sociologist of religion. Widely known for her "believing without belonging" thesis.

KENNETH DEAN British scholar of Daoism.

FRANÇOISE D'EAUBONNE (1920–2005) French feminist. Introduced the term "ecofeminism."

JACQUES DERRIDA (1930–2004) French Algerian Jewish philosopher and linguist. Key figure associated with deconstruction.

RENÉ DESCARTES (1596–1650) French philosopher. Credited with Cartesian dualism. Famous for his phrase "*Cogito, ergo sum*" ("I think, therefore I am").

ANAGARIKA DHAMMAPALA (1864–1933) Sri Lankan Buddhist monk. Represented Theravada Buddhism at the World's Parliament of Religions in 1893. Founded the Mahabodhi Society at Bodh Gaya. Theorized Sri Lankan nationalism. Was exiled by the British.

SOULEYMANE BACHIR DIAGNE Senegalese philosopher. Known for work on logic, epistemology, and Islamic and African philosophies.

WENDY DONIGER American scholar of Hinduism.

MARY DOUGLAS (1921–2007) British anthropologist. Known for *Purity and Danger*.

W. E. B. DUBOIS (1868–1963) African American sociologist of race. Black rights activist.

JACQUES DUPUIS (1923–2004) Austrian Catholic Christian Jesuit theologian.

ÉMILE DURKHEIM (1858–1917) French sociologist. A founding father of sociology.

DIANA ECK Influential American professor of religion. Founded the Pluralism Project at Harvard University.

MIRCEA ELIADE (1907–1986) Romanian historian of religion. Maybe the most influential twentieth-century scholar of religion. Theories are suspect today for bringing theological categories into comparative religion.

FRANTZ FANON (1925–1961) Algerian decolonial thinker. Perhaps best known for *The Wretched of the Earth*. Seen as foundational both for decolonial theory and anti-colonial political activism. Whether he advocated violence as essential in fighting colonial rule is debated, as the first chapter of *The Wretched* suggests it but the final chapter seems to oppose it.

JOHN NICOL FARQUHAR (1861–1929) British Protestant Christian missionary to India. Became the first professor of comparative religion at Manchester University, UK.

DARÍO FERNÁNDEZ-MORERA American scholar of Spanish literature.

ELISABETH SCHÜSSLER FIORENZA American Christian feminist theologian and biblical scholar.

TIMOTHY FITZGERALD British scholar of critical religion.

JEANNINE HILL FLETCHER American Christian feminist theologian.

GAVIN FLOOD British scholar of religion. Focuses on comparative religion and Hindu tantra.

E. M. FORSTER (1879–1970) English novelist. Famous for books on colonial India (e.g., *A Passage to India*), English social and sexuality mores (e.g., *A Room with a View*), and homosexuality in Edwardian Britain (e.g., *Maurice*). His work offered a social critique but reflected many prejudices of his time.

MICHEL FOUCAULT (1926–1984) French philosopher and public intellectual. Wrote landmark books in several areas critiquing established social and intellectual norms. His work on the association of knowledge and power, sexuality, and the genealogy of knowledge has been widely cited.

JAMES G. FRAZER (1854–1941) British folklorist, famous for *The Golden Bough*.

PAULO FREIRE (1921–97) Brazilian educator and philosopher. Famous for *The Pedagogy of the Oppressed*.

SIGMUND FREUD (1856–1939) Austrian psychoanalyst. Argued that religion is a form of neurosis.

CASPAR DAVID FRIEDRICH (1774–1840) German Romantic landscape painter.

AGUSTIN FUENTES American primatologist and anthropologist.

HANS-GEORG GADAMER (1900–2002) German philosopher. Seen as the founder of philosophical hermeneutics.

JOHN LEWIS GADDIS American military historian.

MOHANDAS K. GANDHI (1869–1948) Indian lawyer and political activist. Known for his nonviolent resistance to British rule. Popularly known as Mahatma ("great soul").

ARMIN GEERTZ Danish scholar of religion and anthropologist.

CLIFFORD GEERTZ (1926–2006) American anthropologist.

ARNOLD VAN GENNEP (1873–1957) French ethnographer and folklorist.

RENÉ GIRARD (1923–2015) French sociologist. Known for work on ritual, mimetic theory, and the scapegoat.

ERVING GOFFMAN (1922–1982) Canadian American sociologist and social psychologist.

ANTONIO GRAMSCI (1890–1932) Italian Marxist theorist. Known for his concepts of the subaltern and hegemony.

BEDE GRIFFITHS (1906–1993) British Catholic Christian monk. Lived in India as a Hindu *sadhu*/holy man.

HUGO GROTIUS (1583–1645) Dutch Christian humanist and legal scholar.

RANAJIT GUHA Indian postcolonial theorist. Founder of the Subaltern Studies Collective.

JÜRGEN HABERMAS German political theorist and philosopher. Theorized the concept of public space and known for his work on secularism, among other things.

ANNA HALAFOFF Australian sociologist and scholar of interreligious studies.

STUART HALL (1932–2014) Jamaican-born British sociologist, cultural theorist, and political activist. A cofounder of the Birmingham School of Cultural Studies.

THICH NHAT HANH Vietnamese Zen Buddhist monk. Advocated for civil rights and protested the Vietnam War. Afterward, spent most of his life in exile. Lives and teaches in France.

SAM HARRIS American popular author and public critic of Islam. A New Atheist.

GRAHAM HARVEY British scholar of religion. Focuses on Indigenous studies.

SALLY HASLANGER American philosopher. Leading scholar of social constructionism.

PAUL HEDGES British scholar of religion, interreligious studies, and theology. Author of this book. Currently works in Singapore.

GEORG WILHELM FRIEDRICH HEGEL (1710–1831) German philosopher. His philosophy exemplifies a Euro-centric colonial and racist ideology.

ABRAHAM JOSHUA HESCHEL (1907–1972) American rabbi, Jewish leader, and scholar. Also, a civil rights activist who marched alongside Martin Luther King Jr.

CARTER HEYWARD American theologian and activist. A founder of queer theology.

JOHN HICK (1922–2012) British scholar. Arguably, the most important twentieth-century philosopher of religion. Renowned for theorizing religious pluralism.

HILDEGARD OF BINGEN (1098–1179) German Christian theologian, composer, and mystic visionary.

CHRISTOPHER HITCHENS (1949–2011) British journalist. A New Atheist.

THOMAS HOBBES (1588–1679) British philosopher and political theorist. Early Enlightenment thinker.

BELL HOOKS Black American feminist. She refuses to capitalize her name, arguing it resists patriarchal masculine systems that focus on individuals, thus making her simply one among many (women) working on such issues.

DAVID HUME (1711–1776) Scottish philosopher. Enlightenment thinker. Renowned for his work on miracles, and for probably being an early modern atheist.

LUCE IRIGARAY French feminist scholar.

WILLIAM JAMES (1842–1910) American psychologist. Renowned for his work on religious experience, among other areas.

THOMAS JEFFERSON (1743–1826) American politician. Second president of the US and deist.

JEPPE SINDING JENSEN Danish scholar of religion. Focuses on linguistics and psychology.

JEROME (CA. 342–419) Eastern European Christian saint. Famous as a translator of the Bible into Latin. Lived and worked in Bethlehem.

JESUS (CA. 4 BCE–30 CE) Galilean Jewish rabbi, crucified as a traitor to Rome. Seen as the Messiah by the early Jesus movement and by many later Christians as God. Little, if anything, can be known about his life and teachings. Despite some "mythicist" claims, he almost certainly existed. See box 4.9.

MARK JUERGENSMEYER American scholar of religious violence.

KANGXI (1654–1722) Chinese emperor of the Qing Dynasty.

IMMANUEL KANT (1724–1804) Prussian philosopher. Work is seen as a landmark in modern philosophy, with philosophy often understood as being written, or studied, pre-Kant and post-Kant. Key Enlightenment thinker.

KAPILA (SIXTH TO SEVENTH CENTURY BCE) Indian Hindu thinker, or possibly a number of thinkers, semi-legendary. Seen as "atheist" founder of Samkhya philosophy.

ERNST KÄSEMANN (1906–1998) German biblical scholar and Lutheran theologian.

KHADIJAH (CA. 555–619) Arabian first wife of Muhammed. A business owner and successful trader who was initially Muhammed's employer. Seen as the first believer in Muhammed's revelations.

IBN KHALDUN (1332–1406) Arabian historian. Arguably, first scholar of historiography and sociology.

MARTIN LUTHER KING JR. (1929–1968) American civil rights activist.

RICHARD KING British scholar of religion. Known for *Orientalism and Religion*.

URSULA KING British scholar of religion, feminist scholar, and theologian.

RUDYARD KIPLING (1865–1936) British journalist and writer. Known for *The Jungle Book*. His work often reflects colonial and racist attitudes.

PATTANA KITIARSA Thai scholar of anthropology and Buddhist studies.

KIM KNOTT British scholar of religion.

LILY KONG Singaporean geographer of religion.

HANS KÜNG Swiss Catholic Christian theologian. Known for his Global Ethic.

ERNESTO LACLAU (1935–2014) Argentine political theorist. A founder of post-Marxist political theory.

LACTANTIUS (CA. 250–325 CE) North African Christian apologist.

OSAMA BIN LADEN (1957–2011) Saudi Arabian militant and leader of Al-Qaeda. Organized the 9/11 attack on the Twin Towers in New York.

LAOZI (UNKNOWN) Mythical Chinese founder of Daoism whose biography is drawn from a probable historical figure mixed with legend. However, no Daoist tradition dates to the time any such historical figure lived. See box 4.12.

LOIS LEE British scholar of religion. Specializes in non-religion.

HENRI LEFEBVRE (1901–1991) French philosopher and sociologist. Theorized the production of space.

ODDBJØRN LEIRVIK Norwegian scholar of interreligious studies with a focus on Muslim-Christian dialogue.

EMMANUEL LEVINAS (1906–1995) French philosopher of Lithuanian Jewish ancestry.

CLAUDE LÉVI-STRAUSS (1908–2009) French anthropologist.

LUCIEN LÉVY-BRUHL (1857–1939) French philosopher and anthropologist. Helped develop structuralism.

C. S. LEWIS (1898–1963) British linguist. Famous for his Narnia novels and writings on Christianity.

BRUCE LINCOLN Influential American historian of religion. Author of "Theses on Method."

JOSEPH CHINYONG LIOW Singaporean scholar of international relations, including religious conflict in Southeast Asia.

VINCENT LLOYD American scholar of religion and Black theology.

JOHN LOCKE (1632–1704) British philosopher and political theorist. Early Enlightenment thinker.

AUDRE LORDE (1934–1992) African American feminist and civil rights activist.

LISA LOWE Asian American interdisciplinary scholar. Works on colonialism, race, capitalism, and immigration.

MARTIN LUTHER (1748–1826) German reformer. Reluctantly helped lead the Protestant Reformation. Foundational for Lutheran Protestant Christianity.

GORDON LYNCH British sociologist.

CATHARINE MACKINNON American professor of law.

NURCHOLISH MADJID (1939–2005) Indonesian scholar and intellectual.

MOSES MAIMONIDES (1135–1204) Spanish rabbi. Arguably, the greatest Jewish philosopher. Also, a leading physician, community leader, and expert on Jewish jurisprudence.

BRONISLAW MALINOWSKI (1884–1942) Polish-born British anthropologist. A founder of social anthropology. Known for his hierarchy of needs.

CRAIG MARTIN American scholar of critical religion.

KARL MARX (1818–1883) German sociologist and political theorist. Foundational figure in communism and a founding father of sociology.

MARY (CA. 25 BCE–50 CE) Jesus's mother. Seen as the Virgin Mary in Christian devotion.

TOMOKO MASUZAWA American historian and scholar of comparative literature, notable for *The Invention of World Religions.*

MARCEL MAUSS (1872–1950) French sociologist and anthropologist.

ACHILLE MBEMBE (JOSEPH-ACHILLE) Cameroonian philosopher, theologian, political theorist, and public intellectual.

RUSSELL MCCUTCHEON Influential American scholar of critical religion. Has been called religious studies' theoretical "gadfly."

MEREDITH MCGUIRE British sociologist. Known for work on lived religion.

MENCIUS (FOURTH CENTURY BCE) (Mengzi) Chinese Confucian thinker. Considered the second most significant thinker in Neo-Confucianism.

MARÍA ROSA MENOCAL (1953–2012) Cuban American historian.

MAURICE MERLEAU-PONTY (1908–1961) French phenomenological philosopher. Theorist of embodiment.

NEIL MESSER British Christian ethicist.

WALTER MIGNOLO Argentinian decolonial scholar, historian of ideas, and semiotician. Known for many works, including *Local Histories/Global Designs: Coloniality, Subaltern Knowledges and Border Thinking.*

DANIEL MILLER British anthropologist. Focuses on materiality.

MONICA MILLER American scholar of religion and Africana studies. Known for her work on hip hop and religion.

CHANDRA MOHANTY Indian scholar of women's and gender studies.

MUHAMMAD (571–632) Arabian founder and prophet of Islam. Muslims do not see him as the "founder," believing their tradition stems back to the prophet Adam.

F. MAX MÜLLER (1823–1900) German scholar. Worked at Oxford University. Often termed the "father" of religious studies.

JAWAHARLAL NEHRU (1847–1964) Indian politician and secularist. Congress Party leader and first prime minister after independence from Britain.

JOHN HENRY NEWMAN (1801–1890) British Anglican, later Catholic, Christian theologian. Helped make Catholicism more socially and intellectually acceptable in the UK.

FRIEDRICH NIETZSCHE (1844–1900) German philosopher and critic of Christianity.

AIHWA ONG Malaysian scholar of anthropology.

ROBERT ORSI American scholar of religion.

RUDOLF OTTO (1869–1937) German phenomenologist of religion and theologian known for *The Idea of the Holy.*

EBOO PATEL American Muslim cofounder of the Interfaith Youth Core. A scholar-activist.

PAUL (CA. 4 BCE–64 CE) Jewish rabbi. Became an influential apologist for the Jesus movement.

PHILO OF ALEXANDRIA (CA. 20 BCE–40 CE) Jewish philosopher.

KENNETH PIKE (1912–2000) British linguist known for the concepts emic and etic.

STEVEN PINKER American psychologist and public intellectual.

PLATO (CA. 428–347 BCE) Athenian philosopher. Foundational for modern philosophy.

DOUGLAS PRATT New Zealand scholar of religion and theologian.

ANÍBAL QUIJANO (1928–2018) Peruvian sociologist. Theorized coloniality as distinct from colonialism.

ALAN RACE British Anglican pluralist theologian.

A. R. RADCLIFFE-BROWN (1881–1955) British anthropologist.

WALPOLA RAHULA (1907–1997) Sri Lankan Buddhist monk and scholar of Buddhism.

RAMAKRISHNA (1836–1886) Indian holy man (*sadhu*). Described as the last medieval mystic of India. Devotee of the Goddess. Tried what he saw as Christian and Islamic religious practices and claimed that all of them pointed to the same divine.

RAMANUJA (CA. 1017–1137) Indian Hindu holy man (*sadhu*) and philosopher. Foundational theorist of Dvaita Vedanta.

JOHN RAWLS (1921–2002) American political philosopher.

MATTEO RICCI (1552–1610) Italian Catholic Christian Jesuit missionary to China.

PAUL RICOEUR (1913–2005) French hermeneutical philosopher.

SEN NO RIKYU (1522–1591) Japanese tea master. Considered the most influential figure in transforming tea drinking into a defined ritual and art form.

RICHARD RORTY (1931–2007) American philosopher.

JEAN-JACQUES ROUSSEAU (1712–1778) Swiss philosopher and political thinker. Part of the Romantic movement.

ROSEMARY RADFORD RUETHER American Catholic Christian feminist theologian.

EDWARD SAID (1935–2003) Palestinian literary scholar. Renowned for *Orientalism*.

ALEXIS SANDERSON British Indologist.

BOAVENTURA DE SOUSA SANTOS Portuguese legal scholar and philosopher.

BENOY KUMAR SARKAR (1887–1949) Indian economist and intellectual.

HENRI LE SAUX (1910–1973) French Catholic monk. Set up an *ashram* in India and lived as a Hindu *sadhu*/holy man. Experienced advaita in meditation.

V. D. SAVARKAR (1883–1966) Indian nationalist jailed by the British. Provided a highly significant definition of Hindutva.

KEVIN SCHILBRACK American philosopher of religion.

JOHN SEARLE American philosopher.

ROBERT SEGAL British scholar of religion.

SHANKARA (TRADITIONALLY 788–820) Indian Shaivite Hindu holy man and philosopher. Seen as a foundational theorist of Advaita Vedanta.

ARVIND SHARMA Indian Canadian scholar of religion.

VANANDA SHIVA Indian scholar and environmental activist.

SIMA QIAN (CA. 145–86 BCE) Chinese historian famous for *The Records of the Grand Historians*.

NINIAN SMART (1927–2001) British phenomenologist of religion. Foundational for religious studies in the UK.

JONATHAN Z. SMITH (1938–2017) Influential American historian of religion. Known for work on comparative religion and ritual.

WILFRED CANTWELL SMITH (1916–2000) American scholar of religion. Known for *The Meaning and End of Religion*. Probably the single most influential US scholar of religion.

WILLIAM ROBERTSON SMITH (1846–1894) British biblical scholar.

SOJOURNER TRUTH (CA. 1797–1883) American abolitionist and feminist.

BENEDICT SPINOZA (1632–1677) Dutch Jewish philosopher. Exiled for his critical scholarship on the Tanakh.

GAYATRI CHAKRAVORTY SPIVAK Bengali literary critic and postcolonial scholar. Particularly noted for the essay "Can the Subaltern Speak?" and the concept of strategic essentialism.

ELIZABETH CADY STANTON (1815–1902) American feminist theologian.

GUY STROUMSA Israeli scholar of religion.

ELIZABETH STUART British Christian theologian. Helped theorize queer theology.

WILL SWEETMAN New Zealand historian of religion and scholar of Hinduism.

RABINDRANATH TAGORE (1861–1941) Indian poet and intellectual.

HENRI TAJFEL (1919–1982) Polish social psychologist. Foundational in social identity theory.

STANLEY TAMBIAH (1929–2014) Sri Lankan social anthropologist.

CHARLES TAYLOR Canadian philosopher. Known for work on secularism and diversity.

IBN TAYMIYYAH (1263–1328) Persian Sunni Muslim jurist and reformer. Important for modern conservatives and militant neo-Islamic jihadis. He emphasized a literal reading of the Quran and the supreme authority of early traditions.

TERTULLIAN (CA. 160–220 CE) North African Christian apologist.

BAL (BALASAHEB KESHAV) THACKERAY (1926–2012) Indian politician, Hindutva ideologue, and founder of Shiv Sena.

ROMILA THAPAR Indian historian. Critic of Hindu nationalism.

YI-FU TUAN Chinese American geographer.

BRYAN TURNER British and Australian sociologist.

VICTOR TURNER (1920–1983) British cultural anthropologist.

DESMOND TUTU South African bishop, theologian, and anti-apartheid campaigner. Led South Africa's Truth and Reconciliation Commission after the end of apartheid.

EDWARD BURNETT TYLOR (1832–1917) British anthropologist.

BRAHMABANDHAB UPADHYAY (1861–1907) Indian convert from Hinduism to Catholic Christianity. Sought to develop a Hindu Christian theology.

GIULIO CESARE VANINI (1585–1619) Italian atheist philosopher.

MANUEL VÁSQUEZ Salvadorian scholar of religion and society. Works in the field of religion and embodiment.

RODRIGO DÍAZ DE VIVAR (KNOWN AS EL CID) (CA. 1048–1099) Spanish mercenary who fought for both Muslim and Christian masters. Later a Spanish national hero.

VIVEKANANDA (1863–1902) Indian Hindu holy man, philosopher, and missionary. Influential in spreading Hinduism to the West, especially Advaita Vedanta. Represented Hinduism at the World's Parliament of Religions in 1893. Follower of Ramakrishna.

SHAH WALI ALLAH (CA. 1703–1762) Indian Muslim thinker.

MAX WEBER (1864–1920) German sociologist. A founding father of sociology.

PAUL WILLIAMS British scholar of Buddhism.

DAVID SLOAN WILSON American evolutionary biologist.

KWASI WIREDU Ghanaian philosopher engaged in conceptual decolonization and Akan philosophy.

LUDWIG WITTGENSTEIN (1889–1951) Austrian philosopher and mathematician. Arguably, the most important Western philosopher of the twentieth century. Important in the linguistic turn.

MARY WOLLSTONECRAFT (1759–1797) British feminist known for *A Vindication of the Rights of Women* (1792).

LINDA WOODHEAD British sociologist of religion.

SYLVIA WYNTER Jamaican writer and cultural theorist. Known for interdisciplinary work on race, colonialism, and representations of humanness.

XUNZI (310–215 BCE) Chinese Confucian materialist thinker.

FRANCIS YOUNGHUSBAND (1863–1942) British explorer and author. Founded the World Congress of Faiths.

ZHUANGZI (FIFTH CENTURY BCE) Chinese philosopher who has a book of the same name attributed to him. Sometimes falsely assumed to be part of a legendary school of ancient Daoist philosophy along with Laozi and the mythical Liezi.

ZOROASTER (CA. 1200–1000 BCE) Central Asian founder of Zoroastrianism.

NOTES

INTRODUCTION

1. Paulo Freire, *Pedagogy of the Oppressed* (London: Penguin, 1972), 45–55.
2. Freire, *Pedagogy of the Oppressed*, 60–67.
3. Freire, *Pedagogy of the Oppressed*, 60.
4. Ronald Grimes, "Performance," in *Theorizing Rituals: Issues, Topics, Approaches, Concepts*, ed. Jens Kreinath, Jan Snoek, and Michael Stausberg (Leiden: Brill, 2008), 379–94, 379.
5. See Craig Martin, *A Critical Introduction to the Study of Religion* (New York: Routledge, 2017), xv; Rita Gross, "Where Have We Been? Where Do We Need to Go? Women's Studies and Gender in Religion and Feminist Theology," in *Gender, Religion and Diversity: Cross-Cultural Perspectives*, ed. Ursula King and Tina Beattie (London: Continuum, 2004), 17–27; and Sharon Bong, "An Asian Postcolonial and Feminist Methodology: Ethics as a Recognition of Limits," in King and Beattie, *Gender, Religion and Diversity*, 238–49.
6. Desmond Tutu, "Sanctions vs. Apartheid," *New York Times* (16 June 1986), www.nytimes.com/1986/06/16/opinion/sanctions-vs-apartheid.html.
7. Freire, *Pedagogy of the Oppressed*, 21, 103.
8. Bruce Lincoln, *Gods and Demons, Priests and Scholars: Critical Explorations in the History of Religions* (Chicago: University of Chicago Press), 1–3, http://religion.ua.edu/thesesonmethod.html.
9. See Paul Hedges, "Encounters with Ultimacy? Autobiographical and Critical Perspectives in the Academic Study of Religion," *Open Theology* 4 (2018): 355–72. See also the

special edition "Religion Studies Autobiographies" in *Journal for the Academic Study of Religion* 32.2–3 (2019).

10. For two descriptions, see Paul Hedges, "Interreligious Studies," in *Encyclopedia of Sciences and Religions,* ed. Anne Runehov and Lluis Oviedo (New York: Springer, 2013), 1076–80; and Oddbjørn Leirvik, *Interreligious Studies: A Relational Approach to Religious Activism and the Study of Religion* (London: Bloomsbury, 2014). Importantly, a debate is ongoing over whether interreligious studies is primarily a more confessional/insider narrative or a scholarly/outsider one; see Kate McCarthy, "(Inter)Religious Studies: Making a Home in the Secular Academy," in *Interreligious/Interfaith Studies: Defining a New Field,* ed. Eboo Patel, Jennifer Howe Peace, and Noah Silverman (Boston: Beacon Press, 2018); and Marianne Moyaert, "The Scholar, the Theologian, and the Activist," in *Interreligious Studies: Dispatches from a Field,* ed. Hans Gustafson (Waco: Baylor University Press, 2020), 34–42. Arguably, it is also open to a decolonizing approach; see Paul Hedges, "Decolonizing Interreligious Studies," in Gustafson, *Interreligious Studies,* 164–70.

11. Hedges, "Interreligious Studies," 1077.

12. See Paul Hedges, "Interreligious Studies: Engaged Scholarship as the Study of Religion, or Being a Scholar-Activist," keynote lecture at European Society for Intercultural Theology and Interreligious Studies, University of Münster (April 2017).

13. See Donald Wiebe, *The Politics of Religious Studies* (Basingstoke: Palgrave, 2000). Notably, the separation of theology and the study of religion is challenged by some decolonizing scholarship which argues that secularism, whiteness, and a supposed neutral rationality are conflated forms of discourse used to sideline social justice concerns raised in what Vincent Lloyd terms a Black theology, where he draws from such figures as Achille Mbembe and Sylvia Wynter. See Vincent Lloyd, *Religion of the Field Negro: On Black Secularism and Black Theology* (New York, NY: Fordham University Press, 2017).

14. See Anon., "The Pedagogy of Case Studies," the Economics Network (2018), www .economicsnetwork.ac.uk/handbook/casestudies/12; and Cynthia A. Wei, Minna Brown, and Meghan Wagner, "Pursuing the Promise of Case Studies for Sustainability and Environmental Education: Converging Initiatives," *Case Studies in the Environment* 2.1 (2018): 1–8, doi.org/10.1525/cse.2018.001065.

15. See Pluralism Project, "Case Study Initiative," the Pluralism Project (2019), http:// pluralism.org/casestudy/; and Ellie Pierce, "Using the Case Method in Interfaith Studies Classrooms," in *Interreligious/Interfaith Studies,* Patel, Howe Peace, and Silverman: 72–84.

16. This section is mainly directed at instructors and graduate students. For undergraduate students, it may be most beneficial to read it after having read chapters 2, 5, and 9, though chapters 1, 7, 8, 10, 11, and 18 also strongly relate.

17. See Paul Hedges, "Comparative Theology and Hermeneutics: A Gadamerian Approach to Interreligious Interpretation," *Religions* 7.1 (2016): 1–20, 10.

18. See Bruce Janz, "Hermeneutics and Intercultural Understanding," in *The Routledge Companion to Hermeneutics,* eds. Jeff Malpas and Hans-Helmuth Gander (New York: Routledge, 2015), 474–85, 478–80.

19. Hubert L. Dreyfus and Paul Rabinow, *Michel Foucault: Beyond Structuralism and Hermeneutics* (Chicago: Chicago University Press, 1982), xxiii.

20. See Peter Kemp, review of *"Michel Foucault: Beyond Structuralism and Hermeneutics* by Hubert L. Dreyfus and Paul Rabinow," *History and Theory* 23.1 (1984): 84–105; and Hans Herbert Kögler, *The Power of Dialogue: Critical Hermeneutics after Gadamer and Foucault*, trans. Paul Hendrickson (Cambridge, MA: MIT Press, 1996); Kögler notes that "Foucault . . . misunderstands what Gadamer's linguistic ontology has decisively brought to light: language is at once something in the world, and the world itself, that is, the world-disclosing potential involved in the comprehension of meaning," 195.

21. See Mike Springer, "John Searle on Foucault and the Obscurantism in French Philosophy," *Open Culture* (2013), www.openculture.com/2013/07/jean_searle_on_foucault_and_the_obscurantism_in_french_philosophy.html.

22. See "Steven Pinker on the Case for Reason, Science, Humanism, Progress," *The Rubin Report* (2018), www.youtube.com/watch?v=vK3mm8P21a0. Pinker is, I believe, wrong on the rationale behind these theories, though I agree that humans are not simply blank slates (see chapter 8). Indeed, the origins of such ideas go back to the work of Immanuel Kant (1724–1804) who first noted that our ideas, knowledge, and the world were formed through our mind (see box 5.2).

23. See Lera Boroditsky, "How the Languages We Speak Shape the Ways We Think," UCTV (2014), www.youtube.com/watch?v=VHulvUwgFWo.

24. See "Anil Seth on Why Our Senses Are Fine-Tuned for Utility, Not for 'Reality,'" interview by Nigel Warburton, *Aeon* (30 June 2020), https://aeon.co/videos/anil-seth-on-why-our-senses-are-fine-tuned-for-utility-not-for-reality?fbclid=IwAR0rB_yjKgOk-oFrgt3OS7CPeXK-crvsFXNoGaOkbWDRxKaLu9hu8nra8X6g. In this interview, neuroscientist Anil Seth explains why everything that comes to our brain is filtered through our consciousness. As such, while he argues that things such as color do not exist in the world, he also points out that a solid, physical reality does not get questioned by this. As he notes, getting run over by a train is not dependent on sense perception (or, it may be added, sociolinguistic categorization). Physical reality persists, and acts on us, no matter our how much discourse or non-realist epistemology we throw at it. As discussed in chapters 5 and 9, many biologists, social scientists, and others often claimed as support by non-realists generally disavow it quite explicitly, as Seth does. The idea that physical reality is dependent on sociolinguistic discourse for its interaction with us, or that we never experience it directly (e.g., when it hits us), is simply outside what scholarship, experience, and science tell us.

25. While some scholars will insist that they have the "correct" interpretation of poststructuralism, or that they offer a compelling reading of it, there is much disagreement on what it means. For instance, it has been noted that poststructuralism traces a lineage from Kant (though many poststructuralists will see themselves as avowedly post-Enlightenment and so see what they do as antithetical to Kant's work, often based on a partial and ideological reading of Kant), while Butler (often key to any such lineage) places it with Derrida; for others it is properly seen as stemming from Foucault (Derrida and Foucault were often deeply critical of each other's work). See Bernard E. Harcourt, "An Answer to the Question: 'What Is Poststructuralism?,'" University of Chicago

Public Law and Legal Theory Working Paper 156 (2007), https://chicagounbound
.uchicago.edu/cgi/viewcontent.cgi?article=1029&context=public_law_and_legal_
theory. For an argument against trying to define poststructuralism precisely, see Benoît
Dillet, "What Is Poststructuralism?," *Political Studies Review* 15.4 (2017): 516–27.

26. Margaret Archer et al., "What Is Critical Realism?," American Sociological Association,
Theory Section (23 December 2016), www.asatheory.org/current-newsletter-online
/what-is-critical-realism.

27. See Andrejç Gorazd, *Wittgenstein and Interreligious Disagreement: A Philosophical and
Theological Perspective* (New York: Palgrave Macmillan, 2016).

28. Most would deny that this critique applies to them (and certainly today most theorists
disavow the term "postmodern" and often argue that the term is meaningless); however, some effectively operate as if this were so, that is, refusing any critique of themselves because they rely on "critical" theory techniques, which, they claim, disavow
any foundational stance in their own ideas.

29. See Paul Hedges, "Gadamer, Play, and Interreligious Dialogue as the Opening of
Horizons," *Journal of Dialogue Studies* 4 (2016): 5–26.

30. Souleymane Bachir Diagne, "On the Postcolonial and the Universal?" *Rue Descartes*
78.2 (2013): 7–18, 15.

31. Hedges, "Gadamer, Play, and Interreligious Dialogue."

32. Freire, *Pedagogy of the Oppressed*, 71–2; the term is taken from Vieira Pinto.

33. See, for an accessible overview, "Jacques Derrida," the School of Life (2016), www
.youtube.com/watch?v=HotnHr2dqTs. Note Derrida's statement: "Deconstruction is
justice"; Jacques Derrida, "Force of Law: The 'Mystical Foundations of Authority,'" in
Deconstruction and the Possibility of Justice, ed. Drucilla Cornell, Michel Rosenfeld,
and David Carlson (London: Routledge, 1992), 3–67, 15.

34. Freire, *Pedagogy of the Oppressed*, 27.

35. See Malpas and Gander, eds., *Routledge Companion to Hermeneutics*; and Georgia
Warnke, ed., *Inheriting Gadamer: New Directions in Philosophical Hermeneutics* (Edinburgh: Edinburgh University Press, 2017). It may also be noted that the so-called
Western lineage of philosophy, social science, and science which underlies what has
been described here is not, as some maintain, some "golden road" of (primarily) European (and white, male) thought, but has always drawn from (often unattributed, or
forgetting its origins) a global conversation. Some of this is referenced throughout
this book, but drawing out the way that "Western" thought only exists as part of a
global conversation of ideas would be the work of another book.

CHAPTER 1. RELIGION

1. Wilfred Cantwell Smith, *The Meaning and End of Religion* (London: SPCK, 1978
[1962]).

2. See Julius Lipner, *Hindus: Their Religious Beliefs and Practices*, 2nd ed. (New York:
Routledge), 122–25.

3. This discussion draws heavily from Brent Nongbri, *Before Religion: A History of a
Modern Concept* (New Haven: Yale University Press, 2013), 39–45.

4. This quotation is from the N. J. Dawood translation (London: Penguin, 2003). Italics added.

5. This version is the author's own rendering based on relevant literature on the meaning of the terms noted, but otherwise following Dawood's translation.

6. See Xinzhong Yao, *An Introduction to Confucianism* (Cambridge: Cambridge University Press, 2012), 17.

7. Syed Farid Alatas, "Eurocentrism and the Role of the Human Sciences in the Dialogue among Civilizations," *European Legacy* 7.6 (2002): 759–70, 761–62.

8. Christians outside of Europe had been cognizant of religious diversity for much longer (see chapter 13).

9. Tomoko Masuzawa, *The Invention of World Religions* (Chicago: Chicago University Press, 2005).

10. See Russell McCutcheon, "A Question (Still) Worth Asking about *The Religions of Man*," *Religion and Theology* 25 (2018): 298–311.

11. Rudolf Otto, *The Idea of the Holy* (Oxford: Oxford University Press, 1923).

12. See Mircea Eliade, *Patterns in Comparative Religion,* trans. Rosemary Sheed (London: Sheed and Ward, 1958).

13. For one attempt, with potential criticisms, see Anna King and Paul Hedges, "What Is Religion? Or What Is It We're Talking About?," in *Controversies in Contemporary Religion,* ed. Paul Hedges, vol. 1 (Santa Barbara: Praeger, 2014), 1–30, 14–18.

14. See Willi Braun, "Religion," in *Guide to the Study of Religion,* ed. Willi Braun and Russell McCutcheon (London: Cassell, 2000), 3–18.

15. Russell McCutcheon, "What Is Religion," in *Introduction to World Religions,* 3rd ed., ed. Christopher Partridge (2018), www.augsburgfortress.org/media/downloads/Partridge ShortChapter1.pdf. McCutcheon's suggestion, I assume, is based on people sometimes describing "soccer/football" metaphorically as being their "religion." However, far from showing that this means that "religion" is meaningless, it shows that language users are familiar enough with the term that they believe it can be used as a figure of speech.

16. See Timothy Fitzgerald, *Discourse on Civility and Barbarity: A Critical History of Religion and Related Categories* (Oxford: Oxford University Press, 2007). However, see Paul Hedges, "Discourse on Discourses: Why We Still Need the Terminology of 'Religion' and 'Religions,'" *Journal of Religious History* 38.1 (2014): 132–48.

17. On some of these debates, see the papers in *Implicit Religion* 20.4 (2017) relating to "The Religious Studies Project: Podcast Transcription."

18. W. C. Smith, *Meaning and End,* 154–92.

19. Jonathan Z. Smith, *Imagining Religion: From Babylon to Jonestown* (Chicago: Chicago University Press, 1982), xi.

20. Paul Hedges, "Deconstructing Religion: Where We Go from Here—A Hermeneutical Proposal," *Exchange* 47.1 (2018): 5–24.

21. See Russell McCutcheon, *Manufacturing Religion: The Discourse on Sui Generis Religion and the Politics of Nostalgia* (Oxford: Oxford University Press, 1997); and Nongbri, *Before Religion.*

22. Eva Pascal, "Buddhist Monks and Christian Friars: Religious and Cultural Exchange in the Making of Buddhism," *Studies in World Christianity* 22.1 (2016): 5–21.

23. Walter B. Gallie, "Essentially Contested Concepts," *Proceedings of the Aristotelian Society* S6.1 (1956), 167–98. See Paul Hedges, "Multiple Religious Belonging after Religion: Theorising Strategic Religious Participation in a Shared Religious Landscape as a Chinese Model," *Open Theology* 3.1 (2017): 48–72, 52–53.

24. For a summary of recent research, see Marianna Bolognesi, "How Language Shapes Your Thoughts—What Researchers Know," *Conversation* (26 July 2018), https://theconversation.com/how-language-shapes-your-thoughts-what-researchers-know-96047.

25. Hans-Georg Gadamer, *Theory and Method,* trans. William Glen-Doepl (London: Sheed and Ward, 1979); Paul Ricoeur, *Hermeneutics and the Human Sciences,* ed. and tran. John B. Thompson (Cambridge: Cambridge University Press, 2016). See Paul Hedges, "Deconstructing Religion: Some Thoughts on Where We Go from Here—A Hermeneutical Proposal," *Exchange* 64.3 (2018), 5–24.

26. See Timothy Fitzgerald, *The Ideology of Religious Studies* (Oxford: Oxford University Press, 2000): 159–80.

27. J. Z. Smith, *Imagining Religion,* xi.

28. Fitzgerald, *Ideology of Religious Studies.* His usage of "sacred" was deeply problematic and does not accord with the critical usage herein (see box 18.7).

29. Jeppe Sinding Jensen, *What is Religion?,* 2nd ed. (London: Routledge, 2020), 2.

30. Paul Hedges, *Religious Hatred: Prejudice, Islamophobia, and Antisemitism in Global Context* (London: Bloomsbury, 2021). The way in which we distinguish people within religious or non-religious categories, as well as within particular religions, needs to be seen in relation to Rogers Brubaker's notion of "groupism"; see Rogers Brubaker, "Ethnicity without Groups," *Archives Européenes de Sociologie* 43.2 (2002): 163–89.

31. Martin Riesebrodt, *The Promise of Salvation: A Theory of Religion,* trans. Steven Rendall (Chicago: Chicago University Press, 2010).

32. Gavin Flood, *The Truth Within: A History of Inwardness in Christianity, Hinduism, and Buddhism* (Oxford: Oxford University Press, 2013).

33. Kevin Schilbrack, "A Realist Social Ontology of Religion," *Religion* 47.2 (2017): 161–78.

34. See Schilbrack, "A Realist Social Ontology," and Hedges, "Deconstructing Religion."

35. See Paul Hedges, "Burning for a Cause: Four Factors in Successful Political (and Religious) Self-Immolation Examined in Relation to Alleged Falun Gong 'Fanatics' in Tiananmen Square," *Politics and Religion* 8 (2015): 797–815.

36. See Louis Komjathy, *The Daoist Tradition: An Introduction* (London: Bloomsbury, 2013), 187–224.

37. Benjamin Penny, *The Religion of Falun Gong* (Chicago: Chicago University Press, 2012).

38. Wen-Chen Chang, Li-Ann Thio, Kevin Tan, and Jiunn-Rong Yeh, *Constitutionalism in Asia: Cases and Materials* (London: Hart, 2014), 773.

39. See Paul Hedges, "China," in *Religion and Everyday Life and Culture: Religion in the Practice of Daily Life in World History,* ed. R. D. Hecht and V. F. Biondo, vol. 1 (Santa Barbara: Praeger, 2010), 45–82, 61–63; and BBC, "Confucian Ancestor Worship," video, BBC Radio 4 (2015), www.youtube.com/watch?v=2dZfaU5tsDY.

CHAPTER 2. METHOD

1. See Gavin Flood, *An Introduction to Hinduism* (Cambridge: Cambridge University Press, 1996), 144–45.
2. See Michael Jerryson with Matthew Walton, "Postscript: Buddhist Authority, Politics, and Violence," in *If You Meet the Buddha on the Road: Buddhism, Politics, and Violence* (Oxford: Oxford University Press, 2018), 175–96, 179–84.
3. See Jerryson and Walton, "Postscript," 186–91.
4. See Jerryson and Walton, "Postscript."
5. See George Chryssides, "Insiders and Outsiders," in *The Study of Religion: An Introduction to Key Ideas and Methods,* ed. George D. Chryssides and Ron Geaves, 2nd ed. (London: Bloomsbury, 2017), 67–88; Paul Hedges and Anna King, "Is the Study of Religion Religious? How to Study Religion, and Who Studies Religion?," in *Controversies in Contemporary Religion,* ed. Paul Hedges, vol. 1 (Santa Barbara: Praeger, 2014), 31–56, 33–38; and Marvin Harris, "History and Significance of the Emic/Etic Distinction," *Annual Review of Anthropology* 5 (1976): 329–50.
6. See Russell McCutcheon, *Manufacturing Religion: The Discourse on Sui Generis Religion and the Politics of Nostalgia* (Oxford: Oxford University Press, 1997), 7–15.
7. The most recent theory stresses the inadequacy of seeing insider/outsider as a straightforward binary option; see George Chryssides and Stephen Gregg, eds., *The Insider/Outsider Debate: New Perspectives in the Study of Religion* (Sheffield: Equinox, 2019).
8. Inspired by Russell McCutcheon, "General Introduction," in *The Insider/Outsider Problem in the Study of Religion: A Reader,* ed. Russell McCutcheon (London: Cassell, 1999), 1–11.
9. See Eric Reinders, *Borrowed Gods and Foreign Bodies: Christian Missionaries Imagine Chinese Religion* (Berkeley: California University Press, 2004).
10. See Gavin Flood, *Beyond Phenomenology: Rethinking the Study of Religion* (London: Cassell, 1999), 35–38.
11. Oddbjørn Leirvik, *Interreligious Studies: A Relational Approach to Religious Activism and the Study of Religion* (London: Bloomsbury, 2014), 11.
12. Leirvik, *Interreligious Studies,* 11–12.
13. Boaventura de Sousa Santos, *Epistemologies of the South: Justice against Epistemicide* (New York: Routledge, 2014), 203–4.
14. Sanya Osha, "Kwasi Wiredu," in *The Internet Encyclopedia of Philosophy* (n.d.), www.iep.utm.edu/wiredu/.
15. Hedges and King, "Is the Study of Religion Religious?," 34–35.
16. See Kerry Maloney, "A Few Critical Questions in Multireligious Work," in *Offerings on Interfaith Dialogue,* ed. Harvard Divinity School Office of Student Life (Cambridge: Harvard Divinity School, 2014), 14–17, 14–15, https://hds.harvard.edu/files/hds/files/ifd_2014.pdf.
17. We should not regard figures such as Hirsi Ali as reliable guides, and it is credibly argued that her representation of Islam is distinctly Islamophobic (see box 15.4); see Todd Green, *The Fear of Islam: An Introduction to Islamophobia in the West,* 2nd ed. (Minneapolis: Fortress Press, 2019).

18. See Hedges, "Multiple Religious Belonging after Religion."

19. See Duane Bidwell, *When One Religion Isn't Enough: The Lives of Spiritually Fluid People* (Boston: Beacon Press, 2018); and Paul Hedges, "Strategic Religious Participation in a Shared Religious Landscape: A Model for Westerners?," in *Theology without Walls*, ed. Jerry Martin (New York: Routledge, 2020), 165–71.

20. Paul Williams with Anthony Tribe and Alexander Wynne, *Buddhist Thought: A Complete Introduction to the Indian Tradition*, 2nd ed. (New York: Routledge, 2012).

21. See Coming Home Network, "Dr. Paul Williams: Buddhist Who Became a Catholic Christian—The Journey Home Program," interview, The Coming Home Network International (2014), video, www.youtube.com/watch?v=dUPC_s3i8zU.

22. On debates on this possibility in the Catholic Christian tradition, see Fabrice Blée, "Can Christians Engage in Non-Christian Practices? Eastern Meditation and Contemplative Prayer," in Hedges, *Controversies in Contemporary Religion*, vol. 3, 277–304.

23. Abhistikananda, *Saccidananda: A Christian Approach to Advaitic Experience* (Delhi: International Society for the Promotion of Christian Experience, 1974). *Advaita* means non-dual, or not two, and is the Hindu philosophy that regards the human and divine as essentially a single undivided spiritual essence. See Flood, *An Introduction to Hinduism*, 239–43.

24. For some studies, see Chung Hyun Kyung, "Seeking the Religious Roots of Pluralism," in *Christian Approaches to Other Faiths* (SCM Reader Series), ed. Paul Hedges and Alan Race (London: SCM, 2009), 72–75; Albertus Bagus Laksana, "Multiple Religious Belonging or Complex Identity? An Asian Way of Being Religious," in *The Oxford Handbook of Christianity in Asia*, ed. Felix Wilfred (Oxford: Oxford University Press, 2014): 493–510; Rose Drew, *Buddhist and Christian? An Exploration of Dual Belonging* (New York: Routledge, 2011); Michelle Voss Roberts, "Religious Belonging and the Multiple," *Journal of Feminist Studies in Religion* 26.1 (2010): 43–62; and Diana Eck, "The Pluralism Within," video, *Gifford Lectures*, lecture 6 (2009), www.giffordlectures.org/lectures/age-pluralism.

CHAPTER 3. LIFE

1. Meredith McGuire, *Lived Religion* (Oxford: Oxford University Press, 2008), 3–4.

2. See Jacob Neusner and Bruce Chilton, eds., *The Golden Rule: The Ethics of Reciprocity in World Religions* (London: Continuum, 2008).

3. McGuire, *Lived Religion*, 4.

4. McGuire, *Lived Religion*, 4.

5. McGuire, *Lived Religion*, 16.

6. See Marjorie Wheeler-Barclay, *The Science of Religion in Britain, 1860–1915* (Charlottesville: University of Virginia Press, 2010), 38–70; and Sharada Sugirtharajah, *Imagining Hinduism: A Postcolonial Perspective* (New York: Routledge, 2003), 38–73.

7. McGuire, *Lived Religion*, 41.

8. See McGuire, *Lived Religion*, 19–44.

9. See Syed Farid Alatas, "Academic Dependency and the Global Division of Labour in the Social Sciences," *Current Sociology* 5.1 (2003): 599–613, 602; Samir Amin, *Euro-*

centrism: *Modernity, Religion, and Democracy: A Critique of Eurocentrism and Cultural-ism,* 2nd ed. (Cape Town: Pambazuka Press, 2011), and chapter 7.

10. See Mark Nanos, "Paul and Judaism," in *The Jewish Annotated New Testament,* ed. Amy-Jill Levine and Marc Zvi Brettler (Oxford: Oxford University Press, 2011), 551–54.

11. See Judith Lieu, *Christian Identity in the Jewish and Greco-Roman World* (Oxford: Oxford University Press, 2006).

12. See Cathy Cantwell, *Buddhism: The Basics* (New York: Routledge, 2010), 22–24; and Paul Williams with Anthony Tribe and Alexander Wynne, *Buddhist Thought: A Complete Introduction to the Indian Tradition,* 2nd ed. (New York: Routledge, 2012), 1–15.

13. See Karine Schomer and W. H. McLeod, eds., *The Sants: Studies in a Devotional Tradition of India* (Delhi: Motilal Banarsidass, 1987); and Gavin Flood, *An Introduction to Hinduism* (Cambridge: Cambridge University Press, 1996), 144–45.

14. Stephen Bokenkamp, *Ancestors and Anxiety: Daoism and the Birth of Rebirth in China* (Berkeley: University of California Press, 2007).

15. See Barry Keenan, *Neo-Confucian Self-Cultivation* (Honolulu: Hawai'i University Press, 2011), 11–13.

16. See John Holt, *The Buddhist Visnu: Religious Transformation, Politics, and Culture* (New York: Columbia University Press, 2005). However, labeling these deities "Hindu" is arguably a misnomer as it assumes they "properly" belong to (only) one tradition.

17. See Mark Jurgensmeyer, "Thinking Globally about Religion," in *The Oxford Handbook of Global Religions,* ed. Mark Jurgensmeyer (Oxford: Oxford University Press, 2006), 3–12, 4; and Robert Gulick, *Muhammad the Educator* (Lahore: Institute of Islamic Cultures, 1953), 61.

18. William Harrison, *In Praise of Mixed Religion: The Syncretism Solution in a Multifaith World* (Montreal: McGill-Queens University Press, 2014), 28–31.

19. See Harrison, *In Praise of Mixed Religion;* and Perry Schmidt-Leukel, *Transformation by Integration: How Inter-Faith Encounter Changes Christianity* (London: SCM Press, 2009).

20. Graham Harvey, *Food, Sex and Strangers: Understanding Religion as Everyday Life* (Durham: Acumen, 2013), 38.

21. Harvey, *Food, Sex and Strangers,* 38.

22. Pattana Kitiarsa, "Beyond Syncretism: Hybridization of Popular Religion in Contemporary Thailand," *Journal of Southeast Asian Studies* 36.3 (2005): 461–87, 466.

23. Joseph Winters, "Mestiza Language of Religion: Gloria Anzaldúa," in *Cultural Approaches to Studying Religion,* ed. Sarah Bloesch and Meredith Minister (London: Bloomsbury, 2019), 127–42, 130–31. See also Gloria Anzaldúa, "Mestiza Language of Religion: Gloria Anzaldúa," in *The Bloomsbury Reader in Cultural Approaches to the Study of Religion,* ed. Sarah Bloesch and Meredith Minister (London: Bloomsbury, 2019), 177–90.

24. Mikhail Bakhtin, *The Dialogic Imagination: Four Essays* (Austin: University of Texas Press, 1981), 358, cited in Kitiarsa, "Beyond Syncretism," 46.

25. McGuire, *Lived Religion,* 38.

26. Kitiarsa, "Beyond Syncretism," 484.

27. Kitiarsa, "Beyond Syncretism," 475.

28. Harvey, *Food, Sex and Strangers,* 177–78.

29. Harvey, *Food, Sex and Strangers,* 2.

30. See David Freidenreich, "Food-Related Interaction among Christians, Muslims, and Jews in High and Late Medieval Latin Christendom," *History Compass* 11.11 (2013): 957–66; and Andrea Marion Pinkney, "*Prasāda*, Grace as Sustenance, and the Relational Self," in *The Wiley Blackwell Companion to Religion and Materiality*, ed. Vasudha Narayanan (Chichester: Wiley, 2020), 414–32.

31. See Juhi Ahuja and Paul Hedges, "Interreligious Marriage: Perspectives from the Singaporean Context in Relation to Interreligious Dialogue," *Interreligious Relations*, Occasional Paper series 1 (2019).

32. See Jayeel Serrano Cornelio, "Religious Identity and the Isolated Generation: What Being Catholic Means to Religiously Involved Filipino Students Today" (PhD diss., National University of Singapore, 2011).

33. McGuire, *Lived Religion*, 7.

34. Paul Tillich, *Theology of Culture*, ed. R. C. Kimball (Oxford: Oxford University Press, 1959), 7–8.

35. Robert Orsi, *The Madonna of 115th Street: Faith and Community in Italian Harlem, 1880–1950* (New Haven: Yale University Press, 1985), xvi–xvii.

36. Harvey, *Food, Sex, and Strangers*, 207.

37. McGuire, *Lived Religion*, 7.

38. McGuire, *Lived Religion*, 8.

39. Monica Miller, *Religion and Hip Hop* (London: Routledge: 2011).

40. See Charlene Villaseñor Black, "The Virgin of Guadalupe as an Iconic Image in Mexican Culture," *Oxford Research Encyclopedia of Latin American History*, Oxford Scholarship Online (2016), 1–22, http://oxfordre.com/latinamericanhistory/view/10.1093/acrefore/9780199366439.001.0001/acrefore-9780199366439-e-509.

41. See Francis Johnston, *The Wonder of Guadalupe: The Origin and Cult of the Miraculous Image of the Blessed Virgin in Mexico* (Rockford, IL: Tan Books, 1981), 116–36.

42. María Del Socorro Castañenda-Liles, *Our Lady of Everyday Life: La Virgen de Guadalupe and the Catholic Imagination of Mexican American Women* (Oxford: Oxford University Press, 2018), 1.

43. Sometimes it is grandmothers, and occasionally fathers, who pass on this devotion, though this refers only to the main agent as this devotion is part of a whole familial and community context.

44. Castañenda-Liles, *Our Lady of Everyday Life*, 69.

45. Our Lady of Guadalupe's exact relationship to indigenous religious worldviews is contested; see Nicholas Griffiths, *Sacred Dialogues: Christianity and Native American Religions in the Colonial Americas, 1492–1700* (Morrisville, NC: Lulu, 2017), 270–76.

46. See Alyshia Galvez, *Guadalupe in New York: Devotion and Struggle for Citizenship Rights among Mexican Immigrants* (New York: New York University Press, 2009); see also Castañenda-Liles, *Our Lady of Everyday Life*, 26–27, 77.

47. See Kitiarsa, "Beyond Syncretism," 462.

48. See Kate Crosby, *Theravada Buddhism: Continuity, Identity, and Diversity* (Chichester: Wiley-Blackwell, 2014), 125–29.

49. See Graham Harvey, *Animism: Respecting the Living World*, 2nd ed. (London: Hurst, 2017).

1. John Lewis Gaddis, *The Landscape of History: How Historians Map the Past* (Oxford: Oxford University Press, 2004), 22–23.

2. Gaddis, *The Landscape of History*, 24, italics in original.

3. See Gyanendra Pandey, *Routine Violence: Nations, Fragments, Histories* (Stanford: Stanford University Press, 2006), 41, 199, note 49. This issue is not addressed by Gaddis and is my addition to his three key points.

4. Gaddis, *The Landscape of History*, 25.

5. Gaddis, *The Landscape of History*, 151.

6. See Charles Tilly, "Why and How History Matters," in *The Oxford Handbook of Political Science*, ed. Robert Goodin (Oxford: Oxford University Press, 2011), 522–40; Robert Kroes, "Signs of Fascism Rising: A European Americanist Looks at Recent Political Trends in the U.S. and Europe," *Society* 54.3 (2017): 218–25; and Federico Finchelstein, *A Brief History of Fascist Lies* (Oakland: University of California Press, 2020).

7. See Yao Xinzhong, *An Introduction to Confucianism* (Cambridge: Cambridge University Press, 2000), 49–52.

8. See John Barton, *How the Bible Came to Be* (Louisville: Westminster John Knox Press, 1997), 75–81, where he notes: "Paradoxically, the Protestant attempt to restore the primitive and authoritative Bible succeeded in producing a Bible which no Christian had ever known until that moment," 81.

9. See Paul Hedges, *Towards Better Disagreement: Religion and Atheism in Dialogue* (London: Jessica Kingsley, 2017), 42–44.

10. See Barton, *How the Bible Came to Be*, 15–18.

11. Danièle Hervieu-Léger, *Religion as a Chain of Memory* (Cambridge: Polity Press, 2000), 97.

12. Bodhidharma is considered the 28th Indian Zen patriarch, and the 1st Chinese Zen (Ch'an) patriarch; see John Powers, "Buddhas and Buddhism," in *The Buddhist World*, ed. John Powers (New York: Routledge, 2016), 11–59, 46.

13. See Jonathan Brown, *Misquoting Muhammad: The Challenge and Choices of Interpreting the Prophet's Legacy* (Oxford: Oneworld, 2015), 39–41; and Abdulkader Tayob, *Islam: A Short Introduction* (Oxford: Oneworld, 1999), 19–21.

14. See Eric Hobsbawm and Terence Ranger, eds., *The Invention of Tradition* (Cambridge: Cambridge University Press, 1983).

15. James Lewis and Olav Hammer, eds., *The Invention of Sacred Tradition* (Cambridge: Cambridge University Press, 2007).

16. See MJL, "Jewish Clothing," *My Jewish Learning* (n.d.), www.myjewishlearning.com/article/jewish-clothing/.

17. See Paul Badham, "Contemporary Christianity as a New Religion," *Modern Believing* 40.4 (1999): 17–29.

18. See Michael Cook, *The Koran: A Very Short Introduction* (Oxford: Oxford University Press, 2000), 109–15.

19. See Christopher Driscoll and Monica Miller, *Method as Identity: Manufacturing Distance in the Academic Study of Religion* (Lanham, MD: Lexington Books, 2019), 77–105.

20. Bruce Lincoln, "How to Read a Religious Text: Reflections on Some Passages of the Chāndogya Upanishad," *History of Religions* 46.2 (2006): 127–39.

21. Lincoln, "How to Read," 127.

22. Bryan Van Norden, *Taking Back Philosophy: A Multicultural Manifesto* (New York: Columbia University Press, 2017), 139–42.

23. See Amy-Jill Levine, "Introduction," in *The Historical Jesus in Context*, ed. Amy-Jill Levine, Dale Allison, and John Crossnan (Princeton: Princeton University Press, 2006), 1–39, 3–14.

24. The NIV (New International Version) is well known and so employed here. However, it has been described as an "interpretation" rather than a "translation." For academic study, the RSV (Revised Standard Version) is often preferred. The NRSV (New Revised Standard Version) makes a few corrections but its gender-neutral terminology hides patriarchal structures, making it less suited as an academic text (see chapter 10).

25. See Bart Ehrman, *The New Testament: A Historical Introduction to the Early Christian Writings*, 5th ed. (Oxford: Oxford University Press, 2012), 106–9, 176–79. Note: Scholarly arguments for John's Gospel as the earliest are a minority stance; some scholars argue parts of John are more historically accurate than the synoptics, but even if accepted, this does not make the whole text more reliable.

26. Jaroslav Pelikan, *Jesus through the Centuries: His Place in the History of Culture* (New Haven: Yale University Press, 1985), 9.

27. Ehrman, *New Testament*, 17–28.

28. See Pamela Eisenbaum, *Paul Was Not a Christian: The Original Message of a Misunderstood Apostle* (New York: HarperOne, 2010).

29. See Amy-Jill Levine and Marc Zvi Brettler, eds., *The Jewish Annotated New Testament* (Oxford: Oxford University Press, 2011), 160.

30. See Amy-Jill Levine, *The Misunderstood Jew: The Church and the Scandal of the Jewish Jesus* (New York: HarperOne, 2006), 56–62, 127–31.

31. Levine and Brettler, *The Jewish Annotated*, 58. See also Ehrman, *New Testament*, 302–4.

32. This is also true of Paul's letters read in a Jewish context; see Eisenbaum, *Paul*.

33. Analogies, or overlaps, between Christian concepts and demi-god figures is seen in early Christian funerary art; see Beverly Berg, "Alcestis and Hercules in the Catacomb of Via Latina," *Vigiliae Christianae* 48.3 (1994): 219–34. Note: Popular narratives drawing direct analogies between "Pagan" god-men and Jesus, or asserting that Jesus was simply a copy of some pre-Christian hero/divine figure, are not scholarly arguments. Rather, an ethos existed in which such a divine-human crossover could exist; see Ehrman, *How Jesus Became God*, 11–45. Christian apologetic against any crossover typically targets the popular narratives and not the subtler academic arguments, as seen in Larry Hurtado, *How on Earth Did Jesus Become a God? Historical Questions about Earliest Devotion to Jesus* (Grand Rapids, MI: Eerdmans, 2005), 46.

34. See Cam Howard, "The Pre- and Post-Easter Jesus," *A Portrait of Jesus* (1997–2015), www.aportraitofjesus.org/compare.shtml; and Marcus Borg, "Jesus before and after Easter: Jewish Mystic and Christian Messiah," in *The Meaning of Jesus: Two Visions, Marcus Borg and N. T. Wright*, 2nd ed. (New York: HarperOne, 2007), 53–77.

35. See Robert Henricks, *Lao Tzu's Tao Te Ching: A Translation of the Startling New Documents Found at Guodian* (New York: Columbia University Press, 2000), 1–3, 19–22; and Russell Kirkland, *Taoism: The Enduring Tradition* (New York: Routledge, 2004), 20–73.

36. See Louis Komjathy, *The Daoist Tradition* (London: Bloomsbury, 2013), 3–15; and Kirkland, *Taoism*. See also Komjathy, *Daoist Tradition*, 7; and Harold Roth, *Original Tao: Inward Training (Nei-yeh) and the Foundations of Taoist Mysticism* (New York: Columbia University Press, 1999), 5–9.

37. See Kristofer Schipper, *The Taoist Body*, trans. Karen Duval (Berkeley: University of California Press, 1993).

CHAPTER 5. POWER

1. Taking a religious tradition as a human product in scholarship is different from saying that is all it is (see box 2.4).

2. See Christopher Driscoll and Monica Miller, *Method as Identity: Manufacturing Distance in the Academic Study of Religion* (Lanham, MD: Lexington, 2019).

3. Craig Martin, *A Critical Introduction to the Study of Religion* (New York: Routledge, 2012), xi. For a good example, see Peter van der Veer, *The Value of Comparison* (Durham: Duke University Press, 2016), 12–15, on assuming that tea is Indian.

4. See Leonardo Boff and Clodovis Boff, *Introducing Liberation Theology* (Maryknoll, NY: Burns and Oates, 1989).

5. See Matti Sintonen, ed., *The Socratic Tradition: Questioning as Philosophy and Method* (London: College Publications, 2009). On a contemporary usage in law schools, see www.law.uchicago.edu/socratic-method.

6. See Hu Mei, *Confucius,* film (2010).

7. On Christianity, see Linda Woodhead, *An Introduction to Christianity* (Cambridge: Cambridge University Press, 2004), 51–58. However, monasticism sometimes complemented mundane society, see Cathy Cantwell, *Buddhism: The Basics* (New York: Routledge, 2010), 118–22; and Anthony DeBlasi, "A Parallel World: A Case Study of Monastic Society, Northern Song to Ming," *Journal of Song-Yuan Studies* 28 (1998): 155–75. On monasticism as a way of life, see Giorgio Agamben, *The Use of Bodies,* trans. Adam Kotsko (Stanford: Stanford University Press, 2016).

8. See Rick Roderick, "The Masters of Suspicion," lecture (1993), http://rickroderick .org/301-paul-ricoeur-the-masters-of-suspicion-1993/; see also Andrew Dole, *Reframing the Masters of Suspicion: Marx, Nietzsche, and Freud* (London: Bloomsbury, 2018).

9. See, "A Class Divided," *Frontline,* PBS (1985), www.pbs.org/wgbh/frontline/film/class-divided/.

10. See Teo You Yenn, *This Is What Inequality Looks Like* (Singapore: Ethos Books, 2019), 25–46.

11. Pierre Bourdieu, *Language and Symbolic Power* (Cambridge: Harvard University Press, 1999), 119.

12. Bourdieu, *Language and Symbolic Power,* 119; italics in original.

13. Pierre Bourdieu, *The Logic of Practice* (Stanford: Stanford University Press, 1990), 53; bold added.

14. Jonathan Z. Smith, *Relating Religion: Essays in the Study of Religion* (Chicago: Chicago University Press, 2004), 389.

15. Bourdieu's actual term for our living within our worlds of habitus (what he terms "doxic experience," denoting its embodied nature) is "excellence." He says of our ability to negotiate and adjust within this world that we have "the art of the necessary improvisation which defines excellence." Pierre Bourdieu, *Outline of a Theory of Practice* (Cambridge: Cambridge University Press, 1977), 869. However, Richard Jenkins suggests that "Bourdieu does not help us to understand the absence of 'excellence' in social interaction, let alone the ubiquity of incompetence." Richard Jenkins, *Pierre Bourdieu*, rev. ed. (London: Routledge, 2002), 71. As such, it may be better to speak about "competence," as Jenkins suggests: "Most people, most of the time, exhibit, at best, competence rather than excellence in their dealings with others" (869). Jenkins also suggests that excellence "is a quality which differs from mere competence and is both unevenly distributed and relatively uncommon" (70).

16. See Paul Hedges, *Towards Better Disagreement: Religion and Atheism in Dialogue* (London: Jessica Kingsley, 2017), 36–50.

17. Martin, *A Critical Introduction*, 21–32. Martin notes, "I think discourse constructs both the social and the natural world" (personal email correspondence to author, 2018), a matter discussed in box 5.8.

18. See Cantwell, *Buddhism*, 107–40.

19. See A. C. Graham, *Disputers of the Dao: Philosophical Arguments in Ancient China* (Chicago: Open Court, 1989).

20. See Driscoll and Miller, *Method as Identity*.

21. Craig Martin (personal email correspondence with author, 2018).

22. This lineage is asserted by, for instance, Craig Martin, "Non-Realism," draft unpublished manuscript. For the African context of Derrida, see Biko Agozino, "The Africa-Centred, Activist, and Critical Philosophy of Derrida," *International Journal of Baudrillard Studies* 8.1 (2011), www2.ubishops.ca/baudrillardstudies/vol-8_1/v8–1-agozino.html.

23. See Driscoll and Miller, *Method as Identity*.

24. See the first and second editions of Martin, *Critical Introduction*. However, Martin argues that as a critical standpoint it cannot be maintained, and so now holds it as more of a personal commitment (Martin, personal email correspondence with author, 2018).

25. Bruce Lincoln, "Theses on Method," *Method and Theory in the Study of Religion* 17.1 (2005): 8–10.

26. See Russell McCutcheon, *Studying Religion: An Introduction* (London: Equinox, 2007); and Russell McCutcheon, "A Direct Question Deserves a Direct Answer: A Response to Atalia Omer's 'Can a Critic Be a Caretaker too?,'" *Journal of the American Academy of Religion* 80.4 (2012): 1077–82, 1080.

27. See Peter L. Berger, *The Many Altars of Modernity: Toward a Paradigm for Religion in a Pluralist Age* (Boston: De Gruyter, 2014), 11–12; and Terry Eagleton, *The Illusions of Postmodernity* (Oxford: Blackwell, 1996), who notes that it is a way for Western theorists to maintain or assert control, 124.

28. See Paul Hedges, "The Deconstruction of Religion: So What?," The *Religious Studies Project*, available at www.religiousstudiesproject.com/2016/09/22/the-deconstruction-of-religion-so-what/.

29. See Paul Hedges, "Engaged Scholarship as the Study of Religion, or on Being a Scholar-Activist: Reflections from the Perspective of Interreligious Studies," unpublished paper delivered at the European Society for Intercultural Theology and Interreligious Studies conference, University of Münster (26–29 April 2017).

30. Biko Agozino, *Black Women and the Criminal Justice System: Towards the Decolonisation of Victimisation* (Aldershot: Ashgate, 1997); see also Biko Agozino, "Theorizing Otherness, the War on Drugs and Incarceration," *Theoretical Criminology* 4.3 (2000): 359–76, 363.

31. Romila Thapar, *Talking History* (Delhi: Oxford University Press, 2017).

32. Catharine MacKinnon, *Towards a Feminist Theory of the State* (Cambridge: Harvard University Press, 1989).

33. Driscoll and Miller, *Method as Identity*, xix, 2, 10–22, 25–45.

34. See Hedges, "Engaged Scholarship as the Study of Religion."

35. See Lizzie Wade, "It Wasn't Just Greece: Archaeologists Find Early Democratic Societies in the Americas," *Science* (15 March 2017), www.sciencemag.org/news/2017/03/it-wasnt-just-greece-archaeologists-find-early-democratic-societies-americas.

36. See Waines, *An Introduction to Islam*, 207–10, 228–30; and Mohamed bin Ali, "Salafis, Salafism and Modern Salafism: What Lies behind the Term?," *RSIS Commentary* CO15057 (2015), www.rsis.edu.sg/wp-content/uploads/2015/03/CO15057.pdf.

37. Abdulkader Tayob, *Islam: The Basics* (Oxford: Oneworld, 2003), 13.

38. See Craig Martin, *Capitalizing Religion: Ideology and the Opiate of the Bourgeoisie* (London: Bloomsbury, 2014).

39. Martin, *Capitalizing Religion*, 49, 108–9.

40. Martin, *Capitalizing Religion*, 11.

41. Martin, *Capitalizing Religion*, 11, 35.

42. See Gavin Flood, *The Truth within: A History of Inwardness in Christianity, Hinduism, and Buddhism* (Oxford: Oxford University Press, 2013).

43. Jeremy Carrette and Richard King, *Selling Spirituality: The Silent Takeover of Religion* (London and New York: Routledge, 2004).

44. For one view on Kabbalah water, see Anon, "Kabbalah Water," *Rationalwiki* (2018), https://rationalwiki.org/wiki/Kabbalah_water.

45. See Stephanie Baker, "The Scandal That Should Force Us to Reconsider Wellness Advice from Influencers," *Conversation* (21 May 2019), https://theconversation.com/the-scandal-that-should-force-us-to-reconsider-wellness-advice-from-influencers-117041.

CHAPTER 6. IDENTITY

1. Sheldon Stryker and Peter Burke, "The Past, Present and Future of an Identity Theory," *Social Psychology Quarterly* 63.4 (2000): 284–97, 284.

2. Henri Tajfel, *Social Identity and Intergroup Relations* (Cambridge: Cambridge University Press, 1981), 255.

3. Richard Ashmore, Lee Jussim, and David Wilder, "Introduction: Social Identity and Intergroup Conflict," in *Social Identity, Intergroup Conflict and Conflict Reduction*, ed. Richard Ashmore, Lee Jussim, and David Wilder (Oxford: Oxford University Press, 2001), 3–14, 6.

4. For a classic study, see Samuel Mencher, "Individualism in Modern Western Culture," *Southwestern Social Science Quarterly* 28.3 (1947): 257–63. More recently, see Larry Siedentop, *Inventing the Individual: The Origins of Western Liberalism* (London: Penguin, 2014). See also James Spickard, *Alternative Sociologies of Religion: Through Non-Western Eyes* (New York: State University of New York Press, 2017), 83–86.

5. See Hedges and Coco, "Belonging," 168–69, 183.

6. See Dan Adams and Kate McLean, "Narrative Identity," *Current Directions in Psychological Science* 22.3 (2013): 233–38.

7. See Henri Tajfel and J. Turner, "An Integrative Theory of Intergroup Conflict," in *The Social Psychology of Intergroup Relations*, ed. W. Austin and S. Worchel (Monterey, CA: Brooks/Cole, 1979), 33–47; and Richard Jenkins, *Social Identity*, 4th ed. (New York: Routledge, 2014), 114–19.

8. See Hedges and Coco, "Belonging," 175–76.

9. A good overview is found in Marilynn B. Brewer, "Ingroup Identification and Intergroup Conflict," in Ashmore, Jussim, and Wilder, *Social Identity*, 17–41.

10. On the Trinity, see Alister McGrath, *Historical Theology* (Oxford: Blackwells, 1998), 33–44, 61–72, 305–11; on the *trimurti*, see Gavin Flood, *An Introduction to Hinduism* (Cambridge: Cambridge University Press, 1996), 111; on the *trikaya*, see Paul Williams, *Mahāyāna Buddhism: The Doctrinal Foundations*, 2nd ed. (New York: Routledge, 2009), 172–86.

11. See, e.g., John Milbank, "The End of Dialogue," in *Christian Uniqueness Reconsidered: The Myth of a Pluralistic Theology of Religions*, ed. Gavin D'Costa (Maryknoll, NY: Orbis, 1990), 174–90.

12. On some of the diverging notions, see Bruce Marshall, "Trinity," in *The Blackwell Companion to Modern Theology*, ed. Gareth Jones (Oxford: Blackwell, 2004): 183–203; and Alister McGrath, ed., *The Christian Theology Reader*, 5th ed. (Chichester: Wiley, 2017), 195–97 ("Leonardo Boff on the Trinity as Good News for the Poor"), 215–17 ("Sarah Coakley on Social Models of the Trinity").

13. Jeannine Hill Fletcher, "Religious Pluralism in an Era of Globalisation: The Making of Modern Religious Identity," *Theological Studies* 69 (2008): 394–411, 403.

14. Shelley McKeown, Resshma Haji, and Neil Ferguson, eds., *Understanding Peace and Conflict through Social Identity Theory: Contemporary Global Perspectives* (Basingstoke: Palgrave Macmillan, 2016).

15. See Neil Ferguson and Shelley McKeown, "Social Identity Theory and Intergroup Conflict in Northern Ireland," in McKeown, Haji, and Ferguson, *Understanding Peace*, 215–27.

16. See Samuel Huntington, "The Clash of Civilizations?," *Foreign Affairs*, 72.3 (1993): 22–49.

17. See Ferguson and McKeown, "Social Identity Theory"; and John Alderdice, "The Individual, the Group and the Psychology of Terrorism," *International Review of Psychiatry* 19.3 (2007): 201–9.

18. See Rajeev Bhargava, ed., *Secularism and Its Critics* (Oxford: Oxford University Press, 2005). Tariq Modood and others dispute this. See chapter 16.

19. This was not always so, and the image of Rama as the just king, initially rejected as a suitable figure for reverence by militant Hindu nationalists, has been replaced by the warrior Rama figure. See Kapur Anuradha, "Deity to Crusader: The Changing Iconography of Ram," in *Hindus and Others: The Question of Identity in India Today*, ed. Gyanendra Pandey (New Delhi: Viking, 1993), 74–109.

20. Mary Katzenstein, Uday Mehta, and Usha Thakkar, "The Rebirth of Shiv Sena: The Symbiosis of Discursive and Organizational Power," *Journal of Asian Studies* 56.2 (1997): 371–90.

21. On Islamophobia in militant Hindu nationalist discourse, see Paul Hedges, *Religious Hatred: Prejudice, Islamophobia, and Antisemitism in Global Context* (London: Bloomsbury, 2021), chapter 10.

22. On these dyanamics and wider contexts, see Stephen C. Finley, Biko Mandela Gray, and Lori Latrice Martin, eds., *The Religion of White Rage: Religious Fervor, White Workers and the Myth of Black Racial Progress* (Edinburgh: Edinburgh University Press, 2020).

CHAPTER 7. COLONIALISM

1. See Nicholas Griffiths, *Sacred Dialogues: Christianity and Native Religions in the Global Americas, 1492–1700*, 2nd ed. (Morrisville, NC: Lulu.com, 2017). The magnitude of the death toll may have had dramatic environmental effects; see Chris Brierly, Alexander Koch, Simon Lewis, and Mark Maslin, "European Colonisation of the Americas Killed 10% of World Population and Caused Global Cooling," *Conversation* (31 January 2019), https://theconversation.com/european-colonisation-of-the-americas-killed-10-of-world-population-and-caused-global-cooling-110549.

2. See John Hobson, *The Eastern Origins of Western Civilisation* (Cambridge: Cambridge University Press, 2004).

3. See Kenneth Pomeranz, *The Great Divergence: China, Europe, and the Making of the Modern World Economy* (Princeton: Princeton University Press, 2000). On Britain's destruction of the industrial and economic base of South Asia, see Shashi Tharoor, *Inglorious Empire: What the British Did to India* (London: Penguin, 2017; first published as *An Era of Darkness: the British Empire in India* [Delhi: Penguin, 2016]).

4. See Tomoko Masuzawa, *The Invention of World Religions* (Chicago: Chicago University Press, 2005).

5. David Chidester, *Savage Religion: Colonialism and Comparative Religion in South Africa* (Charlottesville: University of Virginia Press, 1996).

6. See Alison Tweed, *The Civilising Mission and the English Middle Class, 1792–1850: The "Heathen" at Home and Overseas* (Basingstoke: Palgrave Macmillan, 2009). Georg Hegel's (1770–1831) notion of an evolution from "primitive" Asia to "modern" Europe persists; see Balbinder Singh Bhogal, "Sikh Dharam and Postcolonialism: Hegel, Religion and Zizek," *Journal for the Academic Study of Religion* 25.2 (2012): 185–213. The effects of this are ongoing: many have read Friedrich Hegel but not José Rizal, Émile Durkheim but not Nagarjuna, David Hume but not Claude Ake.

7. See Griffiths, *Sacred Dialogues.*

8. Edward Said, *Orientalism* (New York: Pantheon Books, 1978).

9. Rudyard Kipling's (1865–1936) phrase originally asked the US to take up its imperial "duties."

10. See J.J. Clarke, *Oriental Enlightenment: The Encounter between Asian and Western Thought* (London and New York: Routledge, 1997); and Lila Abu Lughod, "Orientalism and Middle East Feminist Studies," in *Feminist Theory Reader,* ed. Carol McKann and Seung-Kyung Kim (New York: Routledge, 2013), 218–26.

11. See Talal Asad, *Genealogies of Religion: Disciplines and Reasons of Power in Christianity and Islam* (London: John Hopkins University Press, 1993); and Richard King, *Orientalism and Religion: Postcolonial Theory, India and "The Mystic East"* (New York: Routledge, 1999), 209.

12. See Lisa Lowe, *Critical Terrains: French and British Orientalism* (Ithaca: Cornell University Press, 1991).

13. See David Smith, *Hinduism and Modernity* (Oxford: Blackwell, 2003), 85–101; and Clarke, *Oriental Enlightenment.* An example might show that not all Western understanding is seen as false by non-Westerners. Once, as a graduate student, I attended a discussion group where a graduate student from Africa mentioned an anthropologist who had written a book on his tribe, at which one scholar piped in: "And, of course, he misinterpreted everything about your people." Somewhat nonplussed, the African student replied: "Actually, we think he described us very accurately." (I recall the event from memory and may not capture the exact words used, but this succinctly expresses the exchange.)

14. See Bruce Sullivan, *Sacred Objects in Secular Spaces: Exhibiting Asian Religions in Museums* (London: Bloomsbury, 2015).

15. See Syed Farid Alatas, "Captive Mind," Wiley Online Library (2016), https://doi.org/10.1002/9781405165518.wbeosc006.pub2.

16. The term "epistemicide" is associated with Boaventura de Sousa Santos, *Epistemologies of the South: Justice against Epistemicide* (New York: Routledge, 2014). But, see also Ramón Grosfoguel, "The Structure of Knowledge in Westernized Universities: Epistemic Racism/Sexism and the Four Genocides/Epistemicides of the Long 16th Century," *Human Architecture Journal of the Sociology of Self-Knowledge* 11.1 (2013): 73–90. Grosfuguel, following Enrique Dussel, traces the belittling of other worldviews to the Cartesian "Cogito, ergo sum" (I think, therefore I am), founded upon a previous conquering vision of the self (this uses the famous phrase of René Descartes (1596–1650). However, a long lineage could be drawn from where John Duns Scotus (1266–1308) distinguished "theology" from "philosophy," which allows the division of ideas Grosfoguel and Dussel speak of. Moreover, Descartes himself, most probably, did not envisage the creation of the "God Eye" "I," that is to say, a detached observer distanced from others, that Grosfoguel critiques. Regardless of how we trace the genealogy, Grosfoguel is right to note that the result of recent Western theory is that "any knowledge that claims to be situated in body-politics of knowledge (Anzaldúa 1987; Frantz Fanon 2010) or geo-politics of knowledge (Dussel 1977) as opposed to the myth of the unsituated knowledge of the Cartesian ego-politics of knowledge is

discarded as biased, invalid, irrelevant, unserious, that is, inferior knowledge" (76–77). Grosfoguel's argument aligns with those made elsewhere throughout this book, especially regarding the problem that much that passes as critical theory is based in assumptions of a view-from-nowhere based in epistemic whiteness (and masculinity, often with a certain class-based presupposition) (see, especially, chapter 5).

17. Gayatri Chakravorty Spivak, "Can the Subaltern Speak?" in *Marxism and the Interpretation of Culture,* ed. Cary Nelson and Lawrence Grossberg (Basingstoke: Macmillan, 1988), 271–313.

18. Homi Bhabha, *The Location of Culture* (New York: Routledge, 1994), 34.

19. Bhabha, *Location of Culture,* 171.

20. While in parts of Asia and Africa skin whitening is seen by many as positive, many Caucasian Westerners seek to get tanned. Part of this is related to socioeconomic factors: in some cultures, the paler skin signifies that one does not have to labor and get exposed to the sun and its effects; in some cultures, the tan signifies leisure, and even foreign travel, that one can be exposed to the sun and is not constantly laboring (in factories or offices, etc.).

21. Bhabha, *Location of Culture,* 71. For an excellent reflection, see Walter Mignolo and Michelle K., "Decolonial Aesthesis: From Singapore, to Cambridge, to Duke University," waltermignolo.com (15 July 2013), https://socialtextjournal.org/periscope_article /decolonial-aesthesis-from-singapore-to-cambridge-to-duke-university/.

22. See Syed Farid Alatas, *Applying Ibn Khaldūn: The Recovery of a Lost Tradition in Sociology* (New York: Routledge, 2015), 26–37. See also James Spickard, *Alternative Sociologies of Religion: Through Non-Western Eyes* (New York: State University of New York Press, 2017), 149–79. Alatas has noted that evidence suggests that many of the early "founders" of "Western" sociology had almost certainly read Ibn Khaldun's work. Further, he suggests that some of their theories could potentially be taken without attribution from Ibn Khaldun, which would give modern sociology roots in an Islamic intellectual.

23. Alatas, *Applying Ibn Khaldūn,* 78.

24. Syed Farid Alatas, "Luxury, State and Society: The Theme of Enslavement in Ibn Khaldun," *Journal of Historical Sociology* 30.1 (2017): 67–76.

25. See Paul Hedges, *Towards Better Disagreement: Religion and Atheism in Dialogue* (London: Jessica Kinglsey, 2017), 138–41.

26. See Paul Hedges, *Religious Hatred: Prejudice, Islamophobia, and Antisemitism in Global Context* (London: Bloomsbury, 2021); and Theodore Vial, *Modern Religion, Modern Race* (Oxford: Oxford University Press, 2016).

27. See Masuzawa, *Invention of World Religions,* 238–39.

28. William David Hart, "Theorizing Race and Religion: Du Boi, Cox, and Fanon," in *Religion, Theory, Critique: Classic and Contemporary Approaches and Methodologies,* ed. Richard King (New York: Columbia University Press, 2017), 563–71, 564.

29. See Hedges, *Religious Hatred.*

30. See Christopher Driscoll and Monica Miller, *Method as Identity: Manufacturing Distance in the Academic Study of Religion* (Lanham, MD: Lexington, 2019).

31. Leon Moosavi, "White Privilege in the Lives of Muslim Converts in Britain," *Ethnic and Racial Studies* 38.11 (2015): 1918–33.

32. Gayraud Wilmore, *African American Religious Studies: An Interdisciplinary Anthology* (Durham: Duke University Press, 1989), xii, cited in Victor Anderson, "Theorizing Black Religious Studies: A Genealogy," in King, *Religion, Theory, Critique*, 579–85, 584. See also Driscoll and Miller, *Method as Identity*, 107–30. For a related argument, see Vincent Lloyd, *Religion of the Field Negro: On Black Secularism and Black Theology* (New York: Fordham University Press, 2017).

33. See Joseph-Achille Mbembé, "Necropolitics," *Public Culture* 15.1 (Winter 2003): 11–40; Walter Mignolo, *The Darker Side of Western Modernity: Global Futures, Decolonial Options* (Durham: Duke University Press, 2011); and Sylvia Wynter, "The Ceremony Must Be Found: After Humanism," *boundary* 2 12.3–13.1 (1984): 19–70. For a reading drawing together thought from some of these and other figures, see Lloyd, *Religion of the Field Negro*.

34. This memorialization, including statues, has been challenged by the Black Lives Matter movement and others; see Paul Hedges, "The Global BLM Movement: Public Memorials and Neo-Decolonisation?," RSIS Commentary CO20127 (2020), www.rsis .edu.sg/wp-content/uploads/2020/06/CO20127.pdf.

35. See Clarke, *Oriental Enlightenment;* and Christopher Beckwith, *Warriors of the Cloister: The Central Asia Origins of Science in the Medieval World* (Princeton: Princeton University Press, 2012). The English term "university" derives from the Latin term *universitas* (denoting something like "the whole" or a "guild" [of scholars]), and so originally named Christian-founded institutions. However, the English system was based upon Islamic models, which used the faculty system (Arabic: *kulliyah*) for differing areas of knowledge (e.g., medicine, law, theology, physical sciences), with academic robes based upon those of Muslim scholars (worn by the early European scholars when they graduated from Islamic institutions). The direct lineage then traces back to Nalanda and other Buddhist universities and institutions which had influenced the development of madrassah. The ancient Greek academies, of for instance Plato (ca. 429–337 BCE) and Aristotle (384–322 BCE), do not form part of this historical chain of development. Chinese influence was largely from the Enlightenment period (see box 16.1).

36. Spickard, *Alternative Sociologies*. Another example of such work is an argument that the Buddhist philosopher Nagarjuna can help shape a decolonized hermeneutical theory; see Paul Hedges, "Theorising a Decolonising Asian Hermeneutic for Comparative Theology: Some Perspectives from Global and Singaporean Eyes," *International Journal of Asian Christianity* 3.2 (2020): 152–168.

37. Samir Amin, *Eurocentrism: Modernity, Religion, and Democracy: A Critique of Eurocentrism and Culturalism*, 2nd ed. (Cape Town: Pambazuka Press, 2011), 219. See also K. N. Chaudhuri, *Asia before Europe: Economy and Civilisation of the Indian Ocean from the Rise of Islam to 1750* (Cambridge: Cambridge University Press, 1991); and V. Y. Mudimbe, *The Invention of Africa: Gnosis, Philosophy, and the Order of Knowledge* (Bloomington: Indiana University Press, 1988).

38. Chen Kuan-Hsing, *Asia as Method: Toward Deimperialization* (Durham: Duke University Press, 2010), 211. This is never simple. Driscoll and Miller's (*Method as Identity*) focus on the US context and its Black-white discourse limits attention to a single hegemonic power center (North America) and thus may sideline other subaltern identities

and theories; see Frank Wu, *Yellow: Race in America beyond Black and White* (New York: Basic Books, 2002). Equally, a focus on Asia may ignore African or Black voices. Indigenous traditions are also often sidelined.

39.   See Leon Moosavi, "The Decolonial Bandwagon and the Dangers of Intellectual Decolonisation," *International Review of Sociology* (2020), DOI: 10.1080/03906701.2020.1776919.

40.   See Hedges, *Religious Hatred*, chapter 1.

41.   See Jessica Frazier, ed., *The Bloomsbury Companion to Hindu Studies* (London: Bloomsbury, 2014), 328; and Barbara Holdrege, "Dharma," in *The Hindu World*, ed. Sushil Mittal and Gene Thursby (London: Routledge, 2007), 213–48, 244–45.

42.   See Gavin Flood, *An Introduction to Hinduism* (Cambridge: Cambridge University Press, 1996), 239.

43.   Will Sweetman, "Against Invention: A Richer History for Hinduism," *Religious Studies Project* (2018), https://religiousstudiesproject.com/podcast/against-invention-a-richer-history-for-hinduism/; and Will Sweetman, *Mapping Hinduism: "Hinduism" and the Study of Indian Religions, 1600–1776* (Halle: Verlag der Franckeschen Stiftungen, 2003).

44.   David Lorenzen, "Who Invented Hinduism?" *Comparative Studies in Society and History* 41.4 (1999): 630–59, 631.

45.   Andrew Nicholson, *Unifying Hinduism: Philosophy and Identity in Indian Intellectual History* (New York: Columbia University Press, 2014).

46.   Alexis Sanderson, "Tolerance, Exclusivity, Inclusivity, and Persecution in Indian Religion during the Early Mediaeval Period," in *Honoris Causa: Essays in Honour of Aveek Sarkar*, ed. John Markinson (London: Allen Lane, 2015), 155–224, 157.

47.   Nicholson, *Unifying Hinduism*, 199.

48.   Pham Quynh Phurong, "Empowerment and Innovation among Saint Trân's Female Mediums," in *Modernity and Re-enchantment: Religion in Post-Revolutionary Vietnam*, ed. Philip Taylor (Singapore: Institute of Southeast Asian Studies, 2007), 221–49, 241–42.

49.   Laurel Kendall, "Gods, Gifts, Markets, and Superstition: Spirited Consumption from Korea to Vietnam," in *Engaging the Spirit World: Popular Beliefs and Practices in Modern Southeast Asia*, ed. Kirsten Endres and Andrea Lausner (New York: Berghahn Books, 2011), 103–20, 114.

50.   David Chidester, *Savage Systems: Colonialism and Comparative Religion in South Africa* (Charlottesville: University of Virginia Press, 1996).

51.   As reviews noted, during the periods when Chidester claimed conflict existed, some labeled traditional systems as "religion," while during periods after conquest the usage of "superstition" remained. See Robert Baum, "Review: *Savage Systems*," *American Ethnologist* 25.3 (1998): 530–31; and Elizabeth Elbourne, "Review: *Savage Systems*," *Journal of Religion in Africa* 29.4 (1999), 504–7.

52.   David Chidester, "Anchoring Religion in the World: A Southern African History of Comparative Religion," *Religion* 26.2 (1996): 141–59, 143.

53.   *Morning Chronicle and London Advertiser* (25 April 1783), cited from *A Sourcebook on the Wreck of the Grosvenor East Indiaman*, ed. Percival R. Kirby (Cape Town: Van Riebeeck Society, 1953), in Chidester, "Anchoring Religion," 144.

54. Chidester, "Anchoring Religion," 149–50.
55. Chidester, "Anchoring Religion," 154.

CHAPTER 8. BRAINS

1. See Justin Barrett and Roger Trigg, "Cognitive and Evolutionary Studies of Religion," in *The Roots of Religion: Exploring the Cognitive Science of Religion*, ed. Roger Trigg and Justin Barrett (New York: Routledge, 2016), 1–15, 3–4; see also Neil Messer, *Theological Neuroethics: Christian Ethics Meets the Science of the Human Brain* (London: Bloomsbury, 2017), 19.

2. See Pascal Boyer, *Religion Explained: The Evolutionary Origins of Religious Thought* (New York: Basic Books, 2001); and Scott Atran, *In Gods We Trust: The Evolutionary Landscape of Religion* (Oxford: Oxford University Press, 2002).

3. See Pascal Boyer and Charles Ramble, "Cognitive Templates for Religious Concepts: Cross-Cultural Evidence for Recall of Counterintuitive Representations," *Cognitive Science: A Multidisciplinary Journal* 25.4 (2001): 535–64; and Ryan Tweney, "What Types of Concepts Make for Great Religious Stories?," in *The Cognitive Science of Religion: A Methodological Introduction to Key Empirical Studies*, ed. D. Jason Sloane and William McCorkle (London: Bloomsbury, 2019), 101–12.

4. See Justin Barrett and Melanie Nyhof, "Spreading Non-natural Concepts: The Role of Intuitive Conceptual Structures in Memory and Transmission of Cultural Materials," *Journal of Cognition and Culture* 1.1 (2001): 69–100. While a recent study suggests there may be some long-term memory retention of certain counterintuitive ideas, it is far from clear what is implied by these and how they are understood; see Aaron C. T. Smith, *Thinking about Religion: Extending the Cognitive Science of Religion* (Oxford: Blackwell, 2014), 45–46.

5. A related theory is the "meme," associated with Richard Dawkins. A meme is a postulated ("false/bad") idea/concept that "fights" to pass itself from one mind to another, as a mind "parasite." However, as there is no evidence for memes, nor an explanation of how they pass themselves on, most scholars reject it as a bad theory; see, e.g., Mary Midgely, "Why Memes?" in *Alas Poor Darwin: Arguments against Evolutionary Psychology*, ed. Hilary Rose and Steven Rose (London: Jonathan Cape, 2000), 67–84.

6. See Roger Trigg, "Human Nature and Religious Freedom," in Trigg and Barrett, *Roots of Religion*, 209–23.

7. Stewart Guthrie, "Animal Animism: Evolutionary Roots of Religious Cognition," in *Current Approaches in the Cognitive Science of Religion*, ed. Ilkka Pyysiäinen and Veikko Anttonen (London: Continuum, 2002), 38–67, 60–61.

8. Justin Barrett, *Why Would Anyone Believe in God?* (Walnut Creek, CA: AltaMira Press, 2004).

9. Deborah Keleman, "Are Children 'Intuitive Theists'? Reasoning about Purpose and Design in Nature," *Psychological Science* 15.5 (2004): 295–301.

10. See Marc Andersen, Thies Pfeiffer, Sebastian Müller, and Uffe Schjoedt, "Agency Detection in Predictive Minds: A Virtual Reality Study," *Religion, Brain, and Behavior* 9.1 (2019): 52–64.

11. Andersen et al., "Agency Detection," 53.

12. Andersen et al., "Agency Detection."

13. See Jesse Bering, "Why Do We See Supernatural Signs in Natural Events?," in Sloane and McCorkle, *Cognitive Science*, 5–14.

14. See Uffe Schjoedt and Marc Andersen, "How Does Religious Experience Work in Predictive Minds?," *Religion, Brain and Behavior* 7.4 (2017): 320–23.

15. See, for instance, the response of Tenzan Eaghll (www.religiousstudiesproject.com /2018/04/26/the-return-of-homo-religiosus/) to an interview and lectures by the anthropologist and primatologist Agustin Fuentes (www.religiousstudiesproject.com /podcast/why-do-we-believe-evolution-primates-and-the-human-niche/) as indicative of the issues.

16. See Smith, *Thinking about Religion*, 4–11.

17. Smith, *Thinking about Religion*, 80.

18. See Ilkka Pyysiäinen, "Religion and the Brain: Cognitive Science as a Basis for Theories of Religion," in *Religion, Theory, Critique: Classic and Contemporary Approaches and Methodologies*, ed. Richard King (New York: Columbia University Press, 2017), 229–36, 230.

19. Vincent Lloyd, *Religion of the Field Negro: On Black Secularism and Black Theology* (New York: Fordham University Press, 2017), 63.

20. See Smith, *Thinking about Religion*, 4.

21. "Module" describes a set of distinct mental functions responsible for a single area of reasoning or thought processes. Sometimes invoked in cognitive science, it is a "folk" category rather than a rigorous analytical one; see Smith, *Thinking about Religion*, 56–57, 59–63, 65–69.

22. See Margaret Boone Rappaport and Christopher Corbally, "Evolution of Religious Capacity in the Genus Homo: Cognitive Time Sequence," *Zygon* 53.1 (2018): 159–97. This is the second in a series of three articles tracing this evolutionary development.

23. See Trigg, "Human Nature and Religious Freedom," especially 216.

24. See Steven Mithen, "Is Religion Inevitable? An Archaeologist's View from the Past," in *The Edge of Reason? Science and Religion in Modern Society*, ed. Alex Bentley (London: Continuum, 2008), 82–94.

25. See Herbert Maschner and Katherine Reedy-Maschner, "The Evolution of Warfare," in Bentley, *Edge of Reason*, 57–64. Indeed, in this sense even something such as genocide could be spoken of as "natural"; see Paul Hedges, *Religious Hatred: Prejudice, Islamophobia, and Antisemitism in Global Context* (London: Bloomsbury, 2021).

26. See David Sloan Wilson, *Darwin's Cathedral* (Chicago: Chicago University Press, 2002).

27. The notion of "social cohesion," what this means, and how it is defined, is much debated. For a recent survey, see Paul Hedges, "Conceptualising Social Cohesion in Relation to Religious Diversity: Sketching a Pathway in a Globalised World," *Interreligious Relations* 16 (2020), www.rsis.edu.sg/research/srp/irr/#.Xtm-nW0zYiI.

28. See Messer, *Theological Neuroethics*, 21.

29. See Linda Woodhead, *An Introduction to Christianity* (Cambridge: Cambridge University Press, 2015).

30. See Benjamin Purzycki, Joseph Henrich, Coren Apicella, Quentin D. Atkinson, Adam Baimel, Emma Cohen, Rita Anne McNamara, Aiyana K. Willard, Dimitris Xygalatas, and Ara Norenzayan, "The Evolution of Religion and Morality: A Synthesis of Ethnographic and Experimental Evidence from Eight Societies," *Religion, Brain and Behavior* 8.2 (2018): 101–32; and Dimitris Xygalatas, "How Do Religious Environments Affect Our Behavior," in Sloane and McCorkle, *Cognitive Science,* 113–21. See also Azim Shariff and Ara Norenzayan, "Does God Make You Good," in Sloane and McCorkle, *Cognitive Science,* 133–43.

31. Gordy Slack, "Why We Are Good: Mirror Neurons and the Roots of Empathy," in Bentley, *Edge of Reason,* 65–72.

32. See sociologist Phil Zuckerman, "Think Religion Makes Society Less Violent? Think Again," *LA Times* (30 October 2015), www.latimes.com/opinion/op-ed/la-oe-1101-zuckerman-violence-secularism-20151101-story.html; see also the Islamicity Index, an assessment of which societies most fulfill in public institutions key Islamic legal (*shariah*) injunctions, which has been topped by predominantly secular countries (http://islamicity-index.org/wp/).

33. Some scholars have hypothesized a shift to a so-called axial age; see Robert Bellah, *Religion in Human Evolution: From the Paleolithic to the Axial Age I* (Cambridge: Belknap Press, 2017). According to axial age theory, human societies shifted ca. 500 BCE to 0 CE from more local polytheistic traditions to an ethical monotheism. However, these changes cover a period from at least 1000 BCE to 1000 CE. Furthermore, the changes occurred very differently in various places. This hypothesis of high gods should not therefore be equated to the axial age notion. However, it could become a more modest and circumspect alternative. For some recent data on the rise of high gods across many regions and centuries, see Harvey Whitehouse, Patrick Savage, Peter Turchin, and Pieter Francois, "Big Gods Came after the Rise of Civilisations, Not Before, Finds Study Using Huge Historical Database," *Conversation* (21 March 2019), https://theconversation.com/big-gods-came-after-the-rise-of-civilisations-not-before-finds-study-using-huge-historical-database-113801?utm_medium=email&utm_campaign=Latest%20from%20The%20Conversation%20for%20March%2020%20 2019%20-%201264011709&utm_content=Latest%20from%20The%20Conversa-tion%20for%20March%2020%202019%20-%201264011709+CID_8cb8a01a59e1 7f70d39f6e4d1e1f9335&utm_source=campaign_monitor_uk&utm_term=Big%20 gods%20came%20after%20the%20rise%20of%20civilisations%20onot%20 before%20finds%20study%20using%20huge%20historical%20database.

34. See Ara Noranzaya, "Does Religion Make People Moral?," *Behavior* 151.2–3 (2014): 365–84; and Azim Shariff and Ara Noranzanya, "God Is Watching You: Priming God Concepts Increases Prosocial Behavior in an Anonymous Economic Game," *Psychological Science* 18.9 (2007): 803–9.

35. See Pascal Boyer, "Explaining Religious Concepts: Lévi-Strauss the Brilliant and Problematic Ancestor," in *Mental Culture: Classical Social Theory and the Cognitive Science of Religion,* ed. Dimitris Xygalatas and William McCorkle (New York: Routledge, 2013), 164–75, 174; and Paul Hedges, *Towards Better Disagreement: Religion and Atheism in Dialogue* (London: Jessica Kingsley, 2017), 26, 173–76.

36. See Harold Koenig and Harvey Cohen, eds., *The Link between Religion and Health: Psychoneuroimmuniology and the Faith Factor* (Oxford: Oxford University Press, 2002), perhaps the most comprehensive survey of studies ever conducted.

37. See David Speed and Ken Fowler, "What's God Got to Do with It? How Religiosity Predicts Atheists' Health," *Journal of Religion and Health* 55.1 (2016): 296–308.

38. Andrew Newberg and Eugene d'Aquili, "The Neuropsychology of Religious and Spiritual Experience," in *Cognitive Models and Spiritual Maps,* ed. Jensine Anderson and Robert Forman (Thorverton: Imprint Press, 2002), 251–66, 259–63. Specific brain areas suggested are the inferior temporal lobe, the inferior parietal lobule, the posterior superior parietal lobule, and the prefrontal cortex.

39. These are diverse, and the literature may sometimes subsume a range of experiences under this heading; see Alison R. Yung and Ashleigh Lin, "Psychotic Experiences and Their Significance," *World Psychiatry* 15.2 (2016), www.ncbi.nlm.nih.gov/pmc/articles/PMC4911755/.

40. Smith, *Thinking about Religion,* 103, citing Peters, McKenna, and Orbach, "Delusional Ideation in Religious and Psychotic Populations," *British Journal of Clinical Psychology* 38 (1999): 83–96.

41. Michel Foucault, *History of Madness,* trans. Jean Khalfa and Jonathan Murphy (New York: Routledge, 2006).

42. Georg Feuerstein, *Holy Madness: The Shock Tactics and Radical Teachings of Crazy-Wise Adepts, Holy Fools and Rascal Gurus* (London: Penguin, 1993).

43. See Anna DeMiller, "Shamanism: A Selected Annotated Bibliography," *ANSS,* https://anssacrl.wordpress.com/publications/bibliographies/annual-program-2002/; and Michael Winkelman, "Shamanism in Cross-Cultural Perspective," *International Journal of Transpersonal Studies* 31.2 (2013): 47–62.

44. Eugene d'Aquili and Andrew Newberg, *The Mystical Mind: Probing the Biology of Religious Experience* (Minneapolis: Fortress Press, 1999). A more recent popular work is Andrew Newberg and Mark Waldman, *How Enlightenment Changes Your Brain: The New Science of Transformation* (New York: Avery, 2016).

45. See Anne Runehov, *Sacred or Neural? The Potential of Neuroscience to Explain Religious Experience* (Goettingen: Vandenhoeck and Ruprecht, 2007).

46. Armin Geertz, "Cognitive Science," in Engler and Stausberg, *Oxford Handbook,* 97–110, 100.

47. Uffe Schjoedt, "The Religious Brain: A General Introduction to the Experimental Neuroscience of Religion," *Method and Theory in the Study of Religion* 21 (2009): 310–39, 313–18.

48. Schjoedt, "Religious Brain," 320–22.

49. Benjamin Purzycki et al., "The Evolution of Religion and Morality," 103.

50. For an example, see Gregory Shushan, "Cultural-Linguistic Constructionism and the Challenge of Near-Death and Out-of-Body Experiences," in *The Study of Religious Experience: Approaches and Methodologies,* ed. Bettina E. Schmidt (Sheffield: Equinox, 2015), 71–87; and Paul Hedges, "Encounters with Ultimacy? Autobiographical and Critical Perspectives in the Academic Study of Religion," *Open Theology* 4.1 (2018), www.degruyter.com/view/journals/opth/4/1/article-p355.xml.

51. See, e.g., Christopher Hitchens, *God Is Not Great: How Religion Poisons Everything* (New York: Twelve, 2007).

52. Peter Harrison, *The Territories of Science and Religion* (Chicago: Chicago University Press, 2015).

53. See Paul Hedges, *Towards Better Disagreement: Religion and Atheism in Dialogue* (London: Jessica King, 2017), 15, 137–59.

54. "Study Shows How College Major and Religious Faith Affect Each Other," *Michigan News* (4 August 2009), https://news.umich.edu/study-shows-how-college-major-and-religious-faith-affect-each-other/.

55. See Rice University, "First Worldwide Survey of Religion and Science: No Not All Scientists Are Atheists," Rice University (3 December 2015), https://news.rice.edu /2015/12/03/first-worldwide-survey-of-religion-and-science-no-not-all-scientists-are-atheists/; and Pew Research Center, "Scientists and Beliefs," Pewforum.org (5 November 2009), www.pewforum.org/2009/11/05/scientists-and-belief. See also Maria Rogińska, "Trajectories of (Non)Belief in the Scientific Community: The Case of Polish and Ukrainian Natural Scientists," *Review of Religious Research* 61 (2019): 389–409.

56. See Hedges, *Towards Better Disagreement*, 96–117, especially 108–10.

57. BBC, "2011 Census: Richard Dawkins Praises Atheism in Wales," *BBC News* (12 December 2012), www.bbc.com/news/uk-wales-20691092.

58. Lois Lee, "Non-religion," in Stausberg and Engler, *Oxford Handbook*, 84–96; and Lois Lee, *Recognizing the Non-religious: Reimagining the Secular* (Oxford: Oxford University Press, 2015).

CHAPTER 9. BODIES

1. See Daniel Miller, "Materiality: An Introduction," in *Materiality*, ed. Daniel Miller (Durham: Duke University Press, 2005), 1–50, 1–2.

2. Manuel Vásquez, *More Than Belief: A Materialist Theory of Religion* (Oxford: Oxford University Press, 2011).

3. For instance, David Chidester, *Religion: Material Dynamics* (Berkeley: University of California Press, 2018); David Morgan, *The Embodied Eye: Religious Visual Culture and the Social Life of Feeling* (Berkeley: University of California Press, 2012); Robert Orsi, *Between Heaven and Earth: The Religious Worlds People Make and the Scholars Who Study Them* (Princeton: Princeton University Press, 2006); and Vásquez, *More Than Belief*.

4. See Marcel Mauss, "Techniques of the Body," *Economy and Society* 2.1 (1973): 70–88. Originally a lecture for the Société de Psychologie (7 May 1934), published in *Journal de Psychologie Normal et Patholigique* 32 (1935): 271–93.

5. See Nick Crossley, "Researching Embodiment by Way of 'Body Techniques,'" *Sociological Review* 55.1 (2007): 80–94.

6. Meredith McGuire, *Lived Religion* (Oxford: Oxford University Press, 2008), 33–34.

7. Sarah Shaw suggests that the Buddhist texts "can be surprisingly silent on . . . the issue of posture," *Buddhist Meditation: An Anthology of Texts from the Pāli Canon* (New

York: Routledge, 2006), 15. But, different forms of posture are prescribed in the Buddhist texts; see Shaw, *Buddhist Meditation*, 15–18, 141–43; and Sarah Shaw, *Introduction to Buddhist Meditation* (New York: Routledge, 2009), 22–24, 130–31, 245–46. See also box 9.5.

8. See Rupert Gethin, *The Foundations of Buddhism* (Oxford: Oxford University Press, 1998), 135–37.

9. Abdulkader Tayob, *Islam: A Short Introduction* (Oxford: Oneworld, 1999), 66–67.

10. Tayob, *Islam*, 62–63.

11. Eric Goffman, *Frame Analysis* (London: Penguin, 1975); and Eric Gombrich, *The Sense of Order* (London: Phaidon Press, 1979).

12. Miller, "Materiality."

13. Hayden Coombs, "Framing Theory," *Hayden Coombs* (blog) (2015), https://hayden-coombs.wordpress.com/2015/09/30/framing-theory/.

14. Bryan Turner, *The Body and Society* (London: Sage, 2008), 15.

15. Vásquez, *More Than Belief*, 43–58.

16. See Elizabeth Stuart and Lisa Isherwood, *An Introduction to Body Theology* (Sheffield: Sheffield Academic Press, 1998), 52–77.

17. Howard Robinson, "Dualism," in *Stanford Encyclopedia of Philosophy* (2016), https://plato.stanford.edu/entries/dualism/.

18. Michel Foucault, *The Foucault Reader*, ed. Paul Rabinow (London: Peregrin, 1984), 123–256.

19. Turner, *Body*, 52.

20. See Michel Foucault, *The History of Sexuality*, trans. Robert Hurley (New York: Vintage, 1981), 139.

21. Turner, *Body*, 37.

22. On the ranking of bodies and religion into racialized categories, see Francisco Bethencourt, *Racisms: From the Crusades to the Twentieth Century* (Princeton: Princeton University Press, 2013); and Paul Hedges, *Religious Hatred: Prejudice, Islamophobia, and Antisemitism in Global Context* (London: Bloomsbury, 2021). See also Sylvester A. Johnson, "Colonialism, Orientalism, and the Body," in Narayanan, *Wiley Blackwell Companion to Religion and Materiality*, 509–29.

23. Syed Hussein Alatas, *The Myth of the Lazy Native* (New York: Routledge, 2010).

24. See Renée de la Torre, "Religion and Embodiment: Religion and the (Latin American) Bodies That Practice It," in *Controversies in Contemporary Religion*, ed. Paul Hedges, vol. 1 (Santa Barbara: Praeger, 2010), 81–112, 88.

25. Michael Rowlands, "A Materialist Approach to Materiality," in Miller, *Materiality*, 72–87, 81.

26. Emily Anderson, *Christianity and Imperialism in Modern Japan: Empire for God* (London: Bloomsbury, 2014), 53–54.

27. See Michelle Mary Lelwica, *Shameful Bodies: Religion and the Culture of Physical Improvement* (London: Bloomsbury, 2017).

28. See David L. McMahan, "Secularism Is Not Secular: Interrogating the Urge to Purge Secularism of Buddhist and Hindu Influence," *Religious Studies Review* 46.2 (2020): 171–72.

29. Torre, "Religion and Embodiment," 88, referencing Merleau-Ponty, *Phenomenology of Perception* (Spanish translation).

30. See Sean O'Neil, "Sapir-Whorf Hypothesis," in *The International Encyclopedia of Language and Social Interaction,* ed. Karen Tracy, Cornelia Ilie, and Todd Sandel (Chichester: Wiley, 2015), https://onlinelibrary.wiley.com/doi/abs/10.1002/9781118611463.wbielsi086. For advocacy of it, see Guillaume Thierry, "The Power of Language: We Translate Our Thoughts into Words, but Words Also Affect How We Think," *Conversation* (27 February 2019), https://theconversation.com/the-power-of-language-we-translate-our-thoughts-into-words-but-words-also-affect-the-way-we-think-111801.

31. Ludwig Wittgenstein, *Philosophical Investigations,* trans. G. Anscombe, P. Hacker, and Joachim Schulte (Oxford: Blackwell, 1953), 610. Wittgenstein's point was how then do we think humans can talk about deity, but we employ his point for a different purpose.

32. Steven Pinker, *The Language Instinct* (New York: Harper, 1994).

33. See Bongrae Seok, *Embodied Moral Psychology and Confucian Philosophy* (Lanham, MD: Lexington Books, 2013).

34. This is argued by, for instance, Karen Barad, *Meeting the Universe Halfway: Quantum Physics and the Entanglement of Matter and Meaning* (Durham: Duke University Press, 2007).

35. See Linda Alcoff, "Cultural Feminism versus Post-Structuralism: The Identity Crisis in Feminist Theory," *Signs* 13.3 (1988): 405–36; and Dorothy Roberts, "The Ethics of Bioscience," Tanner Lecture on Human Values (2016), https://tannerlectures.utah.edu/Roberts%20Manuscript%201%20and%202.pdf.

36. Vásquez, *More Than Belief,* 3. See also Seok, *Embodied Moral Psychology;* and Barad, *Meeting the Universe.*

37. Audre Lorde, "The Master's Tools Will Never Dismantle the Master's House," in *This Bridge Called My Back: Writings by Radical Women of Color,* ed. Cherríe Moraga and Gloria Anzaldúa (New York: Kitchen Table Press, 1983), 94–101.

38. Turner, *Body,* 48, 50–52.

39. David Morgan, "Materiality," in *The Oxford Handbook of the Study of Religion,* ed. Michael Stausberg and Steven Engler (Oxford: Oxford University Press, 2016), 271–89, 273.

40. Morgan, "Materiality," 274.

41. Thomas J. Csordas, *Embodiment and Experience: The Existential Ground of Culture and Self* (Cambridge: Cambridge University Press, 1994), 7; see Torre, "Religion and Embodiment," 88–89.

42. See Vásquez, *More Than Belief.* See also Manuel Vásquez, "The Persistence, Ubiquity, and Dynamicity of Materiality: Studying Religion and Materiality Comparatively," in Narayanan, *Wiley Blackwell Companion to Religion and Materiality,* 1–42.

43. "Miracle" was commonly used by advocates and in the media. While the meaning is contested, it commonly signifies an event which transcends the laws of nature. Most discussions focus on the Western Christian tradition, which frames English usage. See Thomas Aquinas, *Summa Theologiae* (1265–1274), 1.105.aa.6–8, http://inters.org/Aquinas-Theology-Miracles; David Hume, *An Enquiry concerning Human Understanding* (1748), 10.1, "On Miracles," www3.nd.edu/~afreddos/courses/43811/hume-

on-miracles.htm; Malcolm Diamond, "Miracles," *Religious Studies* 9.3 (1973): 307–24; and David Basinger, *Miracles* (Cambridge: Cambridge University Press, 2018).

44. James White, *The Cambridge Movement: The Ecclesiologists and the Gothic Revival* (Cambridge: Cambridge University Press, 1962).

45. The term "Gothic" was first used pejoratively to suggest a barbaric style and was not used by the medieval architects.

46. Simpler items were left by poorer devotees.

CHAPTER 10. GENDER

1. See, for instance, the following report on the situation in the UK: https://trs.ac.uk /wp-content/uploads/2013/11/Gender-in-TRS-Project-Report-Final.pdf.

2. While often cited as evidence of Jewish misogyny, Philo of Alexandria's (ca. 20 BCE–40 CE) ideas were distinct from mainstream Jewish thought; see Daniel Boyarin, "Gender," in *Critical Terms for Religious Studies,* ed. Mark C. Taylor (Chicago: University of Chicago Press, 1998), 117–35. But, today, Orthodox Jews—like Plato—thank God (for Plato, the gods) that they were born male and not female (Plato also thanked the gods he was born free and not enslaved).

3. Elizabeth Stuart, *Gay and Lesbian Theologies: Repetitions with Critical Difference* (Aldershot: Ashgate, 2003), 109.

4. "Sin" is a term that has come to have quite different connotations in Christianity compared to much of the biblical text; see Sarah Johnston, ed., *Religions of the Ancient World: A Guide* (Cambridge: Belknap Press, 2004).

5. See Lisa Isherwood and Elizabeth Stuart, *Introducing Body Theology* (Sheffield: Sheffield Academic Press, 1998), 64–67.

6. This was a trend that began much earlier, with the English queen Elizabeth I (1533–1603) being central in this gender construction.

7. See David Feldman, "Why Do People Blame the Victim?," *Psychology Today* (2 March 2018), www.psychologytoday.com/us/blog/supersurvivors/201803/why-do-people-blame-the-victim.

8. See Cynthia Eller, *The Myth of Patriarchal Prehistory: Why an Invented Past Won't Give Women a Future* (Boston: Beacon Press, 2001).

9. See Sher Banu A. L. Khan, *Sovereign Women in a Muslim Kingdom: The Sultanahs of Aceh, 1641–1699* (Singapore: National University of Singapore Press, 2017).

10. See Gavin Flood, *An Introduction to Hinduism* (Cambridge: Cambridge University Press, 1996), 135–38.

11. See, e.g., Ranjoo Herr, "Confucian Family-State and Women: A Proposal for Confucian Feminism," in *Asian and Feminist Philosophies in Dialogue: Liberating Traditions,* ed. Jennifer McWeeny and Ashby Butnor (New York: Columbia University Press, 2014), 78–98.

12. See Robin Wang, "Dao Becomes Female: A Gendered Reality, Knowledge, and Strategy for Living," in *The Routledge Companion to Feminist Philosophy,* ed. Ann Garry, Serene Khader, and Alison Stone (New York: Routledge, 2017), 35–48.

13. See Catherine Despeux and Livia Kohn, *Women in Daoism* (Cambridge: Three Pines Press, 2003).

14. "Goddess," here, takes a capital, referring to the proper name of the deity worshipped by Goddess traditions.

15. See Alleyn Diesel, "Womanspirit," *Agenda: Empowering Women for Gender Equity* 19 (1993): 71–75; Graham Harvey, *Contemporary Paganism: Religions of the Earth from Druids and Witches to Heathens and Ecofeminists* (New York: New York University Press, 2011); and Starhawk, "Witchcraft and Women's Culture," in *Womanspirit Rising,* ed. Carol P. Christ and Judith Plaskow (New York: Harper and Row, 1979).

16. Anon, "Glastonbury Goddess Temple," Goddesstemple.co.uk (2019), www .goddesstemple.co.uk (capitals in original).

17. Mary Daly, *Beyond God the Father: Towards a Philosophy of Women's Liberation* (Boston: Beacon Press, 1973).

18. See Carolyn De Swarte Gifford, "Politicizing the Sacred Texts: Elizabeth Cady Stanton and *The Woman's Bible,*" in *Searching the Scriptures: A Feminist Introduction,* ed. Elisabeth Schüssler Fiorenza (London: SCM, 1993), 52–63.

19. See Paul Hedges, *Religious Hatred: Prejudice, Islamophobia, and Antisemitism in Global Context* (London: Bloomsbury, 2021), chapter 5. In Protestant Christian–dominated countries it affected not only Jews but also other Christians, especially Roman Catholics.

20. See Judith Butler, *Gender Trouble: Feminism and the Subversion of Identity* (New York: Routledge, 1990); Judith Butler, *Bodies That Matter: On the Discursive Limits of "Sex"* (New York: Routledge, 1993); and Ian Burkitt, *Bodies of Thought: Embodiment, Identity and Modernity* (London: Sage, 1999), 90–98.

21. These colors are a modern, marketized framing of gendered colors. In Europe, traditionally, blue was for girls as it was seen as the color of Jesus's mother, Mary, while pink was for boys.

22. See Rosemary Radford Ruether, "The Emergence of Christian Feminist Theology," in *The Cambridge Companion to Feminist Theology,* ed. Susan Frank Parsons (Cambridge: Cambridge University Press, 2002), 3–22.

23. However, this is still an ongoing battle in many places. See Anon, "An Abortion Ban Prompted by Covid-19 Reaches the Supreme Court," *Economist* (12 April 2020), www .economist.com/united-states/2020/04/12/an-abortion-ban-prompted-by-covid-19-reaches-the-supreme-court.

24. See Germaine Greer, interview, BBC (24 October 2015), www.bbc.com/news/av /uk-34625512/germaine-greer-transgender-women-are-not-women.

25. See Darlene Juschka, "Feminism and Gender Theory," in *The Oxford Handbook of the Study of Religion,* ed. Michael Stausberg and Steven Engler (Oxford: Oxford University Press, 2016), 137–49, 142.

26. Boyarin, "Gender," 130. Scholar Luce Irigaray stated that denying two genders could be seen as "genocide"; Luce Irigaray, *Je, Tu, Nous: Toward a Culture of Difference* (New York: Routledge, 1993), 12, though various interpretations of her meaning exist.

27. Boyarin, "Gender," 125.

28. See Carolyn Burke, Naomi Schor, and Margaret Whitford, eds., *Engaging with Irigaray: Feminist Philosophy and Modern European Thought* (New York: Columbia University Press, 1994).

29. bell hooks, *Ain't I a Woman: Black Women and Feminism* (Boston: South End Press, 1981).

30. Kum-Kum Bhavani and Margaret Coulson, "Transforming Socialist Feminism: The Challenge of Racism," in *Black British Feminism: A Reader,* ed. Heidi Safia Mirza (New York: Routledge, 1997), 59–62.

31. Chandra Mohanty, "Under Western Eyes: Feminist Scholarship and Colonial Discourses," *Feminist Review* 30 (1988), 65–88. See J. Anne Tickner, "Gender in World Politics," in *The Globalization of World Politics: An Introduction to International Relations,* 5th ed., ed. John Bayliss, Steve Smith, and Patricia Owens (Oxford: Oxford University Press, 2011), 262–77, 267.

32. Audre Lorde, "The Master's Tools Will Never Dismantle the Master's House," in *This Bridge Called My Back: Writings by Radical Women of Color,* ed. Cherríe Moraga and Gloria Anzaldúa (New York: Kitchen Table Press, 1983), 94–101.

33. See Serge Guimond, "Psychological Similarities and Differences between Women and Men across Cultures," *Social and Personality Psychology Compass* 2.1 (2008): 494–510.

34. See Carole Mccann, Seung-kyung Kim, eds., *Feminist Theory Reader: Local and Global Perspectives* (New York: Routledge, 2013).

35. See, e.g., Jerusha Lamptey, *Never Wholly Other: A Muslima Theology of Religious Pluralism* (Oxford: Oxford University Press, 2014).

36. Kimberlé Crenshaw, "Demarginalizing the Intersection of Race and Sex: A Black Feminist Critique of Antidiscrimination Doctrine, Feminist Theory and Antiracist Politics," *University of Chicago Legal Forum* 1989.1.8 (1989): 139–67, https://chicagounbound.uchicago.edu/cgi/viewcontent.cgi?article=1052&context=uclf.

37. See Jeannine Hill Fletcher, "Shifting Identity: The Contribution of Feminist Thought to Theologies of Religious Pluralism," *Journal of Feminist Studies in Religion* 19 (2003): 5–24, 16–19.

38. Patricia Hill Collins, *Black Feminist Thought: Knowledge, Consciousness, and the Politics of Empowerment* (Boston: Unwin Hyman, 1990).

39. Francis Beale, *Double Jeopardy: To Be Black and Female* (Detroit: Radical Education Project, 1969).

40. Biko Agozino, "Theorizing Otherness, the War on Drugs and Incarceration," *Theoretical Criminology* 4.3 (2000): 359–76, 363.

41. For an account of this in relation to the Chinese Zhuangzi, see Xinyan Jiang, "What Would Zhuangzi Say to Harding? A Daoist Critique of Feminist Standpoint Epistemology," in *Asian and Feminist Philosophies in Dialogue: Liberating Traditions,* ed. Jennifer McWeeny and Ashby Butnor (New York: Columbia University Press, 2014), 147–66.

42. See Justin Barrett, "What Do We Think about God When We Aren't Careful?," in *The Cognitive Science of Religion: A Methodological Introduction to Key Empirical Studies,* ed. D. Jason Sloane and William McCorkle (London: Bloomsbury, 2019), 15–24, 15–16.

43. See, e.g., Tina Beattie, "Religious Identity and the Ethics of Representation: The Study of Religion and Gender in the Secular Academy," in *Gender, Religion and Diversity: Cross-Cultural Perspectives,* ed. Ursula King and Tina Beattie (London: Continuum, 2005), 65–78.

44. See, e.g., Hilary Rodrigues and John Harding, *Introduction to the Study of Religion* (New York: Routledge, 2009), 112–18.

45. Joan Breton Connelly, *Portrait of a Priestess: Women and Ritual in Ancient Greece* (Princeton: Princeton University Press, 2007).

46. For a feminist reading of "mystic," see Grace Jantzen, *Power, Gender and Christian Mysticism* (Cambridge: Cambridge University Press, 1995).

47. EGMusic Classic, "Hildegard von Bingen Canticles of Ecstasy Medieval Music," video (2017), www.youtube.com/watch?v=6AmpgAoACHg.

48. See Fiona Bowie and Oliver Davies, *Hildegard of Bingen: An Anthology* (London: SPCK, 1995).

49. Maura O'Neill, *Women Speaking, Women Listening: Women in Interreligious Dialogue* (Maryknoll, NY: Orbis Books, 1990), 27–28. See also Helene Egnell, *Other Voices: A Study of Christian Feminist Approaches to Religious Plurality East and West* (Uppsala: Swedish Institute of Mission Research, 2006), 274.

50. Jeannine Hill Fletcher, "Women's Voices in Interreligious Dialogue," *Studies in Interreligious Dialogue* 16.1 (2006): 1–22, 14–15. She develops and critiques ideas found in Enid M. Sefcovic and Diane Theresa Bifano, "Creating a Rhetorical Home for Feminists in the 'Master's House' of the Academy: Toward a Gendered Taxonomy of Form and Content," *Women and Language* 27 (2004): 53–63. For a wider discussion, see Paul Hedges, *Controversies in Interreligious Dialogue and the Theology of Religions* (London: SCM Press, 2010), 208–9.

51. See Hedges, *Controversies in Interreligious Dialogue*, 208.

52. Françoise d'Eaubonne, *Le féminisme ou la mort* (Paris: P. Horay, 1974).

53. Vandana Shiva, *Staying Alive: Women, Ecology and Survival in India* (London: Zed Books, 1988).

54. See Kayla Wheeler, "Women in Religion: Does Gender Matter?," in *Controversies in Contemporary Religion*, ed. Paul Hedges, vol. 2 (Santa Barbara: Praeger, 2014), 1–21, 12.

55. Rita Nakashima Brock, "Feminist Theories," in *Dictionary of Feminist Theologies*, ed. Letty Russell and J. Shannon Clarkson (Loiusville: Westminster John Knox Press, 1996): 116–20, 117.

56. Aihwa Ong, *Spirits of Resistance and Capitalist Discipline: Factory Women in Malaysia* (Albany: State University of New York Press, 1987).

57. Even if other examples come to light, they remain rare and striking.

58. These disputes often concern not the Theravada-Mahayana distinction (doctrinal), but the version of Vinaya interpretation (monastic code of discipline) followed (practice).

CHAPTER 11. COMPARISON

1. Richard King, "The Copernican Turn in the Study of Religion," in *Religion, Theory, Critique: Classic and Contemporary Approaches and Methodologies,* ed. Richard King (New York: Columbia University Press, 2017), 1–20, 1, italics in original.

2. See Eric Sharpe, *Comparative Religion: A History,* 2nd ed. (London: Duckworth, 1986).

3. Jonathan Z. Smith, "In Comparison a Magic Dwells," in *A Magic Still Dwells: Comparative Religion in the Postmodern Age,* ed. Kimberley C. Patton and Benjamin C. Ray (Berkeley: University of California Press, 2000), 23–44.

4. See Peter van der Veer, *The Power of Comparison* (Durham: Duke University Press, 2016).

5. Jeppe Sinding Jensen, "Why Magic? It's Just Comparison," *Method and Theory in the Study of Religion* 16.1 (2004): 45–60, 51. See also Oliver Freiberger, *Considering Comparison: A Method for Religious Studies* (Oxford: Oxford University Press, 2019).

6. Jensen, "Why Magic?," 58.

7. Plato, *Sophist* 231a, cited in J. Z. Smith, "In Comparison a Magic Dwells," 29.

8. Wilfred Cantwell Smith, *What Is Scripture?* (London: SCM, 1993).

9. See John Barton, *How the Bible Came to Be* (Louisville: Westminster John Knox Press, 1998).

10. See Xinzhong Yao, *An Introduction to Confucianism* (Cambridge: Cambridge University Press, 2000), 47–67; and Cathy Cantwell, *Buddhism: The Basics* (New York: Routledge: 2010), 93–106.

11. See Alister McGrath, *Historical Theology: An Introduction to the History of Christian Thought* (Oxford: Blackwell, 1998), 177–85.

12. See Stanley Fish, *Is There a Text in This Class? On the Power of Interpretive Communities* (Cambridge: Harvard University Press, 1982); and Hans-Georg Gadamer, *Truth and Method,* 2nd ed., trans. William Doepel (London: Sheed and Ward, 1979).

13. See Paul Hedges, *Towards Better Disagreement: Religion and Atheism in Dialogue* (London: Jessica Kingsley, 2017), 36–42.

14. See Louis Komjathy, *The Daoist Tradition* (London: Bloomsbury, 2013), 225–42; and Kristofer Schipper, *The Taoist Body,* trans. Karen Duval (Berkeley: University of California Press, 1994).

15. See Klaus Klostermaier, *Hindu Writings: A Short Introduction to the Major Sources* (Oxford: Oneworld, 2000).

16. Robert Campany, "'Religious' as a Category: A Comparative Case Study," *Numen* 65 (2018): 333–76, 37, citing Russell McCutcheon, "A Response to Robert Ford Campany's 'Chinese History and its Implications for Writing 'Religion,'" in *Dynamics in the History of Religions between Asia and Europe: Encounters, Notions, and Comparative Perspectives* (Leiden: Brill, 2011), 295–305, 305.

17. Arvind Sharma, *Religious Studies and Comparative Methodology: The Case for Reciprocal Illumination* (Albany: State University of New York Press, 2005); and Arvind Sharma, "Reciprocal Illumination," in *Interreligious Comparisons in Religious Studies and Theology: Comparison Revisited,* ed. Perry Schmidt-Leukel and Andreas Nehring (London and New York: Bloomsbury, 2016), 178–90.

18. Sharma, "Reciprocal Illumination," 181–82.

19. King, "The Copernican Study," 18.

20. Jonathan Z. Smith, *To Take Place: Toward Theory in Ritual* (Chicago: Chicago University Press, 1987), 14.

21. Oliver Freiberger, "Elements of a Comparative Methodology in the Study of Religion," *Religions* 9.38 (2018): 1–14, 4. For more on his criticism of critics of comparison, see Freiberger, *Considering Comparison.*

22. See David Freidenreich, "Comparisons Compared: A Methodological Survey of Comparisons of Religion from 'A Magic Dwells' to *A Magic Still Dwells*," *Method and Theory in the Study of Religion* 16 (2004): 80–101.

23. See, e.g., Jonathan Z. Smith, *Relating Religion* (Chicago: Chicago University Press, 2004), 92–94.

24. See Campany, "'Religious' as a Category," 335–36.

25. See Freiberger, "Elements of a Comparative Methodology."

26. See David Decosimo, "For Big Comparison: Why the Arguments against Comparing Entire Religious Traditions Fail," *Religion Compass* 12 (2018): 1–18.

27. Mircea Eliade, *Patterns in Comparative Religion*, trans. Rosemary Sheed (London: Sheed and Ward, 1958). Eliade was read by the mythologist Joseph Campbell, who popularized and simplified his work, and Campbell was read by one George Lucas, who used many of the mythological themes in his original *Star Wars* trilogy.

28. See Paul Hedges, "Comparative Methodology and the Religious Studies Toolkit," in Schmidt-Leukel and Nehring, *Interreligious Comparisons*, 17–33, 18–19; and J. Z. Smith, *To Take Place*, 1–23.

29. Gavin Flood, "Religious Practice and the Nature of the Human," in Schmidt-Leukel and Nehring, *Interreligious Comparisons*, 130–41, 131.

30. Jensen, "Why Magic?," 53–54.

31. See Flood, *Truth Within*; and Gavin Flood, *The Ascetic Self: Subjectivity, Memory and Tradition* (Cambridge: Cambridge University Press, 2004).

32. See Douglas Davies, *Death, Ritual, and Belief: The Rhetoric of Funeral Rites*, 3rd ed. (London: Bloomsbury, 2017).

33. Jensen, "Why Magic?," 56.

34. For another recent argument for comparison as a practice in the study of religion, see Freiberger, *Considering Comparison*.

35. Flood, "Religious Practice and the Nature of the Human," 133.

36. Flood, "Religious Practice and the Nature of the Human," 134.

37. See Flood, *Truth Within*, 5–25; and Gadamer, *Truth*.

38. See Campany, "'Religious' as a Category," 369.

39. See Paul Hedges, "Gadamer, Play, and Interreligious Dialogue as the Opening of Horizon," *Journal of Dialogue Studies* 4 (2017): 1–26.

40. Jensen, "Why Magic?," 46.

41. Jensen, "Why Magic?," 49.

42. Jensen, "Why Magic?," 54.

43. Jensen notes that although Otto lamented that language always said things concretely, this is why it may be used; "Why Magic?," 55.

44. Flood, "Religious Practice and the Nature of the Human," 135.

45. See Pascal Boyer, *Religion Explained: The Evolutionary Origins of Religious Thought* (New York: Basic Books, 2001).

46. Flood, "Religious Practice and the Nature of the Human," 136.

47. See Flood, "Religious Practice and the Nature of the Human," 134–38, Luther H. Martin, "'Disenchanting' the Comparative Study of Religion," *Method and Theory in the Study of Religion* 16.1 (2004): 36–44, 41; and Kenneth Rose, "The Singular and the

Shared: Making Amends to Eliade after the Dismissal of the Sacred," in Schmidt-Leukel and Nehring, *Interreligious Comparisons*, 110–29, 110.

48. Hugh B. Urban, "Power Still Dwells: The Ethics and Politics of Comparison in *A Magic Still Dwells*," *Method and Theory in the Study of Religion* 16.1 (2004): 24–35, 26.

49. Barbara Holdrege, "Hindu-Jewish Encounters," in *The Wiley-Blackwell Companion to Inter-Religious Dialogue*, ed. Catherine Cornille (Chichester: Wiley-Blackwell, 2013), 410–37, 423–24.

50. Holdrege, "Hindu-Jewish Encounters," 425, italics in original.

51. See Fabrice Blée, "Can Christians Engage in Non-Christian Practices? Eastern Meditations and Contemplative Prayer," in *Controversies in Contemporary Religion*, ed. Paul Hedges, vol. 3 (Santa Barbara: Praeger, 2014), 277–304.

CHAPTER 12. RITUAL

1. It may even be said that "it is a truth universally acknowledged, that a religious person seeking to fulfill her religious obligations, must be engaged in ritual behavior." With apologies to Jane Austen, I play here on commentators who note the paradox: if it is a truth universally acknowledged, why the need to state it?

2. Bronislaw Malinowski, *The Ethnography of Malinowski: The Trobriand Islands, 1915–18*, ed. Michael Young (London: Routledge and Kegan Paul, 1979).

3. Émile Durkheim, *The Elementary Forms of Religious Life* (Oxford: Oxford University Press, 2001 [1912]).

4. See Dimitris Xygalatas, "Do Rituals Promote Social Cohesion?," in *The Cognitive Science of Religion: A Methodological Introduction to Key Empirical Studies* (London: Bloomsbury, 2019), 163–72.

5. Clifford Geertz, "Ritual and Social Change: A Javanese Example," *American Anthropologist* NS 59.1 (1957): 32–54.

6. See Anantanand Rambachan, "Hinduism," in *Death in World Religions*, ed. Harold Coward (Maryknoll, NY: Orbis, 1997), 66–86.

7. Arnold Van Gennep, *Rites of Passage* (London: Routledge and Kegan Paul, 1960 [1909]).

8. See René Girard, *Violence and the Sacred*, trans. Patrick Gregory (Baltimore: Johns Hopkins University Press, 1977).

9. This episode, which in Islamic tradition involves Ishmael rather than Isaac, is much contested. For a reading via Søren Kierkegaard's (1813–1855) retelling, see Paul Hedges, "What Did Kierkegaard Intend? On the Ethics of Belief and the Failure of Fear and Trembling's Abraham," in *Facing Abraham: Seven Readings of Kierkegaard's Fear and Trembling*, ed. Frederiek Depoortere and Annua Nuntia Lovaniensia (Leuven: Peeters, 2017), 71–97.

10. See Pamela Stewart and Andrew Strathern, *Ritual: Key Concepts in Religion* (London: Bloomsbury, 2014), 59–72.

11. Kathryn McClymond, *Beyond Sacred Violence* (Baltimore: John Hopkins University Press, 2008).

12. Stewart and Strathern, *Ritual*, 98.

13. See Smith, *To Take Place,* 96–103.

14. Jon Mitchell, "From Ritual to Ritualization," in *Religion, Theory, Critique: Classic and Contemporary Approaches and Methodologies,* ed. Richard King (New York: Columbia University Press, 2017), 377–84. Note that Foucault's genealogical and archaeological methods are often seen as synonymous, and are methodologically identical. However, whereas the archaeological is seen as exploring the origins of terms, the genealogical is sometimes seen as an intensification of this where the discourse of power becomes key. It may also signify its contingent nature; see Gary Gutting and Johanna Oksala, "Michel Foucault," in *Stanford Encyclopaedia of Philosophy* (2018), 3.3, https://plato .stanford.edu/entries/foucault/#ArchGene.

15. Talal Asad, *Genealogy of Religion: Discipline and Reasons of Power in Christianity and Islam* (Baltimore: John Hopkins University Press, 2009).

16. See Giorgio Agamben, *The Use of Bodies,* trans. Adam Kotsko (Stanford: Stanford University Press, 2016).

17. For a more technical use of myth, see box 4.3.

18. Robert Segal, "Myth and Ritual," in *The Routledge Companion to the Study of Religion,* ed. John Hinnells, 2nd ed. (New York: Routledge, 2010), 372–96, 387.

19. See Graham Harvey, *Food, Sex, and Strangers: Understanding Religion as Everyday Life* (Durham: Acumen, 2013).

20. On the range of classical theories of myth, see Segal, "Myth and Ritual," 373–84.

21. James Frazer, *The Golden Bough: A Study of Magic and Religion,* Project Gutenberg (2003 [1890]), www.gutenberg.org/files/3623/3623-h/3623-h.htm.

22. Frits Staal, "The Meaninglessness of Ritual," *Numen* 26.1 (1979): 2–22.

23. James Laidlaw and Caroline Humphrey, "Action," in Kreinath et al., *Theorizing Rituals,* 265–83, 265.

24. Ritual theory destabilizes any clear distinction between "religious" and "non-religious" ritual, but nevertheless the social reality (see box 1.9) of these distinctions continues in how people demarcate activities.

25. See Don Saliers, "Artistry and Aesthetics in Modern and Postmodern Worship," in *The Oxford Handbook of Religion and the Arts,* ed. Frank Bruch Brown (Oxford: Oxford University Press, 2014), 403–17, 411–12. See also Davor Džalto, "The Aesthetic Face of the Sacred," *Religions* 10.5.302 (2019), www.mdpi.com/2077-1444/10/5/302/htm, scene 1.

26. Ron Williams and James Boyd, "Aesthetics," in Kreinath et al., *Theorizing Rituals,* 285–305.

27. Erika Fischer-Lichte, *The Transformative Power of Performance: A New Aesthetics* (New York: Routledge, 2008).

28. See Axel Michaels and William S. Sax, "Performance," in *The Oxford Handbook of the Study of Religion,* ed. Michael Stausberg and Steven Engler (Oxford: Oxford University Press, 2016), 304–15, 307. See also Kim Solga, ed., *A Cultural History of Theatre in the Modern Age* (London: Methuen Drama, 2019).

29. While the Jedi religion seemingly began as a protest against census questions on religion, it now has an active following in some places; see Markus Davidsen, "Fiction-Based Religion: Conceptualising a New Category against History-Based Religion and Fandom," *Culture and Religion* 14.4 (2013): 378–95.

30. John L. Austin, *How to Do Things with Words* (Oxford: Clarendon Press, 1962).

31. John Searle, *Expression and Meaning: Studies in the Theory of Speech Acts* (Cambridge: Cambridge University Press, 1979).

32. Erving Goffman, *Interaction Ritual: Essays on Face-to-Face Behavior* (Garden City, NY: Anchor Books, 1967).

33. See Joe Sachs, "Aristotle: Poetics," in *Internet Encyclopedia of Philosophy* (2015), www.iep.utm.edu/aris-poe/.

34. See Habip Turker, "A Discussion of the Aesthetic Views of Ibn Sina and Aristotle on the Basis of Aesthetic Value," in *Classic Issues in Islamic Philosophy and Theology Today,* ed. Anna-Teresa Tymieniecka and Nazif Muhtaroglu (Dordrecht: Springer, 2010), 151–70, 154, 159.

35. Judith Butler, *Notes toward a Performative Theory of Assembly* (Cambridge: Harvard University Press, 2015), 176.

36. See Judith Butler, "Gender Performativity," video, Open Culture (2018), www.openculture.com/2018/02/judith-butler-on-gender-performativity.html.

37. See Stephen Young, "Judith Butler: Performativity," *Critical Legal Thinking* (2016), http://criticallegalthinking.com/2016/11/14/judith-butlers-performativity/#fnref-22068–7.

38. Stanley Tambiah, "A Performative Approach to Ritual: Radcliffe-Brown Lecture," *Proceedings of the British Academy* 65 (1979): 113–69.

39. Ronald Grimes, "Performance," in Kreinath et al., *Theorizing Rituals,* 379–94, 391.

40. See Stausberg, "Ritual Studies," 77–79.

41. See Rumiko Handa, "Sen no Rikyū and the Japanese Way of Tea: Ethics and Aesthetics of the Everyday," *Interiors* 4.3 (2013): 229–47.

42. See Peter Harvey, *An Introduction to Buddhism: Teachings, History and Practices,* 2nd ed. (Cambridge: Cambridge University Press, 2013), 268–78.

CHAPTER 13. DIVERSITY

1. However, diversity is not new in these places, but often hidden or unacknowledged; see Anna Halafoff and Paul Hedges, "Globalisation and Multifaith Societies," *Studies in Interreligious Dialogue* 25.2 (2015): 135–61; and below.

2. See Paul Hedges, "Conceptualising Social Cohesion in Relation to Religious Diversity: Sketching a Pathway in a Globalised World," *Interreligious Relations* 16 (2020), www.rsis.edu.sg/research/srp/irr/#.XuclH2ozYiI.

3. See Mario Pockeski, *Introducing Chinese Religions* (New York: Routledge, 2009), 2–6; Paul Hedges, "China," in *Religion in Everyday Life and Culture,* ed. Richard Hecht and Vincent Biondo, vol. 3 (Santa Barbara: Praeger, 2010), 45–82, 48–57; and Xinzhong Yao and Yanxia Zhao, *Chinese Religion: A Contextual Approach* (London: Continuum, 2010), 6–19.

4. On Daoism, see Russell Kirkland, *Taoism: The Enduring Tradition* (London and New York: Routledge, 2004). On Confucianism, see Anna Sun, *Confucianism as a World Religion: Contested Histories and Contemporary Realities* (Princeton: Princeton University Press, 2013).

5. See Yao and Zhao, *Chinese Religion,* 11–14; and Joachim Gentz, "Religious Diversity in the Three Teachings Discourse," in *Religious Diversity in Chinese Thought,* ed. Perry Schmidt-Leukel and Joachim Gentz (Basingstoke: Palgrave Macmillan, 2013), 123–40. See also Vincent Goossaert and David A. Palmer, *The Religious Question in Modern China* (Chicago: University of Chicago Press, 2011).

6. See Schmidt-Leukel and Gentz, *Religious Diversity in Chinese Thought.*

7. The *dhimmi* system varied considerably over time and place. In general, in return for paying a "poll tax" (*jizya,* theoretically equivalent to the alms [*zakat*] paid by Muslims), the *dhimmi* could worship as they chose, run their own affairs, and were exempted from military service and protected by the caliph. Over time, restrictions became tighter and sometimes they faced more overt oppression. See Paul Hedges, *Religious Hatred: Prejudice, Islamophobia, and Antisemitism in Global Context* (London: Bloomsbury, 2021), chapter 8; Richard Kimball, *The People of the Book* (Bern: Peter Lang, 2019), 148–49; and Youssef Courbage and Philippe Fargues, *Christians and Jews under Islam: From the Arab Conquests to the Lebanese Civil War,* trans. Judy Mabro (London: I. B. Tauris, 2018 [1997]), 14–25.

8. Notably neither "protected people" (*dhimmi*) nor "infidel" (*kafir*) had singular clear meanings. On *dhimmi,* see David Waines, *An Introduction to Islam* (Cambridge: Cambridge University Press, 2003), 52–53; Sydney Griffiths, *The Church in the Shadow of the Mosque: Christians and Muslims in the World of Islam* (Princeton: Princeton University Press, 2008), 14–20; and Anver Emon, *Religious Pluralism and Islamic Law: Dhimmis and Others in the Empire of Law* (Oxford: Oxford University Press, 2008). On "infidel," see Waines, *Introduction to Islam,* 20, 30, 105–8, 126–28; and Jonathan Brown, *Misquoting Muhammad: The Challenge and Choices of Interpreting the Prophet's Legacy* (Oxford: Oneworld, 2014), 82, 207–8.

9. See Reza Shah-Kazemi, *Common Ground between Islam and Buddhism* (Louisville: Fons Vitae, 2010), 14–19; Perry Schmidt-Leukel and Lloyd Ridgeon, eds., *Islam and Inter-Faith Relations* (London: SCM, 2007); and Nasim Hasan Shah, "The Concept of Al-Dhimmah and the Rights and Duties of Dhimmis in an Islamic State," *Journal of Muslim Minority Affairs* 9.2 (1988): 217–22, 219.

10. It should be noted that Europe is spoken of anachronistically in this period. Our current fixed and stable notions of geographic continental markers did not exist, and the boundaries of what would become "Europe," perhaps better spoken of as Western Christendom, were shifting. Importantly, the creation of Europe was also an interreligious distinction, one that exists up until today, with Europe being perceived as both "Christian" and "Western" in contradistinction to an "Islamic" and "Oriental" other. See Franco Cardini, *Europe and Islam,* trans. Caroline Beamish (Oxford: Blackwell, 2001), Roger Ballard, "Islam and the Construction of Europe," in *Muslims in the Margin: Political Responses to the Presence of Islam in Western Europe,* ed. W. A. R. Shadid and P. S. van Koningsveld (Kampen: Kok Pharos, 1996), 15–51. In many ways, for much of the last few millennia, the natural cultural category of much of what we now call Europe has been as part of a wider Mediterranean cultural world; see Monique O'Connell and Eric Dursteler, *The Mediterranean World: From the Fall of Rome to the Rise of Napoleon* (Baltimore: John Hopkins University Press, 2016).

11. See Halafoff and Hedges, "Globalization." This is also not to deny that the medieval European situation was not singular, and certainly around the Mediterranean world, interreligious disputation and coexistence was more of a reality than it was in such areas as northwestern Europe; see Brian Catlos and Alex Novikoff, "Interfaith Dialogue and Disputation in the Medieval Mediterranean," *Medieval Encounters* 24 (2018): 503–9.

12. See Paul Hedges, "Particularities," in *Christian Approaches to Other Faiths*, ed. Paul Hedges and Alan Race (London: SCM, 2008), 112–35.

13. Alan Race, *Christians and Religious Pluralism* (London: SCM, 1983). There he used each term in the singular: "exclusivism," "inclusivism," "pluralism"; here we adopt a later pluralizing of each to emphasize that they describe a range of approaches.

14. Diana Eck, *Encountering God: A Spiritual Journey from Bozeman to Benares* (Boston: Beacon Press, 1993), 166–99.

15. The terms have some equivalence to the sociological concepts of exclusion and inclusion; see Michael A. Peters and Tina A.C. Besley, "Social Exclusion/Inclusion: Foucault's Analytics of Exclusion, the Political Ecology of Social Inclusion and the Legitimation of Inclusive Education," *Open Review of Educational Research* 1.1 (2014): 99–115.

16. It may be useful to suggest how atheist conceptions of diversity may be envisaged by the "theological" markers: an atheist exclusivist might assert that if atheism is true, then religious belief must be false (and, likely, therefore harmful); an atheist inclusivist might suggest that there are many ways that people can make sense of the world that have some utility, but that everybody who has a religious stance is ultimately wrong, and that being religious is not the best option, because atheism alone is right; and an atheist pluralist might assert that the universe is a vast and mysterious place, and while their stance makes sense for them, they cannot completely rule out the possible truths others assert as equally valid ways of making sense of what we experience, and as ways of living an authentic life.

17. See Hedges, *Religious Hatred*.

18. See Daniel Strange, "Exclusivisms: Indeed Their Rock Is Not like Our Rock," in Hedges and Race, *Christian Approaches*, 36–62.

19. For "exclusivistic tendencies" in Buddhism, see Kristine Kiblinger, "Buddhist Stances towards Others: Types, Examples, Considerations," in *Buddhist Attitudes to Other Religions*, ed. Perry Schmidt-Leukel (St. Ottilien: EOS, 2008), 24–46, 26–27.

20. Race, *Christians and Religious Pluralism*, 38.

21. See Paul Hedges, *Controversies in Interreligious Dialogue and the Theology of Religions* (London: SCM, 2010), 24–25.

22. See David Cheetham, "Inclusivisms: Honouring Faithfulness and Openness," in Hedges and Race, *Christian Approaches to Faiths*, 63–84.

23. Perry Schimdt-Leukel argues that Islam is inclusivist to monotheisms but exclusivist to polytheisms, but see above. See Perry Schmidt-Leukel, "Exclusivism, Inclusivism, Pluralism," in *The Myth of Religious Superiority: Multifaith Explorations of Religious Pluralism*, ed. Paul F. Knitter (New York: Orbis Books, 2005), 13–27. See also Mohamed Hassan Khalil, *Islam and the Fate of Others: The Salvation Question* (Oxford: Oxford University Press, 2012).

24. On Buddhism, see Kiblinger, "Buddhist Stances," 27–30; on Hinduism, see Jeffery Long, "Hinduism and the Religious Other," in *Understanding Interreligious Relations,* ed. David Cheetham, Douglas Pratt, and David Thomas (Oxford: Oxford University Press, 2013), 37–63, 55–61.

25. See Perry Schmidt-Leukel, "Pluralisms: How to Appreciate Religious Diversity Theologically," in Hedges and Race, *Christian Approaches,* 85–110, 88–92.

26. See IFYC, "Module 2B: Models of Religious Diversity," Interfaith Youth Core (2016), www .youtube.com/watch?v=slwwRpC29XE&feature=youtu.be&list=PLy-ezZD5S6f3NZ3 ieqmtLwZTrdxgsx007.

27. See Gavin D'Costa, "Changing the Typology? Why Pluralism Should Be Renamed Post-Christian Inclusivism," in *Twenty-First Century Theologies of Religions: Retrospection and Future Prospects,* ed. Elizabeth Harris, Paul Hedges, and Shanthikumar Hettiarachchi (Leiden: Brill, 2016), 128–41.

28. See Schmidt-Leukel, "Pluralisms," 85–86; and Perry Schmidt-Leukel, *Religious Pluralism and Interreligious Theology* (Maryknoll, NY: Orbis, 2017), 32–106.

29. Khalil, *Islam and the Fate of Others,* 7.

30. Khalil, *Islam and the Fate of Others,* 74–109, 26–53, and 48–53, respectively.

31. Guy Stroumsa, *The Making of Abrahamic Religions in Late Antiquity* (Oxford: Oxford University Press, 2017).

32. See Abraham Vélez de Cea, "A Cross-Cultural and Buddhist-Friendly Interpretation of the Typology Exclusivism-Inclusivism-Pluralism," *Sophia* 46.1 (2007): 453–80; and Kiblinger, "Buddhist Stances."

33. Cea, "Cross-Cultural and Buddhist-Friendly," 13.

34. See Hedges, *Controversies in Interreligious Dialogue,* 19–20.

35. On a definition of the typology employing insights from Cea, see Paul Hedges, "The Theology of Religions Typology Redefined: Openness and Tendencies," in Harris et al., *Twenty-First Century,* 76–92.

36. John Nicol Farquhar, *The Crown of Hinduism* (Oxford: Oxford University Press, 1913).

37. See Paul Hedges, *Preparation and Fulfilment: A History and Study of Fulfilment Theology in Modern British Thought in the Indian Context* (Bern: Peter Lang, 2001).

38. See Hedges, *Preparation and Fulfilment,* 334–40.

39. See Jeannine Hill Fletcher "Feminisms: Syncretism, Symbiosis, Synergetic Dance," in Hedges and Race, *Christian Approaches,* 136–54.

40. Stephen David Reicher, Russell Spears, Tom Postmes, and Anna Kende, "Disputing Deindividuation: Why Negative Group Behaviours Derive from Group Norms, Not Group Immersion," *Behavioural and Brain Sciences* 39 (2016), E161, doi:10.1017 /S0140525X15001491.

41. Stuart Hall, "Ethnicity: Identity and Difference," *Radical America* 23 (1989): 9–20.

42. Chris Allen, "'People Hate You Because of the Way You Dress': Understanding the Invisible Experiences of Veiled British Muslim Women Victims of Islamophobia," *International Review of Victimology* 21.3 (2015): 287–301, 300.

43. Samuel L. Gaertner, Mary C. Rust, John F. Dovidio, Betty A. Bachman, and Phyllis A. Anastasio, "The Contact Hypothesis: The Role of a Common Ingroup Identity on Reducing Intergroup Bias," *Small Group Research* 25.2 (1994): 224–49.

44. Stuart Hall, "Introduction: Who Needs Identity," in *Questions of Identity,* ed. Stuart Hall and Paul du Gay (London: Sage, 1996), 1–17.

45. Matthew J. Hornsey, Tina Oppes, and Alicia Svensson, "'It's OK if We Say It, but You Can't': Responses to Intergroup and Intragroup Criticism," *European Journal of Social Psychology* 32.2 (2002): 293–307.

46. On this and recent repudiations, see Ronald Miller, "Judaism: Siblings in Strife," in Hedges and Race, *Christian Approaches,* 176–90.

47. See Pim Valkenberg, "The Dynamics of the Qur'ānic Account of Christianity," in *Routledge Handbook on Christian-Muslim Relations,* ed. David Thomas (New York: Routledge, 2017), 49–56.

48. Scott Steinkerchner asserts the Mahayana argument is different from supersessionism, as Theravada remains a valid vehicle to awakening/nirvana. If supersessionism requires complete annulment of another tradition, this would be correct. However, the logic of supersessionism does not require this and has variations. For instance, while Christians traditionally denied the continued efficacy of Judaism as a system, they did not decry the laws, prophets, and teachings of the Hebrew Bible; rather, they reinterpreted them. See Scott Steinkerchner, "Eckhart and *The Lotus Sutra:* Skilful Means in Speaking What Cannot Be Spoken," *Medieval Mystical Theology* 23.2 (2014): 142–56.

49. See David Langness, "Religion: Renewed Once in about a Thousand Years," Bahaiteachings.org (2016), https://bahaiteachings.org/religion-renewed-thousand-years.

50. The origin of this argument is debated, but see Hemant Mehta, "Ricky Gervais to Stephen Colbert: 'You Don't Believe in 2,999 Gods. I Don't Believe in Just 1 More,'" Patheos.com (2 February 2017), https://friendlyatheist.patheos.com/2017/02/02/ricky-gervais-to-stephen-colbert-you-dont-believe-in-2999-gods-i-dont-believe-in-just-1-more/.

51. Maria Rosa Menocal, *The Ornament of the World: How Muslims, Jews and Christians Created a Culture of Tolerance in Medieval Spain* (New York: Bayback, 2002).

52. No sense of a European identity existed, so we might say the Western end of the Eurasian landmass, or Christendom (see note 10).

53. Jocelyn Hendrickson, "Andalusia," in *Oxford Islamic Studies Online* (n.d), www.oxfordislamicstudies.com/print/opr/t236/e1129.

54. See Kenneth Seeskin, "Maimonides," *Stanford Encyclopedia of Philosophy* (2017), https://plato.stanford.edu/entries/maimonides/.

55. Darío Fernández-Morera, *The Myth of the Andalusian Paradise: Muslims, Christians, and Jews under Islamic Rule in Medieval Spain* (Wilmington, DE: Intercollegiate Studies Institute, 2014).

56. Sarah Pearce, review of *The Myth of the Andalusian Paradise: Muslims, Christians, and Jews under Islamic Rule in Medieval Spain,* by Darío Fernández-Morera (2017), https://wp.nyu.edu/sjpearce/2017/03/17/paradise-lost/.

57. See Aaron Hollander, "Blazing Light and Perfect Death: The Martyrs of Cordoba and the Growth of Polemical Holiness," in *Contested Spaces, Common Ground: Space and Power Structures in Contemporary Multireligious Societies,* ed. Ulrich Winkler, Lidia Fernández, and Oddbjørn Leirvik (Leiden: Brill, 2017), 203–24.

58. It is useful to note that for at least the first century of Islam's existence, its armies were multireligious, with at least Jews, Christians, and Muslims composing the troops. It was only later, as a clearer demarcation of these groups (often resulting from internal Muslim in-group out-group identification which sharpened other borders) emerged, and with it the *dhimmi* system, that Islamic armies became mainly composed of Muslim soldiers.

59. See Malachi Haim Hacohen, *Jacob and Esau: Jewish European History between Nation and Empire* (Durham: Duke University Press, 2019); and Hedges, *Religious Hatred*.

60. On the significance of Vatican II, see John O'Malley, "Opening the Church to the World," *New York Times* (10 October 2012), www.nytimes.com/2012/10/11/opinion /vatican-ii-opened-the-church-to-the-world.html.

61. Vatican, Nostra Aetate (1965), 2, www.vatican.va/archive/hist_councils/ii_vatican_council /documents/vat-ii_decl_19651028_nostra-aetate_en.html.

62. Catholic teaching is embedded in what is termed the magisterium of the church, and various "types" or "levels" of teaching exist which vary from what is seen as infallible and unalterable to those which can be changed. For an explanation from a traditional Catholic stance, see André Marie, "The Three Levels of Magisterial Teachings" (2007), https://catholicism.org/the-three-levels-of-magisterial-teaching.html.

63. Vatican, Dominus Iesus (2000), 22, www.vatican.va/roman_curia/congregations /cfaith/documents/rc_con_cfaith_doc_20000806_dominus-iesus_en.html, italics in original.

64. Jacques Dupuis, *Jesus Christ at the Encounter of World Religions* (Maryknoll, NY: Orbis, 1991).

65. See Sigrid Rettenbacher, "One Text—Different Meanings? The Notification on Jacques Dupuis in the Light of the Second Vatican Council," in *Interreligious Hermeneutics in Pluralistic Europe: Between Texts and People*, ed. David Cheetham, Ulrich Winkler, Oddbjørn Leirvik, and Judith Gruber (Amsterdam: Rodopi, 2011), 3–25; and Edmund Kee-Fook Chia, *Edward Schillebeeckx and Interreligious Dialogue: Perspectives from Asian Theology* (Eugene, OR: Pickwick), 27–31, 36–39.

66. See Fabrice Blée, "Can Christians Engage in Non-Christian Practices? Eastern Meditation and Contemplative Prayer," in *Controversies in Contemporary Religion*, ed. Paul Hedges, vol. 3 (Santa Barbara: Praeger, 2014), 277–304.

67. As associated with comparative theology, see Francis Clooney, *Comparative Theology: Deep Learning across Religious Lines* (Chichester: Wiley, 2010).

68. See Peter Phan, *Being Religious Interreligiously: Asian Perspectives on Interfaith Dialogue* (Maryknoll, NY: Orbis, 2004); see also case study 2B.

69. Jeannine Hill Fletcher, *Monopoly on Salvation? A Feminist Approach to Religious Pluralism* (London: Continuum, 2005), 54.

CHAPTER 14. DIALOGUE

1. Akbar Ahmed, quoted in Alan Race, "Interfaith Dialogue: Religious Accountability between Strangeness and Resonance," in *Christian Approaches to Other Faiths*, ed. Paul Hedges and Alan Race (London: SCM, 2008), 155–72, 155.

2. See Anna Halafoff, *The Multifaith Movement: Global Risks and Cosmopolitan Solutions* (Dordrecht: Springer, 2013), 35–70.

3. See Justin Nordstrom, "Utopians at the Parliament: The World's Parliament of Religions and the Columbian Exposition of 1893," *Journal of Religious History* 33.3 (2018): 348–65, 351–53.

4. See Marcus Braybrooke, *Pilgrimage of Hope: One Hundred Years of Global Interfaith Dialogue* (London: SCM, 1992); and Halafoff, *The Multifaith Movement.*

5. See Marcus Braybrooke, "Francis Younghusband—Explorer, Mystic, Interfaith Pioneer," *Interfaith Observer* (2013), www.theinterfaithobserver.org/journal-articles/2013/6/15/francis-younghusband-explorer-mystic-interfaith-pioneer.html.

6. See Paul Hedges and Mohamed Imran Mohamed Taib, "Singapore's Interfaith Movement: Embedded Autonomy and Precarious Toleration," in *The Interfaith Movement,* ed. John Fahy and Jan-Jonathan Bock (New York: Routledge, 2020).

7. See Paul Hedges and Anna Halafoff, "Globalization and Multifaith Societies," *Studies in Interreligious Dialogue* 25.2 (2015): 135–61.

8. See Clare Amos, "Vatican and World Council of Churches Initiatives: Weaving Interreligious Threads on Ecumenical Looms," in *Contemporary Muslim-Christian Encounters: Developments, Diversity and Dialogues,* ed. Paul Hedges (London: Bloomsbury, 2015), 185–200, and in the Anglican context, see Paul Hedges, "Anglican Interfaith Relations from 1910 to the Twenty-First Century," in *The Oxford History of Anglicanism,* ed. Rowan Strong, vol. 5: *The C20th* (Oxford: Oxford University Press, 2018), 76–97.

9. The classic work is Rosemary Radford Ruether, *Faith and Fratricide: The Theological Roots of Anti-Semitism* (New York: Seabury Press, 1974). For a short survey, see Ronald Miller, "Judaism: Siblings in Strife," in Hedges and Race, *Christian Approaches,* 176–90. For a broader conceptual overview, see Paul Hedges, *Religious Hatred: Prejudice, Islamophobia, and Antisemitism in Global Context* (London: Bloomsbury, 2021).

10. See Deborah Lipstadt, *Denying the Holocaust: The Growing Assault on Truth and Memory* (London: Penguin, 1993).

11. See Amos, "Vatican and World Council."

12. For a discussion of this issue, see Paul Hedges, *Controversies in Interreligious Dialogue and the Theology of Religions* (London: SCM, 2010), 102–8.

13. See Hedges, "Anglican Inter-Faith Relations from 1910 to the Twenty-First Century."

14. See Guardian Opinion, "What Impact Did 9/11 Have on the World?," *Guardian* (5 September 2011), www.theguardian.com/commentisfree/2011/sep/05/9-11-impact-world-al-qaida. Another plane crashed into the Pentagon, outside Washington, DC, and another crashed into the ground in Pennsylvania.

15. Patrice Brodeur, "From the Margins to the Centers of Power: The Increasing Relevance of the Global Interfaith Movement," *Cross Currents* 55 (2005): 42–53.

16. See Halafoff, *Multifaith Movement.*

17. See Eboo Patel and Patrice Brodeur, eds., *Building the Interfaith Youth Movement: Beyond Dialogue to Action* (Lanham, MD: Rowman and Littlefield, 2006).

18. See Hedges and Taib, "Singapore's Interfaith Movement."

19. See Paul Hedges, "The Secular Realm as Interfaith Space: Discourse and Practice in Contemporary Multicultural Nation-States," *Religions* 10.9.498, www.mdpi.com /2077-1444/10/9/498.

20. See Paul Hedges, "Can Interreligious Dialogue Provide a New space for Deliberative Democracy in the Public Sphere? Philosophical Perspectives from the Example of the UK and Singapore," *Interreligious Studies and Intercultural Theology* 2.1 (2018): 5–25.

21. Oddbjørn Leirvik, *Interreligious Studies* (London: Bloomsbury, 2014), 18.

22. See Juhi Ahuja and Paul Hedges, "Interreligious Marriage: Perspectives from the Singaporean Context in Relation to Interreligious Dialogue," RSIS occasional paper series 1 (2019), www.rsis.edu.sg/rsis-publication/srp/interreligious-relations-irr-issue-1/#.Xs1egxNKg3g.

23. Race, "Interreligious Dialogue," 155.

24. See Andrew Holden, *Religious Cohesion in Times of Conflict: Christian-Muslim Relations in Segregated Towns* (London: Continuum, 2009).

25. On the Balkans, see Patrice Brodeur and Ina Merdjanova, *Religion as a Conversation Starter: Interreligious Dialogue for Peacebuilding in the Balkans* (London: Continuum, 2011). On Indonesia, see Sumanto Al Qurtuby, "Reconciliation from Below: Indonesia's Religious Conflict and Grassroots Agency for Peace," *Peace Research* 44–45 (2012): 135–62. Evidence suggests, though, that where good interreligious relations and networks existed before such conflicts, healing was promoted between the communities in some cases.

26. See Hedges, *Controversies in Interreligious Dialogue*, 102–8.

27. See Ingrid Vik, Scanteam, Anne Stensvold, and Christian Moe, "Lobbying for Faith and Family: A Study on Religious NGOs at the United Nations," NORAD Report no. 7 (Oslo, NORAD, 2013), www.oursplatform.org/wp-content/uploads/lobbying-for-faith-and-family.pdf.

28. Russell McCutcheon, "The Costs of Discipleship: On the Limits of the Humanistic Study of Religion," lecture delivered at the University of Toronto (2006), cited in Paul Hedges, "Concerns about the Global Ethic," 10.

29. Ursula King, "Feminism: The Missing Dimension in the Dialogue of Religions," in *Pluralism and the Religions: The Theological and Political Dimensions,* ed. John D'Arcy May (London: Cassell, 1998), 40–55, 43.

30. See Swamy Muthuray, *The Problem with Interreligious Dialogue: Plurality, Conflict and Elitism in Hindu-Christian-Muslim Relations* (London: Bloomsbury, 2016).

31. Mark Owen, "A Buddhist Response to the Christian Theology of Religions," in *Twenty-First Century Theologies of Religions: Retrospective and Future Prospects,* ed. Elizabeth Harris, Paul Hedges, and Shanthikumar Hettiarachchi (Leiden: Brill, 2017), 359–72.

32. Hedges, "Can Interreligious Dialogue."

33. Muthuray, *Problem with Interreligious Dialogue.*

34. See Paul Hedges and Nursheila Muez, "Plural Traditions in Plural Societies: Inclusivity in Inter-Religious Dialogue," RSIS Commentary CO19002 (2019), www.rsis.edu.sg/rsis-publication/rsis/plural-traditions-in-plural-societies-inclusivity-in-inter-religious-dialogue/#.Xs19yBNKg3g.

35. Paul Hedges, "Should Interfaith and Interreligious Dialogue Include Atheists? Towards an Interworldview Perspective," *Interreligious Insight* 15.1 (2017): 38–47. More broadly, see Paul Hedges, *Towards Better Disagreement: Religion and Atheism in Dialogue* (London: Jessica Kingsley, 2017).

36. See Khaleel Mohamed, "Interreligious Dialogue as Lay, Institutional, and Academic: Muslim Perspectives," in Hedges, *Contemporary Muslim-Christian Encounters*, 51–66.

37. See Catherine Cornille, *The Im-Possibility of Interreligious Dialogue* (New York: Crossroad, 2008); and Catherine Cornille, "Conditions for Inter-Religious Dialogue," in *The Wiley-Blackwell Companion to Inter-Religious Dialogue*, ed. Catherine Cornille (Chichester: Wiley-Blackwell, 2013), 20–33.

38. This perspective is not limited to IRD, but is common among secular dialogue theorists such as Martin Buber (1878–1965) and David Bohm (1917–1992).

39. Paul Hedges, "Multiple Religious Belonging after Religion: Theorising Strategic Religious Participation in a Shared Religious Landscape as a Chinese Model," *Open Theology* 3.1 (2017): 48–72.

40. See Hedges, *Controversies in Interreligious Dialogue*, 231–37.

41. Anne Hege Grung, "Gender and Muslim-Christian Dialogue," in Hedges, *Contemporary Muslim-Christian*, 67–82, 78.

42. See Helene Egnell, *Other Voices: A Study of Feminist Approaches to Religious Plurality East and West* (Uppsala: Studia Missionalia Svecana, 2006).

43. Hedges, *Controversies in Interreligious Dialogue*, 206–9.

44. See Leona Anderson and Pamela Dickey Young, eds., *Women and Religious Traditions*, 3rd ed. (Oxford: Oxford University Press, 2015); and Hedges, *Towards Better Disagreement*, 120–23, 124–28.

45. See Wesley Ariarajah, "Power, Politics, and Plurality: The Struggles of the World Council of Churches to Deal with Religious Plurality," in *The Myth of Religious Supremacy*, ed. Paul Knitter (Maryknoll, NY: Orbis, 2002), 176–93.

46. See Tenzin Gyatso, *Towards the True Kinship of Faiths: How the World's Religions Can Come Together* (London: Abacus, 2010), 57–66.

47. Though increased knowledge and contact with the Other are statistically linked to greater appreciation in at least the US, see Robert Putnam and David Campbell, *American Grace: How Religion Divides and Unites Us* (New York: Simon and Schuster, 2012).

48. See Jennifer Howe Peace,, Or N. Rose, and Gregory Mobley, eds., *My Neighbour's Faith: Stories of Interreligious Encounter, Growth, and Transformation* (Maryknoll, NY: Orbis, 2013); and Putnam and Campbell, *American Grace*.

CHAPTER 15. VIOLENCE

1. See James Livingston, *Modern Christian Thought: The Enlightenment and the Nineteenth Century*, 2nd ed. (Minneapolis: Fortress Press, 2006), 270–98; and Paul Badham, *The Contemporary Challenge of Modernist Theology* (Cardiff: University of Wales Press, 1998).

2. See Paul Hedges, *Towards Better Disagreement: A Journey into Religion and Atheism* (London: Jessica Kingsley, 2017), 38–42, especially boxes 2.2 and 2.3.

3. See Keith Ward, "Keith Ward Tears Fundamentalism Apart (Part 1)" (video) (2013), www.youtube.com/watch?v=O9EhYVt-dyw.

4. For a survey, see James Dunn, ed., *Fundamentalisms: Threats and Ideologies in the Modern World* (London: I. B. Tauris, 2015).

5. See Christopher van der Krogt, "The Rise of Fundamentalisms," in *Controversies in Contemporary Religion*, ed. Paul Hedges, vol. 3 (Santa Barbara: Praeger, 2014), 1–38.

6. Martin Marty and Scott Appleby, eds., *Fundamentalisms Observed*, 5 vols. (Chicago: University of Chicago Press, 1991–1995).

7. See Dunn, *Fundamentalisms*.

8. See Krogt, "Rise of Fundamentalisms."

9. Linda Woodhead, "Epilogue," in Dunn, *Fundamentalisms*, 169–79.

10. Douglas Pratt, "Religion and Terrorism: Christian Fundamentalism and Extremism," *Terrorism and Political Violence* 22.3 (2010): 438–56.

11. Scott Appleby, *The Ambivalence of the Sacred: Religion, Violence, and Reconciliation* (New York: Rowman and Littlefield, 2000).

12. See T. Mastnak, *Crusading Peace: Christendom, the Muslim World, and Western Political Order* (Berkeley: University of California Press, 2000), 154–68. Perhaps ironically, Bernard of Clairvaux, who insisted that Muslims must be killed without mercy, is known by the Catholic Christian church as the Doctor of Love in relation to his promotion of what is termed "love mysticism" (speaking of the soul as Jesus's lover).

13. See also Brian Victoria, *Zen at War* (London: Rowman and Littlefield, 2006).

14. See Hagen Berndt, *Non-Violence in the World Religions* (London: SCM, 2000).

15. See Pauline Kollontai, Sue Yore, and Sebastian Kim, eds., *The Role of Religion in Peacebuilding: Crossing the Boundaries of Prejudice and Distrust* (London: Jessica Kingsley, 2018).

16. Mark Juergensmeyer, *Terror in the Mind of God: The Global Rise of Religious Violence*, 4th ed. (Oakland: University of California Press, 2017), 182–203.

17. See Hedges, *Towards Better Disagreement*, 105; see also box 5.2.

18. René Girard, *To Double Business Bound: Essays on Literature, Mimesis, and Anthropology* (Baltimore: Johns Hopkins University Press, 1978).

19. Juergensmeyer, *Terror in the Mind*, 4th ed., 210–12.

20. See Parmjit Singh and Amandeep Singh Madra, *Warrior Saints: Four Centuries of Sikh Military History*, vol. 1, 2nd ed. (London: Kashi House, 2017).

21. See Gerd Lüdemann, *The Unholy in Holy Scripture: The Dark Side of the Bible*, trans. John Bowden (London: SCM, 1997), especially 37–39; and Steven Jacobs, ed., *Confronting Genocide: Judaism, Christianity, Islam* (Lanham, MD: Lexington Books, 2009).

22. See David Whitten Smith and Elizabeth Geraldine Burr, *Understanding World Religions: A Road Map for Justice and Peace*, 2nd ed. (London: Rowman and Littlefield, 2015), 41.

23. Juergensmeyer, *Terror in the Mind*, 4th ed., 25–26.

24. Juergensmeyer, *Terror in the Mind*, 1st ed. (2003), 176, citing Robert Matthews, quoted in "Views of a Racist Anti-Government Leader," *Washington Post* (26 December 1984), 3. On connections between Antisemitism and racism, see Hedges, *Religious Hatred*.

25. See Bruce Lincoln, *Holy Terrors: Thinking about Religion after September 11* (Chicago: University of Chicago Press, 2003), 58–61.

26. Caroline Kennedy-Piper, "Terrorism Studies: What We Have Forgotten and What We Now Know," *Government and Opposition* 53.2 (2018): 356–84.

27. Donald M. Schurman, "Mass Bombing Some Moral and Historical Perspectives," *Canadian Military History* 18.3 (2015): 19–30; and Christopher C. Harmon, *"Are We Beasts?": Churchill and the Moral Question of World War II "Area Bombing"* (Newport, RI: Naval War College, 1991).

28. Peter Neumann, *Radicalized: New Jihadists and the Threat to the West* (London and New York: I. B. Tauris, 2016), 9–52. This draws from the work of David C. Rapoport.

29. Tina Besely and Michael Peters, "Terrorism, Trauma, Tolerance: Bearing Witness to White Supremacist Attack on Muslims in Christchurch, New Zealand," *Educational Philosophy and Theory* (2019), DOI: 10.1080/00131857.2019.1602891.

30. While it may seem "crazy" to many, suicide bombing is arguably a rational tactical tool of asymmetrical warfare. Its modern usage is normally linked to the Tamil Tigers, a secular and political insurgency movement in Sri Lanka, but Japan's so-called kamikaze attacks in WWII, or Russian political dissidents in the nineteenth century, were earlier examples. See Jeffrey Lewis, "The Human Use of Human Beings: A Brief History of Suicide Bombing," *Origins* 6.7 (2013), http://origins.osu.edu/article/human-use-human-beings-brief-history-suicide-bombing; and Michael Horowitz, "The Rise and Spread of Suicide Bombing," *Annual Review of Political Science* 18:1 (2015): 69–84.

31. FBI, *The Radicalization Process: From Conversion to Jihad* ([no place] FBI, 2006).

32. See Paul Hedges, "Radicalisation: Examining a Concept, Its Use and Abuse," *Counter Terrorist Trends and Analyses* 9.10 (2017): 12–18.

33. Marc Sageman, *Leaderless Jihad: Terror Networks in the Twenty-First Century* (Philadelphia: University of Pennsylvania Press, 2008). See also Christian Picciolini, "My Descent into America's Neo-Nazi Movement—And How I Got Out," TEDxMileHigh (2017), www.ted.com/talks/christian_picciolini_my_descent_into_america_s_neo_nazi_movement_and_how_i_got_out?language=en.

34. See, for instance, www.pewresearch.org/fact-tank/2017/08/09/muslims-and-islam-key-findings-in-the-u-s-and-around-the-world/.

35. See Juergensmeyer, *Terror in the Mind*, 4th ed.

36. See Hedges, "Radicalisation." Notably, prison has served as an "incubator"; see Giles Kepel, *Terror in France: The Rise of Jihad in the West* (Princeton: Princeton University Press, 2017), 29–33. Importantly, this refers to those terrorists coming from a primarily northwestern European context. Exact profiles and pathways vary by country and region.

37. See, Sageman, *Leaderless Jihad*; Hedges, "Radicalisation"; Neumann, *Radicalized*; and Olivier Roy, *Jihad and Death: The Global Appeal of Islamic State* (London: Hurst, 2017).

38. See Kumar Ramakrishna, "Countering the Self-Radicalised Lone Wolf? A New Paradigm?," RSIS Commentary CO14019 (2014), www.rsis.edu.sg/rsis-publication/cens/2144-countering-the-self-radicalise/; and Jessica Johnson, "The Self-Radicalization of White Men: 'Fake News' and the Affective Networking of Paranoia," *Communications, Culture and Critique* 11.1 (2008): 100–115. Notably, self-radicalization goes back to nineteenth-century anarchist tactics; see Neumann, *Radicalized*.

39. See Rohan Gunaratna and Sabariah Binte Mohamed Hussin, eds., *Deradicalisation and Terrorist Rehabilitation* (New York: Routledge, 2018).

40. United States Government Accountability Office, "Countering Violent Extremism: Actions Needed to Define Strategy and Assess Progress of Federal Efforts," US Government (April 2017), www.gao.gov/assets/690/683984.pdf.

41. "What Happened at the Bataclan?," BBC News (9 December 2015), www.bbc.com/news/world-europe-34827497; and Maria-Sabina Draga Alexandru, "Global Rhetorics of Disaster: Media Constructions of Bataclan and the 'Colectiv Revolution' in the Wake of 9/11," *Essachess* 10.1 (2017): 129–44.

42. See Stanley Griffiths, The Church *In the Shadow of the Mosque: Christians and Muslims in the World of Islam* (Princeton: Princeton University Press, 2008).

43. See Bassam Tibi, *Islam in Global Politics: Conflict and Cross-Civilizational Bridging* (New York: Routledge, 2012), 167.

44. Samuel Huntington, "The Clash of Civilizations," *Foreign Affairs* 72.3 (1993): 22–49, 35.

45. See Sam Harris, "Islam Is Not a Religion of Peace," video, Fora.tv (30 December 2010), www.youtube.com/watch?v=LfKLV6rmLxE&gl=SG&hl=en-GB.

46. See Tom Anderson's analysis: http://odintext.com/blog/textanalysisbible2of3/.

47. See Khalil, *Jihad,* and note 37.

48. Pew Research Center, "The Changing Global Religious Landscape" Pew Research Center (2017), 1–48, https://www.pewforum.org/2017/04/05/the-changing-global-religious-landscape/ and Green, *Fear of Islam.*

49. Edward W. Said, *Covering Islam: How the Media and the Experts Determine How We See the Rest of the World* (New York: Vintage Books, 1997).

50. See, "Nothing to Do with My Prophet," video, Talk Islam (n.d.), www.facebook.com/talkislam/videos/927607720663026/?pnref=story.

51. BBC, "The End of the Cold War," *BBC Education* (n.d.), www.bbc.com/bitesize/guides/zq63b9q/revision/2.

52. Tracing the exact lineage and source of every group labeled "terrorist" and draws from Islamic resources or claims an Islamic identity, which covers many decades and various parts of the globe, is to recognize the contextual nature of many of these groups. Nevertheless, many have found common ground, have trained together, and first found themselves brought together with US training and finances in Afghanistan. However, some distinctive and particular pathways lie behind various groups, some of which may be ideologically opposed in various ways. A discussion of some pathways is found in Andreas Armborst, "Profile of Religious Fundamentalism and Terrorist Activism," *Defence against Terrorism Review* 2.1 (2009): 51–71; see also Tibi, *Islam in Global Politics*; Kepel, *Terror in France*; Neumann, *Radicalized*; Thomas Hegghammer, *The Caravan: Abdallah Azzam and the Rise of Global Jihad* (Cambridge: Cambridge University Press, 2020); and Fawaz A. Gerges, *The Far Enemy: Why Jihad Went Global*, 2nd ed. (Cambridge: Cambridge University Press, 2009).

53. See Mohamed bin Ali, "Labelling IS Fighters: Khawarij, Not Jihadi-Salafis," RSIS Commentary CO18063 (4 April 2018), www.rsis.edu.sg/rsis-publication/rsis/co18063-labelling-is-fighters-khawarij-not-jihadi-salafis/#.Xs2FUhNKg3g; and "Salafis, Salafism and

Modern Salafism: What Lies Behind a Term?," RSIS Commentary CO15057 (18 March 2015), www.rsis.edu.sg/rsis-publication/srp/co15057-salafis-salafism-and-modern-salafism-what-lies-behind-a-term/#.Xs2FuxNKg3g.

54. See Natana DeLong-Bas, *Wahhabi Islam: From Revival and Reform to Global Jihad* (Oxford: Oxford University Press, 2008).

55. Mohamed bin Ali, *The Roots of Religious Extremism: Understanding the Salafi Doctrine of Al-Wala' wal Bara'* (London: Imperial College Press, 2015).

56. Based on a recorded incident; see Michael Jerryson, *If You Meet the Buddha on the Road: Buddhism, Politics, and Violence* (Oxford: Oxford University Press, 2018), 35.

57. See Jerryson, *If You Meet the Buddha*, 17–48.

58. Stanley Tambiah, *Buddhism Betrayed? Religion, Politics and Violence in Sri Lanka* (Chicago: University of Chicago Press, 1992).

59. Tessa Bartholomeusz, *In Defence of Dharma: Just-War Ideology in Buddhist Sri Lanka* (Richmond: Curzon, 2002).

60. Jerryson, *If You Meet the Buddha*.

61. See Anuruddha Pradeep, "The Political Dimension of Buddhism in Sri Lanka," in *Buddhism in Asia: Revival and Reinvention*, ed. Nayanjot Lahiri and Upinder Singh (Singapore: Institute of South East Asia Studies, 2016), 261–89; and Jude Lal Fernando "Buddhism, Nationalism, and Violence in Asia," in *Controversies in Contemporary Religion*, ed. Paul Hedges, vol. 3 (Santa Barbara: Praeger, 2014), 61–90, 61–76.

62. Alan Strathern, "Why Are Buddhist Monks Attacking Muslims?," BBC News (2 May 2013), www.bbc.com/news/magazine-22356306.

CHAPTER 16. SECULARISM

1. Grace Davie and Nancy Ammerman, "Religions and Social Progress: Critical Assessments and Creative Partnerships," in *Rethinking Society for the 21st Century: Report of the International Panel on Social Progress*, vol. 3, ed. International Panel on Social Progress (Cambridge: Cambridge University Press, 2018), 641–76, 646.

2. See Marion Eggert and Lucian Hölscher, eds, *Religion and Secularity: Transformations and Transfers of Religious Discourses in Europe and Asia* (Leiden: Brill, 2013), especially the chapter by Heiner Roetz, "The Influence of Foreign Knowledge on Eighteenth Century European Secularism," 9–33.

3. See Gertrude Himmelfarb, *Roads to Modernity: The British, French, and American Enlightenments* (New York: Vintage, 2005).

4. Tariq Modood, *Essays on Secularism and Multiculturalism* (London: Rowman and Littlefield, 2019). For an analysis of Modood's (and others') secularism, see Paul Hedges, "The Secular Realm as Interfaith Space: Discourse and Practice in Contemporary Multicultural Nation-States," *Religions* 10.9 (2019), doi.org/10.3390/rel10090498.

5. See Charles Taylor, "Why We Need a Radical Redefinition of Secularism," in *The Power of Religion in the Public Sphere,* ed. Eduardo Mendieta and Jonathan Van Antwerpen (New York: Columbia University Press, 2011), 34–59; Talal Asad, "Reflections on Laïcité and the Public Sphere," *Social Science Research Council* 5.3 (2005): 1–5; and Timothy Fitzgerald, *Discourse on Civility and Barbarity* (Oxford: Oxford University Press, 2007).

6. When British Prime Minister Tony Blair was asked about his Christian faith, his press secretary, Alastair Campbell, replied: "We don't do God"; see Colin Brown, "Campbell Interrupted Blair as He Spoke of His Faith: 'We Don't Do God,'" *Telegraph*, 4 May 2003, www.telegraph.co.uk/news/uknews/1429109/Campbell-interrupted-Blair-as-he-spoke-of-his-faith-We-dont-do-God.html.

7. Rowan Williams, *Faith in the Public Square* (London: Bloomsbury, 2012).

8. Karel Dobbelaere, "Secularization: A Multi-Dimensional Concept," *Current Sociology* 29.2 (1981): 3–153.

9. Silvio Ferrari, "Law and Religion in a Secular World: A European Perspective," *Ecclesiastical Law Society* 14.3 (2012): 355–70.

10. Jeffrey Hadden, "Toward Desacrilizing Secularization Theory," *Social Forces* 65.3 (1987): 587–611, 598.

11. See Peter Berger, *The Sacred Canopy* (Garden City, NY: Doubleday, 1967).

12. On UK statistics, see Steve Bruce, *God Is Dead: Secularization in the West* (Oxford: Blackwell, 2002), 63–73; for recent global statistics, see Ariela Keysar, "Religious/Nonreligious Demography and Religion Versus Science," in Zuckerman and Shook, *Oxford Handbook of Secularism*, 40–54.

13. See Grace Davie, *Religion in Britain since 1945: Believing without Belonging* (Blackwell: Oxford, 1999); Davie and Ammerman, "Religion and Social Progress," 646–48, 657; José Casanova, *Public Religions in the Modern World* (Chicago: University of Chicago Press, 1994); and Peter Berger, *The Desecularization of the World: Resurgent Religion and World Politics* (Grand Rapids: Eerdmans, 1999).

14. Berger, *Desecularization of the World*, 76.

15. See James Miller, *Chinese Religions in Contemporary Societies* (Santa Barbara: Praeger, 2006), 37–38, 57–84, 95–99.

16. Grace Davie, "Religiosity, Secularity and Pluralism in the Global East: Implications for Social-Scientific Theory," keynote lecture, East Asian Society for the Scientific Study of Religion Conference: "Religiosity, Secularity, and Pluralism in the Global East," Singapore (5 July 2018).

17. Vincent Lloyd, *Religion of the Field Negro: On Black Secularism and Black Theology* (New York: Fordham University Press, 2017), 10.

18. Slyvia Wynter, "The Ceremony Must Be Found: After Humanism," *boundary* 2 12.3–13.1 (1984): 19–70. See Lloyd, *Religion of the Field Negro*, 91–94. Lloyd particularly develops an argument that religion/theology is dismissed as part of this racialized secularism, thus seeing a critique of secularism from this lens as justifying a return to theology (see 5–12).

19. See Vineeta Sinha, "Benoy Kumar Sarkar (1887–1949)," in *Sociological Theory beyond the Canon*, ed. Syed Farid Alatas and Vineeta Sinha (Basingstoke: Palgrave Macmillan, 2017), 303–35, 314–15.

20. See Rajeev Bhargava, ed., *Secularism and Its Critics* (New Delhi: Oxford University Press India, 2005).

21. See M. Hakan Yavuz and Ahmet Erdi Öztürk, "Turkish Secularism and Islam under the Reign of Erdoğan," *Southeast European and Black Sea Studies* 19.1 (2019): 1–9.

22. See Bruce, *God Is Dead;* Steve Bruce, *Secularization: In Defence of an Unfashionable Theory* (Oxford: Oxford University Press, 2011); and Johannes Quack, "Identifying (with) the Secular: Description and Genealogy," in Zuckerman and Shook, *Oxford Handbook of Secularism,* 21–39, 27–30.

23. The survey was conducted by the Alister Hardy Research Centre. Importantly, the very different meanings of terms such as "religion" and "spirituality" were considered. See Yao Xinzhong, "Religious Experience in Contemporary China," *Modern Believing* 47.2 (2006): 44–61; Cafer Yaran, "Religious Experience in Contemporary Turkey," *Modern Believing* 51.4 (2010): 45–68; Paul Badham, "Religion in Britain and China: Similarities and Differences," *Modern Believing* 49.1 (2008): 50–58; and Paul Badham and Yao Xinzhong, *Religious Experience in Contemporary China* (Cardiff: University of Wales Press, 2007).

24. The term "post-secular" may denote a number of things, one of which is the supposed return of religion after the secularized age, while others see religion, as it were, haunting the minds of otherwise secular, or atheist, thinkers. It is often associated with the German theorist Jürgen Habermas and his belief that the secularization hypothesis has failed. As a popular example, the atheist British popular philosopher Alain de Botton has argued that religious ways of acting or seeing the world, such as collective ritual, may be revived in museums or other places; see Alain de Botton, *Religion for Atheists: A Non-believer's Guide to the Uses of Religion* (London: Vintage, 2012). Religious themes are also taken seriously by a number of atheist philosophers, such as Slavoj Žižek, Giorgio Agamben, and others. Whether our world is "post-secular," however that is defined, is debated. For some related discussions, see Austin Harrington, "Habermas and the 'Post-Secular Society,'" *European Journal of Social Theory* 10.4 (2007): 543–60; David Cheetham, "Ritualising the Secular? Inter-Religious Meetings in the 'Immanent Frame,'" *Heythrop Journal* (2017), https://doi.org/10.1111/heyj.12491; Charles Taylor, *The Secular Age* (Cambridge: Harvard University Press, 2007); Adam Possamai, "Post-Secularism in Multiple Modernities," *Journal of Sociology* 53.4 (2017): 822–35; and Michael Staudigl and Jason W. Alvis, "Phenomenology and the Post-Secular Turn: Reconsidering the 'Return of the Religious,'" *International Journal of Philosophical Studies* 24.5 (2016): 589–99.

25. Jayeel Serrano Cornelio, "Is Religion Dying? Secularization and Other Trends in the World Today," in *Controversies in Contemporary Religion,* ed. Paul Hedges, vol. 3 (Santa Barbara: Praeger, 2014), 219–45, 234–37. See also José Casanova, "Religion, Secularization, and Sacralization" in *Dynamics in the History of Religions between Asia and Europe: Encounters, Notions, and Comparative Perspectives,* ed. Volkhard Krech and Marion Steinicke (Boston: Brill, 2012), 453–60.

26. See Paul Hedges and Christina Welch, "Charisma, Scriptures, Revelation, and Reason: Sources of Religious Authority," in Hedges, *Controversies in Contemporary Religion,* vol. 1, 57–80.

27. See the International Covenant on Civil and Political Rights (1966); Ghanea and Ahmed, "Religion and Human Rights"; and John Witte Jr. and Christian Green, eds., *Religion and Human Rights: An Introduction* (Oxford: Oxford University Press, 2012).

28. This was introduced under race relations legislation, as Sikhism was first protected as a racial identity in the UK.

29. See Peter Phan and Jonathan Tan, "Interreligious Majority Minority Dynamics," in *Understanding Interreligious Relations,* ed. David Cheetham, Douglas Pratt, and David Thomas (Oxford: Oxford University Press, 2013), 218–40.

30. See Hedges, "The Secular Realm as Interfaith Space."

31. A common stereotype of Satanists is that their worship involves human sacrifice, but this is not the case in modern manifestations (it is unclear if there are any non-modern manifestations); see Asbjorn Dyrendal, James Lewis, and Jesper Petersen, *The Invention of Satanism* (Oxford: Oxford University Press, 2015).

32. See Russel Barsh, "The Supreme Court, Peyote, and Minority Religions: Zero Tolerance," *Wicazo Sa Review* 7.2 (1991): 49–52; and Thomas Maroukis, *The Peyote Road: Religious Freedom and the Native American Church* (Norman: University of Oklahoma Press, 2012).

33. Office for Democratic Institutions and Human Rights, "Guidelines for Review of Legislation Pertaining to Religion and Belief," OSCE (2004), 9, www.osce.org /odihr/13993?download=true.

34. See Elizabeth Bucar, *Pious Fashion: How Muslim Women Dress* (Cambridge: Harvard University Press, 2017).

35. See Paul Hedges, "Women's Bodies as Ideological Battlefield: Fashion, Feminism, and Freedom in France's Burkini Ban," unpublished draft paper (2016), www.academia .edu/28167498/Womens_Bodies_as_Ideological_Battlefield_Fashion_Feminism_ and_Freedom_in_Frances_Burkini_Ban_1. This is an extended version of Paul Hedges, "Fashion, Feminism or Freedom: Dissecting France's Ban on Burkini," *RSIS Commentary* CO16219 (2016), www.rsis.edu.sg/wp-content/uploads/2016/08 /CO16219.pdf.

36. Aheda Zanetti, "I Created the Burkini to Give Women Freedom, Not to Take It Away," *Te Guardian* (24 August 2016), www.theguardian.com/commentisfree/2016 /aug/24/i-created-the-burkini-to-give-women-freedom-not-to-take-it-away.

37. "Paris Attacks: State of Emergency 'to Protect Elections,'" *BBC News* (10 December 2016), www.bbc.com/news/world-europe-38274200; and Shereena Qazi, "French Parliament Approves New Anti-terrorism Law," *Al Jazeera* (4 October 2017), www.aljazeera .com/news/2017/10/anti-terrorism-law-boost-security-france-171002073720302.html.

38. Madeleine Teahan, "Nuns Cannot Wear Their Habits on Our Beaches, Says Deputy Mayor of Nice," *Catholic Herald* (26 August 2016), www.catholicherald.co.uk /news/2016/08/26/nuns-cannot-wear-their-habits-on-our-beaches-says-deputy-mayor-of-cannes/#.V8Kn9TzfyT8.

39. Folly Bah Thibault, "French 'Burkini' Ban: Secularism or Security?," *Al Jazeera* (17 August 2016), www.aljazeera.com/programmes/insidestory/2016/08/french-burkini-ban-secularism-security-160817191824853.html.

40. See Nilüfer Göle and Julie Billaud, "Islamic Difference and the Return of Feminist Universalism," in *European Multiculturalisms: Cultural, Religious and Ethnic Challenges,* ed. Anna Triandafyllidou, Tariq Modood, and Nasar Meer (Edinburgh: Edinburgh University Press, 2012), 116–41, 118.

41. See OHCHR, "France: Banning the Niqab Violated Two Muslim Women's Freedom of Religion—UN Experts," United Nations Office of the High Commissioner on Human Rights (23 October 2018), www.ohchr.org/SP/NewsEvents/Pages/DisplayNews .aspx?NewsID=23750&LangID=E; and Karen Murphy, *State Security Regimes and the Right to Freedom of Religion and Belief* (New York: Routledge, 2013).

42. See Michael D. Barr, "Lee Kuan Yew and the 'Asian Values' Debate," *Asian Studies Review* 24.3 (2000): 309–34.

43. "Appendix A: Government Restrictions Index," PEW Forum (2017), http://assets .pewresearch.org/wp-content/uploads/sites/11/2017/04/07154134/Appendix-A.pdf.

44. Another issue for Singapore is compulsory national military service, which sees Jehovah's Witnesses criminalized for refusing to comply (citing their pacifist stance) (see also case study 18B).

CHAPTER 17. GEOGRAPHY

1. Yi-Fu Tuan, *Space and Place: The Perspective of Experience,* 6th ed. (Minneapolis: University of Minnesota Press, 2008).

2. Henri Lefebvre, *The Production of Space* (Oxford: Blackwell, 1991).

3. Doreen Massey, "Politics and Space/Time," in *Place and the Politics of Identity,* ed. M. Keith and S. Pile (New York: Routledge, 1993), 141–61, 155.

4. Kim Knott, *The Location of Religion: A Spatial Analysis* (New York: Routledge, 2005), 23.

5. Lily Kong and O. Woods, *Religion and Space: Competition, Conflict and Violence in the Contemporary World* (London: Bloomsbury, 2016), 5, citing David Chidester and E.T. Linenthal, "Introduction," in *American Sacred Space,* ed. David Chidester and E.T. Linenthal (Bloomington: Indiana University Press, 1995), 1–11, 6.

6. See Philip Sheldrake, *Spaces for the Sacred* (London: SCM, 2001), 4–20.

7. Marc Augé, *Non-Places: Introduction to an Anthropology of Super-Modernity* (London: Verso, 1997), 77.

8. Lefebvre, *Production of Space,* 142–43.

9. These draw from Kong and Woods, *Religion and Space.*

10. See Kong and Woods, *Religion and Space,* 22–23; Simon Coleman and John Elsner, *Pilgrimage: Past and Present in the World Religions* (London: British Museum Press, 1995), 34–46, 48–51, 69–70, 83–84, 91–99; and Edward Kessler, *Jews, Christians, and Muslims in Encounter* (London: SCM, 2013), 42–58, especially 43–47.

11. See R.R. LaPier, "Why Understanding Native American Religion Is Important for Resolving the Dakota Access Pipeline Crisis," *Conversation* (3 November 2016), https:// theconversation.com/why-understanidng-native-american-religion-is-important- for-resolving-the-dakota-access-pipeline-cris-68032.

12. See Kong and Woods, *Religion and Space,* 74.

13. Michel Foucault, *The Foucault Reader,* ed. Paul Rabinow (London: Penguin, 1986), 206–13.

14. On an argument for this arrangement in the US Baha'i tradition, see Juan Cole, "The Baha'i Faith in America as Panopticon, 1963–1997," *Journal for the Scientific Study of Religion* 37.2 (1998): 234–48. See also, Edward Herman and Noam Chomsky,

Manufacturing Consent: The Political Economy of the Mass Media, rev. ed. (New York: Pantheon Books, 2002).

15. See http://londonmandir.baps.org.

16. See Bindi Shah, Claire Dwyer, and David Gilbert, "Landscapes of Diasporic Religious Belonging in the Edge-City: The Jain Temple at Potters Bar, Outer London," *South Asian Diaspora* 4.1 (2012): 77–94.

17. See Susannah Crockford, "Ecospirituality, Gender and Nature," podcast, Religious Studies Project (1 October 2018), www.religiousstudiesproject.com/podcast /ecospirituality-gender-and-nature/.

18. See Mary Evelyn Tucker and John Grim, "The Movement of Religion and Ecology: Emerging Field and Dynamic Force," in *Routledge Handbook of Religion and Ecology,* ed. Willis Jenkins, Mary Evelyn Tucker, and John Grim (New York: Routledge, 2017), 3–12.

19. Linda Woodhead, *An Introduction to Christianity* (Cambridge: Cambridge University Press, 2004), 53–58.

20. A history marked by global borrowing; see Paul Hedges, *Towards Better Disagreement: Religion and Atheism in Dialogue* (London: Jessica Kingsley, 2017), 69–72.

21. See L. White Jr., "The Historical Roots of Our Ecological Crisis," *Science* 155 (1967): 1203–7.

22. See Marisa Ronan, "Religion and the Environment: Twenty-First Century American Evangelicalism and the Anthropocene," *Humanities* 6.92 (2017): 1–15; and Tony Watling, *Ecological Imaginations in the World Religions: An Ethnographic Analysis* (London: Continuum, 2009), 140–57.

23. Pope Francis I, Laudito Si', Vatican (2015), https://w2.vatican.va/content/Francesco /en/encyclicals/documents/papa=Francesco_20150524_enciclia-laudito-si.html. See Tucker and Grim, "Movement of Religion and Ecology," 3, 11–12.

24. Sarah Bailey, "Why So Many White Evangelicals in Trump's Base Are Deeply Skeptical of Climate Change," *Washington Post* (2 June 2017), www.washingtonpost.com /news/acts-of-faith/wp/2017/06/02/why-so-many-white-evangelicals-in-trumps-base-are-deeply-skeptical-of-climate-change/?noredirect=on&utm_term=.451938df5280.

25. Cited in James Miller, "Is Religion Environmentally Friendly? Connecting Religion and Ecology," in *Controversies in Contemporary Religion,* ed. Paul Hedges, vol. 3 (Santa Barbara: Praeger, 2014), 153–76, 153.

26. Susan M. Darlington, "Translating Modernity: Buddhist Response to the Thai Environmental Crisis," in *TransBuddhism: Transmission, Translation, and Transformation,* ed. Abraham Zablocki, Jay Garfield, and Nalini Bhushan (Amherst: University of Massachusetts Press, 2009), 183–208, 193.

27. S. M. Darlington, "The Ordination of a Tree: The Buddhist Ecology Movement in Thailand," *Ethnology* 37.1 (1998): 1–15, 9.

28. Darlington, "Ordination of a Tree," 2–3, 6–7.

29. See Peter Harvey, *An Introduction to Buddhism,* 2nd ed. (Cambridge: Cambridge University Press, 2012), 52–57.

30. See Darlington, "Ordination of a Tree," 10–11.

31. See Ronald Finucane, *Miracles and Pilgrims: Popular Beliefs in Medieval England* (Basingstoke: Palgrave Macmillan, 1995).

32. See "Protestant Tours," FaithJourneys (2019), http://myfaithjourneys.com/protestant-tours/; note the contrasts with the "Catholic Pilgrimages" on the same site.

33. See Nesma Abdel Azim, "Why Closing Jerusalem's Holy Sepulchre Church Is a Big Deal," *Egypt Today* (25 February 2018), www.egypttoday.com/Article/2/43823 /Why-closing-Jerusalem's-Holy-Sepulchre-Church-is-a-big-deal.

34. See https://gardentomb.com/.

35. See Kristin Romey, "Exclusive: Age of Jesus' Purported Tomb Revealed," *National Geographic* (28 November 2017), https://news.nationalgeographic.com/2017/11/jesus-tomb-archaeology-jerusalem-christianity-rome/.

36. Kong and Woods, *Religion and Space*, 5–8.

CHAPTER 18. POLITICS

1. See Paul Hedges, "Post-Colonialism, Orientalism, and Understanding: Religious Studies and the Christian Missionary Imperative," *Journal of Religious History* 32.1 (2008): 55–75.

2. See Paul Hedges, "Rowland Williams and Missions to the Hindu," in *Religious Dynamics under the Impact of Imperialism and Colonialism: A Sourcebook,* ed. Marion Eggert, Hans-Martin Krämer, Björn Bentlage, and Stefan Reichmuth (Leiden: Brill, 2016), 197–211; and, Paul Hedges, "The Old and the New Comparative Theologies: Discourses on Religion, the Theology of Religions, Orientalism and the Boundaries of Traditions," *Religions* 3.4 (2012): 1120–37.

3. See Walter Mignolo, "Subalterns and Other Agencies," *Postcolonial Studies* 8.4 (2005): 381–407, 383–84; Paul Hedges, *Religious Hatred: Prejudice, Islamophobia, and Antisemitism in Global Context* (London: Bloomsbury, 2021); and Francisco Bethencourt, *Racisms: From the Crusades to the Twentieth Century* (Princeton: Princeton University Press, 2013).

4. Tomoko Masuzawa, *The Invention of World Religions: Or, How European Universalism Was Preserved in the Language of Pluralism* (Chicago: University of Chicago Press, 2005). See also Theodore Vial, *Modern Religion, Modern Race* (Oxford: Oxford University Press, 2016).

5. Franz Fanon, *The Wretched of the Earth* (London: Penguin, 2001 [1963]).

6. Mignolo, "Subalterns," 405–6, note 4.

7. Mignolo, "Subalterns," 386.

8. See Paul Hedges, "Decolonising the Study of Religion (in Relation to the Social and Human Sciences)," logosdao (12 March 2018), https://logosdao.wordpress.com/2018/03/12 /decolonising-the-study-of-religion-in-relation-to-the-social-and-human-sciences/.

9. It is worth noting that Iran was a democracy until 1953, when the American Central Intelligence Agency (CIA), with British assistance, overthrew it and instated the shah, who ruled as an autocratic dictator until 1979; see www.npr.org/2019/01/31/690363402 /how-the-cia-overthrew-irans-democracy-in-four-days. In keeping with the theme of how neocolonial power, including in military operations, affects our world, it is worth noting that Western countries, especially the US (but also the UK, France, and others), have overthrown many democracies and kept dictators in power in many

places, including Iran, Chile, Brazil, Algeria, Syria, Nicaragua, Egypt; see, variously, J. Dana Stuste, "Mapped: The 7 Governments the U.S. Has Overthrown," *Foreign Policy* (20 August 2013, https://foreignpolicy.com/2013/08/20/mapped-the-7-governments-the-u-s-has-overthrown/; Irfan Ahmad, "How the West De-democratised the Middle East," *Al Jazeera* (30 March 2012), www.aljazeera.com/indepth/opinion/2012/03/201232710543250236.html; and David P. Forsythe, "Democracy, War, and Covert Action," *Journal of Peace Research* 29.4 (1992): 385–95.

10. For one perspective, see Hamid Dabashi, *Can Non-Europeans Think?* (London: Zed Books, 2015), 127–93.

11. See Jeffrey Haynes, *An Introduction to International Relations and Religion* (Harlow: Pearson Education, 2013); and Joseph Chingyong Liow, *Religion and Nationalism in Southeast Asia* (Cambridge: Cambridge University Press, 2016).

12. John Kerry, "Faith Based Community Initiatives" (video) C-Span (7 August 2013), www.c-span.org/video/?314438-1/sec-state-kerry-launches-faith-based-community-initiative. See also Madeleine Albright, *The Mighty and the Almighty: Reflections on America, God, and World Affairs* (New York: HarperCollins, 2006).

13. See Naser Ghobadzadeh and Lily Zubaidah Rahim, "Electoral Theocracy and Hybrid Sovereignty in Iran," *Contemporary Politics* 22.4 (2016): 450–68.

14. Anon., "Islamic Politics Show Strength in Massive Anti-Ahok Rally," *Star* (Malaysia) (3 December 2018), www.thestar.com.my/news/regional/2018/12/03/islamic-politics-show-strength-in-massive-jakarta-anti-ahok-rally/.

15. See Michael Jerryson, *If You See the Buddha on the Road: Buddhism, Politics, and Violence* (Oxford: Oxford University Press, 2018); and Liow, *Religion and Nationalism*, 105–14.

16. See Sabrina Rahmet, *Balkan Babel: The Disintegration of Yugoslavia from the Death of Tito to the Fall of Milosevic*, 4th ed. (Boulder, CO: Westview Press, 2002).

17. Jürgen Habermas, *The Theory of Communicative Action*, vol. 1: *Reason and the Rationalization of Society*, trans. T. McCarthy (Boston: Beacon Press, 1984 [1981]); and Jürgen Habermas, *Religion and Rationality: Essays on Reason, God, and Modernity*, ed. E. Medieta (Cambridge: MIT Press, 2002).

18. John Rawls, *A Theory of Justice* (Boston: Harvard University Press, 1971).

19. Dabashi, *Can Non-Europeans Think?*

20. See Paul Hedges and Anna Halafoff, "Globalisation and Multifaith Societies," *Studies in Interreligious Dialogue* 25.2 (2015): 135–61.

21. See David Held and Anthony McGrew, eds., *Globalization Theory: Approaches and Controversies* (Cambridge: Polity Press, 2007); and Thomas Banchoff, ed., *Religious Pluralism, Globalization* (Oxford: Oxford University Press, 2008).

22. Peter Berger, *The Many Altars of Modernity: Toward a Paradigm for Religion in a Pluralist Age* (Berlin: De Gruyter, 2014).

23. See Bhikhu Parekh, *A New Politics of Identity: Political Principles for an Interdependent World* (Basingstoke: Macmillan, 2008); and Liow, *Religion and Nationalism*.

24. Peter Phan and Jonathan Tan, "Interreligious Majority-Minority Dynamics," in *Understanding Interreligious Relations*, ed. David Cheetham, Douglas Pratt, and David Thomas (Oxford: Oxford University Press, 2013), 218–40.

25. See Katayoun Kishi, "Key Findings in the Global Rise of Religious Restrictions," Pew Research Center (21 June 2018), www.pewresearch.org/fact-tank/2018/06/21/key-findings-on-the-global-rise-in-religious-restrictions/.

26. David Brown, *Contemporary Nationalism: Civic, Ethnocultural and Multicultural Politics* (New York: Routledge, 2008).

27. See, e.g., Jason Farr, "Point: The Westphalia Legacy and the Modern Nation-State," *International Social Science Review* 80.3/4 (2005): 156–59; Charles McKelvey, "The Modern Nation State," Global Learning (2013), www.globallearning-cuba.com/blog-umlthe-view-from-the-southuml/the-modern-nation-state; and Andreas Wimmer and Yuval Feinstein, "The Rise of the Nation-State across the World, 1816 to 2001," *American Sociological Review* 75.5 (2010): 764–90.

28. Stanley Tambiah, "The Galactic Polity: The Structure of Traditional Kingdoms in Southeast Asia," *Annals of the New York Academy of Sciences* 293.1 (2006): 69–97.

29. Benedict Anderson, *Imagined Communities: Reflections on the Origin and Spread of Nationalism* (London: Verso, 1983).

30. Charles Taylor, *Modern Social Imaginaries* (Durham: Duke University Press, 2004), 23.

31. See Alexander-Kenneth Nagel, "Religious Pluralization and Interfaith Activism in Germany," *Studies in Interreligious Dialogue* 25.2 (2015): 199–221; and Anna Triandafyllidou, Tariq Modood, and Nasar Meer, "Introduction: Diversity, Integration, Secularism and Multiculturalism," in *European Multiculturalisms: Cultural, Religious and Ethnic Challenges* (Edinburgh: Edinburgh University Press, 2012), 1–29.

32. See Liow, *Religion and Nationalism*, 135–74.

33. See Haldun Gülap, "Secularism as a Double-Edged Sword? State Regulation of Religion in Turkey," in *The Problem of Religious Diversity: European Challenges, Asian Approaches,* ed. Anna Triandafyllidou and Tariq Modood (Edinburgh: Edinburgh University Press, 2017), 273–96; and Ahmed El Amraoui and Faisal Edroos, "Is Turkish Secularism under Threat?," *Al Jazeera* (3 June 2018), www.aljazeera.com/indepth/features/turkish-secularism-threat-180528131157715.html. For a comparative study of Turkey and Israel, see Jocelyne Cesari, "Unexpected Convergences: Religious Nationalism in Israel and Turkey," *Religions* 9 (2018): 1–20.

34. My phrase responds to Steven Weinberg: "With or without religion, you would have good people doing good things and evil people doing evil things. But for good people to do evil things, that takes religion." See Paul Hedges, *Towards Better Disagreement: Religion and Atheism in Dialogue* (London: Jessica Kinglsey, 2017), 105, box 5.2 therein.

35. See Denis Dragovic, "Explainer: ISIS, ISIL, Islamic State or Da'esh?," *Conversation* (6 May 2015), https://theconversation.com/explainer-isis-isil-islamic-state-or-daesh-40838.

36. James Renton, "The Post-Colonial Caliphate: Islamic State and the Memory of Sykes-Picot," *Conversation* (24 February 2016), https://theconversation.com/the-post-colonial-caliphate-islamic-state-and-thememory-of-sykes-picot-52655. For how this led from colonial affairs into contemporary disputes between Jews and Muslims, see Hedges, *Religious Hatred*.

37. See Syed Hussein Alatas, *The Myth of the Lazy Native: A Study of the Image of the Malays, Filipinos and Javanese from the 16th to the 20th Century and Its Function in the Ideology of Colonial Capitalism* (New York: Routledge, 2010 [1977]).

38. See Nicholas Stang, "Kant's Transcendental Idealism," *Stanford Encyclopedia of Philosophy* (2016), 6.1, https://plato.stanford.edu/entries/kant-transcendental-idealism /#PhenNoum. One need not be a Kantian to accept this distinction, which, in various forms, underlies our typical perception of the secular in terms of scholarship (see chapter 16). That is to say, we may study the human social discourses (phenomenal, observable), but we cannot access or know claims beyond this (noumenal, metaphysical), which is part of the distinction sometimes drawn between religious studies (a secular study of human traditions) and confessional theology (based in tradition-specific claims about a posited noumenal). It is sometimes claimed by certain revisionist readings of the work of Georg W. F. Hegel (1770–1831) that this Kantian binary is overcome. However, mainstream Hegelian scholarship offers two readings of Hegel (as two poles of interpretation): either he was a straightforward metaphysician who while claiming to follow Kant had lapsed into the arena that Kant had shown to be untenable (a traditional reading), or he exceeded Kant in showing the metaphysical and ontological assumptions still latent in Kant's own thought and finally formed the basis for a philosophy without metaphysics. In either reading, or with variations, Hegelian thought still follows within the paradigm laid down by Kant. See Paul Redding, "Georg Wilhelm Friedrich Hegel," *The Stanford Encyclopedia of Philosophy*, ed. Edward Zalta (2020), https://plato.stanford.edu/archives/spr2020/entries/hegel/. More recently, some decolonial scholarship such as the work of Vincent Lloyd, *Religion of the Field Negro: On Black Secularism and Black Theology* (New York: Fordham University Press, 2017), has critiqued secularism, though not addressing this Kantian binary as such. However, such theological claims as Lloyd argues for may be equally implicated in racism and discrimination (racism was often founded in religious narratives; see Hedges, *Religious Hatred*), and offer no universal panacea to these problems. Within this book, we have assumed that we study human traditions, for it is not clear how, in any scholarly or academic sense, we may make claims about posited metaphysical realities beyond the human discourse and traditions which we can observe. See Paul Hedges, "Encounters with Ultimacy? Autobiographical and Critical Perspectives in the Academic Study of Religion," *Open Theology* 4.1 (2018): 355–72, https://www.degruyter.com/view/journals/opth/4/1/article-p355.xml.

39. Gordon Lynch, *The Sacred in the Modern World: A Cultural Sociological Approach* (Oxford: Oxford University Press, 2012).

40. Lynch, *Sacred*, 117, citing M. Burleigh, *Sacred Causes: Religion and Politics from the European Dictators to Al Qaeda* (London: Harper Perennial, 2006), 51.

41. Aida Arosoaie, "In the Name of Honour and Freedom: The Sacred as a Justifying Tool for ISIS' and Secular Violence," *Culture and Religion* 18.3 (2017): 278–95.

42. Poem cited in John Esposito, Darrell Fasching, and Todd Lewis, *World Religions Today* (Oxford: Oxford University Press, 2006), 409, referencing H.L. Seneviratne, *The Work of Kings: The New Buddhism in Sri Lanka* (Chicago: University of Chicago Press, 1999), 272–73.

43. See Syed Farid Alatas and Vineeta Sinha, *Sociological Theory beyond the Canon* (London: Palgrave Macmillan, 2017). As discussed in chapters 5 and 7, much that passes for critical religion remains entrapped within white, male, Western circles and may

act to enforce such norms and dismiss nonwhite, non-male, and non-Western scholarship, epistemology, and concepts. However, a critical hermeneutical phenomenology seeks to transcend this version of critical religion (see introduction and passim).

44. On autobiography as methodology, and one narration of the author's own account of this, see Hedges, "Encounters with Ultimacy."

45. Between 2006 and 2016 interethnic marriages rose from 15.5 percent to 21.5 percdent of all marriages; see Juhi Ahuja and Paul Hedges, "Interreligious Marriage: Perspectives from the Singaporean Context in Relation to Interreligious Dialogue," *Interreligious Relations* 1 (2019), www.rsis.edu.sg/wp-content/uploads/2019/02/IRR-Issue-1-February-2019–1.pdf.

46. See Alatas, *Myth of the Lazy Native.*

47. In 1957 the Federation of Malaya attained independence from British Malaya, and Singapore joined them (with Sabah and Sarawak) in 1963 to form Malaysia.

48. MUIS, alongside the Hindu Endowment Board and Sikh Advisory Board, continues an institution of British colonial rule. On Islam, see Rizwana Abdul Azeez, "The Role of Modern Islam in Singapore," in *Singapore: Negotiating State and Society, 1965–2015,* ed. Jason Lim and Terence Lee (New York: Routledge, 2016), 159–71.

49. See Paul Hedges and Mohamed Imran Mohamed Taib, "The Interfaith Movement in Singapore: Precarious Toleration and Embedded Autonomy," in *The Interfaith Movement,* ed. John Fahy and Jan-Jonathan Bock (New York: Routledge, 2019), 139–56.

50. Michael Welch and Jennifer Bryan, "Flag Desecration in American Culture: Offenses against Civil Religion and a Consecrated Symbol of Nationalism," *Crime, Law and Social Change* 26 (1997): 77–93, 77, italics in original.

51. *Texas v. Johnson,* 491 US 397 (1989), 420, cited in Welch and Bryan, "Flag Desecration," 80. That large numbers of US citizens still see defending the flag from being burned as a duty is indicated by the 5 July 2020 hoax burning event in Gettysburg which saw armed militias descend on the area to protect the flag; see Guardian Staff, "Armed Militias Flock to Gettysburg to Foil 'Flag-Burning Protest' That Was All a Hoax," *Guardian* (6 July 2020), www.theguardian.com/us-news/2020/jul/06/gettysburg-militias-flag-burning-protest-hoax.

52. Harold Hongju Koh, "On American Exceptionalism," *Stanford Law Review* 55.5 (2003): 1479–1527.

53. Anon., "Flag Salute, Voting, and Civilian Service," Watchtower Online Library, https//wol.jw.org/en/wol/d/r1/1p-e/1102008085.

54. Welch and Bryan, "Flag Desecration," 85.

55. Jeremy Gunn, "Under God but Not the Scarf: The Founding Myths of Religious Freedom in the United States and Laïcité in France," *Journal of Church and State* 46.1 (2004): 7–24, 15.

INDEX

Art (aesthetics, images): and architecture, 227–228, 295, 409; considered in postcolonial scholarship, 171; as essentially contested concept, 29; and framing, 218; Ibn Sina and persuasion, 292; Islam and, 406; Jesus in, 105*fig*, 243, 406, 496n33; murti, 225–226, 460; Our Lady of Guadalupe, on *tilma*, 81; as physical representation of myth/transcendent, 58*fig*, 105*fig*, 149*fig*, 198*fig*, 209–210, 210*fig*, 237*fig*, 354*fig*; religious art/statues in museums, 169*fig*, 169–170, 406–407; and ritual, 290, 296; and tea ceremony, 294–295; The Wanderer Above a Sea of Fog, 96. *See also* gothic

Asad, Talal, 33, 168, 288, 474

Ashoka, 154, 368, 474

Ataturk, Mustafa Kemal, 383, 406, 432, 474

atheism, 21, 49, 50, 56–57, 125, 126, 193, 195, 201–202, 202–203, 204, 316, 375, 389, 428, 525n50 535n24; and Buddhism, 57, 202, 338; conceptions of (religious) diversity, 307, 523n16; global forms of, 203–204; inclusion/exclusion from interreligious dialogue, 326, 337; and sacred values, 434. *See also* New Atheism

Athos, Mount, 234

Augustine (of Hippo), 136, 234, 308, 320, 359, 461–462, 467, 474

Austin, John, 291–292, 293, 294, 474

awakening (nirvana), 58, 70, 84, 85, 202, 218, 251, 435, 448, 453, 461, 464, 525n48

axial age theory, 447, 508n33

axis mundi, 266, 447

Ayodhya, 156, 404, 405

Babri Masjid. *See* Ayodhya

Baha'i, 316, 447, 537n14

Baptist Church (Baptists), 349, 350

Bartholomeusz, Tessa, 369, 474

Beaman, Lori, 307, 474

Beavoir, Simone de, 240, 474

being-in-the-world, 13, 212, 213, 218, 221–222, 226, 447. *See also* Merleau-Ponty, Maurice

Bell, Catherine, 288, 292, 293, 294, 474

Bellah, Robert, 431, 440, 474, 508n33

Berger, Peter, 11, 130, 381, 474

Bernard of Clairvaux, 353, 475, 530n12

Bhabha, Homi, 75, 76, 78, 173, 178, 475

Bhagavad Gita (Song of the Lord), 102, 358, 447, 458

bhakti. See devotion

bhikkhu (*bhikkuni*). *See* monasticism

Bhargava, Rajeev 156, 383, 475

Bhavani, Kum-Kum 242, 475

Bible, 98–99, 106–110, 243, 249, 258, 259, 261, 308, 309, 447; creation of, 99, 108, 495n8; interpretation of, 106–110, 126, 259, 313, 349; pluralist readings of, 309, 310; translations of, 126, 412–413; and violence, 357, 366, 478. *See also* Hebrew Bible; New Testament

bin Laden, Osama, 330, 479

bodies, 37, 52; as gendered category, 212, 233; as imagined, 221. *See also* Black; China; embodiment; gender; techniques (regimes) of the body

Black (African): bodies, 223; people, 177, 245, 433; scholarship, 132, 177, 178, 486n13; and white/whiteness, 148. *See also* race; religious studies; scholarship; whiteness

Bourdieu, Pierre, 11, 136, 224, 475; on habitus, 123, 498n15; on ritual, 122–123, 287, 290

Brodeur, Patrice, 332, 475, 528n25

Brubaker, Rogers, 148, 152, 453–454, 490n30

Buddha: concept, 448; historical Buddha, teachings of, 84–85, 251, 258, 316, 415, 451, 453; as historical figure, 475

Buddhism (Buddhist), 60–62, 70, 73, 84–85, 128, 177, 218, 251–252, 272–273, 297–298, 342–345, 367–370, 413–416; anthropology of, 216; Buddhist nationalism, 369–370, 416, 425, 435; *chakravartin* (ideal Buddhist ruler), 368, 449; as non-theistic, 20, 25, 202, 338; as oral tradition, 25, 260; women, attitude to, 58, 245, 251–252. *See also* Amida Buddha; Mahayana; meditation; monasticism; Pure Land Buddhism; Thailand (Thai); Theravada; Tripitaka; Zen

burkini, 391–393, 448

Butler, Judith, 11, 240, 241, 293, 475, 487n25

Campany, Robert, 262, 265

Capitalism, 129, 135–136, 137; as religion, 25, 35, 193

captive mind, 170, 172, 407, 448

Carrier, Richard, 107

case study, theory of, 7–8

Castañenda-Liles, María Del Socorro, 81–83, 475

caste, 20, 101, 102, 359, 410, contrasted with class, 263. *See also* Dalit

Catholicism, 71, 77, 81–83, 99, 149, 196, 197, 213, 214, 215, 259, 287–288, 343–345, 393, 448, 526n62; in Asia, 40–41, 79; dialogue and, 328–330, 339; modernity and, 328–329; Nostra Aetate and Dominus Iesus, 320–322; Reformation in, 214. *See also* Christianity; Pope; Reformation(s); Second Vatican Council

Cea, Abraham Vélez de, 311

Certeau, Michel de, 402, 475

charisma, 125, 449

Chatterjee, Partha, 422, 423, 475

Chidester, David, 183–184, 475, 505n51

China (Chinese), 113, 119, 148, 163, 178, 375, 430; bodies, perceptions of, 70, 221; cultural revolution, 429, 450; religion in, 22, 35–39, 40, 60, 168, 198–199, 274, 304, 339–340, 385, 390; secularism in, 374, 376, 381, 429; TCM (traditional Chinese medicine), 215, 222; women, attitudes towards, 238, 410. *See also* acupuncture; Buddhism; Confucianism; Daoism; Falun Gong; filial piety; Hong Kong; mandate of heaven (*tianming*); *sanjiao*; Singapore; strategic religious participation

Christianity: in Asia, 39–41, 320–322; diversity within, 69, 70; as Jesus movement, 109; Judaism, split from, 72, 109; relation to religion, 21, 26, 46, 269; as syncretic, 73, 74; women, attitudes to, 152, 233–234, 239, 240, 245, 248–50, 331, 340–342, 353, 357. *See also* Anglicanism (Episcopalianism, Church of England); Bible; Catholicism; Eucharist; Evangelicalism; Jehovah's Witnesses; Lutheranism; Methodism; Pentecostalism; Protestantism

civilization: in in-group out-group formation, 147; linked to colonial conceptions of religion, 164–165, 167, 183, 184, 219–220; linked to perceptions of Western superiority, 167, 176. *See also* clash of civilizations thesis, decolonial

civil religion, 430, 431, 439, 440, 441

clash of civilizations thesis, 152, 331–332

class, 2, 3, 56, 57, 59, 122, 124, 128, 148, 172, 176, 223, 243, 245, 263, 375, *passim. See also* intersectionality

cognitive science: cognitive revolution, 189

cognitive science of religion (CSR), 33, 188–203, 206–207, 268, 450

Collins, Patricia Hill, 245, 475

colonial difference, 422, 423, 424, 427, 432, 449

colonialism (coloniality, including imperialism): definitions of, 165, 449, 455; Marx not critical of, 172n2; and race, 175–176, 220, 433, 436–437; related to religion, 20, 164–165, 422, 423; Western colonialism, rise of, 163–164. *See* decolonial, postcolonialism

colonial wound, 422, 423, 424, 427, 432, 449

comparative religion: as discipline, 255, 266, 271; critique of, 256; John Kerry on, 424

comparison (comparative): comparative acts, 217, 265, 270–272, 272–275, 294–297, 340–342, 358, 359; concerns about (poor comparison), 255–256, 256–7, 262–264, 275; decolonialism, and, 269, 275; historical comparison, 96; homology and analogy, 264–5; as (natural) human capacity, 256, 268, 275; as illumination, 262–264; as magic, 256–257, 262; methodology, 257–269; and philosophical hermeneutics, 268, 269; typology of, 257. *See also* religious studies

Comte, Auguste, 380, 475

competence: in ritual 290, 296; in social life, 498n15

Confucianism (Confucius), 22–23, 112, 120, 193, 204, 223, 238, 258, 265, 305, 340, 376, 465, 475; Classics, 97, 258, 267; neo-Confucianism, 238, 305, 461; theory of history, 97, 104; women, attitude to, 238. *See also* Analects (Confucian); mandate of heaven

Con-spirando Collective, 248

Constantine (Emperor), 166, 417, 475

Constantinople (Istanbul), 133*fig* 166, 365, 406, 449. *See also* Hagia Sophia

Cornelio, Jayeel Serrano, 79, 386, 387, 475

Cornille, Catherine, 337–340, 345

cosmic war, 37, 353, 449

creationism (intelligent design), 350

Crenshaw, Kimberlé, 243, 475

critical hermeneutical phenomenology, 3, 9–15, 33, 52, 543n43

critical realism, 12–13, 130–131, 449; science
    as supporting, 130, 131n8. *See also*
    non-realism
critical religion, 117–118, 449, 542n43
critical theory, 3, 9, 10, 11, 12, 13, 117, 121, 127,
    128, 129, 132, 176, 194, 225, 449, 503n16
crusade(s), 331, 353, 449
Csordas, Thomas, 225
cult (*xiejiao*), 27, 35–37, 176, 450, 472
culture: as contested and colonial/Orientalist
    term, 94, 175n3, 185; defined as human life
    not biologically determined, 30; seen as
    preferable to religion, 30, 32; distinguished
    from religion, 24–25, 30, 39–41, 194, 271

Dabashi, Hamid, 427, 475
Dalai Lama (14th, Tenzin Gyatso), 329, 343
Dalit, 102, 235, 450
Daly, Mary, 239–240, 476
Daodejing, 111, 112–113, 114, 238, 258, 260, 339,
    450
Daoism: Celestial Masters, 113, 305, 448; origins
    of, 113; as philosophy or religion (false
    dichotomy of), 113, 450; Quanzhen Daoism,
    238, 305, 464; role of Daodejing in, 114,
    260, 304; women, attitudes to, 238. *See also*
    Daodejing; Zhuangzi
darshan, 226, 450, 460
Davie, Grace, 381, 382, 476
Dawkins, Richard, 125, 202, 203, 506n5
decolonial (decolonizing), 2, 101, 128–129, 131, 177,
    223, 225, 269, 383, 450, 542n38; decolonizing
    the curriculum, 178–179, 435; as decolonizing
    not decolonization, 179; and postcolonialism,
    171. *See also* captive mind; colonial difference;
    colonialism; colonial wound; fetish;
    modernity; Orientalism; postcolonialism;
    religion; religious studies; secularism
deconstruction, 15, 28, 32, 33, 117, 450
dehumanization, 312, 363
deindividuation, 312
demerit. *See* merit
Dennett, Daniel, 195, 201, 202
Derrida, Jacques, 10, 128, 211, 476, 487; African
    context, 498n22; on *différance*, 15. *See also*
    deconstruction
Descartes, René, 219, 476, 502n16
detraditionalization, 386, 387, 450

devotion (devotional), 81–82, 83, 85, 86, 180,
    216, 228–229, 260, 274, 339; *bhakti* (Hindu
    devotion), 73, 102, 235, 328, 447; triangle,
    82, 450, 494n43
Dhammapala, Anagarika, 369, 476
dharma, 20, 84, 157, 179, 450; as duty, 20, 263n2,
    358, 359; translated as religion, 20, 31
dhimmi. See protected people
diachronic analysis, 402–403
Diagne, Souleymane Bachir, 14, 476
dialogue (interreligious), 320, 325–347, 358, 390,
    455; classifications of, 333, 334–335; condi-
    tions of, Cornille's, 337–340; critiques of,
    334–337; excluded groups, 337; historical
    development of, 327–332; friendship in
    relation to, 343, 344; not advocated for, 7, 325;
    politics and power dynamics of, 322–333, 343,
    394; storytelling approach, 341; women and
    feminism in relation to, 340–342
discourse (analysis), 117, 118, 451
disenchantment (and reenchantment), 76–77,
    386, 387
diversity (religious): in Chinese context, 304,
    305; classification/typology of attitudes to,
    306–311; distinguished from pluralism, 307,
    451; as factor in secularization, 381; and
    identity, 312–315; Islamic conceptions of,
    304–305, 306; medieval European
    conceptions, 305–306; and multicultural-
    ism, 427; perceived as new, 303, 427
Dogen, 217
Douglas, Mary, 283, 284, 476
Du Bois, W. E. B., 132, 177, 178, 476
dukkha. See suffering
Durga, 236–237, 451
Durkheim, Émile, 280–282, 283, 290, 358, 380,
    431, 434, 476

Eck, Diana, 7, 306, 476
ecofeminism, 248
Eco Monks, 413–416
eidetic vision, 48, 451. *See also* phenomenology
eight-fold path, 85, 451
El Cid, 318–319, 482
Eliade, Mircea, 24, 48, 50, 476; *Patterns in
    Comparative Religion*, 266
embodiment, 10, 13, 221–223, 229, 240–242,
    290, 451; and race/colonialism, 219, 511n22;

unorthodoxy in, 204; relation to Buddhism and Jainism, 73, 204; Sanatana Dharma, 179, 466; as Western creation, 128, 177, 179–80; women, attitude to, 157, 235–237. *See also* Hindutva; Laws of Manu; Puranas; Shri Vaishnavism; Vedanta; Vedas; Vivekananda,

Hindutva, 132, 154–157, 432, 454

history (historical): access to, 95–96; Confucianism and, 97; decolonizing the method, 101; as engaged in this book, 5; future, and 96, 97; historical-critical methodology, 97–100; historical facts, 94, 95, 96, 115; historical texts, how to read, 101–103; methods, differing approaches, 103–104; terminology, 97

history of religion as discipline, 93–94, 101

Hitchens, Christopher, 107, 202, 478

Hobbes, Thomas, 426, 478

Holocaust (Shoah), 308, 329

Hong Kong, 38, 41, 203

hooks, bell, 242, 478

holy: as set apart (*qadosh*), 280, 401, 403, 410, 464. *See also* sacred; space

Humanism, 98, 455; and freedom of religion and belief, 389; and interreligious dialogue, 337

human rights, 27, 375, 388–391, 393–394, 396; contrasted with Asian values, 394. *See also* freedom of religion and belief

Hume, David, 175, 478

Huntington, Samuel: clash of civilizations thesis, 152, 331–332

hybridity, 72–3, 75–79, 87, 88, 243, 455; Homi Bhabha on, 76. *See also* syncretism

idealism, 211, 233, 455

ideal type, 125, 311, 455, 466

identity. *See* identity and conflict; identity salience; narrative identities; social identity theory

identity and conflict, 151–153

identity salience, 151, 154, 157, 313, 455, 466

imagination/imaginary, 148, 430, 455, 468; of Asian feminine, 235; bodies and, 220, 221; Hinduism and Western imagination, 181; nation-state and, 428–430; Protestant, 287–289, 417; race and, 433; religion,

ethnicity, nationalism, connection, 432, 437. *See also* imagined communities; social imaginary

imagined communities, 205, 428–430, 434 455

imperialism. *See* colonialism

indigenous religion, 83, 164–165, 167, 177, 183, 238, 400, 455; Australian Aborigines, 25, 329; indigenous Americans, 183, 329, 391, 404. *See also* shamanism, spirit medium

in-group/out-group, 146–151, 152, 153, 154, 283, 367, 448, 526n58; common-in-group identity, 313; constitutive of religious difference, 312–315; creation of, 148; deindividuation, 312; favoring of in-group, 150; intergroup sensitivity effect, 313, 315; othering, and, 308; and stereotypes, 150; and threat perception, 153. *See also* identity and conflict; social identity theory

inclusivism, 308, 311, 328, 345, 455; social, 308; theological, 309

India, 20, 63, 102, 154–157, 171, 180, 225–227, 263, 375, 409; and gender, 235, 236–237, 243; Indian nationalism, 154; Orientalism and British colonialism, 154, 235, 423, 430; secularism in, 383, 432. *See also* Ayodhya; Hinduism; Hindutva

Indonesia (Indonesian), 331, 334, 365, 383, 425, 429, 528n25

infidel (*kaffir*), 304, 522n8

insider/outsider perspectives, 44–45, 47–49, 51, 54, 56–57, 59–65, 94. *See also* emic-etic

interdisciplinarity, 7–8, 189, 455

intergroup sensitivity effect, 313, 315

interreligious or interfaith, 326

interreligious studies, 7, 455, 486n10

intersectionality, 243, 245, 456. *See also* class, gender, race

intersex. *See* LGBTQI

intrareligious: exclusion and contestation, 337; as majority-minority dynamic, 390

Iran (Iranian, including Persia), 74, 424–425, 539n9. *See also* Bahai, Zoroastrianism

Ireland (Irish), 148; Northern Ireland, 152

Irigaray Luce, 242, 478, 514n26

ISIS (Islamic State in Syria and Iraq, Daesh), 361, 365, 432, 435, 456

legend, 96–97, 106, 457

Leirvik, Oddbjørn, 54, 307, 333, 479

LGBTQI, 172, 178, 335, 425, 457; intersex, 241, 243, 456; queer theory and theology, 242–243, 253, 464; transgender, 241–242, 470. *See also* marriage

liberation theology, 458

liminal (liminality), 283–286, 401, 404, 418, 458

Lincoln, Bruce, 6, 97, 479; "How to Read a Religious Text," 101–104; "Theses on Method," 6, 132

linguistic turn, 10, 12–13, 458

Liow, Joseph Chinyong 479

literalism, 350–352, 458. *See also* fundamentalism

lived environment, 124, 399, 413, 458

lived religion, 68–72, 79–81, 82, 84–88, 180, 225, 246, 266, 335, 381, 458; challenge to notion of religion, 67–68

Lloyd, Vincent, 383, 479, 486n13, 504n32,33, 534n18, 542n38

Locke, John, 332, 389, 426, 479

logocentrism, 13, 131, 211, 219, 223, 225; usage contrasted with Derrida's, 211

Lorde, Audre, 225, 242, 479

Lowe Lisa, 169, 479

Lutheranism, 214, 273, 458; on Eucharist, 288; and Pure Land Buddhism, 149, 343–344

Luther, Martin, 136, 213–214, 479

Lynch, Gordon, 433–434

Madjid, Nurcholish, 383–384, 479

Mahayana, 58, 151, 251–252, 316, 458

magic, 78, 176, 215, 280–282, 218, 458; contrasted with religion, 27, 165, 167, 176, 182, 184, 213, 215, 222; and enchantment/reenchantment, 78, 387; potential usage, 281n1; and science, 215, 222, 280–282. See also *paritta*; superstition

Maimonides, Moses, 317, 479

majority-minority dynamics, 390, 428

Malaysia (Malay), 429, 432; Malay-Muslim identity, 436–438

Malinowski, Branislaw, 279–282, 479

mandate of heaven (*tianming*), 26, 376, 470

marriage, 79, 283, 285–286; across religious borders, 79, 334, 437; Buddhist, 80; ritual of, 285–286; same-sex, 242

Martin, Craig, 119, 127, 128, 129, 130n2, 132, 135–36, 137, 479, 498n24

martyrdom (martyrs), 228, 233; martyrs of Cordoba, 318

Marxism, 25–26, 35, 122, 172, 174

Marx, Karl, 174, 480; on fetish, 129; on religion, 121

masters of suspicion, 55, 119–121

Masuzawa, Tomoko, 33, 174, 422, 480

material culture, 224, 458

material religion, 209–221, 225–229, 266, 271; and colonialism, 219–220, 221; importance for rethinking religion, 211–212; and the regulation of bodies, 219–221; and ritual, 212–216. *See also* embodiment; materiality

materiality (incl. material turn), 10, 13, 33, 131, 209, 212, 218, 221–225, 293, 458, 459

Mauss, Marcel, 212–213, 219, 224, 480

Mbembe, Achille (Joseph-Achille), 177, 194, 480,

McClymond, Kathryn, 263n2, 287

McCutcheon Russell, 132, 263, 480; on the term "religion", 26, 263n1, 489n15; critique of interreligious dialogue, 335

McGuire, Meredith, 68–72, 77–80, 213, 480. *See also* lived religion

meditation, 37, 57, 73, 200, 334, 344; Buddhist, 216–217, 272–274, 510n7; Christian practice of, 63, 274, 321, 344. *See also* Zen (zazen)

megachurch, 290, 386–387, 459

Mencius, 197, 480

Menocal, María Rosa, 316, 318, 480

merit (Buddhist, *punya*), 84, 251, 297, 414–415, 464; demerit (*papa*, Thai: *baap*), 413–414, 416, 462

Merleau-Ponty, Maurice, 213, 219, 222, 224–225, 480

messiah (messianic), 27, 351, 459; first century CE Jewish usage, 109–110; as used by Jesus, 106–107, 305, 315; as Zoroastrian concept, 74

Methodism, 205, 273, 459

methodological agnosticism, 49, 459

methodological atheism, 49–50, 459

methodological polymorphism, 8–9, 49, 170, 459

Mexico, 75, 81–83

Middle East, 163, 166, 361, 365, 424

Mignolo, Walter, 11, 165, 171, 177–178, 422, 480

militant neo-Islamic jihadism. *See* jihad

Miller, Monica, 80–81, 132, 176, 178, 480

Miller, Daniel, 218, 224, 480

mimesis (mimetic desire and mimetic violence), 353–355, 356, 459

minaret. See mosque

minimally counterintuitive idea (MCI), 190, 459

minority. See majority-minority dynamics

mission (missionary), 59, 167, 221, 238, 308, 344, 422, 440; and civilization, 165; and Confucian rituals, 39–40; and dialogue, 320, 327–328, 330, 335, 343; and evolution of world religions paradigm, 46, 164, 271

modernity (modern): associated with Enlightenment, 55, 77, 97, 122, 452; associated with Renaissance, 97–98; and colonialism/ Orientalism/non-Western influences, 98, 163, 165, 168, 175, 177, 178, 219–220, 383, 428, 436, 501n6, 503n22; categories of science, religion, magic, superstition (variously), in, 77–78, 176, 202, 215, 220, 281, 387; category of religion as, 20, 28, 29, 31, 45, 46, 67, 77, 94, 192–193, 383, 471; contrasted with medieval, 213, 219, 294; contrasted with postmodern, 50, 77–78, 173, 463; defined, 460; and fundamentalism, 349–350, 352, 367, 381; political theory and formations of, 426, 428; race and religion in, 174–175, 177, 184, 219–220, 423; racial theories of, 175n2, 219–220, 433; regulation of bodies, in, 219; scholarship and thought of, as Protestant (vs Catholic), 214, 215, 225, 287–289; scholarship of, as textual, 126, 259–260; and secularism, 178, 215, 374, 376, 377, 381–383, 386; women and gender in, 234, 514n21. See also Enlightenment (European); multiple modernities; nation-state; secularism

Mohanty, Chandra, 242, 480

monasticism (monks and nuns), 63, 120, 234, 411, 497n7; Buddhist, 80, 84–85, 143–144, 235, 243, 251–252, 297–298, 367–369, 413–416, 435. See also Vinaya

Modood, Tariq, 374, 533n4

moral disengagement, 363, 364, 460

mosque (minaret), 133, 134, 134–135, 156, 360, 394, 395, 402, 404, 405, 406, 408, 409, 436

Mughal Dynasty, 154, 460

Muhammad, 100–101, 133–134, 260–261, 305, 315–316, 318, 332, 362, 376, 384, 392, 406, 438, 480; sunnah (traditions) of, 124, 342, 366, 469; attitude to women, 244, 341–342

Müller F. Max, 71, 174, 480

multiculturalism, 327, 333–334, 390, 427–428, 431

multidisciplinary, 7–8, 460

multiple modernities, 381–383, 386, 460

multiple religious identities, 59–60, 62, 63, 305. See also strategic religious participation

museums: representation of religion in, 170. See Hagia Sophia.

mysticism, 77, 197–199, 200, 246, 266, 530n12. See also religious experience

myth, 96, 111, 257, 266, 282, 286–287, 289, 293–294, 317, 319; definition of, 97, 460. See also ritual

narrative identities, 145–146, 150, 153

nationalism, 158–159, 431; religious nationalism, 432; types of, 428. See also Buddhism; ethno-nationalism; Hinduism; India

nation-state, 154, 214, 375, 378, 379, 425, 428, 429, 430, 432, 435, 460; potential conflict with religion, 358, 430

natural: embodiment and, 212, 221–222; gender and sexual identities as not, 143, 241, 242; (group) identities as not, 147; 148, 331, 428–430, 433, 453–454; perceptions of religion and/or secular, 24, 26, 60, 72, 373, 374, 388, 463; questioning our world/norms as, 55, 101, 118–123, 124, 218, 451, 454, 455, 498n17; question of religion as, 194, 203; syncretism as, 78, 79; usage here, 460. See also embodiment, materiality

natural law, 197

Neocolonialism, 170, 173, 220, 222, 423, 427, 432, 460, 539n9

New Atheism, 125, 202–203. See also Dawkins, Richard; Dennett, Daniel; Harris, Sam; Hitchens, Christopher

non-realism (anti-realism), 12, 15, 33, 129–131, 461, 487n24. See also critical realism

New Testament, 98–99, 258, 310, 461; Mark 1:1–18, 106–111; Mark 10: 34–36, 357; John 14:6, 314; John's Gospel, 108, 110, 314, 496n25

9/11, 330, 322, 364

nirvana. See awakening (nirvana)

non-dualism. See Vedanta

non-harm. See *ahimsa*

194, 271; as empty signifier, 26, 30; as essentially contested concept, 29–30, 34, 200, 304; etymology of, 21; historical data for, 28–29; as legal category, 27–28, 34, 38, 358, 373–374, 390–391, 396, 425; as Orientalist/racialized concept, 20, 164–165, 174–177, *passim*; as political concept, 26–28, 36, 38, 421, 425; and race, 158–160, 174–177, 183, 185, 422, 423, 435, 436–439, 536n28; related to terms in other languages, 20, 21–22, 31; as social reality, 28, 33, 34, 520n24; as used in this book, 33–34, 465. *See also* cult; culture; decolonial; freedom of religion and belief; magic; Protestantism; race; secularism; superstition; world religions paradigm

religious experience, 24–25, 63, 190, 191, 192, 197–199, 200–201, 218, 334, 385. *See also* god-spot; mysticism

religious studies (study of religion), 3, 7, 48–49, 71, 74–75, 129, 132, 307, 422–424, 435–436, 465, 486n13, 542n38; Black, 177, 178; colonial origins of, 6, 422–424; continued white, colonial, male dominance, 128–129, 176; gender imbalance in, 232; relation to feminism, 246. *See also* comparative religion; history of religion; interreligious studies; secularism; scholarship; theology

Renaissance, 97–98, 164, 375, 465

Ricoeur, Paul, 11, 14, 31, 53, 55, 120–121, 481

Rikyu, Sen no, 295, 481

rites of passage, 122, 283–285, 297

ritual: aesthetic elements of, 290, 295, 296, 471; animals and, 280; and belief, in conception of religion, 271; Buddhist ordination as ritual, 297–298; functional theories of, 279–283; humans as ritual animals, 280; in cognitive science of religion, 193; Islamic prayer (*salat*), 216, 217, 452, 466; myth-ritual theory, 289; as performance, 290–291, 292, 293, 294; Protestant vs Catholic conceptions, 213–216, 287–289; and routine, 278–279; as sacrifice, 285–287; as symbolic, 213–214, 287–289; as technique of the body, 212; theories of, 278–294; Zen and Protestant ritual practices compared, 272–275, 294–297. *See also* Eucharist; liminal (liminality); lived religion; materiality; meditation; purity; ritu-

alization; performance; performativity; rites of passage; techniques of the body

ritualization, 280, 292, 293, 294

role (identity), 123, 141, 143–146, 151, 153, 465

Rousseau, Jean-Jacques, 431, 481

Rudolf, Otto, 24, 48, 50, 268, 480

Ruether, Rosemary Radford, 240, 248, 481

Ruse, Michael, 107

sacralization, 386–387, 414–416, 466

sacred, 33, 216–218, 271, 353, 401, 432–433, 439, 440, 466; as "holy", 155, 401; related to space, 267, 399, 400, 401, 402, 403, 404, 417–418; as sociological concept, 433, 434, 434–435, 435

sacrifice. *See* ritual

Said, Edward. *See* Orientalism

Salafism (Salafi), 126, 466; links to militancy and violence, 367; Wahhabism, 367, 471

sanjiao (three traditions), 304

Sant, 73, 466

Santos, Boaventura de Sousa, 55, 481

Sapir-Whorf thesis, 222, 466

Sarkar, Benoy Kumar, 383, 481

Satanists, 536n31

sati, 180, 466

Savarkar, V. D., 154–155, 481. *See also* Hindutva.

scapegoat, 287, 355, 466

Schechner, Richard, 290–291, 292

Schilbrack, Kevin, 33, 481

Schmidt-Leukel, Perry, 311

scholarship: as political, 1, 2, 5–6, 132, 167, 173, 246, 269, 421, 422–424, 435–436; Black, 132, 177, 178; dominance of West in, 2, 128, 176, 177, 178, 424, 542n43. *See also* Enlightenment; philosophy; secularism; religious studies (study of religion)

science: gender and, 145; global development of, 98, 163, 164, 178, 316–317, 349; hybridity as biological term, 78; modern science, birth/creation/origins of, 97, 215, 281, 474, 488n35; perceived as Western, 167, 174, 178, 411, 488n35; racism, and, 433, 464; relationship to (variously) magic, myth, religion, superstition, 125, 202–203, 215, 222, 280, 281, 282, 289, 466; supportive of critical realism, 130, 131n8, 222–223, 487n24. *See also* cognitive science; cognitive science of religion

transcendence (transcendent), 25, 34, 35, 49, 68, 134, 150, 204, 209, 211, 214, 218, 309, 384, 401, 432; as used here, 35, 470

transgender. *See* LGBTQI

transubstantiation, 213, 288

tribalization, 151–152, 153

Tripitaka, 84, 84–85, 258, 316, 470

Trump, Donald, 158, 159

Turkey, 133*fig*, 198–199, 406; secularism in, 373, 382, 383–385, 385, 432. *See also* Ataturk; Constantinople; Erdogan; Hagia Sophia

turn(s). *See* linguistic turn; materiality (incl. material turn); performance (performative, performativity); reflexive turn (reflexivity)

Turner, Bryan, 219, 225, 482

Turner, Victor, 283, 284, 286, 292, 482

ulama. See jurist

Umayyad Dynasty, 134, 318

UK (United Kingdom, including England, Scotland, Wales, and Northern Ireland)/ Britain, 72, 98, 132, 152, 227, 238, 326, 332, 333, 375, 382, 390, 400, 410, 425, 430; alliance with Ottoman Empire, 365; atheism in, 203; British Empire (colonialism), 20, 102, 154, 164, 179, 181, 243, 423, 436, 437; Canterbury Cathedral, 228–229; Christianity in, 71, 349; secularism in, 374, 376, 378, 385, 429. *See also* Anglicanism (Episcopalianism, Church of England)

US (United States of America), 148, 158–159, 164, 220, 239, 328, 344, 364, 439–441; Black Americans, African Americans, 132, 148, 245; civil religion in, 431, 439, 440, 441; Christianity (incl. Christian (religious) right) in, 99, 158, 350, 424, 425; religious demographics of, 202, 381, 382; secularism in, 373, 374, 378, 383, 429, 440; indigenous/ native Americans, religion of, 183, 329, 391, 404; Abraham Lincoln, temple to, 431*fig*.

Upadhyay, Brahmabandhab, 155, 482

Vásquez, Manuel, 223, 482

Vedanta, 180, 181, 328, 451, 471; Advaita Vedanta, 63, 180, 328, 445

Vedas, 180, 258, 260, 471; *shruti* and *smriti*, 180, 467; Upanishads, 73, 101, 102, 103, 471

veiling (hijab): and feminism, 244–245, 247, 392; Islamic requirements, 244, 391, 392; and *laïcité*, 393

Vietnam, 182, 344, 363

Vinaya (monastic regulation, Buddhist), 80, 243, 297, 368, 414, 471

violence: associated with religion, 330, 331; and Buddhism, 353, 367–370, 435; and Christianity, 152, 331, 353, 357; and fundamentalism, 351, 352; and Hinduism, 154, 156, 157 357–358; and identity, 152; and Islam, 317–318, 361–364, 364–367; legitimated (justified), 357–358, 359, 428, 430, 432, 435; personal reasons for, 361; related to place, 404, 405, 408; religious violence, as complex, 152, 357; in ritual, 285–286; and state and religion, 430, 432; theories of, 352–355. *See also* Ayodhya; crusades; jihad; just war; mimesis; radicalization; terrorism

Vivekananda, 327, 328, 482,

Wahhabism. *See* Salafism

Weber, Max, 27, 79, 124, 125, 174, 199n4, 311, 380, 387, 430, 482

whiteness (white), 148, 173, 175–176, 176–177, 223, 242. 383, 433, 486n13, 503n20; Evangelical, 158–159; in scholarship, 101, 128, 129, 132, 175, 177, 178, 269, 427, 435, 502–503n16; "white man's burden," 167. *See also* Black; race; racialization

Williams, Rowan, 378, 379, 384

Wiredu, Kwasi, 55–56, 482

Wittgenstein, Ludwig, 10, 13, 222, 291, 483

Wollstonecraft, Mary: *A Vindication of the Rights of Woman*, 239, 483

Woodhead, Linda, 196, 483

Women (female): in ancient world, 234; Asian women and strategic essentialism, 172–173; Black (of color), 132, 240, 245; blamed for rape, 234; in Buddhism, 58, 245, 251–252; in Christianity, 152, 233–234, 239, 240, 245, 248–50, 331, 340–342, 353, 357; in Confucianism, 238; constructed (performed), not born as, 241–242, 293; in Daoism, 238; Donald Trump and, 159; Goddess, goddesses, and, 234, 236–237, 238–239; in Greek philosophy, 233, 234, 513n2; in

Hinduism, 157, 235–237; in interreligious dialogue, 329, 335, 340–342; in Islam, 234–235, 242, 244–245, 247, 340–342, 392; mistreatment of, 248, 363; in Paganism, 238–239; perceived differences of men and women, 143, 145, 241–242; and postcolonial scholarship/decolonization, 170, 178; regulation of bodies of, 220, 391, 392–393, 410; as subalterns, 172; women as peacemakers, 152; women's religion as "superstition," 176. *See also* feminism; gender; intersectionality; kyriarchy

world religions paradigm (WRP), 24, 28, 32, 33, 34, 37, 45, 46, 60, 62, 67, 71, 72, 77, 87, 164, 192–193, 200, 217, 256, 258, 265, 270, 271, 304, 305, 306, 335, 340, 383

World Council of Churches, 327–328

World's Parliament of Religion. *See* Parliament of the World's Religions

World War I (WWI), 95

World War II (WWII), 308, 327, 329, 359, 438, 471

Wynter, Sylvia, 177, 383, 483

xiejiao. See cult

Xunzi, 204, 483

yin-yang, 238, 472

yoga, 57, 128, 220, 382, 385, 472

Younghusband, Francis, 327, 483

Zen (zazen), 100, 327, 472; Christians practicing, 344; imagined lineage of, 100; Protestants, comparison with, 272–275, 294–297; satori (experience), 344; sitting in, 217, 272–273. *See also* tea ceremony (Zen)

Zoroaster, 74, 483

Zoroastrianism (Zoroastrians), 28, 73, 74, 304, 310, 472

Founded in 1893,
UNIVERSITY OF CALIFORNIA PRESS
publishes bold, progressive books and journals
on topics in the arts, humanities, social sciences,
and natural sciences—with a focus on social
justice issues—that inspire thought and action
among readers worldwide.

The UC PRESS FOUNDATION
raises funds to uphold the press's vital role
as an independent, nonprofit publisher, and
receives philanthropic support from a wide
range of individuals and institutions—and from
committed readers like you. To learn more, visit
ucpress.edu/supportus.